Frommer's

Greece
day BY day

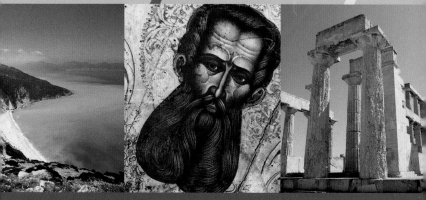

1st Edition

by Stephen Brewer & Tania Kollias

John Wiley and Sons, Inc.

> An Orthodox monk keeps pace with the 21st century at Agia Triada Monastery, in the Meteora region.

Contents

1 **Chapter 1: The Best of Greece**
2 Favorite Moments in Greece
4 The Best Ancient Ruins
6 The Best Museums
7 The Best of the Byzantine Empire
8 The Best Architecture
9 The Best Beaches
10 Favorite Cities & Towns
11 The Best Experiences for Kids
12 The Best Nightlife
13 The Best Dining Experiences
14 Favorite Places to Stay
16 The Best Shopping
17 The Best Outdoor Adventures

18 **Chapter 2: The Best All-Greece Itineraries**
20 Highlights of Greece
24 The Best of Greece in 2 Weeks
30 Exploring Ancient Greece

36 **Chapter 3: Athens**
38 Favorite Moments in Athens
42 The Best of Athens in 1 Day
50 The Best of Athens in 2 Days
54 The Best of Athens in 3 Days
58 Athens for Museum Lovers
64 Athens with Kids
68 Ancient Athens
72 Architectural Landmarks
76 Byzantine Athens
80 Romantic Athens
84 Syntagma to Gazi Neighborhood Walk
88 Plaka, Thissio & Psyrri Neighborhood Walk
92 Athens Shopping Best Bets
93 Athens Shopping A to Z
104 Athens Restaurant Best Bets
105 Athens Restaurants A to Z
112 Athens Hotel Best Bets
113 Athens Hotels A to Z
120 Athens Nightlife & Entertainment Best Bets

PAGE 8

PAGE 23

PAGE 47

121 Athens Nightlife & Entertainment A to Z
130 The South Coast Beaches
134 Athens Fast Facts

136 **Chapter 4: The Saronic Gulf Islands**
138 Favorite Moments in the Saronic Gulf
140 The Saronic Gulf Islands in 1 Day
142 The Saronic Gulf Islands in 5 Days
146 Best Beaches on the Saronic Gulf Islands
148 Aegina
151 Where to Stay & Dine on Aegina
152 *Spotlight: Hellenic Temples*
154 Angistri
155 Where to Stay & Dine on Angistri
156 Hydra
159 Where to Stay & Dine on Hydra
160 Poros
163 Where to Stay & Dine on Poros
164 Spetses
167 Where to Stay & Dine on Spetses
168 The Saronic Gulf Islands Fast Facts

170 **Chapter 5: The Peloponnese**
172 Favorite Moments in the Peloponnese
174 The Peloponnese in 3 Days
178 The Peloponnese in 10 Days
184 Ancient Wonders of the Peloponnese
197 Where to Stay & Dine in Sparta & Olympia
198 *Spotlight: Olympiad*
200 Byzantine Splendors of the Peloponnese
205 Where to Stay & Dine in Mystras & Monemvassia
206 Off the Beaten Path in the Peloponnese
213 Where to Stay & Dine Off the Beaten Path
214 Nafplion
220 Where to Stay in Nafplion
221 Where to Dine in Nafplion
222 Patras
225 Where to Stay & Dine in Patras
226 The Peloponnese Fast Facts

228 **Chapter 6: Crete**
230 Favorite Moments in Crete
232 Crete in 3 Days by Bus

236 Crete in 10 Days
240 On the Trail of the Minoans
248 *Spotlight: Civilization 101*
250 Off the Beaten Path on Crete
257 Where to Stay & Dine Off the Beaten Path on Crete
258 Iraklion
264 Where to Stay in Iraklion
265 Where to Dine in Iraklion
266 Rethymnon
272 Where to Stay in Rethymnon
273 Where to Dine in Rethymnon
274 Hania
282 Where to Stay in Hania
283 Where to Dine in Hania
284 Agios Nikolaos
292 Where to Stay in Agios Nikolaos
293 Where to Dine in Agios Nikolaos
295 Crete Fast Facts

296 **Chapter 7: The Cyclades**
298 Favorite Moments in the Cyclades
300 The Best of the Cyclades in 5 Days
304 The Best of the Cyclades in 10 Days
308 Islands of Gods & Saints: Delos & Tinos
313 Where to Stay & Dine on Tinos
314 *Spotlight: Our Town*
316 Off the Beaten Path on Milos
321 Where to Stay & Dine on Milos & Folegandros
322 Santorini
330 Where to Stay on Santorini
332 Where to Dine on Santorini
334 Paros
341 Where to Stay & Dine on Paros
342 Naxos
349 Where to Stay & Dine on Naxos
350 Sifnos
355 Where to Stay & Dine on Sifnos
356 Mykonos
362 Where to Stay on Mykonos
364 Where to Dine on Mykonos
366 Siros
369 Where to Stay & Dine on Siros
370 The Cyclades Fast Facts

PAGE 286

PAGE 313

PAGE 330

372 **Chapter 8: Rhodes & the Dodecanese**
374 Favorite Moments in the Dodecanese
378 The Island of Rhodes in 3 Days
382 The Dodecanese in 1 Week
386 The Best Dodecanese Beaches
390 Rhodes Town
396 Where to Stay in Rhodes Town
397 Where to Dine in Rhodes Town
398 *Spotlight: Meze*
400 Excursions from Rhodes Town
402 Beach Resorts on Rhodes
405 Where to Stay & Dine in Rhodes Beach Resorts
408 Lindos
411 Where to Stay & Dine in Lindos
412 Symi
416 Where to Stay & Dine in Yialos
418 Kos
422 Kos Beaches & Resorts
426 Where to Stay & Dine on Kos
428 Patmos
432 Patmos Beaches
434 Where to Stay & Dine in Skala
436 Rhodes & the Dodecanese Fast Facts

438 **Chapter 9: Northeastern Aegean Islands**
440 Favorite Moments in the Northeastern Aegean
442 The Best of the Northeastern Aegean in 5 Days
446 The Northeastern Aegean in 7 Days
450 In the Footsteps of the Ancients
456 *Spotlight: Elements of Drama*
458 Samos
464 Where to Stay on Samos
465 Where to Dine on Samos
466 Chios
472 Where to Stay on Chios
473 Where to Dine on Chios
474 Lesbos
480 Where to Stay on Lesbos
481 Where to Dine on Lesbos
482 Northeastern Aegean Fast Facts

484 **Chapter 10: The Sporades**
486 Favorite Moments in the Sporades
488 The Sporades in 6 Days
492 The Sporades in 9 Days
496 The National Marine Park of Alonnisos
   Northern Sporades
500 *Spotlight: Nation of Islands*
502 Skiathos
506 Where to Stay on Skiathos
507 Where to Dine on Skiathos
508 Skopelos
512 Where to Stay & Dine on Skopelos
514 Skyros
518 Where to Stay & Dine on Skyros
520 The Sporades Fast Facts

522 **Chapter 11: Northern Greece**
524 Favorite Moments in Northern Greece
526 The Best of Northern Greece in 3 Days
530 In the Footsteps of Phillip II & Alexander
533 Where to Stay & Dine in Vergina
536 Realm of the Monks: Mount Athos
540 Mount Olympus & Litochoro
542 Where to Stay & Dine Near Mount Olympus
544 *Spotlight: The Pantheon*
548 Thessaloniki
555 Where to Stay in Thessaloniki
558 Where to Dine in Thessaloniki
560 Northern Greece Fast Facts

562 **Chapter 12: Central & Western Greece**
564 Favorite Moments in Central & Western Greece
566 The Best of Central & Western Greece in 3 Days
570 The Best of Central & Western Greece in 1 Week
576 Delphi & Arachova
580 Kalambaka & Meteora Monasteries
582 Meteora Monasteries
584 *Spotlight: Monastic Life*
586 Mountains & Valleys: Metsovo & Zagori
591 Where to Stay & Dine in Metsovo & Zagori
592 Ioannina
596 Where to Stay & Dine in Ioannina
598 Central & Western Greece Fast Facts

PAGE 492

PAGE 528

PAGE 568

600 Chapter 13: Corfu & the Ionian Islands
602 Favorite Moments in the Ionian Islands
604 The Best of Corfu in 3 Days
608 The Best of Corfu & the Ionians in 6 Days
612 *Spotlight: Feta*
614 Kefalonia & Ithaca
617 Where to Stay & Dine on Kefalonia
618 Corfu Town
624 Where to Stay in Corfu Town
625 Where to Dine in Corfu Town
626 Around Corfu
631 Where to Stay & Dine Around Corfu
632 Corfu & the Ionian Islands Fast Facts

PAGE 642

634 Chapter 14: Greece's History & Culture
636 Greece: A Brief History
640 A Timeline of Greek History
642 Greece's Art & Architecture
650 Music, Literature & Cinema
653 Greek Food & Drink

658 Chapter 15: The Best Special-Interest Trips
660 Outdoor Activities & Outfitters
661 Education Travel
662 Multi-Activity Adventures & Outfitters
662 Sustainable & Holistic Travel
664 Cruises

666 Chapter 16: The Savvy Traveler
668 Before You Go
672 Getting There
675 Getting Around
677 Lodgings
678 Travel Tips
678 Traveling with Kids
678 Fast Facts
685 Useful Phrases & Menu Terms

698 Index
709 Photo Credits

PAGE 660

PUBLISHED BY

Wiley Publishing, Inc.

111 River St., Hoboken, NJ 07030-5774

ISBN 978-0-470-58251-0

Frommer's®

Editorial by Frommer's

EDITOR
Maureen Clarke

PHOTO EDITOR
Cherie Cincilla

CARTOGRAPHER
Roberta Stockwell

CAPTIONS
Stephen Brewer

COVER PHOTO EDITOR
Richard Fox

COVER DESIGN
Paul Dinovo

Produced by Sideshow Media

PUBLISHER
Dan Tucker

MANAGING EDITOR
Megan McFarland

PROJECT EDITOR
Kathryn Williams

PHOTO EDITOR
John Martin

PHOTO RESEARCHER
Natalia Roumelioti

DESIGN
Kevin Smith, And Smith LLC

SPOTLIGHT FEATURE DESIGN
Em Dash Design LLC

For information on our other products and services or to obtain technical support, please contact our Customer Care Department within the U.S. at 800/762-2974, outside the U.S. at 317/572-3993 or fax 317/572-4002.

Wiley also publishes its books in a variety of electronic formats. Some content that appears in print may not be available in electronic formats.

MANUFACTURED IN CHINA

5 4 3 2 1

How to Use This Guide

The Day by Day guides present a series of itineraries that take you from place to place. The itineraries are organized by time (The Best of Athens in 1 Day), by region (Kefalonia & Ithaca), by town (Lindos), and by special interest (Realm of the Monks: Mount Athos). You can follow these itineraries to the letter, or customize your own based on the information we provide. Within the tours, we suggest cafes, bars, or restaurants where you can take a break. Each of these stops is marked with a coffee-cup icon ☕. In each chapter, we provide detailed hotel and restaurant reviews so you can select the places that are right for you.

The hotels, restaurants, and attractions listed in this guide have been ranked for quality, value, service, amenities, and special features using a **star-rating system.** Hotels, restaurants, attractions, shopping, and nightlife are rated on a scale of zero stars (recommended) to three stars (exceptional). In addition to the star-rating system, we also use a kids icon kids to point out the best bets for families.

The following **abbreviations** are used for credit cards:

AE American Express	**MC** MasterCard
DC Diners Club	**V** Visa
DISC Discover	

A Note on Prices

Frommer's lists exact prices in local currency. Currency conversion rates fluctuate, so consult www.oanda.com/convert/classic or another source to check up-to-the-minute rates.

How to Contact Us

In researching this book, we discovered many wonderful places—hotels, restaurants, shops, and more. We're sure you'll find others. Please tell us about them, so we can share the information with your fellow travelers in upcoming editions. If you were disappointed with a recommendation, we'd love to know that, too. Please email us at frommersfeed back@wiley.com or write to:

Frommer's Greece Day by Day, 1st Edition
Wiley Publishing, Inc.
111 River Street
Hoboken, NJ 07030-5774

Travel Resources at Frommers.com

Frommer's travel resources don't end with this guide. **Frommers.com** has travel information on more than 4,000 destinations. We update features regularly, giving you access to the most current trip-planning information and the best airfare, lodging, and car-rental bargains. You can also listen to podcasts, connect with other Frommers.com members through our active reader forums, share your travel photos, read blogs from guidebook editors and fellow travelers, and much more.

An Additional Note

Please be advised that travel information is subject to change at any time—and this is especially true of prices. We suggest that you write or call ahead for confirmation when making your travel plans. The authors, editors, and publisher cannot be held responsible for the experiences of readers while traveling. Your safety is important to us, so we encourage you to stay alert and be aware of your surroundings.

About the Authors

Stephen Brewer (chapters 1, 2, 5–7, 9, 10, and 13) is a writer and editor who has worked in magazines, books, radio, and corporate communications for more than 30 years. He stepped off a boat onto the island of Crete 20 years ago, decided he had found his place in the world, and has spent part of each year on the Greek islands and mainland ever since. He is the author of the chapters on the Peloponnese, Crete, the Cyclades, the Northeastern Aegean Islands, the Sporades, and Corfu.

Tania Kollias (chapters 1–4, 8, 11, 12, and 14–16) is a journalist from Vancouver living in Athens, a good and warm base for trips and stories. Her goal in life was to travel, and, after getting a degree, she did, visiting some 32 countries. She has lived in Asia, Australia, and Europe, taking in a range of experiences—from crossing the Arctic Circle in Norway and trekking in Nepal to canoeing the Zambezi River and comparing beaches in India, Thailand, and Zanzibar. She has worked as a writer and editor for 2 decades, drafting reports in Tokyo for an engineering firm, producing books, wearing many hats at a newspaper, running a magazine in Athens, and contributing news and travel articles to major newspapers. This is her fifth work for Frommer's.

Acknowledgments

Stephen Brewer I wish to thank Maureen Clarke, my unfailingly supportive editor at Frommer's, and the many friends and acquaintances in Greece who over the years have introduced me to their beautiful landscapes and enviable lifestyles. Special thanks to the two Giorgioses for many years of friendship, hospitality, and advice.

Tania Kollias I thank Frommer's, friends, and family for their support; my extraordinary father for coming from the most dazzling country in the world; my unconventional British mother and her adventurous stock of explorers, auto pioneers, sea captains, and railway writers for inspiration; and my dear husband and daughter for their patience and much more.

About the Photographers

Award-winning photographer **Georgios Makkas** contributes to major Greek magazines and works on private commissions for various Greek and international clients. His work has been exhibited in the U.K. and Greece, and his pictures are in the permanent collection of the Greek Museum of Photography. To see more of his work, go to www.gmakkas.com.

Athens-based photographer **Yannis Lefakis,** after working for *Exodus* Greek weekly listings magazine for several years, made a shift in his career. For the past 2 years, he has been a portrait photographer for major fashion magazines in Greece.

Based on Skopelos Island, **Vaggelis Mpeltzenitis** has been photographing for hotels and tour operators on Skopelos and the rest of the Sporades Islands for the past 10 years.

One of Greece's best-known concert photographers, **Christos Kissadjekian** has had a career as a photojournalist for the past 21 years contributing to major Greek newspapers. To see more of his work, go to www.livephotographs.com.

1

The Best
of Greece

Favorite Moments in Greece

> *PREVIOUS PAGE The village of Ia on Santorini.*
> *THIS PAGE Stenciled houses in Pyrgi on Chios.*

Losing track of time in modern Athens. Athens may have the Parthenon, that most exquisite achievement of the ancients, but Greece's free, anarchic capital is more than a collection of old monuments. Besides the ancient sites in the compact, historic center, you'll find pedestrian walkways lined with modern cafe-bars and tavernas, where the food is piled high, the barrel wine flows freely, the patrons are animated, and the time is now. See p. 36, chapter 3.

Sitting in Syntagma Square, Nafplion. Life rarely seems as pleasant as it does from a cafe table on a Greek square—especially on the lovely expanse of marble paving on Plateia Syntagma in Nafplion, often called Greece's most beautiful city. Nafpliots and their visitors linger for hours. When it's time to leave, no matter where they're headed, the only way out is to stroll along the beautiful lanes of the Old Town. See p. 214, chapter 5.

Hiking the Samaria Gorge on Crete. In one of the world's most spectacular gorges, eagles float overhead, goats scamper up herb-scented hillsides, and, at one point along the trail, the cleft narrows to only 3m (10 ft.), beneath walls that soar 600m (1,969 ft.) overhead. At the end of the hike, a plunge into the Libyan Sea awaits you. See p. 252, chapter 6.

Sailing into the caldera, Santorini. Approaching Santorini by sea is one of the great Greek experiences. Cliffs rise 300m (984 ft.) from the flooded caldera of a volcano, glimmering in transcendent light, and white villages high atop the rim look like a dusting of snow on what is one of the world's most dazzling islands. See p. 300, chapter 7.

Snacking at a beach taverna, Haraki Bay, Rhodes. All over Greece, there are nearly as many seaside, reed-roofed tavernas as there are beaches. Sitting at a table in the sand, looking out to sea, and tucking into a Greek salad—juicy tomato, thick slab of feta, cucumber, kalamata olives, tangy green peppers, and fresh bread to dip into the virgin olive oil at the bottom of the bowl—is the height of simple pleasure. See p. 403, chapter 8.

Exploring the mastic villages, Chios. Some 20 fortified villages, once wealthy from the mastic they shipped to Turkish harems, are some of the most beautiful monuments of medieval Greece, set amid olive groves and mastic orchards. Pyrgi is especially exotic, with narrow lanes of houses etched with circles, diamonds, stars, other elaborate geometric patterns, and floral motifs. See p. 469, chapter 9.

> On Santorini, dazzling white villages cling to volcanic cliffs.

> Hikers scramble down Crete's 30km-long (19-mile) Samaria Gorge, one of Europe's most spectacular natural wonders.

Wandering through the narrow lanes of Corfu Town, Corfu. One of Greece's most alluring towns is an intoxicating blend of Venetian loggias, Byzantine churches, French arcades, and British palaces and gardens—all awash in Mediterranean ochre and pastels and within sight of shimmering Greek seas. See p. 618, chapter 13.

Sitting on the deck of a ferry en route to a Greek island. There's nothing like propping up your feet on the rails of a big boat deck and appreciating the passing view while you talk, read a book, or play. Although it takes longer to travel this way than by plane, it beats sitting in coach any day.

The Best Ancient Ruins

> *A temple to Athena, crowning the Acropolis Hill above Athens, has exemplified classical perfection since its completion in 432 B.C.*

Parthenon, Athens. The quintessential symbol of classical Greece, the Temple of the Virgin Athena is an architectural masterpiece of order and harmony, built on a human scale, and visible at every other turn in the modern capital. See p. 44, chapter 3.

Corinth and the Acrocorinth, Peloponnese. One of the world's most remarkable fortresses —a lookout post, place of refuge, and shrine since the 5th century B.C.—is surrounded by three rings of mighty walls. Far below are the extensive ruins of the ancient city that once rivaled Athens in wealth, established colonies as far away as Sicily, and frustrated St. Paul with its worldly ways. See p. 184, chapter 5.

Mycenae, Peloponnese. The old palace, humble dwellings, workshops, and other stony remains, cradled by barren peaks and surrounded by sturdy walls, are associated with might and myth and still evoke all the power and wealth of the Mycenaean empire. See p. 188, chapter 5.

Theater at Epidaurus, Peloponnese. It's wondrous enough that you can stand on the stage where actors introduced the Greek classics to ancient audiences jamming the 55 tiers of seats at Epidaurus, but the fact that the 2,000-year-old theater is still perfection is astonishing. Millennia have passed since the Greek traveler Pausanias wondered, "Who can begin to rival the beauty and composition" of Epidaurus? His question still resonates today. See p. 191, chapter 5.

Temple of Apollo at Bassae, Peloponnese. One of the most beautiful and best-preserved temples in Greece stands in splendid isolation atop an Arcadian mountain. Even a protective tent doesn't detract much from the beauty of this marble and limestone wonder. See p. 194, chapter 5.

> *For the ancients, Delphi was the center of the world and a sacred sanctuary where the god Apollo spoke through an oracle.*

Olympia, Peloponnese. Ruins of the stadium, gymnasium, training hall, and dormitories here bring the famous ancient Olympic Games to life, yet temples to Zeus and Hera and the Praxiteles sculpture show that Olympia's glory transcended athletic prowess. See p. 195, chapter 5.

Knossos, Crete. The largest palace complex of the Minoans contained more than 1,300 rooms and was the court of royalty, an important religious and ceremonial center, an administrative headquarters, and a huge warehouse. Today it provides an evocative glimpse into a 4,000-year-old culture. See p. 241, chapter 6.

Delos, Cyclades. One of ancient Greece's most sacred religious sanctuaries, Delos was the legendary birthplace of Apollo, a flourishing center of trade, and onetime headquarters of the Delian League. Today it's one of the most important archaeological sites in the Aegean. See p. 308, chapter 7.

Delphi, Central Greece. Overlooking the Gulf of Corinth and groves of olive and cypress trees, this cliffside sanctuary on Mount Parnassos was considered the center of the earth in ancient times. Apollo spoke through an oracular priestess stationed here, and heads of state and other pilgrims flocked to hear her guidance. The ruins are exceptionally evocative, and the natural setting is as sublime as ever. See p. 577, chapter 12.

Dodona, near Ioannina. The site of the oracle of Zeus and his consort, the goddess of the earth, Dione, was ancient even in antiquity. Climb to the top rows of the theater, look out at the view of the mountains and valley, and feel the power. See p. 595, chapter 12.

The Best Museums

> *Works by the great Praxiteles and other sculptors graced the temples and sports facilities at Ancient Olympia.*

Acropolis Museum, Athens. The enormous concrete-and-glass structure with a stunning view from the top level transformed the area when it opened in 2009 just opposite the Acropolis. Inside, the museum contains a vast collection of beautifully displayed statues and artifacts that were found on the hill. See p. 44, chapter 3.

National Archaeological Museum, Athens. This 19th-century, Ernst Ziller–designed museum houses finds from all the great Greek civilizations—from Minoan and Mycenaean times to the Cycladic, Hellenic, and Roman epochs—plus an Egyptian collection and Trojan pieces found by Heinrich Schliemann. See p. 46, chapter 3.

Archaeological Museum, Olympia. Pride of place belongs to *Hermes Carrying the Infant Dionysus,* purportedly the only work by the great sculptor Praxiteles to survive the centuries. It was once the crowning glory of Olympia's Temple of Hera. See p. 195, chapter 5.

Archaeological Museum, Iraklion. The world's greatest museum of Minoan art brings a long-vanished civilization to life through beautiful frescoes portraying daily activity in an ancient court, elaborate pottery and jewelry, and stones inscribed with ancient script. See p. 240, chapter 6.

Vergina, northern Greece. A rare royal grave, the 4th-century-B.C. burial place of Philip II of Macedonia, father of Alexander the Great, was discovered in 1977 with its treasures intact. Today it's a unique museum: Visitors walk under the tumulus, or burial mound, into the fascinating underworld. See p. 531, chapter 11.

Archaeological Museum, Thessaloniki. This museum houses a beautiful collection of jewelry and other items found in the northern Macedonian region while workers were digging to build roads and railway lines. See p. 551, chapter 11.

The Best of the Byzantine Empire

Panagia Gorgoepikoos Church, Athens. This small 12th-century church is easy to find next to the Metropolitan Cathedral. One of Greece's most charming Byzantine houses of worship, it's built of engraved marble pieces from an ancient temple. See p. 78, chapter 3.

Monemvassia, Peloponnese. One of the best-preserved Byzantine cities in Greece is also one of the most dramatically located cities anywhere, where a maze of stone houses, stepped lanes, domed churches, and patches of gardens are wedged onto the side of a steep rock. See p. 200, chapter 5.

Mystras, Peloponnese. This splendid ghost town of golden stone overgrown with wildflowers and scented herbs was once the second most important city in the Byzantine Empire, after Constantinople. The stony remains of monasteries, churches, and libraries testify to this legacy. See p. 201, chapter 5.

Byzantine and Post-Byzantine Collection, Hania. Mosaics from early basilicas, fragments of wall paintings depicting saints, bronze lamps used during services, and icons evoke the long years of Byzantine presence in Crete. See p. 276, chapter 6.

Palace of the Grand Masters, Rhodes. Damsels and dueling knights in armor come to mind at this 15th-century fortress, the main building within the medieval walls of the Old Town. See p. 392, chapter 8.

Nea Moni, Chios. Naves, the dome, and eight supporting niches of the octagonal *katholikon* are decorated with dazzling Byzantine mosaics depicting saints and sinners—the latter being devoured by fish. See p. 469, chapter 9.

Museum of Byzantine Culture, Thessaloniki. The displays here are as beautiful as the intricate, gem-toned medieval icons and jewelry they showcase. See p. 551, chapter 11.

Osios David Church, Thessaloniki. This northern port city is rich with Byzantine relics and beautiful buildings, but the 6th-century-a.c. Osios David Church, with its unusual

> *Meteora's monasteries appear to float between heaven and earth atop pinnacles of sheer rock called hoodoos.*

mosaic preserved in hiding for centuries, has the most charm. See p. 553, chapter 11.

Meteora, central Greece. Meteora is one of the most spectacular and uplifting regions on earth, with 14th-century monasteries, both occupied and abandoned, clinging to the precipices of sheer-faced rock formations. See p. 581, chapter 12.

The Best Architecture

Parthenon, Athens. This temple of the goddess Athena, built in the 5th century B.C., is the pinnacle of the Doric order. Up on a hill (the Acropolis), it's a landmark indeed, visible at many a turn throughout the sprawling capital, helping modern Athenians find their way. See p. 44, chapter 3.

Koules, Iraklion. This mighty, wave-lapped Venetian fortress once protected Iraklion from attack by sea and provided safe anchorage for the republic's fleets. The view from the ramparts takes in a good swath of coast, the brooding mountains behind, and the inner and outer harbors, which bristled with the trade that made Crete one of Venice's most important outposts. See p. 262, chapter 6.

Arkadi Monastery, Crete. This beautiful monument on a high plateau is revered for its ornate Italianate-Renaissance facade and the events of November 8, 1866, when hundreds of men, women, and children were killed resisting a Turkish assault. See p. 269, chapter 6.

Walls of the Old Town, Rhodes. Sailing into the harbor of Rhodes and seeing the Old Town walls is a memorable experience—especially if you can imagine the Colossus of Rhodes straddling the entryway. See p. 392, chapter 8.

Efpalinio Orygma (Efpalinio Tunnel), Samos. This engineering wonder of the ancient world owes its existence to 6th-century-B.C. tyrant Polycrates and the thousands of slaves who burrowed through Mount Kastro with hammers and chisels for more than a decade to clear this passage. See p. 462, chapter 9.

White Tower, Thessaloniki. The medieval waterfront tower, built by the Turks as part of the fortification walls around the city, has become the easily identifiable symbol of the north and Macedonia in Greece. See p. 551, chapter 11.

The Achilleion, Corfu. Whether you love this garish extravagance or hate it, you're unlikely to forget the palace that Sissi of Austria built to honor Achilles and to escape court life in Vienna. When the excessive statuary becomes overwhelming, turn your gaze to the beautiful sea views. See p. 629, chapter 13.

> *Arkadi is one of Crete's most beautiful and sacred monasteries, where hundreds died fighting Turkish occupation.*

The Best Beaches

A natural sea cave on a bay near Sarakiniko, on Milos.

Aliki, Poros (Galatas). One of the Saronic Gulf's nicest beaches, with views of an offshore islet, is easy to reach, in a small bay just past a lemon grove en route from nearby Poros. See p. 162, chapter 4.

Elafonisi, Peloponnese. A trek down the Laconian Peninsula is rewarded with a short ferry crossing to a quiet isle where fragrant pine groves are ringed by miles of soft sand. See p. 202, chapter 5.

Elafonisi, Crete. A string of little inlets at the southwestern tip of Crete is lined with tamarisk-shaded sands and washed by shallow turquoise waters. See p. 251, chapter 6.

Sarakiniko, Milos. Turquoise coves etched from white volcanic rock are eerily beautiful and enticing. See p. 318, chapter 7.

Plaka, Naxos. These seemingly endless sands, backed by dunes, are nestled along a white and-rimmed coast that extends for 10km (6¼ miles) from Naxos Town to Pyrgaki, an isolated sand spit at the southern tip of the island. See p. 346, chapter 7.

Kambos, Patmos. The longest stretch of sand on the island captures the laid-back allure of Patmian life. White sand and clean, shallow waters are as much a part of the allure as tree-shaded tavernas where a lazy lunch can last all afternoon. See p. 388, chapter 8.

Lindos, Rhodes. The island certainly has quieter beaches, but the harbor and coves at Lindos can't be beat for location. A choice of sands, with tavernas and other amenities, are set against a backdrop of the white-washed village and hilltop acropolis. See p. 388, chapter 8.

Skala Eressos, Lesbos. The ancient poet and teacher Sappho lived on a hillside above this golden beach that stretches for miles and may have composed her poetry while feeling these sands beneath her feet. See p. 479, chapter 9.

Lalaria, Skiathos. The island has sandier beaches, but none can top the sheer beauty of Lalaria, where natural arches frame the pebbly strand and the marble sea bed renders the turquoise waters supernaturally translucent. See p. 504, chapter 10.

Lixouri Peninsula, Kefalonia. Red and golden sands backed by cliffs seem to stretch for miles, interspersed here and there with spectacular rock formations. See p. 615, chapter 13.

Favorite Cities & Towns

> *White houses and dozens of churches climb the hillsides above Skopelos port.*

Nafplion, Peloponnese. In what many admirers claim is Greece's most beautiful city, tall Venetian houses line narrow lanes that surround a marble-paved central square, promenades follow the Bay of Argos, and Byzantine and Venetian fortresses crown the heights above. See p. 214, chapter 5.

Hania, Crete. In this beautiful and exotic city, Venetians created the inner and outer harbors as well as palaces, warehouses, a lighthouse, and a fortress. The Turks added a flourish of mosques and minarets. See p. 274, chapter 6.

Ia, Santorini. This incredibly picturesque village is strung along the rim of the Santorini caldera. Cave houses are etched out of the side of the cliff, and a small fishing fleet bobs in the sparkling Aegean far below. See p. 325, chapter 7.

Hora, Mykonos. Too popular for its own good, the capital of worldly Mykonos never fails to work its charms. Wooden balconies hang from white cubical houses, outdoor staircases are lined with pots of geraniums, and a lopsided seaside church and rows of windmills are among the landmarks. See p. 356, chapter 7.

Old Town, Rhodes. There's something exciting and eye-catching around every corner in this unusual and beautiful town with its mix of the exotic East, mystical antiquity, Rhodian folk culture, and Italian architecture. See p. 378, chapter 8.

Lindos, Rhodes. The Old Town of Lindos is the quintessential island village (*horio*), with narrow lanes and whitewashed, low-rise houses. It's overrun during the height of summer, but the crowds don't detract from its setting, flanked by two bays below the acropolis. See p. 408, chapter 8.

Molyvos, Lesbos. Streets and alleys wind up a hillside from the lively harbor, past houses decked out with hanging geraniums, through shady squares cooled by fountains; at the top is the proud castle the Genoese erected in the 13th century. See p. 478, chapter 9.

Skopelos Town, Sporades. White houses and blue-domed churches (123 in all) climb a hillside to a Venetian Kastro (castle), all set against a backdrop of pine-clad hills. See p. 508, chapter 10.

Corfu Town, Corfu. Various cultures have claimed Corfu as their own, and each has left its mark. A Venetian flavor, with a touch of southern Mediterranean ochre and pastels, pervades the narrow lanes behind the Liston, a cafe-lined French-style arcade, and English gardens and palaces stand next to shimmering Greek seas. See p. 618, chapter 13.

The Best Experiences for Kids

National Gardens Playground, Athens. The beautiful, safe walk through the National Gardens in the center of town leads you down to a small zoo and then to a playground with swings, slides, and a maypole-style ride for bigger kids. See p. 65, chapter 3.

Isthmus of Corinth and Acrocorinth, Peloponnese. If you need to drag the young ones kicking and screaming to ancient sites, go for the wow factor. Stop first at the isthmus to watch slips slide through the narrow canal; then take them up to the Acrocorinth, a remarkable ancient fortress that looms 540m (1,772 ft.) above the coastal plain. See p. 174, chapter 5.

Mystras and Monemvassia, Peloponnese. Adventurous children will love exploring these medieval wonders, clambering through deserted palaces and churches in Mystras, and wandering through lanes and squares before climbing to a mountaintop high above Monemvassia. See p. 201, chapter 5.

Kalavrita Express, Peloponnese. The open-air railway navigates 14 bridges and tunnels, ascends steep slopes, and glides along the rushing Vouraikos River, providing no end of thrills. The beaches of Diakofto are at one end of the route, the pleasantly cool mountain town of Kalavrita at the other. See p. 206, chapter 5.

Cretaquarium and Acquaplus Waterpark, Crete. At one of the largest and most sophisticated aquariums in Greece, jellyfish, sharks, and other fish and marine life swim through beautiful re-creations of Crete's offshore seascapes. But the slides, tunnels, and pools of the nearby water park will be the real kid pleasers. See p. 263, chapter 6.

Spinalonga, Crete. Eerie ruins, pirate legends, beaches, and a boat trip across the Gulf of Mirabello make this little island a hit with young travelers. As the boat passes the nearby islet of Agios Pantes, tell them to keep an eye out for the *agrimi*, also known as the *kri-kri*—a species of long-horned wild goat endemic to Crete. See p. 286, chapter 6.

> *Ships squeeze through the narrow Corinth Canal, opened in 1893.*

Pythagorio, Samos. The 6th-century-B.C. despot Polycrates left behind some remarkable achievements that may intrigue even kids who have had their fill of ruins: a now-submerged jetty, visible beneath the waters of the harbor; a circuit of walls; a spooky water tunnel they can walk through; and a huge temple to Hera. See p. 450, chapter 9.

Skiathos, Sporades. It's not that Skiathos doesn't offer plenty of adult pleasures, but the small island is an especially easy place to keep the little ones amused. Young adventurers can take their pick of sandy beaches, float into Spilia Skotini, a spectacular sea cave, and clamor across the ruins of Kastro, a ghost town at the edge of the sea. See p. 502, chapter 10.

The Best Nightlife

> *Bar-hopping is a long-standing tradition on Mykonos, a favorite getaway for lounge lizards and beachgoers.*

Psyrri, Athens. This central Athens district is buzzing with restaurants, bars, and clubs. Walk down Miaouli Street from the corner of Ermou and Athinas streets toward the square, and you're in the thick of it. See p. 127, chapter 3.

Thissio, Athens. These cafe-bars have elevated the outdoor cafe to a fine art. The awnings have mood lights and even chandeliers, and the view takes in the Parthenon, which is especially magical when lit up at night. See p. 127, chapter 3.

Iraklion, Crete. The busy, chaotic capital of Crete is most pleasant by night, when strollers and cafe sitters take over the city center. The choicest positions are those surrounding the Lions' Fountain on Plateia Venizelou and overlooking the harbor and Venetian Kastro. See p. 265, chapter 6.

Mykonos, Cyclades. The longtime favorite Greek isle of the rich and famous and their followers still throbs with one of Greece's hippest nightlife scenes. An evening can begin with a sunset cocktail in Little Venice, continue with after-dinner drinks on the narrow lanes of Hora, and end with dancing and drinking till dawn on the beach. See p. 365, chapter 7.

Faliraki, Rhodes. This is the granddaddy of foreign youth culture in Greece, a hub of clubs, bars, and rollicking parties since the 1980s. If you're in your 20s or 30s, and partying is the purpose of your beach holiday, come here. See p. 407, chapter 8.

Skiathos, Sporades. A lively club scene transforms Skiathos Town on summer nights, most noticeably on the narrow lanes off Papadiamantis Street in the center of town and on the quays of the old port. Night owls of a more serious bent attend classical Greek dramas and modern dance performances during the summertime Aegean Festival. See p. 507, chapter 4.

Corfu Town, Corfu. The Liston is the place to be on a warm summer night, when orchestras often play in an outdoor pavilion within earshot of sophisticated cafes, and the entire island population seems to be in attendance to soak up the scene. See p. 625, chapter 13.

The Best Dining Experiences

> Cretan favorites are served in a scented garden at Avli, tucked away on the lanes of old Rethymnon.

Archaion Gefseis, Athens. Sample an assortment of *archaion gefseis* (ancient tastes) as the ancients did, reclined at table. All the recipes served here are more than 2,500 years old, yet the ingredients and flavor combinations seem surprisingly contemporary. See p. 105, chapter 3.

Roof Garden, Grande Bretagne Hotel, Athens. This is the best address in Athens, serving Mediterranean cuisine, and the roof garden affords a spectacular view of the Acropolis and sunset. If you're celebrating a special occasion, come here. See p. 108, chapter 3.

Lela's, Kardamyli, Mani, Peloponnese. The charming Lela serves her famous fish soup, oven-baked lamb with mountain herbs, and other homemade specialties on a tree-shaded seaside terrace. See p. 213, chapter 5.

Kronio, Lasithi Plateau, Crete. Welcoming hosts and delicious fare, from thick lamb stews to homemade bread and little cheese-stuffed pies, add a memorable flourish to one of Greece's most remarkable landscapes. See p. 257, chapter 6.

Avli, Rethymnon, Crete. This temple to Cretan cuisine introduces you to the island's freshest bounty, served in a delightful garden and arched dining room. If you're enchanted, there's no need to leave: Avli also offers luxurious, suitelike accommodations. See p. 273, chapter 6.

Selene, Fira, Santorini. One of Greece's most acclaimed restaurants, tucked onto a ledge high above the caldera, serves variations on traditional favorites such as octopus with smoked eggplant and fava balls with capers. See p. 333, chapter 7.

Kiki's, Agios Sostis, Mykonos. Island experiences don't get much better than this: a swim at beautiful Agios Sostis Beach followed by a lazy lunch of grilled fish or meat, served beneath a flowering vine. See p. 364, chapter 7.

O Loutros, Thessaloniki. Thessaloniki, a proper city for a lot longer than Athens, with cultural influences from many ethnic groups, arguably has the best food. For a full-on Greek experience, eat meze outside beside the medieval baths while a musician accompanies the meal with bouzouki music. See p. 559, chapter 11.

Venetian Well, Corfu Town, Corfu. A charming square in the depths of Old Town is a romantic setting in which to tuck into creative pastas and other deftly prepared dishes based on market-fresh ingredients. See p. 625, chapter 13.

Favorite Places to Stay

> *James Bond would feel at home in the high-tech, ultra-luxurious bungalows at the Elounda Beach Hotel on Crete.*

Grande Bretagne, Athens. This is the most famous historic hotel in the country, hosting royalty and heads of state since the 19th century. It's as stately and classy as they come. See p. 116, chapter 3.

Orloff Resort, Spetses. Stay in a beautifully decorated hotel converted from a 19th-century mansion with a swimming pool on this aristocratic holiday island. See p. 167, chapter 4.

Pyrgos of Mystras, Mystras, Peloponnese. You will feel like a pampered Byzantine noble in this beautifully decorated stone country house just outside the ruined city. See p. 205, chapter 5.

Kyrimai Hotel, Gerolimenas, Mani, Peloponnese. In converted centuries-old warehouses at the end of a rocky promontory, comfortable, appealing stone-walled rooms and suites overlook the sea and waterside terraces. See p 213, chapter 5.

Doma, Hania, Crete. Simple yet elegant and character-filled accommodations in a seaside mansion face the sea or a delightful garden. See p. 282, chapter 6.

Elounda Beach, Elounda, Crete. This luxurious getaway sets the standard for all large Greek resorts, providing accommodations in dozens of variations, from villas with private pools to charming suites nestled above the shoreline. Amenities include lovely beaches, watersports, spa treatments, a variety of dining experiences, and top-notch service. See p. 292, chapter 6.

Elounda Mare, Elounda, Crete. Elegant Cretan style and relaxed hospitality distinguish this intimate and stylish retreat. It's one of Europe's finest resorts, with rooms, suites, and bungalows tucked into beautiful seaside gardens. See p. 292, chapter 6.

Esperas, Ia, Santorini. You'll feel like a cliff dweller as you take in the stupendous views from your terrace and hot tub at this welcoming enclave of traditional houses teetering on the edge of the caldera. See p. 330, chapter 7.

Astra Apartments, Imerovigli, Santorini. Dramatic eagle's-eye views over the caldera and the Skaros promontory set the scene for stylish and distinctive accommodations that surround terraces and a beautiful pool. See p. 330, chapter 7.

Cavo Tagoo, Mykonos. Chic island style prevails at this sophisticated hideaway outside Hora. A sumptuous outdoor lounge surrounds the infinity pool, and stunning rooms and suites, many with pools of their own, have large terraces that face the sea. See p. 362, chapter 7.

Petali Hotel, Apollonia, Sifnos. Roomy accommodations, tucked into terraces and gardens high above Apollonia, provide an airy retreat on one of Greece's most beautiful isles. See p. 355, chapter 7.

Iapetos Village, Symi. Families and lovers of Symi will be happy staying in one of the roomy suites at this modern complex, set back into the village, with a pool in the courtyard. See p. 416, chapter 8.

Perleas, Kambos, Chios. Fragrant citrus orchards surround a stone mansion and outbuildings filled with antiques and carefully chosen artwork. See p. 472, chapter 9.

Safeti, Dion. You'll feel right at home in an eco-friendly studio at this charmed establishment across from the ancient site at Dion. The industrious owners, who sell their own handmade wares from a store on site, may inspire you to learn a new craft during your stay. See p. 533, chapter 11.

> Casual yet chic Cavo Tagoo on Mykonos makes for a sophisticated seaside getaway.

Villa Pantheon, Litochoro. This beautiful and peaceful hotel in the base camp of Mount Olympus is secluded with a view out to sea. The hotel itself seems more like a big house. See p. 543, chapter 11.

Casa Lucia, Corfu. At one of the island's most idyllic getaways, cozy bungalows and small villas are well equipped for settling in for a spell, amid verdant gardens. See p. 631, chapter 13.

The Best Shopping

> *In her eponymous shop in old Hania, Carmela shows her own work along with that of fellow Greek jewelers and sculptors.*

Shoes on Ermou Street, Athens. Even if you're not a footwear fanatic, you'll appreciate browsing up and down this pedestrian street in search of a beautiful pair of leather shoes. See p. 56, chapter 3.

Gold or silver jewelry, Athens. As you can see just by walking down Adrianou Street in Plaka, Athens has its share of beautifully crafted precious metal jewelry for sale, and it's much cheaper here than elsewhere. Come prepared to buy. See p. 90, chapter 3.

Greek wine and crafts, Nafplion. As you wander around the narrow lanes of Old Town, stock up on wines from the nearby Nemea vineyards at 150-year-old Karonis, buy a new string of worry beads at the Komboloi Museum, or select jewelry and handicrafts from the enticing shop run by the Peloponnesian Folklore Foundation Museum. See p. 219, chapter 5.

Old and new crafts, Hania. Two side-by-side shops on Anghelou near the Venetian Harbor introduce shoppers to fine Greek artistic traditions. Carmela displays the work of contemporary jewelers and sculptors from throughout Greece. Cretan Rugs and Blankets is filled with fine examples of top-quality work, much of it antique and handwoven, from around the island. See p. 283, chapter 6.

Woven goods, Mykonos. This island's distinctive textiles have attracted well-heeled travelers for decades, inspired international couturiers, and shown up in clothing by local designers including Yiannis Galatis, Dimitris and Orsalia Parthenis, and Ioanna Zouganeli. See p. 363, chapter 7.

Honey from Rhodes. Artisanal honey is made all over Greece, but the flower-based honey from Rhodes is unforgettable. It's especially good from the village of Siana, which also makes *tsipouro* (grappa).

Handmade silver, Ioannina. Craftsmen in this city have made silverware for centuries. Fine specimens are for sale from shops in the Turkish bazaar or from the Traditional Handicraft Center. See p. 569, chapter 12.

The Best Outdoor Adventures

> *Much of the south coast of Crete, including the village of Loutro, is accessible only on foot or by sea.*

Sailing through the National Marine Park of Alonissos Northern Sporades. The largest marine park in the Mediterranean encompasses 2,200 sq km (849 sq. miles) of sea, eight islands, and 22 rocky outcroppings, home to falcons, dolphins, wild goats, and many other species of flora and fauna. You probably won't sight the most famous denizen, the highly endangered monk seal, but it's no less thrilling just to float, swim, and snorkel through the pristine waters. **See p. 498, chapter 4.**

Hiking along the south coast of Crete. Paths follow the rugged coast and the beautiful gorges that cleave through the White Mountains to little-visited bays and beaches. You'll take in some of Europe's most spectacularly unspoiled landscapes and a remote village or two. **See chapter 6.**

Swimming on Milos. Mykonos, Paros, and Naxos are justly famous for their beaches, but the many long stretches of sand on Milos are more beautiful and much less discovered. **See p. 316, chapter 7.**

Walking on Sifnos. Walks along *monopati* (mule tracks) can take you to every corner of one of the most beautiful islands in the Aegean—through the cluster of six villages clinging to the hills around Apollonia, along the coast to the monastery at Chrysopigi or the one atop Profitas Elias o Pilos, and to the beautiful bay at Vathy. **See p. 350, chapter 7.**

Trekking Hellas, Central Greece. Climb Mount Olympus, rappel in Meteora, or learn to sculpt on the island of Tinos through this domestically based organization. **See p. 581, chapter 12.**

2
The Best
All-Greece
Itineraries

Highlights of Greece

You'll see just a fraction of Greece in a week, but these 7 days should fascinate you and lay the groundwork for future excursions farther into the mainland or to more remote islands. You'll gain a strong sense of Athens and visit the Acropolis, Delphi, and some of the other remarkable remnants of ancient Greece. You will also do some island-hopping and experience the beauty of Santorini, the medieval might of Rhodes, and the quiet simplicity of Symi. This itinerary does not require a car.

> PREVIOUS PAGE *Symi's neoclassical houses surround one of Greece's most welcoming ports.*
> THIS PAGE *Treasuries in Delphi were once filled with offerings to Apollo.*

START **From Athens International Airport, take the bus or metro into central Athens (about a 1-hr., 35km/22-mile trip).** TRIP LENGTH **1 week.**

1 Athens. As soon as you set foot in central Athens, you will be met by astonishing views of the Acropolis. It's hard to resist the urge to climb to the world's most famous classical monument as soon as you see it, but we recommend that you start your day with breakfast on **Thissio Square** instead, followed by an exploration of the **Ancient Agora.** From both places you'll have fabulous views of the **Acropolis** before you make your way up there,

following the route detailed in The Best of Athens in 1 Day (p. 42). Spend your second day as recommended in the Best of Athens in 2 Days. ⏱ 2 days, 2 nights.

Your hotel or just about any travel agency in Athens can help you arrange a day trip to Delphi. The excursion usually begins with an early-morning pickup and ends with a mid-evening drop-off back in Athens.

2 Delphi. As you make your way to this hillside temple complex, you will be following in the footsteps of the ancients, who traveled from all over the Aegean world to visit the sanctuaries of Apollo and Athena and

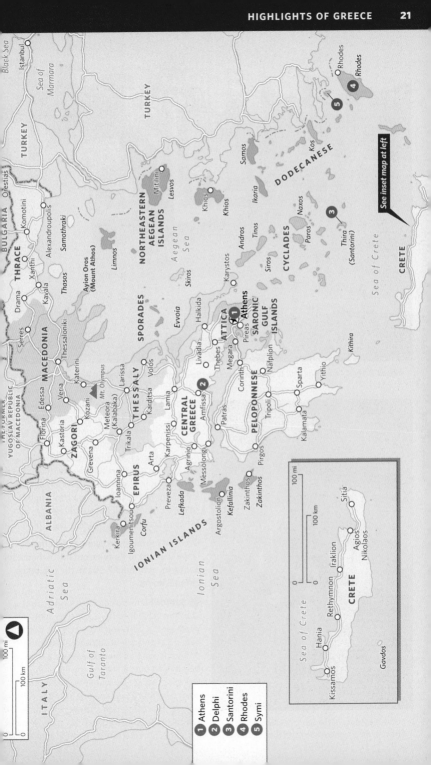

1 Athens
2 Delphi
3 Santorini
4 Rhodes
5 Symi

> *Athens' Roman Agora was built to accommodate overflow from the nearby Ancient Agora.*

> *Inside the Palace of the Grand Masters on the Street of the Knights in medieval Rhodes Town.*

to attend athletic contests held here every 4 years. They also famously sought advice from the oracle of Apollo, who spoke from deep within an inner chamber. The views are mesmerizing, encompassing the temples, gymnasium, stadium, and theater tucked into terraces on the herb-scented mountainsides. Return to Athens in time for a good night's sleep in order to catch the early boat to Santorini on Day 4. See p. 576. ⏱ 1 day.

On most mornings a couple of fast boats leave the port of Piraeus, outside Athens, for Santorini at around 7:30am; the trip takes about 5 hours.

❸ **Santorini.** If you catch a morning boat, you'll be in Santorini by early afternoon. As you near the port, you'll sail into the flooded caldera of an ancient volcano, a natural phenomenon that lends the island a unique beauty and puts it high on the list of the world's great scenic wonders. You will not want to venture too far away from the caldera on your first afternoon and evening on the island. For that matter, you can spend the next 2 nights immersed in this setting, in one of the

traditional island houses clinging to the side of the cliffs hundreds of feet above the sea; it will likely be among the most memorable places you'll ever stay. Spend part of the afternoon walking 10km (6¼ miles) along a cliff-top path from busy **Fira,** the island capital, to **Ia,** a village at the far southern end of the island. You'll also want to be near the edge of the caldera to witness the island's legendary sunsets.

On Day 5, tear yourself away from the caldera to explore the island's ancient past at **Akrotiri,** a remarkably well-preserved city settled 4,000 years ago, and **Ancient Thera,** on a headland high above the sea. You will also want to partake in some of Santorini's more hedonistic pleasures—lying on a lava beach or sipping the island's distinctive wine at one of the many vineyards. For more on Santorini, see p. 322. ⏱ 2 days.

4 Rhodes. A night boat or short flight delivers you to Rhodes, distinguished not by great natural beauty—though the verdant, mountainous island is certainly attractive—but by its remarkable medieval monuments. The Knights of St. John settled the island after the Crusades, in the 13th century, and the Old Town is little changed since they built the magnificent **Palace of the Grand Masters** and their many smaller palaces. The Turks, who eventually chased the knights off the island, left behind mosques and Ottoman houses, and the entire **Old Town** is surrounded by a vast circuit of walls. The island has other appealing spots as well, including a string of beautiful beaches and the ancient acropolis at Lindos, rising high above a beautiful medieval seaside town. For more on Rhodes, see p. 390. ⏱ 1 day, 2 nights.

5 Symi. On Day 7, make the short crossing to this small, ruggedly beautiful island with a town distinguished by 19th-century neoclassical mansions and a coastline etched with coves. Symi will introduce you to a side of Greek island life that is much quieter and more authentic than what you'll encounter on Santorini or Rhodes. Return to Rhodes in time for dinner and one last stroll through Old Town. For more on Symi, see p. 412. ⏱ 1 day.

From Rhodes you can easily fly back to Athens or directly to London and many other European cities.

> On Symi, waterside walks follow the coast from the port to secluded coves.

The Best of Greece in 2 Weeks

In 14 days, you can see Greece's two biggest cities, Athens and Thessaloniki, and one of its most beautiful, Nafplion. Other stops lead you in the footsteps of Philip II of Macedonia and Alexander the Great; into the realm of monks in Meteora and of the ancients at Delphi, Olympia, and Mycenae; and to the beautiful landscapes of Arcadia. For a sample of island life at its most scenic, you will visit Santorini and Hydra. You will need a car for sections of this route.

> The only way to get around Hydra is on foot or by donkey.

START Athens. TRIP LENGTH 2 weeks, 1,020km/634 miles overland (excluding two boat trips).

1 Athens. For the first 2 days, follow the Athens itineraries we recommend in The Best of Athens in 1 Day and 2 Days. See p. 42, 50. ⏱ 2 days.

2 Thessaloniki. On the morning of Day 3, fly or take the express train to Greece's second city, leaving the afternoon and evening to explore this ancient cultural crossroad.

Your focus in so short a visit should be the **Archaeological Museum** and the **Museum of Byzantine Culture,** the **Upper City,** with its many churches, and the harbor front. For a daylong itinerary, see p. 526, **1**. For an in-depth tour, see p. 548. ⏱ 1 day.

From Thessaloniki to Pella, head westbound on Egnatia St./Monastiriou St. through Konstantine Karamanlis Ave. to Rte. 2/E86 on the Thessaloniki-Edessa road till you reach Pella. 40km/25 miles, 40 min.

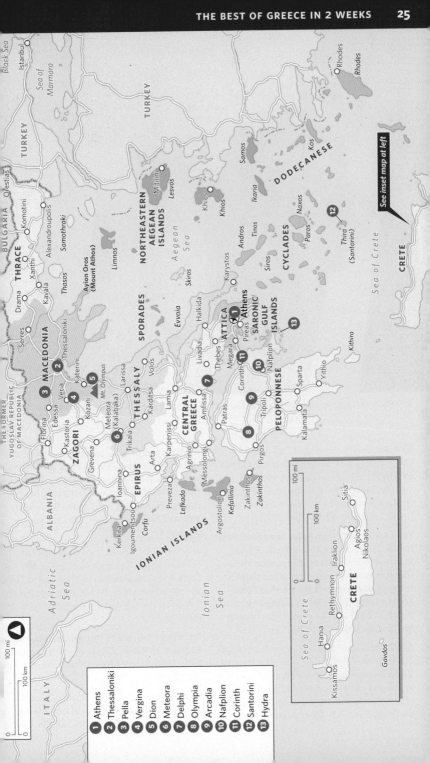

1 Athens
2 Thessaloniki
3 Pella
4 Vergina
5 Dion
6 Meteora
7 Delphi
8 Olympia
9 Arcadia
10 Nafplion
11 Corinth
12 Santorini
13 Hydra

> *Thessaloniki's Byzantine treasures include these rich mosaics in the Church of Agios Dimitrios.*

❸ Pella. On the morning of Day 4, pick up a car and make arrangements to leave it in Athens, because you won't be returning to Thessaloniki. Set out for Pella, the ancient capital of Macedonia and birthplace of Alexander the Great. See p. 530, ❶. ⏱ At least 1 hr.

To reach Vergina from Pella, head southeast to Rte. 2/E86 on the Thessaloniki-Edessa road and follow signs for the road to Veria (Beroia), turning southwest. Head south at the town of Alexandria for the road to the Egnatia Odos (E90). Take it southwest, turning off at Exit 14 at Rte. 4 southeast bound for Vergina. 63km/39 miles, 1 hr.

❹ Vergina. Don't miss the magnificent Royal Tomb of Macedonian King Philip II in Vergina. Visitors descend into the tomb itself for a look at Philip's solid gold casket and crown, among other treasures befitting the sire of Alexander the Great. See p. 531, ❷. ⏱ At least 1 hr.

From Vergina to Dion, backtrack onto Rte. 4 to the Egnatia Odos/E90/A2 and the national road (Rte. 1) south toward Athens. Then take the exit for Dion (or Diou), following the B-road signs, heading right on the Diou-Karitsas road 100km/62 miles, 1 hr. 10 min.

❺ Dion. Continue through Dion, where Philip and Alexander trained their armies on the flanks of Mount Olympus (see p. 532, ❸). Drive up the mountain to pay homage to Zeus and then continue to the Meteora region, settling in for the evening in Kalambaka. ⏱ At least 1 hr.

From Dion, follow E75 through Larissa, then E92 west to National Road 6, north to Kalambaka; total distance from Dion is about 90km (56 miles).

❻ Meteora. Even if Meteora's magnificent pinnacles were not topped with monasteries, the region would seem holy (p. 581, ❸). Giant

Inscribed temple columns suggest the sacred mysteries of Delphi.

sandstone formations, etched by the elements, rise from the plain. Monasteries cling precariously to the tops of these rocky spires, giving the Meteora its name (*meteoros* means "suspended in air"), and lending an almost mystical aura to one of the most fascinating corners of Greece. Spend Day 5 visiting the monasteries and exploring the surrounding countryside; then make the late afternoon drive to Delphi and spend the night there. ⏱1 day.

Drop down to Delphi on E92 and E65; total distance is about 200km (124 miles).

7 Delphi. On the morning of Day 6, you will visit the center of the world as decreed by Zeus (p. 576, **2**). Legend had it that the god released two eagles from Mount Olympus to locate the earth's center, and they met here on the slopes of craggy Mount Parnassus, above the Gulf of Corinth. Ancients revered the spot and established a sacred sanctuary on it. Delphi's famous oracle spoke from an inner chamber within the Temple of Apollo, uttering famously ambiguous prophecies: "Invade and you will destroy a great empire," she told Croesus, king of Lydia. Croesus followed her advice and declared war on the Persians and did indeed destroy an empire—his own. The sacred and mysterious surroundings at Delphi include the **Sanctuary of Apollo,** the **Castalian Spring,** the **Sanctuary of Athena,** and the **museum.** These will keep you busy well into the afternoon, when you should set out for Olympia. ⏱1 day.

The trip from Delphi to Olympia is 230km (143 miles) on E65 and E55, and passes through Patras.

> Hoodoos, the natural rock formations of the Meteora, are as magnificent as the monasteries that cap them.

> *Cliff-hanging towns teeter above the rim of a flooded volcano on Santorini.*

⑧ Olympia. Crossing the Rion Bridge, you will enter the Peloponnese, the huge peninsula that forms the southern mainland of Greece. Your first stop will be Olympia, the mountain town where the famous ancient games were inaugurated in 776 B.C. Spend 2 nights, so you have all of Day 7 to explore the site (p. 195, ⑮). The stadium, gymnasium, training hall, and dormitories at the foot of the Kronion Hill lie in fascinating ruin. Olympia is also a sacred place, originally founded as a sanctuary of Zeus. The magnificent *Hermes* of Praxiteles and other sculptures created to adorn these structures are on view in the Archaeological Museum. ⏱ 2 nights, 1 day.

From Olympia, follow well-marked mountain roads in the direction of Megalopolis to Andritsena, about 70km (43 miles) east of Olympia.

⑨ Arcadia. The drive on Day 8 will take you across the mountainous interior of the Peloponnese. Just east of Olympia, you will enter the mountainous province of Arcadia, a wild, forested terrain of craggy peaks and deep ravines, where medieval stone villages cling to the hillsides. **Andritsena** is a string of houses clinging to the steep mountainside high above the Alpheios River. On a remote mountaintop some 15km (9 miles) above Andritsena is one of the most spectacularly located ancient monuments in Greece, the **Temple of Apollo at Bassae. Karitena,** 30km (19 miles) southeast, is topped by a massive castle built by the Franks in the early 13th century. **Stemnitsa** and **Dimitsana** are other beautiful stone and tile-roofed mountain villages just north of Karitena. (For more details, see p. 206, Off the Beaten Path.) ⏱ 1 day.

Continue from Dimitsana on well-marked roads through Megalopolis and Tripoli, and from there, on National Rte. 7 to Nafplion. Nafplion is about 115km (71 miles) from Dimitsana.

⑩ Nafplion. Arrive on the evening of Day 8 in time for a walk out the Promenade to **Arvanitia,** the town beach, for a plunge into the waters of the Gulf of Argos. Not only is Nafplion the most beautiful city in Greece, but it is surrounded by some of the most fascinating remnants of the ancient world. Spend the morning of Day 9 getting to know the **Old Town,** where Venetian houses, neoclassical mansions, churches, and mosques line streets around the marble expanses of **Plateia Syntagma** (Constitution Sq.), and climb to the fortresses, the **Acronafplia** and the **Palamidi.** In the afternoon and on the following day, you will want to make short excursions across the

The streets of Nafplion are enchanting on a balmy summer night.

Argolid Plain to some of the classical sites that surround Nafplion. In the short time you have, set your sights on **Mycenae,** capital of the civilization that dominated much of the Mediterranean world from around 1500 to 1100 B.C. and whose stony ruins still evoke might and power. **Epidaurus,** one of the best-preserved classical Greek theaters in the world, is also a exquisite stop. See p. 214. ⊕ 2 nights, 1 day.

Corinth is 65km (40 miles) north of Nafplion on E65.

⓫ **Corinth.** After a final leisurely morning in Nafplion on Day 11, head north to Corinth. This ancient city once rivaled Athens in wealth, and the temples, agora, fountains, and other sprawling ruins of the Greek and Roman city, one of the mightiest in the ancient world, seem to sprawl forever. Above them is the Acrocorinth, the acropolis of the ancient city, a lookout post, place of refuge, and shrine surrounded by three rings of massive fortifications that ramble across the craggy mountaintop. Leave Corinth for Piraeus in time to catch a late afternoon or night boat to Santorini. See p. 184, ❶. ⊕ Half-day.

Athens (Piraeus) is 80km (50 miles) east of Corinth on E94.

⓬ **Santorini.** In Piraeus, board a late afternoon boat that will get you to Santorini shortly after midnight or a night boat for an early morning arrival on Day 12. Whichever one you take, be on deck as you approach the island to experience the beauty of a volcanic archipelago. The bay is the flooded caldera of a volcano, and towns and villages line the rim, white clusters practically teetering on the sides of the cliffs. Follow the itinerary in Best of the Cyclades in 5 Days (p. 300) to enjoy the island over the next two days. Your head will be spinning by the time you sail away. Time here includes getting an eyeful of the caldera and visiting two remarkable ancient sights, **Akrotiri** (p. 327, ❽), a beautifully preserved Minoan settlement from around 2000 B.C., and **Ancient Thera** (p. 328, ❾), an ancient city on a rocky headland. ⊕ 2 days.

Return to Piraeus from Santorini and make the trip out to Hydra.

⓭ **Hydra.** Once you've experienced island life, you'll probably want a bit more. So, after you dock again in Piraeus, board a boat for the short trip to Hydra. The beautiful harbor, surrounded by an amphitheater of stone and pastel mansions, is welcoming, and you'll soon discover the island has no motorized traffic. Donkeys clamber up the cobblestone streets, and footpaths follow the shoreline. The island is so idyllic that you will regret having only a day and evening to spend here. You may decide not to leave, or at least vow to return. See p. 156. ⊕ 1 day.

Exploring Ancient Greece

The Acropolis and National Archaeological Museum will prepare you for a journey into the world of the ancient Greeks, as their myths and many artistic accomplishments spring to life. You'll take in the wonders of Greece's 5th-century-B.C. Golden Age in Athens, encounter the oracle in Delphi and ancient athletes in Olympia, and travel 1,500 years back in time to the Minoan towns and palaces on Santorini and Crete. A car is necessary for parts of this itinerary.

> *The Odeon of Herod Atticus began hosting ancient dramas in A.D. 160 and continues to do so today.*

START Athens. **TRIP LENGTH** 710km/441 miles (excluding boat passages), 2 weeks.

❶ Athens. You will encounter classical Greece as soon as you set foot in central Athens and look up to the **Acropolis.** Spend 2 days exploring the ancient **Agora,** the **Herodes Atticus Theater,** and the capital's other classical sights, following the recommendations in the Best of Athens in 1 Day (p. 42) and 2 Days itineraries (p. 50). You will want to spend at least half a day in the **National Archaeological Museum,** where you'll come across art and artifacts from many of the sites you will be visiting on the rest of the tour. In the afternoon of Day 2, board a bus for the 2-hour trip to the **Temple of Poseidon at Sounion,** which is at its scenic best at sunset (p. 53, ❿). ⏱ 2 days.

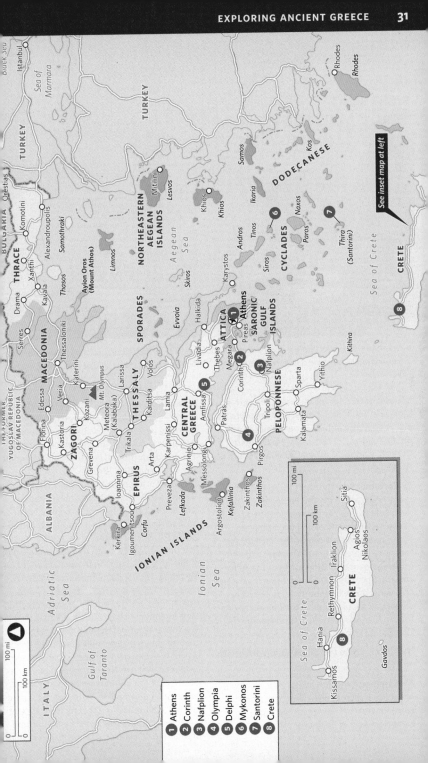

> *THIS PAGE The perfectly preserved Theater at Epidaurus still seats 55 rows of spectators for summertime performances of the classics. OPPOSITE PAGE Corinth was one of the wealthiest cities in the ancient world.*

You will need a car for the next part of this itinerary. You'll find it most convenient to pick it up at the airport, where you can get on the roadway network and zip down to Corinth. Corinth is 80km (50 miles) south of Athens on E94.

2 Corinth. Make the short trip south across the isthmus and enter the Peloponnese, the peninsula that forms the southern part of mainland Greece. Greeting you at the top of the Peloponnese is Corinth, the ancient city that once rivaled Athens in wealth, and its remarkable mountaintop fortress, the **Acrocorinth.** Spend half a day exploring the extensive ruins; then continue south to Nafplion, where you should settle in for 3 days, making trips to the many classical sights nearby (p. 184, **1**). ⏱ 1 day.

Nafplion is 65km (40 miles) south of Corinth on E65.

3 Nafplion. One of the most beautiful towns in Greece is also a convenient base from which to visit Tiryns, Argos, Mycenae, Ancient Nemea, and Epidaurus. The town beach,

Arvanitia, is a great place to cool off after a hot day amid dusty ruins. To explore the following ancient sites on the plains around Nafplion, follow the time recommendations and driving directions in the Ancient Wonder tour in chapter 5, p. 184.

Homer praised "mighty-walled **Tiryns,**" a Mycenaean hill fort that was the legendary birthplace of Hercules; you may have seen frescoes from the palace in the National Gallery in Athens. At **Argos,** once a powerful city that rivaled Sparta, scant remains include one of the largest theaters in the ancient world. **Mycenae** was capital of the short-lived Mycenaean civilization, and from the city that Homer links with power, riches, and tragedy, King Agamemnon launched the Trojan War. The Mycenaeans left behind many magnificent treasures that are now among the holdings of the National Archaeological Museum in Athens. Ancient **Nemea** was famous for its games, and a stadium remains largely intact, as well as the Temple to Zeus. The most magnificent, well-preserved theater from ancient Greece is at **Epidaurus,** where summertime dramas are still staged. ⏱ 3 nights in Nafplion.

> *Emperor Theodosius destroyed Delphi in the name of Christianity in 390, but columns and other ruins still stand.*

> *Elegant frescoes attest to the sophistication of the ancient Minoan civilization on Crete.*

The trip from Olympia to Delphi is 230km (143 miles) on E55 and E65, and passes through Patras.

5 **Delphi.** After a morning in Olympia, drive north to Rion and cross the beautiful Rion suspension bridge, which leaves you within a short drive east to Delphi. Settle in and enjoy an evening walk through the **Sanctuary of Apollo;** then spend the next morning in the ruins and excellent museum, where a bronze figure, *The Charioteer of Delphi,* commands pride of place among statuary and other treasures. Make the drive to Athens. If you've had your fill of classical sites, conclude your itinerary here. If not, continue to Mykonos by air or on a late-afternoon boat. ⏱ **2 days.**

From Delphi, the fastest route to Athens (Piraeus) is on National Roads 48 and 3 to E75; Athens is 190km (118 miles) southeast of Delphi. Whether you are flying or taking a boat to Mykonos, you will find it most convenient to return your rental car to the airport. From there you can take a bus to Piraeus or, better, to nearby Rafina to get a boat from there.

Andritsena is 145km (90 miles) west of Naf-plion; the route will take you first to Tripoli, and from there on well-marked mountain roads through Megalopolis to Andritsena. Olympia is another 70km (43 miles) west of Andritsena.

4 **Olympia.** Spend the day crossing the mountains of Arcadia to Olympia, home to the famous games and acclaimed for its sacred sanctuary to Zeus and Hera as well. On the way, stop outside the village Andritsena and the **Temple of Apollo at Bassae.** One of the most beautiful and best-preserved temples in Greece, dedicated to Apollo Epikourios, it stands in splendid isolation atop an Arcadian mountain. Arrive in Olympia in time for a walk through the pine-scented ruins; then return to the site in the morning to continue your explorations and to visit the museum, where *Hermes Carrying the Infant Dionysus,* by the great sculptor Praxiteles, is on display. ⏱ **2 days.**

6 **Mykonos.** Don't let the island's free-living ways tempt you: You're here to see ruins, remember? So set off in the morning by boat to Delos, one of the most important archaeological sites in the Aegean. Delos was one of ancient Greece's most sacred religious sanctuaries, a flourishing center of trade, and headquarters of the Delian League, the confederation of Greek city-states. You'll have the late afternoon for a swim on one of Mykonos's famous beaches, and the evening to stroll through Hora. ⏱ 1 day.

7 Santorini. Take a morning boat to Greece's most scenic island. The flooded caldera of an ancient volcano steals the show on Santorini, but the island was also home to the ancient civilizations that left behind the cities of Ancient Thera and Akrotiri. Follow the itinerary in Best of the Cyclades in 5 Days (p. 300) to make the most of the next 2 days, paying special attention to the two archaeological sites and museums. **Akrotiri** is the so-called Minoan Pompeii, settled by Minoans who sailed over from Crete as early as 3000 B.C. and buried deep in ash during the eruption of 1600 B.C. The more than 40 stores, warehouses, and houses that line Akrotiri's main street are remarkably well preserved. Magnificent frescoes are in the National Archaeological Museum in Athens, but you can see stunning reproductions of them at the **Thera Foundation** in **Fira.** Ancient Thera,

> *Knossos was the largest and most elaborate Minoan palace.*

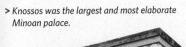

set atop a rocky headland at the north of the island, was settled in the 9th century B.C. Since then, Egyptian palaces, Greek temples, Roman baths, and Byzantine walls have risen atop the seaside cliffs. Enjoy a swim from Kameri, a dramatic swath of silky black sand below the promontory. ⏱ 2 days.

8 Crete. A morning boat will take you south to Iraklion, Crete, in an hour or so. You will spend most of the day here exploring the sophisticated accomplishments of this vanished civilization, showing just how advanced these peaceable people were. Spend the morning in the **Archaeological Museum** (p. 240, **1**), where frescoes of court ladies, ivory figures, vessels in the shape of a bull's head, and beautifully crafted jewelry bring the gifted artistry of the Minoans to light. Spend the afternoon at nearby **Knossos,** the largest of the Minoan palace complexes and one of the most captivating archaeological sites in the world. On the following day, cross the island to **Phaestos** (p. 244, **4**), the second-most important Minoan palace, another vast complex of royal apartments, ceremonial spaces, and storehouses atop a hill looking out across the Messara Plain toward the Libyan Sea. The Phaestos Disk, found here during excavations a century ago and now in the Archaeological Museum in **Iraklion,** is covered with yet-to-be-deciphered symbols, presenting one of the great unsolved mysteries of archaeology. Spend the rest of the day relaxing on one of the beaches around **Matala,** a low-key retreat famous for its seaside cliffs etched with caves (p. 255, **13**). ⏱ 2 days.

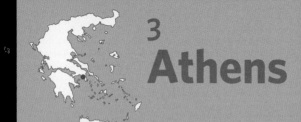

3
Athens

Favorite Moments in Athens

With its sidewalk cafes, Athenian Riviera beaches, neighborhood tavernas, and anarchic atmosphere, Athens is ideal for youth. But all ages take part in the city's outdoor lifestyle, and the generations aren't only civil to one another, they're outright affectionate. Wander the streets and you'll stumble across remarkable remnants of the past; visit one of the city's numerous museums; shop for handcrafted jewelry, linens, or pottery sold by expert clerks in specialist shops; or stroll up a centrally located hill to see the famed Attic sky and gaze out to sea, past the ancient port city of Piraeus.

> PREVIOUS PAGE Few sights are more romantic than the moonlit Parthenon. THIS PAGE The Odeon of Herod Atticus is one of the city's many outdoor theaters.

1 Gazing at the Acropolis. There is no comparison anywhere to the wonder that is the Acropolis, topped by the Parthenon—Greece's pride and joy since antiquity. Ancient Greeks were as distracted by its beauty as we are today. Eyes are drawn to it, streets lead to it, and thankfully, given its location, it's easy to catch a glimpse of it from just about anywhere. It's absolutely spectacular at night. See p. 44, 4.

2 Experiencing an outdoor theater. You could visit a neighborhood **open-air cinema** to see a first-run movie, complete with a glass of wine at intermission, in a breezy garden on a warm evening. For live action, head to the Athens Epidaurus Festival in summer for an **ancient theater** performance of The Winter's Tale or a play by Euripides. See p. 125, p. 669.

3 Strolling along the pedestrian walkway around the Acropolis. With its breathtaking views, it's a peak experience even for Athens residents—especially if you stop en route at a cafe to savor the spectacle along with a drink or a snack. See p. 42, 3.

4 Browsing the neighborhood farmer's market. Known as *laiki*, these markets are set up once a week all over Athens—each neighborhood on a different day. You can buy fresh fruits and veggies, fish, kitchenware, flowers, and even carpets. See p. 54, **1**.

5 Looking out from Pnyx. Amid all the concrete in Athens, you'll welcome the natural setting of this historic hill where the world's first democratic assembly convened. It's worth a visit if only for the views of the Parthenon, sea, and sunset. See p. 42, **3**.

6 Sipping coffee at Thissio Square. Sitting here with friends or family at an outdoor cafe is relaxing, especially for parents. (Kids can play without fear of traffic.) This is where you get that million-dollar view of the Acropolis and Lycabettus Hill. See p. 42, **1**.

7 Spotting a find at the Gazi flea market. The Monastiraki flea market has the more upscale estate contents, but the market that starts from opposite the ancient Kerameikos Cemetery on Sunday is the real deal. See p. 101.

8 Taking in Monastiraki's Adrianou Street. There are two Adrianou streets, and this one is great for sitting at an outdoor cafe and people-watching. The view of the Acropolis and the Thisseion Temple in the Ancient Agora across the Metro line won't hurt your eyes either. See p. 87, **8**.

9 Experiencing Psyrri by night. Quality of life in Athens is directly related to the fact that you can set out on foot at any hour and not worry about personal safety. The Psyrri district is full of bars, clubs, and restaurants, and the atmosphere rightly feels like a carnival. This is life as it should be. See p. 91, **8**.

10 Wandering the mom and pop hardware and supply shops off Athinas Street. Athens is hearteningly full of independent businesses, with many conveniently grouped by what they sell. (Looking for kitchenware? Go to Vissis St.) Many of these shop-filled lanes lie off Athinas Street, a main artery. See p. 91, **9**.

11 Finding a cultural gem. There are so many museums and galleries in Athens that you could see something new and interesting every Sunday afternoon. State museums are free

> *Brimming with souvenirs and shoppers, the Plaka is tacky, exhilarating and quintessentially Athenian.*

in winter—a great public gesture. Finding one in a charming neighborhood followed by a coffee makes for a red-letter day. See p. 58.

12 Shopping for shoes on Ermou. There are so many shoe stores on the pedestrian **Ermou Street** that finding the perfect pair is practically a sport. They're all well priced, so you can comparison-shop for the high-quality leather shoes that suit you best. See p. 86, **3**.

13 Admiring the souvenirs on Adrianou Street. Items fashioned in olive wood and handmade pottery are as popular now as they were in antiquity, when they were coveted by the Romans. These and other local wares are sold on this heavily touristed street in Plaka. See p. 90, **4**.

14 Eating souvlaki on "Kebab Street." The bottom of **Mitropoleos Street,** at the Monastiraki Metro station, is lined with tables from grill tavernas, so you can sit down in the middle of your shopping and have a souvlaki meal or skewers and a beer. See p. 56, **6**.

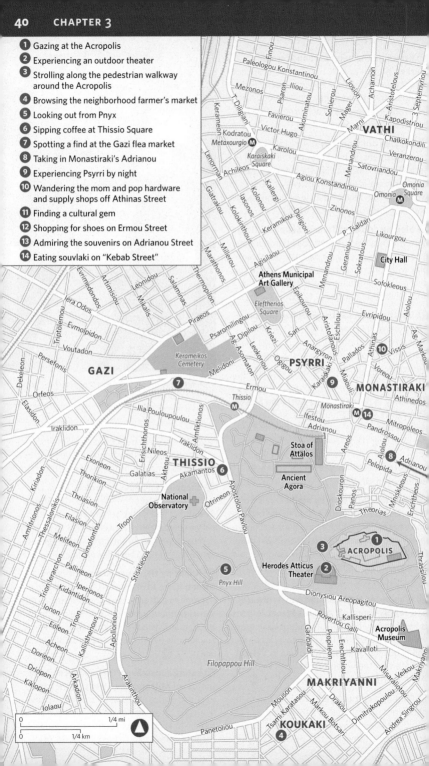

1. Gazing at the Acropolis
2. Experiencing an outdoor theater
3. Strolling along the pedestrian walkway around the Acropolis
4. Browsing the neighborhood farmer's market
5. Looking out from Pnyx
6. Sipping coffee at Thissio Square
7. Spotting a find at the Gazi flea market
8. Taking in Monastiraki's Adrianou
9. Experiencing Psyrri by night
10. Wandering the mom and pop hardware and supply shops off Athinas Street
11. Finding a cultural gem
12. Shopping for shoes on Ermou Street
13. Admiring the souvenirs on Adrianou Street
14. Eating souvlaki on "Kebab Street"

The Best of Athens in 1 Day

If you've got only a day in town, wear comfortable shoes, pack a camera, fill your water bottle, and get moving. In this ambitious itinerary, you will focus on the greatest of all Greek monuments, the Acropolis; the surrounding antiquities and museum; and the National Archaeological Museum, which houses stunning Mycenaean antiquities, Cycladic sculptures, and Minoan frescoes. It should make for a full but rewarding day.

> For 2,400 years, a climb to the Acropolis has proven to be a peak experience for visitors.

START Metro to Thissio.

① 🍽 ★★★ **Thissio Square.** Stop at this square near the Metro for your morning coffee and a "toast" (a grilled cheese or grilled ham-and-cheese sandwich). Try for a table at **Athinaion Politeia** (33 Apostolou Pavlou and 1 Akamantos sts.; ☎ 210/341-3795), far into the square toward the Ancient Agora at the back (east), and behold the spectacle of both the Acropolis and Lycabettus Hill. Apostolou Pavlou and Iraklidon sts.

SITE GUIDE PAGE 45

② ★ kids **Ancient Agora.** Once the center of commercial life in ancient Athens—with temples, gymnasiums, odeons, markets, and council houses where the *vouli* (parliament) legislated for the world's first democracy—the Agora is now a collection of broken columns strewn among crumbling foundations interspersed with olive, pink oleander, cypress, and palm trees.

③ ★★★ **Acropolis Walkway.** The stroll along this cobblestone walkway connecting the

1 Thissio Square
2 Ancient Agora
3 Acropolis Walkway
4 Acropolis
5 Acropolis Museum
6 Hadrian's Arch
7 Plaka
8 National Archaeological Museum
9 Exarchia Square

> *The new Acropolis Museum is a stunning showcase for some of Greece's greatest treasures.*

ancient sites in the historic center is grand, alive with street sellers and buskers. Quieter spots and nooks are popular with courting couples, who sit along the low walls that line the route. Meander past or even through the pine, olive, and cypress groves, and take in the views of the Acropolis, Lycabettus Hill, the Observatory on Pnyx Hill, and the Filopappou Monument atop Filopappou Hill on your way to the Acropolis. **Apostolou Pavlou/Dionysiou Areopagitou sts.**

SITE GUIDE PAGE 47

④ ★★★ kids **Acropolis.** The beloved, 2,400-year-old temple to the city's patron saint, Athena, is an architectural masterpiece. It was intact until 1687, when the Venetians tried to dislodge the long-ruling Turks. A major controversy revolves around the friezes that originally decorated the Parthenon. At the nadir of the scramble to amass antiquities while Greece was under occupation in the early

19th century, Britain's Lord Elgin, who had permission only to draw the pediment sculptures, hastily chiseled them off instead. They are now displayed in the British Museum as Greece continues to claim that, as part of the national symbol, they should be returned. The Acropolis Museum was built to house them. It now displays copies.

⑤ ★★ kids **Acropolis Museum.** The new museum, opened in 2009, faces the Acropolis on Dionysiou Areopagitou Street. Some 300 marble statues weighing up to 2.5 tons each were moved off the hill for the first time in 2006 and 2007. Four of the original six caryatids (sculptures of women taking the place of columns or architectural supports) from the Erechtheion (p. 153) have been moved here (one had disappeared during Ottoman rule; another is in the British Museum). The collection from the old museum includes sculptures from the Parthenon burnt by the Persians, statues of *kourai* (maidens) dedicated to

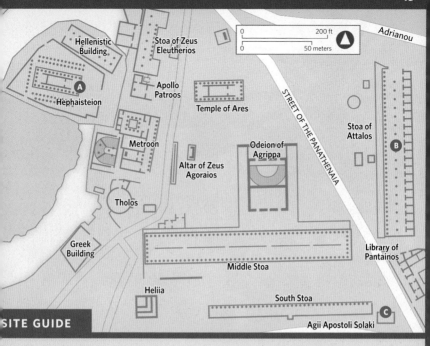

2 Ancient Agora

Communal life in early Athens revolved around the Ancient Agora, although you'd be hard-pressed to reconstruct the layout of this market from the mind's eye. The **A Thisseion** (more properly Hephaisteion, but not referred to as that) dates from 449 B.C. and is one of the world's best-preserved Greek temples, owing to protection from the Greek Orthodox Church, which used it as a house of worship from the 7th century to 1834. The 1950s **B Stoa of Attalos** is a reconstruction of the 2nd-century-B.C. version, where businesses set up shop, philosophers debated, and people just hung out. The Stoa museum contains fascinating artifacts that show how the ancients carried out early democratic processes. Jurors voted by ballot: They cast a bronze disk with a solid axle if they believed the defendant was innocent, and cast a hollow one if they believed the story rang hollow. A marble *kleroterion*, an early version of the lotto machine, was used to select citizens for jury duty. The **C Agii Apostoli Solaki** medieval church is the only other structure intact on the site, built in the 11th century. Everything else was

demolished by either the invading Herulians in A.D. 267 or the private housing put up during the Roman and Byzantine eras. The area was still residential through the 1950s, when it was razed again—to dig for archaeological remnants of the original Agora. ⏲ 1 hr. Entrances on Adrianou St. and Agiou Filippou, Monastiraki; west end of Polygnotou St., Plaka; and Thissio Sq., Thissio. ☎ 210/321-0185. www.culture.gr. Site and museum 4€ adults. May–Oct daily 8am–7pm, Nov–Apr daily 8:30am–3pm. Closed Jan 1, Mar 25, Orthodox Easter Sun, May 1 and Dec 25-26. Metro: Monastiraki or Thissio.

> *The absence of car traffic and the classic view make Plaka a rewarding place for lunch.*

Athena, figures of *kouroi* (young men), and many other finds from the Acropolis; there are some 4,000 works altogether in the new museum—10 times the number previously on display. The view from the top floor is stunning, and the display for the anticipated return of the Elgin marbles is poignant (p. 44, ④). ⏰ At least 1 hr. 15 Dionysiou Areopagitou St. ☎ 210/900-0900. www.theacropolismuseum.gr. Admission 5€. Year-round Tues–Sun 8am–8pm. Closed Jan 1, Mar 25, Orthodox Easter Sun, May 1, Dec 25–26. Metro: Akropoli.

⑥ Hadrian's Arch. Facing Plaka and the Acropolis is Hadrian's triumphal arch, on a main Athens thoroughfare (Amalias Ave.). This gate from the "old" city of Athens to the "new" Roman one is made of Pentelic marble (from nearby Mount Pendeli) with Corinthian capitals, built in A.D. 131 in honor of Emperor Hadrian. It bears two inscriptions: facing west (toward the old town), THIS IS ATHENS, ONCE THE CITY OF THESEUS; and facing east (toward the new town), THIS IS HADRIAN'S, AND NOT THESEUS'S CITY. Amalias Ave. and Dionysiou Areopagitou St.

⑦ 🎭 ★★★ kids Plaka. Stop for lunch in this old quarter, most of which is now a pedestrian zone; the food is nothing special but the atmosphere makes up for it. Shop for some souvenirs, too, along Adrianou (Hadrian's) and Pandrossou streets, before or after wandering through the island-village-like alleys of Anafiotika, an area within Plaka. Adrianou and Kydathineon sts.

You will probably want to take the Metro (to Victoria Station) or trolley to the museum, but the walk through Omonia introduces you to the bustle of downtown Athens.

SITE GUIDE
PAGE 49

⑧ ★★★ National Archaeological Museum. Most recently renovated in 2004 following damage from a 1999 earthquake and in anticipation of the Olympic Games, this handsome 1880 neoclassical building houses some of the most significant archaeological remains of ancient Greece. It has had many alterations and will undergo more, but the facade is courtesy of

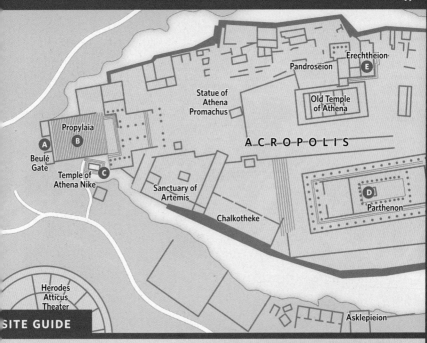

Propylaia

Statue of Athena Promachus

Pandroseion

Erechtheion **E**

Old Temple of Athena

A **B**

Beulé Gate

Temple of Athena Nike **C**

Sanctuary of Artemis

A C R O P O L I S

D

Parthenon

Chalkotheke

Herodes Atticus Theater

Asklepieion

SITE GUIDE

4 Acropolis

After the ticket entrance, you first pass through the **A** **Beulé Gate**—built by the Romans in A.D. 267 but known by the name of the French archaeologist who discovered it in 1852. Beyond lies the **B** **Propylaia,** the monumental 5th-century-B.C. entranceway. The little **C** **Temple of Athena Nike** (Athena Victory), a beautifully proportioned Ionic temple built in 424 B.C., where citizens prayed for success, is perched above the Propylaia. It was restored in the 1930s and has been rebuilt once more. Off to the left of the **D** **Parthenon,** the Temple of Athena, is the **E** **Erechtheion,** which the Athenians honored as the tomb of Erechtheus, a legendary king. ⏱ 1 hr. Dionysiou Areopagitou St. ☎ 210/321-0219. www.culture.gr. Coupon booklet 12€ adults (many categories, including archaeology students, are admitted free; ask or check website for free-admission days) valid for 4 days; includes the Acropolis, Ancient Agora, Theater of Dionysos, Kerameikos Cemetery, Roman Forum/Hadrian's Library, and the Temple of Olympian Zeus. Elevator for the disabled. Year-round daily 8am–4:30pm, closes 1–3 hr. later in summer. Metro: Akropoli or bus no. 230.

> *Adrianou and many other streets in Plaka are pedestrian-only.*

> *The student quarter of Exarchia has long inspired revolutionary zeal and exuberant graffiti.*

Ernst Ziller. The museum is divided into sections—the Prehistoric Collection; the Santorini findings; sculptures, vases, and minor objects; metallurgy; the Stathatos Collection; the Vlastos Collection; Egyptian art; and Near Eastern antiquities. Artifacts range from the Neolithic period (8500–5500 B.C.) to the 1st century B.C. Highlights include Trojan pieces excavated by German treasure-hunter Heinrich Schliemann, Mycenaean gold work (also uncovered by Schliemann), and Cycladic sculptures.

9 Exarchia Square. You'll probably want to head back to your hotel to collapse, but if you still have energy, walk to the nearby student zone Exarchia, just south of the museum. This area's proximity to the Polytechnic and its anarchic reputation make it a magnet for artists (both fine and graffiti), intellectuals, and students, who frequent the cafe-bars around the square. Also check out the interesting Boho shops, especially on Themistokleous, Emmanouil Benaki, and Zoodochou Pigis streets. **Stournari and Themistokleous sts.**

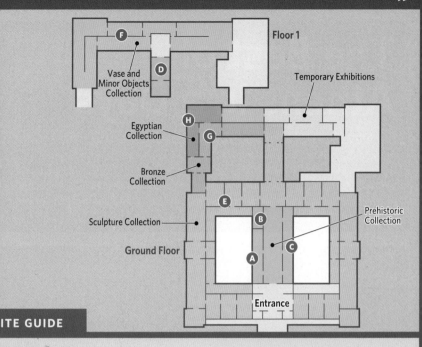

Floor 1

Vase and Minor Objects Collection

Temporary Exhibitions

Egyptian Collection

Bronze Collection

Sculpture Collection

Ground Floor

Prehistoric Collection

Entrance

ITE GUIDE

8 National Archaeological Museum

he museum's **A** **Neolithic Collection** houses eramic pottery and figurines that date from 800 B.C. Grouped with the Neolithic is the **B** **Mycenaean Collection,** highlighted by the olden "Mask of Agamemnon." Uncovered in a rave at Mycenae, this royal funeral mask was iitially thought to be for Agamemnon, the king who led the Greeks to battle in Troy, but it may ctually predate him. Follow this collection to he razor-planed marble figurines of the **C** **Cy-adic Collection.** Amazingly, these modern-ooking, milky-white statues were carved some ,000 to 5,000 years ago. The **D** **Thera Col-ection** of circa-1700-B.C. frescoes from Akrotiri n the isle of Santorini, preserved following a olcanic eruption, emphasizes that settlement's nks to Minoan Crete. For an island town, Ak-otiri—Greece's much older "Pompeii"—had a ide network of external relations. The large **E** **Sculpture Collection** shows the progression om the wooden Egyptian to the fluid classical, he angular to the anatomically correct. Also pstairs, represented in the **F** **Vase and Minor bjects Collection,** is the famed red-figure and lack-figure Attic pottery. Exquisite jewelry and

silver are also found here. The **G** **Metals Collection** contains the bronze *Horse and Jockey* and *Poseidon* (or *Zeus*) *of Artemision* statues, from the 2nd century B.C. There is also a Virgin Mary look-alike, *The Lady of Kalymnos.* Finally, the **H** **Egyptian Collection** covers that civilization from 5000 B.C. up to the Roman conquest. ⏱ 2 hr. 44 Patission St. (signposted 28th Oktovriou) ☎ 210/821-7717. Admission 7€ adults, 18 & under free, discounts for students and seniors. Apr–Oct Mon 1:30–8pm, Tues–Sun and holidays 8:30am–8pm; Nov–Mar Mon 1:30–8pm, Tues–Sun 8:30–3pm. Metro: Victoria or trolley no. 2, 3, 4, 5, 6, 7, 8, 9, 11, 13, or 15.

The Best of Athens in 2 Days

On Day 2, devote the morning and early afternoon to seeing more of the central city, this time at a slightly more leisurely pace. Begin with a bird's eye view from the top of Lycabettus Hill and then descend through the pleasant Kolonaki neighborhood to visit more of the antiquities and other sights of central Athens. In the late afternoon, make the trip out to Sounion to view the sunset from the Temple of Poseidon.

> *The highest point in Athens, Lycabettus Hill rises above the Kolonaki quarter.*

START Walk along Didotou or Skoufa streets into Kolonaki, or take bus 22, 60, or 200 to the Teleferik (cable car).

1 ★ kids **Lycabettus Hill.** Board the cog railway, and head up for a look at the city view from the highest hill in town. See p. 66, ⑨.

② ☕ ★ **Kolonaki Square.** This posh area of central Athens is the definition of Athenian cafe society, where the restaurants facing the square don't seem to have changed since the 1960s, where the movers and shakers live, where beautiful people have to be seen, and where the arty

items in basement shops look as if they're on display more to indulge the proprietors than to actually sell. If you want to be seen as well, **DaCapo** is a good spot, with fine coffees, snacks, and cocktails. 1 Tsakalof St. 210/360-2497. $.

3 ★★ **Benaki Museum.** Housed in the mansion of one of Athens's most prominent families, this excellent private museum contains artifacts from the Neolithic era to the 20th century. The folk-art collection (including costumes and icons) is superb, as are two rooms decorated in the style of 18th-century

1. Lycabettus Hill
2. Kolonaki Square
3. Benaki Museum
4. Syntagma Station
5. Changing of the Guard, Syntagma Square
6. National Gardens
7. Zappeion Gardens
8. Temple of Olympian Zeus
9. Panathenian Stadium
10. The Temple of Poseidon

northern Greek mansions, with ancient bronzes, gold cups, Fayum portraits, and rare early-Christian textiles. A new wing has doubled the exhibition space of the early-20th-century neoclassical house. The Benaki's massive collection of Islamic art is housed in a museum near the Thissio Metro station, and large exhibitions are held at its annex at 138 Piraeos Street (bus no. 049), which also has a gift-bookshop and cafe. ⏰ At least 1 hr. Koumbari st. and Vas. Sofias Ave. ☎ 210/367-1000. www.benaki.gr. Admission 6€ adults, 3€ seniors, free on Thurs and for children 17 & under; see website for other discounts. Mon, Wed, Fri–Sat 9am–5pm; Thurs 9am–midnight; Sun 9am–3pm; closed Tues and holidays. Metro: Syntagma.

④ ★ kids **Syntagma Station.** This station and nearby fenced-in open-air sites display archaeological finds from Metro excavations. Exhibitions include well-preserved Roman baths, with sections dating from the 5th and 3rd centuries A.D. ⏰ 10 min. Vas. Georgiou, Othonos and Filellinon sts., and Amalias Ave.

⑤ ★★ kids **Changing of the Guard.** The Presidential Guard keeps watch over the Tomb of the Unknown Soldier, and two soldiers engage in ceremonial exercises on the hour. See p. 64, ②.

> *Soaring columns still pay homage to the supreme god at the Temple of Zeus.*

⑥ 🔊 kids **National Gardens.** The 16 hectares (40 acres) of crisscrossing paths, quiet little dead ends, a fenced playground, and ponds among giant trees in the former Royal Gardens behind Parliament (once the palace) in the city center are a great place to escape the concrete jungle that surrounds it. Some 7,000 trees and 40,000 plants from Greece and abroad have taken root here since the mid-1800s, when Queen Amalia brought over a Bavarian gardener to redesign her backyard. It was nationalized in 1923. Stop at the **cafe**, 4 Irodou Attikou Street (☎ 210/723-2820), for refreshment. ⏱ 20 min. Syntagma Sq.; entrances from Zappeion Gardens, Amalias Ave., Vas. Sofias, or Irodou Attikou sts. Year-round daily 8am–sunset.

⑦ **Zappeion Gardens.** Adjacent to the National Gardens is the 14-hectare (35-acre) Zappeion, bequeathed in the 1880s by philanthropist Evangelias Zappas to kick-start the Olympic movement. Still resembling Henry Miller's description of it as the "quintessence of park," it contains a small but important exhibition hall, a cafe-restaurant, and Aigli, Athens's oldest open-air movie theater. You can still picture parasol-twirling women and children in sailor suits on the broad, tree-lined promenade, and the regular contingent of pensioners debating politics and playing tavli (backgammon). ⏱ 20 min. Entrances from the National Gardens, Amalias Ave., Vas. Olgas, or Vas. Konstantinou sts.

⑧ **Temple of Olympian Zeus.** Construction on this giant temple to the top god began with the tyrant Peisistratos in the mid-500s B.C., and then stopped and started a few times during its 650-year building schedule as commissioners came and went. The stockpiled building materials were used elsewhere (in the Themistoclean Wall and the Capitoline Temple in Rome, for example). Hadrian finally completed the 4,785 sq.-m (51,500-sq.-ft.) temple and installed inside a statue of himself and a replica of one of the Seven Wonders of the Ancient World, Phidias's statue of Zeus. The temple is located at an ancient outdoor

The National Gardens are a welcome retreat from the noise and haste of modern Athens.

nctuary dedicated to Zeus, and the columns one tower at 17m (56 ft.) high. ⏱ 45 min. 1 as. Olgas St. and Amalias Ave. ☎ 210/922-330. www.culture.gr. Admission 2€ or part of cropolis ticket. Daily Apr–Oct 8am–8pm, Nov–b 8:30am–3pm. Metro: Syntagma or Acropoli.

Panathenian Stadium. Also called the Kali-armaro (Beautiful Marble) and Panathinaiko adium, this track was reconstructed in marble Herodes Atticus in A.D. 143, after the original a. 330 B.C.), where the Panathenian Games ok place every 4 years. It was again rebuilt for e first modern Olympics in 1896 by benefac- George Averoff, and today it's the venue for ajor events, including the finish line for the riginal) long-distance run that begins in Mara-on. It measures 1 stade (an ancient Greek easurement equal to 180m/600 ft.), hence e word stadium, and it originally held 50,000 ople—like the Roman Coliseum. For the 004 **Olympic Stadium,** 37 Kifissias Avenue : 210/683-4060; www.oaka.com.gr), with e roof designed by Santiago Calatrava, head the Irini Metro station. For a guided tour (for oups of more than 15 people, 3€ per person) x requests to 210/683-4021. ⏱ 10 min. Vas. nstantinou and Irodou Atikou sts. ☎ 210/ 2-2985-6. www.hoc.gr. Admission 3€, 1.50€ idents, free under 7. Open daily Mar–Oct 8am–m, Nov–Feb 8am–5pm.

union is 70km (42 miles) south of Athens; u can take an organized tour or easily reach e temple by bus (see below).

⑩ ★ The Temple of Poseidon. If time allows, consider a trip to the Temple of Poseidon at Cape Sounion, a promontory at the south-ern tip of the Attica Peninsula and one-time lookout point for guarding the Saronic Gulf. It's high up on most tourists' lists, so it'll be crowded in late afternoon or early evening for the sunset, but the views of the temple, hills, and sea are spectacular. Six-meter (20-ft.) columns are all that remain of the majestic 5th-century-B.C. temple where mythical King Aegeus waited for his son, Theseus, to return from slaying the Cretan Minotaur. A white sail on Theseus's ship meant he lived; a black one meant he had died. Theseus forgot to change the sail on his return journey, and the king jumped from the cliff in sorrow (the Ae-gean Sea was named for him). You can take an organized tour (p. 673) for about 40€, or see it on your own. The bus terminus is near the Archaeological Museum and stops close to the temple (*Nao*) in Sounion. ⏱ 5 hr. ☎ 229/203-9363. Admission 4€. Year-round daily 9:30am–sunset, Orthodox Easter Sat and Mon 8:30am–3pm. Closed Jan 1, Mar 25, May 1, Orthodox Easter Sun, Dec 25–26. Bus: 2 hr. (69km/43 miles). KTEL Attikis bus terminus: Patission St. at Aigyptou Sq. ☎ 210/880-8080. www.ktelattikis.gr. Tickets 5.70€. Buses leave Athens hourly 6:40am–5:30pm and depart Sounion from 8am–7pm.

The Best of Athens in 3 Days

Day 3 begins at Athens's main farmers' market, on bustling Athinas Street. Gawk at all the produce and seafood and pick up some dried fruit or nuts to tide you over until mealtime. Then head back into the historic center, setting your sights on Monastiraki, Psyrri, and Thissio. The quarter is compact and easy to orient yourself in, as the Acropolis is visible from just about anywhere. Join the rest of Greece by taking an afternoon rest, and then head back out to experience the lively streets and squares by night.

> Athenians stock up on fresh fish and other staples at Central Market.

START Metro to Omonia.

1 ★★ Central Market. Farmers' markets set up in neighborhoods around town (on Fri on Xenokratous St. in Kolonaki, and Zacharitsa or Matrozou sts. in Koukaki), but the main meat, fish, and vegetable market of Athens is here 6 days a week on Athinas Street near Omonia Square. Fresh cheeses, dried nuts, and herbs are also plentiful here. It opens at 6am, so we recommend starting your day here. See p. 101.

2 ★★★ Psyrri. Psyrri, where bars and restaurants are crammed on narrow pedestrian streets, is the liveliest of the central districts of Athens. You will want to return in the evening, when the neighborhood is positively hopping and you can sit outside and watch Athenians coming and going to and from their favorite night haunt.

1 Central Market
2 Psyrri
3 Iraklidon Street
4 Kerameikos Cemetery
5 Ermou Street
6 Thanasis
7 Tower of the Winds
8 Dioskouri
9 Dora Stratou Theater
10 Thission Open-Air Cinema
11 Technopolis

> *Trendy Psyrri is bustling with night spots, boho shops, and street vendors peddling jewelry and other wares.*

❸ Iraklidon Street. From Psyrri, walk to Iraklidon Street in Thissio (walk across Ermou St. and up the cobblestone walkway past the Thissio Metro station to Thissio Sq., and down Iraklidon), which is abuzz with outdoor cafe-bars. If it's winter, get cozy under a gas heater, and in summer cool off under mist machines and fans. Drinks are expensive, but you can sip (and sit) for hours. **Iraklidon and Apostolou Pavlou sts.**

❹ Kerameikos Cemetery. If you have time, continue down Athinas Street to Ermou Street, and take Ermou west to this site, which includes the Sacred Gate and the ancient Kerameikos Cemetery, funerary avenues of graves and monuments of famous ancient Athenians. (Pericles delivered his funeral oration for the soldiers of the Peloponnesian War here in 431 B.C. In reference to Athens's constitution, he said, "We are rather a pattern to others than

imitators ourselves.") The on-site museum houses organized exhibits with interesting finds, mainly related to burial customs, such as urns and monuments. **See p. 87, ⓫** .

❺ ★★★ Ermou Street. You can't leave Greece without buying a pair of stylish leather shoes, or at least the iconic sandals. Pedestrianized Ermou (Hermes) Street has always been one of Athens's busiest, and all the main chain stores are here, alongside Greek shoemakers. The street goes from Parliament all the way down (west) past the Monastiraki and Thissio Metro stations to the ancient Kerameikos Cemetery and old-gasworks-turned-cultural-center Technopolis in Gazi. **Ermou and Athinas sts.**

⑥ 🍢 Thanasis. One of three or four grills, or *psistaries,* at the end of the pedestrian section of Mitropoleos Street (aka "Kebab St."), Thanasis spills out into Monastiraki Square, selling minced-meat souvlaki in a pita to go for 2.20€. Or eat at an outdoor table amid the throngs at this bustling corner of Plaka and Monastiraki. **69 Mitropoleos St. ☎ 210/324-4705. $.**

❼ Tower of the Winds. Built by astronomer Andronikos Kyristes, the octagonal 1st-century-B.C. Tower of the Winds at the end of Aeolou Street (Street of the Winds), inside the **Roman Agora** (a marketplace constructed under the reign of Julius Caesar and Augustus), depicts the eight wind deities. Once containing a water clock and topped by a weather vane, this unique monument gives the area, Aerides, its name. In the 18th century, whirling dervishes danced in the tower. The surrounding ruins of the Agora also contain the photogenic 15th-century **Fetiye Mosque,** built to commemorate Mehmet II, the Conqueror's visit to Athens in 1458.

Take the rest of the afternoon off. If it's summer, and if your hotel has a pool, you know where to plant yourself. However you relax, get a bit of rest so you are ready to explore Athens by night. Any or all of the following stops will fill an evening. ⏱ **20 min. Aeolou and Pelopida sts. ☎ 210/324-5220. Admission 2€ or w/Acropolis ticket. May–Oct daily 8am–7pm, Nov–Apr daily 8:30am–3pm. Closed Jan 1, Mar 25, Orthodox Easter Sun, May 1, and Dec 25–26. Metro: Monastiraki.**

> *Busy Ermou is one of the city's main shopping streets, best known for its shoe stores.*

⑧ 🍽 **Dioskouri.** Begin the evening by walking to the promenade behind (south of) Monastiraki Station across from the Metro line that runs to Thissio. Your reward will be a view of the Acropolis above the Ancient Agora—and the low prices at this meze restaurant and cafe that is always full. Look for the ancient-ship logo on the awnings (the sign's only in Greek). **37–39 Adrianou St. ☎ 210/325-3323 or 3333. $$.**

⑨ ★★ **Dora Stratou Theater.** One of the most unusual experiences in Athens is to see traditional Greek dancers performing in folk costume in the outdoor theater on Filopappou Hill. It's an adventure to walk there (there's a footpath leading there from opposite the entrance to the Acropolis, beside Dionysus restaurant), and it's memorable to watch and listen to the live singers and musicians as you're sitting under the stars. Look out for bats as they dart in and out of the light. **See p. 125.**

⑩ ★★★ **Thission Open-Air Cinema.** The Thission theater is one of the few places where you can still see a film under the stars in licensed comfort—with a view of the Acropolis in the distance. Like drive-ins, most theaters such as Thission, dating from the 1950s and '60s, have been declared cultural sites and cannot be used for any other purpose. Big movie chains have bought in, screening first-run films as well as classic movies. Buy popcorn and a beer or glass of wine during the intermission, and bring them to your cafe table interspersed between directors' chairs in the breezy garden. **See p. 125.**

⑪ ★★ **Technopolis.** If you hear muffled music in Thissio, chances are there's an open-air concert at Technopolis, the former-gasworks-turned-exhibition-and-event-space run by the City of Athens. The old brick smokestacks glow red at night and provide an orienting beacon, as does the Acropolis. Restaurants, cafe-bars, and clubs have sprung up in the surrounding area known as Gazi, especially alongside Kerameikos Metro Station. ⏱ **2 hr. 100 Piraeos St. at Persefonis St. ☎ 210/346-7322. Metro: Kerameikos.**

Athens for Museum Lovers

Greece cherishes its cultural artifacts and encourages respectful appreciation of its heritage from as many people as possible. Many excellent state-run and private museums are free or have low entrance fees. National museums and sites are free on Sundays from November 1 through March 31 and offer reduced admission rates for many categories of visitors. But they close early, and hours change each April and October. Check www.culture.gr or call ahead.

> *The Cycladic Art Museum pays homage to a culture that flourished as early as 3,200 B.C.*

START Metro to Monastiraki.

1 Tzisdarakis Tzami. One of the remaining vestiges of 400 years of Ottoman rule, the big 18th-century mosque overlooking the square has been restored and now houses the Ceramic Folk Art Museum. There are some beautifully crafted pieces here, including charming animals for children made by a little-known artist, Dimitrios Migdalinos, who died poor and unknown in 1949 or 1950. ⏱ **20 min.**

1 Areos St. at Monastiraki Sq. ☎ 210/324-2066. Admission 2€. Year-round Wed–Mon 9am–2:30pm. Metro: Monastiraki.

2 ★ kids **Museum of Greek Popular Musical Instruments.** Tambourines, drums, horns, bagpipes, and goat bells are just some examples of instruments informatively displayed alongside photos, diagrams, and earphones with which to hear them. The museum is also a musicology center and features occasional performances (check the board). ⏲ 30 min. 1–3 Diogenis St. ☎ 210/325-0198. Free admission. Year-round Wed noon–6pm, Tues and Thurs–Sun 10am–2pm. Closed Mon. Metro: Monastiraki.

❸ **Loutro ton Aeridon (The Bathhouse of the Winds).** Named for Aeolus, god of wind, this 15th-century hamam (Turkish bath) is now restored as a museum. Buy the brochure (2€) for information in English, or listen to the 23-minute audio guide, skipping to room nos. 4 and 5 for evocative, firsthand accounts of what it was like inside, according to diaries and letters from the period. ⏲ At least 15 min. 8 Kyrisstou St. ☎ 210/324-4340. Admission 2€. Year-round Wed–Mon 9am–2:30pm. Metro: Monastiraki.

❹ **Athens University Historical Museum.** The pre-Ottoman residence of town planner and architect Stamatis Kleanthis is where the first classes for Athens's oldest university took place from 1837 until 1841, before moving to the Panepistimiou Street location still in use today. Beautifully restored, it contains various items relating to the history of Greece's National and Kapodistrian University of Athens. ⏲ 30 min. 5 Tholou St. at Klepsydras St. ☎ 210/368-9502 or 9504. www.history-museum.uoa.gr. Free admission. Oct–May Mon–Fri 9:30am–2:30pm; June–Sept Tues and Thurs–Fri 9:30am–2:30pm, Mon and Wed 9:30am–2:30pm and 6–9pm. Metro: Monastiraki.

❺ **Folk Art Museum.** It looks like it hasn't been updated since 1973, but the displays of modern Greek objects here are charming: Upstairs are nice collections of traditional buckles and costumes, with maps of where they're from, but the star is the complete room of frescoes by naïve artist Theophilos Hatzimihail. ⏲ At least 30 min. 17 Kydathineon St. ☎ 210/322-9031. Admission 2€. Year-round Tues–Sun 9am–2pm. Metro: Syntagma.

❻ **Jewish Museum of Greece.** Jewish communities have been present in Greece since Hellenistic times. At this museum, some 8,000 remnants of Greek Jewish life spanning 4,000 years have been amassed, including 600-year-old textiles, with displays on nine levels, including some temporary exhibitions. ⏲ At least 30 min. 39 Nikis St. ☎ 210/322-5582.

> If you've fallen under the spell of Greek music, hum your way through the Museum of Greek Popular Musical Instruments.

www.jewishmuseum.gr. Admission 5€, students 3€. Year-round Mon–Fri 9am–2:30pm, Sun 10am–2pm. Metro: Syntagma.

❼ ★★ kids **Acropolis Museum.** This sleek and minimalist new building houses sculptures and fragments, including frieze fragments from the Parthenon and original caryatids from the Erechtheion. See p. 44, ❺.

❽ ★ **Lalaounis Jewelry Museum.** You don't need to be a jewelry lover to covet prolific designer Ilias Lalaounis's gold collection, inspired by different epochs and cultures. ⏲ At least 30 min. 4 Karyatidon and 12 Kalliperi sts. ☎ 210/922-1044. Admission 5€, reduced 4€ (for seniors, students, and groups). Year-round Wed 9am–9pm, Thurs–Sat 9am–4:30pm, Sun 11am–4pm. Closed Mon–Tues. Metro: Akropoli, or bus no. 230.

1. Tzisdarakis Tzami
2. Museum of Greek Popular Musical Instruments
3. Loutro ton Aeridon (The Bathhouse of the Winds)
4. Athens University Historical Museum
5. Folk Art Museum
6. Jewish Museum of Greece
7. Acropolis Museum
8. Lalaounis Jewelry Museum
9. Kentrikon
10. City of Athens Museum
11. National History Museum
12. Numismatic Museum
13. Benaki Museum
14. Cycladic Art Museum
15. Byzantine and Christian Museum
16. War Museum
17. National Archaeological Museum

VATHI

Finou
Paleologou Konstantinou
Mezonos
Iliou
Psaron
Ioannion
T. Diligani
Favierou
Kerameon
Victor Hugo
Kodratou
Metaxourgio Ⓜ
Karolou
Karaiskaki Square
Achileos
Agiou Konstandinou
Lenorman
Giatrakou
Kolonou
Iasonos
Kolokinthous
Keramikou
Millerou
Marathonos
Thermopilon
Agisilaou
Piraeos
Psaromilingou
Ag. Dipilou
Iera Odos
Evmolpidon
Voutadon
Triptolemou
Persefonis
Kerameikos Cemetery
Melidoni
Dekeleon
Orfeos
GAZI
Iraklion
Elasidon
Kinadon
Ilia Pouloupoulou
Amfiktionos
Erisichthonos
Nileos
Iraklidon
Akteou
Thorikion
Exoneon
Galatias
Akamantos
Amfitrionos
Thessalonikis
Filasion
Meliteon
Dimofontos
Pallineon
Trion Ierarchon
Kidantidon
Iperionos
Ionon
Troon
Eoleon
Acheon
Kallisthenous
Apolloniou
Dorieon
Driopon
Kiklopon
Iolaou
Arakinthou

Iliou
Liosion
Acharnon
Aristotelous
Mager
3 Septemb
Senierou
Akominatou
Kapodistriou
Marni
Menandrou
Chalkokondi
Veranzerou
Satovriandou
Zinonos
Deligiorgi
Omonia Square
Omonia Ⓜ
Likourgou
P. Tsaldari
Geraniou
Sokratous
City Hall
Sofokleous
Evripidou
Aiolou
Ag. Asomaton

Athens Municipal Art Gallery
Eleftherios Square
Menandrou
Epikourou
Sari
Anargyron
Aristofanous
Eschillou
Pallados
Athinas
Vissis
Voreou
Ag. Filou
PSYRRI
Miaouli
Karaiskaki

MONASTIRAK

Monastiraki Ⓜ
Ermou
Thissio
Ⓜ
Athinedo
Ifestou
Adrianou
Mitropoleo
Pandrossou
❶
Areos
Aiolou
Pelopida
❷
Adrian
❸
Minisikleous
Erichthiou
Dioskouron
Panos
❹
Theorias

THISSIO
National Observatory
Otrineon
Apostolou Pavlou

Stoa of Attalos
Ancient Agora

ACROPOLIS

Herodes Atticus Theater

Pnyx Hill

Dionysiou Areopagitou
Rovertou Galli
Kallisper
❽
Garibaldi
Acropolis Museum
❼
Popileon
Erechthiou
Kavalloti
Misaras
Veikou
Mak

Filopappou Hill

MAKRIYANNI

Stisikleous
Arakinthou
Mouson
Drakou
Tsami Karatasou
Markou Botsari
Dimitrakopoulou
Andrea Singrou
Panetoliou
KOUKAKI

0 ————— 1/4 mi
0 ————— 1/4 km

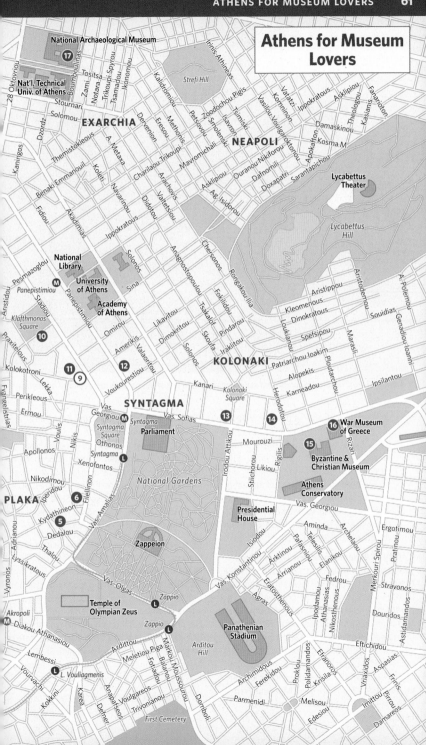

Athens for Museum Lovers

> *Anthony Benaki donated his house and collections to create one of the capital's most colorful museums.*

⑨ 🍽 **Kentrikon.** Come in off the streets to the arcade beside the shoe store (under the big KENTRIKON sign) to this old-fashioned, lunch-only (Mon–Sat noon–6pm) diner in the middle of the shopping district, where you can eat a full meal or just stop for a drink. Long menu, good food, unpretentious service. 3 Kolokotroni St. (opposite the National History Museum in the arcade). ☎ 210/323-2482. $$.

⑩ **City of Athens Museum.** This modest 1830s home of King Otto and Queen Amalia (where they lived while the royal palace-Parliament was being built) re-creates life in the royal household and features a superb collection from Byzantine times to the 19th century, including foreigners' impressions of Athens when the population was 25,000 (it's now 4 million). ⏱ At least 30 min. 7 Paparigopoulou St. ☎ 210/323-1397. www.athenscitymuseum. gr. Admission 3€. Year-round Mon and Wed–Fri 9am–4pm, Sat–Sun 10am–3pm. Metro: Panepistimiou.

⑪ **National History Museum.** Known as the Palaia Vouli, or Old Parliament (used 1875–1935), this museum explores Greece's history from the fall of Constantinople (1453) to World War II. A helmet and sword that reputedly belonged to Lord Byron rest here. ⏱ At least 30 min. 13 Stadiou St. at Kolokotroni St. ☎ 210/323-7617. Admission 3€, free on Sun. Year-round Tues–Sun 9am–2pm. Metro: Syntagma.

⑫ **Numismatic Museum.** With its entrance via a pretty courtyard, Iliou Melathron (Ilium Mansion, Ilium being another name for Troy) was the home of eccentric archaeologist Heinrich Schliemann, who famously excavated that site, as well as ancient Mycenae and Tiryns. His house now attractively displays some 600,000 coins dating from 700 B.C. A **cafe** is on site. ⏱ 30 min. 12 Panepistimiou St. ☎ 210/364-3774. Admission 3€. Year-round Tues–Sun 8:30am–3pm. Metro: Syntagma.

⑬ ★★ **Benaki Museum.** Anthony Benaki collected artifacts for over 35 years and then

> *Greece's ancient and modern battles are portrayed at the War Museum.*

donated his house and collection to the state in 1931. It features antiquities, costumes, relics from Asia Minor, and El Grecos, plus Lord Byron and War of Independence memorabilia. The gift shop has reproductions in silver and terra cotta, jewelry, books, and icons. See p. 50, **3**.

⑭ ★★ Cycladic Art Museum. This private museum with the grand corner entrance has one of the best collections of Cycladic and ancient art dated 3200 to 2000 B.C., donated by Nicolas and Aikaterini Goulandris. The galleries are small and well lit. You'll probably enter via the **Stathatos Mansion** (1 Herodotou St. and Vas. Sofias Ave.), which has retained its turn-of-the-20th-century decor and is used to host temporary exhibits. ⏱1 hr. 4 Neophytou Douka St. ☎210/722-8321 or 8323. www.cycladic.gr. Admission 7€ Wed–Sun (Mon 3.50€); reduced 3.50€ seniors, 2.50€ students; kids 18 & under free. Year-round Mon, Wed, Fri–Sun 10am–5pm; Thurs 10am–8pm. Closed Tues. Metro: Syntagma or Evangelismos.

⑮ ★ Byzantine and Christian Museum. Historic relics and treasures of the early Church are displayed in the new wings of the Tuscan-style 1848 villa of Sophie de Marbois, duchess of Plaisance (1785–1854). The collection demonstrates the transition from paganism to Christianity, including a few representations of the lyre-playing animal lover Orpheus as Christ. ⏱1 hr. 22 Vas. Sofias Ave. ☎210/721-1027. www.byzantinemuseum.gr. Admission 4€. May–Sept Tues–Sun 8am–8pm, Oct–Apr Tues–Sun 8:30am–3pm. Metro: Evangelismos.

> *The home of noted archaeologist Heinrich Schliemann now houses the Numismatic Museum, filled with ancient coins.*

⑯ kids War Museum. This cheerful armed forces museum has a collection from Greece's military past, from antiquity to the 20th century. The exhibits include battle plans, weaponry, uniforms (including a samurai outfit), etchings, aircraft, and memorabilia from Phil-hellenes who came to fight in the 19th-century War of Independence (from the Ottomans), and who cheered again when Greece scored the first major land victory against an Axis power (Italy) in World War II. ⏱1 hr. 2 Rizari St. at Vas. Sofias Ave. ☎210/724-4464. Admission 2€. Year-round Tues–Sun 9am–2pm. Metro: Evangelismos.

⑰ ★★★ National Archaeological Museum. It's tempting to skip it now that there's the Acropolis Museum at the bottom of the hill, but the best originals from all over the country are still here. See p. 46, **8**.

Athens with Kids

Children are practically worshiped in Greece. You can take
kids almost anywhere, including tavernas, restaurants, and alcohol-serving
cafe-bars, given that the concept of a neighborhood baby-sitter is nonexistent.
Athens's sidewalks, however, are not stroller-friendly; most people use the
roads. Keep this in mind as you follow the tour below, which includes age-
appropriate activities for tykes, tweens, and teens.

> *Syntagma Square supplies no end of amusements for young travelers.*

START Metro to Syntagma.

1 ★ **Syntagma Station.** Show older kids
the antiquities inside and outside the Metro
station on Amalias Avenue, which provides
a window into more than 25 centuries of the
city's buried past. They will enjoy the layers of
the ancient city discovered during construction. Inside are graves and the remains of an
ancient aqueduct used to bring water from
Mount Hymettus to Athens in the 5th century
B.C. Outside are 1,800-year-old Roman baths
covered by a nonglare glass roof—one of several free open-air museum exhibits around
the center displaying finds uncovered during

Metro work. ☉ 45 min. Amalias Ave. and Vas.
Georgiou St. Year-round daily 5:30am–midnight.
Metro: Syntagma.

2 ★★ **Changing of the Guard.** In front of
Parliament at Syntagma Square, two Evzones
(traditionally dressed soldiers of the Presidential Guard) keep watch at the 1932 Tomb of
the Unknown Soldier. Every hour on the hour,
the guards do some fancy footwork in front
of the tomb. A much more elaborate duty-
rotation ceremony occurs on Sunday at 11am.
☉ 15 min. Amalias Ave. and Vas. Georgiou St.
Metro: Syntagma.

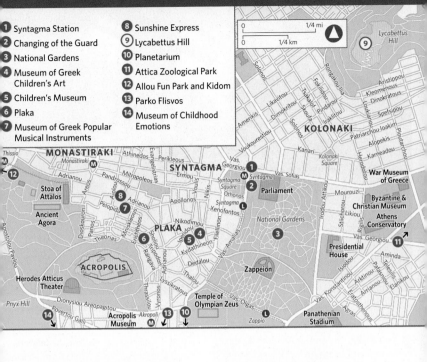

① Syntagma Station
② Changing of the Guard
③ National Gardens
④ Museum of Greek Children's Art
⑤ Children's Museum
⑥ Plaka
⑦ Museum of Greek Popular Musical Instruments
⑧ Sunshine Express
⑨ Lycabettus Hill
⑩ Planetarium
⑪ Attica Zoological Park
⑫ Allou Fun Park and Kidom
⑬ Parko Flisvos
⑭ Museum of Childhood Emotions

③ **National Gardens.** The one-time Royal Gardens are the city's great escape. Wander along trails lined with some 500 plant varieties to the duck and turtle ponds, the small zoo (birds, wild goats, and a donkey), and beyond, and then rest on benches or at the **cafe,** 4 Irodou Attikou Street (☎ 210/723-2820). Children can read, play chess, or paint at the **"child library"** (☎ 210/323-6503; year-round Tues–Sat 8am–2:30pm). The librarian will baby-sit children who are older than 3 if they can quietly do their own thing. Continue through to the **Zappeion Gardens** (p. 52, ⑦) and the **Panathenian Stadium** (p. 53, ⑨). See p. 52, ⑥.

④ **Museum of Greek Children's Art.** The only one of its kind in Greece and one of few in the world, this museum displays the naïve and surprisingly skillful artwork of children ages 5 to 14 from around the country. A selection have been made into unique postcards. ⏱ 20 min. 9 Kodrou St. at Voulis St. ☎ 210/331-2621 or 2750. www.childrensartmuseum.gr. Adults 2€, free for children and students up to age 18. Sept–July Tues–Sat 10am–2pm, Sun 11am–2pm. Closed Aug, holidays. Metro: Syntagma.

⑤ ★ **Children's Museum.** Watch how simple objects such as stones, siphons, tubes, and water hold young children's attention as well as the latest gadget. Don't forget to go downstairs to the market. Some Greek-made toys are available at the shop. ⏱ 1 hr. 14 Kydathineon St. ☎ 210/331-2995. www.hcm.gr. Free admission. Year-round Tues–Fri 10am–2pm, Sat-Sun 10am–3pm. Metro: Syntagma.

Children of Greece

Children are put on a pedestal in Athens, and many venues, public and private, cater to them with well-maintained and fenced neighborhood playgrounds frequented by families living in the surrounding apartment blocks. Many parents take their children to the local square when the siesta is over and the heat of the day abates, at around 7pm in summer. State-run child-care centers accept children as young as 40 days free of charge for working mothers, and education through college is free for every Greek citizen.

> *"Little Trains" ply a route through the city center, making it easy for kids and their adult companions to take in the sights.*

⑥ ★★★ **Plaka.** The area of Anafiotika in Plaka is like an island village. In fact it was named for the islanders of Anafi who originally came to Athens to build the king's palace in the 19th century. Children will enjoy wandering through the narrow streets. ⏰ 1 hr. Various approaches; one is from Stratonos St. Metro: Syntagma or Akropoli.

⑦ ★ **Museum of Greek Popular Musical Instruments.** Kids with a musical bent will like this museum, where they can listen to the tambourines, lutes, lyres, drums, and clarinets on display. See p. 58, ②.

⑧ ★ **Sunshine Express.** Prevent your kids from tiring out, get your bearings, and pass by Athens's main sites on this *trenaki* (little train), which makes a circuit around pedestrian central roads on car tires, not a track. An alternative with a hop-off-hop-on component is the **Happy Train,** Areos and Adrianou streets, Monastiraki (☎ 210/725-5400). ⏰ 40 min. Terminal: Aeolou and Adrianou sts., Plaka. www. sunshine-express.gr. Adults 6€, children 9 & under 4€. Winter Sat–Sun and holidays 11am to dark; summer Mon–Fri 11:30am–2:30pm and 5pm–midnight, Sat–Sun 11am–midnight. Metro: Monastiraki.

⑨ 🚠 ★ **Lycabettus Hill.** Take the **teleferik** (cable car) up this 295m (968-ft.) hill for a fabulous view of the city, and have a pricey ice cream (10€) at the **cafe** on top. Then run or walk back down the hill on one of the many paths. Buses no. 022, 060, and 200 go near the base station, but it's a hard uphill hike just to get to that point. (Take the bus from Akademias St., Kanari St., or Kolonaki Sq. and get off at Loukianou or Marasli sts.) Teleferik: Aristippou and Ploutarchou sts. ☎ 210/721-0701. Daily every 30 min. 9am–3am. Adults 6.50€ round-trip, 3.20€ one-way; age 2–3 half-price; under age 2 free. Only return tickets can be purchased at the base. Bus no. 022, 060, and 200 go near the base.

⑩ ★ **Planetarium.** With a 25m (82-ft.) large-format iWerks dome screen (like IMAX)—10 times larger than conventional movie projections and more than two basketball courts in size—the 40-minute productions here take the audience on intergalactic, undersea, or overland journeys with a 360-degree view. Book ahead for children's shows on busy winter weekends. ⏰ 1 hr. Eugenides Institute, 387 Syngrou. ☎ 210/ 946-9600. www.eugenfound.edu.gr. Adults 6€

regular screen or 8€ big screen, children and college students w/ID 4€ and 5€ respectively. Bus no. B2, 126 (from Piraeus), or 550.

⑪ ★★★ **Attica Zoological Park.** This 19-hectare (47-acre) zoo near the airport is easy to get around and houses the third-largest collection of birds in the world (some 2,000), as well as big-game African animals, endangered native ponies, and even beasts they can ride. ⊙ 3 hr. Yalou, Spata. ☎ 210/663-4724. www.attica park.com. Admission 14€ adults, 10€ children 3–12 and seniors. Year-round daily 9am–sunset. Bus no. 319 (from Doukissis Plakentias Metro Station, Christoupoli-bound), or take the Attiki Odos national road from the airport to exit 18 (Spata) or from Elefsina to exit 16P (Rafina).

⑫ **Allou Fun Park and Kidom.** In out-of-the-way Rendi (20 min. away by bus), this big amusement park has a lot of rides—and not just for teens. Adrenaline pumpers include the 40m-drop (131-ft.) Shock Tower. Kidom is for the little ones. ⊙ At least 1 hr. Kifissou and Petrou Ralli aves., Agios Ioannis-Rendi. Kidom: ☎ 210/425-2600. Allou: ☎ 210/425-6990. www.alloufun park.gr. Free entrance. Unlimited rides 23€, individual rides 1€–10€. Allou: Year-round Mon–Thurs 5pm–midnight, Fri 5pm–1am, Sat 10am–1am, Sun 10am–midnight. Kidom (ages 3–9): Mon–Thurs 5pm–11pm, Fri 5pm–midnight, Sat 10am–midnight; Sun 10am–11pm. Bus no. B18, Γ 18, or 21.

⑬ **Parko Flisvos.** You can reach the "biggest and best playground in Greece," or so the sign says, in 10 minutes by taxi down Syngrou Avenue, or in about a half-hour on the tram. A bus, whose terminus is behind the swish new **Flisvos Marina** (www.flisvosmarina.com), also gets you there. Pick up an ice cream and coffee, and then it's a 10- to 15-minute walk along the mega-yacht-moored promenade to the playground, but your kids will love it. If you only see one set of slides, keep going—it ends at the "rope tree." ⊙ At least 1 hr. Poseidonos Ave., Paleo Faliro. Free admission. Winter daily 9am–9pm, summer 9am–11:30pm. Tram: Parko Flisvos. Bus no. 550.

⑭ **Museum of Childhood Emotions.** This museum, a Hands on Europe Museum Association member, encourages family participation through interactive exhibits and activities for children ages 4 to 12. Weekend workshops start at 1pm, as does storytelling, which takes place on the first Saturday of the month. ⊙ 1hr. 7 Karatza and Tsamikaratasou sts., Makriyanni/Koukaki. ☎ 210/921-8329. www.mce.gr. Entrance 4€, 2€ for toddlers accompanying family. Year-round Sat–Sun 10am–2pm, weekdays by appt. for groups. Bus no. 230. Trolley no. 1, 5, or 15. Metro: Syngrou-Fix.

> *Kidom, an amusement park just outside the city center, caters to young thrill seekers.*

Ancient Athens

Athenians are reaping the rewards of a 40-million-euro urban renewal and archaeological-site reunification project implemented in 2004. It's a revised version of an 1832 plan by Greek and Bavarian architects who laid out the then-fledgling modern Greek capital. The project links up the ancient sites, monuments, green areas, and squares in Athens's historic center along a pedestrian walkway that roughly corresponds to ancient pathways. Building facades were also restored and billboards removed. The change in appearance and quality of life has been nothing short of stellar.

> *The Acropolis Walkway skirts the bottom of the Acropolis Hill and connects many of the city's ancient sights.*

START **Metro to Akropoli.**

❶ Hadrian's Arch. Start a tour from this 2nd-century gate built for Emperor Hadrian, who went through it en route to the newly completed Temple of Olympian Zeus. See p. 46, ❻.

❷ Temple of Olympian Zeus. Greece's largest temple took some 650 years to build, between 515 B.C. and A.D. 132. It measures 96 by 40m (315 x 131 ft.), but only 15 of the original 104 columns are still standing, each 17m (56 ft.) high. See p. 52, ❽.

❸ ★★★ Acropolis Walkway. Start walking up pedestrian Dionysiou Areopagitou Street, along this walkway around the Acropolis. See p. 42, ❸.

❹ Theater of Dionysos. Dating to the 6th century B.C., this is the first and oldest theater in Athens. The Assembly met here after they moved off Pnyx Hill in the 3rd century B.C. Competitions for the best dramas took place here in honor of the god of pleasure, Dionysus. In its heyday, it could hold some 17,000 spectators. Plays by Aeschylus, Aristophanes,

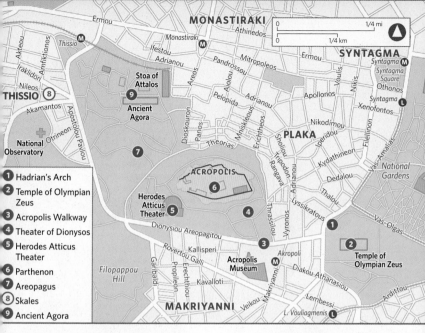

1. Hadrian's Arch
2. Temple of Olympian Zeus
3. Acropolis Walkway
4. Theater of Dionysos
5. Herodes Atticus Theater
6. Parthenon
7. Areopagus
8. Skales
9. Ancient Agora

> The Temple of Zeus.

Sophocles, and Euripides were performed here in classical times; gladiator and mock sea battles took place in Roman times. Also on the site are the **Panagia Chrysospiliotissa Church;** the ruins of the 5th-century-B.C. **Pericles Odeon,** used for musical performances; the **Asklepion,** a sanctuary and clinic dedicated to the god of medicine; and the 2nd-century-B.C. **Stoa of Eumenes,** once a covered walkway to the nearby **Herodes Atticus Theater,** built by the Pergamene king Eumenes II (198–159 B.C.). You can still walk along it en route to the **Acropolis.** ⏱ 1 hr. Thrassilou and Dionysiou Areopagitou sts. ☎ 210/322-4625. www.culture.gr. Admission 2€ or part of Acropolis ticket. Apr–Oct daily 8am–7:30pm, Nov–Mar 8am–3pm. Metro: Akropoli.

⑤ ★★★ **Herodes Atticus Theater.** Built in the 2nd century A.D. by Athens benefactor Herodes Atticus in honor of his wife, Regilla, the once cedar-roofed odeon at the foot of the Acropolis hosts Athens Festival performances on balmy evenings. The marble seating dates from the 1950s, and up to 5,000 people squeeze in for popular performances, but the ambience is worth it. See p. 125.

> *The Agora, the commercial hub of the ancient city, became so congested that an annex, the Roman Agora, was built nearby.*

6 ★★★ **Parthenon.** Walk around, admire the view, and soak up the atmosphere around Greece's most iconic national treasure. See p. 44, **4**; p. 80, **1**.

7 ★ **Areopagus.** Continue on your way around the pedestrian walkway, now called Apostolou Pavlou (Apostle Paul's). Opposite the Thission theater is an entrance to Areopagus (Ares Hill), where trials were held in classical times. Ares himself was tried here by the pantheon of gods for the murder of Poseidon's son, according to myth. The apostle Paul preached here much later, in A.D. 51, as noted on an embedded tablet opposite the entrance to the Acropolis. On this side of the hill, a bucolic **path** runs alongside the Ancient Agora from Thissio to Plaka. ⏱ 20 min. Continuation of Theorias St. opposite Acropolis entrance. Metro: Akropoli or bus no. 230.

8 🍵 **Skales.** Sit down for a coffee at an outdoor cafe on Thissio Square, or get something stronger across the street to go with a filling plate of *pikilia* (hot or cold mixed appetizers) at Skales (pronounced *ska*-less, meaning "steps"), a meze restaurant next to the stairs between Nileos and Akamandos streets. 1 Nileos St. ☎ 210/346-5647. $$.

9 ★ 🧒 **Ancient Agora.** Walk across the street through Thissio Square to the ruins of what was once the capital's business center. See p. 42, **2**.

> *From the Areopagus, it's easy to find a rocky perch from which to contemplate the past while taking in the sprawl of modern Athens.*

Architectural Landmarks

The Athens basin may be a sprawl of concrete blocks, but the city has managed to protect the beautiful 19th- and early-20th-century buildings in the historic center. Central Panepistimiou Street, which connects Omonia and Syntagma squares, is the headquarters for many private enterprises and offers a great sampling of modern Greek architecture that is impressively lit-up at night.

> Parliament is housed in the 1843 palace built for Otto, first king of a united Greece.

START Metro to Syntagma.

❶ Parliament. The biggest landmark in the city center, the 1842 former royal palace of Bavarian-born King Otto (1833–62) has Munich architects to blame for its plain neoclassical design. A *London Illustrated News* correspondent lamented "the ugliness of the palace. . . . It is invariably compared by travelers to a huge manufactory, while the interior plan is, if possible, in worse taste than the exterior." It was then bigger than Buckingham Palace, and its Pompeian-style decor was damaged in a 1909 fire. It has housed Greece's parliament since 1935. The **Tomb of the Unknown Soldier,**

guarded by two highly photogenic soldiers in traditional *foustanellas* (ceremonial skirtlike garments), fronts the building. ⏱ 15 min. Amalias Ave. and Vas. Georgiou St. at Syntagma Sq. Metro: Syntagma.

❷ Zappeion. This semicircular exhibition hall is a classical public building associated with many historic events, such as the signing of Greece into the European Union. It was originally bankrolled by expat Evangelias Zappas in his quest to spark the modern Olympic Games, which took place after his death at the nearby Panathenian Stadium in 1896. The 1888 construction by Theophilos Hansen, the

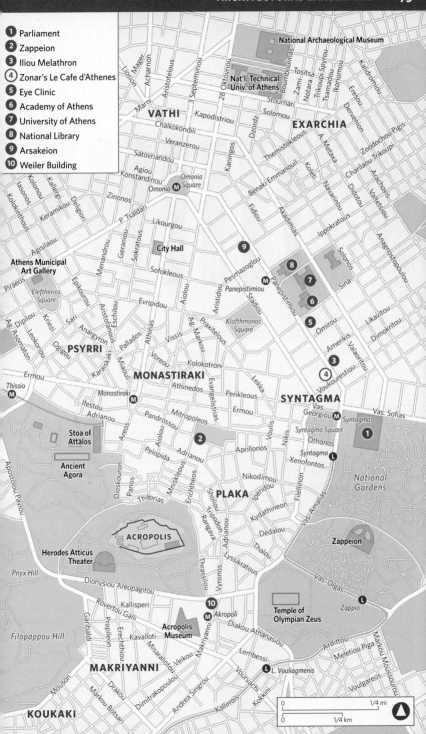

1 Parliament
2 Zappeion
3 Iliou Melathron
4 Zonar's Le Cafe d'Athenes
5 Eye Clinic
6 Academy of Athens
7 University of Athens
8 National Library
9 Arsakeion
10 Weiler Building

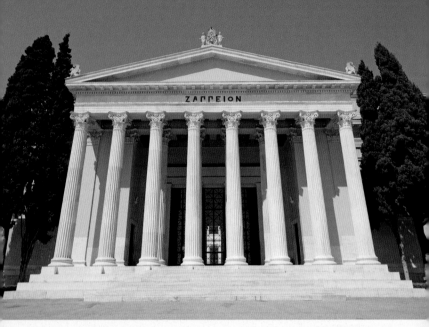

> *In 1981, Greece's entry into the European Union was signed into effect in the 19th-century Zappeion.*

Athens Academy and Library architect, was plagued by indecision over its design. It was renovated in 1959 and remodeled in 1982 for Greece's EEC presidency. See p. 52, **7**.

Architecture in Brief

After Greece's 1821 War of Independence had captured the imaginations of Romantic Victorians (and many antiquities had been captured by avid "Philhellenes"), the capital was moved to Athens from Nafplio. Bavarian King Otto and his architects planned for a town of 40,000, not 4 million—which explains the haphazard layout and crowded streets—with public buildings designed in the neoclassical style to honor the culture they idealized. The interwar period also saw eclectic, Art Nouveau, modernist, and Bauhaus architecture, and buildings taller than the usual two or three stories. The uniformly dull concrete blocks that dominate many neighborhoods, however, are the pragmatic result of a mass influx of rural migrants in the 1950s.

3 Iliou Melathron. The Numismatic Museum, with coins dating from 700 B.C., is housed in the Renaissance-style Ilium Mansion, built in 1878 as the home of fabled German archaeologist Heinrich Schliemann, who excavated Mycenae and Troy (aka Ilium). Behind gates adorned with the swastika (which was an ancient symbol of well-being long before the Nazis appropriated it for their nefarious causes), it may be the best-known building by royal-court architect Ernst Ziller. See p. 62, **12**.

④ **Zonar's Le Cafe d'Athenes.** Zonar's, a beloved aristocratic pastry shop, was closed in 2001, when the 1930s building in which it resided was overhauled and opened as Attica, the department store, four years later. In 2007, the coffee shop reopened in a corner of the building and is more packed (and posh) than ever. Panepistimiou and Voukourestiou sts. ☎ 210/321-1158. $$.

5 Eye Clinic. The Ophthalmological Clinic (built 1847–51) was originally designed in the style of the "neoclassical trilogy" of the Hansen brothers (the Academy, University, and Library), but was redesigned in a Byzantine style by Lissandros Kafantzoglou at the request of King Otto. Another story was added in 1869 to keep eye-diseased patients separate so as not to infect other patients; more sections were built in 1881. It has belonged to the University of Athens's Faculty of Medicine since 1869. ⏱ 10 min. Panepistimiou and Sina sts. Metro: Panepistimiou.

⑥ **Academy of Athens.** Built in two phases (1859–63 and 1868–85), this neoclassical structure with its Ionic columns and entrance based on the eastern Erechtheum was built by royal-court architect Theophilos Hansen (1813–91). Bankrolled by Baron Georgios Sinas (1783–1856), who has a statue in the hall, it's an example of mature (some would say mad) neoclassical design. Athena and Apollo top the columns. The nonlending library is open to the public. ⏱ 10 min. 28 Panepistimiou St. ☎ 210/360-0207 or 366-4700. www.academyofathens.gr. Metro: Panepistimiou.

⑦ **University of Athens.** On Eleftherios Venizelos Street (its name in signs only; Panepistimiou, or University, is how the street is known), this neoclassical building designed by Christian Hansen (brother of Theophilos) is plain compared with the Academy. The portico is Ionic Pentelic marble, with frescoes of ancient Greek authors. The statues include likenesses of British Prime Minister William Gladstone and Ioannis Kapodistrias, the first modern president of the country, for whom the university is named. ⏱ 10 min. 30 Panepistimiou St. No switchboard. www.uoa.gr. Metro: Panepistimiou.

⑧ **National Library.** Another building by Theophilos Hansen (who also designed Viennese public buildings), and financed by Panagis Valianos (who has a statue in front), this nonlending library of university and state holdings is another enthusiastic nod to antiquity. Built from 1887 to 1891 of Pentelic marble, it contains 10th- or 11th-century illuminated gospels. ⏱ 10 min. 32 Panepistimiou St. No switchboard. www.nlg.gr. Free admission. Year-round Mon–Thurs 9am–8pm, Fri–Sat 9am–2pm. Manuscripts: Year-round Mon–Fri 9am–2pm. Metro: Panepistimiou.

> *Statuary surrounds the Iliou Melathron, home of Heinrich Schliemann, the archaeologist who unearthed Mycenae.*

⑨ **Arsakeion.** Originally a girls' school founded by Apostolos Arsaki in 1836 (now a network of coed private schools throughout Greece), the neoclassical complex with the silver domes was rebuilt in 1848 by Greek architect Lissandros Kafantzoglou, and again by Constantine Maroudis in the early 20th century. It now houses the Council of State, the Education Society, and a book arcade. ⏱ 15 min. 47 Panepistimiou St. at Arsaki St. ☎ 210/371-0097. www.ste.gr. Metro: Panepistimiou.

⑩ **Weiler Building.** The 1830s Rundbogenstyle building, now overwhelmed by the New Acropolis Museum, was designed as a military hospital by Wilhelm von Weiler, an architect in the Bavarian army. Used as both police and partisan army headquarters during the post–World War II civil war, it was the Center for Acropolis Studies for 20 years and now houses offices of the Archaeological Service and New Acropolis Museum. ⏱ 10 min. 2-4 Makriyanni St. ☎ 210/923-9381. Metro: Akropoli.

Byzantine Athens

Athens has been linked with Christianity since the earliest days of the church—from the era of Christ, when the apostle Paul preached here, through the reign of Constantine, when Athens was a small, provincial town in the shadow of Constantinople, capital of the Eastern Roman (aka Byzantine) Empire. Athens still encompasses a large number of Eastern Orthodox houses of worship constructed from the 9th through the 13th centuries. Fortunately, newer constructions have marched around rather than over many of these unique medieval Attica-style churches.

> Athens has grown up around 11th-century Kapnikarea, which now rises right out of the middle of Ermou Street.

START Metro to Thissio.

1 Agii Asomati. With an Athenian-style dome, this cruciform church from the 11th century, sunken in the road at Ermou Street beside the Thissio Metro station, is eclectic but forlorn. Its original Byzantine structure was altered in the 1950s, and it's only open on special occasions. Life goes on around it as if it were invisible, as suggested by its name, Saints of the Disembodied. ⏱ 5 min. Agion Asomaton and Ermou sts. Metro: Thissio.

2 ★★ Agios Dimitrios Loumbardiaris. The lovely 14th-century Church of St. Dimitrios the Bombardier is nestled in a copse on Pnyx Hill. Legend tells that on October 26, 1645, the Ottoman commander of the Acropolis garrison, Yusuf Aga, planned to massacre Christians gathered here for name-day celebrations by bombarding the church with cannon fire from the Propylaia on the Acropolis. The night before the attack, lightning exploded the gunpowder there, killing Aga and his family, except his Christian daughter. ⏱ 45 min. Apostolou Pavlou St., on the path opposite (south of) the entrance to the Acropolis. Metro: Akropoli, or bus no. 230.

3 Agii Apostoli Solaki. On the site of the Ancient Agora, this four-columned cruciform Church of the Holy Apostles of Solakis is a very early (ca. 1020), beautiful example of Athenian/Attic Byzantine architecture. Restored in the 1950s by the Samuel H. Kress Foundation of New York, it has pseudo-Kufic decorations, the oldest Arab calligraphy, and unusual multiple apses (the semicircular vaulted protrusion from the main building that usually houses the altar). The 17th-century wall paintings are from a demolished church. ⏱ 10 min. Entrances on Adrianou St. and Agiou Filippou, Monastiraki; west end of Polygnotou St., Plaka; and Thissio Sq., Thissio, in the Ancient Agora. Metro: Monastiraki.

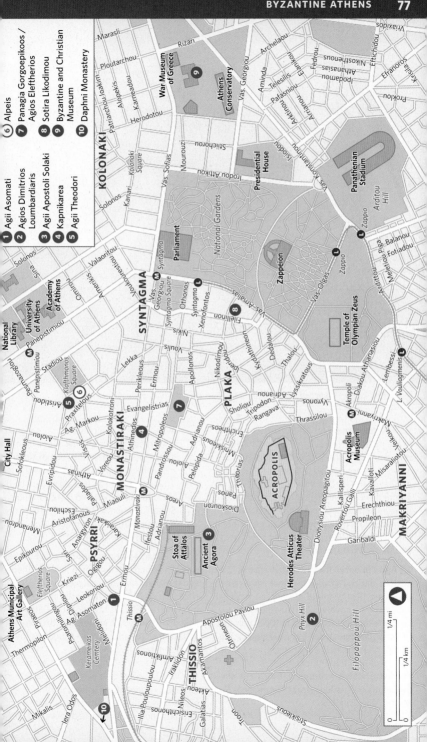

① Agii Asomati
② Agios Dimitrios Loumbardiaris
③ Agii Apostoli Solaki
④ Kapnikarea
⑤ Agii Theodori
⑥ Alpeis
⑦ Panagia Gorgoepikoos / Agios Eleftherios
⑧ Sotira Likodimou
⑨ Byzantine and Christian Museum
⑩ Daphni Monastery

> *The 10th-century Church of Agii Apostoli Solaki rises amid the ruins of the Ancient Agora.*

④ ★ **Kapnikarea.** This little cruciform church, in the middle of Ermou Street near Monastiraki, dates from the 11th to 13th centuries. Town planners wanted to demolish it in 1834, but Bavarian King Ludwig (King Otto's father) stepped in to preserve it. It occupies the site of an ancient temple to Athena (or possibly Demeter), but the dome is dedicated to the Virgin Mary. ⏱10 min. Ermou and Kapnikarea sts. Metro: Monastiraki.

⑤ **Agii Theodori.** It's easy to bypass this 12th-century church on Evripidou Street, though it's one of the most beautiful in Athens. It was built with much care on the site of another older structure that was renovated in 1065 (perhaps to repair damage caused by an earthquake), as marble tablets over the door attest. It sustained damage during the 19th-century War of Independence but was restored in 1840. ⏱10 min. Evripidou and Aristidou sts. at Klafthmonos Sq. Metro: Panepistimiou.

⑥ 🍴 **Alpeis.** Grab a cheap, quick souvlaki, a full meal, or a cold drink at this cafe, and sit outside in front of one of Athens's most beautiful Byzantine churches, Agii Theodori. It's on a pleasant square near the Central Market and Panepistimiou Street landmarks. **7 Palaion Patron Germanou St. at Klafthmonos Sq.** ☎ 210/331-0384. $.

⑦ ★★ **Panagia Gorgoepikoos/Agios Eleftherios.** A small church dedicated to St. Eleftherios and the Virgin Mary Gorgoepikoos (She Who Hears Quickly), it is overpowered by the unremarkable, mid-1800s Metropolitan Cathedral next door. It was built in the late 12th century and constructed entirely with antiquities from an ancient temple founded some 400 years earlier on the site by Empress Irene. Also called the "little Metropolis," it was the official Episcopal See of Athens after Orthodox bishops were expelled by Franks and Ottomans in turn from the Parthenon, which they had converted into a

> Many shops sell replicas of Byzantine icons.

> Engaging reliefs of flora and fauna adorn the small, 12th-century Panagia Gorgoepikoos, built from remnants of an ancient temple.

church. Note the beautiful relief carvings of flora and fauna around the perimeter as well as inside, if you're lucky enough to pass by when it's open. ⏱ 10 min. Mitropoleos and Agias Filotheis ts. at Mitropoleos Sq. Metro: Monastiraki.

8 Sotira Likodimou. Generally known as the "Russian church" after the Russian Orthodox Church took over its administration, it is also known as the Church of St. Nicodemus. The Byzantine structure is the biggest medieval church in Athens. Founded before 1031 by Stefan Likodimou, it's a copy of Osios Loukas Monastery in Boeotia. The Russians bought and restored the derelict church in the mid–19th century and added a bell tower, with a beautiful-sounding bell that was a gift from the czar. The interior was painted by noted Bavarian artist Ludwig Thiersch and Greek Nikiforos Lytras. ⏱ 10 min. 21 Filellinon St. ☎ 210/323-1090. Metro: Syntagma.

9 Byzantine and Christian Museum. The museum holds one of the best collections of early Christian art and artifacts. See p. 63, **15**.

10 Daphni Monastery. If only the walls could talk at this monastery, founded in the 6th century on the site of an ancient sanctuary. Originally a rare three-aisled basilica, it underwent many structural changes: Ionic columns from the Temple of Apollo (destroyed by Goths in A.D. 395) were used in its construction—and then removed by Lord Elgin (one remains). In the 11th century, it was dedicated to the Dormition of the Virgin. It became a monastery for Frankish Cistercian monks (rare in Greece) in the 1200s; it was returned to the Orthodox Church by the Turks in 1458; Greeks used it as a garrison during the 1820s War of Independence; and Bavarian troops camped out here when their king's son was installed a decade later. From 1883 to 1885, it was used as a psychiatric asylum. It suffered earthquake damage a few years later, when the site was also first excavated (1892). The area once held an annual wine festival, and then the site closed for many years. The actual church is decorated with unique 11th-century mosaics, and if you can't climb the steps to see them yourself, get a sense of their beauty from the slide show in the small museum. Daphni is about 10km/6¼ miles west of Athens; allow plenty of travel time. Buses leave from Koumoundourou Square. ⏱ 2 hr. Iera Odos, Attica. ☎ 210/581-1558. Free admission. Year-round daily 8:30am–3pm. Bus no. B16, Γ 16, 801, 836, 845, 865, or 866.

Romantic Athens

Athens has become a popular weekend getaway for European couples, and lovebirds from around the world travel here for honeymoons and other extended stays. The city's nightlife and sultry weather make a romantic backdrop for some of the world's most astonishing and important historic monuments. Many engaged or just-married couples arrive en route from a wedding in the Greek islands, but the capital itself is no less romantic or fun, with its surplus of outdoor cafes, shops, sights, and, of course, the Acropolis. At the end of the day, nothing says forever like the Parthenon.

> *Filopappou Hill is a rejuvenating perch for a quick retreat from the city below.*

START Metro to Syntagma.

❶ ★★★ The Parthenon and Acropolis. Anywhere with a view of the Sacred Rock is going to be special—which is pretty much everywhere, given that it towers some 156m (512 ft.) over the capital ("acropolis" means "the highest city"). It looks especially magical at night, when the temple ruins and the surrounding wall are dramatically floodlit. Plenty of restaurants and hotels are nearby, affording many opportunities to snag rooms or tables within sight of it to suit a range of budgets and tastes. You must also, of course, visit it while here, likely getting there via Plaka. Dionysiou Areopagitou St. See p. 44, ❹.

❷ ★★★ Plaka. Wander through the white-washed, island-village-like paths in **Anafiotika.** Then imagine yourself living in one of those beautifully restored 19th-century mansions around the east face of the Acropolis. This area is one of the most expensive and it shows, but so does its charm. See p. 66, ❻.

> *Despite crowds of shoppers, the narrow lanes of Plaka retain some small-village charm.*

③ 🚶 ★ **Filopappou Hill.** If you're in Athens when the weather's comfortable (from late Mar to May and late Sept to Nov), make yourself a picnic lunch and head for the hill. Go toward **Agios Dimitrios Church** (see p. 76, ➋), a favorite for weddings, opposite the entrance to the Acropolis. Veer left (east) on the trails up Filopappou Hill and find yourself a shady spot to clink glasses and gaze at the Parthenon—a day you will always remember.

④ ★★★ **Acropolis Walkway.** Walk along the cobblestone pedestrian roads that link up ancient sites, from Parliament down through the shopping district (Ermou St.), to Kerameikos and Gazi, back to Thissio (Apostolou Pavlou St.) and around toward the Acropolis entrance (Dionysiou Areopagitou St.). Do as the Greeks do and stake out a special viewing spot, in secluded areas near the entrance and around towards Thissio. The Sanctuary of the Nymph, where in antiquity brides-to-be made offerings for a happy marriage, is located near the Herodes Atticus Theater and the entrance to the Acropolis. See p. 42, ➌.

A Spa Experience

For lovers who'd rather relax than explore, try the award-winning luxury spa right in the center of town: The ★★★ **Grande Bretagne Hotel Spa** in Syntagma Square (☎ 210/333-0799; www.gbspa.gr) will give both of you face or body treatments, followed by side-by-side massages, among a range of other options, from a quickie express massage to half-day and full-day wedding packages. They also have an indoor pool with hydrojets, a sauna, and various steam rooms. Or go next door, where you can spend all day luxuriating in the indoor pool, Jacuzzi, steam-room or sauna at the **King George Palace Hotel Spa,** 3 Vas. Georgiou Street (☎ 210/322-2210; www.classicalhotels.com), for 25€; use them all for 50€. They also have various beauty treatments and massages. For a quick stop, the aptly named **Quick Spa,** 50–52 Aeolou and 31 Miltiadou streets (☎ 210/325-5545; www.quickspa.gr), is centrally located and offers massages, facials, manicures, and pedicures for him and her at non-deluxe prices.

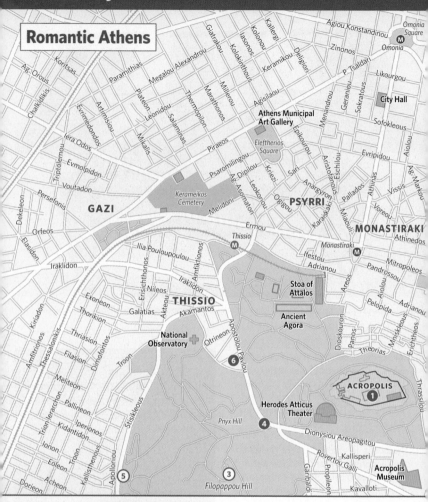

Romantic Athens

ACROPOLIS **1**

Stoa of Attalos

Ancient Agora

National Observatory

Herodes Atticus Theater **4**

6

Pnyx Hill

Filopappou Hill **3**

5

Acropolis Museum

Athens Municipal Art Gallery

Eleftherios Square

Kerameikos Cemetery

GAZI

PSYRRI

MONASTIRAKI

THISSIO

City Hall

> In the Zappeion Gardens, it's easy to find a secluded corner graced by romantic statuary.

5 🍴 **To Koutouki.** For a rustic Greek experience, climb the steep steps to the roof of this grill taverna on **Pnyx Hill,** where the waiters read off a list of specialties for the day, from hot and cold salads and dips to lamb (by the kilo), pork, or steak specialties. Order the house wine, sit back, catch the breeze, and glance over at the Parthenon, getting an unusual and beautiful west-facing view. Dinner hour is 10pm, so be there an hour before or after to get a terrace table. 9 Lykeio St. at Agia Sotira Church on Filopappou ring road. ☎ 210/345-3655. $$.

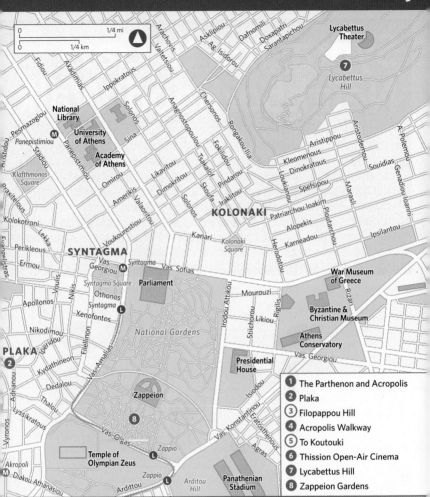

1. The Parthenon and Acropolis
2. Plaka
3. Filopappou Hill
4. Acropolis Walkway
5. To Koutouki
6. Thission Open-Air Cinema
7. Lycabettus Hill
8. Zappeion Gardens

6 ★★★ **Thission Open-Air Cinema.** Watch a classic or memory-making first-run film (don't worry—they're subtitled) under the stars in a garden setting. Then head to a very contemporary outdoor cafe-bar on Iraklidon Street, complete with mood-enhancing chandeliers attached to the awnings. See p. 125.

7 ★ **Lycabettus Hill.** Everything seems more romantic from on high, so make your way up this 277m (909-ft.) hill for the best panoramic view of the city. You can huff and puff it up the trail, or take the cog railway. The **cafe** at the top serves Mediterranean cuisine; it's cheaper than the **restaurant** but still takes advantage of the captive market. See p. 66, 9.

8 **Zappeion Gardens.** This oasis of the city is adjacent to the National Gardens, originally the private garden of Greece's first queen, Amalia. It's perfect for a refreshing break in the hot summer months. It doesn't close, so if you end up here for some predawn smooching, you might find yourself in the company of fellow trysters. If you're just in the mood for a coffee, **Aigli** (☎ 210/336-9363), the very chic, very pricey bistro next to the hall, has a cafe, so you can sip one at your table inside or outside on the veranda. See p. 52, 7.

Syntagma to Gazi Neighborhood Walk

You'll have plenty of company on this walk, as it follows the main shopping thoroughfare along Ermou, where you can find a great pair of shoes. Then veer into Monastiraki to pick up some souvenirs, see some sites, and admire the Acropolis from a cafe. Start in Syntagma Square, the main hub of Athens; then continue west down Ermou Street and through Monastiraki, with its youth-oriented shops, cafes, and a Sunday flea market; pass Psyrri to the north, where the race to replace traditional tinsmiths and tanneries with cafes, bars, and restaurants has slowed for the time being; and finally end your walk in Gazi, named after the gasworks plant that dominates the area, now the latest trendy scene.

> *The changing of the guard takes place hourly in front of Parliament on Syntagma Square.*

START Metro to Syntagma.

1 Syntagma Square. Parliament faces the city's main square, forming a point of the commercial triangle (with Monastiraki and Omonia) in the historic center where you can find major banks, travel agencies, and hotels. The 1830s-era square has three parts: the Tomb of the Unknown Soldier, the Metro exit, and the top of Ermou Street. It has hosted massive protest rallies, New Year's celebrations, and major historic events in the life of the country,

starting with its namesake: the *syntagma* (constitution). The people demanded it in 1843 from the reluctant Bavarian King Otto, who was installed by the Great Powers—the United Kingdom, France, and the Russian Empire—following the War of Independence. Now a Wi-Fi hot zone, it's a good place to stop for a rest or to check your guidebook on a bench or at a cafe near the central fountain. ⏲ 20 min. Amalias and Vas. Georgiou sts. Metro: Syntagma.

1. Syntagma Square
2. Ariston
3. Ermou Street
4. Kapnikarea
5. Aeolou Street
6. Pandrossou Street
7. Tzisdarakis Tzami
8. Monastiraki Square
9. Ifestou Street
10. Abyssinia Square
11. Kerameikos
12. Technopolis
13. Gazi district

> *A Turkish bazaar thrived along Pandrossou during Ottoman rule, and the alleyway's current incarnation is not much different.*

Ermou leads off the west end of the square. Follow it only a block or so, then turn right onto Voulis.

② 🥟 **Ariston.** It's perfectly acceptable in Athens to eat crumbly pies while on the go. You can get your daily nutrients cheaply here, one of the oldest pita bakeries, which makes vegetable-and-meat-pie combinations such as chicken, leek, and eggplant for 1.70€. Takeout only. 10 Voulis St. ☎ 210/322-7626. $

Retrace your steps to Ermou and turn right.

③ ★★★ **Ermou Street.** A busy commercial strip since the 19th century, Ermou Street was pedestrianized in the 1990s to the protests of some misguided shopkeepers who thought they'd lose business. Do your shoe shopping here. See p. 56, ⑤.

As you follow Ermou west, you can't miss the church—it's right in the middle of the street.

④ ★ **Kapnikarea.** This charming church dating from 1050 has typical Athenian-style domes. While dedicated to the Virgin Mary, it has been called various names over the years, but the one that stuck likely refers to a Byzantine-era tax or to the surname of the church's sponsor. See p. 78, ④.

Aeolou is just a block beyond the church.

⑤ ★ **Aeolou Street.** Veer left for 2 blocks on the 1830s street named for Aeolus, god of wind, which leads to the **Tower of the Winds** (p. 56, ⑦). But don't follow the road all the way to the tower; turn right before you reach it, so you can see Pandrossou Street.

⑥ **Pandrossou Street.** This pedestrian alley was the Turkish bazaar, one of the last vestiges of 400 years of Ottoman rule, which ended in the 1820s. No longer the flea market as the banner over the street at Mitropoleos Square suggests, it has long since gone up-market with souvenir and jewelry shops. Pandrossou St. at Mitropoleos Sq.

Souk-like Pandrossou ends at one of Athens' former mosques.

⑦ **Tzisdarakis Tzami.** The Turkish *viovode* (governor) felled an Olympian Zeus temple column to plaster his namesake mosque in 1759. The remaining columns are said to have noisily mourned their sister's loss until the governor, exiled by his superior for the vandalism, was killed. It was used as a prison before being converted in 1918 to a museum, now the Ceramic Folk Art Museum. See p. 58, ①.

Monastiraki Square is in front of you.

Technopolis, which once supplied gas to light the city, is now a hip performing arts venue.

⑧ ★★ Monastiraki Square. The square in ront of Monastiraki Station is named for ne **Little Monastery,** a badly restored 10th-entury church that belonged to a Greek Orodox convent. The square has had multiple celifts; the latest opened up a section of the ncient Iridanos River, which has been long aved over. Stop for a coffee or souvlaki at one f the cafe-restaurants here, or around the orner on **Adrianou Street,** where you'll also et a view of the Acropolis over the Ancient gora. Ermou and Athinas sts.

estou runs offs the west side of the square, ıst beyond the Metro station.

⑨ Ifestou Street. This alley is full of shops atering to youths (beads, boots, shirts), ourists (souvenirs, jewelry), and antique/ ea-market lovers (miscellaneous junk), plus ne odd shop thrown in, like one that sells cycles. Ifestou St. at Monastiraki Sq.

ollow Ifestou west for a few blocks.

⑩ ★ Abyssinia Square. This name may refer ⁻ Ethiopians who lived here, but the square is so known as Paliatzidika (the "secondhand-ıop district"), as this is where a flea market

and a few household-goods auctions are held on Sunday. Ermou, Normanou and Kinetou sts.

Continue west on Ifestou until you see Ermou, then follow that west for several blocks.

⑪ Kerameikos. Located in what was the pottery district of classical Athens, this ancient cemetery has burial artifacts dating from the 11th century B.C. to the 2nd century A.D. It also contains ruins of the 5th-century-B.C. Long Walls, which provided a corridor from Athens to the sea outlet of Piraeus, and the Dipylon Gate (the main entrance to ancient Athens). Sections of Iera Odos (Sacred Way), an important road that led from Athens to Demeter's temple in ancient Eleusis, now modern Elefsina (22km/14 miles away), are also here. Kerameikos is one of the lesser-known sites in Athens, but it's beautiful nonetheless: Despite the busy location, it's peaceful to meander among the monuments. The museum is interesting too. ⏱ 1 hr. 148 Ermou St. ☎ 210/346-3552. Part of the 12€ Acropolis ticket package. Museum and site 2€. May–Oct daily 8am–8pm, Nov–Apr daily 8:30am–3pm. Museum: Mon 11am–3pm. Metro: Thissio.

From the cemetery, get back on Ermou, follow that a block or so until it ends at Piraeos, and turn left. The Technopolis complex and the Gazi district will be on your right.

⑫ ★★ Technopolis. Lovers of industrial design and the film *Metropolis* will appreciate this unique converted gasworks. Dating from 1862, with additions in 1896 and the mid-1900s, it fueled the city's network of lights with gas. The site and its unusual mix of buildings now host concerts, exhibitions, and the City of Athens radio station. There's a cafe on site. At night, the smokestacks are lit up as if they're red hot. See p. 57, ⑪.

⑬   🍽 ★ **Gazi district.** Go inside the **Technopolis** complex, the old gasworks, where there's a **cafe** (☎ 210/347-0981; daily 9:30am–11pm) in one of the buildings on the grounds. Or stop for a meal at one of the many restaurants along Persefonis Street, toward the Kerameikos Metro station, or at one of numerous, über-trendy cafe-bars on the parallel road opposite the station. See p. 127.

Plaka, Thissio & Psyrri Neighborhood Walk

Experience a slice of life in Athens by wandering through the districts where the locals shop—the area reaffirming that expertise-driven, mom-and-pop shops can thrive in mixed zoning, with Sundays off. Start in the historic Plaka zone, with its stately 19th-century buildings and tourist stores; then head through ancient parks into the cafe-lined streets of Thissio with its excellent views of the Acropolis. Turn northeast into vibrant Athinas Street, with its central food market and DIY shops, as well as the streets leading off it, through Psyrri, and back eastward up to where you started.

> *Major avenues, and at times what seems like most of Athens' 4 million residents, converge on Syntagma.*

START **Metro to Syntagma.**

① Syntagma Square. Central Syntagma, the main square in town in front of Parliament, is the heart from which the arterial avenues of Athens branch out. This should be your starting point. See p. 84, **①**.

As you follow Ermou off the square, Nikis is first street you'll come to.

② Nikis Street. The first cross street west of Syntagma, often confused with Voulis Street (the next one down), Nikis is getting trendier by the day, with a busy organic food store tha

1. Syntagma Square
2. Nikis Street
3. Plaka
4. Adrianou Street
5. Hill Memorial School
6. Roman Agora
7. Thissio
8. Psyrri
9. Athinas Street
10. Perikleous Street

also sells lunches, colorful jewelry shops, and Asian restaurants. It leads into Kydathineon Street, named after the ancient municipality in Plaka. Nikis and Ermou sts.

As you head south on Nikis, you'll be entering the Plaka district.

❸ ★★★ kids **Plaka.** This is the oldest and most expensive part of town, hugging the north and east slopes of the Acropolis. There are both ruins and historic buildings to gawk at here, including the unusual **Lysicrates** monument. Built to display trophies for the best play productions at the Dionysos Theater around the corner, it's named after the patron whose performance won top prize in 334 B.C. Ancient Tripodon Street, which still exists, was lined with similar monuments. Continue to Kydathineon and turn right, then left on Selly. Backtrack onto Tripodon and turn left into any small street to reach **Anafiotika.** The area was settled by Cycladic island migrants, especially from the island of Anafi, who came to build the modern capital in the mid-1800s. Apart from the view of the city, the atmosphere can only be described as that of an Aegean island village. See p. 46, ❼.

Turn right (north) onto Adrianou.

❹ **Adrianou Street.** This is the main street in Plaka, the long-inhabited area north of the Acropolis. It's lined with attractive 19th-century buildings with ground-floor tourist shops. The mansion that is believed to be the city's

oldest, a rare relic that dates at least from Turkish rule in the 17th century, is behind the wall at no. 96, at the top of Palaiologou Benizelou Street, named for its owner (a magistrate). Thought also to be the ancestral home of an Athens-born saint, Filothei (1522–89), it is being restored by the Archdiocese of Athens, which also has her relics.

Turn right on Nikodimou and left on Thoukididou to see an American landmark.

❺ **Hill Memorial School.** American John Henry Hill (1791–1882) opened a school for underprivileged girls here in 1831, receiving many awards for the effort. It now operates as a coed private school. 9 Thoukididou St. ☎ 210 323-5298. www.hill.gr.

Get back on Adrianou, turn right, and follow it west through the Plaka to Aeolou. Turn left and walk south a block to the Agora.

❻ **Roman Agora.** The "new" Roman Agora was funded and built by Julius Caesar in 51 B.C. (and finished by Octavian Augustus in 19 B.C.), after wealthy, Athens-loving Romans had moved into the Ancient Agora site and built larger edifices there, thus crowding out merchants. It was larger than what we see now (much of it is now buried under buildings). The most visible remains are the 1st-century B.C. **Tower of the Winds,** a unique ancient water clock built by the astronomer Andronikos Kyristes, and the gate entrance to the market dedicated to Athena

> *Julius Caesar began construction of the Roman Agora in 51 B.C.*

rchegetis (Athena the Leader) around 11 B.C. Without a minaret, the forlorn but beautiful **etiye Mosque** on the site was built in 1458 to ommemorate then Turkish ruler Mehmet II's sit to Athens. See p. 56, **7**.

ollow the Agora around to its southern oundary on Polygnotou.

) ★★★ Thissio. Follow the top (south) boundary of the Roman Agora westward on Polygnotou Street (where some graffiti shows real talent) until you come to the Ancient Agora entrance. There's a lovely green area here where you can explore the north slope of the Acropolis. Continue on the **path** past the fenced-off Agii Apostoli Church till you reach Thissio. Turn right (north), stop at one of the many outdoor **cafes** for refreshment, and marvel at the view of both the Acropolis and Lycabettus Hill. See p. 42, **2**.

hissio Square is on the edge of Pyssri.

) ★★★ Psyrri. Continue into Psyrri, where ou can stroll through the narrow streets inerspersed with traditional small manufacturrs—mostly tinsmiths, basket weavers, and eather craftsmen specializing in bags and hoes. At night, the area gets a second life when estaurants, bars, and clubs open. In 1809, poet nd Greek War of Independence fighter Lord yron boarded at 11 Agias Theklas Street (now nondescript warehouse). He romanticized the wner's 12-year-old daughter, Teresa Makris, in Maid of Athens." See p. 54, **2**.

> *Central Market overflows with produce and comestibles, and shops on nearby streets ply tools, twine, and other domestic staples.*

Head east on any street to reach Athinas and turn left.

9 ★ Athinas Street. Get in touch with your inner handyman on Athinas Street, which anchors shops selling tools, hardware, and other supplies, from votive candles to live chickens. It leads to the **Central Market,** where vendors sell meat, fish, vegetables, nuts, dried fruit, and other bulk foods. Veer right from Evripidou (Euripides) Street (which has a plethora of cheese shops near Athinas) onto **Polykleitou,** lined with more interesting specialty shops, including some that sell nothing but string, rope, and twine. **Athinas St. at Evripidou or Sofokleous sts.**

From Polykleitou, head east on Vissis to Aeolou, turn right, and head south to Athinaidos.

10 Perikleous Street. Make your way across to Perikleous, one street north of central Ermou Street. It changes names four times: It's Karageorgi Servias, Perikleous, Athinaidos, and Agias Eirinis before it reaches Athinas Street, and Vas. Georgiou A (King George I) on the other side of Stadiou Street. It doesn't have Ermou's international chain stores, but it has undergone gentrification, and more funky and upscale shops and cafes are moving in. You'll find ethnic items, polished stones, and every kind of bead imaginable with which to create your own earrings, necklaces, or bracelets.

Follow Perikleous up (east), and you're back at central Syntagma Square.

Psyrri's Charms

Psyrri is an ideal showcase for a typical night out in Athens. It's a busy working neighborhood by day, but its narrow pedestrian streets are a magnet for nightlife-loving Athenians. Patrons sit at tables lining the sidewalks around the squares, interrupted by the odd car trying to gain passage, a Roma child selling flowers, or an accordion troupe making its way from table to table. A mix of Greek restaurants, cafes, alternative bars and clubs, art galleries, theaters, and shops, Psyrri is one of Athens's prime entertainment zones.

Athens Shopping Best Bets

Best Original Art
Astrolavos-Dexameni 11 Xanthippou St. (p. 93)

Best Folk Art
★ **Amorgos** 3 Kodrou St. (p. 98)

Best Spice & Herb Shop
★ **Bahar** 31 Evripidou St. (p. 97)

Best Museum Reproduction Gifts
★ **Benaki Museum Gift Shop** 1 Koumbari St.
(p. 98)

Best Bookstore
Eleftheroudakis 17 Panepistimiou St. (p. 95)

Best Sunday Flea Market
★★ **Gazi Flea Market** Ermou and Pareos sts.
(p. 101)

Best Traditional Greek Textiles
★ **ISPS Arts & Crafts** 14 Filellinon St. (p. 99)

Best Place for Designer Shoes
Kalogirou 4 Patriarchou Ioakim St. (p. 103)

Best Magazine Shop
★★ **Kiosk** 18 Omonia Sq. (p. 95)

Best Selection of Silverware
Konstantopoulou 23 Lekka St. (p. 99)

Best Place for Skin Care Products
Fresh Line 10 Skoufa St. (p. 94)

Best-Known Athenian Jeweler
★ **Lalaounis** 6 Panepistimiou St. (p. 101)

Best Place for Worry Beads
★ **Mala** 1 Praxitelous St. (p. 99)

Best Place for Musical Instruments
Philippos Nakas Conservatory 44 Panepistimiou St. (p. 102)

Best One-Stop Shop
★★★ **Shopping Center Plaka** 1 Pandrossou St.
(p. 100)

> *The Benaki Museum gift shop.*

Athens Shopping A to Z

Antiques & Collectibles

Antiqua SYNTAGMA
Buy museum pieces such as 19th-century watercolors, pistols, and enormous belt buckles at this high-end antique store, which carries furniture from Greece and abroad as well as *objets d'art*. 2 Amalias Ave. ☎ 210/323-2220. www.antiqua.gr. AE, DC, MC, V. Metro: Syntagma. Map p. 95.

Old Prints, Maps & Books SYNTAGMA
For as little as 10€, purchase a beautiful, original 19th-century gravure of Athens or other destinations in Greece. Old maps, books, and drawings of birds and plants are also for sale here. 15 Kolokotroni St. ☎ 210/323-0923. www.oldprints.gr. AE, DC, MC, V. Metro: Syntagma, or bus no. 200. Map p. 95.

Art

Astrolavos-Dexameni KOLONAKI
This gallery sells fresh, accessible, and unique work by Greek artists. Displays range from temporary exhibitions of art to bric-a-brac and furniture for sale. The overriding quality is whimsical, especially at the 11 Irodotou Street location (☎ 210/722-1200) near Kolonaki Square. Also at 140 Androutsou Street, Piraeus (☎ 210/412-8002). 11 Xanthippou St. ☎ 210/729-4342 or 4343. www.astrolavos.gr. AE, DC, MC, V. Metro: Syntagma. Map p. 95.

Grekas Ekklesiastika Eidi MONASTIRAKI
This shop lies outside the neighborhood where most ecclesiastical accouterments are sold (Apollonos St.), but it's conveniently located near Agia Eirini Church. In the large showroom and workshop onsite, the artist can make an icon of any saint in silver, wood, or other materials. 9 Agias Eirinis St. ☎ 210/325-2047. AE, DC, MC, V. Metro: Monastiraki. Map p. 94.

A vendor in Monastiraki.

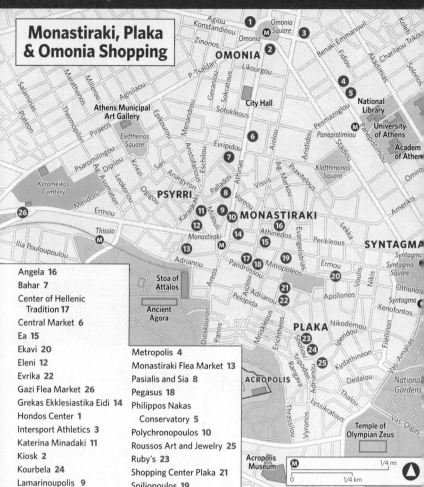

Monastiraki, Plaka & Omonia Shopping

Angela 16
Bahar 7
Center of Hellenic Tradition 17
Central Market 6
Ea 15
Ekavi 20
Eleni 12
Evrika 22
Gazi Flea Market 26
Grekas Ekklesiastika Eidi 14
Hondos Center 1
Intersport Athletics 3
Katerina Minadaki 11
Kiosk 2
Kourbela 24
Lamarinoupolis 9

Metropolis 4
Monastiraki Flea Market 13
Pasialis and Sia 8
Pegasus 18
Philippos Nakas Conservatory 5
Polychronopoulos 10
Roussos Art and Jewelry 25
Ruby's 23
Shopping Center Plaka 21
Spiliopoulos 19

Beauty & Toiletries

Apivita KOLONAKI

This manufacturer of natural beauty products, including Propoline hair care made from bee products and herb extracts, is popular in 16 countries and sold in major pharmacies throughout Greece. 26 Solonos St. ☎ 210/364-0560. www.apivita.com. MC, V. Metro: Panepistimiou, or bus no. A5, E7, 060, or 224. Map p. 95.

Fresh Line KOLONAKI

Beauty products and pyramids of colorful, soaps with rice, seaweed, honey, and other all-natural organic ingredients look good enough to eat. 10 Skoufa St. ☎ 210/364-4015. www.freshline.gr. MC, V. Metro: Syntagma. Map p. 95.

Hondos Center OMONIA

The flagship store of this toiletries chain has all the grooming items you'll ever need, with lavish perfume counters, complete product lines, accessories, and even luggage. Come here when you need to restock or get sunscreen; then go to the 10th floor and enjoy the view of the city over lunch or coffee. 4 Omonia Sq. ☎ 210/528-2800. www.hondos.gr. AE, DC, MC, V. Metro: Omonia. Map p. 94.

Korres PANGRATI

Used by the likes of the Beckhams and Nicole Kidman, this reasonably priced skin-care line was developed by an herbal pharmacist using natural products. The products are

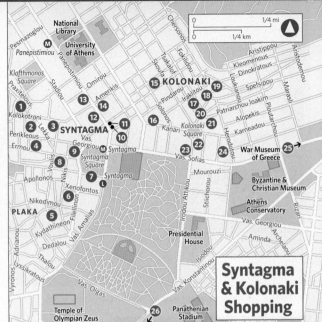

morgos **5**
ntiqua **7**
pivita **15**
strolavos-Dexameni **19**
ttica **12**
enaki Museum Gift Shop **23**
leftheroudakis **13**
ena Votsi **18**
resh Line **17**
PS Arts & Crafts **6**
alogirou **21**
arakou Gulluoglu **8**
ombologadiko **22**
onstantopoulou **2**
orres **26**
ozatsa Creations **16**
alaounis **11**
apin House **4**
Iala (Komboloi Club) **1**
he Mall **25**
Mastihashop **10**
Museum of Cycladic Art **24**
Old Prints, Maps & Books **3**
rasini **20**
ublic **9**
santilis **14**

Map labels: National Library, University of Athens, Panepistimiou, KOLONAKI, SYNTAGMA, Syntagma Square, PLAKA, Presidential House, War Museum of Greece, Byzantine & Christian Museum, Athens Conservatory, Kolonaki Square, Temple of Olympian Zeus, Panathenian Stadium

Syntagma & Kolonaki Shopping

biquitously available in Greece, sold at pharmacies, Attica Department Store, and the lagship shop in Pangrati, but you can also find he brand in many other countries and purchase products online. **8 Ivikou St. at Erathoshenous St.** ☎ **210/722-2774. www.korres.com. AE, DC, MC, V. Metro: Syntagma. Map p. 95.**

Books & Magazines

Eleftheroudakis SYNTAGMA
ind English titles on any subject in the eighttory Panepistimiou location, which has a whole floor devoted to travel books, as well s a cafe-restaurant to rest in after hours of browsing. **17 Panepistimiou St.** ☎ **210/325-440. www.books.gr. AE, DC, MC, V. Metro: Panepistimiou. Map p. 95.**

★★ Kiosk OMONIA SQUARE
Athens's best-stocked foreign-press *periptero* kiosk) never closes, which is fortunate for lesperate or jet-lagged news and magazine unkies. It's my favorite place to buy obscure magazines. **18 Omonia Sq. at Athinas St., in ront of Everest (fast food).** ☎ **210/322-2402. No credit cards. Metro: Omonia. Map p. 94.**

> *Perfume purveyor Hondos.*

> *Astrolavos-Dexameni shows the work of contemporary Greek artists.*

Where to Get It

Jewelry, shoes, and edibles are standout merchandise in Greece. For hip and **cool fashions,** head to the streets around youthful Exarchia Square or Ifestou Street in Monastiraki. Kolonaki is the **upmarket designer** district, while **shoes** and **chain stores** are on central Ermou Street. **Souvenirs** and **jewelry** are mainly on Adrianou Street in Plaka, down to Pandrossou Street in Monastiraki. For **goods made in Greece,** go to the streets leading off Athinas. Running from Athinas toward Stadiou Street are shops grouped together by merchandise, such as **textiles** (Athinaidos St.) and **church-related supplies** (Apollonos St., near the Mitropoleos Cathedral). Abyssinia Square in Monastiraki is a **flea market** that also sells **used and antique furniture.** Be aware that the Latin spelling for street names can be different, street names may change from one block to the next, and many districts use the same name. Plaka and Monastiraki both have an Adrianou Street, for example, while Eleftherios Venizelos has his name on numerous streets, but not all are known as that, including central Panepistimiou Street. Keep an open mind while map-reading.

Department Stores

Attica SYNTAGMA

In the middle of town, this eight-floor "shop-in-shop" department store (a mall-like collection of individual designer and brand-name shops under one roof) sells a range of wares, from perfumes to home products and, most of all, clothes. You can purchase garments by up-and-coming Greek designers here, such as Eleftheriadis at Collage Sociale, Erotokritos at Eros, and Celia Kritharioti at 5226 by Celia Kritharioti. It's best to buy in August and January, when the sales are on. 9 Panepistimiou St. ☎ 211/180-2600. www.atticadps.gr. AE, DC, MC, V. Metro: Syntagma. Map p. 95.

The Mall MAROUSSI

Greece's largest mall was built here in 2005 by one of the shipping dynasties (Latsis). It has four levels, some 200 shops, a food court, an entertainment complex, and a convenient Metro station entrance. 35 Andrea Papandreou St. ☎ 210/630-0000. www.themallathens.gr. Metro or Proastiakos (suburban train): Nerantziotissa. Map p. 95.

Public SYNTAGMA

This very centrally located high-tech department store sells everything to do with gadgets, from cameras and memory cards to

> *Greek designer wear at Tsantilis.*

toys, books, CDs, and laptops. The music and English-language books won't set you back too far either. 1 Nikis and Karageorgi Servias sts. ☎ 210/324-6210. www.public.gr. AE, DC, MC, V. Metro: Syntagma. Map p. 95.

Fashion

★ Kourbela PLAKA

Comfy, reasonably priced, and eco-friendly linen-, silk-, and-cotton-blend unisex clothing, including Earth Collection garments, is sold at this signless corner shop alongside Greek-made classic knits. I can't get enough of them. 109 Adrianou St. ☎ 210/322-4591. AE, DC, MC, V. Metro: Syntagma or Monastiraki. Map p. 94.

Tsantilis SYNTAGMA

This shop has various branches around town that also sell material. It's well known for stocking good-quality fabrics and designer clothing at reasonable prices. 6 Panepistimiou St. at Voukourestiou St. ☎ 210/360-6815. www.tsantilis.gr. AE, DC, MC, V. Metro: Syntagma. Map p. 95.

Food & Wine

★ Bahar AGORA

Take home big bags of oregano, mountain tea, and many more obscure herbs that make

welcome, inexpensive gifts. 31 Evripidou St. ☎ 210/321-7225. www.bahar-spices.gr. No credit cards. Metro: Omonia or Monastiraki, or bus no. 025, 026, 027, 035, 049, 200, or 227. Map p. 94.

Olde Athens

Even today, numerous old-world craftsmen front their own shops on the streets of this modern European capital. And while many thrive, some skills will die out for lack of apprentice interest or because the wares can be imported cheaper. Browse and—better yet—buy from these charming places on the verge of extinction, found here listed under Art, Gifts, Home, Handbags & Hats, and Shoes. Salespeople still have expert knowledge of their wares, and they welcome browsing (unlike larger establishments with hired staff expected to shadow customers and push for a sale). For the best of this nostalgic side of Athens life, start by walking through Psyrri and east of Athinas Street to Polykleitou, Praxitelous, Agiou Markou, and Perikleous sts.

> *Lalaounis re-creates ancient and Byzantine jewelry.*

Karakou Gulluoglu SYNTAGMA
This shop sells irresistible Turkish pastries and puddings. Their horseshoe-shaped shortbread cookies dipped in chocolate are addictive—but sold only in winter so they don't melt. The dainty spinach pies are good too. 10 Nikis St. ☎ 210/321-3959. MC, V. Metro: Syntagma. Map p. 95.

Mastihashop SYNTAGMA
The island Chios is known for its coveted medicinal mastic tree gum. It's a unique flavor, and here the resin is made into a variety of products and packaged in attractive, old-fashioned tins. The *loukoumi* (Turkish Delight) is a standout. Panepistimiou and Kriezotou sts. ☎ 210/363-2750. www.mastihashop.gr. AE, MC, V. Metro: Syntagma. Map p. 95.

Gifts

★ **Amorgos** PLAKA
At the entrance to Plaka, where the street goes pedestrian, this shop sells Greek-made antique and folk items as well as linen and embroidery. 3 Kodrou St. ☎ 210/324-3836. AE, DC, MC, V. Metro: Syntagma. Map p. 95.

★ **Benaki Museum Gift Shop** KOLONAKI
The museum stocks a variety of exhibit reproductions of gold and silver jewelry, textiles, and ceramic bowls, as well as a good selection of translated books on Greece. 1 Koumbari St. at Vas. Sofias Ave. ☎ 210/367-1000. www.benaki.gr. AE, DC, MC, V. Map p. 95.

Center of Hellenic Tradition MONASTIRAKI
This shop is a good place to find genuine folk arts and crafts from around Greece, including pottery, decorative roof tiles, and old-fashioned painted-wood shop signs. 36 Pandrossou and 59 Mitropoleos sts. ☎ 210/321-3023. MC, V. Metro: Monastiraki. Map p. 94.

★ **Ekavi** MONASTIRAKI
Here you'll find handmade *tavli* (backgammon) board games—the *kafeneion* (cafe) brigade's game of choice—or chess sets, with pieces resembling Olympic athletes, Greek gods, and so on, created in wood, metal, or stone. 36 Mitropoleos St. ☎ 210/323-7740. AE, DC, MC, V. Metro: Monastiraki or Syntagma, or bus no. 025, 026, or 027. Map 94.

vrika PLAKA
ick up official shirts and other mementos of
Greek football (soccer) teams such as Pan-
thinaikos, Olympiakos, and AEK, as well as
Athens 2004 souvenirs from this ex-Olympic
store outlet. **69 Adrianou St.** ☎ 210/325-1935.
E, DC, MC, V. Metro: Monastiraki or Syntagma.
Map p. 94.

ISPS Arts & Crafts ZAPPEION
or traditional Greek designs made in Greece,
ome to this store. It sells carpets, tapestries,
nd beautifully embroidered linens made by
isadvantaged women around the country.
Prices start at 20€ for a small embroidery. **14
ilellinon St.** ☎ 210/325-0240. www.oikotexnia-
kpa.gr. AE, DC, MC, V. Metro: Syntagma. Map
. 95.

Kombologadiko KOLONAKI
Bone, stone, wood, and antique amber are
used to make these globally sourced *komboloi*
(worry beads) at the most exclusive branch of
his store (don't even try to say the name).

Tony Kolonaki
Perfectly coiffed, shod, and clothed Athenians can be found in **Kolonaki.** It's full of
old-fashioned coffee bars that are proud to
stay that way, chic designer shops, pedestrian streets, expensive apartments, and
denizens of Athens's upper echelons who
aim to impress. **Voukourestiou Street** has
the most exclusive shops (Tod's shoes and
Baccarat crystal, to name two), and streets
that lead off it are lined with outdoor cafes
(turn right on Skoufa or Tsakalof sts.).

> *Angela outfit kids in high style.*

6 Koumbari St. ☎ 212/700-0090. www.
kombologadiko.gr. AE, DC, MC, V. Metro: Syntagma. Map p. 95.

Konstantopoulou SYNTAGMA
A large silverware store among many along
"Silver Alley," it sells bowls, candlesticks,
lamps, cutlery, and the like. **23 Lekka St.**
☎ 210/322-7997. AE, DC, MC, V. Metro: Syntagma. Map p. 95.

★ Mala (Komboloi Club) SYNTAGMA
You'll find a beautiful selection of amber worry
beads for any budget at this inviting shop on a
street that sells all kinds of beads. **1 Praxitelous
St.** ☎ 210/331-0145. www.komboloiclub.com.
MC, V. Metro: Panepistimiou. Map p. 95.

★ Museum of Cycladic Art KOLONAKI
Purchase Cycladic figurines, art posters,
jewelry, and other reproductions from this

> *Ea sells toys, housewares, and other goods for the home.*

museum's collection. 4 N. Douka St. at Vas. Sofias Ave. ☎ 210/722-8321 or 8323. www. cycladic.gr. AE, DC, MC, V. Metro: Syntagma. Map p. 95.

Roussos Art and Jewelry PLAKA
For porcelain Greek dolls made at a workshop in western Athens, come to this shop at the main Plaka intersection; they start at 45€. You'll also find many other handcrafted, Greek-made trinkets, such as silver jewelry and ceramics. 121 Adrianou St. at Kydathineon St. ☎ 210/322-6395. AE, D, MC, V. Metro: Akropoli. Map p. 94.

★★★ Shopping Center Plaka MONASTIRAKI
Do all your souvenir shopping in one go at this superstocked three-level store that straddles the Ermou, Plaka, and Monastiraki districts. It's also one of the few places that stocks writing paper (including some with a Greek motif). 1 Pandrossou St. ☎ 210/324-5405. www. shoppingplaka.com. AE, MC, V. Metro: Monastiraki. Map p. 94.

Handbags & Hats
Katerina Minadaki MONASTIRAKI
Katerina and her husband make beautiful, soft leather and cloth handbags (60€–120€)—a

rarity, as most of the craftsmen make ● hard leather bags. They also make the● order but prefer to see an actual exam● what you're looking for rather than a p● 3rd floor, 9 Miaouli St. (through the arca● ☎ 210/321-5903. DC, MC, V. Metro: Mo● raki. Map p. 94.

Polychronopoulos MONASTIRAKI
This men's hat shop opened up right n● to one that's been around for years, wh● perhaps a good sign. Men of a certain ● pick up their Bermudas, while the Gree● erman's hat makes a useful Greek sou● and it's only 7€. 15 Voreiou St. (end of K● troni St.) at Athinas St. ☎ 210/321-4510● Monastiraki. Map p. 94.

Home
Lamarinoupolis MONASTIRAKI
Psyrri still has a few tinsmiths who sell ● lightweight items, such as typical tave● barrel wine jugs, miniwatering cans, ar● in all sizes (from 3€). Venture carefully● the steep steps to see more wares and ● workshop. 17 Athinas and 2 Kakourgodi● sts. (beside Cyprus Bank). ☎ 210/324-8● credit cards. Metro: Monastiraki. Map p.●

Pasialis and Sia MONASTIRAKI

This bric-a-brac shop with wares along the sidewalk should be renovated by the time you read this review. The store sells all kinds of merchandise, from wine barrels to fake flowers to tin vases and wine jugs, as well as basketry and woven goods, including handy reed slippers, which can do double duty at the beach. 5 Pallados St. ☎ 210/321-4200. MC, V. Metro: Monastiraki. Map p. 94.

Jewelry

Elena Votsi KOLONAKI

Popular with celebrities who want to make a statement, Votsi's jewelry is as heavy as your neck, wrist, or finger can stand. She also has an outlet on the island Hydra. 7 Xanthou St. ☎ 210/360-0936. www.elenavotsi.com. AE, DC, MC, V. Metro: Syntagma. Map p. 95.

★ Lalaounis SYNTAGMA

A luxury brand, Lalaounis is perhaps the best known among many superb jewelers for crafting ancient and Byzantine reproductions as well as modern creations. 6 Panepistimiou St. at Voukourestiou St. ☎ 210/361-1371. Museum: 12 Karyatidon St., Makriyanni. ☎ 210/922-1044. www.lalaounis-jewelrymuseum.gr. AE, DC, MC, V. Metro: Akropoli. Map p. 95.

Ruby's PLAKA

High-quality jewelry that won't break the bank is made on site at this long-established shop. They can also fabricate your own designs, do engravings, or change your ring size while you wait. 105 Adrianou St. ☎ 210/322-3312. AE, DC, MC, V. Map p. 94.

Kids

kids Angela MONASTIRAKI

You can't walk by without noticing the cutest christening dresses in the window. Get one, or the whole baptism package needed for the ceremony. There's a sweet selection of baptism favors (*boubouniera*). 9 Kalamiotou St. at Kapnikareas St. ☎ 210/323-8448. www.angela.gr. AE, D, MC, V. Metro: Monastiraki. Map p. 94.

kids Ea MONASTIRAKI

Find whimsical piggy banks, fairies, dolls, and other toys, plus unique knickknacks and home decorations in this spacious shop on a street parallel to pricey Ermou. 9 Agia Irinis Sq. at Aeolou and Athinaidas sts. ☎ 210/321-8562. DC, MC, V. Metro: Monastiraki. Map p. 94.

kids Lapin House SYNTAGMA

This Greek chain offers up really nice, good-quality kids' clothes—but with a price tag to match. 21 Ermou St. ☎ 210/324-1316. www.lapinhouse.com. AE, DC, MC, V. Metro: Syntagma. Map p. 95.

Markets

★★ Central Market OMONIA

This is one of the best things about Athens. Farmers' markets appear once a week in neighborhoods around town, but the main one for more than a century is the Varvakio Agora—a visual, aural, and olfactory jolt. Athinas St. at Sofokleous St. Year-round Mon–Thurs 6am–3pm, Fri-Sat 6am–6pm. Metro: Omonia or Monastiraki, or bus no. 025, 026, 035, 049, 100, 200, 227, or 400. Map p. 94.

★★ Gazi Flea Market GAZI

The "down-market" flea market sets up here on Sundays at the foot of Ermou Street opposite Gazi, near the ancient Kerameikos

> *The Sundays-only Gazi fleamarket extends for blocks.*

> *The fish section of Central Market.*

Cemetery, and extends up Ermou Street to Thissio Station, merging into Monastiraki's flea market. It's mainly junk set out on blankets, but who knows, you might find a treasure and it's fun to have a look. **Ermou and Piraeos sts.** Year-round Sun early morning to 3 or 4pm. Metro: Thissio or Kerameikos. Map p. 94.

Monastiraki Flea Market MONASTIRAKI
Shops in the narrow alleys of the Monastiraki district, particularly Pandrossou and Ifestou streets, have long gone up-market, but you'll still find secondhand and antique estate contents in Abyssinia Square, while the alleys leading to it get covered by flea market merchandise every Sunday. You'll find dusty books, military uniforms, coins and stamps, light fixtures, plates, cutlery, and furniture. **Abyssinia Sq. at Ermou, Normanou, and Kinetou sts.** Year-round daily 9am–9pm, best on Sun. Metro: Monastiraki. Map p. 94.

Music
Metropolis OMONA
The city's best-known department store for music sells concert and event tickets and hosts performances on the premises. They carry an extensive selection of all kinds of music as well as books and games. **54 Panepistimiou St.** ☎ 210/380-8549. www.metropolis.gr. AE, DC, MC, V. Metro: Omonia. Map p. 94.

Pegasus MONASTIRAKI
Genuine handmade bouzouki instruments (starting at 150€) are the best-selling items, but this shop also sells stringed *taboura* (a type of lute) and small, hand-held *touberlekia* (bongo drums). The 26 Pandrossou Street store sells only instruments while the other shop sells instruments, jewelry, and art as well. **26 Pandrossou St.** ☎ 210/324-2036. **92 Adrianou St.** ☎ 210/324-2601. www.pegasusgreece.com. AE, DC, MC, V. Metro: Monastiraki. Map p. 94.

Philippos Nakas Conservatory OMONA
Buy an instrument or sheet music at this serious chain of music stores, or buy online from their catalog. If this outlet is closed, try the main shop, nearby at 13 Navarinou Street (☎ 210/364-7111). **44 Panepistimiou St.** ☎ 210/361-2720. www.nakas.gr. AE, DC, MC, V. Metro: Panepistimiou. Map p. 94.

> At Kozatsa Creations, you can buy shoes custom-made or off the rack.

Shoes

Eleni MONASTIRAKI

Prada? Gucci? Manolo Blahnik, anyone? Fashionistas who don't have the budget to match their tastes can get beautifully crafted designer-reproduction shoes for 100€ to 150€ made to order on the premises (allow 7–10 days). Have a look at their sample shoes too. 9 Miaouli St. (on the ground floor in the Singer arcade). ☎ 210/322-7678. No credit cards. Metro: Monastiraki. Map p. 94.

Intersport Athletics OMONIA

This shop on "Runner Alley" has the best selection of trainers in town. 3 Themistokleous St. ☎ 210/330-3997. www.intersport.gr. AE, DC, MC, V. Metro: Omonia. Map p. 94.

Kalogirou KOLONAKI

This shop has its own label but carries designer shoes as well. Branches are located in the best districts, including a shop that sells stock at half-price or less (best for odd sizes) in Plaka/Monastiraki (12 Pandrossou St.; ☎ 210/335-6410). 4 Patriarchou Ioakim St.

☎ 210/335-6401. AE, DC, MC, V. Metro: Syntagma, or bus no. 022, 060, or 200. Map p. 95.

Kozatsa Creations KOLONAKI

Before the shoemaker retires, order custom leather shoes or buy house styles (with pretty, non-teetering heels) for 130€ to 150€. 11 Kanari St. ☎ 210/362-7592. No credit cards. Metro: Syntagma. Map p. 95.

Prasini KOLONAKI

One of the main shoe sellers on Tsakalof Street carries a nice selection of designer shoes and bags. 7–9 Tsakalof St. ☎ 210/364-6258. AE, DC, MC, V. Metro: Syntagma. Map p. 95.

Spiliopoulos MONASTIRAKI

This stock shoe store is another place to find designer labels at good prices, but it's best for very big or very small feet. The nicest pairs in average sizes go quickly. Also wallets, purses, and a huge selection of bags. 63 Ermou St. ☎ 210/322-7590. AE, DC, MC, V. 50 Adrianou St. ☎ 210/321-9096. DC, MC, V. Metro: Monastiraki. Map p. 94.

Athens Restaurant Best Bets

Best Exotic Food
★ **Altamira** 36A Tsakalof St. (p. 105)

Best Novel Greek Dining Experience
★ **Archaion Gefseis** 22 Kodratou St. (p. 105)

Best Highbrow Evening Out
★ **Benaki Museum Restaurant's Thursday night buffet** 1 Koumbari St. (p. 105)

Best French Bistro
★ **Chez Lucien** 32 Troon St. (p. 106)

Best Place for Romance
★★ **GB Roof Garden** Grande Bretagne Hotel, Syntagma Sq. (p. 108)

Best Place for Budget Romance
Filistron 24 Apostolou Pavlou St. (p. 106)

Best Vegetarian Diner
★ **Health-Ecology** 57 Panepistimiou St. (p. 109)

Best Panorama of the City
Orizontes Aristippou and Ploutarchou sts. (p. 109)

Best Meze
★★ **Rozalia** 58 Valtetsiou St. (p. 110)

Best Grill
★★★ **Telis** 86 Evripidou St. (p. 111)

Best Seafood
★ **Varoulko** 80 Piraeos St. (p. 111)

Best Mince Souvlaki
Thanasis 69 Mitropoleos St. (p. 56)

> *Altamira serves cuisines from around the world.*

Athens Restaurants A to Z

★ **Altamira** KOLONAKI *EXOTIC*
Crocodile, wild boar, or ostrich, anyone? This bar-restaurant also serves dishes with Arabian, Indian, Mexican, and Asian pedigrees and fusions. Their duck filets are especially popular; ask about the chef's daily special, too. 36A Tsakalof St. ☎ 210/361-4695 or 363-9906. www.altamira.com.gr. Entrees 15€–25€. MC, V. Sept-June Mon–Sat lunch & dinner. Closed July and Aug. Metro: Syntagma, or bus no. 200. Map p. 106.

★ **Archaion Gefseis** METAXOURGIO
TRADITIONAL GREEK Patrons sample *archaion gefseis* (ancient flavors), such as ambrosia of the gods, at this theme restaurant that re-creates the ancient Greek dining experience. Servers wear togas, and you can too. Hits include *tyros* (cheese with berry sauce) and *kreokakavos* (pork pancetta). 22 Kodratou St. ☎ 210/523-9661. Entrees 12€–17€. AE, DC, MC, V. Year-round Mon–Sat dinner, Sun lunch & dinner. Map p. 108.

> *Café Avissinia serves Greek favorites amid old world surroundings.*

★ **Athinaikon** OMONIA *MEZE TAVERNA*
This is one of three authentic Athenian meze restaurants in the heart of town. The others on this pedestrianized block are Petrino and Andreas, and they're all good. Athinaikon, opposite the Titania movie theater, has been around since 1932, and it's still busy all the time. The starters are excellent, many of them seafood-based. 2 Themistokleous and Panepistimiou sts. ☎ 210/383-8485. Entrees 6.50€–14€. MC, V. Year-round Mon–Sat lunch & dinner. Metro: Omonia. Map p. 106.

★ **Benaki Museum Restaurant** KOLONAKI
EUROPEAN Rest midtour with a quiche and an expansive view of Athens. The Thursday-night (8:30pm–midnight) buffet (40€ without drinks) is very popular; reservations are recommended. 1 Koumbari St. at Vas. Sofias Ave. ☎ 210/367-1000. www.benaki.gr. Entrees 12€. AE, DC, MC, V. Year-round daily breakfast & late lunch. Closed holidays. Metro: Syntagma. Map p. 106.

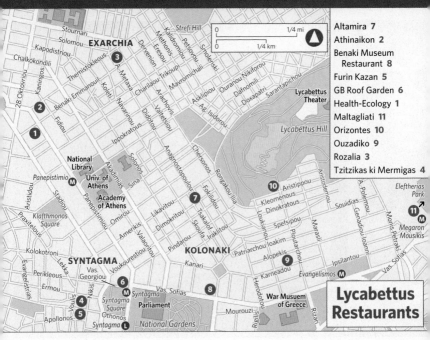

Altamira **7**

Athinaikon **2**

Benaki Museum Restaurant **8**

Furin Kazan **5**

GB Roof Garden **6**

Health-Ecology **1**

Maltagliati **11**

Orizontes **10**

Ouzadiko **9**

Rozalia **3**

Tzitzikas ki Mermigas **4**

Lycabettus Restaurants

★★ **Café Avissinia** MONASTIRAKI *TAVERNA* Unusual Greek dishes, a view of the Acropolis from upstairs, a lively atmosphere, and a location off the main restaurant strip (near the flea market) are the attractions at this mahogany-and-polished-copper cafe. 7 Kinetou St. at Abyssinia Sq. ☎ 210/321-7047. www.avissinia.gr. Entrees 9.50€–16.50€. MC, V. Sept–July Tues–Sun lunch. Closed Aug. Metro: Monastiraki. Map p. 108.

★ **Chez Lucien** ANO PETRALONA *FRENCH* This tiny restaurant with a completely set table affixed to the ceiling is a dining experience—so much so that the owners opened another one, which serves only seafood, next door. It's so small you're likely to share a table, but the country-French food is delicious. Most people order the set 3-course meal for 22€; a 3-course at

Restaurant Tip

Fish in Athens restaurants may not be fresh if it's not a specialty item on the menu. Athens's port city of Piraeus, 10km (6¼ miles) away, has a plethora of restaurants where seafood is always fresh, especially along the marina in Microlimani.

Chez Lucien LaMaree (seafood) is 25€. 32 and 30 Troon St. ☎ 210/346-4236. Entrees 14€–17€. No credit cards. Daily dinner. Chez Lucien LaMaree closed Sun–Mon, both closed Christmas week. No reservations, except for orders (4 minimum) for bouillabaisse. Bus no. 227. Map p. 107.

★ **Edodi** KOUKAKI *CONTEMPORARY* This is one of Athens's best restaurants, where the foodie chef brings ingredients to your table for precooking inspection, then gauges your tastes and prepares them accordingly. The style is a fusion of Greek and French. **Note:** The restaurant is at the top of a steep staircase. 80 Veikou St. ☎ 210/921-3013. www.edodi.gr. Entrees 25€. AE, DC, MC, V. Sept–June Mon–Sat dinner. Closed July–Aug. Reserve ahead. Metro: Syngrou-Fix, or trolley no. 1, 5, or 15. Map p. 107.

★ **Filistron** THISSIO *REGIONAL GREEK* This fits the bill in the romantic department: It's one of the best places in town to see the million-dollar view of the Acropolis and Lycabettus Hill while eating. 24 Apostolou Pavlou St. ☎ 210/346-7554. www.filistron.com. Entrees 14€. DC, MC, V. Sept–June Tues–Sun lunch & dinner, July–Aug Tues–Sun dinner only. Metro: Thissio. Map p. 107.

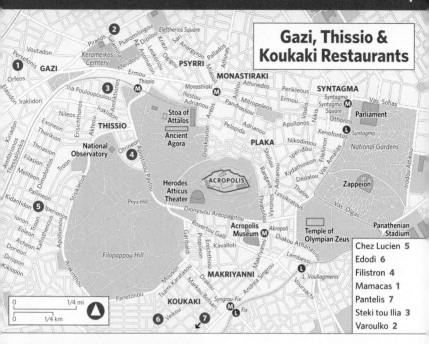

Gazi, Thissio & Koukaki Restaurants

Chez Lucien 5
Edodi 6
Filistron 4
Mamacas 1
Pantelis 7
Steki tou Ilia 3
Varoulko 2

Restaurant Tips

Dining out is a national pastime in Greece, and fresh ingredients are the staples piled high on multiple meze plates. Athenian restaurants are sometimes divided by neighborhood (for instance, you can easily find a good midday or early-evening souvlaki on "Kebab Street," at the foot of Mitropoleos St., at Monastiraki Sq.; in the Psyrri district, you can dine later, at 10pm, to the tune of live *bouzouki* music). Most restaurants, except those in hotels and others that cater to tourists, are usually closed on either Sunday, Monday, or Tuesday, as well as on Christmas, New Year's Day, Orthodox Easter Sunday, and around August 15 (the Assumption of the Virgin Mary). Unless stated otherwise, the closing times listed are when the kitchen closes, not the restaurant—it is a rare proprietor who would kick out a patron. As for tipping, restaurants may include a service charge, but an extra 10% to 15% for the waiter or busboy is appreciated.

> A meze platter at Altamira.

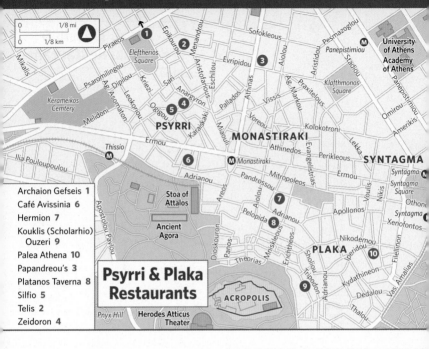

Archaion Gefseis **1**
Café Avissinia **6**
Hermion **7**
Kouklis (Scholarhio)
   Ouzeri **9**
Palea Athena **10**
Papandreou's **3**
Platanos Taverna **8**
Silfio **5**
Telis **2**
Zeidoron **4**

Psyrri & Plaka Restaurants

> Simple salads burst with flavor in Greece.

Furin Kazan SYNTAGMA *JAPANESE*
Get your Japanese-food fix at this well-placed restaurant that straddles the town center and Plaka. It's got an extensive menu and reasonable prices, even if the portions are smaller than you may be used to. 2 Apollonos St. ☎ 210/322-9170. Entrees 8€–22€. AE, DC, MC, V. Year-round Mon–Sun lunch & dinner. Metro: Syntagma. Map p. 106.

★★ **GB Roof Garden** SYNTAGMA *MEDITERRANEAN* This is a destination restaurant with a to-die-for view favored by politicians from nearby Parliament and those about to leave singledom behind. It's open year-round for breakfast, lunch, and dinner on the eighth floor of the city's most prestigious hotel. The Italian chef makes pastas, plus fish and steak, and there are homemade desserts. Or just come for the sunset and have a drink at the translucent backlit bar, which is open-air in summer. Grande Bretagne Hotel, Syntagma Sq. ☎ 210/333-0000. www.grandebretagne.gr. Entrees 19€–45€. AE, DC, MC, V. Year-round daily breakfast, lunch, & dinner (limited hours Dec 24, Dec 25, Dec 31, Jan 1). Metro: Syntagma. Map p. 106.

> Diners sample meze at Kouklis Ouzeri.

★ **Health-Ecology** OMONIA *VEGETARIAN*
This cafeteria has been serving cheap, Greek-style dishes and fresh juices for years. There's an adjacent health-food store with organic fresh fruit and vegetables that accepts credit cards (MC, V), unlike the restaurant. 57 Panepistimiou St. ☎ 210/321-0966. Entrees 4.50€–7€. No credit cards. Year-round Mon–Sat breakfast, lunch, & early dinner; Sun late breakfast & lunch only. Closed holidays. Metro: Omonia. Map p. 106.

★ **Hermion** MONASTIRAKI/PLAKA *TAVERNA*
This elegant taverna with cloth tablecloths and discreet service opens into its own enclosed garden. An old Athenian standby, it's frequented by ladies who lunch, businessmen, and people wanting to meet up in a central location or after shopping. 15 Pandrossou St. ☎ 210/324-7148. www.hermion.gr. Entrees 8€–14€. AE, MC, V. Year-round daily lunch & dinner. Metro: Monastiraki. Map p. 108.

Kouklis (Scholarhio) Ouzeri PLAKA *MEZE/TAVERNA* Choose from a tray of appetizers at this tourist-oriented taverna, nicknamed the Scholarhio for the nearby school. Ten dishes, a liter of wine (or a substitute), mineral water, and dessert go for 14€ per person for a group of four or more. 14 Tripodon St. ☎ 210/324-7605. www.sholarhio.gr. Meze 3€–6€. MC, V. Year-round daily lunch & dinner. Metro: Syntagma or Monastiraki. Map p. 108.

★★ **Maltagliati** PANORMOU *ITALIAN*
A small trattoria in Panormou draws a crowd with its homemade pastas and many other delicacies from across the Adriatic. 6 Varnakioti St. ☎ 210/691-6676. www.maltagliati.gr. Entrees 15€–17€. No credit cards. Mon–Sat 8pm–midnight. Closed Aug. Metro: Panormou. Map p. 106.

Mamacas GAZI *MODERN GREEK*
This upscale taverna garners great reviews, more for its location than anything. Dishes are out of the ordinary, and you can dine on the sidewalk beside the Kerameikos Metro station in trendy Gazi. 41 Persefonis St. ☎ 210/346-4984. www.mamacas.gr. Entrees 10€–15€. Year-round daily 1:30pm–1:30am. AE, MC, V. Metro: Kerameikos. Map p. 107.

Orizontes KOLONAKI *CONTINENTAL*
See the city in all its vastness and gaze out to sea, freighters and all, atop Lycabettus Hill at this seafood restaurant that also serves Kobe beef. **Cafe Lycabettus,** a

> *Palea Athena, meaning Old Athens, serves old-fashioned favorites.*

Mediterranean-cuisine bar-restaurant with a cheaper menu and an outdoor terrace, is on the same site. **Aristippou and Ploutarchou sts.** ☎ 210/721-0701. www.kastelorizo.com.gr. Entrees 23€–70€, cafe entrees 14€–27€. AE, D, MC, V. Year-round daily noon–2am; cafe 9am–2am. Last cable car at 3am. Bus no. 022, 060, or 200 to the cable railway. Map p. 106.

Ouzadiko KOLONAKI *MEZE*
The shopping mall location may be odd, especially since there are no shops in it, but this lively *ouzeri* (meze restaurant) has a wide variety of food and, of course, ouzo. **Lemos International Centre, 25–29 Karneadou St.** ☎ 210/729-5484. Entrees 8€–25€. AE, DC, MC, V. Year-round Mon–Sat noon–12:30am. Closed Dec 25, Jan 1, Orthodox Easter Sun, and Aug. Metro: Evangelismos. Map p. 106.

Palea Athena PLAKA *TAVERNA*
At this old-fashioned Athenian restaurant, the prices are just fine and the selection is wider than usual—including an item missing from most menus here: soup. **46 Nikis St.** ☎ 210/324-5777. Entrees 6€–13€. AE, DC, MC, V. Year-round Mon–Sat noon–12:30am. Metro: Syntagma. Map p. 108.

★★ Pantelis PALAIO FALIRO *TURKISH-GREEK*
It's well worth the trip to this restaurant serving *politiki* (city) cuisine (the city in question being Constantinople, though *Politiki Kouzina* is also the Greek title of the popular foodie film *A Touch of Spice*). Indulge in *yaourtlou* kebabs—skewers of meat and veggies on pita with a yogurt sauce, *kazandibi* (deliberately burnt rice pudding), and other dishes from "the city." **96 Naiadon St.** ☎ 210/982-5512. Entrees 7.50€–12.50€. No credit cards. Sept–July Tues–Fri 8pm–midnight, Sat noon–5pm and 8pm–midnight, Sun noon–6pm. Closed holidays and Aug. Tram: Panagitsa. Map p. 107.

★★ Papandreou's AGORA *TAVERNA*
This *mageiria* (cookhouse) serves big portions of soups, stews, and square meals round-the-clock near one of the meat-market entrances at the Central Market. Customers range from surly loners to loud clubgoers who happily rub shoulders in the name of taste. **1 Aristogeitonos St. at Evripidou St. (inside the agora meat market).** ☎ 213/008-2242. Entrees 6€–9€. No credit cards. Year-round daily 24 hr. Metro: Omonia, Panepistimiou, or Monastiraki. Map. 108.

Platanos Taverna PLAKA *TAVERNA*
Platanos is a simple classic Greek taverna on a quiet street near the Tower of the Winds. You can eat inside or outside. **4 Dioyenous St.** ☎ 210/322-0666. Entrees 4€–10€. No credit cards. July–Feb Mon–Sat lunch & dinner, Mar–Jun lunch & early dinner daily. Closed 2 weeks in Aug. Metro: Monastiraki or Syntagma. Map p. 108.

★★ Rozalia EXARCHIA *MEZE/TAVERNA*
Take your choice of meze from a tray and/or order entrees in the enclosed garden (opposite the taverna or under the overhead vines in the pedestrian street at this busy restaurant off Exarchia Square. **58 Valtetsiou St.** ☎ 210/330-2933. Entrees 6€–15€. MC, V. Daily lunch & dinner. Closed Jan 1, Dec 25. Metro: Omonia. Map p. 106.

Silfio PSYRRI *MODERN GREEK*
The cat-and-moon-silhouette logo is a beacon in the Psyrri maze: It's notably reliable for big portions, tasty food, and good service. **24 Taki St.** ☎ 210/324-7028. Entrees 11€–22€. AE, DC, MC, V. Year-round Tues–Sun lunch, daily dinner. Closed Orthodox Easter. Metro: Thissio. Map p. 108.

★ Steki tou Ilia THISSIO *TAVERNA*

A duo of traditional tavernas under one name on the same pedestrian street, this place is full both winter and summer, when tables are set up across the road. This is Greek food where Greeks eat—order your lamb chops by the kilo. 5 Eptahalkou St. ☎ 210/345-8052; 7 Thessalonikis St. ☎ 210/342-2407. Entrees 8€–12€. No credit cards. 5 Eptahalkou St.: Mon–Sat dinner, Sun lunch & early dinner. 7 Thessalonikis St.: Tues–Fri dinner, Sat–Sun lunch & dinner. Eptahalkou closed last 2 weeks in Aug, Thessalonikis closed first 2 weeks in Aug. Both closed Jan 1, Orthodox Easter Sun, and Dec 25. Metro: Thissio. Map p. 107.

★★★ Telis PSYRRI *GRILL*

Within moments of your taking a table at Telis, a stack of pork chops the size of steaks appears. They're possibly the best anywhere, and the ultimate for hungry carnivores. Getting there might be an adventure though; the area's a bit seedy these days. 86 Evripidou St. at Koumoundourou Sq. ☎ 210/324-2775. Entrees (a stack plus bread) 9€. No credit cards. Sept–July Mon–Sat lunch & dinner. Closed Aug. Bus no. 100, or 200. Map p. 108.

★ Tzitzikas ki Mermigas SYNTAGMA *MODERN GREEK*

With the look of an old grocery store, this restaurant serves cooked, baked, or grilled chicken and shrimp, as well as other Greek standards. Patrons dine indoors or outside on the sidewalk. Tables have butcher paper on top and drawers storing flatware and napkins. 12–14 Mitropoleos St. ☎ 210/324-7607. Entrees 12€–18€. MC, V. Mon–Sat lunch & dinner. Closed holidays, 2 weeks in Aug. Metro: Syntagma. Map p. 106.

★ Varoulko KERAMEIKOS *SEAFOOD*

This is a well-known restaurant in the Athens scene and cited among the city's best. It's known from its longtime location at the port of Piraeus, but the Michelin-starred chef moved it in 2004 to this rather out-of-the-way place beside the Eridanus Hotel within walking distance of three Metro stations, and on the main route from the port. 80 Piraeos St. ☎ 210/522-8400. www.varoulko.gr. Entrees 22€–32€. AE, DC, MC, V. Year-round Mon–Sat dinner from 8:30pm. Metro: Kerameikos, Thissio, or Omonia. Map p. 107.

> Tables at Steki tou Ilia spill onto the street.

Zeidoron PSYRRI *MEZE*

Choose from a wide variety of wine, beer, and ouzo, plus excellent meze and heartier fare, at this restaurant better known for its central Psyrri locale. Try their seafood assortment, or ask about the daily special. 10 Taki St. at Agia Anargyron St. ☎ 210/321-5368. Entrees 9.50€–15€. AE, D, MC, V. Fri–Sun lunch, daily dinner. Closed Jan 1, Orthodox Easter weekend, 1 week in Aug, and Dec 25. Metro: Monastiraki. Map p. 108.

Athens Hotel Best Bets

Best Quiet Hotel Near the Acropolis
Acropolis View Hotel 10 Webster St. (p. 113)

Best Supersize Luxury Hotel
Athenaeum InterContinental 89–93 Syngrou Ave. (p. 114)

Best Hostel
★★ **Athens Backpackers** 12 Makri St. (p. 114)

Best Budget Lodging for Families
★★★ **Athens Studios** 3A Veikou St. (p. 115)

Best Hotel with Conveniently Located Parking
★ **Central Athens Hotel** 21 Apollonos St. (p. 116)

Best All-Around
★★★ **Electra Palace** 18 Nikodimou St. (p. 116)

Best Old-World Luxury Hotel
★★★ **Grande Bretagne** Syntagma Sq. (p. 116)

Best Midsize Hotel Near the Acropolis
★★ **Herodion Hotel** 4 Rovertou Galli St. (p. 117)

Best Iconic Luxury Hotel
★ **Hilton Athens** 46 Vas. Sofias Ave. (p. 117)

Best Stay in a Greek Neighborhood Hotel
★ **Art Gallery** 5 Erechthiou St. (p. 114)

Best Conveniently Located Budget Hotels
★ **Hotel Attalos** 29 Athinas St. (p. 118)

★ **Adonis Hotel** 3 Kodrou St. (p. 113)

Best Boutique Hotel
★ **O&B** 7 Leokoriou St. (p. 119)

Accommodations Booking Services

The private travel agencies at the arrivals hall of the Athens International Airport, Amphitrion (☎ 210/353-0162) and Pacific Travel (☎ 210/353-0160), are open 24 hours and can book hotels and tours.

> *The rooftop pool at the Grande Bretagne.*

Athens Hotels A to Z

Acropolis House Hotel PLAKA
This popular budget hotel occupies a restored 150-year-old house on a quiet pedestrian street that straddles Syntagma and Plaka. The old wing has the old Athenian touches. Rooms without air-conditioning are cheaper. 6–8 Kodrou St. ☎ 210/322-2344. www.acropolishouse.gr. 19 units. Doubles 61€–91€ w/breakfast. MC, V only to reserve (pay in cash). Metro: Syntagma. Map p. 117.

Acropolis View Hotel KOUKAKI
On a quiet side street close to the Acropolis and the walkway in a residential area, it has small, clean rooms, some with balconies facing the Parthenon, as well as a roof terrace. 10 Webster St. at Rovertou Galli St. ☎ 210/921-7303 or 7305. www.acropolisview.gr. 32 units. Doubles 70€–110€ w/breakfast. MC, V. Metro: Akropoli or Syngrou-Fix, or bus/trolley no. 1, 5, 15, or 230. Map p. 114.

★ **Adonis Hotel** PLAKA
This hotel is a good value on a quiet street in a great location, near the shopping district and Syntagma Square. Rooms are spartan, but some have big balconies, and the rooftop cafe (good for breakfast and evening drinks) has a view of the Acropolis. 3 Kodrou St. ☎ 210/324-9737. www.hotel-adonis.gr. 26 units. Doubles 60€–95€ w/breakfast. AE, MC, V. Metro: Syntagma. Map p. 117.

★ **Adrian Hotel** PLAKA
Catty-corner to a cafe-lined square on Plaka's main pedestrian street, the Adrian allows you to eat breakfast or lounge in the garden with a view of the Acropolis, or soak up the atmosphere across the street. Rooms are updated and airy. 74 Adrianou St. ☎ 210/322-1553. www.douros-hotels.com. 22 units. Doubles 85€–140€ w/breakfast. MC, V. Metro: Monastiraki. Map p. 117.

> *A view of the Parthenon from the Divani Palace Acropolis.*

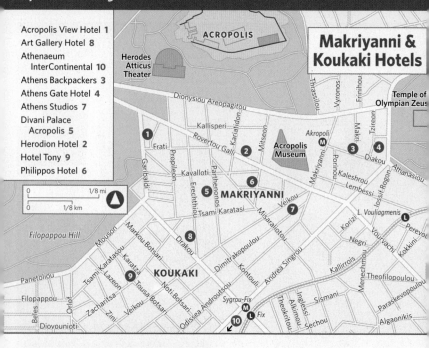

Acropolis View Hotel **1**
Art Gallery Hotel **8**
Athenaeum
    InterContinental **10**
Athens Backpackers **3**
Athens Gate Hotel **4**
Athens Studios **7**
Divani Palace
    Acropolis **5**
Herodion Hotel **2**
Hotel Tony **9**
Philippos Hotel **6**

Makriyanni & Koukaki Hotels

Lodging Tips

Athens is a tourist town awash in hotels. There are countless good ones—particularly in the historic center around the Acropolis and other neighborhoods popular with travelers, such as Syntagma, Plaka, Monastiraki, Thissio, Makriyanni, and Koukaki. These are the best areas covered here, so you don't have to worry about staying in a hotel far from the sites or in areas that are dodgy, although they do offer incredible rates, especially for online booking. Many hotels have also been renovated in the past 10 years in the run-up to the 2004 Olympics. To find particularly good deals, book online or ask about off-the-rack-rate rooms during the off-season (often July and Aug), for multiple-night stays, or with cash payment. Hotels outside the center may also be a bargain, especially since the efficient Metro (another Olympics-related development project) runs all over town. Finally, hotels can request an advance payment of up to 25% of the total for a multiple-night stay, or not less than 1 night's rate, and some may accept cash only.

★ kids **Art Gallery Hotel** KOUKAKI
If you want to see what it's like to live in an average Greek neighborhood but still be near the Acropolis and a Metro stop, this hotel in a converted 1950s house, the former home of an artist, is conveniently located. 5 Erechthiou St. ☎ 210/923-8376. www.artgalleryhotel.gr. 21 units. Doubles 70€–100€. No credit cards. Metro: Syngrou-Fix, or bus/trolley no. 1, 5, 15, or 230. Map p. 114.

kids **Athenaeum InterContinental** NEOS
KOSMOS When only no-fuss, American-size luxury will do, stay here (Bill Clinton did). Athens's biggest luxe hotel is efficient with large rooms, a 24-hour restaurant, a pool, a spa, and a nearby movie complex. It's a 15-minute walk from the city center, but there's a shuttle. 89–93 Syngrou Ave. ☎ 210/920-6000. www.intercontinental.com. 543 units. Doubles 220€–245€. AE, DC, MC, V. Metro: Syngrou-Fix; or bus/trolley no. 9, A2, B2, E2, E22, 040, 450, 550, or 126; or tram: Neos Kosmos. Map p. 114.

★★ **Athens Backpackers** MAKRIYANNI
Always full, this bunk-bed hostel organizes tours and BBQs. It's lively, and the staff is friendly. The rooftop bar has a view of the

Syntagma & Kolonaki Hotels

Athens Cypria Hotel **2**
Grande Bretagne **5**
Hilton Athens **7**
Hotel Achilleas **1**
King George Palace **4**
NJV Athens Plaza **3**
Periscope **6**

Acropolis. 12 Makri St. ☎ 210/922-4044. www.
backpackers.gr. 60 units. Price per bed: 17€–
25€. AE, MC, V. Metro: Akropoli. Map p. 114.

Athens Cypria Hotel SYNTAGMA

On a narrow street with outdoor cafes just 3
blocks from Syntagma Square, this popular
business hotel is relatively empty during low
season, July and August. It's cheerful, too, with
bright white walls. Room nos. 603 to 607 overlook the Acropolis. Book ahead. 5 Diomias St.
☎ 210/323-8034 or 0470. www.athenscypria.
com. 115 units. Doubles 98€–120€ w/breakfast.
AE, MC, V. Metro: Syntagma. Map p. 115.

Athens Gate Hotel MAKRIYANNI

In a central location on an arterial eight-lane
street, this midsize hotel has clean rooms, top-
notch service, and a rooftop breakfast area
and restaurant with superb views. 10 Syngrou
Ave. ☎ 210/923-8302. www.athensgate.gr. 99
units. Doubles 135€–175€ w/breakfast. AE, DC,
MC, V. Metro: Akropoli. Map p. 114.

★★★ kids Athens Studios MAKRIYANNI

Backpackers often upgrade from the Backpackers hostel (p. 114) to these Ikea-kitted,
self-catering apartments, also ideal for

> *A room at the Adrian in Plaka.*

families. There is a sports bar and a self-service laundry downstairs. 3A Veikou St. ☎ 210/
923-5811. www.athensstudios.gr. 35 units. Apt
for 2–3 people 70€–120€. AE, MC, V. Metro:
Akropoli. Map p. 114.

> *Roomy quarters have kitchenettes at Athens Studios.*

★ kids **Ava Hotel** PLAKA
Ava's spacious, clean, and comfortable studios with kitchenettes, on a quiet street in the Old Town within sight of Hadrian's Arch, are great for families and businesspeople staying in Athens for a while. Check with the hotel for special offers. 9–11 Lyssikratous St. ☎ 210/325-9000. www.avahotel.gr. 15 units. 130€–390€. AE, MC, V. Metro: Akropoli. Map p. 117.

★ **Central Athens Hotel** SYNTAGMA
Modern furnishings, attentive service, perfect location: This midprice hotel hits all its marks. Twin rooms at the back have Acropolis views, while bigger front rooms have balconies and king-size beds. There's also a rooftop lounge and parking. 21 Apollonos St. ☎ 210/323-4357. www.centralhotel.gr. 84 units. Doubles 93€–155€ w/breakfast. AE, DC, MC, V. Metro: Syntagma. Map p. 117.

Divani Palace Acropolis MAKRIYANNI
This large anchor hotel is in a quiet residential neighborhood, though it caters mainly to tour groups. It has an outdoor pool and a rooftop restaurant (with an extensive breakfast buffet), and rooms are big if bland, with balconies. 19–25 Parthenonos St. ☎ 210/928-0100. www.divanis.gr. 253 units. Doubles 143€–440€ w/

breakfast. AE, DC, MC, V. Metro: Syngrou-Fix. Map p. 114.

★★★ **Electra Palace** PLAKA
The luxury Electra is the biggest hotel in Plaka and the best choice for convenience. Higher floors here have smaller rooms but bigger balconies with views of the Acropolis and are farther up from the busy narrow street. Amenities include indoor and outdoor pools, a gym, and a steam room. The rooftop pool and bar/restaurant have views of the Acropolis. 18 Nikodimou St. ☎ 210/337-0000. www.electrahotels.gr. 150 units. Doubles 166€–267€ w/breakfast. AE, DC, MC, V. Metro: Syntagma. Map p. 117.

★★★ **Grande Bretagne** SYNTAGMA
This 160-year-old landmark hotel is *the* Athens address. Now part of the Starwood Luxury Collection, it has an Acropolis-view rooftop bar-restaurant, an award-winning spa, an indoor pool, and an outdoor rooftop pool, not to mention immaculate service, beautiful rooms, and a lobby bar. Syntagma Sq. ☎ 210/333-0000. www.grandebretagne.gr. 321 units. Doubles 362€–690€. AE, DC, MC, V. Metro: Syntagma. Map p. 115.

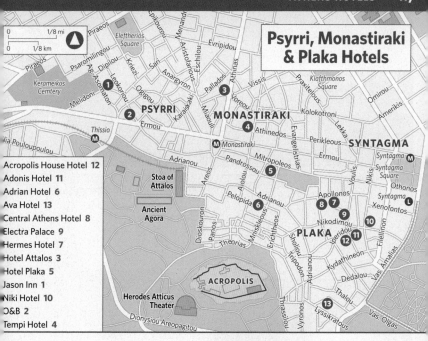

Psyrri, Monastiraki & Plaka Hotels

Acropolis House Hotel 12
Adonis Hotel 11
Adrian Hotel 6
Ava Hotel 13
Central Athens Hotel 8
Electra Palace 9
Hermes Hotel 7
Hotel Attalos 3
Hotel Plaka 5
Jason Inn 1
Niki Hotel 10
O&B 2
Tempi Hotel 4

Hermes Hotel SYNTAGMA

One of three hotels on perfectly located Apollonos Street—walking distance from Syntagma Square (and the Metro to the airport), the shopping area, and Plaka—this renovated hotel has spacious rooms by city standards. 19 Apollonos St. ☎ 210/323-5514 or 2706. www. hermeshotel.gr. 45 units. Doubles 95€–150€ w/breakfast. AE, DC, MC, V. Metro: Syntagma. Map p. 117.

★ Herodion Hotel MAKRIYANNI

This modern midsize hotel is in a quiet neighborhood near the New Acropolis Museum, which is also a great central location. The rooms are large, the staff is helpful, and you can use the rooftop Jacuzzi for 5€. 4 Rovertou Galli St. ☎ 210/923-6832. www.herodion.gr. 90 units. Doubles 130€–250€. AE, DC, MC, V. Metro: Akropoli. Map p. 114.

kids Hilton Athens HILTON

Athens's iconic landmark hotel, on the point between two arterial roads, has a huge outdoor and indoor pool and spa, great restaurants, and a roof-top bar, Galaxy. The artwork on the facade is by Yiannis Moralis. 46 Vas. Sofias Ave. ☎ 210/728-1000. www.athens. hilton.com. 508 units. Doubles 217€–525€ w/

> *The Electra Palace garden.*

> *An old stunner steals the show at the stylish, contemporary O&B.*

breakfast. AE, DC, MC, V. Metro: Evangelismos. Map p. 115.

Hotel Achilleas SYNTAGMA

You can't go wrong at this business hotel with minimalist decor and helpful staff on a quiet street close to Syntagma Square in the main shopping area. If you can get a room, that is— it's a popular choice for the location and price. 21 Lekka St. ☎ 210/323-3197. www.achilleas hotel.gr. 34 units. Doubles 80€–130€ w/break-fast. AE, MC, V. Metro: Syntagma. Map p. 115.

★ Hotel Attalos MONASTIRAKI

This very popular budget hotel is on lively Athinas Street near Monastiraki Station, which is also on the Metro line to the airport. There's a roof-terrace snack bar as well as Acropolis-view rooms. 29 Athinas St. ☎ 210/321-2801. www.attaloshotel.com. 80 units. Doubles 60€–94€; 10% discount for Frommer's readers. AE, MC, V. Metro: Monastiraki. Map p. 117.

Hotel Plaka MONASTIRAKI

The rooms seem small at this convenient hotel close to Monastiraki Station, the shopping area, Plaka, and Mitropoleos Cathedral, but it's nonetheless popular. Request an Acropolis view. 7 Kapnikareas St. at Mitropoleos St. ☎ 210/322-2096. www.plakahotel.gr. 67 units. Doubles 95€–145€ w/breakfast. AE, DC, MC, V. Metro: Monastiraki, or bus no. 025, 026, or 027. Map p. 117.

kids Hotel Tony KOUKAKI

A pink building on a residential street, Tony's is a budget hotel in a bedroom neighborhood, renovated with some deluxe studios that are well suited for families or longer stays. There's also a roof garden. 26 Zacharitsa St. ☎ 210/923 0561 or 5761. www.hoteltony.gr. 21 units. Doubles 60€. No credit cards. Metro: Syngrou-Fix, or trolley no. 1, 5, or 15. Map p. 114.

Jason Inn PSYRRI

You can Acropolis-gaze over breakfast from the roof garden at this moderate hotel that's perfect for nightlife sampling on the edge of trendy Psyrri, Thissio, and Monastiraki, with their restaurants, bars, and sidewalk cafes. And it's just a short walk to even trendier Gazi. 12 Agion Asomaton St. ☎ 210/325-1106.

eservations ☎ 210/520-2491. www.douros-
otels.com. 57 units. Doubles 75€–95€ w/
reakfast. MC, V. Metro: Thissio. Map p. 117.

King George Palace SYNTAGMA

his modern hotel in the most central part of
own has a comfy lounge-bar-restaurant, an
ndoor pool and sauna, and a gorgeous Acrop-
lis view from the 7th-floor Tudor Hall res-
aurant serving Greco-French cuisine. 3 Vas.
eorgiou St. ☎ 210/322-2210. www.classical
otels.com. 78 units. Doubles 270€. Metro:
yntagma. Map p. 117.

iki Hotel PLAKA

his hotel on a quiet, convenient, and trendy
treet has small rooms and bathrooms, but
his is Europe. Higher floors have balconies
nd there's a bar-lounge downstairs. 27 Nikis
t. ☎ 210/322-0913. www.nikihotel.gr. 23 units.
oubles 80€–107€ w/breakfast. AE, DC, MC, V.
Metro: Syntagma. Map p. 117.

NJV Athens Plaza SYNTAGMA

ocated in the busiest yet central and conve-
ient part of town at Syntagma Square, this
rge, bustling luxury hotel draws crowds of
cals to its upstairs lounge. Syntagma Sq.
210/335-2400. www.njvathensplaza.gr. 182
nits. Doubles 160€–215€ w/breakfast. AE, DC,
C, V. Metro: Syntagma. Map p. 115.

O&B PSYRRI

ou'll have dinner and drinks on your door-
tep if you stay at this plush and minimalist
outique hotel right in the nightlife district,
entrally located between Thissio and Mo-
astiraki Metro stations. 7 Leokoriou St.
210/331-2950. www.oandbhotel.com. 22
nits. Doubles 105€–190€ w/breakfast. AE, MC,
. Metro: Thissio or Monastiraki. Map p. 117.

Periscope KOLONAKI

ou can designer-shop, join cafe society, party,
nd then sleep at this minimalist hotel in the
icest Athens district. A bar/restaurant on the
remises serves light meals, including chicken
d steaks. 22 Haritos St. ☎ 210/729-7200.
ww.periscope.gr. 21 units. Doubles 150€–190€
/breakfast. AE, DC, MC, V. Metro: Syntagma, or
us no. 022, 060, or 200. Map p. 115.

hilippos Hotel MAKRIYANNI

he sister hotel of the Herodion around the
orner has more of a boutique feel, with sleek

> Hotel Tony in posh Kolonaki.

polished wood. The entrance is on the staircase landing, so it's not for those with mobility
issues. 3 Mitseon St. ☎ 210/922-3611. www.
philipposhotel.gr. 50 units. Doubles 85€–110€.
AE, DC, MC, V. Metro: Akropoli. Map p. 114.

Tempi Hotel MONASTIRAKI

This popular budget hotel is on a pedestrian
street that leads to the Roman Agora. It's in
the shopping area and faces a flower market.
It's central, friendly, clean, and quiet, with
communal kitchen facilities and Wi-Fi. 29
Aeolou St. ☎ 210/321-3175. www.tempihotel.gr.
24 units. Doubles 45€–64€. AE, MC, V. Metro:
Monastiraki. Map p. 117.

Athens Nightlife & Entertainment Best Bets

Best Place to See Greek Folk Dance
★★ **Dora Stratou Theater** Filopappou Hill (p. 125)

Best Highbrow Evening Out
★★★ **Herodes Atticus Theater** or **Epidaurus Theater** Acropolis or Epidaurus (p. 125)

Best Lowbrow Evening Out
★★ **Stamatopoulos** 26 Lissiou St. (p. 129)

Best Outdoor Movie Theater
★★★ **Thission Open-Air Cinema** 7 Apostolou Pavlou St. (p. 125)

Best Glamorous Seaside Lounge
★ **Akrotiri Boutique** B5 Vas. Georgiou St. (p. 121)

Best Hotel Bar
★ **Alexander's Bar** Hotel Grande Bretagne, Syntagma Sq. (p. 124)

Best Place to Go Clubbing
★ **Vega** 3 Agias Eleousis St. (p. 126)

Best Bar with a Panoramic View
★ **Galaxy Bar** Hilton Athens, 46 Vas. Sofias Av (p. 124)

Best Cafe-Bar for People-Watching
Jackson Hall 4 Milioni St. (p. 121)

Best Irish Pub to Watch Sports
★★ **James Joyce** 12 Astiggos St. (p. 124)

Best Urban Watering Hole
★★ **Kafeneion Pente Dromous** Themistokleous and Koletti sts. (p. 124)

Best Place to See a Big-Name Greek Singer
★ **Rex** 48 Panepistimiou St. (p. 128)

Best Authentic *Bouzoukia*
★ **Romeo** 1 Ellinikou St. (p. 129)

Best Cafe-Bar for Rock Music
★ **Stavlos** 10 Iraklidon St. (p. 121)

> View classic tragedy in an ancient setting at the Herod Atticus Theater.

Athens Nightlife & Entertainment A to Z

Bar- & Club-Restaurants

Akrotiri Boutique AGIOS KOSMAS

The food at this glam seaside lounge-club-restaurant is various and artful, ranging from lamb to caviar, as is the music, which runs from Greek to hip-hop and R&B. Guest DJs and live performances are scheduled on weekends. It's about 6.8km (4¼ miles) from central Athens, along the coast. B5 Vas. Georgiou St., Kalamaki. ☎ 210/985-9147. www.akrotirilounge.gr. The cover varies from 10€–20€. Mid-Apr to Oct daily. Tram: Kalamaki, or bus no. A2 (third Kalamaki stop). Map p. 122.

Cubanita Havana Club PSYRRI

Cuban cuisine and the perfect mojito are coupled with Latin music played live each night by a house band with accompanying animation and dancers. This place isn't warehouse-size, but it's the spot for salsa. 28 Karaiskaki St. at

Psyrri Sq. ☎ 210/331-4605. www.cubanita.gr. 15€ cover (includes one drink) Fri–Sat, Tues–Thurs and Sun 10€. Closed Aug. Metro: Monastiraki. Map p. 122.

Jackson Hall KOLONAKI

The best-known bar-cafe-restaurant in dress-up Kolonaki is dedicated to American memorabilia and simple American-style food such as burgers and steaks, plus there's a seafood restaurant upstairs. The crowd, however, is fashionably European. Sit out on the pedestrian sidewalk near the main square to people-watch. 4 Milioni St. ☎ 210/361-6098. www.jacksonhall.gr. Metro: Syntagma. Map p. 122.

★ Stavlos THISSIO

This easygoing rock/house/mainstream bar, restaurant, and outdoor cafe, converted from the former royal stables, is an anchor on cafe-lined Iraklidon Street. The small bar is a fine place to

Dance to ethnic music by candlelight at Thirio.

Athens Entertainment & Nightlife

National Archaeological Museum

Nat'l. Technic
Univ. of Athe

Finou
Paleologou Konstantinou
Pilou
Platonos
Palamidiou
Alamanas
Astrous
Iliou
Psaron
Sonierou
Mager
Acharnon
Aristotelous
3 Septemvriou
28 Oktovriou
Solomou
Kapodistriou

Mezonos
Favierou
Victor Hugo
Akominatou
Marni
VATHI
Chalkokondili
Veranzerou

Timneou
Monastiriou
Mirtidiotou
Alikarnassou
Kimonos
Kodratou
T Dilegan
Kerameon
Karolou
Karaiskaki
Square
Menandrou
Satovriandou

Keratsiniou
Serron
Leoforos Konstantinoupoleos
Peanieon
Lenorman
Achileos
Agiou Konstandinou
Zinonos
Omonia
Square
Omonia

Naousis
Daniil
Koritsas
Giatrakou
Kolokinthous
Iasonos
Keramikou
Deligion
P. Tsaldari
Likourgou
Geraniou
Sokratous

Chalkidikis
Paramithias
Platon
Megalou Alexandrou
Marathonos
Thermopilon
Milerou
Agisilaou
Menandrou
City Hall
Sofokleous

Naousis
Artimisiou
Leonidou
Salaminas
Athens Municipal
Art Gallery
Eleftherios
Square
Epikourou
Evripidou
Aiolou
Aristidou
Panepistimiou

27
26
Iera Odos
Evmedondos
Mikalis
Piraeos
Psaromlingou
Ag. Asomaton
Dipilou
Leokoriou
Sari
Anargyron
Aristotelou
Eschilou
Athinas
Vissis
Praxitelous
Ag. Markou
Klafthmonos
Square

Triptolemou
Voutadon
Persefonis
GAZI
Orfeos
Kerameikos
Cemetery
Melidoni
Ermou
PSYRRI
31
32
29
Pallados
Karaiskaki
Voreou
Kolokotroni
MONASTIRAKI
30
Athinedos
Evangelistrias
Lekka

Iraklidon
Ilia Pouloupoulou
Amiktionos
Iraklidon
Thissio
Ifestou
Adrianou
28
Monastiraki
Pandrossou
Mitropoleos
Ermou
Perikleous

Kriadon
Thessalonikis
Ersichthonos
Nileos
THISSIO
25
Stoa of
Attalos
Areos
Aiolou
Pelopida
Adrianou
Apollonos

Exoneon
Thorikion
Galatias
Akteou
Akamantos
Ancient
Agora
Dioskouron
Panos
Theorias
24
Miniskelou
Erichtheos
23
13
Nikodimo
speridon
PLAKA

Filason
Meliteon
Dimofontos
Pallineon
Otrineon
Apostolou Pavlou
22
ACROPOLIS
14
Kydathinon
Dedalo
Thalou

Troon Ierarchon
Iperionos
Kidantidon
National
Observatory
Herodes
Atticus
Theater
Thrassilou
Vyronos
Lyssikratous

Iohon
Eoleon
Acheon
Dorieon
Apolloniou
21
Pnyx Hill
Dionysiou Areopagitou
Kallisperi
Rovertou Galli
Propileon
Erechthiou
Kavaloti
Acropolis
Museum
Makriyanni
Akropoli
Diakou Athanasio

Drioon
Kiklopon
Iolaou
Kallisthepous
Araknthou
Filopappou Hill
Garibaldi
Mouson
Misaralitou
Veikou
20
Diakou
Lembessi
L. Vouliagmenis
L

MAKRIYANNI
Tsami Karatasou
19
18
Drakou
Dimitrakopoulou
Andrea Singrou
Kallirois
Kokkini

Akrotiri Boutique 19	Cine Paris 14	Half Note Jazz Club 16
Alexander's Bar 11	Coronet Theatre 15	Jackson Hall 9
Athens Epidaurus Festival 5	Cubanita Havana Club 29	James Joyce Irish Pub 28
Athens Sports Bar 20	Dora Stratou Theater 21	Joy 32
Badminton Theater 8	Galaxy Bar 7	Kafeneion Pente Dromous 2
Bo 17	Greek National Opera 3	Kalua 10

Megaron Mousikis **6**
Mostrou **24**
Rex **4**
Romeo **18**
S-cape **27**

The 7 Jokers **13**
Sodade **26**
Stamatopoulos **23**
Stavlos **25**
T-Palace **12**

Terra Vibe **1**
Thirio **31**
Thission Open-Air
  Cinema **22**
Vega **30**

> *One of the capital's many outdoor cinemas.*

rock out, though it's only ever as good as the DJ. 10 Iraklidon St. ☎ 210/346-7206 or 345-2502. www.stavlos.gr. Metro: Thissio. Map p. 123.

Bars & Lounges

★ **Alexander's Bar** SYNTAGMA

An 18th-century tapestry depicting Alexander the Great dominates this classic hotel piano

---

Athens by Night

It would be a shame to miss out on Athens nightlife while you're in town. Cafes, bars, and clubs are almost as common as eating establishments, and it's one of the safest cities in the world for walking at night, provided you're careful in traffic. Weekly listings magazines such as *Athinorama* (www.athinorama.gr) are published in Greek, but foreign acts or DJs are usually noted in Latin letters. Also try websites such as **www.athensnights.gr** to see who's playing where (your best bet is in the Gazi area), or try taking the **Athens Bar Crawl,** which meets in Plaka (www.athensbarcrawl.com). A few final words of advice: If you see people drinking bottled beverages, follow suit and don't drink the hard stuff, which may be a cheap substitute and cause a serious hangover.

---

bar where you can order Dom Pérignon by the glass (though it'll set you back 40€). It's been cited as one of the best hotel bars in the world by Forbes.com, watering a regular clientele from the upper echelons. Hotel Grande Bretagne, Syntagma Sq. ☎ 210/333-0000. www.grande bretagne.gr. Metro: Syntagma. Map p. 122.

★ **Galaxy Bar** HILTON

A gorgeous view of the Acropolis, smart decor, perfect cocktails, and a spot on the top floor of the city's most iconic hotel distinguish this celebrity-frequented wood-bedecked bar. Hilton Athens, 46 Vas. Sofias Ave. ☎ 210/728-1000. www.hilton.com. Metro: Evangelismos. Map p. 122.

James Joyce Irish Pub MONASTIRAKI

This large pub has been embraced by expats and foreigners as well as Greeks in its very central if incongruous location in the ramshackle flea-market part of Monastiraki. Its rustic interior has **big screens for sports,** a full-on restaurant, and Guinness on tap. 12 Astiggos St. ☎ 210/323-5055. www.jjoyceirish pubathens.com. Daily from noon till late. Metro: Monastiraki or Thissio. Map p. 122.

★ **Joy** PSYRRI

This fun little modern-art bar is on the third floor of a neoclassical building, above the Bee cademy restaurant (open Tues–Sun). Its arious rooms have sparse industrial decor shades of gray. Don't show up before midight. 18 Sarri and 2 Sachtouri sts. ☎ 210/322-038. Fri–Sat 10pm till late, Sun 6pm till late. Metro: Monastiraki or Thissio. Map p. 122.

★ **Kafeneion Pente Dromous** EXARCHIA
his buzzing bar-cafe is full of young Athe-ans both inside and at tables outside on the dge of the student zone in Exarchia. It also erves meze. Themistokleous and Koletti sts. ☎ 210/380-0642. Daily 10am till late. Metro: monia. Map p. 122.

he 7 Jokers SYNTAGMA
his intimate (read: small) bohemian bar osts clubbers as well as a regular contingent vho stay on for the night, chilling out to a ange of funk, soul, and rock music. It opens rom 8:30am (when people actually drink cof-ee), and snacks are served. 7 Voulis St. ☎ 210/21-9225. Mon–Sat 8:30am till late, Sun from pm. Metro: Syntagma. Map p. 123.

★★ **Thirio** PSYRRI
his unusual casual bar covers two levels. he myriad seating is divided into cubbyhole paces, room after room, lit by candles and ecorated with African tribal artifacts. There's ven some space to dance to the ethnic music. Lepeniotou St. ☎ 210/321-7836. Daily 9pm till ate. Metro: Monastiraki. Map p. 123.

-**Palace** SYNTAGMA
he redecorated space inside the King George alace has added sushi to its menu and is pen all day and into the evening. The lounge s a classy central place to meet (it's on Syn-agma Sq.). King George Palace Hotel, 3 Vas. Georgiou St. at Syntagma Sq. ☎ 210/325-8970. Metro: Syntagma. Map p. 123.

Cinema

★★★ **Cine Paris** PLAKA
Athens has multiplexes, but it's a great ex-erience to watch a film under the stars. The creen here is in the roof terrace garden at his open-air summer cinema opposite Plaka's nain square. Most movies are in English with Greek subtitles, and there's a bar on site. The uilding becomes a live performance venue n winter. 22 Kydathenion St. ☎ 210/322-2071. Metro: Syntagma. Map p. 122.

★★★ **Thission Open-Air Cinema** THISSIO
There are many great outdoor summer movie theaters (see Cine Paris, above), but this popular garden theater is particularly charm-ing, on the main pedestrian street near the Acropolis, and screens old favorites as well as new releases. 7 Apostolou Pavlou St. ☎ 210/347-0980. Metro: Thissio. Map p. 123.

Classical Music, Opera & Dance

★★★ **Athens Epidaurus Festival** PANEPISTI-MIOU Ancient drama, opera, symphonies, ballet, and modern dance all appear in Ath-ens at the ancient outdoor **Herodes Atticus Theater** (☎ 210/324-2121 or 323-2771) and **Lycabettus Theater** (☎ 210/722-7233), and in Epidaurus at the ancient **Epidaurus Theater** (☎ 275/302-2026), which you can reach by bus or boat. Box office: 39 Panepistimiou St. ☎ 210/327-2000 or 928-2900. www.greek festival.gr. May–Oct. Ticket prices vary. Metro: Panepistimiou. Map p. 122.

★★ **Dora Stratou Theater** FILOPAPPOU
Since 1953, traditional Greek folk dances have been staged here on Filopappou Hill. The Dora Stratou troupe is an institution in Athens. Various dances are performed, together with live music, at the outdoor theater. Box office: 8 Scholiou St. ☎ 210/324-4395. Theater: Filopap-pou Hill. ☎ 210/921-4650. www.grdance.org. Tickets 15€. Performances: June–Sept Tues–Sat 9:30pm, Sun 8:30pm. Ticket office (at the the-ater): 7:30–10:30pm. Metro: Petralona, or bus/trolley no. 15 or 227. Map p. 122.

Greek National Opera OMONIA
From September to June, opera and ballet per-formances for adults take place at the **Olympia Theatre,** while the **Akropol Theatre** chiefly hosts operettas for children. Olympia Theatre: 59–61 Akademias St. ☎ 210/364-3725. Akropol: 9–11 Ippokratous St. ☎ 210/364-3700. www.nationalopera.gr. Ticket prices vary. Box office daily 9am–9pm. Metro: Omonia. Map p. 122.

★ **Megaron Mousikis** EMBASSY
The acoustics at this modern concert hall are excellent, as is the classical music program that runs from September to July. Vas. Sofias and Kokkali sts. ☎ 210/7282-000. Central ticket kiosk: 8 Omirou St. ☎ 210/324-3297 or 331-1183. www.megaron.gr. Ticket prices vary. Box of-fice: Mon–Fri 10am–6pm; Sat 10am–2pm; until

> *Megaron Mousikis is the city's modern concert hall.*

8:30pm on performance nights, including Sun 6–8:30pm. Kiosk (8 Omirou St.): Mon–Fri 10am–4pm. Metro: Megaron Mousikis. Map p. 123.

Casino Action

Greeks love to gamble, and there are two casinos near Athens. One is the **Club Hotel Casino Loutraki,** on 48 Poseidonos Ave. (☎ 274/406-0300; www.clubhotel loutraki.gr or www.casinoloutraki.gr), in the seaside resort town of the same name, 80km (50 miles) from Athens. There are 80 games, 1,000 slot machines, an elegant hotel, a restaurant, and a spa. The Casino Express bus to and from Athens is 15€ (☎ 210/523-4188 or 4144) and includes casino admission, drinks on the gaming floors, and a meal at the Neptune restaurant. The **Regency Casino Mont Parnes,** on Mount Parnitha (☎ 210/242-1234; www.regency.gr), is recovering from the devastating fires of 2007 and is still publicity-shy. It has 53 table games and more than 500 slot machines. There's also a restaurant. You can take a cable car from the mountain base in Aharnon in northern Athens (18km/11 miles from central Athens), or drive there (30km/19 miles).

Dance Clubs

★ **Bo** VOULA

This club on the south coast operates year-round on weekends. It appeals to a European and Greek clientele with a musical mix that includes house, R&B, and Greek music. 14 Karamanlis St. ☎ 210/895-9645. Sun, Tues–Thurs 10am–2am (café-bar); Fri–Sat (club nights) 11pm–5 or 6am. Tram: Voula. Map p. 122.

Kalua SYNTAGMA

One of the city's oldest clubs, this busy basement club-disco is located on its own in downtown Athens, but that hasn't dampened its popularity. 6 Amerikis St. ☎ 210/360-8304 Cover 12€ Tues–Thurs, 15€ Fri–Sat. Tues–Sat from midnight. Metro: Syntagma. Map p. 122.

★ **Vega** PSYRRI

This big mainstream club that took over from Envy caters to well-off, trendy youth. It plays hip-hop and R&B on Wednesdays, and Greek music on Sundays. The other days feature house, dance, hip-hop and Greek music. Like Athenians, it moves to the south coast in summer. Monastiraki Center, 3 Agias Eleousis St. ☎ 210/331-7801. Wed, Thurs, Sun 10€ cover; Fri–Sat 15€. Wed–Sun midnight–5 or 6am. Metro Monastiraki. Map p. 123.

Gay & Lesbian

S-cape GAZI

This is one of the best-known gay clubs and plays a range of music, from Greek nights to karaoke. If you're early, you can go across Iera Odos (main road) to the gay-friendly **Rages,** a multispace theater-cafe-bar under the same ownership. 139 Megalou Alexandrou St., Gazi.

☎ 210/341-1003. Daily from 11pm. Rages (Rails): 82 Konstantinopoleos St., Gazi. ☎ 210/345-2751. Daily 6pm–2am. Metro: Kerameikos. Map p. 123.

Sodade GAZI

This bar-club-lounge plays cool music on two stages in the gay-friendly district Gazi. One plays disco (though Mon is Greek night), and

Nightlife Districts

Most of the city center seems just as lively at night as by day, at least on weekends. You'll find a heavy student crowd around **Exarchia Square,** behind the Polytechnic, while in **Kolonaki,** on Milioni Street and at the end of Haritos Street, you'll see a sophisticated, dressed-up clientele. **Plaka** has low-key cafe-bars at its squares on Kydathenion Street and Adrianou Street (Agora Sq.), but the best places to see and be seen are in **Thissio,** where the year-round outdoor cafes along pedestrian Iraklidon Street have mood-lit chandeliers under their awnings. The latest trendy cafe-bar area of Athens is **Gazi,** first (and still) popular with gays. It has restaurants, bars, and clubs, especially alongside

the Kerameikos Metro station. **Psyrri,** however, has been the dining and nightlife district for all ages for the past few years. It attracts coffee-sipping cafe-goers during the day, and at night you may struggle to hear above the din, with all its jampacked restaurants, bars, clubs, and even more cafes. The **Ilissia** area (near the Hilton), **Alexandras Avenue** (between the Metro station and Kifissias Ave.), and **Kifissia,** in the northern suburbs, also host vibrant bar scenes, and there are many English or foreign bars around Grigoriou Lambraki Street in **Glyfada,** a southern suburb of Athens. In summer, the big dance clubs move to locations on the coast along **Poseidonos Avenue.**

> Bouzoukia *nights are best when fueled by an ouzo or two.*

an electro-progressive music stage opens on weekends. 10 Triptolemou St. ☎ 210/346-8657. www.sodade.gr. 8€ cover (includes one drink). Mon–Thurs 11:30pm–4am, Fri–Sat 11:30pm–6am. Closed Good Fri. Metro: Kerameikos. Map p. 123.

Jazz Music
Half Note Jazz Club METS

The Half Note has hosted jazz majors and minors from across the pond for 30 years, but it still feels fresh. This is where to go for live shows. 17 Trivonianou St. ☎ 210/921-3310. www.halfnote.gr. Tickets 30€ (includes one drink), tables 35€ or 40€. Mon–Sat 10:30pm till late, Sun 9pm till late. Bus no. A3, B3, or 057. Map p. 122.

Live Greek Music
Mostrou PLAKA

This *laika,* a popular urban "stage" club, is big for Plaka but small for its purpose: hosting well-known Greek performers. For a bit of fresh air, there's a roof garden bar and restaurant. 22 Mnissikleos St. at Lysiou St. ☎ 210/322-5558 or 5337. A la carte dinner 30€, drinks 15€. Mid-Apr through Oct daily 8pm–2am or later (live music begins at 8:15pm); performances Nov–Apr Fri–Sat 10pm–4am; Sun 1:30–8pm. Metro: Monastiraki. Map p. 123.

★ Rex OMONIA

The current show home of Greek singers Michalis Hatziyiannis (from the Eurovision song contest) and catchy breakout group Onirama is conveniently located downtown. 48 Panepistimiou St. ☎ 210/381-4591. 20€ cover (includes one drink). Daily Nov–Apr Thurs–Sat, from 10:30pm. Metro: Omonia. Map p. 123.

A Night at the *Bouzoukia*

The bouzouki, a stringed instrument, is played at many restaurants in the Psyrri and Plaka districts. For a sampling of a few, you can take an organized tour that includes dinner and dancing. Some of the better-known tour operators are **CHAT Tours,** 4 Stadiou Street (☎ 210/322-3137 or 3886; www.chatours.gr), and **Key Tours,** 4 Kallirois Street (☎ 210/923-3166; www.keytours.gr), which both offer "Athens by Night" tours for about 60€ (including dinner). If you venture out on your own, keep in mind that for big *bouzoukia* clubs, you need deep pockets, as the norm is sharing a 100€ to 300€ bottle of whiskey with friends while settling in for a long night. Also note that buying baskets of flowers to throw at the songsters has replaced plate-smashing.

★ Romeo ELLINIKO

You can get up and dance on the tables at this low-cost and fun Greek-music dance hall on the coast. If that's not your style, buy baskets of flowers to throw on the singers and impromptu dancers. 1 Ellinikou St. ☎ 210/894-5345 or 1893. 15€ cover (includes one drink). Thurs–Sun. Tram: Ellinon Olympionikon, or bus no. A2 (fifth Ellinikou stop). Map p. 123.

★★ Stamatopoulos PLAKA

The walls of this taverna are painted with murals of Greek revelers characteristic of old Athens. Greeks go to listen to the live bouzouki music, and tourists get up to dance. 26 Lissiou St. at Flessa St. ☎ 210/322-8722. www.stamatopoulostavern.gr. Daily 4pm–2am. Metro: Syntagma. Map. 123.

Sports

Athens Sports Bar MAKRIYANNI

This bar on the ground floor of the Athens Backpackers building gets quite lively. Watch your team on wide-screen TVs. You may even catch them live, given the opening hours. 3A Veikou St. ☎ 210/923-5811. www.athensstudios.gr. Daily 7:30am–midnight. Metro: Akropoli. Map p. 122.

For the Sports Fan

The main Greek clubs have teams for multiple sports; the biggest among them are eternal enemies **Panathinaikos FC** (☎ 210/870-9000; www.pao.gr) and **Olympiakos Piraeus** (☎ 210/414-3000; www.olympiakos.gr). These two teams meet at Olympiakos's Karaiskaki Stadium at Neo Faliro Metro station, or at the distinctive Calatrava-designed **Olympic Athletic Center of Athens** (☎ 210/683-4060; www.oaka.com.gr), aka the Olympic stadium, where both Panathinaikos and **AEK Athens** (Athletic Union of Constantinople; ☎ 210/612-1371; www.aekfc.gr), the other major Athens club, play for the time being. You can see if horse races are taking place at the **Athens Race Track** at Markopoulo (☎ 22990/81000; minimum bet .50€), while there's an 18-hole **golf course in coastal Glyfada,** at Terma Pronois Street (☎ 210/894-6820; shop ☎ 210/894-2180; www.athensgolfclub.com).

> *The Badminton Theater hosts internationally renowned performances.*

Terra Vibe MALAKASA

This outdoor park for big-name pop and rock acts is the venue for the multiday Rockwave Festival. Shuttle buses bring the crowds. Lamia National Rd. at Malakasa Junction. ☎ 210/882-0426. www.didimusic.gr or www.rockwavefestival.gr. Train: Sfendali Station. Map p. 123.

Theater

★ kids Badminton Theater GOUDI

A 2,000-seat former Olympic venue hosts a variety of family entertainment, including dance performances, concerts, and musicals such as *West Side Story, Beauty and the Beast,* and *Singin' in the Rain.* Alsos Stratou (Army Park). ☎ 211/101-0020. www.badmintontheater.gr. Tickets: www.ticketnet.gr. Ticket prices vary. Metro: Katehaki. Map p. 122.

kids Coronet Theatre PANGRATI

This wintertime venue showcases live variety acts that appeal to international audiences of all ages, including magic shows and children's plays. 11 Frinis St. at Imittou St. ☎ 210/701-2123. www.coronet.gr. Tickets 18€–23€. Sept–Mar. Trolley no. 4 or 11. Map p. 122.

The South Coast Beaches

Temperatures in the city can exceed 100°F (40°C) between June and August, so Athenians make a beeline for the beach at the flimsiest excuse on summer weekends and holidays. You'll be in plenty of company at the organized beaches along the south coast of Athens, especially during the two weeks around August 15—a national holiday, when hardly anybody stays in town. Here are some popular beaches along the Apollo Coast with amenities, such as restrooms and umbrellas, for a fee. Note that drinking is encouraged, but topless sunbathing isn't.

> *With plenty of places to relax and socialize, Yabanaki Varkiza and other south coast beaches are a haven for Athenians.*

kids Asteria Glyfada. This beach across from the main seaside resort-suburb of Glyfada (17km/11 miles from Athens) was very popular when the old Athens airport was in the area. Glyfada is also the shopping, restaurant, and nightlife hub for suburbs farther along the coast. In addition to the beach, the complex includes bars, lounges, and a pool. The beach has a Miami vibe, with a wide swath of sand, overstuffed beach chairs and umbrellas, and a garden backing it. The Balux House Project is a year-round **bar-cafe-restaurant**

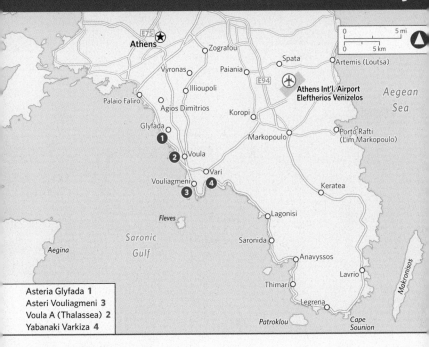

Asteria Glyfada **1**
Asteri Vouliagmeni **3**
Voula A (Thalassea) **2**
Yabanaki Varkiza **4**

entrees 10€–25€; ☎ 210/898-3577), but there are also summer-only restaurants and poolside bars, as well as the **Balux nightclub** (☎ 210/894-1620). An exotic thatched-roof **bar beside the pool** (14 years and up) is surrounded by daybeds with diaphanous privacy drapes, and servers will deliver drinks to your lounge chair. ⏱ 2 hr. 58 Poseidonos Ave. ☎ 210/894-1620. www.asterascomplex.com. Admission 6€ weekdays, 7€ weekends and holidays, 3€ ages 4–12. Daily 8:30am–8pm, beach bars 9am–2 or 3am. Tram: Metaxa Agg. or Kolymbitirio, Asteria (Glyfada) stop. Bus no. A2 or E22.

★ kids **Asteri Vouliagmeni.** This beach is where I send visiting family and friends. Vouliagmeni is a beach resort, and this beach is near the Astir Palace Hotel, just across the street from the yacht club. They charge twice as much as other nearby beaches, but the payoff is cushioned teak beach chairs, curtained daybed areas, nice changing facilities, and warm showers. Shops on site sell food, coffee, books, toys, snacks, sunglasses, and swimwear. The water is shallow, warm, and gentle, even though the bay is quite big. The sea floor is clean, and the water is super-clear, so you can see the schools of fish that nip at your ankles. Water-skiers and large yachts anchored offshore may distract you from your reading or your drink, but overall the atmosphere is low-key, with no booming music or loud noises. I thought the ruins of the on-site temple were fake, but they're real, and little ones can squidge their toes in the mud while looking for frogs. ⏱ 2 hr. Astir Beach, 40 Apollonos St. ☎ 210/890-1621. www.astir-beach.com. Entrance May–Oct Mon–Fri 15€, kids under 12 8€; Sat–Sun 25€, under 12 13€. Nov–Apr Mon–Fri 10€, under 12 free; Sat–Sun 12€, under 12 free. Bus no. A2, B3, or E22 to Glyfada, Tram: Glyfada (Voula-bound) from Akademias St., then bus no. 114 from Glyfada. Better (but more expensive) to take a taxi (p. 134).

kids **Voula A (Thalassea).** Twenty-somethings and teenagers flock to this big, busy beach at the end of the tram line, 19km (12 miles) south of Athens in Voula, a suburban residential area neighboring the glitzy commercial area Glyfada. The beach is sandy and, in a few spots, pebbly, but shade is scarce, so try to snag an umbrella. Amenities include a snack

> *Suburban Glyfada has a Miami vibe, with a sandy beach backed by bars and lounges.*

bar, bars, and a market, plus water slides, watersports gear (skis, tubes, and boards), pedal boats, and equipment for parachuting, racquetball, beach volleyball, and minisoccer. The same company runs Voula B, a smaller, quieter beach half a mile (¾km) farther down the coast, but it may or may not be operational after recent renovations. Call and check before setting out for it. ⏱ 2 hr. 4 Alkyonidon St. ☎ 210/895-9632. www.astir-beach.com www.thalassea.gr. Admission 5.50€ adults (weekdays), 6.50€ (weekends); 3.50€ kids 6–12 and 65 and over. Daily 8am–sunset (beach closes); beachfront cafe and other facilities stay open at night. Tram: Asklipiou Voulas St., or bus no. A2 or E22.

kids **Yabanaki Varkiza.** The farthest organized beach from Athens (30km/19 miles away) on the road to Sounion, this stretch of sand in the seaside resort Varkiza is one of the nicest in terms of seawater, sand, and gradient. It's very popular, with rows of beach chairs and blaring cafe-bars, and features cabanas, a self-service restaurant, a taverna, three beach bars, a water park, beach volleyball, windsurfing, water-skiing, and free parking. The drive to Varkiza affords a spectacular view of the Attic Peninsula's cliffs, while the return trip inland through Vari features a number of roadside tavernas serving roast lamb on a spit. Rocky coves, past Varkiza along the route to Cape Sounion, are unsupervised but great for snorkeling or swimming. ⏱ 3 hr. Sounion Ave., Vari. ☎ 210/897-2414. www.yabanaki.gr. Admission 7€ Mon–Fri; 8€ Sat–Sun; 4.50€ children 6–12, students, and seniors; 5 & under free. Fri–Sun 5€ beach chairs, umbrellas. Open June–Aug daily 8am–8pm. Bus no. E22.

> *The coastal drive to Varkiza Beach is spectacular.*

Athens Fast Facts

Arriving

For local (OASA) bus schedules, dial ☎ 185; for long-distance (KTEL) bus schedules, call ☎ 14505. For (OSE) train info, call ☎ 1110. For flight info, call the airport at ☎ 210/353-0000. For domestic ship info, call ☎ 1441 or 210/414-7800 (recording in Greek). Also see p. 672, "Getting There," in Fast Facts Greece.

ATMs/Cashpoints

Nearly all banks have after-hours ATMs that work with global banking systems.

Currency Exchange

See p. 681, Fast Facts Greece.

Doctors & Dentists

Most doctors speak English, but you can call your embassy for lists of English-speaking doctors and dentists, or call the 24-hour **SOS Doctors** (☎ 1016; www.sosiatroi.gr) or **Homed** (☎ 1144; www.hospitalathome.gr), who make house calls. Most of the larger hotels have doctors they can call in an emergency.

Emergencies

A first-aid clinic is at the corner of 3 Piraeos (P. Tsaldari) and Socratous sts., near Omonia Square (☎ 213/204-4000; www.polykliniki.gr). **Euroclinic** (9 Athanasiadou St., Ambelokipi; ☎ 210/641-6600; www.euroclinic.gr) is a private hospital. Also see p. 680, Fast Facts Greece.

Getting Around

Tickets are good for all modes of public transport for 90 minutes, and must be validated in the time-stamp machine upon boarding, or before boarding the Metro or tram. Tickets are 1€ bought in advance from kiosks or bus-ticket booths. A 3€ ticket buys you 24 hours; a 15€ "tourist" ticket gets you 3 days and includes airport travel and the sightseeing bus no. 400. These can be purchased at bus-ticket booths, kiosks, and tram, Metro, and Proastiakos stations. See the **Metro** (www.amel.gr) and **OASA** (www.oasa.gr) websites for more options. **Athens Urban Transport Organization** (OASA; ☎ 185; www.oasa.gr) puts out a route map, and you can check it online. **BY BUS** Local buses and trolleys run from about 5am to 10pm, occasionally to midnight, depending on the line. **BY METRO** There are three lines: the much older **green Line 1** (run by ISAP), the **red Line 2,** and the **blue Line 3.** The trains aren't color-coded—just the signage. **BY TRAM** The tram (www.tramsa.gr; Sun–Thurs 5am–1am, Fri–Sat 24 hr.) runs from Syntagma to Neo Faliro or along the coast (and beaches) to Voula. **BY TAXI** Taxis are yellow and more expensive than they used to be, since meter rates doubled in 2010. The flag rate, normally posted on the dashboard, is 1.16€ to start, with a minimum charge of 3.10€. Beyond the city limits (except the airport) and after midnight until 5am, the meter rate of .72€ per km jumps to 1.20€. Small-change add-on charges include runs to the airport or pickup from a port or bus station, heavy luggage, tolls, and time. Round up, usually to the nearest euro. You can share a taxi with others traveling the same route, but each party pays separately. You have the right to refuse co-passengers if you enter the cab first, but sharing helps keep the rates down. Taxis can be difficult to find at times, especially around 3pm (shift change) and 11:30pm (when they wait for the higher tariffs they'll earn from midnight to 5am). For an extra 2.50€ to 5€, you can call for a cab or schedule a pickup from **Attika** (☎ 210/341-0553) or **Proodos** (☎ 210/345-1200), among others. **BY CAR** Driving is not recommended, as traffic is heavy, and parking is difficult. A slew of car-rental offices are situated at the top of Syngrou Avenue (Metro: Akropoli). **ON FOOT** All the main sites in Athens are best seen on foot (watch your step on slippery, broken, or blocked sidewalks and while crossing roads) or in one or two short Metro stops. Much of the historic and commercial center is pedestrianized, including touristy Plaka, while a scenic walkway links up the main archaeological sites. **Note:** Drivers rarely yield to pedestrians, so don't blindly step into the road even if the little green man is lit. Always look both ways before crossing the street, including one-way streets and pedestrian roads.

Internet & Games

Most hotels provide Internet access, and

many also offer Wi-Fi, either free or for a fee. Wi-Fi is also free at many cafes such as Starbucks (39 Mitropoleos St. is one location), and at the airport, Syntagma Square, Kotzia Square (in front of Town Hall on Athinas St.), Thissio Station, and Thissio Square. Internet cafes also exist around town. Four are: **Arcade** (5 Stadiou St., Syntagma; ☎ 210/322-1808; daily 9am–11pm; minimum charge 1.80€ for 30 min.); **Cafe 4U,** a 24-hour bar-café (44 Ippokratous St., Exarchia; ☎ 210/361-1981; minimum charge 1€); **E-Zone,** 24-hour, where you can also make CDs or DVDs (Veikou and Orlof sts., Koukaki; ☎ 210/922-0431; minimum charge 1.50€). **Blaster.Net** (29 Nileos St., Thissio; ☎ 210/341-7703; www.blaster.net.gr) is open 24 hours. Minimum charge 1€.

Pharmacies

A round-the-clock pharmacy can be found by dialing ☎ 14944 (in Greek), by picking up a copy of the *Athens News, Athens Plus,* or *Kathimerini* (IHT), or looking online (www.ekathimerini.com). See p. 682, Fast Facts Greece.

Police

In an emergency, dial ☎ **100** or **112.** For help dealing with taxi drivers, hotels, restaurants, or shop owners, call the Tourist Police (☎ **171;** 24 hr.). 43 Veikou St., Koukaki. ☎ 210/920-0724. Daily 7:30am–10pm.

Post Office

The main post office is on Syntagma and Mitropoleos Street (☎ 210/331-9500; Mon–Fri 7:30am–8pm; Sat 7:30am–2pm; Sun 9am–1:30pm). If you're shipping parcels that weigh more than 2 kilos (4.4 lb.), take them unsealed for inspection to 60 Mitropoleos Street (☎ 210/321-8156 or 8143; Mon–Fri 7:30am–8pm).

Safety

Touts often try to lure single men to unscrupulous bars with beautiful women or to hotel room "parties." The visitor is then forced to pay the bill for all. Don't accept offers of food or water, and put your hand over the keypad at ATMs when you enter your PIN. Although Greece has a low crime rate and you can safely walk the streets well into the night, pickpocketing can happen on public transport especially during busy times, and motorcycle thieves target seniors and the unwary by pulling off shoulder bags and, often, pulling over the victim. Take precautions.

Telephones

Most phone booths only accept phone cards (*tilekartes*), available at newsstands and kiosks for 4€ and 10€. The card works for 100 short local calls (fewer long-distance or international calls). Widely available prepaid calling cards (kiosks, exchange bureaus, and the like) start at about 3€ and can be much cheaper, often the charge of a local call. Some kiosks still have metered phones; you pay what the meter records. Local phone calls cost .03€ for the first 2 minutes or part thereof, and a similar rate for each additional minute. You can phone home directly by contacting AT&T (☎ 00/800-1311), MCI (☎ 00/800-1211), or Sprint (☎ 00/800-1411). For the international operator, dial ☎ 139.

Toilets

Metro stations do not have toilets, but some have coin-operated ones nearby. Some squares have public toilets, but most people use the facilities at restaurants and cafes.

Tours

Many travel agencies offer city tours. Two bus tours are the hop-on **public sightseeing bus (no. 400,** www.oasa.gr for details) that goes to all the main sites in 80 to 90 minutes, but the 5€ ticket is good for 24 hours on all city public transport. Or you can book ahead on the open-top **City Sightseeing Bus** (www.city-sightseeing.com), which goes on a 90-minute, 15-stop tour, leaving every 30 minutes from 9am to 5pm (winter) or 6pm (summer). It starts at Syntagma Square and costs 18€ for adults and 8€ for ages 5 to 15.

Visitor Information

The Greek National Tourism Organization Information desk is at 26 Amalias Street, Syntagma (☎ 210/331-0392; www.gnto.gr). A booth operates at the arrivals terminal of Athens International Airport (☎ 210/353-0445; Mon–Fri 9am–7pm, Sat–Sun 10am–3pm).

4
The Saronic Gulf Islands

Favorite Moments in the Saronic Gulf

As the island group closest to Athens, the archipelago in the Saronic Gulf appeals equally to day-trippers from the mainland, who cross over on a regular basis for a swim and a seaside meal in Angistri, and long-term visitors on a beach holiday in Spetses, which is farthest from the bustle of Athens. Aegina and Poros are known for their compelling archaeological sites, and glamorous Hydra has what is often considered the most beautiful port in the country. Because of their proximity to Athens, all five Saronic Gulf Islands remain relatively lively year-round, offering plenty of options for off-season visitors.

> PREVIOUS PAGE *The port at Perdika, Aegina.* THIS PAGE *The Pirate Bar is a longstanding presence on Hydra's port.*

① **Exploring the Doric Temple of Aphaia at close range, Aegina.** It's smaller than the Parthenon in Athens but older, with pockmarked tufa columns, and it sits alone atop the mountain. See p. 150, **⑥**.

② **Awaiting nightfall at a taverna table in the sand at Lekkas, Aegina Town.** Watch a ferry sail away at twilight as the sky and clouds darken and the boat's night lights twinkle on. See p. 151.

③ **Watching the sun set in Aegina Town's lively harbor.** Catch a glimpse of the sun sinking in the distance, through the yacht masts and fishing boats, as horse-drawn carriages clip-clop past behind you. See p. 148, **①**.

④ **Munching on taverna snacks at Agia Marina Beach, Aegina.** Few simple pleasures beat lying on a beach chair and eating small fish and deep-fried zucchini slices out of a cardboard cup from Galaris, at Agia Marina Beach, Aegina. See p. 150, **⑦**.

⑤ **Spending a lost weekend on the beach at Skala, Angistri.** You'll lose all sense of time here, with little to do besides fingering through perfectly formed seashells that are nearly as tiny as grains of sand. See p. 154, **①**.

⑥ **Quenching your thirst with spring water, Zoodochos Pigi Monastery, Poros.** Fill your bottles at the chapel just before you reach the monastery, and then you can drink up while you're admiring the view from the monastery terrace. See p. 161, **③**.

⑦ **Taking the little ferry across the strait in Poros.** Poros's cheery atmosphere will put a smile on your face whatever you do. The

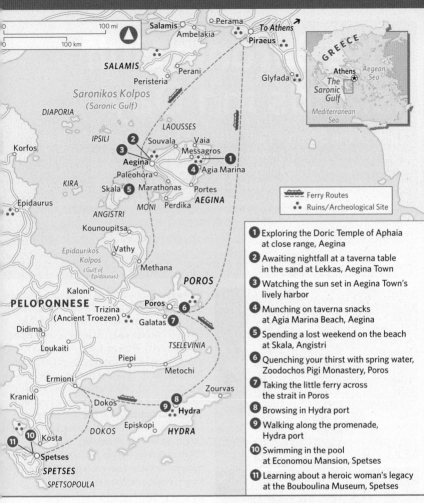

1. Exploring the Doric Temple of Aphaia at close range, Aegina

2. Awaiting nightfall at a taverna table in the sand at Lekkas, Aegina Town

3. Watching the sun set in Aegina Town's lively harbor

4. Munching on taverna snacks at Agia Marina Beach, Aegina

5. Spending a lost weekend on the beach at Skala, Angistri

6. Quenching your thirst with spring water, Zoodochos Pigi Monastery, Poros

7. Taking the little ferry across the strait in Poros

8. Browsing in Hydra port

9. Walking along the promenade, Hydra port

10. Swimming in the pool at Economou Mansion, Spetses

11. Learning about a heroic woman's legacy at the Bouboulina Museum, Spetses

ride to Aliki Beach, through the unmistakably Greek countryside, is especially pleasant. See p. 160, **1**.

8 Browsing in Hydra port. Hydra's harbor has such a uniquely beautiful setting, from the Venetian and Genoese-style mansions to the mottled flagstones underfoot. The shops are twee, but the merchandise is fun to ogle, as are the museum objects and the people parading past the portside cafes. See p. 143, **2**.

9 Walking along the promenade, Hydra port. Lots of water taxis ferry back and forth, but the walkway is fragrant and scenic. On a clear night, you might see a low orange moon,

appearing huge as it hovers just above the mountain, casting its reflection on the water. See p. 158, **5**.

10 Swimming in the pool at Economou Mansion, Spetses. It's heated to just the right temperature—a rarity in Greece. The breakfast is scrumptious too. See p. 167.

11 Learning about a heroic woman's legacy at the Bouboulina Museum, Spetses. Laskarina Bouboulina's conduct during the War of Independence deserves even more credit and exposure than Greece gives it—which is already considerable. See p. 165, **3**; p. 166.

The Saronic Gulf Islands in 1 Day

Each of the Saronic Gulf Islands has its own distinctive character, and you can experience three of them in one day without feeling rushed or unsatisfied. Aegina, the favorite getaway for weekending Athenians, is the biggest of the group, with the most transportation links and some notable ancient treasures. Poros is the most lush, separated from the Peloponnese by a narrow channel (*poros* means "strait" or "fjord"), with its own stash of archaeological finds and ruins. Hydra is distinguished by an island-wide prohibition on cars, tony residents and repeat guests, and handsome mansions that rise from the beautiful harbor in Hydra port.

> With its beautiful port town and ban on motorized traffic, Hydra is one of the most pleasant islands in all of Greece.

START Aegina Town Harbor. In Athens, take the Metro to Piraeus for ferry service to Aegina. **TRIP LENGTH** 30 min.–75 min. from Piraeus to Aegina.

❶ Aegina. Known for its pistachios, Aegina is the biggest island of the Saronics group, and it's the one most easily viewed from Athens, 28km (17 miles) away. After entering Aegina Town's pretty 19th-century harbor, you'll find nice beaches along the way to picturesque **Perdika** (9km/5⅔ miles from Aegina Town), a fishing village with seafood tavernas. Most tourists try to squeeze in a stop at the **Doric Temple of Aphaia,** near the port of Agia Marina on the east coast, a busy beach resort catering mainly to Athenians. See p. 148. 🕑 Crossing from Athens 30–70 min. In summer, hydrofoil or catamaran every half-hour, car ferry hourly; reduced winter service.

❷ Poros. This green enclave (57km/35 miles from Athens) is often crowded with Athenians on weekends, especially in July and August, but its beaches can be a fun place for teenagers who like watersports. It's separated at its narrowest point from the mainland by 150m to 350m (492–1,148 ft.), and frequent ferry crossings close the distance. The ancient site of **Trizina** is worth a look, as is the **Monastery of Zoodochos Pigi** (Source of Life), with its curative springs. Athenian orator Demosthenes (a dissident on the run from the Macedonian king of Athens) is believed to be buried in the courtyard. See p. 160. 🕑 1 hr. by hydrofoil, 2½ hr. by car ferry. In summer, hydrofoil every half-hour, car ferry hourly; reduced winter service.

❸ ★★ **Hydra.** Celebrated by writers and artists, the tumble of cubist, neoclassical *archontika* (mansions) at the stunning port of Hydra (68km/42 miles from Athens) are favored by old Athenian families and publicity-shy celebrities. They're painted in browns, instead of the more familiar Greek whitewash. Hydra's shoreline is beautiful, and cars are prohibited throughout the island. See p. 156. ⏲ 1½ hr. by hydrofoil. In summer, hydrofoil every half-hour; reduced winter service.

Getting There & Around

The easiest way to reach the Saronic Islands is via an organized three-island cruise to Aegina, Poros, and Hydra for 98€, which includes lunch served onboard (www.hydraiki.gr, or book through a travel agent). You can also venture out independently: Hydrofoils from the mainland stop at Aegina, Angistri, Poros, Methana, Hydra, Spetses, and Porto Heli. See www.gtp.gr and www.openseas.gr for sailings from Athens's port of Piraeus. See p. 168 for details.

The Saronic Gulf Islands in 5 Days

A five-day passage through the Saronic Gulf Islands introduces you to beautiful port towns, classical ruins, and some pleasant beaches. Begin on Spetses, the most southerly of the group, and work your back, one island per day, through the archipelago. The islands are relatively close to one another, and boat service among them is frequent, so island-hopping is a relatively easy adventure. Athenians flock to the Saronics on weekends, year-round, so you'll find the islands less crowded and more relaxed during the week.

> Horse-drawn carriage is a popular mode of transport on Spetses, where lanes are lined with mansions.

START Spetses. From Athens, take the Metro to Piraeus for ferry service to Spetses. **TRIP LENGTH** From Piraeus to Spetses 2 hr. by hydrofoil, 4 hr. by ferry.

❶ **Spetses.** Start your 5-day tour of the Saronics in **Dapia and environs** (p. 164, ❶). Walk or take a horse-and-buggy along the coastal road past stately mansions in the leafy area known as Kounoupitsa. Notice the **Anargyrios and Korgialenios College** (ca. 1927), which was modeled on Eton—a likeness touted by British author John Fowles, who taught here in 1950. It's now run by a foundation and used for special events. Check the tour times for the **Bouboulina Museum** (p. 165, ❸) and learn about the swashbuckling heroine who fought for Greece during

1 Spetses
2 Hydra port
3 Poros
4 Aegina
5 Angistri

To Athens ↗

Salamis
Ambelakia
Perama
Piraeus

SALAMIS
Perani
Glyfada

Peristeria

Saronikos Kolpos
(Saronic Gulf)

DIAPORIA

LAOUSSES

IPSILI
Souvala   Vaia
Messagros

Korfos

Aegina **4**
Paleohora   Agia Marina

KIRA
Skala   Marathonas   Portes

Epidaurus
5   *MONI*   Perdika   **AEGINA**
ANGISTRI

Kounoupitsa

Epidaurikos
Kolpos   Vathy
(Gulf of
Epidaurus)   Methana

POROS

Kaloni
Poros **3**

PELOPONNESE   Trizina
(Ancient Troezen)   Galatas

Didima

TSELEVINIA

Loukaiti
Piepi

Ermioni   Metochi

Kranidi
Zourvas

Dokos
Hydra **2**

Kosta   Episkopi
DOKOS   **HYDRA**

Spetses **1**
SPETSES

SPETSOPOULA

GREECE

Athens ★
Aegean
Sea
The
Saronic
Gulf

Mediterranean
Sea

Ferry Routes
Ruins/Archeological Site

0 ____ 100 mi
0 ____ 100 km

ts War of Independence from the Ottoman Turks in the 1820s. On the Greek side, Lord Byron and Napoleon's nephew Paul-Marie Bonaparte were among the casualties. You can also visit the **Spetses Museum** (p. 164, **2**) either the same day or the next morning, before catching the boat to Hydra. If you want to forgo history and jump in the sea instead, take a water taxi to the beach nearest the port, **Agia Marina** (p. 150, **7**), or one farther around the island. In the evening, head over to the Old Harbor to see the yachts and have a meal or a nightcap. See p. 164. ⏱ 1 day.

Hydrofoils run all day from Spetses to Hydra (30 min.).

2 Hydra port. Take a boat to Hydra, and be sure to have your camera ready. The turn into the small **harbor** takes you by surprise, and the view is one of the world's most beautiful: Cubist-like mansions in the colors of the hills fall sharply to the water's edge at portside (p. 156, **1**). You'll see a lot of yachts and boats tied up, as well as a couple of sleepy donkeys waiting to take supplies here and there. Settle into a hotel and then head to the nearest beach, which is off the rocks and cement platforms at Spilia, or Sunset cafes on the west side of the port. Another option is to take a water taxi or walk for about half an hour (if it's not too hot) in the other direction to Mandraki

> *The sands at Aegina's Agia Marina make for a perfect day at the beach.*

Bay, where the **Mira Mare bungalows** (p. 159) are right on the beach. Maybe you'll want to stay the night. Afterwards, find yourself a cafe or taverna on the port where you can sit and watch the goings-on. Prices on the island are reasonable, and service is good. Lots of water taxis ferry back and forth, but the **cliff-hugging walkway** (p. 158, ❺) is a gorgeous and romantic alternative. Many memorable weddings take place here; the bride and groom often arrive by water taxi after taking a few spins around an islet offshore. If you have time, if history interests you, or if you can't sit a moment longer at a cafe, tuck inside the **Historical Museum** (p. 158, ❹) on the east side of the port and check out the displays, including paintings, ship models, and costumes. In the evening, head to a cafe or **bar** (p. 158) where you can sit and unwind or rev up to dance the night away. See p. 156. ⏱ 1 day.

Hydrofoils run often between Hydra and Poros (30 min.).

❸ **Poros.** First, get oriented. Boats bring you to the small island Sphaeria, named after Hermes's son, a charioteer said to be buried here. The mythology gets complicated but includes the Ionian goddess Athena, Poseidon, Theseus, and Saron, the gulf's namesake (p. 544). The main attraction on Sphaeria is the actual **port and town** (p. 160, ❶). It's separated by a narrow strait from Galatas on the Peloponnesian mainland (frequent boats make the 5-minute trip). Sphaeria is also joined by a bridge to another island, Kalavria;

both are referred to as Poros, part of a conglomerate region united by shared history and government even today. You can visit the ruins at **Trizina** (p. 162, ❻) on the Galatas side, as well as the superlative beach, **Aliki** (p. 162, ❼). Past Askeli beach resort on Kalavria is the **Monastery of Zoodochos Pigi** (Source of Life, p. 161, ❸), with its curative springs. Poros is also popular with walkers. Trek around **Russian Bay** (p. 161, ❺) or try watersports. Megalo Neorio's water-ski school is a popular meeting place for youth. The area is named for the state shipyards that used to be here; it later became home to Asia Minor refugees. Hotels and tavernas line the waterfront, site of the imposing Villa Gallini, where Henry Miller and Greek poet George Seferis stayed. See p. 160. ⏱ 1 day.

Car ferries run often between Poros and Aegina (1 hr. 25 min.).

❹ **Aegina.** It's worth spending a couple nights on Aegina, the biggest island, if you want to swim at leisure and see the **Temple of Aphaia** (p. 150, ❻), the main archaeological site. Stay overnight in the tiny beach resort at **Marathonas** (p. 149, ❹) or the fishing village **Perdika** (p. 150, ❺), 5km (3 miles) farther along the road. Aegina Town (p. 148, ❶) has a broader selection of lodgings, restaurants, and things to do: Browse in shops along the narrow lanes, watch the boats come and go, or visit the Kolona archaeological site (p. 148, ❷) when it's open. On Day 2, head to the small Doric **Temple of Aphaia** (p. 150, ❻). En route check

> *The Temple of Aphaia on Aegina is one of the most intact complexes to survive from ancient Greece.*

out the enormous **Agios Nektarios** Church, also known for healing, or explore the abandoned village **Paleochora.** Another worthwhile stop is the busy but fine, pine-backed sandy beach at **Agia Marina** (p. 150, ❼), 2km (1¼ miles) down the hill from the temple and 15km (9⅓ miles) from Aegina Town (40 min. by bus). From the port here, you can go back to Aegina Town or, in summer months, Piraeus. See p. 148. ⏲ 1 day.

Boats run every half-hour from Aegina to Angistri (10 min. by hydrofoil, 20 min. by ferry).

❺ **Angistri.** If you want to see the entire group, whip over here (a 9-min. ride from Aegina), where there's nothing to do but read, sunbathe, and swim. The beach is only a few feet from the dock at **Skala** (p. 154, ❶), with umbrellas and beach chairs for rent and tavernas and cafes across the walkway. See p. 154. ⏲ 1 day.

Angistri is an hour away by hydrofoil, and 2 hours by regular ferry from Piraeus.

> *Quiet beaches are just steps away from the port on tiny, often-overlooked Angistri.*

Book Ahead

If you plan to spend the night on the Saronics in summer, make reservations well in advance.

Best Beaches on the Saronic Gulf Islands

The Saronic Islands are mainly used as beach getaways close to Athens. They don't afford the remote, rustic experience that attracts most visitors to the Greek islands, but they provide a quick and easy way to bathe in warm, clear waters and escape from city life, if only for the day. These are your best bets.

> *Clear, shallow, inviting waters wash against the sandy headlands around Skala on Angistri.*

Agia Marina, Aegina. If we were staying in Athens and wanted to escape to a beach for the day, we'd hop on the next boat to Aegina. The nice sandy beach provides food, facilities, beach chairs, and umbrellas; and the water is lovely to swim in. See p. 150, ⑦. Direct service (hydrofoil, ferry) from Piraeus.

Agia Marina, Spetses. This is the nearest beach to town, and it's easily accessible by taxi and water taxi. By my standards, it's got it all: It's sandy with a shallow gradient, umbrellas and beach chairs, and an upscale cafe/

bar/restaurant (**Paradisos;** ☎ 22980/74963). The downside is that it's also the busiest beach. If that's a big issue, then take the water taxi farther out, to the pebble and sand beaches of **Agii Anargyri** or **Agia Paraskevi.** 2km (1¼ miles) southeast of Dapia.

★★ Aliki, Poros (Galatas). Aliki is the nicest beach in the region, but it's also busy. It's beautiful and sandy, and it has facilities, a bartaverna, and an islet in the bay to admire from a distance. On **Kalavria,** one of the islands that make up Poros, there are beaches at Megalo

Agia Marina, Aegina **1**
Agia Marina, Spetses **5**
Aliki, Poros (Galatas) **4**
Marathonas, Aegina **2**
Skala, Angistri **3**

and Mikro Neorio, where teenagers gather at the watersports wharf; **Calypso Bay;** pine-shaded Love Bay (a sweet little beach); **Russian Bay** with its naval ruins; and secluded **Vayionia,** which is good except when a north wind blows; **Askeli;** and **Monastery Beach.** See p. 162, **7**. 4km (2½ miles) from Poros port.

★ **Marathonas, Aegina.** Take the boat to Aegina Town and, from there, a taxi to Marathonas. The beach is small but fine for swimming, and it has food, facilities, and some beach chairs and umbrellas. You can be settled on the beach in an hour and 20 minutes from the time the hydrofoil sets sail,

which is comparable to a trip down the south coast of Attica, but it eliminates the hassle of driving and traffic. See p. 149, **4**. 4km (2½ miles) south of Aegina Town.

kids ★ **Skala, Angistri.** The water around the port and headland is clear and shallow, and if you closely examine the sand, you'll make out the tiniest, perfectly proportioned seashells, which fascinate children. The beach is narrow but fronted by beach chairs, cafes, and restaurants, and you can watch the boats come and go. See p. 154, **1**. Skala port, Angistri (1 hr. from Piraeus).

Aegina

Aegina is a relatively big island playground at 87,410 sq. km (33,749 sq. miles), just 29km (18 miles) from Athens; its distinctive Mount Ellanio (aka Oros) is a familiar sight from the south-coast mainland. Now known mainly for producing pistachios, Aegina has a long and complicated history. At loggerheads with Athens in antiquity, the island had a formidable navy, produced pottery, and introduced coinage to the western world around 700 B.C. It's an easy Greek Island Lite experience, with a friendly port town lined with neoclassical buildings and outdoor tavernas, pedestrianized streets, and opportunities for horse-and-carriage rides. It has its own ancient temple and fine beaches too.

> *Pine-shaded beaches line the west coast around Marathonas.*

START Aegina Town Harbor. In Athens, take the Metro to Piraeus for ferry service to Aegina. **TRIP LENGTH** 30 min.–75 min. from Piraeus to Aegina.

① ★ **Aegina Town.** Not too crowded and not too small, Aegina Town is lovely and old-fashioned. It has flagstone alleys to wander; boutiques to browse; and a lively port scene with a promenade, boats and yachts coming and going, horse-and-traps trotting by, people selling colorful fruit from caiques, and good-quality cafes and tavernas. ⊕ At least 1 hr.

② **Kolona Site & Archaeological Museum.** Besides the town beach, little remains at the cape where the 6th-century Temple of Apollo was located, except for a single Doric column, aptly called Kolona. There's evidence of human habitation from as early as 3500 B.C. Some walls were repeatedly rebuilt, and parts of a wall and ruins date to 1600 B.C. Other

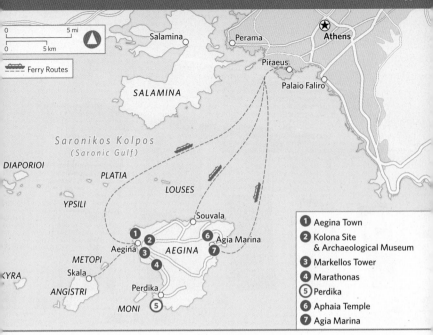

1 Aegina Town

2 Kolona Site
   & Archaeological Museum

3 Markellos Tower

4 Marathonas

5 Perdika

6 Aphaia Temple

7 Agia Marina

uins include Byzantine-era buildings and a emple to Artemidos. Gold jewelry discovered ere is held by the British Museum in London. ⏱ 1 hr. ☎ 22970/22248. Tues–Sun 8:30am–3pm. Admission 3€.

3 Markellos Tower. It may not look like much, but it's a rare example of Venetian architecture remaining in these parts. Believed o date from the 1600s, this building was one of the last defenses to fall to the Ottomans n 1718. Tradition says revolutionary leader Spyros Markellos used it to house the modern state's first government (1826–27) before it moved to Nafplion and, later, Athens. It was also used as the police chief's office and the national treasury. ⏱ 10 min. Thomaidou and Aiakou sts., Aegina Town.

4 ★ Marathonas. This tiny resort is on a shallow beach by a tree-lined sand pit. It has a bakery and supermarket, a taverna (**Tassos; ☎** 22970/24040), a bar and meze place (**Ammos; ☎** 22970/28160), a snack bar with rooms to rent, and free beach chairs (**La Palma; ☎** 22970/27980). A canteen has

> *Popular lore dates Markellos Tower to the 19th-century War of Independence, but it's actually an older remnant of Venetian rule.*

> *Although the exact origins are unknown, the Temple of Aphaia reputedly honored a sea nymph who took refuge on Aegina.*

showers. A second **Marathonas Beach,** 500m (1,640 ft.) toward Perdika, is also shallow, with beach chairs and umbrellas (7€). **Aeginitissa Beach** near Perdika is popular with youth and has a beach bar. ⏱ 1–2 hr. 4km (2½ miles) south of Aegina Town.

⑤ 🍽 ★ **Perdika.** This attractive fishing village has an islet (Moni) right in front of the cove marina and beach. Protected by a headland, it's a relaxing place to visit for a meal or an entire weekend, and the number of hotels is growing. Try **Antonis Taverna** (☎ 22970/61443; www.venetia. gr; year-round) or **Saronis Taverna** (☎ 22970/61501; year-round). ⏱ 1 hr. 9km (5⅔ miles) south of Aegina Town.

❻ ★★ **Aphaia Temple.** The lone structure at the top of a hill, this temple dates to 500 B.C. Dedicated to an unknown goddess, it's smaller than the Parthenon, but you can get closer to the Doric limestone columns, which were re-erected in the 1950s, for a better sense of how it was in ancient times. The sculpture pediments were removed in 1811 and reside in the Glyptothek Museum in Munich. There's a small museum on site, and a souvenir shop and canteen in the parking lot. ⏱ At least 30 min (site and museum). 13km (8 miles) east of Aegina Town, 2km (1¼ miles) north of Agia Marina. ☎ 22970/32398. Nov–Mar site daily 8am–5pm, museum Tues–Sun 8am–2:15pm; Apr–Oct site daily 8:30am–7:30pm, museum Tues–Sun 8am–2:15pm. Tickets 4€. Bus runs from Aegina Town daily 6:30am–8pm, every 90 min. (some via Agios Nektarios Church, a local pilgrimage site).

❼ **Agia Marina.** The beach at this old-fashioned resort is sandy but narrow and busy in summer, as boats go direct from here to Piraeus. Walk past the sliver of sand until it opens up after **Galaris snack bar** (☎ 22970/32369). Established in 1950, it serves old-style seaside food such as battered and fried small fish, zucchini, and eggplant slices. For a full meal at a good price with views of the sea, try **Neromylos** (☎ 22970/32198; Apr–Sept daily breakfast, lunch & dinner), with the water wheel. ⏱ At least half-day. 15km (9⅓ miles) east of Aegina Town.

Where to Stay & Dine on Aegina

★ Aeginitiko Archontiko AEGINA TOWN

This 19th-century stone mansion has lodged some famous Greek guests, including President Pavlos Kountouriotis and Saint Nektarios. The walls in the upstairs suites are .6m (2 ft.) thick, built to guard against pirates, and the ceilings still bear original artwork. The downstairs rooms are a bit dark and noisy. 100m (330 ft.) from the port. Ag. Nikolaou and 1 Thomaidou sts. ☎ 22970/24968. www.aeginitikoarchontiko.gr. 11 units. Doubles 75€ w/breakfast. AE, DC, MC, V. Year-round.

★ kids Crownview Suites MARATHONAS

These self-catering apartments at the tiny resort of Marathonas have clean rooms and kitchenettes. It's gated, just opposite a shallow beach. About 4km (2½ miles) down the Aegina-Perdika road. ☎ 22970/28470 or 69444/21763. 18 units. Doubles 95€–105€ w/breakfast. AE, MC, V. Apr–Sept.

Hippocampus Hotel PERDIKA

The rooms have standard-issue pine furniture, but the location is good for staying over in the village. A chapel in the bougainvillea-draped garden was restored in the 1920s by the owner's grandfather, when the site was a summer home. Main road into the village. ☎ 22970/61363. www.hippocampus-hotel-greece.com. 20 units. Doubles 50€–65€ w/breakfast. MC, V. Year-round.

★ Maridaki AEGINA TOWN *GREEK*

True to its Athenian clientele, this taverna serves everything from moussaka to meze to seafood. Sunsets are lovely from this portside location. Directly opposite the caiques selling fruit, in front of the church. ☎ 22970/25869. Entrees 5€–7€. AE, DC, MC, V. Mon–Sat breakfast, lunch & dinner; open past midnight July–Aug.

★★ O Batis AEGINA PORT *GREEK*

Better known as Lekkas, the name on the awning across the street, this restaurant is on the water-front side, and some tables sit right in the sand. You can literally watch ships sailing off into the sunset from here. Overall it's good value, serving hefty portions of decent slow-cooked food. Service is very quick, and they also do takeout, which is convenient if you need to catch a ferry.

> *Old-fashioned favorites and sunset views are staples at Maridaki.*

4 Kazantzaki Ave. ☎ 22970/22527. Entrees 6€–10€. No credit cards. Breakfast, lunch & dinner daily. Closed Dec to mid-Feb.

★ kids Rastoni Hotel AEGINA TOWN

You can laze in the lovely garden at this hotel built in a pistachio tree orchard, set above the archaeological site Kolona at the water's edge of the main town. Each room has its own style; one called the Rama has a mezzanine with extra beds. Along the port from where the boats dock for 200m (656 ft.) toward Kolona Park and then right, a little uphill. 31 Petriti St. ☎ 22970/27039. www.rastoni.gr. 12 units. Doubles 80€–90€ w/breakfast. MC, V. Apr–Nov.

★ To Dromaki AEGINA TOWN *MEZE*

This cheerful meze restaurant occupies a tiny street just back from the port. Especially good are the moussaka, lasagna, beef in red sauce, and *ladero* (vegetarian meze in oil). Between Aristofanous and Ioulias Katsa sts. 2 Myrtidiotissis St. ☎ 22970/24445. Entrees 6€–9€. MC, V. May–Oct daily lunch & dinner, Nov–Apr Wed–Mon lunch & dinner. Closed Dec 25, Jan 1, Easter.

HELLENIC TEMPLES

BY TANIA KOLLIAS

TEMPLES TO THE GODS are the epitome of Ancient Greek architecture. Open only to priests, the interiors typically housed a statue of the namesake god and votive offerings. The temple reached its apotheosis during the Golden Age in Athens's Parthenon (p. 44, ❹), the temple of Athena Parthenos. The Golden Age ruler Pericles wanted to showcase Athens's strength and wealth and used the most beautiful and enduring material—marble—to build it. In a comparable effort to project stability, order, and integrity, Europeans and Americans revived the classical style in 18th and 19th-century banks, government offices, and other public structures built to inspire trust and prevail over the ravages of time.

TEMPLE OF ZEUS, OLYMPIA
Built of stuccoed limestone, this is an early Doric temple from 470 to 56 B.C., with columns more than 2m (6½ ft.) in diameter at the base. It contained a 12m (40 ft.) wood, gold, and ivory statue of Zeus, a wonder of the ancient world sculpted by Phidias, who also created the Parthenon friezes. The artist of the frieze and pediment sculptures is in dispute.

RECHTHEION, ATHENS
masterpiece attributed to Mnesicles and built under Pericles in 409 B.C., his split-level Ionic temple was dedicated to Athena and Poseidon-Erechheus. Her sacred olive tree and Poseidon's well were housed inside. The outhern portico with six caryatids—columns of maidens modeled on women rom Karyes in Laconia—is one of the most famous icons of classical Greece.

SANCTUARY OF ATHENA, DELPHI
Theodoros of Phocis wrote a book on how he built his 4th century B.C. *tholos*—a circular building with an external colonnade that combined elements of classical architecture. A frieze and 20 Doric columns surrounded the rotunda's exterior (3 were re-erected in 1938); Corinthian columns, marble in blue and two shades of white, ornaments, and waterspouts decorated the interior, thought to house a statue of Athena.

PORTARA, NAXOS
The 530 B.C. door frame is all that remains of an enormous but unfinished Ionic temple to Apollo that faces sacred Delos on an islet at the port entrance of Naxos. Reaching 8m (26 ft.), the 20-ton marble slabs were too heavy for the Venetians to cart away when they pillaged the rest of the temple to build a castle.

TEMPLE OF APOLLO EPICURIUS, BASSAE, PELOPONNESE
This remote temple (420 B.C.) on a hillside near Andritsena is the only one that combines Doric, Ionic, and Corinthian orders—including the oldest known example of the latter. Covered by a protective tent, it's dedicated to Apollo the Helper and may have been designed by the Parthenon's architect, Iktinos. Its friezes, now in the British Museum, depict battles with Amazons and Centaurs.

Myths in Marble

Temples were decorated with sculptures showing the exploits of the gods and heroes, and scenes often related to the building or site. **Olympia's Temple of Zeus** (p. 195, ⑮), for example, depicted Olympic contests with Zeus as the judge on one pediment (the triangular section over the entrance). On the portico, in a popular theme showing Greeks prevailing over barbarians, Apollo presides over a wedding party where the Centaurs get too raucous. The frieze around the sides of the temple depicted muscleman Hercules' Twelve Labors.

Made to Order

Characteristic elements of temples, mausoleums, and public buildings, were classified into orders by the 1st century B.C. engineer, Vitruvius, who said that "without symmetry and proportion, there can be no principles in the design of any temple." Identifiable by the decoration at the top of exterior columns, the oldest style is the simple ① **Doric order**, from about 600 B.C., named after the austere ancient Greek tribe called the Dorians; the rings *(annuli)* around the column tops are thought to represent cords used to keep the original reed columns in place. The Ionians of Asia Minor introduced the taller and more delicate ② **Ionic order** in the 6th century B.C. The leaf-motif capital decoration of the

③ **Corinthian order**, seen from the 5th century B.C., was favored by the Romans and is attributed to architect Callimachus's inspired invention.

Temple pediments and friezes were painted and decorated with ornaments and sculptures that usually depicted heroes and mythological battles.

Angistri

Beaches are the main attraction on the quiet, green 13sq. km (5 sq. mile) islet of Angistri, also spelled Agistri, and it's close enough to Athens to make for an easy weekend jaunt. One stretch of sand is right beside the port, Skala, where most visitors base their stay. Nearby Skliri, on the bluff about a 10-minute walk away, is near a more secluded beach. There are also a few coves around the island where yachts can drop anchor.

> *The Church of Agii Anargyri dominates the profile of Skala Port.*

START The port in Skala. **TRIP LENGTH** 1 hr. from Piraeus, Athens, by hydrofoil; 10 min. from Aegina.

❶ ★ Skala. The port area has newly built studios with simple kitchenettes, well-stocked supermarkets, family-run hotels, and rooms to rent. Fortunately the vicinity can't be developed much more than it already is because of land-use restrictions. A sidewalk that runs around the shallow, sandy **beach** and the headland is backed by a handful of tavernas and cafes. The path ends at a road with more shops, tavernas, and the **Church of Agii Anargyri,** which dominates the port. ⊕ At least 2 hr.

❷ Skliri. The area west of the port, barely distinguishable from it, is called Skliri, backed by a pine-covered hill with the residential settlement of Metohi above it, and with cliff-side hotels and restaurants along the path. **Halikiada,** a secluded pebble beach at the end of the road at the bottom of the bluff, attracts nudists. Notorious assassin Dimitris Koufodinas, of the far-left terrorist group known as November 17, camped

out here in 2002 before turning himself over to police after they arrested several members of his group. It's a steep descent to the beach, accessible via a goat path to the left of the ridge. ⊕ At least 2 hr. 10 min. walk east of Skala.

❸ Milos/Megalohori. If you have time to kill, come to the sleepy administrative center Milos (aka Megalohori, meaning Big Village), where the ruins of an ancient hot-spring bath are discernible amid the rocks along the road. There's a narrow, pebbly **beach** here as well, a couple of seaside tavernas, and places to stay. A minitrain (summer only) or half-size bus that operates on the boat schedule can bring you here from Skala in 5 minutes, or to the village of **Limenaria,** 6.5km (4 miles) away, leaving from the port or from a bus stop on the road behind the landmark Agii Anargyri Church in Skala. Milos also has its own **port (Myli),** redeveloped for hydrofoil traffic (Aegean Flying Dolphins; ☎ 21041/21654; www.aegeanflyingdolphins. gr), an hour from Piraeus, Athens. ⊕ At least 1 hr. 1.5km (1 mile) northwest along the coast.

- 1 Skala
- 2 Skliri
- 3 Milos/Megalohori

> *The Agistri Club is one of many small, informal getaways on the island.*

Where to Stay & Dine on Angistri

★ **Agistri Club** SKLIRI *TAVERNA/MEZE*
This hotel, restaurant, and bar run by a jovial Welshman attracts an eclectic mix of staff and guests, though most are British. It's on a ridge overlooking the sea. For a superb evening meal, walk 10 minutes heading left (east) as you arrive at the port to the taverna at the end of the road, where patrons graze from a tray of various specialty meze. ☎ 22970/91242 or 69326/07308. www.agistriclub.com. 15 units. Doubles 70€–90€. Entrees 12€–15€. AE, D, MC, V. Hotel May–Oct. Restaurant May–Oct daily dinner.

★ kids **Ilios Hotel** SKALA
The rooms at this hotel are spacious and clean with lots of drawers and nice big balconies that accommodate a table and a couple of chairs. All the rooms are studios with kitchenettes, but there's also a cafe in the lobby. A souvenir shop sells beach toys, too. ☎ 22970/91029. 11 units. Studios 30€–45€. AE, DC, MC, V. Year-round.

★ kids **Rosy's Little Village** SKLIRI
A 5-minute walk from the port toward Skliri, these village-style lodgings include family rooms. The on-site restaurant serves local specialties using local products, as well as local wine. A big buffet breakfast is an additional 6.50€. ☎ 22970/91610. www.rosys littlevillage.com. www.agistrigreece.com. 18 units. Doubles 48€–70€. AE, MC, V. Mar–Oct.

Hydra

Hydra's shoreline is mostly rocky, but the deep waters around it make for good swimming and a very active port, considered by many to be the most beautiful harbor in Greece. Vehicles are prohibited throughout its 52sq.-km (20 sq.-mile) territory, so the monasteries inland, accessible by donkey or on foot, plus a couple of villages on the inhospitable coast don't draw too many people away from the glitzy harbor. Hydra's star began to rise again in the 1950s, when Greek artist Nikos Hadjikyriakos-Ghikas moved here, and *Boy on a Dolphin* (1957), starring Sophia Loren, and other films were set here. Today it continues to attract international celebrities, such as Leonard Cohen and Mick Jagger, as well as wealthy Greeks.

> Hydra has long been a haven of artists and celebrities, but it retains its unspoiled beauty and charm.

START Hydra port. **TRIP LENGTH** 1½ hr. by ferry from Piraeus, Athens.

❶ **Hydra port.** Known as Hydrea in antiquity, Hydra is the most famous island of the Saronic group. Celebrated by writers and artists, it's the summer home of fashionable Athenian families and international celebrities drawn to its aesthetic, grand houses, pretty port, absence of cars, and proximity to the capital, right on the Dolphin run. Hydra is a charmer, with its mansions tumbling down the hillside in shades of brown rather than blinding white. The view upon entering the tiny concave port,

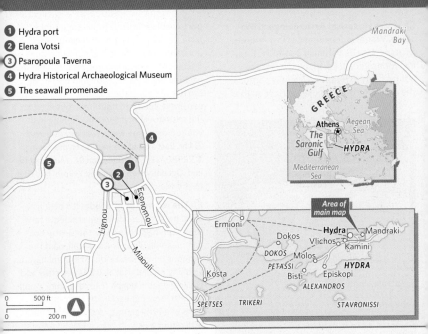

1 Hydra port
2 Elena Votsi
3 Psaropoula Taverna
4 Hydra Historical Archaeological Museum
5 The seawall promenade

0 500 ft
0 200 m

whether you're looking straight ahead, left, or right is just like the cubist renditions you see in galleries: Little boutiques flank one side, restaurants and village stores occupy the middle, and the far side of the quay fronts cafes. Farther along the distinctive gray and rust-colored flagstone pavement is the museum. ⏲ At least 1 hr.

2 Elena Votsi. The jeweler who redesigned the permanent side of Olympic medals has a shop here selling super-size semiprecious stones set into rings and necklaces. Shoppers who want their jewelry to make a bold statement flock here from New York and London as well as Athens. ⏲ 10 min. 3A Economou St., port. ☎ 22980/52637. www.elenavotsi.com. AE, D, MC, V. Year-round.

3 🍴 kids Psaropoula Taverna. This seafood taverna right on the port sets tables out in front of the yachts, water taxis, and tethered donkeys. You can grab a quick and casual meal, including alternatives to the expensive fresh fish on the menu. Service is friendly. **Central harbor front.** ☎ 22980/52360. www.psaropoula.com. $$ Mar–Oct.

> Transport is by two or four legs on Hydra, where even bicycles are banned.

4 Hydra Historical Archaeological Museum. War of Independence hero Andreas Miaoulis may be buried in Zoodochos Pigi Monastery in Poros, but he literally left his heart in Hydra, as it's now part of the collection at this museum right on the

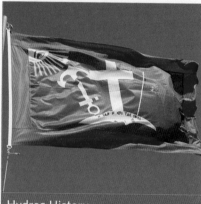

port. Displays include interesting trinkets from the 18th and early 19th centuries, portraits, ship models, old currency, and documents—including one that forbade the wearing of garments with gold thread, at the risk of deportation for life. History buffs can easily spend an hour here, but even for the casual visitor, it's worth popping in if you're killing time while waiting for a boat. ⏱ 1 hr. East side of the harbor, Hydra Town. ☎ 22980/52355. Admission 5€. Mid-May to mid-Oct daily 9am–4pm and 7–9pm; mid-Oct to mid-May 9am–4pm.

5 The seawall promenade. It's best to stroll the promenade when residents take their evening strolls, after the siesta. You can meander along the sea wall, past the cannons on the west side, to Kamini harbor, a fishing hamlet that also has a narrow and shallow pebble **beach** (Mikro Kamini, popular with families) backed by the restored ruins of a 19th-century arsenal. ⏱ 30 min. with return walk.

Hydrea History

Once known for its springs (hence its name, which was shortened from Hydrea), Hydra, evidence suggests, supported shepherds 3,000 years ago. Later settled by refugee Samians and then by Troezenians, it was again a grazing outpost in 1204 when it came under Venetian then Turkish rule, when the Arvanites from the neighboring Peloponnese moved over in the 15th and 16th centuries. By the 18th century, it was wealthy from shipping and trade aided by the Napoleonic Wars, and Genoese and Venetian architects built the shipowners' flat-roofed, pirate-resistant mansions at the port, to our eternal gratitude. In the early 1800s, the islanders used their wealth (and some 100 ships) to fight in the War of Independence, but they were unable to recover from the losses, and turned to fishing, sponge-diving, and the merchant marine, where they made excellent seamen. Hydriots built a school for naval officers here in the 19th century. In the mid-20th century, international films such as *Boy on a Dolphin* (1957) introduced the world to Hydra's striking harbor, and the island became a tourist magnet, attracting artists and fashionable Greeks and internationals who stay on for all or part of the year.

Night Crawl

To start your night out in Hydra, try dining around 9pm to beat the 10pm crush. Perhaps start out at **Sunset** (p. 159) or down the steps at **Spilia** (☎ 22980/54166); then head straight in from Alpha Bank about 100m (328 ft.) till you reach **Amalour** (Tombazi St.; ☎ 69774/61357), a club playing a mix of ethnic, jazz, and Latin music in a landmark early-1800s mansion. For more, backtrack to the port and over to the west side's **Pirate Bar** (☎ 22980/52711; www.pirate.gr), which has been sliding drinks down the bar for more than three decades. It's open from March through October, and, like many bar-cafe-clubs in Greece, it operates as a cafe by day, serving light snacks and desserts until the 9pm cocktail hour. You might find yourself closing the place at 6am as it morphs into a dance club playing mainstream music, house, and R&B, and then ending with rock standards. Most visitors stay on here, but if you want to hear some modern Greek music as well, try **Red** (☎ 69722/60864), near the Pirate Bar.

Where to Stay & Dine on Hydra

The gardenside pool at Bratsera Hotel, a former sponge factory.

★ Bratsera Hotel PORT
This hotel received an award for its conversion of a 19th-century sea-sponge industry building. It retains the traditional Hydriot architecture, with high ceilings and liberal amounts of wood and also has a pool in the garden beside a wisteria-shaded breakfast area. **2 min. walk from the port. Tombazi St.** ☎ 22980/53971. www.bratserahotel.com. 26 units. Doubles 135€–160€ w/breakfast. AE, D, MC, V. Mar–Oct.

★ Hotel Mira Mare MANDRAKI BEACH
These bungalows are just yards from the sea on the beach at Mandraki, 1.5km (1 mile) from town (30 min. on foot, 10 min. via water taxi). They have standard-issue pine furniture and flagstone floors. The owners have their own boat and run island tours for guests. They also organize beach activities, Greek nights, and other diversions. **Mandraki Beach.** ☎ 22980/52300. www.miramare.gr. 28 units. Doubles 60€–150€. MC, V. Apr–Sept.

★ Mistral Hotel PORT
This traditional stone mansion houses elegantly appointed rooms that vary considerably in size. Each room is equipped with a mini-fridge, and breakfast is served in the courtyard. **200–300m (656–984 ft.) from the port.** ☎ 22980/52509 or 53411, winter ☎ 21096/

80233. www.hotelmistral.gr. 17 units. Doubles 90€–120€ w/breakfast. AE, MC, V. May–Oct.

★ kids Phaedra Hotel PORT
This charming small hotel in a former tapestry factory is set back in a quiet area. All the rooms are spacious with kitchenettes for preparing snacks and drinks (in order to minimize strong food odors, the hotel discourages guests from cooking full meals). There's also an interconnecting room for families with two or three children. Eat on the terrace or in the courtyard. **3 min. walk from the port.** ☎ 22980/53330 or 69722/13111. www.phaedrahotel.com. 6 units. Doubles 100€–200€ w/breakfast. MC, V. Year-round.

★ Sunset Restaurant PORT *TAVERNA/ SEAFOOD/BAR* This popular restaurant with a reputation for quality and presentation has been around for years, catering to everyone from casual diners to wedding parties. They serve traditional taverna fare, but most come for the seafood and the romantic sunset view. Live Greek music in summer, and a bar. **Portside, next to the cannons on the cliff over the swimming area.** ☎ 22980/52067. www.sunsethydra.com. Entrees 8€–26€. AE, D, MC, V. Lunch & dinner daily Apr–Oct.

Poros

The boat ride into Poros is like a "deep dream," wrote Henry Miller in *The Colossus of Maroussi*. "Suddenly the land converges on all sides and the boat is squeezed into a narrow strait. . . . The men and women of Poros are hanging out of the windows, just above your head. You pull in right under their friendly nostrils, as though for a shave and haircut en route." It's indeed a whimsical place, with lush surroundings, a sensual atmosphere, and a unique history, as the site where the British, French, and Russians met in 1828 to help decide how the modern nation of Greece would be run.

> The monastery of Zoodochos Pigi, popular for its curative spring, overlooks Poros port.

START Poros port. **TRIP LENGTH** 1 hr.–2½ hr. by ferry from Piraeus, Athens.

1 ★★ **Poros port.** Boats deliver you to the small island of Sphaeria, cut off when a volcano erupted in nearby Methana in 273 B.C. This is the port with all the tavernas and activities along the waterfront, with many tied-up sailing yachts. Residents' homes are built up the hill from the waterfront. Sphaeria was also joined to pine-clad Poros proper, known as Kalavria. A small, bridged canal dug in 1877 separates the two near

the Greek naval training school, once the site of a Russian base station built during the Russo-Turkish War of 1806–12. The beaches are here, along with the Temple of Poseidon and Zoodochos Pigi Monastery. Frequent ferries make the 5-minute crossing across the strait, just 150m (492 ft.) at its narrowest point, to the distinctive area called Galatas on the mainland Peloponnese. Fragrant **lemon groves** are there (10 min. by taxi), as well as the ancient site of Trizina, where the Decree of Themistocles was discovered. It's also the way to Aliki Beach. ⏲ At least 1 hr.

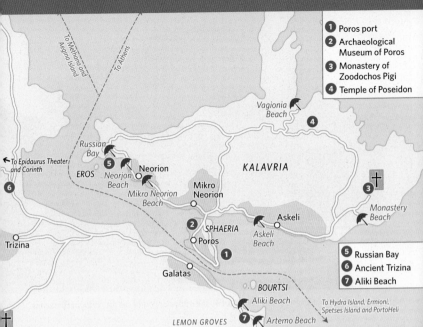

1. Poros port
2. Archaeological Museum of Poros
3. Monastery of Zoodochos Pigi
4. Temple of Poseidon

5. Russian Bay
6. Ancient Trizina
7. Aliki Beach

2 Archaeological Museum of Poros. This little museum from the 1960s houses artifacts from the Mycenaean era to Roman times, with finds from the Temple of Poseidon and the wider region—including ancient Trizina and nearby Methana—such as geometric pottery, funeral steles, figurines, and bronze vessels. ⏱ 30 min. Koryzi Sq., Poros port. ☎ 22980/ 23276. Admission 2€. Tues–Sun 8:30am–3pm.

3 Monastery of Zoodochos Pigi. Don't forget to bring some empty bottles to the Source of Life Monastery, a pilgrim magnet believed to have curative spring waters. Built between 1726 and 1732 at the top of a winding, tree-lined road, the monastery includes a small chapel, **Agii Anargyri,** by the fountain at the roadside. Passing through the entrance, the chapel is on the left, where the 17th-century carved wooden screens around the walls (*iconostasis*) are reputed to be from Cappadocia, once home to a thriving monastic Orthodox community. The Virgin Mary icon is by Italian painter and founder of the Academy of Fine Arts in Athens, Rafael Ceccoli, and is said to resemble his daughter, who died at age 21. She is buried in the monastery's courtyard, as is Admiral Andreas Miaoulis, a War of

Independence hero, and Athenian orator Demosthenes. ⏱ 1 hr. 3km (2 miles) from Poros port, Kalavria. ☎ 22980/22926. May–Sept daily 8am–1:30pm and 4:30–8:30pm, Oct–Apr daily 8am–1:30pm and 4:30–5:30pm.

4 Temple of Poseidon. Only the foundations of the ancient temple remain, so it's hard to reconstruct how it once looked from the diagram, but this is where the seven maritime powers of the Kalavrian League met in the 7th century B.C.: Athens, Aegina, Epidaurus, Hermioni, Prassies (Attica, succeeded by Sparta), Nafplion (succeeded by Argos), and Orchomenos (Boeotia). The stones were carted off to Hydra for mansion building. The view from up here is superbly panoramic. Both forks in the road lead to the summit, where the site is fenced but open. ⏱ 30 min. 5km (3 miles) from Poros port, Kalavria.

5 Russian Bay. Taking the road in the other direction, past the **Neorio** area (another beach resort a number of inviting bays later), you reach Russian Bay, site of the Russian naval station ruins that were moved here between 1834 and 1836 and abandoned after the Bolshevik Revolution in 1917. There are beach

> *A 19th-century Russian dockyard fronts Poros harbor, still a popular port of call for northern Europeans.*

> *Poros Town climbs the hillsides of Sphaeria, a volcanic islet separated from the rest of Poros by a narrow strait.*

chairs, umbrellas, and a canteen. Daskalio is the small islet with the chapel (Assumption of the Virgin). ⏲ At least 15 min. 2km (1¼ miles) from Poros port, Kalavria.

⑥ ★ Ancient Trizina. The site on the Galatas side is more interesting than the Temple of Poseidon, though there are still scant remains. Ancient Trizina (Troezene) includes a tower with a medieval top and ancient bottom; remains of what was likely a temple to Asklepios; foundations of Byzantine churches; an aqueduct leading to the naturally formed Devil's Bridge across a ravine to a ruined sanctuary of Pan; and a Frankish castle of Damala, then the region's powerful town. It's also the legendary birthplace of Theseus, and events connected with Poseidon and Orestes took place here, commemorated in Euripides' tragedies 2,450 years ago (p. 456). ⏲ 2 hr. Galatas. 10km/6¼ miles from Poros port.

⑦ ★★ Aliki Beach. Take the 5-minute ferry over to Galatas, then a 10-minute taxi ride to this lovely beach on a bay, past the lemon groves. The sandy seashore is also on a "spit" that backs onto a lake. A beach bar can call a taxi when you're ready to return. ⏲ At least 2 hr. 4km (2½ miles) from Poros port, Galatas.

Where to Stay & Dine on Poros

★ kids **Kathestos Taverna** PORT TOWN *GREEK*
There are opportunities to eat everywhere in
Poros, and this is one of the better options—a
good, traditional taverna right at the harbor
front, between the post office square and the
National Bank. You can book your table online,
too. ☎ 22980/24770. Entrees 6€–14€. AE, D,
MC, V. Breakfast, lunch & dinner daily.

★★ **Sto Roloi Hotel** PORT TOWN
Marie Luis is an Austrian architect who has
lovingly done up traditional houses with
beautiful details. You won't believe your luck
if you choose to stay at one of her unique
properties, one of which has a pool. All are
studios and have their own kitchens. You'll be
met at the port, so let them know when you
arrive. 34–36 Kostelenou St. ☎ 22980/25808 or
69324/27267. www.storoloi-poros.gr. 7 units.
55 €–100€. MC, V. Year-round.

★★ kids **Villa Dolphins** ASKELI, KALAVRIA
The Villa Dolphins is a great place for families,
with two-bedroom apartments, a swimming
pool, a big garden with a fountain, many amenities, and, of course, a beach 180m (590 ft.)

> *Villa Dolphins is popular with families.*

Poros in Modern History

Trizina (aka Troezene) was the site of important events leading up to Greece's birth
as a nation. Rival assemblies still skirmish-
ing with Turks and their Egyptian allies
in battles against the Ottoman Empire
agreed to meet here in the Third National
Assembly in 1827. They hammered out
a constitution; agreed to intervention by
Russia, Britain, and France as guarantor nations; and elected Ioannis Kapodistrias, an
advisor to the czar in Russia, Greece's first
governor for a 7-year term. A year later, the
ambassadors of the Great Powers in Constantinople (modern-day Istanbul) also
met here with Kapodistrias to work out the
new country's boundaries and to incorporate broader, and thus less democratic,
control under Kapodistrias's mandate. He
was assassinated in 1831.

away. A multitude of watersports will keep
older kids entertained. Frequent buses and
taxis go to Poros port, or you can walk there in
20 minutes (1km/⅔ miles). ☎ 22980/23751.
www.villadolphins.com. 13 units. Doubles
(apartments) 50€–75€. AE, D, V, MC.
Year-round.

★★ **White Cat Restaurant** MICRO NEORIO,
KALAVRIA *GREEK* This restaurant is also known
by its Greek name, Aspros Gatos, which is also
the name of the area. The owner's grandfather
opened it in 1909. It has the most romantic
setting on the water, with a sparkling evening
view of the town and the goings-on in the
strait. The specialty is lobster (expect a whole
kg/2.2 lb.) with pasta. There's also a buffet
every Thursday evening, 10 €–12€. 49 Lambraki
St. ☎ 22980/25650. Entrees 6€–40€. MC, V.
Breakfast, lunch & dinner daily Apr–Oct, closing
earlier in shoulder seasons.

Spetses

Private cars are forbidden on this small, high-society island whose native sons and daughters played a galvanizing role in Greece's War of Independence. The island is only 6.5km (4 miles) long, so it's easy to get around on foot or by horse-and-buggy, public bus, car, taxi, bicycle, motorbike, or the water taxi that runs to the beaches. It takes 2 hours to reach by hydrofoil and 4 hours by ferry from Piraeus.

> *Spetses Town climbs a hillside above two ports, modern Dapia and the Venetian Old Harbor.*

START Dapia harbor. **TRIP LENGTH** 2–4 hr. by ferry from Piraeus, Athens.

❶ **Dapia & environs.** Aristocrats at the turn of the 20th century built the mansions with white balustrades; thick, pirate-defying walls; and attractive, pebble-mosaic entrances on Dapia's harbor. Kounoupitsa is an exclusive area past the Poseidonion Hotel. In the other direction, the Old Harbor is good for dining and nightlife. ⏱ Half-day.

❷ ★ **Spetses Museum.** The former home of statesman Hatzigiannis Mexis (1754–1844) also houses relics of the 1821 War of Independence, including the bones of heroine Laskarina Bouboulina. The **Archaeological, Folklore and Historic Museum of Spetses** houses 4 centuries' worth of finds from the island, but the main collection relates to the modern war, including the revolutionary flag. ⏱ 30 min. Behind the clinic, Spetses Town. ☎ 22980/72994. www.culture.gr. Admission 3€, E.U. citizens 65 and over and non-E.U. students 2€. Tues–Sun 8:30am–2:30pm.

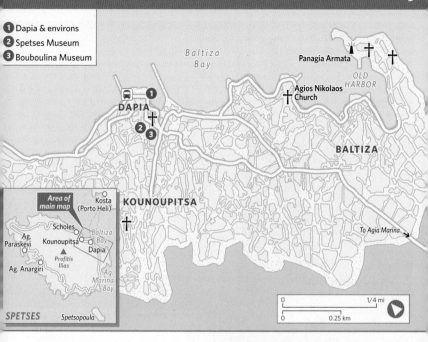

1 Dapia & environs
2 Spetses Museum
3 Bouboulina Museum

Baltiza Bay

Panagia Armata

OLD HARBOR

Agios Nikolaos Church

DAPIA

BALTIZA

Area of main map

Kosta (Porto Heli)

KOUNOUPITSA

Scholes

Ag. Paraskevi

Kounoupitsa

Baltiza Bay

Dapia

Profitis Ilias

Ag. Anargiri

Ag. Marina Bay

To Agia Marina

SPETSES   *Spetsopoula*

0   1/4 mi
0   0.25 km

3 ★★ **Bouboulina Museum.** Spetses's most famous daughter is the 1821 War of Independence heroine Laskarina Bouboulina (p. 166), whose statue dominates the square in front of the Poseidonion Hotel. The museum was her home, and her heirs still live there, allowing scheduled tours of the exhibition spaces displaying interesting artifacts, an ornately carved ceiling, and famous paintings of Bouboulina, complete with cowering boatmen. ⏱ 40 min. Spetses Town. ☎ 22980/72416 or 72077. www.bouboulinamuseum-spetses.gr. Admission 5€, students 3€, children ages 6–18 2€, children under 6 free. Open Mar–Oct at tour times (see website for details).

Getting Around

A water taxi can take you to the beaches at Agia Marina, Agii Anargyri, and Agia Paraskevi. You can also swim around Dapia, the port, and along the coastal road toward the former boarding school, Anargyrios and Korgialenios College (1927), where John Fowles, author of *The Magus*, taught.

> The cannons that ring Dapia Harbor on Spetses are reminders of the island's role in the Greek War of Independence.

Bouboulina & the Armada Battle

On Poseidonion Square, the prominent statue of a woman looking seaward depicts Spetsiot heroine Laskarina Bouboulina (1771–1825), whose role in the Greek struggle for independence is part of an epic tale.

Born in a Constantinople prison where her father was held by the ruling Ottomans, Laskarina grew up in Spetses, where her mother remarried to a prominent sea captain. Laskarina married two sea captains herself, but both were killed fighting pirates, who continually harassed the wealthy shipbuilding and trading Spetsiots.

Laskarina was widowed the second time in 1811, leaving her to raise seven children and four stepchildren.

She used her vast fortune to help instigate the fight for Greek Independence, including construction of Greece's first fighting boat, the *Agamemnon*. In 1821, at the age of 50, she herself took to the battlefield, leading her fleet of eight ships to aid the siege of the formidable Ottoman fortress at Nafplion.

Spetses's finest hour came on September 8, 1822, when an armada of Turkish and Egyptian ships sailed through Greece intent on destroying the seafaring capability of Spetses, Hydra, and Psara, another island that provided brigs for the cause. The vastly outnumbered and outsized Greek fleet managed to rout the enemy, following a 6-hour exchange of cannon fire, when a single fire ship targeted the Turkish flagship carrying the *capitan pasha* (admiral) and drove it away along with its fleet—an event re-enacted at the harbor each September during the Armata Festival.

Where to Stay & Dine on Spetses

Economou Mansion KOUNOUPITSA
This renovated house from 1851 has brass beds with French roll pillows and mosquito nets, and a small, inviting pool in the courtyard. Do not miss the wonderful traditional homemade breakfast by the pool. They maintain an office at the port (Yachting Club office). Coastal road to Kounoupitsa. ☎ 22980/3400. www.spetsesyc.gr. 8 units. 105€–185€ w/breakfast. AE, MC, V. Year-round.

Nissia Spetses Hotel KOUNOUPITSA
This converted cotton factory from the 1920s houses luxurious apartments right on the waterfront. Once owned by industrialist D. Dasalakis, the heritage building is on the coastal road overlooking the sea and coastline of the Peloponnese peninsula. ☎ 22980/75000. www.nissia.gr. 31 units. Doubles 155€–255€ w/breakfast. AE, DC, MC, V. Apr-Oct.

★ Orloff Resort OLD HARBOR, ANALYPSI
Rooms in this hotel, including the 19th-century Orloff mansion, are beautiful, done in minimalist style, and the courtyard pool is inviting. It's about a 10-minute walk from the port (walk east toward the Old Harbor and then ask directions), but staff will pick up guests if necessary. ☎ 22980/75444. www.orloffresort.com. 22 units. Doubles 120€–210€ w/breakfast. MC, V. Apr-Oct.

Kids Philippos DAPIA *PIZZA*
Right near the disembarkation point from the ferry in Dapia, this cafe serves up pizza, spaghetti, and salad. It's ideal for families waiting for a boat or landing. ☎ 22980/75500. Pizzas 8.50€–14€. No credit cards. Breakfast, lunch & dinner daily.

★★ Poseidonion Grand Hotel DAPIA
Near the central port, the landmark Poseidonion is widely photographed, with its unique French Colonial architecture. Built by Spetses benefactor Sotirios Anargyros between 1911 and 1914, it was one of the first establishments to accommodate foreign and Greek guests and dignitaries at a time when tourism was practically unknown here. Guests and diners

> Tables on the terrace at Trehadiri overlook Spetses Town's Old Harbor.

gather on the veranda for evening meals in front of Poseidonion Square, where Spetsiots and visitors converge at dusk. Reopened in 2009 after a four-year renovation, it includes a spa (*hamam*/steam room and indoor pool), a restaurant, and a brasserie. ☎ 22980/74553. www.poseidoniongrace.com. 52 units. Doubles 195€–305€ w/breakfast. MC, V. Mar-Oct.

★ Trehadiri Bar Restaurant PALEO LIMANI
GREEK For a romantic night out, try this bar and restaurant with top-notch food and service on the coastal road to Paleo Limani. The sign is hard to discern in English (it says TPEX-ANTHPI in Greek), but the bar and restaurant is around the corner and upstairs from a pizzeria bar. The late shipping magnate Stavros Niarchos—whose island, Spetsopoula, is not far away—was a visitor. Old Harbor. ☎ 22980/29413. Entrees 12€–22€. AE, DC, MC, V. Apr-Sept lunch & dinner daily, Oct-Mar Fri-Sun. Closed Dec.

The Saronic Gulf Islands Fast Facts

> *A fleet of ferries and hydrofoils departs Piraeus for the Saronic Gulf Islands almost hourly.*

Arriving

From Athens, ferries and hydrofoils sail daily every hour or two to the Saronic Gulf Islands from the main port of Piraeus (Athens Port Authority ☎ 21041/47800), opposite the Metro station. For sailing timetables, see www.gtp.gr or www.openseas.gr. Sailing time to **Aegina** is 30 to 75 minutes (Aegina Port Authority ☎ 22970/22328). To **Angistri,** Milos, the crossing takes 55 minutes. To **Poros** it's a 1 to 2½-hour sail (Poros Port Authority ☎ 22980/22274). The crossing to **Hydra** takes 90 minutes (Hydra Port Authority ☎ 22980/52279). You can buy tickets from booths at the port or from travel agencies.

The main boat companies are **Hellenic Seaways Ferries** (☎ 21041/17341), **Hellenic Flying Dolphins** (☎ 21041/90200; www.hellenicseaways.gr), **Aegean Flying Dolphins** (☎ 21041/21654; www.aegeanflyingdolphins.gr), **ANES** (Aegina; ☎ 22970/25625; www.anes.gr), **Nova** (Aegina; ☎ 21041/26181 or 22970/24200; www.novaferries.gr), and **Hydraiki** (3-island cruise; ☎ 21032/30100; www.hydraiki.gr).

To reach **Spetses** (Spetses Port Authority ☎ 22980/72245), a KTEL bus (☎ 21051/34588 or 14505; www.ktel.org) runs from the long-distance terminal in Athens to Kosta, Peloponnese (2½ hr. one way). From there you can ferry across or take a water taxi for the 15-minute crossing.

Currency Exchange

See p. 681, Fast Facts Greece.

Doctors & Dentists

AEGINA For doctors, contact the **Ag. Dionysos Hospital** (☎ 22970/24489) or the **Medical Center** (☎ 22970/22886). POROS **Galatas Medical Center** (☎ 22983/20300) is open 24 hours daily. HYDRA Call the **Koulourio Hospital** (☎ 22980/53150 or 53151). SPETSES contact the **Health Center** (☎ 22980/72472).

Emergencies

AEGINA For emergencies, dial ☎ 22970/22172. POROS Dial ☎ 22980/35599. SPETSES Dial ☎ 199. **The European Emergency Call Number** (☎ 112) puts callers in contact with the appropriate emergency service in any E.U. country, including local police, firefighters, or emergency medical technicians. The service is restricted to genuine emergencies but free from pay phones, mobile phones, and land lines.

Getting Around

AEGINA Aegina (☎ 22970/22787) has frequent bus service, bike rental shops, and taxis near the port. For taxi service try **Aegina Radio taxi** (☎ 22970/22010 or 22635). ANGISTRI For water taxis, try ☎ 69445/35659. POROS Poros is easy to navigate on foot, but is served by buses and taxis (for taxis, dial ☎ 22980/23003). HYDRA Hydra is navigable only on foot or on bicycle; water taxis run to the beaches. SPETSES Spetses has limited bus service, a few taxis, and horse-and-buggy operators (☎ 22980/73171). Bicycling is popular, and the terrain is easy to bike. Water taxis ☎ 22980/72072) are the most popular means of reaching the island's best beaches. For the Port Authority on each island, see "Arriving," above.

Internet

See p. 681, Fast Facts Greece.

Pharmacies

See p. 682, Fast Facts Greece.

Police/Tourist Police

AEGINA For help from the police or tourist police, dial ☎ 22970/22100. ANGISTRI Call ☎ 22970/91201. POROS Call ☎ 22980/22462. HYDRA Phone ☎ 22980/52205. SPETSES Dial ☎ 22980/73100. Also see p. 682, Fast Facts Greece.

Post Office

AEGINA The post office (☎ 22970/22398) is on Plateia Ethatneyersias, around the corner from the hydrofoil pier. POROS The post office (☎ 22980/23451) is on the waterfront. HYDRA The post office (☎ 22980/52262) is off the harbor on Ikonomou. SPETSES The post office (☎ 22980/72228) is near the police station on Boattassi. Also see p. 682, Fast Facts Greece.

Telephones

See p. 683, Fast Facts Greece.

Toilets

There's usually a public toilet at the port. Look for standard restroom icons or WC. You can usually use the facilities inside archaeological sites or in cafes if you purchase a drink.

Visitor Information

See the tourist police numbers listed above for each island. AEGINA The tourist office is in the Town Hall (☎ 22973/20000 or 20026). ANGISTRI Angistri's (☎ 22970/91260) is in the town hall as well. POROS **Family Tours** (on the port; ☎ 22980/23743) organizes excursions and makes hotel bookings. HYDRA On the harbor, **Saitis Tours** (☎ 22980/52184) offers a number of basic tourist services. SPETSES **Mimoza Travel** (☎ 22980/73426) supplies all kinds of information. PIRAEUS At Piraeus Port in Athens, you'll find an information booth at the Saronic hydrofoil gate (☎ 21041/94000; summer season Mon–Fri 9am–9pm, Sat–Sun 10am–6pm). For general tourist information, contact the **Greek National Tourism Organization** (☎ 1572; open Mon–Fri 8am–8pm).

Favorite Moments in the Peloponnese

Ancients, Byzantines, Franks, Venetians, and Turks all left their traces on this landscape, scattering their fascinating cities and monuments throughout the Peloponnese. Nature has graced the terrain too, affording travelers views of mountains, beckoning forests, and seascapes at many a bend in the road. Here are some especially satisfying ways to experience the man-made and natural splendors of one of Greece's most wondrous regions.

> PREVIOUS PAGE *The Church of Agia Sofia atop Monemvassia.* THIS PAGE *Byzantines, Franks, Venetians, and Turks once laid claim to lovely Nafplion.*

① **Strolling on the Nafplion Promenade.** It's hard to believe that the Old Town is only a few steps behind you as you make your way along the Gulf of Argos, with the blue water shimmering and gentle waves crashing onto the rocks below you. At the end of the walk you can dip into the sea beneath the Acronafplia Fortress at Arvanitia—one of the most beautiful town beaches anywhere. See p. 219, **⑧**.

② **Entering the Monemvassia Gate.** The name of this Byzantine city means "single entrance," and you appreciate how apt that moniker is as you make your way through the one tunnel-like gate, dug out of rock. Suddenly the darkness gives way and you emerge onto a stage set, a medieval town clinging to the rock face high above the crashing surf. See p. 200, **①**.

③ **Driving down the Mani Peninsula.** The mountains are barren, the rocky shoreline seems inhospitable, and the villages of stone tower houses are formidable. Unwelcoming as it may seem when you first encounter the center peninsula, of the three that dangle from the Peloponnese, you soon discover that the landscapes, customs, and sights of this remote region are fascinating. See p. 210, **⑨**.

④ **Exploring the fortress in Methoni.** Massive fortifications built to protect Venetian sea lanes seem wonderfully extravagant, rising as they do today from a quiet seaside village. Walk past ruined arsenals through vast, overgrown courtyards to the sea, and a vision appears—a minuscule, elegant octagonal castle perched just offshore on a tiny islet. See p. 210, **⑧**.

⑤ **Walking through Karitena.** The ubiquitous stone—of the castle, the bridge, the houses, the old streets—evokes the Middle Ages, when Frankish knights claimed the surrounding mountaintops as their fiefdoms. Then, as now, not much disturbs the tranquillity besides a cacophony of goat bells. See p. 208, **④**.

⑥ **Walking beneath the pines in Olympia.** The sports arenas, temples, magnificent sculpture, and lore of the famous games are what bring visitors to this popular ancient city, but another discovery awaits as well. The

0   50 mi
0   50 km

Rio-Antirio Bridge
Patras
Aighio
Kyllini
Kalavryta
P E L O P O N N E S E
Pyrgos
6 Olympia
5
Dimitsana
Andritsena
Temple of Apollo at Bassae
Megalopolis
Kparissia
Messene (Ithomi/Mavromati)
Medieval city of Mystras
Nestor's Palace
Pylos (Pilo/Navarino)
4
Methoni
Koroni
Kardamyli
Korinthiakos Kolpos (Corinthian Gulf)
Perachora
Corinth
7
Loutraki
Isthmia
Corinth Canal
Megara
Nemea
Mycenae **8**
9 **Epidaurus**
Argos
Tiryns
Tripoli
1 **10**
Nafplion
Argolikos Kolpos (Argolic Gulf)
HYDRA
Leonidi
SPETSES
Sparta
Mt. Taygetos
Kalamata
Gythion
Monemvassia
2
Areopolis
Caves of Pyrgos Dirou
3
Messiniakos Kolpos (Messenian Gulf)
Lakonikos Kolpos (Laconian Gulf)
THE MANI
KYTHIRA
Kythira
Mediterranean Sea

Kyparissiakos Kolpos (Cyparissian Gulf)

GREECE
Aegean Sea
Athens
Peloponnese
CRETE

1 Strolling on the Nafplion Promenade
2 Entering the Monemvassia Gate
3 Driving down the Mani Peninsula
4 Exploring the fortress in Methoni
5 Walking through Karitena
6 Walking beneath the pines in Olympia
7 Looking out from the Acrocorinth
8 Descending into the cistern at Mycenae
9 Standing in the theater at Epidaurus
10 Sitting in Syntagma Square

roves of pine and meadows beside rushing
orrents prove yet again that the ancients had
 knack for finding the most beautiful settings
r their creations. See p. 195, **15**.

7 Looking out from the Acrocorinth. Atop
ne of the world's most remarkable fortresses,
igh above the isthmus and the Corinth Plain,
ou seem to be sharing time and place with
he Greek and Roman inhabitants of one of the
most cosmopolitan cities in the ancient world. In
hose less polluted days, they had a more far-
eaching view—all the way to the gleaming col-
mns of the Acropolis in Athens. See p. 186, **2**.

3 Descending into the cistern at Mycenae.
 climb down into this vast, dark cavern

reveals the genius of a 3,500-year-old engineering feat. See p. 188, **6**.

9 Standing in the theater at Epidaurus. Even
the hordes of *American Idol* wannabes belting
out show tunes don't detract from the thrill of
standing on the stage where ancient actors
performed the Greek classics when they were
new. See p. 191, **8**.

10 Sitting in Syntagma Square. Life rarely
seems as pleasant as it does from a cafe table
on this lovely expanse of marble paving. Nafpliots and their visitors linger for hours, and when
it comes time to leave, no matter where you're
going, the only way out is to stroll along the
beautiful lanes of the Old Town. See p. 214, **1**.

The Peloponnese in 3 Days

Even with just three days in the Peloponnese, the southern-most part of the Greek mainland, you'll see ancient ruins; monuments left behind by the Franks, Venetians, and Ottomans; and rugged, mountainous landscapes. You should also catch your breath every once in awhile and sip coffee in Nafplion's beautiful central square, Plateia Syntagma, and stand still amid the ruins of Olympia to take in a whiff of pine-scented air while listening for the sound of goat bells from the surrounding hills.

> *Seven of 38 original columns still surround Corinth's Temple of Apollo.*

START Isthmus of Corinth. From Athens, follow E65 south to the Isthmus of Corinth, 75km (47 miles) and less than 1 hr. away.
TRIP LENGTH Total distance traveled, with day trips from Nafplion, 316km (196 miles).

1 kids **Isthmus of Corinth.** You will enter the Peloponnese over this narrow neck of land, only 6.3km (4 miles) wide, which connects the region to the rest of mainland Greece. Before the Corinth Canal was dug across the isthmus in the 1890s—indeed making the Peloponnese, which means "Pelops Island," a bona fide island—ships were forced to sail an extra 400km (240 miles) around the Peloponnese. This inconvenience inspired numerous attempts at shortcuts over the millennia. The ancient Greeks built a stone road, the Diolkos, to cart goods and small ships between the Gulf of Corinth to the west of the isthmus and the Saronic Gulf to

1 Isthmus of Corinth
2 Acrocorinth & Ancient Corinth
3 Nafplion
4 Mycenae
5 Epidaurus
6 Olympia

he east. Portions of the stone ramp still run alongside the modern canal. The Romans attempted to dig a canal several times but eventually settled for rolling ships across he isthmus on logs, similar to the way the

Getting There

You will need a car to cover this much ground in so short a time. If you are coming from Athens, rent a car at the airport, from where you can easily connect with Hwy. E65 south to Corinth (for rental information, see p. 227).

Egyptians had transported blocks of granite across the desert to build the Great Pyramids. The Emperor Nero revived attempts in A.D. 67 and set 6,000 slaves to work with spades, but that endeavor, too, was soon determined to be too costly and impractical. It was not until the Suez Canal was completed in the 1870s that interest turned again to digging a similar water route across the isthmus, and a Greek team completed the job in 1893. You can observe the canal, the ship traffic, and, most impressively, the 86m-high (282-ft.) walls of rock through which the canal was cut from a well-marked overlook. ⏲ 30 min.

> *At Epidaurus, a stage whisper in the ancient theater can be heard from any of the 14,000 limestone seats.*

Ancient Corinth is 7km (4⅓ miles) south of the isthmus, well marked off E65.

2 🧒 **Acrocorinth & Ancient Corinth.** The Peloponnese was at the forefront of the ancient Greek world—a fact that comes to light as soon as the **Acrocorinth** (p. 186, **2**) comes into view, looming 540m (1,700 ft.) above the coastal plain. One of the world's most remarkable fortresses, it defended the Peloponnese from any army that attempted to march across the isthmus and ensured the safety of the city of **Corinth** below (p. 184, **1**). This ancient city once rivaled Athens in wealth, and the luxury the citizens enjoyed is reflected in the so-called Corinthian Order of architecture—an ornate style with elaborately decorated columns. As early as the 7th century B.C., under the tyrant Periander, Corinth had established colonies on the islands of Sicily and Corfu, in present-day Albania, and elsewhere. In the minds of many travelers, Corinth is most famously associated with the apostle Paul. He lived there for 18 months, around A.D. 51 and 52, and wrote his famous epistles to the Corinthians, to vent his frustration about trying to establish Christianity in such a wealthy, cosmopolitan city. Corinth has since then been ruled by the Byzantines, granted to the Franks after the Fourth Crusade in the 13th century, and handed back and forth between the Turks and the Venetians. Yet the temples, agora, fountains, and other sprawling ruins of the Greek and Roman city, one of the mightiest in the ancient world, most capture our interest. See p. 178, **1**. ⏱ 3 hr.

Take E65 for 65km (40 miles) south (less than 1 hr.) to the Nafplion exit.

3 **Nafplion.** Settle into Nafplion—Greece's loveliest city, with some of the most fascinating remnants of the ancient world—for two nights in order to visit Mycenae and Epidaurus. Byzantines, Franks, Turks, and Venetians all left their mark on the **Old Town,** crowded onto a narrow peninsula that juts into the Bay of Argos. Their once-mighty forts and castles are now spectacular viewpoints. The fortifications of the **Acronafplia** have stood at the southeastern heights of Nafplion for some 5,000 years and incorporate several castles scattered among the pines. The massive walls of the **Palamidi Fortress** ramble across a bluff some 200m (656 ft.) above the sea and the city, and the **Bourtzi,** a 15th-century island fortress, commands the harbor. Elegant Venetian houses, neoclassical mansions, churches, and mosques line the streets that surround the marble expanses of **Plateia Syntagma** (Constitution Square), where Nafpliots sit at cafe tables to sip coffee, chat, and watch the parades of passers-by. The excellent **Archaeological Museum,** in a sturdy Venetian storehouse at one end of the square, is filled with treasures from Mycenae, and the **Peloponnesian Folklore Foundation,** in an old mansion around the corner, shows off life in the region as it once was. Promenades follow the rocky shore around the tip of the peninsula, opening every so often to gardenlike terraces carved out of the cliff face above coves and pebbly beaches. See p. 214. ⏱ 2 nights.

Mycenae is 22km (14 miles) northwest of Nafplion, well-marked on the Nafplion-Corinth road.

Mycenae. In the morning on your second day, visit this storied city associated with might and myth. From around 1500 to 1100 B.C, the Mycenaen civilization dominated much of the southern Mediterranean from here. The dramas surrounding King Agamemnon and the ruling House of Atreus that transpired within the sturdy walls led to the Trojan War and inspired some of the most poignant Greek tragedies, retold again and again in the *Iliad* and the *Odyssey* and in classical drama. These legends, along with the exquisite death masks and other artifacts on display in the small **museum,** bring the old palace, humble dwellings, workshops, and other stony remains to life. Plan to visit early in the day, before the sun is too hot; shade is scarce amid the ruins, and your explorations will include some uphill climbs. See p. 188, ⑥. ⏱ Half-day.

Epidaurus is 25km (16 miles) east of Nafplion on the Nafplion–Epidaurus road.

⑤ kids **Epidaurus.** One of the best-preserved classical Greek theaters in the world is a magnificent arrangement of 14,000 limestone seats set into a hillside. Pausanias, the 2nd-century-A.D.- Greek traveler and chronicler, commented, "Who can begin to rival . . . the beauty and composition?" Or, he might have added, the acoustics? They are so perfect that a whisper onstage can be heard at the top of the 55 tiers, as demonstrated at productions of the summertime **Hellenic Festival** (p. 190). If your visit coincides with the festival, consider attending an evening performance in the **ancient theater** (p. 191, ⑧). To the ancients, Epidaurus was best known for the **Sanctuary**

> *Hermes Carrying the Infant Dionysus, attributed to Praxiteles, is part of the treasure trove of statuary unearthed at Olympia.*

of **Asklepios** (p. 191, ⑧), a healing center where dream interpretation and the flickering caress of serpent tongues were among the remedies practiced. ⏱ Half-day.

From Nafplion, drive through Argos 35km (22 miles) to Hwy. E65 south toward Tripoli for 16km (10 miles). Turn onto E55 west, the Tripoli–Pyrgos road, for 125km (78 miles) to Olympia. Olympia is 170km (106 miles, a 3-hr. drive) west of Nafplion.

⑥ kids **Olympia.** On Day 3, make the morning drive to Olympia, leaving time to visit the ruins and museums in the afternoon and early evening. One of the most popular archaeological sites in the world, the **stadium, gymnasium, training hall,** and **dormitories** at the foot of the Kronion Hill evoke the city's famous ancient games, inaugurated in 776 B.C. Olympia is also a sacred place, originally founded as a sanctuary of Zeus, and **temples** and **public buildings** litter the wooded terrain. Many of the sculptures, metopes, and frescoes created to adorn these structures—including the magnificent *Hermes of Praxiteles*—are on view in the **Archaeological Museum.** See p. 195, ⑮. ⏱ 1 day.

To return to Athens, retrace your steps to Hwy. E65 north (265km/165 miles, 4 hr. total).

Tips on Accommodations

True Greece (☎ 210/612-0656; www.truegreece.com) can provide a fine selection of comfortable hotels with character throughout the Peloponnese and arrange personalized, distinctive itineraries. **CHAT Tours** (☎ 210/323-0827; www.chatours.gr) will also book hotels and share knowledge about well-traveled parts of the region.

The Peloponnese in 10 Days

Ten days allow time to sample the many pleasures of the Peloponnese, not exactly at leisure, but at least at a pace that will enable you time to appreciate the region's riches, even if you don't have time to plumb them all. And what a bounty there is—from the classical temples at Corinth and Bassae to the stone tower houses of the Mani, from the mighty walls of Tiryns and Mycenae to the formidable curtain of the Taygetos Mountains, and from the Byzantine strongholds of Mystras and Monemvassia to the mountain villages of Arcadia.

> *Vathy, at the southern tip of the stark Mani Peninsula, is a ghost town of stone tower houses.*

START Corinth, 80km (50 miles) from Athens. **TRIP LENGTH** 990km (615 miles). You will need a car for this itinerary.

❶ Ancient Corinth & Acrocorinth. Antiquity will confront you almost as soon as you cross the **Isthmus of Corinth** (p. 174, ❶) and enter the Peloponnese. The imposing **fortress** of Acrocorinth (p. 186, ❷), crowning a craggy mountaintop, testifies to the power and importance of Ancient Corinth on the plain below. As home to the Temple of Aphrodite's

1,000 sacred prostitutes, the Acrocorinth was also a beacon of Corinth's free-wheeling life style, which vexed St. Paul when he came to preach Christianity in the 1st century A.D. With two ports, **Corinth** (p. 184, ❶) was one of the richest cities in the Greek world and an important Roman outpost rebuilt by Julius Caesar in A.D. 44. ⏰ 3 hr.

Take E65 south to Nafplion (65km/40 miles total, less than 1 hr).

0   50 mi
0   50 km

Rio-Antirio
Bridge
Aighio
Patras
Kyllini
PELOPONNESE
Kalavryta
Perachora
Megara
Corinth
Loutraki
1
Isthmia
Corinth Canal
Nemea
6
Mycenae
5
Pyrgos
9 Olympia
Dimitsana
Argos
3 **Epidaurus**
7
Tiryns
4
2 Ayia Moni
Convent
*Kyparissiakos
Kolpos*
10
Andritsena
Tripoli
Nafplion
(Cyparissian Gulf)
Temple of Apollo
at Bassae
*Argolikos
Kolpos*
HYDRA
Megalopolis
*(Argolic
Gulf)*
Kparissia
SPETSES
**Messene
(Ithomi/Mavromati)**
**Medieval city
of Mystras**
13 **Sparta**
Leonidi
Nestor's
Palace
14
Mt. Taygetos
Pylos
(Pilo/Navarino) **11**
Kalamata
Methoni
Koroni
Kardamyli
*Messiniakos
Kolpos*
(Messenian Gulf)
Gythion
Monemvassia
Areopolis
15
Caves of
Pyrgos Dirou
*Lakonikos
Kolpos*
12
(Laconian Gulf)
THE MANI

KYTHIRA

Kythira

1 Ancient Corinth
& Acrocorinth
2 Nafplion
3 Epidaurus
4 Tiryns
5 Mycenae
6 Ancient Nemea
7 Argos
8 Diakofto & the Vouraikos
Gorge
9 Olympia
10 Andritsena & mountain
villages
11 Pylos & Methoni
12 Kardamyli & the Mani
13 Sparta
14 Mystras
15 Monemvassia

Mediterranean Sea

GREECE
*Aegean
Sea*
★ **Athens**
Peloponnese
CRETE

> *Venetian and neoclassical houses surround Syntagma Square, in the center of Nafplion's Old Town.*

② **Nafplion.** While you will want to explore the great monuments of ancient Greece that litter the Argolid Plain outside Nafplion, also take time to soak in the ambience of this gracious city, the onetime capital of Greece, with imposing hilltop fortresses and palm-shaded seaside promenades. Enjoy a frappe on **Plateia Syntagma** (Constitution Sq.); wander into the galleries of the **Archaeological Museum** and the **Peloponnese Foundation;** and amble through the narrow streets of the **Old Town.** It's easy to dip into the **Gulf of Argos** at Arvanitia and other swimming spots, a welcome tonic after a day of wandering through the dusty **ruins** nearby (p. 214). Spend three nights here, making day trips to the ancient sites nearby. See p. 214. ⏱ **3 nights.**

Take the Nafplion–Epidaurus road east 25km (16 miles).

③ **Epidaurus.** A half-day excursion the morning of Day 2 takes you east to an exquisite **theater,** buried in mud in antiquity and perfectly preserved for close to two millennia. Even when a performance is not on the bill (for details about the Hellenic Festival, see p. 190), you can

experience the theater's phenomenal acoustics as an endless chorus of visitors climbs to the stage to whisper snippets that can be heard from the top of the 55 tiers of seats. The adjoining **Sanctuary of Asklepios** was one of the ancient world's most important healing centers. See p. 191, **⑧**. ⏱ Half-day.

Backtrack to Nafplion; then follow the coast road to Tiryns 5km (3 miles) north of Nafplion.

④ **Tiryns.** Before settling back into Nafplion for the evening, make a short stop at this Mycenaean stronghold, a formidable place even in its ruined state. The **walls** are 20m (66 ft.) thick and constructed of rough-cut stones weighing 14 tons apiece. They evoke Homer's reference to "wall girt" Tiryns—or, for that matter, the 20th-century writer Henry Miller' comment that Tiryns "smells of cruelty, barbarism, suspicion, isolation." A visit to Tiryns (p. 188, **④**) sets the mood for your visit to the even more powerful city of Mycenae the following day. On Day 3, visit Mycenae and nearby Ancient Nemea. ⏱ Half-day.

Take the well-marked Nafplion–Corinth road northwest to Mycenae, 22km (14 miles) from Nafplion.

5 Mycenae. On your third day, visit Mycenae and Ancient Nemea. Three experiences in Mycenae will shed vivid light on the Mycenaean civilization that flourished from around 1400 to 1100 B.C. The might of these war-prone people becomes apparent as you walk through the elaborate **Lion Gate** and stand close to the massive walls; a descent into the vast **cistern** reveals their building prowess and architectural accomplishments; and a look at the **museum,** glittering with reproductions of the gold death masks and jewels unearthed in tombs at Mycenae, testifies to the fabled Mycenaean wealth. See p. 188, **6**. ⊕ Half-day.

Continue north from Mycenae on the Nafplion–Corinth road about 18km (11 miles) for the well-marked turnoff to Ancient Nemea; Ancient Nemea is 40km (25 miles) from Nafplion.

6 Ancient Nemea. Like Olympia, this ancient city drew visitors from throughout the ancient world to a **Temple of Zeus** and to its famous sporting events, the **Nemean Games,** held in a remarkably well-preserved stadium (p. 190, **7**). ⊕ Half-day.

Leave Nafplion on Day 4 and stop in Argos before taking E65 north and west to Diakofto, at the mouth of the Vouraikos Gorge. Argos is 12km (7½ miles) northwest of Nafplion.

7 Argos. On Day 4, visit this farm town wrapped up in everyday business but with evidence of the ancient past around every corner. A **Roman theater** is the most impressive monument, and the **Archaeological Museum** shows off mosaics, statues, and other artifacts of the Mycenaeans, Romans, and other civilizations. See p. 188, **5**. ⊕ Half-day.

Diakofto is 125km (78 miles) northwest of Argos. From Argos, get on E65 and follow it north toward Corinth, then northwest toward Patras.

8 Diakofto & the Vouraikos Gorge. An open-air train chugs from seaside Diakofto up mountainside to **Kalavrita,** on the flanks of Mount Helmos. Along the way are wooded glades, rushing torrents, and one of Greece's

> Corinth exported black figure pottery throughout the ancient world.

oldest monasteries, **Mega Spileo.** Arrive in Diakofto in time to board the last run of the day, at 2pm. See p. 206, **1**. ⊕ Half-day.

From Diakofto, take E65 through Patras, 55km (34 miles) west of Diakofto, and continue west then south on E65 and its continuation, E55, 110km (68 miles) to Olympia.

9 Olympia. Your arrival in Olympia on Day 5 puts you in league with the spectators, touts, and athletes who began descending on this mountain town some 2,500 years ago to participate in what have become some of the world's most famous athletic events. You will want to divide your time between the **ruins** (scant as they are, they still evoke the great athletic contests); the **Altis,** the sacred precinct of Zeus; and the handsome **museum** where the works of Praxiteles and other great ancient artists come to life (p. 195, **15**). ⊕ 1 day.

From Olympia, follow the mountain roads in the direction of Megalopolis to Andritsena, about 70km (43 miles) east of Olympia. Stop in Andritsena to visit the Temple of Apollo at Bassae. Continue to Karitena, and from there to Stemnitsa and Dimitsana.

> *Olympia's evocative ruins are scattered among pines on the banks of the rivers Kladeos and Alphios.*

⑩ Andritsena & mountain villages. On Day 6, the itinerary leads through the mountain villages of Arcadia before dropping down to the southeastern coast. East of Olympia rises the mountainous province of **Arcadia,** where medieval stone villages cling to the hillsides. On a remote mountaintop some 15km (9⅓ miles) above **Andritsena** (p. 208, ❸) is one of the most spectacularly located ancient monuments in Greece, the **Temple of Apollo at Bassae** (p. 194, ⑭). **Karitena** (p. 208, ❹), 30km (19 miles) southeast, is topped by a massive castle built by the Franks in the early 13th century. **Stemnitsa** (p. 208, ❺), 16km (10 miles) north of Karitena, was the capital of Greece for a week in 1821, following the insurrections against the Turks that year. **Dimitsana** (p. 209, ❻), 10km (6¼ miles) north of Stemnitsa, helped fuel the revolutionary fervor with its School of Greek Letters. ⊕ Half-day.

From Dimitsana, backtrack to Karitena and then drop down 16km (10 miles) to Megalopolis. Continue south 60km (37 miles) to Kalamata. Head west on the well-marked Kalamata–Pylos road 50km (31 miles) to Pylos.

⑪ Pylos & Methoni. The relaxed air of these two pretty seaside towns belie their important and often turbulent pasts. The Bay of **Pylos** (p. 209, ❼), protected by two fortresses, witnessed the sinking of the Ottoman fleet in 1827, which led to Greek Independence. **Methoni** (p. 210, ❽), 14km (8⅔ miles) south of Pylos, was an important way station on the Middle Eastern trade routes and was protected by a massive seaside fortress and castle. Spend the night in either town. ⊕ Half-day.

Backtrack through Pylos and Kalamata to Kardamyli, 30km (19 miles) southeast of Kalamata. Settle into Kardamyli or continue to Gerolimenas, 62km (37 miles) south.

Not much remains of Ancient Sparta, but a statue of Leonidas evokes the might of the city-state that defeated Athens.

12 Kardamyli & the Mani. You'll spend Day 7 on the Mani—the middle of the three peninsulas that dangle from the southern Peloponnese. This region has always been a land apart, with a history of blood feuds and vendettas. From Kardamyli, the northwestern entrance to the Mani, the seaside road heads down the peninsula into the stony gray landscape. An air of mystery persists in Vathia and other villages of stone tower houses that rise above the rockbound coast (p. 210, **9**). 1 day.

Head up the eastern coast of the Mani for a brief stop in Gythion, the northeastern gateway to the region; then follow E65 to Sparta, 40km (25 miles) north.

13 Sparta. Start your eighth day in Sparta. Little remains of one of the most powerful cities of the ancient world. A huge **statue of Leonidas,** the great warrior king and hero of the Battle of Thermopylae in 480 B.C., helps fuel the imagination, as do a ruined **theater** and a **sanctuary to Artemis** (p. 191, **9**). Spend the night here or in Mystras, where you'll while away the afternoon. Half-day.

Mystras is 4km (2½ miles) west of Sparta off the Sparta–Kalamata road.

> *The magnificent Church of Pantanassa is one of many remnants of Byzantine Mystras, once second only to Constantinople.*

14 Mystras. This ghost town of golden stone evokes the last days of the Byzantine Empire. Churches and monasteries still preserve rich frescoes, exquisite examples of medieval art (p. 201, **3**). Half-day.

Make the trip to Monemvassia, 97km (60 miles) southeast of Sparta on the Monemvassia–Sparta road.

15 Monemvassia. Spend your last day and evening here. Passing through the single gate into the labyrinth of cobbled lanes, narrow stone staircases, and sunny squares that hang high above the sea is like stepping back into the Middle Ages. Monemvassia, wedged onto the side of a small, steep rock, was then a major port on the trade routes between Europe and the Middle East, and a prize possession for the Byzantines and Venetians and later the Turks. See p. 200, **1**. 1 day.

Ancient Wonders of the Peloponnese

The mountains and valleys of the Peloponnese nurtured some of the world's greatest ancient civilizations. In your travels through the region, you will encounter the Mycenaeans, who once dominated the southern Mediterranean from their citadel of Mycenae; warlike Spartans, who left not much more than their fearsome reputations behind; and the classical Greeks, who created the theater at Epidaurus, the temples, games arenas, and sculptures at Olympia, and so many other monuments.

START Ancient Corinth, 5km (3 miles) west of modern Corinth. TRIP LENGTH About 625km (388 miles); you should be able to visit the major ancient sites in 7 days.

SITE GUIDE PAGE 187

① ★★★ kids **Ancient Corinth.** A settlement that began to take shape as early as 5,000 B.C. flourished as one of the most important and wealthiest cities of classical Greece. Corinth was a major trading center with two ports—Lechaion on the Gulf of Corinth, a gateway to the Greek colonies in Italy, and Kenchreai on the Saronic Gulf, connecting Corinth with

trading routes throughout the Middle East. Boats were hauled between the two ports on the Diolkos, a stone-paved ramp. Among the city's chief exports was black figure pottery, the most common style of ancient Greek vases in which figures turn black after firing.

Corinth fought in the Trojan and Persian wars, was a major sea power that established a huge colony at Siracusa on the island of Sicily, and hosted the Isthmian Games, held every two years to honor the sea god Poseidon, alternating with the games at Olympia, Nemea, and Delphi. In myth, it was at Corinth that Jason abandoned his wife, the sorceress Medea, who wreaked

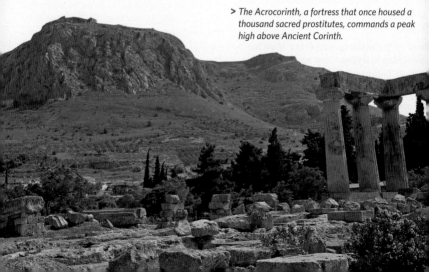

> *The Acrocorinth, a fortress that once housed a thousand sacred prostitutes, commands a peak high above Ancient Corinth.*

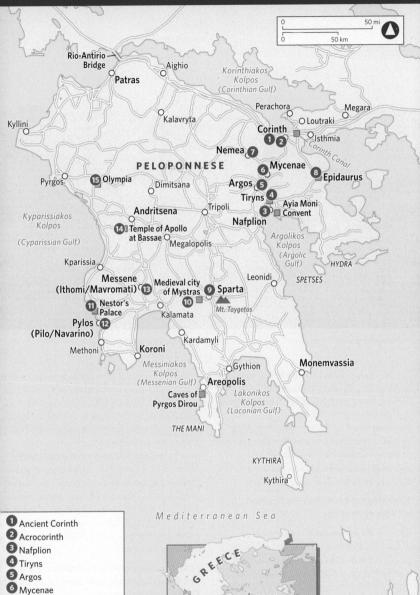

Rio-Antirio Bridge
Aighio
Patras
Korinthiakos Kolpos (Corinthian Gulf)
Perachora
Kalavryta
Megara
Kyllini
Corinth ①②
Loutraki
Isthmia
Nemea ⑦
Corinth Canal
PELOPONNESE
Mycenae ⑥
Olympia ⑮
Pyrgos
Dimitsana
Argos ⑤
Mycenae
Epidaurus ⑧
Tiryns ④
Ayia Moni ③ Convent
Kyparissiakos Kolpos
Andritsena
Tripoli
Nafplion
(Cyparissian Gulf)
Temple of Apollo ⑭ at Bassae
Megalopolis
Argolikos Kolpos (Argolic Gulf)
HYDRA
Kparissia
Leonidi
SPETSES
Messene (Ithomi/Mavromati) ⑬
Medieval city of Mystras
Sparta ⑨
Nestor's ⑪ Palace
Mt. Taygetos
Pylos ⑫ (Pilo/Navarino)
Kalamata
Methoni
Kardamyli
Koroni
Monemvassia
Gythion
Messiniakos Kolpos (Messenian Gulf)
Areopolis
Caves of Pyrgos Dirou
Lakonikos Kolpos (Laconian Gulf)
THE MANI
KYTHIRA
Kythira
Mediterranean Sea

① Ancient Corinth
② Acrocorinth
③ Nafplion
④ Tiryns
⑤ Argos
⑥ Mycenae
⑦ Ancient Nemea
⑧ Epidaurus
⑨ Sparta
⑩ Langada Pass
⑪ Nestor's Palace, Hora
⑫ Pylos
⑬ Ancient Messene
⑭ Temple of Apollo at Bassae
⑮ Olympia

GREECE
Aegean Sea
Athens
Peloponnese
CRETE

> *The enormous stones that gird Tiryns inspired Homer to call the city "mighty walled."*

her murderous revenge. The Romans destroyed much of Corinth when they overran Greece in the 2nd century B.C., and Julius Caesar ordered the reconstruction of the city in A.D. 52. Two centuries later Corinth was a bustling city of 100,000 inhabitants. ⏱ 2 hr. 5km (3 miles) west of modern Corinth. ☎ 27410/31443. www.culture.gr. Admission 6€. Apr–Oct daily 8:30am–8pm, Nov–Mar daily 8am–5pm.

A winding road connects the Acrocorinth with the ancient city.

② ★★★ kids **Acrocorinth.** The acropolis of Corinth, standing sentinel some 540m (1,772 ft.) above the coastal plain, has been a lookout post, place of refuge, and shrine since the 5th century B.C. Byzantines, Franks, Venetians, and Turks all added to the ancient walls. These three rings of massive fortifications, pierced by gates, ramble across the craggy mountaintop—a formidable deterrent to armies attempting to cross the Isthmus of Corinth, the narrow strip of land separating mainland Greece from the Peloponnese. The ruins of the **Temple of Aphrodite** stand atop the highest reaches of the peak, and in ancient times the reward for the climb to these heights was the company of one of the temple's 1,000 prostitutes. Trekkers who make the 3-hour ascent now settle for a look at one of the world's most remarkable fortresses, views that sweep across the sea to the east and west, and a broad swath of landscape that, in less polluted times, extended north all the way to the gleaming columns of the Acropolis in Athens. The less adventurous can make the ascent in a car or in one of the taxis that wait at the bottom of the peak. ⏱ 1 hr. www.culture.gr. Free admission. Apr–Oct daily 8:30am–7pm, Nov–Mar daily 8am–3pm.

From Corinth, continue to Nafplion, 65km (40 miles) south and less than 1 hr. following E65 to the Nafplion exit.

③ ★★★ **Nafplion.** This lovely city is rooted not in antiquity but in the more recent past, graced by monuments built by the Franks, Venetians, and Turks. The surrounding **Argolid Plain,** however, is littered with ancient ruins. Nafplion is a convenient base from which to visit Tiryns, Argos, Mycenae, Ancient Nemea, and Epidaurus. See p. 214. ⏱ 3 nights.

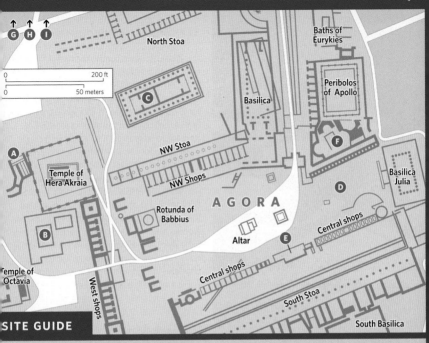

North Stoa

Baths of
Eurykies

Basilica

Peribolos
of Apollo

C

0 — 200 ft
0 — 50 meters

A

Temple of
Hera Akraia

NW Stoa

NW Shops

F

Basilica
Julia

D

AGORA

Rotunda of
Babbius

B

Altar

E

Central shops

Temple of
Octavia

West shops

Central shops

South Stoa

South Basilica

SITE GUIDE

① Ancient Corinth

Glauke, daughter of the king of Corinth, allegedly threw herself into the **A** **Glauke Fountain**
when Medea, the scorned wife of Jason, presented her with a wedding dress that burst into
flames. Just beyond is the **B** **museum,** a treasure trove of black figure pottery. The **C** **Temple of Apollo** retains 7 of its original 38 Doric
columns. Most of the city that remains is Roman. Shops line the streets and plazas of the
D **Forum,** and more shops stretch along the
marble-paved 12m-wide (39-ft.) Lechaion
Road, which ran from the market to the port at
Lechaion. The **E** **Bema,** a raised platform for
public speaking, stands amid the ruins of the
lower forum. It was here that St. Paul went before the Roman prosecutor Gallio in A.D. 52. The
F **Fountain of Peirene,** rebuilt by the Romans
with arches and arcades, surrounds a spring
that allegedly began to bubble forth when Peirene, a Greek woman, wept at the death of her
son until she dissolved into a stream of water.
The Romans also refurbished the **G** **Greek
Theater** so it could be flooded for naval battles.
Just to the north is the **H** **Asklepion,** the sanctuary of the god of healing. The ill came here,

bearing votive offerings fashioned in the shape
of their ailing body parts, and refreshed themselves in the beautiful **I** **Fountain of Lerna**
near the entrance.

> Roman baths are among the scant remains of ancient Argos, once one of the most powerful cities in the Mediterranean world.

Tiryns is 5km (3 miles) north of Nafplion on a well-marked road that follows the Gulf of Argos toward Argos.

④ ★★ **Tiryns.** A jumble of massive stones—some, known as Cyclopean, weighing as much as 15 tons—were once part of the walls surrounding this Mycenaean hill fort. Homer praised the city as "mighty-walled Tiryns," and the sheer power the place exudes gave rise to the ancient belief that it was the birthplace of Hercules. A modern observer, the writer Henry Miller, observed that the ruined city "smells of cruelty, barbarism, suspicion, isolation." Not all about Tiryns is barbaric: Within the fortifications is a **palace** that was once decorated with splendid frescoes of women riding chariots and other scenes that are now in the National Gallery in Athens. ⏱ 1 hr. Off Nafplion–Argos road. ☎ 27520/22657. www.culture.gr. Admission 2€. Apr–Oct daily 8:30am–7pm, Nov–Mar daily 8am–5pm.

Argos is 7km (4⅓ miles) northwest of Tiryns and 12km (7½ miles) northwest of Nafplion on the Nafplion–Argos road.

⑤ ★★ **Argos.** One of the most powerful cities of the ancient Peloponnese saw its heyday in the 7th century B.C., under the tyrant Phaedon, until it was eventually eclipsed by Sparta. The scant remains scattered around the modern market town include a **theater** that, with room for 20,000 spectators in 89 rows of seats, was one of the largest in the ancient world. The Romans re-engineered the arena so it could be used for mock naval battles and channeled the water into the adjacent baths. A small **Archaeological Museum** (Plateia Agios Petros; ☎ 27510/68819; admission 2€; Tues–Sun 8:30am–3pm) shows off local finds; among them is a clay figure of a squat, heavy-thighed woman, unearthed at nearby Lerna and thought to be the earliest representation of the human body yet to be found in Europe. Two ancient **citadels** (free admission; daily 8am–6pm), the Aspis and the much higher Larissa, are perched on adjacent peaks above Argos, accessible via a circuitous road or a steep path. ⏱ 2 hr.

Mycenae is 10km (6¼ miles) north of Argos on the well-marked road to Corinth and 22km (14 miles) northwest of Nafplion.

SITE GUIDE PAGE 189

⑥ ★★★ **Mycenae.** The short-lived Mycenaean civilization dominated much of the southern Mediterranean from around 1500 to 1100 B.C. Its greatest city is cradled on a bluff above the fertile Argolid Plain and surrounded by deep ravines between two barren craggy peaks—a somber setting for this citadel-palace that Homer linked with power, riches, and tragedy. Agamemnon, King of Mycenae, launched the Trojan War when the beautiful Helen, wife of his brother, Menelaus, was abducted by the Trojan prince Paris. Upon Agamemnon's return from Troy, his wife, Clytemnestra, and her lover Aegisthus, killed him. Agamemnon's son and daughter, Orestes and Electra, slew Aegisthus in turn. Aeschylus, Sophocles, and Euripides wrote about these events, and the Mycenaeans left behind many magnificent treasures that Heinrich Schliemann unearthed in the 1870s and that are now among the holdings of the **National Archeological Museum** in Athens (p. 46, ⑧). So steeped in legend is Mycenae that it is difficult to separate fact from fiction; even Schliemann was convinced

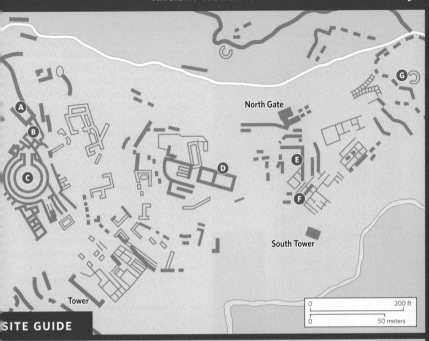

North Gate

Ⓐ
Ⓑ
Ⓒ
Ⓓ
Ⓔ
Ⓕ
Ⓖ

South Tower

Tower

0		200 ft
0		50 meters

SITE GUIDE

⑥ Mycenae

You'll enter **Mycenae** through the Ⓐ **Lion Gate** (see photo, right), topped by a relief of two lions, now headless, who face each other with their paws resting on a pedestal that supports a column. Holes for the pivots that once supported a massive wooden door sheathed in bronze are still visible, and an adjacent round tower provided a vantage point from which guards could unleash arrows on invaders who breached the gate. A Ⓑ **granary** was used to store massive quantities of wheat that, with the citadel's water supply, provided insurance against a long siege. Just beyond is a Ⓒ **grave circle** where, beneath six **stone slabs,** Heinrich Schliemann found face masks, cups, and jewelry, all fashioned from gold—14 kilos (31 pounds) worth. The ruins of houses cover a nearby slope, and at the top is the Ⓓ **main palace,** surrounding a courtyard. Traces of a central hearth and supporting columns are still visible in the throne room, and Schliemann conjectured that a small bathtub in an apartment adjoining the ceremonial hall was the very one in which King Agamemnon was slain by his wife, Clytemnestra. Beyond are the

Ⓔ **artisan workshops** and the Ⓕ **House of the Columns,** where a row of columns surrounds the central court. You can descend a wooden staircase into a vast subterranean Ⓖ **cistern** to appreciate the enormous amount of water, delivered by a secret channel, that could be stored. The largest and grandest Mycenaean tomb, the so-called Ⓗ **Treasury of Atreus,** is just off the entry road. A narrow passageway, fashioned out of massive blocks, leads to a high domed chamber; already robbed in antiquity, the tomb was the final resting place of the ruling House of Atreus and may well have been the grave of Agamemnon himself.

> Athletes at the ancient Nemean Games took time off from the field to pay homage at the famous Temple of Zeus.

Olympia, and Corinth, they attracted athletes from throughout the Greek world. Coins from every Greek city have been unearthed among the ruins and, along with athletic gear and other artifacts, are on display in a small **museum.** Legend has it that the games were founded to honor Hercules, who slew a ferocious lion lurking in a den outside Nemea, the first of the 12 labors he was assigned in penance for killing his own children. According to another myth, the games were founded to honor Opheltes, son of the Nemean king. The oracle at Delphi predicted health for the young prince if he remained off the ground until he could walk. One day his nursemaid set him down in a bed of parsley while she showed soldiers marching toward Thebes the way to a spring, and in her absence a serpent strangled the boy. Judges at the games wore black in mourning, and the victor was crowned with a wreath of parsley. Nemea was also famous for its **Temple to Zeus,** surrounded by several remaining columns but mined extensively for a Christian basilica nearby. The 4th-century-B.C. **stadium** is still largely intact, and a **vaulted tunnel** leads from a locker room to a running track where ancient races were run and modern ones still are, under the auspices of the Society for the Revival of the Nemean Games (www.nemeagames.gr). The tunnel is one of the great marvels of ancient engineering and sheds new light on the development of the arch. Once thought of as a Roman innovation, this arch present in a pre-Roman structure suggests that troops traveling with Alexander the Great during his India campaign in 326 B.C.

that a golden death mask he found in a tomb was that of Agamemnon, though the mask predates the king by many centuries. Some of these artifacts are in a small museum near the entrance, and seeing them and learning the stories behind this fabled place will bring the stony ruins to life. ⊕ 3 hr. Off Nafplion-Argos and Corinth-Argos roads. ☎ 27510/76585. www.culture.gr. Admission 8€, includes Treasury of Atreus. Apr–Oct daily 8:30am–7pm, Nov–Mar daily 8:30am–3pm.

Ancient Nemea is well marked off the Argos–Corinth road, 18km (11 miles) north of Mycenae and 40km (25 miles) north of Nafplion.

❼ ★★ **Ancient Nemea.** Gently folded into the foothills of the Arcadian Mountains and surrounded by the famous Nemean vineyards, this once-great city was famous throughout the ancient world for the **Nemean Games** held every two years. Like those at Delphi,

Hellenic Festival

Classical drama is performed in the ancient theater at Epidaurus from June through September on most Saturdays and Sundays at 9pm. For schedules and tickets, contact the Hellenic Festival Box Office in Athens, 39 Panepestimiou (☎ 21092/82900; www.hellenicfestival.gr), or the box office at the theater (☎ 27530/22006). Travel agencies in Athens and Nafplion also sell tickets, and special buses run to the theater from Nafplion on nights of performances. Tickets run from 12€–35€—a small price to pay for a once-in-a-lifetime experience.

Spartan Habits

Who would have guessed it? Leonidas became Hollywood's golden boy with the release of *300*, a pumped-up blockbuster-film version of the heroic battle in which 300 Spartans put up a brave and suicidal fight against the Persians at Thermopylae. Some of the most memorable lines from the film come right out of the annals of history. The 5th-century-B.C. historian Herodotus recorded the Spartan response to learning that thousands of Persian archers were about to unleash so many arrows in their direction that they would blot out the sun: "Then we will fight in the shade." Spartan women sent their men off to battle with the words "Come back with your shield, or on it," a reference both to the Spartan practice of carrying the dead from the battlefield on their shields and to the shame of dropping a shield in battle—a cowardly act punishable by death or banishment.

> *Epidaurus, most famous for its theater, was also a center of healing, where remedies included the flicker of serpents' tongues.*

may have introduced the architectural concept to the Mediterranean world. ⏱ 2 hr. Outside modern Nemea. ☎ 27460/22739. www.nemea.org. Admission includes stadium and museum, 7€. May–Oct Tues–Sun 8am–7pm, Nov–Apr Tues–Sun 8:30am–3pm.

Epidaurus is 25km (16 miles) east of Nafplion on a well-marked road.

8 ★★★ 𝐤𝐢𝐝𝐬 **Epidaurus.** The **Sanctuary of Asklepios** at Epidaurus was, with the Asklepion on Kos (see p. 420, **9**), one of the most famous healing centers in the Greek world. Asklepios, son of Apollo and god of medicine, was worshiped in the beautiful temple at Epidaurus (like much of the sanctuary, undergoing restoration) by cure-seekers who were housed in an enormous guesthouse, the **Kategogeion.** They were treated in the **Abaton,** where Asklepios came to them in their drug-induced dreams and dispensed advice on cures. The round **Tholos** appears to have housed the labyrinthine chambers for the healing serpents that could allegedly cure ailments with a flicker of the tongue over an afflicted body part. Chillingly evocative of ancient medicine are the 2,500-year-old medical instruments on view in the small **museum,** but given the large

number of votives and inscriptions of thanks offered by grateful patients, the pine-scented surroundings may have offered some relief. The magnificent **theater** at Epidaurus is one of the best preserved from the ancient world. Buried for close to 1,500 years, the 55 tiers of seats and the stage remain much as they were, and acoustics are so sharp that a stage whisper can be heard at the top of the house. ⏱ 2 hr. Off Rte. 70, outside Ligouria; follow signs to Ancient Theater. ☎ 27530/22009. www.odysseus.culture.gr. Admission 6€, includes theater, sanctuary, and museum. May–Oct daily 8am–7pm, Nov–Apr daily 8:30am–3pm.

Sparta is 115km (69 miles) south of Nafplion on E65.

9 ★ **Sparta.** Travelers are likely to be disappointed if they visit Sparta in search of vestiges of the most powerful city-state in ancient Greece. Modern Sparta, laid out on

> *The rugged Taygetos Mountains once isolated the southern Peloponnese from the rest of Greece.*

orange-tree-shaded avenues along the River Eurotas, is animated and affable, but very little remains of the city that had the might to conquer Athens in the Peloponnesian War. The militaristic Spartans never created a monumental city. As Thucydides, the 5th-century-B.C. Greek historian, prophetically observed: "If the city . . . were destroyed, and its temples and the foundations of its buildings left, remote posterity would greatly doubt whether their power were ever equal to their renown. Their city is not built continuously, and has no splendid temples or other edifices." A **theater** from the 2nd century B.C. and other scant remains of ancient Sparta are scattered about a park at the north end of town. Near the entrance stands a **statue of Leonidas,** the king who led 300 warriors in a heroic stand against the 250,000-man Persian army at the pass of Thermopylae in 480 B.C.

Adolescent boys from the elite warrior class were initiated into the Spartan ethic during rituals at the **Sanctuary of Artemis Orthia,** farther north along the river. They were whipped until the marble altar was splashed with their blood. Romans revived the practice as a spectator sport and built the 3rd-century amphitheater to accommodate travelers who came from throughout the empire to witness the spectacles (off Tripoli road; unattended; free admission). Spartans were as ambivalent about art as they were about architecture, and some bas-reliefs and a bust of Leonidas said to be from his tomb are among the relatively few works from ancient Sparta on view in the town's modest **Archaeological**

Museum (off Agios Nikolaos; ☎ 27310/28575; admission 2€; Tues–Sat 8:30am–3pm, Sun 8:30am–12:30pm). More imposing are the **Taygetos Mountains** looming just to the west, snowcapped well into June; their presence impressed even the Spartans, who felt that the tall range set them far apart from the rest of the world. From Sparta you may wish to visit Monemvassia and Mystras; see the "Byzantine Splendors" tour, p. 200. If not, after visiting Sparta, continue west to Nestor's Palace and plan to spend the night in Pylos or Methoni. ☺ 1 day.

From Sparta, cross the Langada Pass to Kalamata, 70km (43 miles) west.

10 Langada Pass. This route through the Taygetos Mountains is one of the most scenic drives in Greece, climbing through stands of evergreens to the summit at 1,524m (5,000 ft.). The most dramatic segment begins about 20km (12 miles) west of Sparta, where the road clings to the cliffs of the Langada Gorge. From these heights, the Spartans threw babies deemed physically unable to become soldiers.

From Kalamata, continue 50km (31 miles) west to Hora and Nestor's Palace. The most direct route takes you to a well-marked turnoff for Hora from Pylos and north from there.

11 ★★ Nestor's Palace, Hora. Mycenaean King Nestor built his palace around 1400 B.C., and the two-story structure was destroyed about a hundred years later in a fire that was no doubt fueled by vast quantities of oils kept in large clay vases in a warren of storerooms. We know much about old King Nestor and the palace, known to the ancients as Pylos, from Homer. In the *Iliad* and the *Odyssey,* he portrays Nestor as a wise elder statesman given to telling long- winded stories to his guests. Among these visitors was Telemachus, who came to the palace seeking news of the whereabouts of his father, Odysseus. Because of these ancient associations with hospitality and the extent of the well-preserved remains (parts of the walls still stand), the palace is more welcoming than the stony rubble of Mycenae (p. 188, **6**) or Tiryns (p. 188, **4**). The king conducted state business in a large **throne room** that surrounded a circular hearth and was decorated with colorful frescoes. His adjoining

> *At ancient Messene, the most extensive fortifications in the Greek world enclose ruins that include a beautifully preserved theater.*

apartments include a **bathroom** still equipped with a terra cotta bathtub, including a step that the king, 110 years old in Homer's accounts, may have used to get in and out. An enormous **wine cellar** and golden drinking vessels have been unearthed at the palace, a legacy of the king's legendary hospitality, but the most important finds are 1,200 **clay tablets** inscribed with Linear B script, a form of early Greek. These are the only examples of Linear B to be found on the mainland, and the discovery links the mainland Mycenaeans with Minoan Crete, where Linear B was prevalent (p. 240, **1**). Some of the tablets, as well as enticing palace frescoes, are in the **Archaeological Museum** in nearby Hora. ☺ 2 hr. for visit to palace and museum. ☎ 27630/31437. www.culture.gr. Admission 3€ each for palace and museum. May–Oct daily 8am–7pm, Nov–Apr daily 8:30am–3pm.

Backtrack along the well-marked road 25km (16 miles) south to Pylos.

12 Pylos. Spend the night in this pleasant and historic seaside town (p. 209, **7**), or continue a bit farther to even quieter Methoni (p. 210, **8**), 40km (25 miles) south of Nestor's Palace.

Take the Pylos-Kalamata road east to modern Messene and follow signs for about 20km (12 miles) north to Ancient Messene. Distance from Pylos to Ancient Messene is 80km (50 miles).

13 ★★ Ancient Messene. The most extensive **fortifications** in the Greek world ramble for 9km (5⅔ miles) across the rolling foothills

> *Corinthian columns, with their elaborate capitals, first appeared at the Temple of Apollo at Bassae in the Arcadian mountains.*

of Mount Ithomi amid olive groves and pine forests. The Thebans built the walls as a deterrent to their war-hungry neighbors, the Spartans, whom they had finally defeated in 369 B.C. after centuries of warfare. The walls are interspersed with **four gates** that are like miniature fortresses in themselves, 9m (30 ft.) high and punctuated with slits for launching arrows on the lower levels. The **Arcadian Dipylon** is a double gate, flanked by square towers and with portals leading into and out of an interior courtyard rutted with the wheels of chariots. A small village, **Mavromati,** has sprung up within the walls, and around it are scattered the ruins of a theater, a temple, a sanctuary of Asklepios, and a Synedrion, or meeting hall for town officials. From the site, a road ascends to the summit of **Mount Ithomi,** where a view across what seems to be all of southern Greece is enhanced by the ruins of a temple to Zeus and an abandoned medieval monastery. ⏱ 2 hr. North of modern Messene. ☎ 27240/51201. www.culture.gr. Free admission. Daily dawn–dusk.

From Ancient Messene, take the Kalamata–Tripoli road to Megalopolis. From there, a winding, well-marked route through the mountains brings you to the village of Andritsena. The Temple of Apollo is 15km (9⅓ miles) south via a narrow mountain road. Total distance is 40km (25 miles).

⓮ ★★★ kids **Temple of Apollo at Bassae.** One of the most beautiful and best-preserved temples in Greece is dedicated to Apollo Epikourios and stands in splendid isolation atop an Arcadian mountain. The word Epikourios means "helper" in Greek, and the nearby village of Phylagia commissioned the temple in 420 B.C. in thanks to Apollo for deliverance from an outbreak of the plague. It's been conjectured and contested that the architect of the temple was Iktinos, who designed the Parthenon in Athens; whether or not this is the case, the temple is remarkable for several elements, including the first use of Corinthian columns and a north–south orientation, a departure from the east–west orientation of most Greek temples and a concession to the steep slope. Unfortunately, you will not be able to enjoy some of the temple's greatest visual splendors: a frieze depicting battles with the Amazons and the Lapiths and other works was long ago removed to the British Museum in London, and the temple is currently wrapped in a white tent as protection against the elements as restoration work drags on year after year. Even so, coming upon this glorious marble and limestone jewel box tucked away on its aerie is one of the great pleasures of traveling in the Peloponnese. ⏱ 45 min. ☎ 27240/22529. www.culture.gr. Admission 3€. May–Oct daily 8am–7pm, Nov–Apr daily 8:30am–3pm.

From the temple, continue to Olympia, about 25km (16 miles) west of Andritsena, reached off the well-marked road to Pyrgos.

SITE GUIDE
PAGE 196

⑮ ★★★ kids **Olympia.** Some of the most storied ancient ruins in the world, host to the famous games, are surrounded by rolling countryside carpeted with pine and hardwoods. Plan to spend the night in Olympia and explore the ruins by day. The Alpheios and Kladeos rivers rush past the remains of the sanctuary and city founded around the 10th century B.C. to honor Zeus and his older sister and wife, Hera. The **Temple of Zeus** once housed a statue of the god, sculpted by the great Phidias, sheathed in gold, and one of the Seven Wonders of the Ancient World. The **Temple of Hera** was graced with *Hermes Carrying the Infant Dionysus,* the only work by the great sculptor Praxiteles to survive the centuries, now in Olympia's **Archaeological Museum.**

The superheroes who bring most visitors to Olympia are not gods but ancient athletes. Remnants of the city's games, inaugurated in 776 B.C., are copious; the **stadium, gymnasium, training hall,** and **dormitories** are scattered around the foot of the Kronion Hill. Legend tells us that Hercules, assigned 12 labors for slaying his children, rerouted the Alpheios to clean out the stables of King Augeas. Then he relaxed by mapping out the stadium with his toe and running the length without taking a breath 192m (630 ft.) to work off steam, and in so doing, established the city and the games. Athletes from throughout Greece were granted safe passage to the games under the Ekecheiria, a truce that promoted the notion of a united Greece. In their footsteps came spectators, touts, vendors, poetry reciters, entertainers, and prostitutes, and the 5-day festivities were both a forum where city-states could commingle peaceably and, in part, a wine-fueled bacchanal. The **Museum of the History of the Olympic Games in Antiquity** tells the story of the ancient contests; the

Museum of the Olympic Games chronicles the modern games, resurrected in 1896; and the **Museum of the History of the Excavations** in Olympia documents the excavations, beginning with 1766, when British antiquarian Richard Chandler discovered the ruins. For more on Olympia and the games, see p. 198. Ancient site: ⏱ 4 hr. ☎ 26240/22517. www.culture.gr. Admission 6€, combined ticket with Archaeological Museum 9€. May–Oct daily 8am–7pm, Nov–Apr daily 8:30am–5pm. Archaeological Museum: ⏱ 1 hr. ☎ 26240/22742. www.culture.gr. Admission 6€, combined ticket with ancient site 9€. May–Oct Mon 11am–7pm, Tues–Sun 8am–7pm; Nov–Apr Mon 10:30am–5pm, Tues–Sun 8:30am–3pm. Museum of the History of the Olympic Games in Antiquity: ⏱ 1 hr. ☎ 26240/22529. Free admission. May–Oct Mon noon–7pm, Tues–Sun 8am–7pm; Nov–Apr daily 10:30am–5pm. Museum of the History of the Excavations in Olympia: ⏱ 1 hr. ☎ 26240/20128. Free admission. May–Oct Mon noon–7pm, Tues–Sun 8am–7pm; Nov–Apr daily 10:30am–5pm.

> *Olympia's Archaeological Museum shows off sculpture from the site's many temples, some of the finest works from classical Greece.*

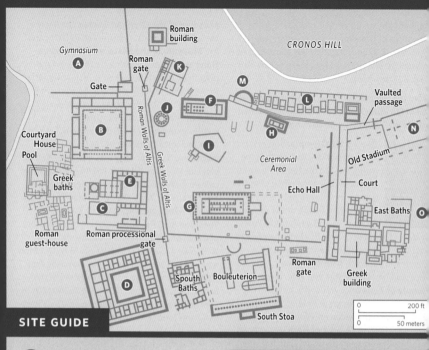

Roman building

Gymnasium

Ⓐ

CRONOS HILL

Roman gate

Ⓚ

Gate

Ⓜ

Ⓕ

Ⓛ

Vaulted passage

Ⓙ

Ⓝ

Roman Walls of Altis

Greek Walls of Altis

Courtyard House

Pool

Ⓗ

Ⓘ

Ceremonial Area

Old Stadium

Greek baths

Ⓔ

Echo Hall

Court

Ⓖ

East Baths

Ⓞ

Ⓒ

Roman guest-house

Roman processional gate

Roman gate

Greek building

Ⓓ

Spouth Baths

Bouleuterion

South Stoa

| 0 | 200 ft |
| 0 | 50 meters |

SITE GUIDE

⓯ Olympia

Fifth-century Roman Emperor Theodosius II, ruling that the games were pagan rituals, cleared much of ancient Olympia, and earthquakes and mudslides over the centuries finished the job. Enough rubble remains to lend a sense of the layout and magnificence of the ancient city. The entrance is just west of the modern village, across the Kladeos River. The first ruins are those of the **Ⓐ gymnasium,** a field surrounded by porticoes where athletes could train in bad weather, and the **Ⓑ Palaestra,** a training ground for wrestlers and runners. Just beyond is the **Ⓒ Workshop of Phidias,** where the great sculptor crafted his gold-sheathed statue of Zeus; archaeologists found the sculptor's tools here, along with a cup inscribed with "I belong to Phidias." The **Ⓓ Leonidaion** was a luxurious hostel for visiting dignitaries, next to the **Ⓔ Theokoleon,** chambers of the priests who oversaw the Altis, the sacred precinct of Zeus. Within this complex were the **Ⓕ Temple of Hera** and the **Ⓖ Temple of Zeus,** once surrounded by 36 columns, one of which was re-erected in honor of the 2004 Athens Olympic Games. The famous statue of a seated Zeus that once rose 13m

(43 ft.) above the temple floor was carted off to Constantinople in the 5th century, where it was destroyed in a fire. The **Ⓗ Metroon** is shrine to Rhea, mother of the gods, and the **Ⓘ Pelopeion** honors Pelops, legendary king of the Peloponnese; his altar was drenched nightly with the blood of a black ram. Philip of Macedonia erected his own shrine when he overran Greece in 338 B.C., the **Ⓙ Philippeion.** A perpetual flame burned in the **Ⓚ Prytaneion,** a banqueting hall where victorious athletes were feted. The most powerful city-states stored their equipment and valuables in the 12 **Ⓛ treasuries,** and next to it isthe **Ⓜ Nymphaeum,** a grandiose, column-flanked fountain house from which water waschanneled throughout the city. To the east of the Altis are the **Ⓝ stadium** and **Ⓞ hippodrome.**

Where to Stay & Dine in Sparta & Olympia

> *The Europa tops a hill above Olympia's ancient ruins.*

★ **Diethnes** SPARTA *GREEK*
This popular stop on the tourist-bus circuit also has a loyal following among Spartans, who appreciate the lamb with lemon sauce and other old-fashioned favorites, served in the large rear garden in good weather. 105 Paleologou. ☎ 27310/28636. Entrees 7€–12€. No credit cards. Lunch & dinner daily.

★★★ kids **Europa Best Western** OUTSIDE OLYMPIA The most luxurious accommodations in Olympia are the large and well-appointed rooms at this airy hilltop retreat. The many amenities include a pleasant garden surrounding a large pool, and the hotel's outdoor taverna can't be beat for a meal on a summer evening. Oikismou Drouba, above modern town. ☎ 26240/22650. www.hoteleuropa.gr. 80 units. Doubles 80€–100€ w/breakfast. AE, MC, V.

★★★ **Hotel Pelops** MODERN OLYMPIA
The most appealing and friendly lodgings in the modern town are on a quiet back street, an easy walk away from the ruins and museums. Small terraces off the attractive rooms overlook the surrounding hills, the Spiliopoulou family is on hand with gracious hospitality, and a delicious Peloponnesian feast is served at dinner upon request. 2 Varela. ☎ 26240/22543. www.hotelpelops.gr. 26 units. Doubles 62€ w/breakfast. MC, V.

★ **Maniatis Hotel** SPARTA
In the guest rooms, contemporary style and soothing colors put a new spin on the concept of Spartan decor. The in-house restaurant, Zeus, is one of the best in town. 72 Paleologou. ☎ 27310/22665. www.maniatishotel.gr. 80 units. Doubles 120€ w/breakfast. MC, V.

★ **Menelaion Hotel** SPARTA
Though not as chic as the Maniatis across the street, this popular old hostelry is very comfortable and has the advantage of a swimming pool that sparkles in the courtyard. 91 Paleologou. ☎ 27310/22161. www.menelaion.gr. 48 units. Doubles 100€ w/breakfast. AE, MC, V.

★ **Pantheon** SPARTA *GREEK*
What began as a simple street-side stand has grown into a big operation, owing to the high quality of its Greek specialties, especially the grilled meats and gyros—deftly prepared and served with garden-fresh vegetables. 106 Vrasidou. ☎ 27310/23767. Entrees 4€–6€. No credit cards. Lunch & dinner Mon–Sat.

★★ **Taverna Bacchus** ANCIENT PISSA *GREEK*
This popular countryside taverna also has extremely comfortable guest rooms, with in-room Wi-Fi, a swimming pool, and other amenities, as well as beautiful views over the rolling hills. The ruins are a pleasant hike away through the woods, and delicious home-cooked meals are served in the attractive dining room and terrace. Ancient Pissa, 3km (2 miles) outside Olympia. ☎ 26240/22298. www.bacchustavern.gr. 6 units. Doubles 80€–100€ w/breakfast. AE, MC, V.

OLYMPIAD

The Thrill of Victory, the Agony of Defeat

BY STEPHEN BREWER

FOR THE ANCIENTS, the Olympic Games were the greatest show on earth, staged every 4 years in honor of Zeus (p. 546), king of the gods. For nearly 12 centuries, they drew athletes from as far as the shores of the Black Sea, and behind them followed prostitutes, pushy vendors, orators, and tens of thousands of spectators, including diehard fans such as Plato and the tyrant Dionysus of Syracuse. Conditions were primitive, but most attendees were happy to sleep under the stars to watch the world's greatest athletes perform and to curry favor with Zeus and the other gods who were worshiped during the proceedings. In the earliest years, the only event was a simple foot race on a straight strip of grass the length of the stadium—a unit of measure known as a *stade* (185m/610 ft.). By 500 B.C., wrestling, boxing, discus throwing, and more than 50 events took place over the course of 5 days in the hippodrome, gymnasium, stadium, and other arenas now in ruin beneath the pines of Olympia.

Ancient Champs

Greece's most famous boxers were **Diogaras of Rhodes**, who claimed to be the son of Hermes (p. 546), and his offspring. Three generations of his clan won in Olympia.

Polydamas, a champ of the *pankration* was as famous for his exploits off the field as on. He slew a lion with his bare hands, stopped a speeding chariot in its tracks, and single-handedly defeated a trio of Persia's mightiest warriors.

One brave female, **Kallipateira**, dressed as a trainer to watch her son compete but accidentally revealed her sex while climbing over a wall. Her life was spared, but from then on trainers, like athletes, were not allowed to wear clothes.

Milo of Croton, a 6th-century-B.C. wrestling champ, won many victories but died showing off, attempting to rip a tree in half. His hands got stuck in the trunk, and a pack of wolves devoured him.

When Sparta was banned from participating in the games of 420 B.C. for waging war, **Lichas of**

Sparta entered his chariot in the name of Thebes. He was caught and flogged.

Roman Emperor Nero demanded that the Games take place a year early, in A.D. 67, when his schedule would allow him to travel from Rome to compete. After bribing officials to disqualify competitors, he won six events—including a chariot race he didn't finish after falling from his chariot.

The Games Through the Ages

776 B.C.
The first *stadion* (foot race) takes place at Olympia in honor of Zeus. Koroibos, a cook, is the winner.

684 B.C.
Games are extended from 1 day to 3. In the 5th century B.C., they are extended again to 5 days.

445 B.C.
The sculptor Phidias completes a 13m-tall (43-ft.) gold and ivory statue of Zeus, one of the Seven Wonders of the Ancient World, to commemorate the games and establish Olympia as the center of Zeus worship.

396 B.C.
Kyniska of Sparta becomes the first female Olympic victor, as owner of the team that won the notoriously brutal four-horse chariot race, which somtimes left drivers trampled to death.

A.D. 393
Christian Emperor Theodosius bans the games as a pagan rite.

A.D. 1898
The first modern Olympic Games take place in Athens.

A.D. 2004
The Olympics return to Greece.

Rules of Engagement

> Regardless of social status, any free, Greek-speaking male without a criminal record could enter the games.

> To kick off the ceremonies, a hundred oxen were sacrificed.

> Athletes competed naked, though boxers were allowed to wear metal knuckle bands to add sting to their punches.

> Competitors rubbed themselves with olive oil and sand, an ancient sunscreen.

> Ground lizard skins stood in for steroids.

> Victors won money, tax emption, free meals for life, laurel wreaths, the favor of the gods, and the services of *Hetaeras*, high-class escort girls, at the victors' table.

> Women-only Olympics called the Heraea Games (in honor of the goddess Hera, wife of Zeus) took place just before the main Olympics.

> Only virgins and certain priestesses could attend the men's games. Trespassers, if caught, were tossed from a cliff.

> The *pankration*— *mano a mano* combat between two men (opposite page)—had only two rules: no biting or eye gouging. Strangulation was perfectly acceptable. The game ended when one athlete quit, passed out, or died.

Byzantine Splendors of the Peloponnese

The Byzantine Empire began exerting control over the Peloponnese in the 9th century, lost the region to Frankish knights briefly in the early 13th century, and won it back 50 years later. While the Byzantine Empire was dying out in Constantinople and elsewhere, the last flames flickered most brightly here in the Peloponnese, especially in the enlightened city of Mystras.

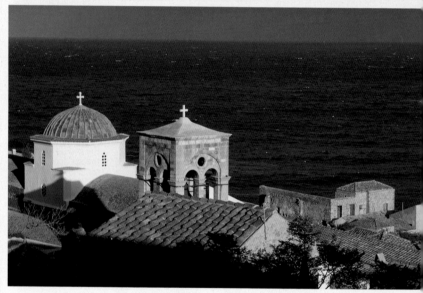

> Byzantine Monemvassia, often called the "Gibraltar of the East," clings to the sides of a steep rock high above the Aegean.

START Monemvassia, 224km (139 miles) southeast of Corinth; 304km (189 miles) southeast of Athens. TRIP LENGTH 114km (71 miles), 2–3 days.

1 ★★★ kids Monemvassia. Monemvassia is undeniably one of the most dramatically located cities in Greece, if not the world, wedged onto the side of a small, steep rock 300m (984 ft.) high and 1.8km (1 mile) long, linked to the mainland by a causeway 200m (656 ft.) long. This setting has earned Monemvassia

the nicknames "Gibraltar of the East" and "The Rock," and protected the town from Slavic, Arab, and Norman invasions. With its strategic position on the Mediterranean sea lanes, Monemvassia was a major trading center on the trade routes between Europe and the Middle East for the Byzantines and later became a prize possession for the Venetians and Ottomans. Malmsey, a sweet Madeira wine made from Malvasia grapes grown on the surrounding mainland, proved to be an especially lucrative commodity for the Venetians.

1 Monemvassia
2 Geraki
3 Mystras

From many vantage points on the mainland, the steep rock rising from the sea appears to be uninhabited. The town only makes its presence known once you have followed the causeway from Gefyra, the modern village that hugs the coast, to the dark, narrow entrance gate that gives Monemvassia (Single Entrance) its name. Inside are a labyrinth of cobbled lanes, narrow stone staircases, and sunny squares that hang high above the sea.

Several Byzantine churches rise above small, tile-roofed houses and a patchwork of walled gardens. The ruined 13th-century Church of Myrtidotissa is lit by a lone candle flickering on the stone altar, and a former mosque on Plateia Dsami houses the modest collections of the **Archaeological Museum** (free admission; daily 8am–7pm; limited hours in winter). The main monument is the hilltop fortress, a jumble of ruins and sections of defensive walls crowning the mountaintop. Standing amid the ruins is the domed Church of Agia Sofia. The solid beauty of this 13th-century octagon is enhanced by the vast vista of the sea and coast, stretching south into the mountains of the Mani Peninsula (p. 210, 9). 1 day.

Geraki is 69km (43 miles) west of Monemvassia, off the Monemvassia–Sparta road.

2 ★ **Geraki.** A crumbling ruin in mountainous terrain midway between Monemvassia and Mystras, this smaller, now all but unknown Byzantine city was never as large or as important

as its two neighbors. Geraki is nonetheless older, established as long as 4,000 years ago as Geronthrai. The site was resettled in 1245 by the Franks, who built the imposing fortress, and Geraki thrived for several centuries under the Byzantines. Their legacy is the dozen or so small chapels scattered among the ruins. 🕐 1 hr. 4km (2½ miles) outside the modern village of Geraki. For entrance to chapels, ask to see the caretaker in the modern village.

Mystras is 4km (2½ miles) west of Sparta off the Sparta–Kalamata road, 45km (27 miles) west of Geraki, and 101km (63 miles) west of Monemvassia. You may want to stop in Sparta for a look at the scant remains of the once mighty city-state, or use the city as a base for visiting Mystras.

SITE GUIDE PAGE 204

3 ★★★ kids **Mystras.** A splendid ghost town of golden stone overgrown with wildflowers and scented herbs was for many centuries one of the most important cities in southern Greece, a center of learning, culture, and political intrigue. Guillaume de Villehardouin, a Frankish prince, built a castle at Mystras in 1249 as

Travel Tip

You can see Monemvassia and Mystras in 2 days, but you may want to do the tour in 3, adding time to enjoy the beaches at Elafonisi and make the stop at Geraki.

> *The Church of San Giovani Evangelista is one of a dozen or so Byzantine chapels in Geraki.*

> *Ruined palaces and monasteries evoke 13th- and 14th-century Mystras, when the city was one of the Byzantine empire's last holdouts.*

part of his strategy to exert control over the Peloponnese after the Franks took the territory from the Byzantines during the Fourth Crusade in 1204. These efforts were thwarted when the Byzantines regained control of the region in 1262. The story goes that Villehardouin was defeated in battle and, in the guise of a peasant, took refuge under a haystack. He was betrayed by his famously protruding buck teeth, held for ransom, and forced to hand Mystras over to the Byzantines as part of his payment. Ongoing battles between the Franks and Byzantines

proved to be beneficial to Mystras, as the local populace took refuge within the walls and the well-fortified city became a center of power

Slip Away to a Desert Isle

Monemvassia is at the top of the Laconian Peninsula, the easternmost of the three Peloponnesian peninsulas. Few travelers venture into this relatively remote region of orchards and farms, and one of the rewards for the trip is the chance to get away from it all on **Elafonisi.** This small, sandy island, 35km (22 miles) south of Monemvassia, is forested in pine and ringed by some of Greece's most spectacular beaches. You reach the island by one of the car ferries that make the 15-minute crossing from the village Viglafia. Ferries leave about every half-hour and charge 8€ for cars and 2€ for foot passengers. The island has a few tavernas and rooms for rent.

Frescoes at the Perivleptos Monastery in Mystras depict scenes from the New Testament.

nd commerce. Mystras came under the rela-
ively enlightened rule of the despotate (as
ons, brothers, and other near relatives of the
Byzantine emperors were known). Philosophy
nd arts thrived, and Mystras became a great
enter of culture—by the late 13th century, the
econd most important city in the Byzantine
Empire after Constantinople. Chrysolaras and
other Byzantine men of letters who taught and

studied in Mystras were influential in spread-
ing classic Greek philosophy and literature
through the West. As you wander through the
hillside ruins, the stony remains of monasteries,
churches, and libraries will testify to this legacy.
⏱ 4 hr. Ano Chora. ☎ 27310/23315. www.culture.
gr. Admission 5€. June–Sept daily 8am–7pm,
May and Oct daily 8am–6pm, Nov–Apr daily
8:30am–3pm.

Holdouts of the Byzantine Empire

Vestiges of the Roman Empire lingered well
into the Middle Ages as the Byzantine Empire,
ruled from Constantinople, encompassed
far-ranging territories that included the Peloponnese. The Byzantines weathered war after
war, invasion after invasion, until 1204, when
crusaders from western Europe, on their way
to conquer Muslim-controlled Jerusalem, set
their sights on Constantinople instead. The
empire was divided among the conquerors,
with much of the Peloponnese going to the
Franks. They briefly established the Princi-
pality of Achaea, reinforcing their holdings
with the formidable Frankish castles that still
crown many a hilltop in the Peloponnese. The
Byzantine Empire, however, was not dead. The
so-called Palaiologan emperors, descended
from a noble Greek family, recaptured

Constantinople in 1261 and re-established the
Byzantine Empire. In Frankish Achaea they
established the Despotate of Morea, with its
capital in Mystras. The region and the city
became especially prosperous under Michael
Kantakouzenos, who ably ruled the Morea in
the early 14th century, and whose son, John,
followed him as governor of Morea and later
became emperor of the Byzantine Empire.
The last Byzantine emperor, Constantine XI,
was also governor of Morea before ascending
the throne. But by the late 15th century, Constantinople and most of the Byzantine Empire,
including the Morea, had fallen to the Ottoman Turks. Mystras and Monemvassia, the
two most important cities of the Morea, were
passed between the Turks and Venetians over
the next 4 centuries.

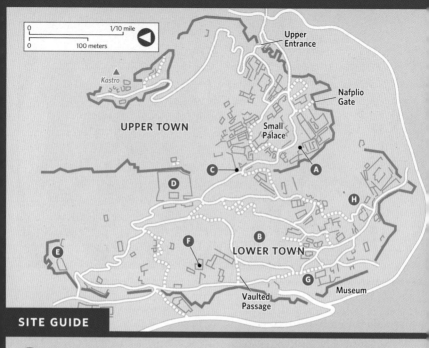

3 Mystras

In the **A Palace of the Despots,** an enormous audience hall is lit by eight elaborately framed windows and warmed by eight hearths. The palace chapel, Agia Sofia, retains some of its frescoes, though frescoes of the monasteries and churches of the **B Lower Town,** reached through the **C Monemvassia Gate,** are much more elaborate and better preserved—a virtual feast of Byzantine art at its finest. Behind the elaborately carved stone facade of the **D Convent of Pantanassa** are several rooms decorated with especially rich, 15th-century scenes, including a *Raising of Lazarus,* that are some of the finest examples of late Byzantine art. Frescoes in the nearby **E Perivleptos Monastery** are a vivid visual retelling of the New Testament, beginning with *The Birth of Christ.* The well-preserved scenes have served as an invaluable key to Byzantine religious symbolism. The **F Laskaris Mansion** is a typical Byzantine house, the home of a merchant, with stables on the ground floor and living quarters above. **G Agios Dimitrias** was founded in 1291 as the *mitropolis,* the city's cathedral; Constantine XI, the last Byzantine emperor, was crowned here

in 1449 seated atop a marble slab inscribed with a two-headed eagle, the symbol of the empire. A small museum houses sculpture and icons from the city's churches. The **H Vrontokhion Monastery** is the burial place of many of the despots who ruled the Morea from Mystras, and its church of Panagia Hodegetria, or Afendiko, is richly frescoed.

Where to Stay & Dine in Mystras & Monemvassia

Savor meatballs and other traditional favorites at Marianthi.

★ **Byzantino** MONEMVASSIA

Rooms and suites are tucked away in old houses round town, and vary considerably in size and outlook. All have character, and many are embellished with fireplaces, terraces, and sea views. Breakfast, snacks, and drinks are served at a bar on the main street. ☎ 27230/61351. www.yourgreece.com/hotel/en/byzantino.html. 25 units. Doubles 90€–135€ w/breakfast. MC, V.

★ **Malvassia** MONEMVASSIA

Recently built from old stones and timbers, this getaway at the end of the main street offers modern comforts and a great deal of character. Many of the large rooms have sea-facing terraces and kitchenettes. ☎ 27230/61323. www.malvasia-hotel.gr. 16 units. Doubles 85€–130€ w/breakfast. AE, MC, V.

★ **Marianthi** MONEMVASSIA GREEK

A homey, stone-walled dining room that spills into street-side tables in good weather is the setting for delicious preparations of old favorites, from salads of fresh mountain greens, spinach and cheese pies, to potatoes fried in olive oil and spicy meatballs. ☎ 27320/61371. Entrees 6€–9€. No credit cards. Lunch & dinner daily.

★★★ **Pyrgos of Mystras** MYSTRAS

You will feel like a pampered Byzantine noble in this beautiful stone country house at the edge of the modern village. Guest rooms and public spaces overlook a lush garden and are beautifully and comfortably decorated. Service is extremely attentive, and a lavish breakfast and afternoon snack are served. 3 Manousaki. ☎ 27310/20870. www.pyrgosmystra.com. 7 units. Doubles 220€ w/breakfast. AE, MC, V.

★ **Stelakos** NEAR MYSTRAS GREEK

Parori, just east of Mystras off the road to Sparta, is a charming little village in the foothills of the Taygetos Mountains. Many Spartans come here to stroll around the *plateia*, where a waterfall cascades down one side, then enjoy the grilled chicken and other country-style fare at Stelakos. Parori, 2km (1N mile) east of Mystras. ☎ 27310/83346. Entrees 6€–9€. No credit cards. Lunch & dinner daily.

★★ **Ta Kellia** MONEMVASSIA

An old monastery tucked away near the Church of Panagia Chrissiffitissa is a quiet getaway, with views out to sea and over the tile roofs of the old town. Accommodations are simple but comfortable, and some rooms have cozy sleeping lofts. The hospitable hosts go out of their way to ensure a pleasant stay. ☎ 27320/61520. www.kellia.gr. 11 units. Doubles 90€–100€ w/breakfast. No credit cards.

Watch Your Step

Monemvassia is not geared to travelers with limited mobility. When booking a hotel, remember that the town is accessible only by foot, and reaching any accommodation will require a trek over uneven stone streets and up and down steps.

Off the Beaten Path in the Peloponnese

Travelers cannot live by culture alone—at least not in a place as enticingly beautiful as the Peloponnese. Craggy mountains, deep forests, and isolated beaches washed by warm waters beckon, as do small mountain hamlets scented with herbs and seaside villages where fishing boats fill the horizon. No small part of the allure is a homemade meal enlivened with local wine and enjoyed under the stars, and genuine Greek *filoxenia* (hospitality).

> *Venetians and Turks guarded their sea routes from a wave-battered fortress and castle at Methoni.*

START Diakofto, on the north shore 80km (50 miles) west of Ancient Corinth off Hwy E65. **TRIP LENGTH** About 600km (373 miles); allow at least 4 days (5 at a leisurely pace).

1 ★★★ kids **Vouraikos Gorge.** According to legend, Hercules cleared this dramatic cleft in the mountains so he could easily stride from the heights to the seashore and meet up with his beloved, Voura. Late-19th-century French engineers found the pine-scented alpine valleys and narrow passages between towering cliffs to be a handy route for a narrow-gauge cog railway they built to carry ore out of the mountains. The open-air Kalavrita Express still operates, chugging up the mountain between seaside Diakofto and mountainside Kalavrita to provide passengers with large doses of scenery and thrills as it navigates 14 bridges and tunnels, ascends steep slopes, and glides along the rushing Vouraikos River. At the riverside hamlet of Zakhlorou, tucked into a wooded glade about halfway along the route, you can alight to make

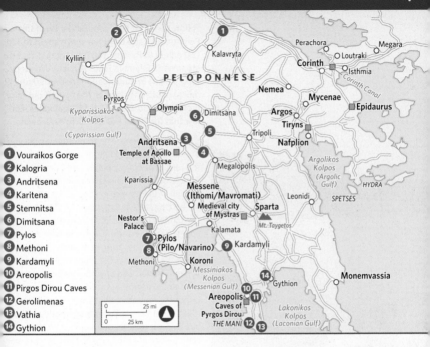

1 Vouraikos Gorge
2 Kalogria
3 Andritsena
4 Karitena
5 Stemnitsa
6 Dimitsana
7 Pylos
8 Methoni
9 Kardamyli
10 Areopolis
11 Pirgos Dirou Caves
12 Gerolimenas
13 Vathia
14 Gythion

the easy trek to **Mega Spileo** (admission 2€; daily 8am–6pm), one of Greece's oldest monasteries. Two wandering, 4th-century monks, so the story goes, followed a clue from a visionary shepherdess and, deep within a cave, found an icon painted by St. Luke the Evangelist. They built Mega Spileo into the cliff around the face of the cave, and the icon is today the monastery's prize possession. Kalavrita, at the end of the route, is perched at 600m (2,000 ft.) on the flanks of Mount Helmos. A pleasantly cool getaway in the summer and a spirited ski resort in the winter, the mountain town is best known as the scene of one of Greece's worst World War II atrocities. On December 13, 1943, occupying German forces executed every man and boy in the village over the age of 15, and the event is commemorated by the clock on the church tower, permanently stopped at 2:34pm, the time of the mass murder.

The best way to experience the Vouraikos Gorge is to spend the night in Diakofto, where you can swim from the town beaches, take an early morning train to Zakhlorou, make the hike to Mega Spileo, then continue to Kalavrita and take a stroll around the square before descending back to Diakofto in early afternoon.

> The Kalavrita Express, an open-air cog railway, chugs up the magnificent Vouraikos Gorge.

Follow the coast road around the tip of the Peloponnese and continue south about 80km (50 miles) to Pyrgos. You may want to make a stopover in Olympia (see "Ancient Wonders" tour, p. 184) or continue for another 20km (12 miles) south of Pyrgos to the turnoff onto the mountain road east toward Megalopolis. Follow that for 70km (43 miles) to Andritsena.

3 ★★ **Andritsena.** The mountainous province of Arcadia rises and falls across a wild, forested terrain of craggy peaks and deep ravines. Medieval villages cling to mountainsides topped with Frankish castles and goats, and sheep clog the winding roads. As you travel the mountain passes east from the coast, you'll pass only a few villages, and none are as appealing as this string of stone houses clinging to the steep mountainside high above the Alpheios River. The beautiful village square is shaded by plane trees, and a spring bubbles out of the mountainside. Some 15km (9⅓ miles) south is the **Temple of Apollo at Bassae** (p. 194, **14**), beautiful in its isolation on a remote mountaintop. Spend the morning exploring the temple but plan to spend the night in Andritsena. ⏱ 3 hr. with visit to temple.

Follow the mountain roads 30km (19 miles) southeast to Karitena.

4 ★ **Karitena.** The so-called Toledo of Greece was a thriving city of 20,000 during the Middle Ages, protected by a massive hilltop castle built by the Franks who took the region after the Byzantine Empire toppled in the early 13th century. A climb to the picturesque ruin affords stunning views of the surrounding mountains and, far below, the magnificent Frankish stone bridge that spans the deep gorge of the Alpheios River. The Byzantine Church of Agios Nikolaos is richly decorated with colorful frescoes. ⏱ 1 hr.

Stemnitsa is 16km (10 miles) north of Karitena on a well-marked mountain road.

5 ★★ **Stemnitsa.** After the insurrections of 1821, this beautiful village of tile-roofed stone houses was the capital of Greece for a few weeks, the seat of the revolutionary parliament. A well-marked path from the village square leads through meadows and copses of chestnut trees to the beautiful Byzantine **Church of Moni Agiou Ioannitou,** with beautiful 14th- and

> The sands at Kalogria are backed by groves of fragrant pines and eucalyptus.

⏱ 1 night and half the following day. Train: Diakofto Station. ☎ 21032/36747. 8€ round-trip. June–Aug: 4 round-trips daily, leaving Diakofto at 8am, 10am, noon, and 2pm; less frequent service in May and Sept–Oct; schedules vary and service is sometimes curtailed for construction on the route; for information, check with the Chris-Paul Hotel, p. 213).

From Diakofto, take E65 through Patras, about 55km (34 miles) west of Diakofto, to Kalogria, another 30km (19 miles) beyond Patras.

2 ★★★ kids **Kalogria.** One of the most beautiful beaches in the northern Peloponnese is a long stretch of sand backed by stands of eucalyptus and a tidal estuary. Brisk winds howling in from the Ionian Sea make the waters popular with windsurfers but can transform the beach into a Sahara of blowing sand. ⏱ 2 hr.

Medieval Andritsena and its Arcadian neighbors cling to mountainsides above deep ravines.

5th-century frescoes (only open occasionally; sk in the village). ⏱ 1 hr.

Dimitsana is 10km (6¼ miles) north of Stemnitsa on a well-marked mountain road.

⑥ ★★ **Dimitsana.** On a mountainside high above the Lousios Gorge, Dimitsana was at one time a center of the early-19th-century Greek nationalism that flourished in these remote reaches of the Peloponnese. The village's **School of Greek Letters** (Plateia; ☎ 27950/31217; admission 2€; Tues–Sat

Towers & Blood Feuds

Forced to eke substance out of the unforgiving, waterless landscape, cold in the winter and blisteringly hot in the summer, Maniots developed long-standing blood feuds over the little cultivable land there was. Clans built tower houses, often 20m (66 ft.) or even taller, as residences and hideouts. Each level contained a single room, reached by an interior ladder. Windows were scarce but the houses were well equipped with slits through which arrows could be shot, boiling oil poured, and stones hurled. Truces were called during harvest but invariably resumed until a family died out or surrendered, passing a tower house to the victors. More than 800 of these tower houses still stand, forlorn sentinels in the lonely landscape.

9am–2pm) was instrumental in fueling the revolutionary fervor against Turkish occupation, and the remarkable library is filled with more than 35,000 manuscripts that helped keep Greek culture alive at a time when reading or speaking the native language was forbidden. The **Open-Air Water Power Museum** (south of village; ☎ 27950/31630; admission 2€; Wed–Mon 10am–6pm) is a celebration of the early 20th century, with a water-powered flour mill, tannery, and other undertakings that once drove the rural economy. ⏱ 2 hr.

From Dimitsana, backtrack to Karitena, and then drop down 16km (10 miles) to Megalopolis. Continue south to Kalamata, about 60km (37 miles); then head west 50km (30 miles) to Pylos.

⑦ ★★ **Pylos.** The deep Bay of Pylos has been the scene of some decisive moments in Greek history. In 425 B.C., during the Peloponnesian War, beleaguered Spartans made an ill-fated stand against the Athenians on Skiatheria Island, at the mouth of the bay. In 1825 Ibrahim Pasha, the brilliant Egyptian general who commanded an army for Sultan Mahmud II of the Ottoman Empire, assembled the Turkish navy in the bay to quell the growing movement for Greek Independence. A combined British, Russian, and French allied fleet sailed in on October 20, 1827, to negotiate a peace treaty. The Turks inadvertently lobbed a volley of shots, the allies retaliated, and when the firing was over, the Turks had lost 53 ships and 6,000 men. The sultan signed the truce that led to Greek Independence in 1831. From the quays near the shady *plateia,* tour boats sail over the sunken hulls of Turkish warships and past such landmarks as Sfaktiria islet and Tsichli-Baba, a rocky outcropping that was an infamous pirate's lair for many centuries (tours are about 25€. The Paleokastro, the fortress the Venetians erected on the north end of the bay in the 13th century, is now a romantically crumbling ruin. The 17th-century **Turkish Neokastro** (southern edge of village; admission 3€; daily 9am–dusk) still retains its thick walls, from which the views take in a large swath of Roman aqueduct that crosses the coastal plain. ⏱ 3 hr.

Methoni is 14km (8⅔ miles) south of Pylos on a well-marked road.

> *Frankish knights built a castle above Karitena, when the medieval stronghold sheltered 20,000 souls.*

⑧ ★★★ **Methoni.** This quiet, out-of-the-way village at the southeastern tip of the Peloponnese was once an important Venetian way station on the trade routes to the Middle East and a stopover for pilgrims on their way from Europe to Jerusalem. The Venetians constructed a massive **seaside fortress,** and the Turks added a remarkable flourish—a minuscule, **octagonal castle** atop a wave-battered islet (free admission; daily 8:30am–dusk). The sturdy fortress walls are a colorful backdrop to Methoni's long, sandy beach and a scattering of tile-roofed houses surrounded by garden plots and the vineyards with which Methoni has been linked since antiquity. Homer tells how Agamemnon offered the town, "rich in vines," to appease Achilles, in a rage when his beloved Briseis was carried off during the Trojan War. The name is said to derive from the *onoi* (donkeys) who became *methoun* (drunk) from the grapes they carted. Spend the night here or backtrack to Pylos. ⏱ 2 hr.

Backtrack through Pylos and Kalamata to Kardamyli, 30km (19 miles) southeast of Kalamata.

⑨ ★★★ **Kardamyli.** The west coast of the Mani, the central peninsula of the southern Peloponnese, begins at Kardamyli. This western coast is the Messinian Mani, and the eastern coast, across the narrow spur of mountains that runs the length of the peninsula, is the Laconian Mani. The Mani has always been isolated, set apart from the rest of the mainland by the thick wall of the Taygetos Mountains; Kardamyli and other villages along the rockbound, cove-etched coasts were accessible only by boat until well into the 20th century. The foothills of the craggy Taygetos are quite verdant here in the so-called Outer Mani. In Kardamyli's lovely Old Town, tall stone tower houses are nestled among fragrant pines and cypress. A pebbly strand just north of town is one of the most popular beaches in the Mani. From Kardamyli, the seaside road heads down the peninsula into the stony gray landscape. ⏱ 2 hr.

Areopolis is 40km (25 miles) south of Kardamyli on the single road that follows the west coast of the Mani.

⑩ ★★ **Areopolis.** As befits a town named for the ancient Greek god of war, Areopolis is

> Quiet Dimitsana was a hotbed of early 19th-century revolutionary fervor against Turkish occupation.

> In Areopolis, on the stark Mani Peninsula, narrow lanes lined with stone houses lead to the Church of the Taxarchos.

an austere place, a collection of stone tower houses lining narrow lanes on a rocky promontory high above the sea. The Church of the Taxiarchos is one of the Mani's finest, and the facade is beautifully engraved with the signs of the zodiac, saints, and armies of warring archangels. Inland are bleak hillsides and barren mountains; Areopolis marks the beginning of the Inner Mani, as the more desolate, southern portion of the peninsula is known. The town's hero is Petrobey Mavromichalis, leader of the Maniots in their insurrection against the Turks. His statue stands in the central square, near the spot where he raised his flag on March 17, 1821, launching the Greek War of Independence. Though Mavromichalis settled into a successful career in the Greek senate, he was never too far removed from the Maniot way of taking care of business: His brother and his son murdered Ioannis Kapodistrias, the first head of an independent Greek government, when Mavromichalis clashed with Kapodistrias over administrative policy. ⏲ 1 hr.

The Pirgos Dirou Caves are 10km (6¼ miles) south of Areopolis, well marked off the coast road.

⑪ ★★ kids Pirgos Dirou Caves. A boat trip across lakes and underground rivers, past wild and colorful formations of stalagmites and stalactites, provides just a hint of the full scope and beauty of this amazing network of subterranean caverns that may extend as far as 70km (43 miles), all the way to Sparta. The caves are known to have been inhabited by Paleolithic and Neolithic inhabitants of the region, but they have never been explored in their entirety. A small museum displays artifacts that Pirgos Dirou's prehistoric cavemen left behind. ⏲ 1 hr. South of Areopolis on Vathia Road. ☎ 27330/52222 or 52223. Admission 12€. Nov–Mar daily 8:30am–3pm, Apr–Oct daily 8:30am–5:30pm.

Gerolimenas is 12km (7½ miles) south of the Pirgos Dirou Caves on the coast road.

> *Gythion, at the top of the Mani, is a busy fishing port and the octopus capital of Greece.*

⑫ ★★ Gerolimenas. A long natural harbor put Gerolimenas on the map as an important port through much of the 19th century, when vessels sailing to and from North Africa and the Middle East pulled in to take on supplies. With a small beach and low-key hotels and tavernas, Gerolimenas is still a welcome stopover. From Stavri, about 3km (2 miles) north, a trek past salt flats along a rocky spur ends at the **Castle of Mina,** built by the Franks in the mid–13th century and hard to distinguish from the boulder-littered terrain that surrounds it. ⊙3 hr. with hike to the castle.

Vathia is 10km (6¼ miles) south of Gerolimenas on the coast road.

⑬ ★★ Vathia. A cluster of tower houses on a rocky promontory is a forlorn ghost town. Cobblestone lanes and squares are overgrown, and the wind howls through the narrow windows and openings that residents once used to launch attacks on their neighbors. Nearby Cape Tenaro is even more barren, as befits the ancient belief that a small seaside cave was the entrance to the Underworld. From the cape, you see across the Gulf of Laconia to the east and the Gulf of Messinia to the west. ⊙1 hr.

Gythion is 80km (50 miles) north of Vathia on the road that follows the east coast of the Mani.

⑭ ★★ Gythion. Classically minded travelers may find this port at the northeastern end of the Mani the most romantic place on earth. It was here that Paris, prince of Troy, brought Helen, wife of King Menelaus of Sparta, after he abducted her and in so doing launched the Trojan War. The pair set sail for Troy from Marathonisi, a tiny islet connected to the mainland by a causeway. Gythion is famous throughout Greece for octopus, and tentacles are hung out to dry in the sun along the waterfront. ⊙1 hr.

From Gythion, head north 40km (25 miles) to Sparta. From there follow the Sparta–Tripoli road north to Tripoli and onto E65 north to Corinth and Athens; Athens is a 4–5-hour drive from Gythion.

Where to Stay & Dine Off the Beaten Path

★★ Amalia METHONI

Simple, large rooms overlooking the sea, the town, and the fortress are surrounded by pretty flower gardens. If you are lucky enough to be here on one of the evenings when a Greek feast is served on the terrace, by all means partake. On hillside off coastal road outside Methoni. ☎ 27230/31129. 34 units. Doubles 75€ w/breakfast. MC, V. Closed Nov to mid-Mar.

★★ Avgerinou Syrrakou ANDRITSENA

Two village houses have been converted to a welcoming inn, with stone-walled rooms and a large terrace—a perfect base for exploring the nearby Arcadian villages and Temple of Apollo at Bassae. ☎ 26260/22314. 9 units. Doubles 65€–95€ w/breakfast. No credit cards.

★★ kids Chris-Paul Hotel DIAKOFTO

Pleasant rooms overlook the garden and pool, and the village center and train station (where you'll board the Kalavrita Express) are just steps away. ☎ 26910/41715. www.chrispaul-hotel.gr. 24 units. Doubles 65€. DC, MC, V.

★★ Kyrimai Hotel GEROLIMENAS

Centuries-old warehouses at the end of a rocky promontory have been converted into a distinctive getaway. Rooms are embellished with stone walls and old timbers and offer all the modern comforts. Sea views, waterside terraces, a swimming pool, and a wave-washed swimming jetty set a nautical theme. The dining room is excellent. Even breakfast is a lavish feast, and snacks are available all day. ☎ 27330/54288. 26 units. Doubles 110€–250€. AE, MC, V.

★★ Lela's KARDAMYLI *GREEK*

At her seaside taverna, the charming Lela serves her famous fish soup, oven-baked lamb with mountain herbs, and other homemade specialties, enjoyed on a tree-shaded seaside terrace. Upstairs are five simple but comfortable rooms. ☎ 27210/73541. 5 units. Doubles 70€. Entrees 7€–15€. No credit cards.

★★ To Limeni LIMENI *SEAFOOD*

The fish is so fresh and served so close to the water's edge that you may get the feeling your

> *Lela serves her famous lamb seaside in Kardamyli.*

meal jumped right onto the table. Ask to be shown what's fresh, and your selection will be cleaned then grilled to perfection. Waterfront. ☎ 27330/51327. Entrees 8€–20€. No credit cards. Lunch & dinner daily; closed some days in winter.

★★ Ulysses METHONI

Trim and well-equipped rooms are just steps from the beach and fortress, and all have small balconies. The air-conditioning is a godsend on hot summer nights, and a breakfast of homemade cakes and local cheeses is served in a lovely garden. ☎ 27230/31600. 12 units. Doubles 55€ w/breakfast. No credit cards.

Nafplion

Nafplion is more than just pretty. For a few years after
Greece achieved independence in 1828, Nafplion was the nation's first capital. For years, Byzantines, Franks, Venetians, and Turks fought over the city, strategically placed on the Gulf of Argos. Even without this provenance, Nafplion would be notable for its proximity to Epidaurus, Mycenae, and some of the other most magnificent remains of the ancient world; it's a delightful place to spend time while visiting the nearby sites.

> The Bourtzi, on an islet in the Bay of Argos, is one of three Venetian-Ottoman fortresses that once defended Nafplion.

START Plateia Syntagma, Nafplion (146km/91 miles from Athens). **TRIP LENGTH** About 1½ days to explore the city in depth; you'll probably want to stay at least several days to visit the nearby archaeological sites.

SITE GUIDE
PAGE 216

❶ ★★★ **Old Town.** Wedged onto a narrow promontory between the sea and the heights dominated by the Acronafplia and Palamidi fortresses, old Nafplion is a delightful place. Tall, proud Venetian town houses line narrow lanes that lead off lovely Plateia Syntagma (Constitution Sq.), and two broad, airy seaside promenades, the Bouboulinas and Akti

Miaouli, are lined with cafes and patisseries. Palaces, churches, and mosques are remnants of the Venetians and Turks who occupied the city for centuries, and other monuments are from Nafplion's brief tenure as the first capital of Greece, from 1829 to 1834, when King Otto moved the capital to Athens. ⏱ 4 hr.

❷ ★★ **Archaeological Museum.** A thick-walled Venetian storehouse exhibits artifacts from the many ancient sites that surround Nafplion. The Mycenaeans steal the show with their splendid craftsmanship, unearthed at Mycenae, Tiryns, Dendra, and other nearby settlements. These include a bronze suit of armor consisting of 15 sheets of bronze so heavy

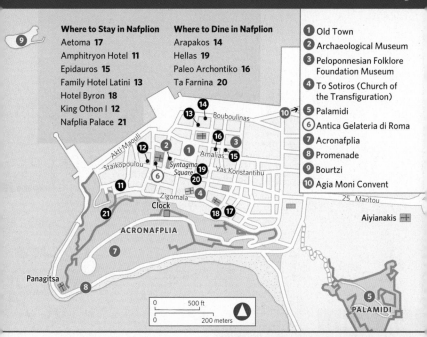

Where to Stay in Nafplion

Aetoma **17**
Amphitryon Hotel **11**
Epidauros **15**
Family Hotel Latini **13**
Hotel Byron **18**
King Othon I **12**
Nafplia Palace **21**

Where to Dine in Nafplion

Arapakos **14**
Hellas **19**
Paleo Archontiko **16**
Ta Farnina **20**

1. Old Town
2. Archaeological Museum
3. Peloponnesian Folklore Foundation Museum
4. To Sotiros (Church of the Transfiguration)
5. Palamidi
6. Antica Gelateria di Roma
7. Acronafplia
8. Promenade
9. Bourtzi
10. Agia Moni Convent

at scholars have concluded the wearer could
ave fought only while riding in a chariot.
eath masks and offerings from the extensive
etwork of tombs at Mycenae are also on dis-
lay. ⏱ 1 hr. Plateia Syntagma. ☎ 27520/27502.
dmission 2€. Daily 8:30am–3pm.

**⑧ ★★★ Peloponnesian Folklore Founda-
on Museum.** In this handsome neoclassical
ouse in the Old Town, the emphasis is on
eautiful textiles, along with looms and other
quipment used to make clothing—harking
ack to the days when just about all everyday
ems were made at home. Peloponnesian
milies donated many of the dowry items and
mbroidery, though the holdings come from
l over Greece and include such rarities as
erveri, tents that surround bridal beds in the
odecanese. Especially evocative are re-cre-
cions of the overstuffed drawing rooms from
e homes of well-to-do 19th-century Nafpli-
s, affording a glimpse into the comfortable
ves of the bourgeoisie. These are all the more
scinating given Nafplion's 19th-century fas-
nation with European styles, then in fashion
s Otto of Bavaria and other Western royalty
ssumed the throne of the new kingdom
: Greece. ⏱ 2 hr. 1 Vasileos Alexandrou.

> *A domestic scene at the Peloponnesian Folklore Foundation Museum.*

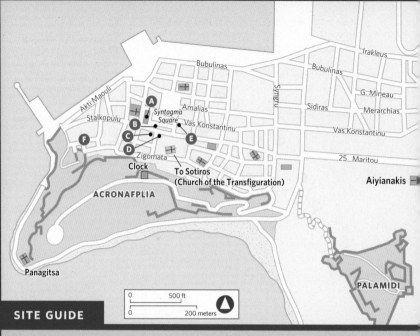

SITE GUIDE

1 Old Town

Syntagma Square was once dominated by the 16th-century residence of the Turkish commanders of the Peloponnese, and a Venetian storehouse, now the  **A** **Archaeological Museum** (p. 214, **2**), flanks one end; nevertheless, the plaza is most associated with Greek nationalism. One of Greece's favorite heroines is **Psorokostaina,** an impoverished woman who in 1826 attended a rally held beneath the plane tree that then grew in the middle of the square and donated her sole possessions, a silver ring and a cross, to help fund the new nation. In front of the **B** **National Bank of Greece,** built in the 1930s in the style of a Mycenaean palace, stands a statue of **Kalliopi Papalexopoulos,** who in the 1860s led the movement to establish greater independence from foreign monarchs.

The **C** **former mosque of Aga Pasha** has since 1825 been known as the Parliament Building, when it was refurbished to house the first meetings of the Greek National Assembly.

The city's oldest mosque is at the east end of the square and is now known as the **D** **Trianon,** for the cinema that the domed building

housed for much of the 20th century. Farther east is **E** **St. Spyridon Church,** associated with the dark events of September 27, 1831: Ioannis Kapodistrias, the first governor of an independent Greece, was shot and stabbed by two political opponents, Konstantinos and Georgios Mavromichalis. One of the bullets is still imbedded in the wall next to the door.

The stepped streets of the **F** **Psaromachalas Quarter** have been home to fishermen and merchants since the beginning of the 13th century. The *plateia* at the center of the neighborhood is still associated with a hospital for the poor, of which only the chapel of **Agia Sofia** remains, that stood here from 1394 until it was demolished in the late 1940s.

Syntagma Square is Nafplion's living room, and its cafes are busy from early morning until well into the night.

⑤ ★★ kids **Palamidi.** The mightiest of the three fortresses that defended Nafplion is Venetian, completed in 1714 and surrounded by massive walls and eight bastions that ramble across a bluff some 200m (660 ft.) above the city. So secure were the Venetians with these defenses that upon completing the Palamidi they left only 80 soldiers in Nafplion, and the Turks easily seized the Palamidi just one year later. Greek rebels then took the fortress from the Turks during the War of Independence in 1821. Leading the siege was Gen. Theodoros Kolokotronis, who later ran afoul of the new government and was imprisoned in the Palamidi for 15 months. His stark cell demonstrates the harsh conditions that awaited prisoners, who were forced to cut the 999 steps that climb the cliff face from Polyzoidhu Street in the town below. ⏱ 2 hr. Above Old Town. ☎ 27520/28036. Admission 3€. Apr–Oct Mon–Fri 8am–7pm, Sat–Sun 8am–3pm; Nov–Mar daily 8am–3pm.

⑥ 🍨 **Antica Gelateria di Roma.** Traditional gelato, better than most you'd find in Italy, is dispensed to appreciative crowds here, along with panini and superb espresso. 3 Farmakoupoulou. ☎ 27520/23520. $.

www.pli.gr. Admission 4€ day, 3€ evening. ☎ 27520/28947. Wed–Sat and Mon 9am–3pm and 6–9pm, Sun 9am–3pm.

④ ★ **To Sotiros (Church of the Transfiguration).** The oldest church in Nafplion began as a convent for Franciscan nuns during the 13th-century Frankish occupation, fell into disrepair under the Venetians, and was refurbished as a mosque by the Turks. A distinctly Christian presence has prevailed since 1839. That's when Otto, the Bavarian king who served as monarch of a united Greece, presented the church to Greek Catholics and the so-called Philhellenes, the foreigners who fought alongside Greeks for independence from the Turks. Otto named the church in honor of the Transfiguration of Christ, the miracle in which Christ was addressed by God as "son" to show the power of the divinity—an apt symbol for the emergence of a free and unified Greece. The names of the Philhellenes, among them the British poet and adventurer Lord Byron, are inscribed on the columns. ⏱ 30 min. Zigomala. Daily 8am–7pm.

Gulf of Argos Beaches

The beautiful waters of the Gulf of Argos can be tested from several places around Nafplion. **Arvanitia,** a section of diving platforms and a pebbly beach at the base of the Acronafplia fortress, is only a short, lovely walk from the Old Town along the Promenade; **Karathonia,** about 1km (⅔ mile) farther south at the foot of the Palamidi, is sandy and washed by shallow waters that are popular with families. **Tolo,** 11km (7 miles) southeast of Nafplion and reached by frequent bus service, follows a perfect crescent of a beach that is packed with sunburned visitors from northern Europe; paddle boats, as well as snorkeling, windsurfing, water-skiing, and jet-skiing gear, are available for rental. At **Asine,** about 2km (1¼ mile) north of Tolo, you can take time from the beach to explore Mycenaean walls, Roman baths, and a Venetian fortress.

> *Nafplion's town beach is tucked onto the shoreline beneath the Acronafplia Fortress.*

> *The Promenade skirts the entire Nafplion peninsula, providing an eyeful of sea views.*

7 ★★ kids **Acronafplia.** Fortifications have stood at the southeastern heights of Nafplion for some 5,000 years. Until the Venetians arrived in the 13th century, the entire town lived within the walls, out of harm's way from pirates. Scattered among the pine-scented hilltops are the ruins of several castles and forts, a testament in stone to the Byzantine, Frankish, and Venetian powers who fought for control of Nafplion and the rest of the Peloponnese. The Turks referred to the Acronafplia as Iç Kale, or Inner Castle, a reference to building a fortress within a fortress, a practice they adopted throughout the Ottoman Empire. A well-fortified Venetian castle, the **Castello del Torrione,** is the best preserved of the fortifications, and nearby is the **Castello dei Franchi** (Castle of the Franks) and the **Castello dei Greci** (Castle of the Greeks). You can make the climb to the Acronafplia on a stepped path that begins at a gate embellished with the head of a Venetian lion off Potamianou Street, at the southern end of the Old Town. You can also make the ascent in an elevator, reached through a tunnel off Kostouros Street; this will leave you outside the Nafplia Palace (p. 220), a luxurious hotel built into the Acronafplia ruins. ⏱ 2 hr. Public parkland. Free admission.

8 ★★★ **Promenade.** All that remains of the lower walls, constructed in 1502 to encircle the city, is one bastion—the so-called Five Brothers, intended to defend the harbor and named for five Venetian cannons, all bearing the Lion of St. Mark. A beautiful seaside promenade beyond the Five Brothers skirts the southeastern tip of the peninsula, following a ledge between the Acronafplia above and the rocky shore below. About halfway along, a small church, Santa Maria della Grotta, clings to the rocks and is a favorite place for prayer and reflection among Nafpliots. **Arvanitia** (see p. 217), at the end of the promenade, is popular with residents, who gather here to chat and swim from the rocks and the pebbly beach. ⏰ 1 hr. for walk to Arvanitia and back.

9 ★ kids **Bourtzi.** This picturesque 15th-century island fortress in the harbor has witnessed pirate attacks and Venice's massacre of the Turkish garrison, housed the revolutionary government in the days following Greek independence, served as headquarters for the town executioners, and was once equipped with a massive chain that the Turks could draw across the harbor to block entry. Boats chug out to the Bourtzi from the Akti Maouli, the town quay, but the island and its storied past are best appreciated from the shore, from which the crenellations and sturdy hexagonal watchtower look like a mirage shimmering across the water. ⏰ 1 hr. for trip out, visit, and return trip. Boat is usually about 5€.

Agia Moni is set amid olive groves off the Epidaurus Road, 3km (2 miles) northeast of Nafplion.

10 ★ **Agia Moni Convent.** This Byzantine convent is dedicated to virgins in both the pagan and Christian traditions. In a shady courtyard within the walls is the Spring of Kanathos, channeled into a fountain. Legend has it that Hera, the wife of Zeus, bathed in the waters annually to renew her virginity and refire the god's ardor for her. Leo, bishop of Nafplion, chose this spot to build a monastery to honor the Virgin Mary in atonement for his sins. The resident nuns make beautiful embroidery and sell it to visitors. ⏰ 1 hr. Daily 9am–1pm and 4–6pm. Free admission.

Shopping in Nafplion

Souvenir shills hawk their wares on just about every street in Nafplion, but several shops stand out. To find **Agynthes** (10 Siokou; ☎ 27520/21704), just follow the sound of the clacking looms, from which emerge beautiful natural woolens, often woven into exquisite scarves. Nafpliots shop for their spirits and wines at **Karonis** (4 Siokou; ☎ 27520/22329), in business for 150 years. The shop sells many fine wines from the Nemea vineyards that are being planted with fervor across the nearby countryside. Complement your selections with honey, candied fruit, wild herbs, and other local foodstuffs at **Nektar and Ambrosia** (6 Farmakopoulou; ☎ 27520/43001). The **Komboloi Museum** (25 Staikopoulou; ☎ 27520/21618) displays antique worry beads and sells exquisitely fashioned new designs, and **Nafplio tou Nafplio** (56A Staikopoulou) is famous throughout Greece for its icons. **Odyssey** (Plateia Syntagma; ☎ 27520/23430) is well stocked with English-language periodicals and books and sells maps and guidebooks along with a good selection of stationery. The shop of the **Peloponnesian Folklore Foundation Museum** (1 Vasileos Alexandrou; ☎ 27520/28947) sells beautiful jewelry and other accessories based on its holdings, making it a good stop for Peloponnesian handicrafts.

Where to Stay in Nafplion

> *A swim with a view across the Gulf of Argos is among the luxuries on offer at the Nafplia Palace.*

★★★ Aetoma OLD TOWN

In this lovely neoclassical mansion, delightful rooms have balconies looking up to the Palamidi Fortress, and the penthouse has a wraparound terrace. Reserve well in advance. Plateia Spiridomas. ☎ 27520/27373. www.nafplionhotel.gr. 5 units. Doubles 110€. MC, V.

★★ Amphitryon Hotel OLD TOWN

All the extremely stylish and comfortable guest rooms here open to teakwood decks overlooking the harbor, and public spaces are chic yet welcoming; the lounge is one of the city's best night spots. The Old Town is just steps away, as is the elevator that ascends to the Nafplia Palace, a related property where guests have use of the pool and gardens. Spiliadou St. ☎ 27520/70700. www.amphitryon.gr. 45 units. Doubles 240€–290€ w/breakfast. AE, MC, V.

★ Epidauros OLD TOWN

Not too long ago this simple inn in the center of the Old Town was one of the very few hotels in Nafplion. Other hotels may be fancier and offer more amenities, but for the budget-conscious, these clean, simple rooms still fit the bill. 2 Kokkinou. ☎ 27520/27541. 35 units. Doubles 55€. No credit cards.

★★★ Family Hotel Latini OLD TOWN

This stylish little hotel in a former sea captain's mansion has a prime location near the port, steps from Syntagma Square. Rooms are large and bright, many have balconies, and a welcoming bar- breakfast room opens to a sidewalk terrace. 47 Othonos. ☎ 27520/96470. www.latinihotel.gr. 10 units. 95€ w/breakfast. AE, MC, V.

★★ Hotel Byron OLD TOWN

This old-fashioned inn on the back streets near the Church of Agiou Spiridona has long been a favorite of archaeologists and repeat visitors to Nafplion. Some of the rooms are small, but all have character and share a delightful terrace set atop an old Turkish *hamam*. 16 Platonos. ☎ 27520/26338. www.byronhotel.gr. 18 units. Doubles 50€–70€. AE, MC, V.

★★ King Othon I OLD TOWN

This neoclassical mansion near the sea has plain and comfortable rooms; most are reached via a graciously curved staircase. Breakfast is served in a side garden, a welcome retreat after a day of visiting the nearby ruins. 4 Farmakopoulou. ☎ 27520/27585. www.kingothon.gr. 11 units. Doubles 90€ w/breakfast. MC, V.

★★ Nafplia Palace ACRONAFPLIA

The best thing going for this luxury hotel, tucked into the Acronafplia ruins, is its dramatic perch high atop the city. Dramatic views and pine-scented grounds are best appreciated from one of the new villas or renovated rooms in the main building, equipped with sumptuous bathrooms, all manner of electronic gadgetry, and, in some cases, private pools; older rooms are showing their age, as are the vast public spaces. ☎ 27520/28981. 100 units. Doubles 250€–350€. AE, MC, V.

Where to Dine in Nafplion

> *A street in Old Town provides an atmospheric backdrop for a meal at Paleo Archontiko.*

★★ **Arapakos** OLD TOWN *SEAFOOD*
In a string of fish tavernas along the waterfront, this favorite among discerning Nafpliots stands out for the high quality of its fish. Meals include such traditional favorites as delicately fried eggplant and dolmades with lemon sauce, served for much of the year on a pleasant seaview terrace. 79 Bouboulinas. ☎ 27520/27675. Entrees 8€–20€. No credit cards. Lunch & dinner daily; closed Tues in winter.

★ **Hellas** OLD TOWN *GREEK*
One of the oldest restaurants in Nafplion commands one end of Plateia Syntagma with a large terrace and high-ceilinged, old-fashioned dining room. The traditional Greek cuisine is as straightforward as the surroundings, and reliably well prepared. Plateia Syntagma. ☎ 27520/27278. Entrees 8€–12€. MC, V. Lunch & dinner daily.

★★★ **Paleo Archontiko** OLD TOWN *GREEK*
The "old mansion," with its terrace on the quiet street in front, provides one of Nafplion's most pleasant dining experiences. Slow-cooked stews and other traditional meals are often served to the strains of wandering musicians. Siokou St. ☎ 27520/22449. Entrees 8€–12€. No credit cards. Lunch & dinner daily.

★★★ **Ta Farnina** OLD TOWN *GREEK*
This old Nafplion favorite is the standout among the tourist haunts along busy Staikopoulou Street. Locals count on the moussaka and other traditional dishes, served under a flowering arbor. 13 Staikopoulou. ☎ 27520/27141. Entrees 6€–10€. MC, V. Lunch & dinner daily.

Patras

Greece's third largest city and one of the country's major ports is more of a place to pass through than to linger. Most travelers hop on and off the ferries connecting Patras with Italy or Corfu, or the other Ionian Islands, without casting so much as a glance beyond the shabby waterfront. If you do—when you have a few hours or even an evening to kill between connections—you'll find some gracious squares, a few monuments, and the characteristically friendly exuberance that makes spending time in any Greek city a pleasure.

> Patras looks best from the hilltop Kastro, a good place to pass time while waiting for an outbound ship.

START **Plateia Olga, Patras (215km/133 miles from Athens). TRIP LENGTH About half a day.**

① ★★ **Plateia Olga.** Tree-shaded Plateia Olga and the city's other two main squares—Plateia Yioryiou and Plateia Maritou 25—recall Patras's more gracious, 19th- and early-20th-century heyday. Earthquakes and neglect have laid waste to much of the city's former beauty, though these squares and the arcaded streets that surround them are greatly appreciated by residents, who crowd them on warm evenings. The neoclassical theater and the Art Nouveau Galabopoulos House, both facing Plateia

Yioryiou, are two especially appealing remnants of 19th-century Patras. ⏱ 1 hr.

② ★ **Kastro.** The Franks built this castle on a hilltop high above the city, and the Venetians embellished the fortifications. Within the massive walls is a large park, and views over the harbor from the grounds reward a climb up the many flights of stairs. It's a good way to spend time while waiting for an outbound ferry. ⏱ 1 hr. with walk up from center and back. Above city center, at top of Agios Nikolaos stairs. Free admission. Daily 8am–8pm.

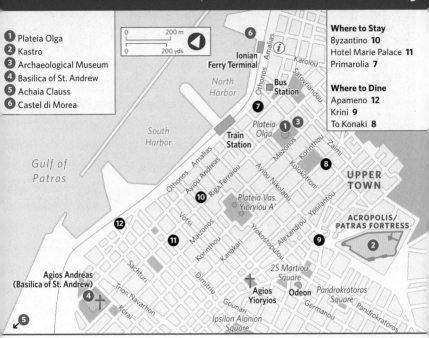

1 Plateia Olga
2 Kastro
3 Archaeological Museum
4 Basilica of St. Andrew
5 Achaia Clauss
6 Castel di Morea

Where to Stay
Byzantino **10**
Hotel Marie Palace **11**
Primarolia **7**

Where to Dine
Apameno **12**
Krini **9**
To Konaki **8**

3 ★ **Archaeological Museum.** Patras was an important Mycenaean city that also flourished under the ancient Greeks and was a major harbor for the Romans. This past is remembered in newly renovated exhibits that show off some exquisite Mycenaean funerary objects and mosaics found in Roman houses. Many of the objects were uncovered while digging out the Roman Odeon, a beautiful open-air theater off Plateia Maritou 25, where the Summer Festival takes place (p. 668). ⏲ 1 hr. 42 Mezonos. ☎ 26102/20829. Free admission. Tues–Sun 8:30am–5pm.

4 ★ **Basilica of St. Andrew.** This vast, early-20th-century church is built over the spot where the apostle St. Andrew was martyred; as such, it holds a special place in the hearts of thousands of pilgrims who descend upon Patras to pay homage. Andrew spread Christianity throughout Greece and was crucified in Patras, next to an ancient spring, on an X-shaped cross in A.D. 60. The church is now the repository of the saint's head, which has traveled widely—it was carried off to Constantinople in the 4th century and 1,000 years later moved to Rome, where it was enshrined

> *Arcaded avenues are a holdover from more gracious 19th-century heydays in Patras.*

> *Patras' crowded streets give way to Plateia Olga and two other tree-shaded main squares.*

in St. Peter's Basilica until the prized relic was returned to Patras in 1964. An annual ceremony takes place on his feast day, November 30. ⏱ 30 min. Trion Navarhon. Free admission. Daily 8am–8pm.

Achaia Clauss is 8km (5 miles) west of Patras, off E65. Take exit 3, from which signs lead to the hilltop winery.

❺ ★★ Achaia Clauss. Greece's oldest winery, founded by Bavarian Gustav Clauss in 1861, is surrounded by fragrant pines on a hilltop west of the city center. The winery is best known for Mavrodafni—a sweet dessert wine aged in oak vats that Clauss installed and named for his beloved, who died young. The operation also produces many noted reds and whites from grapes grown on the property and throughout Greece. Tours show off the winemaking process, and the grounds and views over the rural surroundings provide a relaxing respite from busy Patras. ⏱ 1 hr. Outside Patras. ☎ 26105/80100. Free admission, visits by tour only. May–Oct daily 9am–7:30pm, Nov–Apr daily 9am–5pm.

The Castel di Morea is 5km (3 miles) east of Patras, on E65.

❻ ★★ Castel di Morea. A forest of oil storage tanks and the Rion suspension bridge, which floats across the narrows of the Gulf of Corinth to connect the Peloponnese with the rest of mainland Greece, provide desultory surroundings for this spectacular castle that the Turks built in 1499. A twin, the Castel di Roumeli, guards the narrows from the opposite shore. The Castel di Morea (Morea was then the name for the Peloponnese) was captured by the Venetians at the end of the 17th century but retaken by the Turks shortly afterward. It was the scene of the Turks' last stand in the Peloponnese in 1828, when Ottoman soldiers holed up in the castle for three weeks before surrendering to Anglo-French forces. ⏱ 30 min. Near foot of Rion bridge. Free admission. Daily 8am–7pm.

Danger in the Fast Lanes

Rte. E65, the highway that connects Patras and Corinth and the major artery between Patras and Athens/Piraeus, is one of the most dangerous roads in Greece. Given that Greece has one of the highest accident rates in Europe, that's saying quite a bit about the perils of this roadway, which is almost always crowded with drivers speeding to and from the Patras ferries. Although it's two lanes wide for much of its length, trucks and cars also speed along the shoulders. Approach this stretch slowly and cautiously, or, safest yet, not at all: If you are coming to Patras from the southern Peloponnese, do so on the safer route that comes up the western shore of the region.

Where to Stay & Dine in Patras

The Byzantino occupies a richly embellished old mansion near the city center.

★ Apameno WATERFRONT *SEAFOOD*
The Patras waterfront is not terribly inviting, but that doesn't stop locals from seeking out fresh seafood here. Apameno is one of the top choices, serving notably fresh fish as well as a delicious fish soup. 107 Othos. ☎ 2610/671588. Entrees 7€–15€. MC, V. Lunch & dinner daily.

★ Byzantino CITY CENTER
Some of the most charming accommodations in Patras occupy an old mansion near the city center and include pleasant, high-ceilinged rooms and extremely attractive lounges and a bar downstairs. 106 Riga Ferraiou. ☎ 26102/43000. 0 units. Doubles 100€–110€. MC, V.

★ Hotel Marie Palace CITY CENTER
Pleasant, businesslike, and conveniently located for ferry, bus, and train connections, this city center hotel is perfectly adequate for a night's stay; you'll get a better night's sleep if you request a room to the side or rear, away from the busy avenue in front. 6 Gounari. ☎ 26103/31302. 36 units. Doubles 80€. MC, V.

Krini NEAR KASTRO *GREEK*
This atmospheric, publike wine bar at the top of the steps near the Kastro is as popular with locals as it is with the few tourists who make the climb up from the port. The garden is a delightful spot on a summer evening, and the simple menu is perfect for grazing on meze. 5 Pandokratoros. No phone. Entrees 5€–10€. No credit cards. Lunch & dinner daily.

★★ Primarolia WATERFRONT
The snazziest lodgings in town occupy an old distillery on the waterfront, and some rooms have balconies hanging over the busy harbor. Public areas are filled with contemporary art, the guest rooms are stylish and comfortable, and the restaurant and bar are sophisticated haunts for those stranded in Patras overnight. 33 Othonos Amalias. ☎ 26106/24900. www.arthotel.gr/primarolia. 14 units. Doubles 200€–250€. AE, DC, MC, V.

★★ To Konaki CITY CENTER *GREEK*
This local favorite set under the arcades of the Old Town is well known for traditional fare such as homemade vegetable pies and savory casseroles and for the traditional music played by family members on weekend evenings. The restaurant closes in summer, when the operation moves to the beach about 10km (6¼ miles) east of Patras. 44 Aratou and Karaiskai. ☎ 26102/75096. Entrees 7€–10€. No credit cards. Lunch & dinner daily. Closed May–Aug.

The Peloponnese Fast Facts

> *The Isthmus of Corinth, a neck of land bisected by a canal, connects the Peloponnese with mainland Greece*

Arriving

You'll most likely reach the Peloponnese by car, train, or bus, probably through the Isthmus of Corinth. **BY CAR** You can make the trip from Athens on the E65 toll road in an hour; on this route, Corinth is just 75km (47 miles) south of Athens, and Nafplion is 140km (85 miles) south. If you're driving from Delphi or another part of central Greece, you will cross the Gulf of Corinth near Patras on the Rion–Antiron suspension bridge. **BY TRAIN** Trains depart from the **Larissa Station** in Athens, Theodorou Diligianni, off Plateia Karaiskaki (the adjacent Peloponnissos station is closed for the time being).The fastest option is the high-speed commuter train to Corinth, which also leaves from the Athens airport, and make the 1-hour run every hour between 8am and 8pm. From Corinth you can connect to Nafplion, Tripoli, or Patras, and from Patras continue to Kalamata (with the option of changing at Pyrgos for Olympia). The newly organized Greek Railways Organization is not terribly forthcoming with information; check with the tourist information office in Athens or another GNTO branch, with the information booths at Larissa Station, or at one of the stations in the Peloponnese. **BY BUS** The Peloponnese is extremely well served by bus; service runs between Athens and Corinth and Athens and

Patras every 30 minutes; buses leave from Terminal A on the outskirts of Athens at 100 Kifissou. From Corinth, you can connect to service to Nafplion and many other towns in the Peloponnese, and in Patras to Olympia and other places along the west coast. Buses also run directly from Athens to Tripoli, Sparta, Gythion, and other towns in the region. For more information on bus service, contact one of the offices of the Greek National Tourist Office (GNTO). **BY BOAT** Many travelers arrive in Patras on one of the many ferries that cross the Adriatic from Ancona, Bari, and Venice in Italy. Patras is also a port for boats to and from Corfu and the Ionian Islands. **Superfast** (☎ 21096/91100; www.superfast.com) and **Minoan** (☎ 28103/99800; www.minoan.gr) are the major lines connecting Patras and Italian ports; numerous companies make the runs to the Ionians (p. 633). **BY AIR** The Peloponnese has only a few small and underserved airports. The airport outside Kalamata in the southern Peloponnese is served by a daily **Olympic Airlines** flight from Athens (☎ 80111/44444 reservations within Greece).

Dentists & Doctors

You will find clinics in almost every town, and an excellent medical center at the **University of Patras** (☎ 26109/97120), in outlying Rion. Most hotels will be able to refer you to a local doctor or dentist who speaks English.

Emergencies

See p. 680, Fast Facts Greece.

Getting Around

BY BUS If you have time, you can get around the Peloponnese by bus. Even the remotest villages in the Arcadian Mountains and the Mani are served by bus, operating out of Sparta, Tripoli, Kalamata, Patras, Nafplion, and other hubs around the region. From Nafplion, you can visit many of the ancient sites as well as Olympia by bus. **BY CAR** We recommend touring by car to save time, explore at your own speed, and get off the beaten track. Expect to pay about 30€ to 40€ a day, even in the busy August tourist season. You will find agencies in every town of any size in the Peloponnese.

Two major agencies are **AutoEurope,** 22 Karalou, Patras (☎ 800/1157/40300; www.autoeurope.com), and **Europcar,** 6 Andreou, Patras (☎ 306/21362; www.europcar.com). If you are coming from Athens, you will probably want to rent a car there (for driving tips, see p. 676). Buy a good map and keep an eye on the gas gauge, as it can be hard to find a station in some parts of the region.

Internet Access

Internet cafes, where you can log on for 4€ to 5€ an hour, are common in Nafplion, Patras, Sparta, and other major towns, where many cafes and coffee shops also offer free Wi-Fi. Also see p. 681, Fast Facts Greece.

Pharmacies

See p. 682, Fast Facts Greece.

Police

See p. 682, Fast Facts Greece.

Post Office

See p. 682, Fast Facts Greece.

Safety

The biggest danger in any city in the Peloponnese is traffic; most have pedestrian zones, but once outside these precincts, be extremely careful when crossing streets. In Patras, keep an eye on your belongings; pickpocketing is rare but not unheard of there. Also see p. 682, Fast Facts Greece.

Visitor Information

The Peloponnese has a fairly limited network of tourist information offices, operated either by municipalities or the Greek National Tourist Organization, and service is uneven at best. The best offices are the GNTO outlets in the following cities. **OLYMPIA** 75 Praxitelous Kondili (☎ 26240/23100; daily 9am–8pm, with shorter hours in winter). **PATRAS** 6 Filopomenos (☎ 26106/20353; daily 10am–7pm). Patras also has an excellent municipal tourist office, 6 Amalias (☎ 26104/61740; Mon–Fri 8am–8pm). **NAFPLION** The municipal tourist office, 25 Maritou (Mon–Fri 9am–1pm and 5pm–8pm) is often closed and not especially helpful when it is (many staff members do not speak English).

6
Crete

Favorite Moments in Crete

Be prepared to succumb. Crete can easily overwhelm you with its spectacular natural beauty, in the Samaria Gorge and elsewhere; its residents' distinct respect for traditional life, which still thrives in places such as the Lasithi Plateau; and its wealth of artifacts from the ancient Turks, Venetians, and other bygone civilizations, including the fascinating Minoans.

> PREVIOUS PAGE *Mountains hem in the tidy fields and orchards of the Lasithi Plateau.* THIS PAGE *At Elounda Beach, you'll have a room with a view and maybe a private pool.*

1 Hiking the Samaria Gorge. Yes, it will seem that you share the trail with just about every other traveler on the planet, but finding yourself in canyons only 3m (10 ft.) wide and 600m (1,969 ft.) deep is a profound experience nonetheless. See p. 253, **7**.

2 Cruising along the southwestern coast. The craft is no sleeker than the public ferry, but you will feel like Odysseus or another intrepid explorer as you chug past the mouths of mountain gorges, groves of cypress, hidden coves, and, every so often, a white-clad village

1. Hiking the Samaria Gorge
2. Cruising along the southwestern coat
3. Gazing at the Venetian Harbor in Hania
4. Walking down to the sea at Moni Gouverneto
5. Enjoying a meal under the stars
6. Ambling through the Amari Valley
7. Regarding the Minoan frescoes in the Archaeological Museum in Iraklion
8. Descending onto the Lasithi Plateau
9. Exploring the Elounda Peninsula

tucked far away from the modern world. See p. 252, **5**.

3 Gazing at the Venetian Harbor in Hania.

Find a spot on the western side of the harbor, maybe the terrace of the Firkas, the waterside fortress the Venetians built—and take in the view. The shimmering sea, a lighthouse, and waterside palaces are rendered even more exotic by the presence of mosques and minarets the Turks left behind. See p. 276, **5**.

4 Walking down to the sea at Moni Gouverneto.

Crete is generously graced with beautiful monasteries, but this one on the Akrotiri Peninsula adds a bit of a thrill—a walk that begins in a tranquil courtyard and descends through a ravine etched with millennia-old hermitages to an isolated cove where a swim seems almost spiritual. See p. 280, **13**.

5 Enjoying a meal under the stars.

You can experience this pleasure anywhere on Crete, and the food is almost always delicious. My first choice of venue would be a taverna in one of the farming villages around Matala. The sea is nearby, the pace is easygoing, and the spectacle of everyday small-town life buzzing around you is endlessly entertaining. See p. 255, **13**.

6 Ambling through the Amari Valley.

Few outings are more pleasant than an easygoing drive through this verdant valley, where fields and orchards are interspersed with stands of

aspen and pine, and tidy villages are clustered around little churches graced with Byzantine frescoes. It's not hard to believe that Zeus was reared in a cave on Mount Ida, rising high above this idyllic place. See p. 270, **8**.

7 Regarding the Minoan frescoes in the Archaeological Museum in Iraklion.

The subjects seem to reach across the millennia and touch us—so palpably you can understand why a modern French archaeologist looked at a 4,000-year-old scene of flounce-skirted court ladies and exclaimed, *"Les Parisiennes!,"* giving the fresco its name. See p. 240, **1**.

8 Descending onto the Lasithi Plateau.

First the road climbs and climbs; then suddenly you reach the summit of the pass and at your feet spreads a high haven of orchards and fields, studded with windmills and protected by a tidy ring of mountains. Your explorations can include the cave that is one of the alleged birthplaces of Zeus, but the biggest pleasure of being up here is simply experiencing a slice of rural Cretan life. See p. 256, **15**.

9 Exploring the Elounda Peninsula.

The vistas of barren hillsides meeting the turquoise sea are all the more beautiful amid the presence of Spinalonga, the Venetian stronghold, and the sunken city of Olus below the clear waters. Some of Greece's most luxurious resort getaways line the shores, heightening the allure of this enchanting landscape. See p. 286, **5**.

Crete in 3 Days by Bus

A mere 72 hours gives you enough time to experience the three most distinctive aspects of Crete—relics of the ancient Minoan past in and around Iraklion; the influence of the Venetians and Turks in Rethymnon and Hania; and the island's rugged natural beauty in the Samaria Gorge.

> *Hania's beautiful harbor is largely Venetian, with Turkish flourishes.*

START Iraklion. **TRIP LENGTH** Total distance traveled, with the excursion through the Samaria Gorge, is about 220km (136 miles). You will not need a car for this itinerary and can easily get around by bus.

① **Iraklion.** Most visitors come to Crete's largest city and capital in pursuit of the Minoans, the remarkable people whose culture flourished on the island from 1900 to 1200 B.C. You will spend most of your day here exploring the considerable remnants left behind by this long-vanished civilization.

The sophisticated accomplishments of the Minoans come to light in the city's **Archaeological Museum** (p. 240, **①**), where frescoes of court ladies, ivory figures, vessels in the shape of bull's heads, and beautifully crafted jewelry show just how accomplished these peaceable people were. You will want to spend the morning in the museum, preparing for an afternoon visit to Knossos, the largest of the Minoan palace complexes and one of the most captivating archaeological sites in the world. City buses make the trip out to the

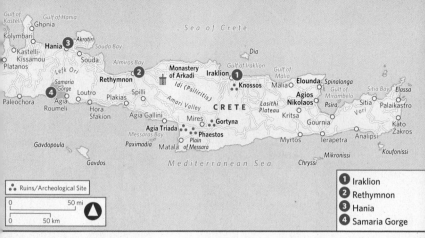

Gulf of Kastelli
Gulf of Hania
Ghonia
Kolymbari
Hania ❸
Akrotiri
Souda Bay
Sea of Crete
Dia
Kastelli-Kissamou
Platanos
Souda
Almiros Bay
Monastery of Arkadi
Iraklion ❶
Gulf of Iraklion
Gulf of Malia
Elounda
Spinalonga
Sitia Bay
Elassa
Lefk Ori
Rethymnon ❷
Knossos
Malia
Agios Nikolaos
Gulf of Mirombelo
Sitia
Samaria Gorge ❹
Loutro
Plakias
Spilli
Idi (Psiliritis)
Psira
Vori
Palaikastro
Paleochora
Agia Roumeli
Hora Sfakion
Amari Valley
CRETE
Lasithi Plateau
Kritsa
Gournia
Kato Zakros
Agia Gallini
Mires
Gortyna
Myrtos
Ierapetra
Analipsi
Gavdopoula
Agia Triada
Phaestos
Plain of Messara
Paximadia
Matala
Messaras Bay
Koufonissi
Gavdos
Mediterranean Sea
Chryssi
Mikronissi

•• Ruins/Archeological Site
0   50 mi
0   50 km

❶ Iraklion
❷ Rethymnon
❸ Hania
❹ Samaria Gorge

alace, 5km (3 miles) south of Iraklion, about very 15 minutes from the front of the Archaelogical Museum.

More than 1,300 rooms at **Knossos** (p. 241, ❸)—a maze of artisans' workshops, storerooms, royal apartments, courtyards, and ceremonial courts—present a glimpse into Minoan life. The palace is all the more evocative given that, for better or worse, parts of the complex have been recreated, and artists have recreated many of the frescoes.

What you see at Knossos and what we now of the Minoans is largely the work of ne man, Sir Arthur Evans. Heir to a paper mill fortune, this amateur archaeologist became fascinated with the notion that another great ancient civilization pre-dated the Mycenaeans, who flourished on the Greek mainland beginning around 1600 B.C. (p. 248). Using is own funds, Evans began excavating at Knossos in 1900. Evans linked the mazelike arrangement of the rooms he unearthed to the King Minos legend (p. 245), and he gave the civilization he was bringing to light the name of this mighty king of myth. Even without these associations with myth, the physical remains of the Minoan civilization you see at the Archaeological Museum and here at Knossos work a great deal of magic on their own.

You will spend the rest of the afternoon and evening in Iraklion, where another discovery waits. This bustling city, the fifth largest in Greece, is not as immediately appealing as other cities on Crete but soon reveals considerable charm. You'll probably want to spend your time strolling, like many Irakliots, beginning in **Ta Liontaria** (Lion's Square; p. 258, ❶), named for the Venetian fountain that rises to one side. A few steps south bring you to **Odos 1866** (p. 260, ❺), a road lined with market stalls all the way to Plateia Kornarou, with two more fountains, one Venetian and one Turkish. A walk farther south becomes a literary pilgrimage. Crete's most famous man of letters, Nikos Kazantzakis, is buried within the **Martinengo Bastion,** part of the massive fortifications the Venetians built around the city they called Candia (p. 261, ❼). If you make your way back through the Old City to the sea, you will see the Venetian seaside defenses and harbor, the Koules (p. 262, ❾). These wharves and warehouses (*arsenali*) once bustled with the commerce that made Crete such a valuable possession for Venice. Another discovery awaits you nearby: Crete was the birthplace of Domenikos Theotocopoulos (aka El Greco) and two of his paintings hang in the **Historical Museum of Crete** (p. 261, ❽). ⏱ 1 day.

More on Iraklion, Rethymnon & Hania

For detailed coverage of sights, hotels, and restaurants in Iraklion, see p. 258; for Rethymnon, see p. 266; for Hania, see p. 274.

> *A bazaarlike atmosphere prevails on the narrow lanes of Rethymnon.*

Venetian Crete

The walls that surround Iraklion, the fortress in Rethymnon, the harbor in Hania, and many other monuments around the island are the legacy of four centuries of Venetian occupation. Crete was a prize for Venice, awarded to the Republic after Constantinople was sacked in 1204 and the holdings of the Byzantine Empire were disbursed. Crete provided Venice with agricultural bounty, timber for shipbuilding, and a strong presence in the southern Mediterranean. Venice lost control of Crete to the Ottoman Turks in the middle of the 17th century.

Rethymnon is 80km (50 miles) west of Iraklion. Buses leave every 30 min. and the trip takes 90 min. You can leave luggage at the bus station as you explore.

❷ **Rethymnon.** Start Day 2 in Rethymnon. This little city has been inhabited for at least four millennia but owes its extremely attractive appearance to the Venetians. Their greatest monument, the massive seaside *fortezza* (fortress), rises above the narrow streets of the **Old Town** (p. 266, ❶). The Turks who took the city in the 16th century added a distinctive Ottoman element to the Venetian houses, including wooden balconies surrounded by distinctive latticework to protect women's privacy, and minarets on churches they had converted to mosques. ⏱ Half-day.

Hania is 70km (42 miles) west of Rethymnon. Buses run every half hour, and the trip takes less than an hour.

❸ **Hania.** Continue by bus to Hania for the afternoon. The second largest city in Crete, it's one of the most beautiful in Greece.

Tips on Accommodations

An excellent source for travel in Crete is **CreteTravel.com** (☎ 28250/32693; www.cretetravel.com). This online service provides excellent and frank descriptions of hotels, restaurants, and sights across the island, and visitors can book hotels on the site. They refreshingly veer off the beaten path to introduce you to less traveled parts of the island. **Diktynna Travel**, on 6 Archontaki, Hania (☎ 28210/43930; www.diktynna-travel.gr) provides distinctive accommodations in choice hotels and villas. Tourist information offices (see "Fast Facts") can give you lists of hotels and rooms to rent.

important to classical Greeks, Byzantines, Venetians, and Turks, it was capital of an independent Cretan State from 1898 to 1913. The Venetians left the greatest mark on Hania, and their many landmarks include the beautiful harbor (p. 276, ⑤). A walk around this great basin—from the **Firkas fortress** (p. 276, ⑥) in the west to the arsenal in the east—skirts mosques, Venetian and Turkish enclaves, the stone wharves where galleons were once loaded with goods for Venice, and the base of the Kastelli Hill, atop which a sizable Minoan settlement once thrived. ⏱ Half-day, 2 nights.

⑦ Samaria Gorge. Crete's most noted natural spectacle is one of Europe's longest gorges—a deep cleft running south to the Libyan Sea from the Omalos Plateau, high in the White

> A narrow gash in the mountainous southern coast, the Samaria Gorge provides one of Greece's most spectacular hikes.

Samaria Gorge Excursions

Just about every tour operator in Hania offers Samaria Gorge excursions, and these are by far the easiest way to make the trek. Most include a morning pickup at your hotel, transfer to the starting point of the hike at the Xyloskala (a steep wooden staircase that provides access to the gorge), pickup by boat at the mouth of the gorge at Agia Roumeli, and bus transfer back to Hania, usually from Hora Sfakion. You will be back in Hania by late afternoon, in time for a stroll and further exploration into the evening. For more on hiking the gorge, see p. 252.

Mountains about 30km (19 miles) south of Hania. Other spots in the rugged west of the island are as beautiful, but few can match the Samaria for sheer drama. Cliffs rise as high as 600m (1,969 ft.) from the canyon floor, only 3m (10 ft.) wide in places. A trek along the crowded trail through the 15km (9⅓-mile) gorge is not a solitary experience, but it's nonetheless exhilarating. One thrill you are not likely to experience, however, is a sighting of the shy kri-kri, the wild Cretan mountain goat for whom the gorge was declared a refuge, as a national park, in 1962. See p. 253, ⑦. ⏱ 1 day.

Crete in 10 Days

With a little more than a week, you can deepen your sense of Crete's extraordinary richness: You will encounter Minoans in Iraklion and Romans in Gortyna, experience traditional rural Cretan life in the villages along the south coast and the Lasithi Plateau, and behold the Venetian elegance of Rethymnon and Hania and the rugged natural beauty of the Amari Valley and Samaria Gorge. For a steep price, you can cavort in the lap of luxury at fabled resorts on the Elounda Peninsula.

> Romans and Byzantines left their mark at Gortyna.

START Iraklion. **TRIP LENGTH** Total distance traveled is about 900km (559 miles). Pick up a car, necessary for this itinerary, on Day 2 when you are ready to leave Iraklion.

1 Iraklion. Day 1 on Crete takes you back in time almost 4,000 years, when the Minoan culture began to flourish on the island. The world's finest collection of Minoan artifacts, from sensuous figures of snake goddesses to frescoes of youths leaping over bulls, are in the **Archaeological Museum** (p. 240, **1**). A walk through the newly renovated galleries prepares you for the extraordinary spectacle

of the **Palace of Knossos,** the largest of several elaborate complexes the Minoans built on Crete (p. 241, **2**). You can then spend the late afternoon and evening wandering through Iraklion and exploring more recent history, beginning with the year 1204, when Venetians arrived and set about building the magnificent **city walls** (p. 261, **7**) and walled harbor, the **Koules** (p. 262, **9**). ⏲1 day.

Gortyna is 45km (28 miles) south of Iraklion, just outside Agil Deka, on the Mires–Timpaki road.

1 Iraklion
2 Gortyna
3 Phaestos
4 Matala

5 Moni Preveli
6 Rethymnon
7 Arkadi Monastery
8 The Amari Valley

9 Akrotiri Peninsula
10 Hania
11 Samaria Gorge
12 Lasithi Plateau

13 Agios Nikolaos
14 Spinalonga
15 Sitia
16 Moni Toplou

Gortyna. Begin Day 2 with visits to more vestiges of the island's lengthy past. First stop is Gortyna, an ancient city that has seen the presence of Minoans, ancient Greeks, and Romans, who designated Gortyna the capital of their far-reaching province Cyrienacia. Later, in the Christian era, Gortyna witnessed the construction of a 6th-century Byzantine basilica built in honor of St. Titus, who converted the Cretans to Christianity in the 1st century. See p. 246. ⏱ 2 hr.

Continue another 20km (12 miles) west through Mires to Phaestos on a well-marked road.

3 **Phaestos.** The second most important Minoan palace—another vast complex of royal apartments, ceremonial spaces, and storehouses, atop a hill overlooking the Messara Plain toward the Libyan Sea—was at one time an important center for trade with Africa. The Phaestos Disk, found here during excavations a century ago, is covered with yet-to-be-deciphered symbols and presents one of the great unsolved mysteries of archaeology. See p. 244. 4. ⏱ 3 hr.

Matala is just 10km (6¼ miles) west of Phaestos on a well-marked road.

4 **Matala.** Spend Day 3 at this low-key retreat that drew ancient Roman legionnaires and 1960s dropouts alike with its seaside cliffs etched with caves (p. 255, 13). Matala and several nearby villages make it easy to relax

on south-coast beaches and then escape the midday sun at the **Museum of Cretan Ethnology** in Vori, a fascinating collection of folk objects (p. 255, 14). ⏱ 1 day.

On Day 4, head north on the road through Timpaki and Agia Gallini toward Rethymnon.

5 **Moni Preveli.** As you leave the Messara Plain, the road ascends into beautiful mountainous terrain. About 30km (19 miles) beyond Agia Gallini, just before the village of Spilli, follow signs for a short drive through spectacular mountain and valley scenery west to Moni Preveli. This beautiful and remote seaside monastery was a refuge for freedom fighters in the 19th-century revolution against Turkish rule and a rallying point for Allied soldiers stranded on the island during German occupation during World War II (p. 639). A scramble down the cliffs below the monastery leads to **Palm Beach,** one of the most beautiful stretches of sand on the island (p. 269, 7). ⏱ Half-day.

Retrace your steps to Spilli and continue to Rethymnon, 30km (19 miles) north and well marked.

More on Iraklion, Rethymnon & Hania

For detailed coverage of sights, hotels, and restaurants in Iraklion, see p. 258; for Rethymnon, see p. 266; for Hania, see p. 274.

> *Moni Preveli Monastery.*

6 **Rethymnon.** Like many Cretan towns, Rethymnon has been settled for millennia but owes much of its appearance, including a massive fortress, to the Venetians. An early evening arrival allows time for a leisurely amble through the **Old Town** (p. 266, **1**). You can continue your explorations the morning of Day 5, leaving some time to wander into the surrounding countryside before heading to Arkadi Monastery. ⏱ Half-day.

Arkadi is 25km (15 miles) southeast of Rethymnon. Take the national highway east to Maroulas, then the road to Arkadi.

7 **Arkadi Monastery.** One of Crete's most beloved landmarks, this monastery is associated with the events of November 8, 1866, when hundreds of Cretans gave their lives in the fight for freedom from Turkish rule. See p. 269, **6**). ⏱ 1 hr.

Take the beach road east 5km (3 miles) to Platanias. Drive south to Apostoli, then to Thronos, into the Amari Valley. Thronos is 20km (12 miles) south of Rethymnon.

8 **The Amari Valley.** Beautifully frescoed churches and tidy villages are nestled in the shadow of Mount Ida. Zeus was allegedly reared in a cave on the mountain's flanks. See p. 270, **8** . ⏱ At least 4 hr.

On Day 6, head west to Hania on the national highway, detouring onto the Akrotiri Peninsula en route. Drive onto the peninsula at Souda, 65km (40 miles) west of Rethymnon.

9 **Akrotiri Peninsula.** What draws travelers to the end of the peninsula are two adjacent monasteries surrounded by olive groves. At **Agia Triada,** an elaborate Venetian gate leads into an exotic flower-filled courtyard. At **Gouverneto,** a descent into a ravine leads past caves that served as 11th-century hermitages for St. John the Hermit and his followers. See p. 280, **12** and **13** . ⏱ At least 4 hr.

Well-marked roads lead west off the peninsula into the outskirts of Hania.

10 **Hania.** An afternoon and evening spent around the Venetian Harbor (see p. 276, **5**), past palaces, chapels, and mosques, introduce you to Hania's rich Venetian and Turkish legacy. See p. 274. ⏱ Half-day, 1 night.

On Day 7, make an excursion into the Samaria Gorge. Dozens of companies in Hania arrange tours (see p. 252).

11 **Samaria Gorge.** You will hike through Crete's most popular natural attraction in the company of eagles, goats, and outdoor enthusiasts from all over the world. Despite the crowds, it's a memorable experience. ⏱ 1 day. See p. 253, **7** .

On Day 8, head east across the north coast toward Agios Nikolaos. Leave by mid-morning to reach the Lasithi Plateau in time for lunch. Signs mark the turnoff up to the plateau about 210km (130 miles) east of Hania, outside Chernossios. (Allow 6 hr. for the trip to Agios Nikolaos, 300km/186 miles including the side trip to the Lasithi Plateau.)

12 **Lasithi Plateau.** This lovely high haven, a patchwork of fields and orchards studded with windmills, keeps a tight hold on traditional rural Cretan life. Enjoy lunch and soak in the bucolic atmosphere before descending to the worldly pleasures of Agios Nikolaos and Elounda. See p. 256, **15** . ⏱ 3 hr.

The Venetian harbor in Rethymnon.

> *The Archaeological Museum in Agios Nikolaos.*

ollow the signs for the road down to Neapoli nd Agios Nikolaos; allow 45 min. for the 0km (25 mile) trip along the winding road ack down to the coast.

3 Agios Nikolaos. This little coastal town is icturesque and amiable but more attuned to ttracting tourists than retaining even a sem- lance of Greek character. The town's one great ttraction is **Lake Voulismeni** (p. 284, **1**), the egendary bathing spot of the goddess Artemis. he most famous resident is a 2,000-year-old oman legionnaire whose wreath-encircled kull is on display at the worthy little **Archaeo- ogical Museum** (p. 284, **3**). **The Elounda eninsula** (p. 286, **5**) extends into the Gulf of Mirabello (Gulf of the Beautiful View) just north f town. It's an ideal natural complement to gios Nikolaos—a spectacular landscape un- bashedly given over to hedonism, provided by ome of Greece's most luxurious resorts.

Over the next 2 days, you can easily make wo excursions: one to Spinalonga, the capti- ating island accessible via boat from Agios likolaos, Elounda, and Plaka; and one east to itia (p. 287). ⏲ **2 days.**

ou can reach Spinalonga on boat trips from gios Nikolaos and Elounda.

14 Spinalonga. This forbidding little outcrop- ping has been home to ancient Greeks, Vene- tians, Turks, and lepers. A visit to the ruins of their various habitations is incomplete without a swim in the gulf's pristine waters. See p. 286, **6**. ⏲ 2 hr.

Sitia is about 70km (43 miles) east along the north coast from Agios Nikolaos.

15 Sitia. Not too much in this easygoing and attractive town demands your attention, but shady promenades invite a stroll, and old lanes lead up to a monumental Venetian fortress (p. 289, **12**). ⏲ 2 hr.

Drive 20km (12 miles) farther east on the coast road to Toplou.

16 Moni Toplou. Forbidding and forlorn, this monastery has held its own against attacks by pirates, Turks, and German soldiers. Today, however, it's a peaceful haven surrounding shady courtyards. The monastery's icons are some of the finest on the island. See p. 290, **13**. ⏲ 2 hr.

On the Trail of the Minoans

One of Europe's oldest civilizations flourished on Crete from around 2700 to 1450 B.C. The Minoans left behind palaces and towns at Knossos, Phaestos, Gournia, Kato Zakros, and elsewhere around the island, along with a bounty of frescoes and other sophisticated artifacts. Exploring the vestiges of this ancient civilization is one of the great pleasures of visiting Crete. You'll begin the tour at the Archaeological Museum in Iraklion (where most of the significant treasures unearthed on the island are on display) and at the great palace at Knossos just outside Iraklion, and then travel to other Minoan sites around the island by car.

> *Minoan frescoes show the culture's refinement and fondness for the sport of bull leaping.*

START Iraklion. **TRIP LENGTH** At least 4 days. Total distance 300km (186 miles).

1 ★★★ **Archaeological Museum, Iraklion.** The world's greatest museum of Minoan art houses many of the finds from the Palace of Knossos and other monuments of the Minoan

civilization that thrived in Crete some 4,000 years ago. A walk through the museum, a mandatory first stop on a tour of Crete's many Minoan sites, brings to light the remarkable accomplishments of this sophisticated culture. Large round "seal" stones, inscribed with an early form of Greek known as Linear B script,

1. Archaeological Museum, Iraklion
2. Palace of Knossos
3. Tylissos
4. Phaestos
5. Agia Triada
6. Palace of Malia
7. Agios Nikolaos
8. Gournia
9. Palaikastro
10. Palace of Kato Zakros

Ruins/Archeological Site

...ave revealed a wealth of information about ...e Minoans. However, one of the most elabo-...tely inscribed stones, called the Phaestos ...isk, for the palace near the southern coast ...here it was unearthed, remains a mystery: ...e large circular stone is elaborately in-...cribed in Linear A, a script predating Linear B ...at has yet to be deciphered.

A look at the art of these ancient peoples ...rovides glimpses into a long-vanished civili-...ation remarkable for its nearly photographic ...nd exuberant depictions of life: Beautiful ...escoes portray proceedings at a Minoan ...ourt; *The Prince of the Lilies* depicts an athletic ...riest-king, wearing a crown with peacock ...eathers and a necklace decorated with lilies, ...eading an unseen animal to slaughter; other ...vorks show muscular men and trim women ...eaping over bulls—either a religious rite or ...n athletic contest. A whimsical fresco of ...ourt ladies in skirts, in the Palace of Knossos, ...arned the nickname *Les Parisiennes* for its ...ubjects' resemblance to ladies on the grand ...oulevards of the French capital.

As early as 2000 B.C., Minoan craftsmen ...vere producing pottery known as Kamares ...vare. Other decorative pieces are made of ...tone, ivory, and a kind of glass paste known ...s faience. Many pieces illustrate life in Mi-...oan towns and palaces. One vase depicts a ...arvest ceremony, another a boxing match. A ...are-breasted faience goddess holds writh-...g snakes, perhaps part of a religious ritual. ...ythons, vases for pouring libations, are carved

in the shape of bulls' heads and other elabo-rate designs—yet more evidence that this long-vanished culture had a sophisticated flair for living. ⏱ 2 hr. Plateia Eleftherias. ☎ 2810/224630. www.culture.gr. Admission 4€; com-bined ticket for museum and Palace of Knossos 10€. Apr to mid-Oct daily 8am–7:30pm; mid-Oct to Mar daily 8am–5pm.

To reach Knossos from Iraklion, take bus no. 2, departing every 15 min. from Odos Evans in the city center; the fare is 1.15€.

SITE GUIDE PAGE 243

2 ★★★ kids **Palace of Knossos.** These dramatic and enticing ruins once made up the center of Minoan culture and contained more than 1,300 rooms. Cretan merchant and archaeologist Mi-nos Kalokarinos discovered the remains of the largest Minoan palace complex atop Kephala Hill in 1878, and the British ar-chaeologist Sir Arthur Evans began excavating the site in earnest in 1899, soon after Crete was liberated from three and a half centuries of Turkish occupation. Employing an enor-mous workforce, Evans brought the complex

Tip

You'll want to spend at least a day and a night in Iraklion, allowing yourself time to see the Archaeological Museum and Knossos, as well as the other sights of this millennia-old city (p. 258).

> *Reconstruction of the throne room and other parts of the Palace of Knossos show what life at a Minoan court was like.*

to light in relatively short order. His work showed that the palace was originally built around 1900 B.C., rebuilt after an earthquake around 1700 B.C., and taken over by the Mycenaeans around 1400 B.C.

The palace was the center of Minoan culture in every way—not just the court of royalty and an important religious and ceremonial center, but also an administrative headquarters and a huge warehouse where the Minoans stored everything from the honey they cultivated; to the wheat, figs, and barley they grew; to the elephant tusks and saffron they imported from Africa and the Middle East. As you tour the palace, you'll see ample evidence of these various functions: tall clay jars in which wine, oil, and grain were stored; a splendid grand staircase that ascends from a ceremonial court up four flights through a light well; and the elaborate apartments of the queen, complete with a bathtub and toilet that would have drained into the palace's elaborate sewage system. What's missing from Knossos and other Minoan palaces and towns are defensive walls. This culture seems to have been peace-loving and unconcerned about invasion—for better or for worse. While the decline of the Minoans remains a mystery, it has been attributed to attacks from outsiders as well as earthquakes and tsunamis after the eruption of the nearby Santorini volcano. Evidence suggests that Mycenaeans from mainland Greece took over the palace and other parts of Crete around 1400 B.C., but by 1200 B.C., they too had vanished.

Evans rebuilt parts of the palace, reconstructing the courtyards and rooms as they were under the Minoans and painting them vibrant colors—a sacrilege to purists that nonetheless richly re-created Minoan life for today's visitors. ⏱ 2 hr. Knossos Rd., 5km (3 miles) south of Iraklion. ☎ 2810/231940. www.culture.gr. Admission 6€; combined ticket for Knossos and Archaeological Museum in Iraklion 10€. Apr to mid-Oct daily 8am–7:30pm; mid-Oct to Mar daily 8am–5pm.

From Iraklion, follow the national highway west for 7km (4⅓ miles) to Gazi; from there follow signs 5km (3 miles) south to Tylissos.

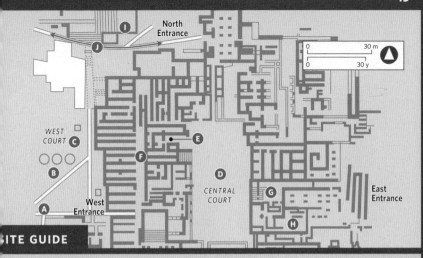

North Entrance

WEST COURT **C**

CENTRAL COURT

West Entrance

East Entrance

2 Knossos

Visitors to the palace follow the well-marked walkway, first passing a statue of **A** **Sir Arthur Evans,** a wealthy Englishman who bought the site in the late 19th century to pursue his interest in archaeology. Just beyond are vast **B** **underground silos,** which may have been used to store grain and other valuable foodstuffs. Altar bases on the nearby **C** **west court** suggest that this large space near the entrance to the palace was used for public ceremonies; the Minoans worshiped many gods and goddesses, and evidence suggests they may have engaged in human sacrifice. Fresco-lined hallways lead to the **D** **central court,** 49.5m (162 ft.) wide and 24m (79 ft.) long. The so-called **E** **throne room,** on the west side of the Central Court, houses a black gypsum chair that is claimed to be the oldest throne in Europe but may have served more mundane functions (it also may be Mycenaean rather than Minoan). Much of the **F** **west wing** was given over to store rooms, where wine, oil, olives, and other commodities were stored in brightly painted clay jars called *pithoi.* The royal apartments, reached by a **G** **grand staircase,** were in the east wing of the palace. The **H** **queen's apartments** were lavishly decorated with a dolphin fresco and equipped with running water and plumbing. At the northwest end of the complex is the **I** **theatrical area,** also used for ceremonies.

From here the **J** **Royal Road,** the oldest roadway in Europe, leads west into the surrounding countryside.

> *Minoans stored oil, wine, olives, and other goods in* pithoi, *elaborately decorated clay vessels.*

③ ★ Tylissos. Three Minoan villas and storerooms, outside this modern village surrounded by vineyards and farms are more than 4,000 years old. The halls, staircases, kitchens, and a central court reveal an intriguing look at day-to-day domestic Minoan life. Archaeologists have unearthed many clay human and animal figures, used as votives (some of which are on display in the Archaeological Museum in Iraklion) as well as an elaborate system of terra cotta pipes. These carried water from a spring to a cistern and faucets throughout the villa complex. Beekeeping is still a major undertaking in the village, just as it was for the Minoans. 🕐 1 hr. Tylissos village. ☎ 2810/831372. Admission 2€. Daily 8:30am–3pm.

From Iraklion, take the Mires-Timpaki road south for 50km (31km) across the island's mountainous spine; you'll descend onto the Messara Plain to Mires. From there, follow the signs west to Phaestos, about 60km (37 miles) south of Iraklion. Spend at least a night in this unspoiled part of Crete.

④ ★★★ Phaestos. Italian archaeologists began unearthing Phaestos, the second-greatest Minoan palace, about the same time Sir Arthur Evans was excavating Knossos. Unlike Evans, though, the Italian team left the ruins much as they found them, and the overall results evoke Minoan life even more effectively than reconstructed Knossos. Lavish apartments, ceremonial areas, granaries, and warehouses suggest the importance of the palace complex, probably a key center of trade with Egypt and other parts of northern Africa, just across the Libyan Sea. The **Phaestos Disk** was found, encased in a vault of mud brick, at the palace during the Italian excavations. The purpose of this stone, elaborately inscribed on both sides in Linear A script and covered with concentric circles filled with four distinct symbols, is unknown, making the stone one of the great mysteries of archaeology. Theories abound, ascribing the disk and its symbolism to everything from a prayer wheel to a board game; the Phaestos Disk is on display at the Archaeological Museum in Iraklion. 🕐 1 hr. Off Mires-Timpaki rd. ☎ 28920/42315. www.culture.gr. Admission 4€, 6€ combined ticket with Agia Triada. May–Oct daily 8:30am–8pm, Nov–Apr daily 8am–5pm.

Agia Triada is 3km (2 miles) west of Phaestos on a well-marked, narrow road.

⑤ ★ Agia Triada. This small complex around the hill from Phaestos continues to stir debate about what its function may have been. Was it a small palace? A settlement used for shipping wares from Phaestos? A summer retreat for patricians? Evidence suggests that Agia Triada may have been all three. Elaborate villas and pleasure-oriented frescoes (including one of a cat chasing a pheasant in a garden now in the Archaeological Museum in Iraklion) suggest that the settlement was at least in part a place of leisure. Below the villas are warehouses that once brimmed with grain, oil, and other precious commodities. ⏱ 30 min. Off Mires-Timpaki rd. ☎ 28920/42315. www.culture.gr. Admission 4€, 6€ combined ticket with Agia

> *Agia Triada was both a Minoan port and summer retreat for nobility.*

Triada. May–Oct daily 10am–4pm, Nov–Apr daily 8:30am–3pm.

Take the Iraklion road back to the north coast. From Iraklion, take the national highway east for 40km (25 miles) to Malia.

6 ★★ **Palace of Malia.** Another palace, outside the atrociously overdeveloped resort town of the same name, was once a beach-head of Minoan administration on the eastern end of the island. The ruins of this third-largest Minoan palace on Crete are not as overwhelming as those at Knossos or Phaestos, yet they richly evoke a Minoan settlement. As you walk through the ruins, you'll get a good sense of how the Minoans were both practical and highly ceremonial, placing storage, administrative, religious, and living facilities side by side throughout the palace complex. Granaries and storerooms surround large courtyards that were probably used for public gatherings and religious ceremonies. A limestone *kernos*, a large table etched with hollows in which seeds and other offerings were placed, stands near

A Bit of Cretan Mythology

Legend has it that Knossos was once home to King Minos, son of Zeus and Europa. Minos prayed to Poseidon to send him a white bull from the sea as a sign that he had the blessing of the gods to rule; he would sacrifice the bull in thanksgiving. The bull appeared, but Minos could not part with the beautiful creature; his wife, Pasiphae, too, was smitten, and she seduced the bull and gave birth to the Minotaur. Minos ordered the architect Daedalus to build a labyrinth to imprison this monstrous half-man, half-bull creature. Meanwhile, the Athenians killed Minos's son, Androgeos, and Minos demanded the city send him seven boys and seven girls every nine years to be sacrificed to the Minotaur. Ariadne, the daughter of Minos, fell in love with one of these youths, Theseus. She gave Theseus a sword to slay the Minotaur and a ball of red fleece he could unravel to find his way out of the maze. Minos blamed Daedalus for the escape and imprisoned him in a tower, but the architect crafted a pair of wings for himself and his son, Icarus. The pair made an airborne escape, but Icarus failed to heed his father's advice and flew too close to the sun: His wings melted, and he fell into the azure waters now known as the Icarian Sea. Nor does the unhappiness end there: Theseus abandoned Ariadne on the island of Naxos as they made their way to Athens. Ariadne put a curse on Theseus, and under her spell, he changed the sails of his ship to black. His father, Aegeus, saw the black-sailed ship approaching, assumed his son was dead, and leapt from a cliff into the sea that to this day bears his name.

A Step Forward in Time

Gortyna, about 10km (6¼ miles) east of Phaestos, was a small Minoan settlement that flourished under the Greeks. By the 5th century B.C., the citizens enjoyed a civilized society governed by laws they literally set into stone—the Code of Gortyna, on display in a small building at the site. A small Greek theater and other structures remain, but most of what you see at Gortyna is Roman. The Romans conquered Crete in 69 B.C., after years of bloody warfare against the Greeks, and made Gortyna the administrative center of Cyrenaica, a province that included Crete as well as parts of Northern Africa. Under their jurisdiction, roads, aqueducts, and other public works soon appeared throughout Crete. When the Roman Empire divided into East and West regions in the 4th century, Crete came under the rule of Byzantium. A Roman bath and theater stand amid the rubble of what was once a city of 10,000. The most intact remains belong to a later era, the 6th century, when Christianity had gained a stronghold across the island under the Byzantine Empire. The ruins of a magnificent Byzantine basilica, destroyed during 9th-century Arab raids, stand on the site of a simple church erected in the 1st century by St. Titus, dispatched by Paul to convert the Cretans. Outside Agii Deka, on the Iraklion-Mires road. ☎ 28920/3114. www.culture.gr. Admission 4€. Apr–Oct daily 8am–7:30pm, Nov–Mar daily 8:30am–3pm.

the **central court,** once lined with porticos and from which a large staircase, a hallmark of most Minoan palaces, ascends to terraces and more ceremonial spaces. Domestic apartments were located off the **northern court.** The sea laps against the northern side of the settlement, and the brooding Lasithi Mountains loom just a mile or so to the south—a natural setting that lends Malia a sense of timelessness despite the clutter of nearby resorts. ⏱1 hr. 3km (2 miles) east of Malia off the national road. ☎ 2897/31597. www.culture.gr. Admission 4€. July–Oct Tues–Sun 8am–7:30pm, Nov–June Tues–Sun 8:30am–3pm.

From Malia, it's another 30km (19 miles) on the national road to Agios Nikolaos.

❼ ★★ Agios Nikolaos. This attractive town (p. 284) and the resorts on the nearby Elounda Peninsula are good bases from which to explore the Minoan sites of eastern Crete.

Gournia is 20km (12 miles) east of Agios Nikolaos on the national road.

❽ ★★ Gournia. This small town is often called the Minoan Pompeii, because the well-preserved ruins surrounding a small governor's palace so richly evoke everyday life in ancient times. Harriet Boyd-Hawes, an American archaeologist, began to excavate the site in 1901, and her work unearthed olive presses, carpenter's tools, a coppersmith's forge, and other artifacts that yield clues to the sorts of enterprises that once kept the 4,000 inhabitants busy. Stepped streets climb hilly terrain and cross two major avenues that run at right angles to each other. They are lined by stone houses with workrooms or shops open to the street and ladders inside that lead to storage rooms below and living quarters above ground level. Gournia is near a narrow neck where the island is only 12km (7½ miles) wide, so the fishermen-trader inhabitants could either embark from the town's harbor or make their way to the south shore and set sail from there. ⏱1 hr. Just off the national highway. ☎ 28410/22462. www.culture.gr. Admission 2€. May–Oct daily 8am–7:30pm, Nov–Apr daily 8:30am–3pm.

Palaikastro is 70km (43 miles) east of Gournia at the far eastern end of the island. Take the national highway east to Sitia (p. 289, ⑫) and then follow signs to Palaikastro.

Palaikastro and other Minoan settlements on the east coast may have bustled with trade with Egypt.

⑨ ★ **Palaikastro.** This wonderfully evocative jumble of ruins was once a thriving Minoan town, a busy agricultural center where inhabitants harvested the fields and orchards that thrived on the surrounding coastal plain. A palace or temple has never been unearthed at Palaikastro, so you don't come across the ceremonial spaces that you find at the Minoan palace sites. Even so, the gridlike arrangement of streets lined with the ruins of shops and houses are haunting. ⏰ 1 hr. Outside village of Palaikastro. ☎ 28410/22383. www.culture.gr. Free admission. May–Oct daily 8am–7:30pm, Nov–Apr daily 8:30am–3pm.

Kato Zakro is 20km (12 miles) south of Palaikastro on a well-marked road.

⑩ ★ **Palace of Kato Zakro.** Given its position on the eastern tip of the island, this small palace, the fourth of the main Minoan administrative centers, may well have been a trading post on the lucrative sea routes with Egypt and other parts of the Middle East and Africa. Elephant tusks, copper, and other items of exotic origin found during excavations suggest just how far-roaming the Minoans must have been. A ramp leads from the harbor into the palace, where royal apartments, banqueting halls, and shrines surround the series of courtyards typical of Minoan palaces. Unique to Kato Zakro are burial caves, carved out of the sides of the so-called Ravine of the Dead, which cuts through the settlement. ⏰ 2 hr. Near Kato Zakro harbor. ☎ 28410/22462. Admission 3€. July–Oct Tues–Sun 8am–7:30pm, Nov–June Tues–Sun 8:30am–3pm.

CIVILIZATION 101
The Cultures That Shaped Greece

BY STEPHEN BREWER

		STOMPING GROUNDS	DEFINING MOMENT
	CYCLADICS 3000 B.C.–2000 B.C.	Central Aegean islands	Began to establish towns (2500 B.C.)
	MINOANS 2000 B.C.–1150 B.C.	Crete and nearby islands	A massive eruption on nearby Santorini destroyed Knossos and other Minoan palaces on Crete (1600 B.C.)
	MYCENAEANS 1600 B.C.–1100 B.C.	Peloponnese and other parts of mainland, extending as far as Crete, Sicily, and Asia Minor	According to legend, Mycenae won the Trojan War (13th or 12th century B.C.), led by King Agamemnon
	CLASSICAL GREEKS 1100 B.C.–146 B.C.	Greek mainland and islands, and colonies as far afield as Sicily, southern Italy, and Asia Minor	The Golden Age gave rise to some of the greatest cultural achievements the world has ever known (5th century B.C.)
	BYZANTINES A.D. 324–1204	Greek mainland and islands	Emperor Theodosius made Christianity the official religion and banned Olympic Games and other observances as pagan rituals (394)
	VENETIANS 1100s–1400s	Crete and Central Aegean islands	Venetian bomb hits the Parthenon, winning 5-month rule (1687)
	OTTOMANS 1453–1827	All of Greece	Ottoman general Ali Pasha establishes independent domain in Ioannina (1788)

OR MILLENNIA BEFORE GREECE BECAME AN INDEPENDENT NATION IN 1832, the nainland and islands gave rise to some of history's earliest civilizations—beginning vith the Cycladic people, who left traces of advanced farming and metalworking echniques from as far back as 3200 B.C. Even as their territories were parceled into ity-states and usurped by foreign powers, these cultures retained distinctive raits that are easy to identify in the artifacts they left behind. Here are some clues ɔ help you tell their works apart as you travel through Greece.

LAIMS TO FAME	WHERE TO ENCOUNTER THEM
aised wheat, barley, goats, and pigs; speared sh from boats and cruised the Aegean in 0-man canoes; made tools, ornaments, and eapons from lead, silver, and copper	Distinctive, flat, marble female idols that re- semble Modern sculpture; Athens's **National Archaeological Museum** (p. 46, ❽); **Museum of Cycladic Art** (p. 63, ⓮)
eveloped a sophisticated, non-military culture cen- red around elaborate palaces with fluid, dynamic et frescoes, while Egyptians were still painting em dry; created exquisite pottery and metalware, hich they traded on the mainland and throughout sia Minor and North Africa; developed script inear A) unrelated to any known language	Linear A script (predating Greek) found on frescoes, pottery, jewelry, and seal stones in **Archaeological Museum, Iraklion** (p. 240, ❶); **Knossos** (p. 241, ❷); **Phaestos** (p. 244, ❹); and other palaces on Crete
uilt a powerful, warlike empire based in the city f Mycenae; inspired some of the world's greatest erature: the *Iliad* and the *Odyssey*'s account of e Trojan War and the murderous exploits of e cursed royal house of Atreus in the plays of eschylus, Sophocles, and Euripides	Lion Gate, defensive walls, and other ruins in **Mycenae** (p. 188, ❻), **Tiryns** (p. 188, ❹), and **Ancient Messene** (p. 193, ⓭); gold death masks and carved ivory statues from the **royal Mycenaean tombs** (p. 188, ❻); **National Ar- chaeological Museum** in Athens (p. 46, ❽)
eveloped cornerstones of Western civiliza- on in their advanced principles of democracy, hilosophical thought, scientific reasoning, erature, drama, and art; developed loosely nited, democratically administered city states ith shared mythology and legends	**Parthenon** (p. 44, ❹), **Acropolis Museum** (p. 44, ❺), and **National Museum of Archaeol- ogy** (p. 46, ❽) in Athens; **Delphi** (p. 576); theater at **Epidaurus** (p. 191, ❽); tombs of Philip and Alexander the Great at **Vergina,** Macedonia (p. 531, ❷)
s part of the Byzantine Empire, centered in onstantinople (Byzantium), Greece embraced astern Orthodox Christianity and saw a flour- hing of religious art and architecture	**Agia Sofia** (p. 550, ❹) and **Agios Dimitrios** (p. 552, ⓰) basilicas, **Rotunda** (p. 552, ⓭), and **Byzantine Museum** (p. 551, ❾) in Thes- saloniki
stablished lucrative trading centers in rete and elsewhere	In the architecture of **Corfu** (p. 618); the fortresses, walls, and harbors in **Iraklion, Rethymnon,** and **Hania,** on Crete; in **Nafplion,** the Peloponnese; and on **Naxos** and elsewhere in the Cyclades
eljuk Turks who came to be known as Ottomans eized Constantinople and, over the course of two enturies, established a vast empire that extended to the Middle East and throughout Greece; reek language and Hellenistic culture preserved monasteries and secret schools and libraries	**Aslan Mosque** (p. 594, ❹), **Aslan Pasha Cami, Its Kale** (p. 594, ❻), and **Turkish bazaar** (p. 569, ❽) in Ioannina

Off the Beaten Path on Crete

Tourism has wrought greater change in parts of Crete over the past several decades than waves of invaders did over millennia. Much of the island, however, remains unspoiled, spectacularly beautiful, and deeply rooted in traditional ways. The west and south of the island are especially rewarding getaways, but you will discover quiet corners just about anywhere on Crete.

> *A steep scramble is required to reach Palm Beach and other remote stretches of sand on the south coast.*

START Polyrinia, about 45km (28 miles) west of Hania. TRIP LENGTH About a week. Total distance covered by car is 470km (292 miles), plus excursions by boat and on foot.

Take the national highway from Hania 40km (25 miles) west to Kastelli and the road south from there for 5km (3 miles) to modern Polyrinia. A path from the village leads to ancient Polyrinia.

1 ★ Ancient Polyrinia. One of the most important Greek city-states of western Crete tops a remote hillside, a half-hour walk from the modern village of Polyrinia through meadows ablaze with wildflowers in spring. Legend has it that Agamemnon stopped at Polyrinia on his way back to Mycenae from Troy. He entered the city to make a sacrifice at the city's famous Temple to Artemis, but the proceedings were cut short when the king saw that his prisoners of war had set fire to his ships, anchored far below. The city still commands a view of much of the northwestern coastline, and stone from the temple was used to construct the 19th-century **Church of the Holy Fathers,** incongruously and sturdily standing amid the ruins. 🕑 1 hr. Free admission. Daily dawn to dusk; site is unattended.

1 Ancient Polyrinia	6 Sougia	11 Hora Sfakion
2 Falasarna	7 Samaria Gorge	12 Frangokastello
3 Moni Chrysoskalitissa	8 Loutro	13 Matala
4 Elafonisi	9 Vrisses	14 Vori
5 Paleochora	10 Kare & Imbros gorges	15 Lasithi Plateau

Falasarna is 25km (15 miles) northwest of Polyrinia. Retrace your steps to Kastelli and take the road west from there.

2 ★★ **Falasarna.** Travelers who make it to the far western edges of Crete discover a long white-sand beach, washed by crystal-clear waters and interspersed with boulders. Just behind the beach are the scant remains of an ancient Greek harbor, once protected within thick walls. Due to shifts in sea levels over the past 2,500 years, the old stones are now scattered across a dry, rugged landscape several hundred feet from the shore. ⏱ 2 hr.

A narrow, winding road follows the west coast. Moni Chrysoskalitissa is 35km (21 miles) south of Falasarna.

3 ★★ **Moni Chrysoskalitissa.** The name of this beautiful, whitewashed monastery, appearing like a mirage atop an outcropping above the rugged coast, means "golden stair." Legend has it that one of the 90 stairs ascending to the monastery from the sea below is made of gold, but only those without sin can see it—which may explain why the stair has never been sighted in the 600 or so years since the hermitage was established. As many as 200 monks and nuns once lived at Chrysokalitissa, but today only two remain. ⏱ 30 min. Free admission. Daily 9am–7pm.

Elafonisi is 5km (3 miles) south of Moni Chrysoskalitissa. The narrow road is well marked.

> *Moni Chrysoskalitissa, the "Golden Stair" Monastery, sits in splendid isolation above the sea.*

4 ★★ **Elafonisi.** A remote location at the southwestern tip of the island does not deter summertime beachgoers. This string of little inlets, lined with tamarisk-shaded sands and washed by shallow turquoise waters, rewards the long overland journey or the boat trip

Hiking the Samaria Gorge

Organized tours of the Samaria Gorge operate out of almost every town on the island. Many trekkers set off on Samaria Gorge tours from Hania and Rethymnon. Most tours provide a bus trip to the drop-off at the Xyloskaka entrance to the gorge; transfer by boat at the end of the hike from Agia Roumeli to Hora Sfakion, Paleochora, or Sougia; and a return trip from one of those places by bus. Fees begin at about 30€, though at that price you should expect to be part of a large group. Out of Hania, we recommend **Diktynna Travel,** notable for its small groups and knowledgeable and personable guides; tours start at about 45€. Contact Diktynna at 6 Archontaki Street, Hania (☎ 28210/43930; www.diktynna-travel.gr).

If you decide to hike the gorge on your own, you can take the morning bus from Hania or Rethymnon to Xyloskala or from Paleochora to Xyloskala (as we recommend in this itinerary). From the mouth of the gorge at Agia Roumeli, boats will take you to Hora Sfakion, Sougia, or Paleochora, and from there you can catch a bus back to Hania or Rethymnon, with connections to other towns on the island.

The gorge is open from mid-April through mid-October, depending on weather conditions; rains raise the risk of flash floods, and winds have been known to send rocks careening from great heights toward hikers. Entry is allowed from 6am to 4pm, and the entrance fee is 6€; you will be asked to show your ticket as you leave the gorge (this way, park personnel can keep track of numbers entering and leaving and launch a search for errant hikers if necessary). The trek takes 5 or 6 hours, and boulders can make for some rough going in places. Mandatory gear includes sturdy hiking shoes, sunscreen and a hat, and a bathing suit, for a well-deserved swim in the sea at the end of the hike. You'll want to bring a snack, but don't load yourself down with too much water, because you'll come upon several freshwater springs along the way. Any tourist office on Crete can provide additional information on this phenomenal attraction.

from Paleochora (see below). A sandbar, sometimes submerged, links the shoreline to a narrow islet, where another, less frequented tree-shaded beach faces the open seas. ⏱ 2 h

To reach Paleochora from Elafonisi, head back north to Stomio, then continue through Vathi and Elos toward Vlatos. There, a road heads south to Paleochora. Total distance is 50km (31 miles). Make Paleochora your base for the next 3 days.

⑤ ★ Paleochora. It's been a long time since hippies wandering through southern Europe discovered this once-isolated fishing village, but the years have not been unkind. Paleochora's setting is as appealing as ever—a rambling collection of whitewashed houses is tucked into the end of a stubby peninsula, with a pebbly beach on one flank, a carpet of soft sand on the other, and a picturesquely ruined 13th-century Venetian fortress at the end. A quiet, out-of-the-way atmosphere still prevails, and some of Greece's most beautiful and unspoiled coastline scenery can be easily explored from Paleochora by ferry boat. A pleasant walk of about 5km (3 miles) into the hills north of Paleochora ends at **Anidri,** where the simple little chapel is beautifully frescoed with images of St. George. From there, you can scramble down the steep hillside for a swim in one of several idyllic coves. ⏱ 3 nights.

Paleochora is the port for a daily ferry that plies the southwest coast, calling at several ports. From Paleochora, you can make day trips to Sougia and to Loutro.

⑥ ★★ Sougia. The ancient Greeks erected a temple at Lissos to the west of Sougia, and the Romans established the port of Elyros, the ruins of which lie just to the east. Today, though, Sougia is a quiet and unassuming place, where it seems unlikely that anything of too much import ever transpired. The attractive little village is home to no more than a few dozen families and is best known for its long, wide beach backed by cave-etched cliffs. Sougia is a popular outing from Hania, 75km (47 miles) to the north and connected by road or with hikers who have made the trek through the Samaria Gorge. The **temple at Lissos,** a 3km (2-mile) walk along a spectacular seaside path, was dedicated to Asklepios, god of

The village square in Sivas, an agricultural community on the Messara Plain.

ealing, and a spring that bubbled forth into a fountain that was reputedly therapeutic. Romans sought cures from the waters as well, and their small settlement, of which a few ruined houses remain, catered to ill legionnaires and colonists who made the sea journey to Lissos from throughout Crete. ⏱ 1 day.

A morning bus will take you to the Xyloskaka entrance to the Samaria Gorge. You will emerge from the gorge at Agia Roumeli, where you can catch the boat back to Paleochora.

⑦ ★★★ kids Samaria Gorge. Although it's tucked away on the remote southwestern coast, the longest gorge in Europe is one of the most traveled places in Crete. Every morning from spring through fall, eager trekkers get off the bus at the head of the gorge on the Omalos Plateau and descend the Xyloskaka, the wooden steps, to begin their 15km (9⅓-mile) walk to the sea at Agia Roumeli. While other gorges on the southern coast offer more solitude, none can match the Samaria for spectacle—the canyon is only 3m (10 ft.) wide at the narrowest passage, the so-called **Iron Gates,** and the sheer walls reach as high as 600m (1,969 ft.). Copses of pine and cedar and a profusion of springtime wildflowers

carpet the canyon floor, where a river courses through a rocky bed, fed by little streams and springs. *Kri-kri*, the shy, endangered Cretan wild goat, can sometimes be sighted on the flanks of the gorge, and eagles and other raptors soar overhead. Samaria has been a national park since 1962, and the only sign of habitation is the now-deserted village of Samaria and a church dedicated to its namesake, St. Maria. You will, of course, be partaking of this natural paradise with hundreds of other enthusiasts, but the experience will be no less memorable. See box, "Hiking the Samaria Gorge." ⏱ 1 day.

Reach Loutro by boat from Paleochora.

⑧ ★★ Loutro. One of the loveliest villages in Crete sits above a perfect semicircle of a bay and is accessible only on foot or by boat. A blessing for travelers in search of a getaway, its remoteness was hardly a hindrance to the Romans, Venetians, and 19th-century Cretan freedom fighters who made use of Loutro's well-protected anchorage. The village's shady taverna terraces and clear waters are its biggest draws, but it's also the starting point for some rewarding hikes. A half-hour coastal walk leads east to **Sweetwater Beach,** named

> *The 15km- (9½-mile) trek down the Samaria Gorge is not a solitary experience, but it's still thrilling.*

for the springs that bubble forth from the rocks. A more strenuous half-day excursion leads from **Marmara Beach,** east of Loutro, into the **Aradena Gorge,** a deep, oleander-scented cleft in the White Mountains. The walk ends at the abandoned village of Aradena, where half-ruined houses surround a sturdy, 14th-century Byzantine chapel. ⏱ 1 day.

After walking from Loutro to Paleochora, head north to Hania, 75km (47 miles), on a well-marked road. Then take the national highway east 30km (19 miles) to Vrisses.

9 ★★ **Vrisses.** This pretty village rests its fame on thick, creamy yogurt, topped with local honey and savored at a cafe table beneath the shade of plane trees alongside a rushing stream. Two of Crete's most beautiful churches are in the countryside just outside of Vrisses. The 11th-century, honey-colored

church at Samonas rests atop a knoll in a green valley, and inside are some well-preserved frescoes of the Virgin and Child. The **Church of the Panayia** in Alikambos is surrounded by orange groves and houses some o the finest fresco cycles in Crete, a vivid telling of the Bible story, from Adam and Eve to the Crucifixion, painted in 1315. ⏱ 1 hr. Churches are usually open daily 8am–5pm.

The drive from Vrisses to Hora Sfakion is 40km (24 miles) on a well-marked road.

10 ★★ **Kare & Imbros gorges.** From Vrisses, a road heads south across the White Mountains to Hora Sfakion, following the fertile Kare Gorge into the rugged landscapes of the Imbros Gorge. The road follows the cliffs atop the gorges, providing some hair-raising views, and you can hike into the narrow canyon from the village of Imbros. On even a short scramble, you can experience the drama of the gorges, flanked by steep cliffs and forested with oak and cypress. Or, you can traverse the 11km (7-mile) length of the gorges, emerging on the south coast at Hora Sfakion after a few hours of fairly easy walking.

11 ★ **Hora Sfakion.** This rather forlorn-looking little fishing village is enlivened by summertime hikers, who emerge here from the Imbros Gorge or pass through as they come and go from the Samaria Gorge on the ferries that ply the south coast. You might take a moment to ponder the fact that the little port was the stage for a massive evacuation of Allied troops after Germans took the island in the Battle of Crete (see p. 670).

Frangokastello is 10 km (6¼ miles) east of Hora Sfakion on a narrow road along this part of the south coast.

12 ★ kids **Frangokastello.** You'll encounter the slightly more distant past east along the coast at this mighty Venetian fortress, erected on the flat coastal plain in 1371 as a defense against pirate raids and the rebellious local populace. The fortress is most famously associated with one of Crete's favorite folk heroes, Ioannis Daskalogiannis. He is largely credited as the father of the movement to free Crete from the Turks, leading an uprising against the island's Ottoman administrators in 1770. Turkish troops suppressed the insurrection

> *Caves above the beach at Matala have sheltered everyone from Roman soldiers to 1960s hippies.*

n fairly short order, and Daskalogiannis gave himself up outside the Frangokastello fortress, saving the lives of most of his 1,300 followers. He was taken to Iraklion and skinned alive, suffering the ordeal in dignified silence. The surrounding landscape has not been altered much in the intervening centuries, and the sandy beach and shallow waters in front of the fortress are especially popular with families. ⏱ 30 min. Admission 2€. Daily 9am–4pm (hours vary).

The drive to Matala is 70km (43 miles), through beautiful mountainous terrain to Spilli and from there south onto the Messara Plain to Matala; follow the signs to Mires and from there to Matala.

⓭ ★★ **Matala.** This bland little beach resort has been popular with visitors for millennia. Legend has it that Zeus, taking the form of a white bull, wooed Europa on the beach at Matala, and that Brutus was among the Romans who encamped in the caves that riddle a seaside bluff. These same caves housed hippies during the 1960s and now present a picturesque backdrop to a fine sandy beach. Matala is a good place to relax for a few days, but the surrounding farm villages on the Messara Plain are even more pleasant—**Pitsidia, Kamilari,** and **Sivas** offer an especially nice taste of rural Crete. **Phaestos** (p. 244, ❹), **Agia Triada** (p. 244, ❺), and **Gortyna** (p. 246) are within easy reach. So is the fine beach at **Kommos,** 3km (2 miles) north of Matala off the road to Phaestos, and **Red Beach,** reached by a 20-minute hike over a headland on the south side of Matala. ⏱ 3 days.

Vori is 10km (6¼ miles) north of Matala off the road to Mires and well marked.

⓮ ★★ **Vori.** This pleasant and unspoiled farming village on the Messara Plain is home to the island's finest collection of folkcraft, the Museum of Cretan Ethnology. Handsome displays provide an intriguing look at farm equipment, basketry, pottery, weavings, and furnishings.

> *More than 7,000 windmills bring water to the Lasithi Plateau, a high haven in the Dikti Mountains.*

🕐 1 hr. Village center. ☎ 28920/91112. www.cretanethnologymuseum.gr. Admission 3€. Daily 10am–6pm.

Head to Iraklion, 70km (43 miles) north on the well-marked road to the north coast. From there, take the national highway east. Outside Chernossisos, follow signs to the road to Lasithi Plateau, 70km (43 miles) past Iraklion.

⓯ ★★★ kids **Lasithi Plateau.** Few experiences on Crete top the sensation of making the final steep, vertiginous ascent over the crest of the Dikti Mountains and getting your first glimpse of the Lasithi Plateau. At your feet, a tidy patchwork of orchards and fields with more than 7,000 windmills spreads out to the encircling hills. A road skirts the rim of the plateau, passing through small villages and the largest town, Tzermiado. Residents of the plateau are famous on Crete for their deft weaving and embroidery, executed in front of the fire on winter evenings, and they ply these wares to the busloads of daytime visitors who arrive from resort towns on the north coast. You can see some especially fine examples of their finger work at the **Cretan Folk Museum** in Agios Giorgios (admission 3€, mid-April to mid-Oct daily 10am–4pm). By midafternoon, the plateau is quiet again, caught up in working the land that has been cultivated since the Minoans. Votive offerings suggest these ancient residents worshiped in the **Psychro Cave,** outside the village of the same name. According to some legends, the cave was the birthplace of Zeus, though the sacred associations of the cavern are lost amid the touts and shills who crowd the entrance (admission 4€, June and Sept daily 8:30am–3pm, July–Aug daily 8am–7pm). A walk along any of the paths that crisscross through the orchards and fields quickly restores a sense of the sheer loveliness of this high haven. 🕐 1 day.

Where to Stay & Dine Off the Beaten Path on Crete

> *Taverna Sigelakis in Sivas.*

★★★ Kronio LASITHI PLATEAU *GREEK*
This cozy establishment is the best restaurant on the plateau. All the dishes, from thick lamb stews to homemade bread and cheese-stuffed pies, are memorable. The proprietors, Vassilis and Christine, are gracious hosts and willing advisors on how to see the best of the plateau. Tzermiado. ☎ 28440/22375. Entrees 5€–10€. No credit cards. Lunch & dinner daily. Closed Nov–Mar.

★★ On the Rocks Hotel PALEOCHORA
Quirky accommodations range from small but bright rooms to huge penthouse suites. All are as comfortable as accommodations get in Paleochora. The bar and terrace are popular, and the beach is steps away. ☎ 28320/41713. 16 units. Doubles 95€ w/breakfast. No credit cards. Closed Nov–Mar.

★★★ Portokali Studios VORI
Lovely and comfortable apartments surround a flowery terrace outside one of the region's most appealing villages. Hostess Gudrun Krasagaki is on hand to see to your needs and help you explore southern Crete. ☎ 28920/91188. http://portokali.messara.de/english.html. 4 units. Doubles 50€. No credit cards.

★ Rea Hotel PALEOCHORA
One of the many comfortable, no-frills hotels in Paleochora, Rea offers some nice amenities, including balconies, sea views, and a shady little garden. Near the beach. ☎ 28230/41307. 14 units. Doubles 60€. No credit cards. Closed Nov–Mar.

★★ Shivas Village Hotel SIVAS
The beautifully furnished rooms and suites, all with kitchenettes, and such amenities as a pool, gym, and tennis court are a bit out of keeping with the rustic village surroundings, but they make a comfortable base for your explorations. ☎ 28920/42750. www.shivas.com. 24 units. Doubles 70€ w/ breakfast. AE, DC, MC, V. Closed Nov–Apr.

★★★ Taverna and Studios Sigelakis SIVAS
GREEK Excellent meals, accompanied by friendly service and complimentary homemade *raki,* are served on the terrace or in a stone-walled dining room. Down the road, attractive and comfortable studios, with kitchens, living and sleeping areas, and terraces, are surrounded by gardens and olive groves. 6km (3½ miles) northeast of Matala. ☎ 28920/42748. www.sigelakis-studios.gr. 8 units. Doubles 50€. Dinner daily. Entrees 6€–10€. MC, V.

Iraklion

Many visitors linger in Crete's busy capital, the fifth largest city in Greece, just long enough to visit the remarkable remnants of the Minoan civilization in the Archaeological Museum and the outlying Palace of Knossos. Give the city a little time, however, and you'll discover a large Old Quarter that's enclosed within massive walls and filled with animated streets and squares and remnants of the city's Venetian and Turkish past.

> *The old Venetian fountain, Ta Liontaria, is the hub of busy Iraklion.*

START Ta Liontaria, city center, Iraklion. Iraklion is the first stop for many visitors to Crete, with an international airport and port for ferries and cruise ships. It's also off the national highway in the middle of the north coast, making it easy to reach the rest of the island by car. Buses connect Iraklion with towns across Crete; see p. 295. **TRIP LENGTH** 2 days.

1 ★★ **Ta Liontaria.** The busy hub of Iraklion is officially listed as **Plateia Eleftheriou Venizelou,** for the Crete-born revolutionary and ever-popular prime minister (from 1910 to 1920 and again from 1928 to 1932), often considered the father of modern Greece. Any

Irakliot, however, refers to the square as Ta Liontaria (the Lions), in honor of the Venetian fountain that graces one side. The *plateia* has been the center of island life since the 9th century, when the Arab rulers of the island staged a large slave market here; its central importance then endured many centuries of rule by the Byzantines, the Venetians, and the Turks. Today a spot at one of the square's many cafe tables affords the chance to admire some of Iraklion's most important landmarks. The famous fountain is adorned with four leonine symbols of the Venetian Republic, and the water that once streamed from their

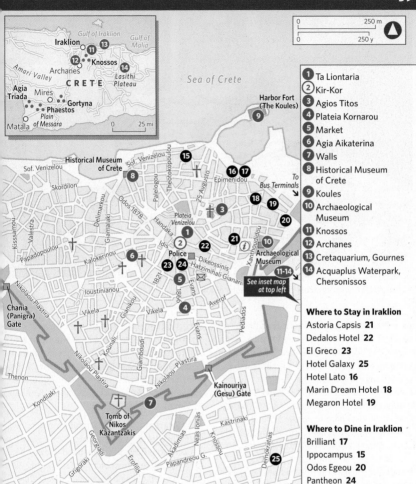

①	Ta Liontaria
②	Kir-Kor
③	Agios Titos
④	Plateia Kornarou
⑤	Market
⑥	Agia Aikaterina
⑦	Walls
⑧	Historical Museum of Crete
⑨	Koules
⑩	Archaeological Museum
⑪	Knossos
⑫	Archanes
⑬	Cretaquarium, Gournes
⑭	Acquaplus Waterpark, Chersonissos

Where to Stay in Iraklion

Astoria Capsis 21
Dedalos Hotel 22
El Greco 23
Hotel Galaxy 25
Hotel Lato 16
Marin Dream Hotel 18
Megaron Hotel 19

Where to Dine in Iraklion

Brilliant 17
Ippocampus 15
Odos Egeou 20
Pantheon 24

mouths filled a basin that is ornately carved with mythological figures. Handsome 13th-century **Agios Marcos Church** is named for the patron saint of Venice and houses art exhibitions. The adjacent 17th-century **Loggia**—a replica of architect Andrea Palladio's elegant basilica in Vincenza—was the seat of Venice's island government and is now Iraklion's city hall. ⏱15 min.

② 🍽 **Kir-Kor.** At Iraklion's famous *bougatsa* shop, you can enjoy flaky pastry filled with sweet cream custard or soft cheese while watching the comings and goings around the Lions Fountain. Eleftheriou Venizelou. $

③ ★ **Agios Titos.** This handsome church, just east of the Loggia, honors Crete's favorite saint, Titus. Titus appears in scripture alongside Paul in Ephesus, Corinth, and Rome; in the 1st century A.D., Paul commissioned him to convert Crete to Christianity and ordained him Bishop of Gortyna, then the Roman capital (p. 246). Founded in the 10th century, this church was destroyed in an earthquake in 1856 and rebuilt over the next few years as a mosque (Crete was then Turkish). The minaret was removed in the 1920s when the structure was rededicated as a church. A silver vault houses one of the island's most sacred artifacts, the skull of Titus, who died in A.D. 107 at the age of 95. ⏱15 min. 25 Avgostos. Daily 8am–7pm.

> *An outdoor market stretches through the center of town.*

④ ★ Plateia Kornarou. This busy square south of Ta Liontaria is named for Vitsentzos Kornaros (1553–1617), a Cretan who is widely acclaimed as one of Greece's greatest poets. Even though you may not be familiar with his epic work, *Erotokritos*—a 10,000-verse romance of love, honor, friendship, and courage that is not dissimilar to *Romeo and Juliet*—you may well encounter segments of the poem in your Cretan travels: The verses are often set to folk music and sung at performances of traditional music. A statue honors the work's eponymous hero, who is on horseback bidding farewell to his beloved, Aretousa. Many residents still refer to the square as Falte Tzami,

a corruption of the Turkish Valide Camil, or Queen Mother. This was the name of a church-turned-mosque that once dominated the square and was demolished in the 1960s. This history is still reflected in the square's two fountains, one Turkish and one Venetian. ⏱ 15 min.

⑤ ★ Market. One long outdoor market stretches from Ta Liontaria to Plateia Kornarou, Odos 1866. Stalls are piled high with fresh produce grown on the island, along with thick Cretan olive oil and *raki,* the fiery digestive for which every Cretan household has a special recipe. ⏱ 30 min.

⑥ ★ Agia Aikaterina. This small 15th-century church to the east of Eleftheriou Venizelou and Kornarou squares, named for St. Katherine, houses a museum of icons, most by Cretan artists. Under the Venetians, Crete became an important center of religious art, and many islanders were sent to Venice to perfect their craft (p. 291). The most famous Cretan artist of all, Domenikos Theotocopoulos, best known as El Greco, allegedly studied at the church's monastery school and soon became known for his skillful blending of Byzantine and Western traditions. He left the island forever in 1570 and perfected his distinctive expressionist style in Rome, Venice, and, finally, Toledo, Spain, where

Iraklion Essentials

You can easily navigate the center of Iraklion on foot, and outlying Knossos is served by frequent city bus service. Parking and driving in the center are difficult, so wait to pick up a rental car until you are ready to leave town to tour the rest of the island. The tourist information office, opposite the Archaeological Museum at 1 Xanthoudidou Street (☎ 28102/28225; open Mon–Fri 8am–2:30pm), is a good source for brochures and other material on Minoan sites across the island.

> *Slow and easy is the best pace for a stroll in the colorful city center.*

he died in 1614. Despite the painter's long exile from his native land and his widespread acclaim as El Greco, he continued to sign his works with the Greek letters of his given name; his only two works in Crete hang in the Historical Museum (p. 261, **8**). ⏱ 45 min. Kyrillou Loukareos. Admission 5€. Mon–Sat 10am–1pm; Tues, Thu–Fri, also 4–6pm.

7 ★★ kids **Walls.** The mighty walls that still surround much of old Iraklion are a sturdy remnant of the past amid the untidy sprawl of the modern city. Venetians began building the walls soon after they arrived in the 13th century, eventually erecting a circuit 5km (3 miles) long and up to 40m (131 ft.) thick atop a network of defensive ditches that the city's Saracen and Byzantine inhabitants dug. In the middle of the 17th century the Venetian fortifications almost thwarted the vast Ottoman armies—in the longest siege in European history, Iraklion held out for 21 years after the Ottomans overran the rest of the island, finally surrendering in 1669. The Turks allegedly lost 100,000 men, the Venetians 30,000. When the Venetians finally agreed to lay down their arms, they were allowed to leave the city in ships laden with their belongings and important documents. Two elegant gates still punctuate the walls, the **Hania Gate** (also known as the Pantocrator Gate or Panigra Gate) in the west and the **Kainouryia Gate** (Gate of Gesu) in the southeast. At seven points, the walls thicken into arrowhead-shaped defenses known as bastions. The southernmost of these, **Martinengo Bastion,** is the final resting place of Nikos Kazantzakis (1883–1957), the Cretan author of *Zorba the Greek* and other modern classics who was born and died in Iraklion and lies beneath a simple stone inscribed with his own words: "I expect nothing, I fear nothing, I am free." Irakliots come to pay tribute and take in the airy views across the straggling outskirts to the mountainous interior of the island, dominated by the craggy peak of Mount Iouktas, attributed in legend to be the head of Zeus. ⏱ 1 hr. Open sunrise–sunset.

8 ★★ **Historical Museum of Crete.** Fascinating artifacts from Crete's long and colorful past fill the rooms of this neoclassical mansion near the harbor. *The Baptism of Christ* and *View of Mount Sinai and the Monastery of St. Catherine,* by Crete-born artist Domenikos Theotocopoulos (El Greco), the only works by the artist in Crete, take their place among ceramics, sculpture, icons, and artifacts from the island's Roman, Byzantine, Venetian, and Ottoman past. Several rooms document the bloody revolutions against Turkish rule in the 18th and 19th centuries and the very brief period when Crete was an independent state in the first years of the 20th century. Especially evocative are the re-creations of the library and study of novelist Nikos Kazantzakis and a simple farmhouse interior still typical of the island today. ⏲ 2 hr. 27 Sofokli Venizelou. ☎ 28102/83219. www. historical-museum.gr.

⑨ ★★ Kids Koules. The Venetians put up this mighty, wave-lapped fortress between 1523 and 1540 to protect the city from attack by sea and assure safe harbor for the fleets that constantly made the 3-week journey between Crete and Venice. Within the thick walls topped by rambling ramparts are workshops, warehouses, and vaulted *arsenali* where ships were repaired and outfitted, as well as officers' quarters and a prison. An inscription over the main entrance announces that the fortress stands on the remains of a fort erected by the Genoese in 1303, and in your wanderings you will come upon three plaques bearing the telltale symbol of the Venetian republic, a lion. The view from the ramparts takes in a good swath of coast, the brooding mountains behind, and the inner and outer harbors, jammed today with pleasure craft, fishing boats, and the ferries coming and going from the mainland and islands. ⏲ 30 min. Old Harbor. ☎ 2810/246211. Admission 1.50€. July–Oct daily 8am–9:30pm, Nov–June daily 9am–3pm.

⑩ ★★★ Archaeological Museum. The Minoans, whose civilization thrived on Crete some 4,000 years ago, come spectacularly to life in the world's most extensive collection of the artifacts they left behind. See p. 240, **①**.

⑪ ★★★ Knossos. One of the world's most remarkable archaeological treasures—controversially reconstructed in part—spreads across a low hill just east of Iraklion and evokes Minoan Crete. See p. 241, **②**.

If you're traveling by car, follow the road to Knossos and continue another 3km (2 miles) to the Archanes turnoff; follow the road 5km (3 miles) to the village. Buses to Archanes run about every 30 minutes from Iraklion's central station.

⑫ ★ Archanes. Cretans barely recognize this village near Iraklion in the heart of the island's grape-growing region after a recent makeover with funds from the European Union. Fresh paint, newly laid cobblestones, and blooming flower boxes have lent new life to the steep streets of neoclassical houses. One pleasure, enjoying a glass of local wine in the beautiful *plateia,* remains the same. ⏲ 1 hr.

> *Venetians built Iraklion's ramparts atop defenses laid by the Saracens and Byzantines before them.*

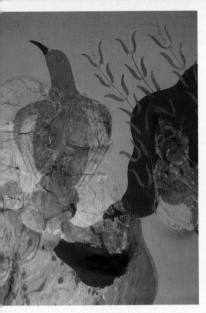

▶ *Iraklion's Archaeological Museum is the world's foremost treasure trove of the Minoan civilization.*

The aquarium is in Gournes, 16km (10 miles) east of Iraklion on the national highway. Regular bus service runs directly to the aquarium from Iraklion's central station.

⓭ ★★ kids Cretaquarium, Gournes. Jellyfish, sharks, and 2,500 species of fish and other marine life that thrive in the Mediterranean swim through beautiful re-creations of Crete's offshore seascapes. Submersible periscopes and other high-tech gizmos make a walk past the 60 enormous tanks, designed by the Hellenic Center for Marine Research, fun as well as enlightening. ⏱ 2 hr. Outside Gournes. ☎ 28103/37788. www.cretaquarium.gr. Admission 8€ adults; 6€ seniors, children 17 and under, and students. June–Sept 9am–9pm, Oct–May 9am–7pm.

The water park is about 25km (15 miles) east of Iraklion outside Chersonissos, to the south; follow the national highway to Chersonissos and follow signs. Frequent bus service runs from Iraklion's central station to Chersonissos, where you can transfer to a local bus to the water park.

> *Pleasure crafts bob in a protected harbor that provided safe anchorage for Venetian galleys.*

⓮ ★ kids Acquaplus Waterpark, Chersonissos. You might not see why the slides, tunnels, and pools of this 23-hectare (57-acre) water park outside the hideously overbuilt resort town of Chersonissos are any more appealing than Crete's lovely seas, but your young traveling companions certainly will. At times it seems as if every youngster in Greece has converged on this popular place, so if you're in the mood for peace and quiet, go elsewhere. ⏱ 4 hr. About 25km (15 miles) east of Iraklion, outside Chersonissos. ☎ 28970/24950. www.acquaplus.gr. 20€ adults, 12€ children 5 and older, children under 5 free. May to mid-Oct 9am–sunset.

Where to Stay in Iraklion

> *The Megaron Hotel.*

★★ Astoria Capsis CITY CENTER
This hotel's location, across animated Plateia Eleftherias from the Archaeological Museum, is one great asset. The rooftop swimming pool is another, especially for summer guests who spent the day sightseeing. Other perks are the soothingly modern rooms, all with balconies, and a 24-hour bar/coffee shop off the lobby. Plateia Eleftherias. ☎ 28103/43080. www.capsishotels,gr. 130 units. Doubles 120€–140€ w/breakfast. AE, MC, V.

★ Dedalos Hotel CITY CENTER
A convenient location at a low price makes this aging and very modest old standby a perennial favorite among the budget-conscious. Those looking for even a hint of luxury should look elsewhere; here the amenities don't extend much beyond a view over the rooftops to the sea and the ease of being in the heart of the Old Quarter. 15 Daidalou. ☎ 28102/44812. 58 units. Doubles 45€–55€. MC, V.

★★ El Greco CITY CENTER
This comfortable old inn is not luxurious, but the location, just steps from Ta Liontaria, can be beat, nor can the price. Rooms are a bit outdated but large; those overlooking the interior garden are blessedly quiet. 4 Odos 1821. ☎ 28102/81071. www.elgrecohotel.gr. 90 units. Doubles 75€–85€ w/breakfast. MC, V.

★★ Hotel Galaxy CITY CENTER
A sleek modern style prevails at one of the city's largest hotels. The best rooms have sea-facing balconies, and amenities include a swimming pool and a pastry shop that's a popular gathering spot. 75 Leoforos Dimokratias. ☎ 28102/38812. www.galaxy-hotel.com. 137 units. Doubles 125€–130€ w/breakfast. AE, MC, V.

★★★ Hotel Lato CITY CENTER
Everything about this excellent small hotel seems geared to soothe—from the pleasing decor to the Jacuzzi and steam room. A perch above the Venetian Harbor ensures wonderful sea views from most rooms and the roof terrace, making it an even better value. 15 Epimenidou. ☎ 28102/28103. www.lato.gr. 58 units. Doubles 85€–100€ w/breakfast. MC, V.

★★ Marin Dream Hotel CITY CENTER
One of this comfortably small hotel's best assets is its extremely helpful staff. Its location is another, within easy reach of the port, bus station, Archaeological Museum, and other city sights. Request one of the top-floor rooms that overlook the harbor. 12 Doukos Mpofor. ☎ 28103/00018. www.marinhotel.gr. 50 units. Doubles 75€–85€ w/breakfast. MC, V.

★★★ Megaron Hotel CITY CENTER
An abandoned office building high above the harbor has been revamped as a stylish and luxurious getaway, with extremely handsome guest rooms and public spaces. A rooftop terrace and swimming pool are among the many indulgences on offer. 9 Beaufort. ☎ 28103/05300. www.gdmmegaron.gr. 46 units. Doubles 150€–190€ w/breakfast. AE, MC, V.

Where to Dine in Iraklion

★★ **Brilliant** CITY CENTER *GREEK*
The excellent Lato Hotel provides Iraklion's most chic dining experience, in a sleek room accented in shiny black and red. Fresh Cretan ingredients appear in inventively delicious creations, accompanied by wines from the island. 15 Epimenidou. ☎ 28103/34959. Entrees 20€-25€. AE, DC, MC, V. Dinner Wed-Sat.

★★★ **Ippocampus** SEAFRONT *GREEK*
You will dine in the Greek fashion at this deservedly popular *mezederia,* where you will assemble a memorable meal from a wide choice of meze, such as zucchini fritters, delicately fried baby squid, and such perennial staples as tzatziki and other spreads. 3 Mitsotaki. ☎ 28102/82081. Entrees 3€-5€. No credit cards. Lunch & dinner Mon-Fri.

★★ **Odos Egeou** VENETIAN HARBOR *SEAFOOD*
Iraklion's best choice for fresh fish also offers one of the city's most pleasant dining experiences, along with wonderful views across the harbor and excellent service. Egeou and Spinaki. ☎ 28102/88266. Entrees 10€-25€. MC, V. Lunch & dinner daily.

★ **Pantheon** CITY CENTER *GREEK*
Diners are assured an authentic Cretan dining experience at this local favorite, tucked away in the covered market (also unappetizingly known as Dirty Alley). The offerings—spit-roasted lamb is usually available—are as simple as the surroundings and invariably delicious. 2 Theodosaki. ☎ 28102/41652. Entrees 7€-9€. No credit cards. Lunch & dinner Mon-Sat.

Cafe Society

Dozens of cafes line the narrow streets between Plateia Eleftheria and Plateia Venizelou. Many are on Korai, a narrow passage just south of Dedalou, the main passageway through the center; these are perfect if you enjoy shouting to be heard above pumping dance music and the cacophonous clatter of what must be the entire student body of the Iraklion-based University of Crete. Some of the choicest perches are those surrounding the Lions' Fountain on Plateia Venizelou, and none provide a better view than the **Four Lions Roof-Garden Cafe** (☎ 28102/22333). Down toward the seafront, **Cafe Veneto,** Epimenidou (☎ 28102/23686), affords wonderful views of the harbor and the Venetian fortress through its tall windows and from the terrace.

Rethymnon

Old Rethymnon, crowded onto a peninsula, is an inviting maze of Venetian and Turkish houses, mosques, and a massive seaside fortress, all looking as they have for centuries. Narrow lanes, shady squares, and a long sandy beach invite lingering, and magnificent mountain and valley scenery, monasteries, and other distinctly Cretan landmarks are within easy reach.

> *The Venetian Harbor, once a way station on sea routes between Iraklion and Hania, is a popular spot for waterside dining.*

START Plateia Plastira, at the edge of Old Town, Rethymnon. Rethymnon is off the national highway that skirts the north coast, making it easy to reach the city by car or bus from Iraklion, 80km (50 miles) east, and Hania, 70km (44 miles) west. You will want to rent a car to visit some of the sights around Rethymnon. **TRIP LENGTH 3 days.**

❶ ★★★ Old Town. The maze of narrow lanes and squares that crisscross a narrow peninsula jutting into the Sea of Crete is enticing and exotic, a warren of Venetian palaces, wooden Ottoman houses, mosques, and fountains. Rethymnon was inhabited by Minoans and Mycenaeans and later by ancient Greeks, Romans, and Byzantines. The historic city that remains today is largely the creation of the Venetians and Turks, who occupied Rethymnon for almost 800 years, until the late 19th century. For Venetians, the city was an important way station on the sea route between Iraklion and Hania, and they left many landmarks. The Turks built fewer monuments, though wooden balconies, surrounded by lattice work to ensure the privacy of Muslim women, project from many of the old houses. Rising high above the tile roofs is the minaret of the Mosque of the Nerantzes, converted from a former monastery and church when the Turks

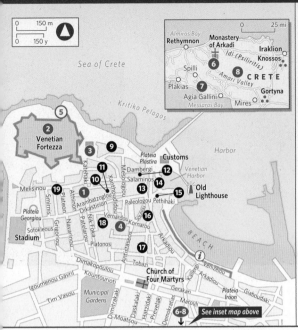

1 Old Town
2 Fortezza
3 Archaeological Museum
4 Historical and Folk Art Museum
5 Thalassographia
6 Arkadi Monastery
7 Moni Preveli
8 Amari Valley

Where to Stay in Rethymnon

Avli Lounge Apartments 10
Fortezza Hotel 19
Hotel Ideon 9
Hotel Leo 16
Palazzino di Corina 12
Vetera Suites 17

Where to Dine in Rethymnon

Avli 11
Cavo D'Oro 14
Kyria Maria 13
Myrogdies 18
Othonos 15

.ook Rethymnon in 1646. (Nerantzes now
houses a school and music school, open only
when concérts are performed; the minaret
can be climbed Mon–Fri 11am–7:30pm and
Sat 11am–3pm, closed in Aug.) Two Venetian
remnants are nearby: the Rimondi Fountain,
where streams of water gush from the mouths
of three lions, symbols of the republic, and the
oggia, once the meeting house of Venetian

Rethymnon Essentials

Free parking is available along the seaside
road that skirts the Fortezza. A lot off Plateia Plastira, next to the Old Harbor, charges about 2€ an hour and is free for the first
half-hour, handy for dropping off baggage
at Old Town hotels. Buses connect Rethymnon with Iraklion and Hania about every
half-hour throughout the day, and the fare
is about 14€ from each. The bus station is
to the west of the Old Town near the sea at
Akti Kefaloyianithon (☎ 28310/22212).
You'll find the tourist office on waterfront
Venizelou, to the east of the Old Town
(☎ 28310/29148; open in summer Mon–Fri
8am–3pm, often later).

> Venetian and Ottoman houses line the narrow
lanes of the Old Town.

> *A mighty seaside fortress kept pirates at bay but proved defenseless against the invading Turkish navy in 1664.*

nobility. The Venetian Harbor, at the eastern edge of the Old Town, is surrounded by a high breakwater and overlooked by a 13th-century lighthouse. Rethymnon never became a major port for Venice, in part because this claustrophobically small harbor was not well suited to large Venetian galleys. Today, a jumble of cafe tables crowd the quayside and a fleet of colorful fishing boats are moored chockablock against one another. ⏱ 4 hr.

❷ ★★ **Fortezza.** Rethymnon's most prominent landmark rises next to the sea on a high promontory at the northern end of the Old Town. Ancient Greeks built a Temple of Artemis and a Sanctuary of Artemis on the hill,

Hit the Beach

To the east of the Old Town, Rethymnon stretches along several miles of sandy beach. The hotels and apartments of recent vintage that now line the waterfront are not terribly attractive, but the sand and water are clean and welcoming. Much of the beach is taken up by concessionaires, from whom you can rent two beach lounges and an umbrella for about 12€ a day. You can also plop yourself down on the sand for free.

and the Venetians erected a small fortress that proved useless in defending the city against pirates who attacked with 40 galleys in 1571. The Venetians rebuilt the fortress with a labor force of more than 100,000 Cretans conscripted for the task, but the thick walls, bastions, and embrasures were ineffective in stopping the Turks who overran Rethymnon in 1646. The vast rock-strewn space is now overgrown and barren. Inside the massive battlements are two simple churches, a mosque, and several former barracks that served in later years as the town brothels. Every summer, the forlorn atmosphere is enlivened during the musical and theatrical performances of the **Rethymnon Renaissance Festival** (contact the tourist office, p. 267, for details). ⏱ 1 hr. Above the sea at the edge of Old Town. Admission 3€. Daily 8:30am–7pm.

❸ ★ **Archaeological Museum.** Built by the Turks next to the Fortezza gate as part of the town defenses, and later used as a prison, this sturdy stone pentagon now houses a smattering of ancient artifacts unearthed in caves and other ancient sites around Rethymnon. Here you will not come across the Minoan frescoes and jewels that bedazzle visitors to the Archaeological Museum in Iraklion, but the prehistoric stone tools, igurines, Roman oil lamps, and other finds warrant a passing glance, if only as intriguing reminders that Crete has been inhabited or millennia. ⏲ 45 min. Next to main gate of Fortezza. ☎ 28310/29975. Admission 2€. Daily 8:30am–3pm.

④ ★★ Historical and Folk Art Museum. A restored Venetian mansion is the setting for beautiful basketry and hand-woven textiles, along with farm implements, traditional costumes, and old photographs that pay homage to Cretan traditions. These well-displayed collections are not merely a repository of the past. Many items—from lyres and other musical instruments to embroidery fashioned from techniques that date back to the Byzantines—are still a widespread part of island life. ⏲ 45 min. 30 Vernardou. ☎ 28310/23398. Admission 3€. Mon–Fri 10am–2pm.

⑤ 🦑 Thalassographia. The apt name of this place, clinging to the seaward flanks of the fort, means "seascape." The terrace is a good place to stop for a drink, snack, and fabulous view. 33 Kefalogianhidou. ☎ 28310/52569. $

Arkadi is 25km (15 miles) southeast of Rethymnon. Take the national highway east to Maroulas, then the road to Arkadi. You can also reach the monastery by regular bus service from Rethymnon.

⑥ ★★★ kids Arkadi Monastery. The ornate Italianate-Renaissance facade of this monastery, built on a high plateau under Venetian rule in 1587, rises out of pretty pastureland in a high valley at the base of Mount Ida. As serene as the setting is, Arkadi was the seat of Cretan revolutionary fervor, acclaimed for the events of November 8, 1866. By that time, rebellious zeal against the occupying Turks was at fever pitch across Crete. Arkadi and many other monasteries across the island supported the rebels, and hundreds of men, women, and children took refuge there. A Turkish force of some 15,000 men besieged the monastery, but the Cretans refused to surrender. Just as the Turks broke through the gate and swarmed the compound, the abbot ordered that the gunpowder store be ignited. The explosion killed hundreds of Cretans and Turks, and the event has become synonymous with Crete's

> *Crete's revolutionary heroism against the Turks at Arkadi Monastery is celebrated every November 8.*

long struggle for independence. November 8 is celebrated as a holiday in Crete, and Arkadi is a place of pilgrimage for many Cretans. ⏲ 3 hr. Admission 2€. Daily 8am–8pm.

Preveli is 40km (25 miles) south of Rethymnon. Take the road south into the mountains to the town of Spilli. About 5km (3 miles) past town, a turnoff on the right leads onto the well-marked narrow road that cuts through magnificent gorges and coastal mountains to the remote monastery.

⑦ ★★★ kids Moni Preveli. One of Crete's most beautiful and beloved monasteries is perched

> *Monks at Moni Preveli hid Allied soldiers trapped on Crete by German forces during World War II.*

in isolation high above the south coast, due south of Rethymnon. The Preveli monastic community is more than a thousand years old and long enjoyed the direct patronage of the Patriarch of Constantinople. The monastery's widespread fame, though, arises from the role it played in 19th- and 20th-century resistance movements—against the Turks, as early as 1821, when the abbot organized and outfitted the first rebels to take up arms against the Ottoman occupiers, and then against the Germans who invaded the island in 1941. During those long World War II years, the monastery became a rallying point for the Allies, sheltering British, Australian, and New Zealand soldiers left behind when Germans occupied the island in the aftermath of the Battle of Crete. Many of these men were saved by the monks and the residents of neighboring villages, who hid them until they could be picked up by submarine from the beach below. A memorial on the hillside just outside the monastery gates commemorates the Allied soldiers, Cretan resistance fighters, and others who lost their lives in the war. Today the peaceful monastery terraces look across olive-studded hillsides to the Libyan Sea. **Palm Beach,** reached by a steep path from the monastery grounds, is one of the most beautiful stretches of sand on Crete, enclosed within rocky cliffs and shaded by palms that grow along the banks of the Potamas River as it flows

into the sea. ⏱ 30 min., longer with a stop on the beach. Monastery: Admission 2€. Daily 9am–7pm

From Rethymnon, take the beach road east 5km (3 miles) to Platanias. Drive south to Apostoli, then to Thronos, with its beautiful view of the valley.

SITE GUIDE PAGE 271

8 ★★★ **Amari Valley.** It is easy to get a taste for rural Crete and some of the island's most beautiful scenery in this highland valley just to the south of Rethymnon. As you travel the narrow roads, you'll pass through lovely small villages, come upon Byzantine churches, and be surrounded by rugged peaks, including Mount Ida, where Zeus was allegedly raised in the Idaian Cave. Rhea, Zeus's mother, hid him in the cave out of harm's way from Kronos, his father. Kronos had already eaten five of his offspring—Hades, Poseidon, Hera, Hestia, and Demeter—in an effort to outwit a prophecy that one of his sons would rob him of power. Zeus later gave Kronos an emetic that caused him to regurgitate the five siblings, and in turn, they appointed their brother the god of gods. Even without such an important legend to its credit, the Amari Valley would cast a spell on you with its vineyard- and orchard-covered mountain slopes, lovely little villages, and the omnipresence of tinkling goat bells. ⏱ At least 4 hr.

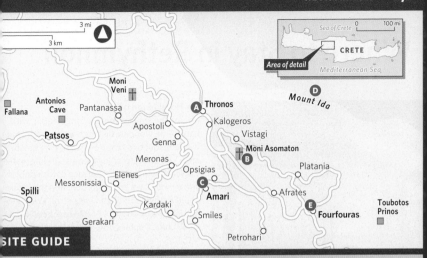

SITE GUIDE

❽ Amari Valley

The village of Ⓐ **Thronos** surrounds a little church decorated with 14th-century frescoes and, on the exterior, a mosaic from a 4th-century Byzantine church that originally stood on the spot. A path from the village center leads to Sivrita, an early Greek settlement that is now being excavated; rough and unpolished, the site gives you the sense that you're stumbling upon an ancient town in its original state. Ⓑ **Moni Asomaton** is about 5km (3 miles) south. It was founded in the 10th century, but its present building dates from the Venetian period. Walled and fortified, it's a remnant of the fierce resistance the monastery once put up to Turkish occupation; many objects from the 15th-century church are in the Historical Museum of Crete in Iraklion (p. 261, ❽). Ⓒ In **Amari,** about 2km (1¼ mile) west, a Venetian clock tower looms over the main square, and the Church of Agia Anna is decorated with some of the oldest church frescoes in Crete, from 1225. Ⓓ **Mount Ida,** at more than 2,600m (8,530 ft.) the tallest mountain on Crete, looms just across the valley. (The mountain is also called Psiloritis, which means "highest" in Greek.) The splendid sight may draw you to Ⓔ **Fourfouras,** perched on the flanks of the mountain amid beautiful alpine scenery. From Fourfouras, serious hikers can begin the ascent to the summit, a strenuous climb that takes about 8 hours. Your own vehicle or a hired taxi is a must for this drive, unless of course you arrange a tour through a travel agency. We recommend independent exploration, but you'll need a good map of Crete. You'll find tavernas and cafes in some of the villages; you won't find many English speakers.

Where to Stay in Rethymnon

> The Palazzino di Corina.

★★★ Avli Lounge Apartments OLD TOWN
One of Crete's most renowned restaurants (p. 273) offers suite-sized accommodations that also generate excited raves. Decor is gorgeous and full of flair, rooms are enormous, and such amenities as soaking tubs and a rooftop terrace and whirlpool add a final flourish. 22 Xanthoudidou. ☎ 28310/58250. www.avli.gr. 8 units. Doubles 120€–150€ w/breakfast. AE, MC, V.

★★ Fortezza Hotel OLD TOWN
Many visitors to Rethymnon swear by this comfortable and convenient choice in a quiet part of the Old Quarter. Rooms are fairly standard, but a pool sparkles in the courtyard, ample parking is nearby, and the staff is most helpful. 10 Melisinou. ☎ 28310/55551. www.fortezza.gr. 52 units. Doubles 75€–90€ w/breakfast. AE, MC, V.

★★ Hotel Ideon OLD TOWN
Rooms are conventionally comfortable, with handsome wood furnishings, and most come with a distinctive feature—sea-facing balconies. You can also enjoy these sparkling water views from the popular terrace cafe; a pool is surrounded by a shady garden, and the sights of old Rethymnon are an easy stroll away. Plateia Plastira. ☎ 28310/28667. www.hotelideon.gr. 52 units. Doubles 85€–95€ w/breakfast. AE, MC, V.

★★★ Hotel Leo OLD TOWN
A former home from 1450 is now a character-filled and intimate inn on a quiet side street. Stone walls, beamed ceilings, and a handsome blend of antiques and contemporary furnishings provide comfort and style. Amenities include a pleasant bar and sidewalk cafe, where an excellent breakfast is served. Vafe and Arkadiou. ☎ 28310/26197. www.leohotel.gr. 8 units. Doubles 80€–100€ w/breakfast. AE, MC, V.

★★★ Palazzino di Corina OLD TOWN
Several of Rethymnon's old Venetian palaces have been converted to hotels, and this one, tucked away on a quiet back street near the seafront, is among the best. Rooms vary in size, and all are comfortable and attractive. A lovely courtyard with a small pool are among the many luxuries. 7-9 Dambergi. ☎ 28310/21205. www.corina.gr. 21 units. Doubles 120€–150€ w/breakfast. AE, MC, V.

★★★ Vetera Suites OLD TOWN
No end of care has gone into creating these distinctive lodgings in a centuries-old Venetian/Turkish house, where much of the old wood- and stonework remains. Modern conveniences, such as bathrooms and kitchenettes, are tucked into alcoves, and sleeping lofts are nestled beneath high ceilings. 39 Kastrinogiannaki. ☎ 28310/23844. www.vetera.gr. 4 units. Doubles 100€–150€. MC, V.

Where to Dine in Rethymnon

★★★ Avli OLD TOWN GREEK

This veritable temple to Cretan cuisine introduces you to the freshest island ingredients—fish and lamb, of course, appear in many different guises, as do mountain greens and other fresh vegetables, all served in a delightful garden and arched dining room. Avli also operates an enoteca that offers a wide choice of serious Greek wines and a shop selling local foodstuffs, along with an excellent hotel (p. 272). 22 Xanthoudidou. ☎ 28310/28310. Entrees 15€–30€. AE, DC, MC, V. Lunch & dinner daily.

★★ Cavo D'Oro VENETIAN HARBOR SEAFOOD

The best of the many restaurants crowded alongside Rethymnon's miniscule harbor upholds its long tradition of serving the freshest fish and other seafood specialties. Patrons dine on a waterside terrace or in a paneled medieval cavern once used for storage. 42 Nearchou. ☎ 28310/24446. Entrees 10€–20€. MC, V. Lunch & dinner daily.

★ Kyria Maria OLD TOWN GREEK

Excellent, plain cooking and friendly service are the hallmarks of this old favorite, where tables are set along a narrow lane beneath a trailing grape vine. Even a simple salad is a treat, as are the array of generously sized appetizers. Moshovitou. ☎ 28310/29078. Entrees 5€–10€. MC, V. Lunch & dinner daily.

> Avli puts innovative twists on the freshest Cretan ingredients.

★★ Myrogdies OLD TOWN GREEK

A beautiful walled garden, shaded by fruit trees, and a pleasant white room are the settings for a huge selection of deftly prepared meze, perfect for a casual meal. 32 Vernadou. ☎ 69726/95170. Entrees 5€–10€. MC, V. Lunch & dinner daily.

★★ Othonos OLD TOWN GREEK

It would be easy to walk by what looks like another Old Town tourist trap, but looks can be deceiving. Locals pour in for the excellent lamb and other traditional dishes, known for the freshest ingredients. 27 Plateia Pethihaki. ☎ 28310/55500. Entrees 5€–15€. MC, V. Lunch & dinner daily.

Down by the Sea . . .

Rethymnon residents like to relax next to the sea in Koumbes, a little enclave just west of Old Town; on foot or in a car, follow the seaside road west past the Venetian fortress. A string of tavernas line the shore, offering drinks, coffee, and seafood meals. Among the most popular are **Tabakario,** 93 Stamathioudaki (☎ 28310/29276), and **Maistros,** 7 Akrotiriou (☎ 28310/25492). The seaside terraces at both sit just above the surf crashing onto the rocks below.

Hania

One of the most beautiful cities in Greece has been settled for nearly 4,000 years, and it has plenty of evidence to demonstrate the number of times power changed hands here. Much of today's city is Venetian and Turkish; minarets rise above tile roofs and bell towers, life still centers around a remarkable harbor built to foster Venice's power here in the southern Mediterranean, and Byzantine monasteries and Roman ruins litter the surrounding countryside.

> Hania's harbor was fortified by the Venetians in the 14th century.

START Hania Market, at the edge of the Old Town surrounding the Venetian Harbor. Hania is off the national highway that skirts the north coast, making it easy to reach the city by car or bus from Rethymnon, 80km (50 miles) east, and Iraklion, 150km (93 miles) west. TRIP LENGTH 3 days.

❶ ★ **Market.** Hania's handsome, cross-shaped covered market opened in 1913 as part of the celebrations surrounding the island's unification with Greece. The dozens of stalls are enticingly packed with typically Cretan products—olive oil, *raki,* honey, wild herbs and teas, *gravouria* and other mountain cheeses. Several small cafes serve spinach pie and other snacks. Just outside the west entrance is an outdoor extension of the market along Odos Skirdlof, where dozens of jampacked little shops sell Cretan leather goods. ⏱ 30 min. Mon–Sat 8am–1:30pm; Tues, Thu, Fri also 5–8pm.

② 🍴 **Enomayirio.** Freshness is guaranteed at this no-frills collection of tables in the middle of the market that serves seafood and other offerings from the surrounding stalls. Market. $

❸ ★ **Archaeological Museum.** Hania and the surrounding lands of western Crete have passed through the hands of the Minoans, Greeks, Romans, Genoese, Venetians, and Turks, and remnants of this tumultuous past are on display in the former 16th-century Church of San Francesco. The artifacts here are more likely to charm than to overwhelm: a stone carved with Minoan houses standing next to the sea; a toy dog found in the tomb

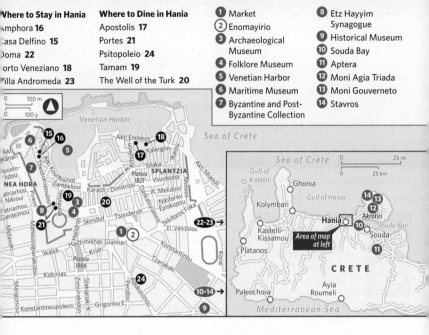

Where to Stay in Hania	Where to Dine in Hania
Amphora **16**	Apostolis **17**
Casa Delfino **15**	Portes **21**
Doma **22**	Psitopoleio **24**
Porto Veneziano **18**	Tamam **19**
Villa Andromeda **23**	The Well of the Turk **20**

1 Market
2 Enomayirio
3 Archaeological Museum
4 Folklore Museum
5 Venetian Harbor
6 Maritime Museum
7 Byzantine and Post-Byzantine Collection
8 Etz Hayyim Synagogue
9 Historical Museum
10 Souda Bay
11 Aptera
12 Moni Agia Triada
13 Moni Gouverneto
14 Stavros

of a Greek boy; several colorful mosaics that once carpeted the floor of a Roman town house. A small garden, embellished with a 10-sided Turkish fountain and a Venetian doorway, is one of the most delightful retreats in town. Just across the street is a remarkable-looking assemblage of 12 domes sitting atop what looks like a stone box. Under the Turks, this was Hania's largest *hamam* (baths). The city's Muslim inhabitants built their facility on the site of Roman baths, fed by a fresh supply of spring water; the *hamam* in turn became part of the Venetian Monastery of Saint Clara and is now a bronze foundry. ⊙ 30 min. 30 Halidron. ☎ 28210/90334. Admission 2€, combined ticket with Byzantine and Post-Byzantine Collection 3€. Tues–Sun 8:30am–3pm.

4 ★ **Folklore Museum.** Cretan traditions are captured in artifact-filled re-creations of farm and domestic scenes. You'll find more orderly presentations of the island's important folk heritage elsewhere on Crete, but the casual, overstuffed feel of this cramped space, filled to bursting with furniture, farm implements,

looms, and traditional clothing, imparts a strong appreciation for a way of life quickly disappearing. ⊙ 30 min. Akti Kountourioti. ☎ 28210/90816. Admission 2€. Mon–Sat 9am–3pm and 6–9pm.

Hania Essentials

Free parking is available along the sea to the west of the harbor; follow the signs as you enter town. One lot is for visitors and one is reserved for residents with permits, as is much of the street parking; observe signs carefully. Buses connect Hania with Rethymnon and Iraklion and run about every half-hour throughout the day. The fare is about 14€ to Rethymnon, and 22€ to Iraklion; buses also connect Hania with towns throughout western Crete. The bus station is south of the Old Town, off Plateia 1866 at 25 Kidonias; ☎ 28210/93306. The **tourist office** is nearby at 40 Kriari, ☎ 28210/92943; it is open Mon–Fri 8am–3pm, sometimes later in summer.

> *A small slip near the lighthouse was once the only means of entering Hania.*

SITE GUIDE
PAGE 277

5 ★★★ Venetian Harbor. The Venetians, obviously accustomed to the beauty of their native city, lavished considerable care when they set about rebuilding the Byzantine town to their needs and tastes, renaming it Canea. First and foremost, they fortified the outer and inner harbors, enclosing the natural inlet within thick walls that could be entered only through one well-protected, narrow slip at the foot of a sturdy lighthouse. Around the outer harbor rose the palaces of well-to-do officials who reaped considerable profits from the timber for shipbuilding and other raw materials the island supplied, as well as from the lucrative trade routes to which Crete provided easy access. The inner harbor, lined with wharves, was a place of business where goods were stored and ships outfitted in massive *arsenali* (warehouses). The Turks added their own impossibly picturesque element—a mosque with a large central dome surrounded by 12 smaller domes. Rising on the east side of the outer harbor, it lends a whiff of exoticism to the surroundings (open occasionally for temporary exhibitions). ⏱ 2 hr.

6 ★★ Maritime Museum. The Firkas, the waterside fortress the Venetians built to keep a watchful eye on the sea lanes and their harbor, is the setting for models of prehistoric and Minoan boats and riveting renderings of the great naval battles of the Persian and Peloponnesian wars. The quirky and intriguing collections veer beyond the long history of Cretan and Greek shipping, however. Attention is paid to Crete's struggle for independence and unification with Greece, which was celebrated here when King Constantine hoisted the Greek flag above the Firkas on December 1, 1913, and photographs and artifacts chronicle the Battle of Crete during World War II. A scale model re-creates the 17th-century Venetian city, and a step outside onto the ramparts reveals that palaces, sea walls, churches, and other landmarks remain remarkably intact. ⏱ 1 hr. Akti Kountourioti. ☎ 28210/26437. Admission 2€. Apr–Oct daily 9am–2pm, Nov–Mar daily 9am–4pm.

7 ★ Byzantine and Post-Byzantine Collection. Christianity took root as early as the 1st century in Crete, and the Franciscan Monastery of San Salvatore, established by the Venetians next to the Firkas, houses many religious works that appeared on the island in the centuries that followed. Many of the pieces here—mosaics from early basilicas, fragments of wall paintings of saints, bronze lamps used during services, and icons—were fashioned when Crete was under Byzantine and even Venetian rule, when Byzantine art continued to thrive on the island (p. 291). 82 Theotokopoulou. ☎ 28210/96046. Admission 2€, combined ticket with Archaeological Museum 3€. Tues–Sun 8:30am–3pm.

8 ★ Etz Hayyim Synagogue. Beginning in the 17th century, Evraiki, the neighborhood of tall houses and narrow lanes just south of the Firkas, was Hania's sizable Jewish ghetto. German authorities arrested and deported the residents in May 1944, and all but a few

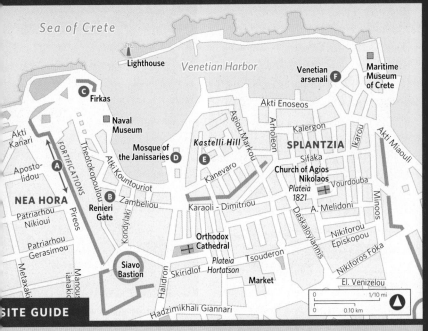

Sea of Crete

Lighthouse · Venetian Harbor · Venetian arsenali **F** · Maritime Museum of Crete

C Firkas · Akti Enoseos

Naval Museum · *Kastelli Hill* · Kalergon · SPLANTZIA

Akti Kanari · Mosque of the Janissaries **D** · **E** · Sifaka

Aposto-lidou · Church of Agios Nikolaos · Vourdouba

A FORTIFICATIONS · Kanevaro · *Plateia 1821* · A. Melidoni

NEA HORA · Renieri Gate **B** · Karaoli - Dimitriou · Nikiforou Episkopou

Patriarhou Nikioui · Zambeliou

Patriarhou Gerasimou · Orthodox Cathedral · Nikiforos Foka

Metaxaki · Siavo Bastion · Skiridlof · *Plateia Hortatson* · Tsouderon · El. Venizelou

Halidron · Market

Hadzimikhali Giannari

0   1/10 mi
0   0.10 km

SITE GUIDE

5 Venetian Harbor

A Thick **fortifications** once surrounded the landward side of the Old Town. These walls did not repel the Turks who invaded in 1645, but the Venetian defenses were so hard to topple that the invaders lost 40,000 men, an indignity for which the Turkish commander lost his head upon returning to Constantinople. The Turks fortified the walls, but no amount of brick and mortar could withstand the German bombs that rained down upon the city during the Battle of Crete in 1941, sparing only the western and eastern flanks. One of the most graceful remnants of the Venetian presence is the **B** **Renieri Gate,** the entranceway to the palace and chapel of one of the city's most prominent 15th-and 16th-century families. Many tall Venetian palaces line the warren of narrow stepped lanes of the surrounding Topanas Quarter. Follow Akti Kountourioti past the entrance to the **C** **Firkas** (p. 276, **6**) to the quay and take in the view of the **D** **Mosque of the Janissaries** across the water, the only mosque the Turks built from scratch, rather than converting a church to their purposes. The exotic-looking structure, now used for exhibitions, was intended as a place of worship for the Janissaries, an elite corps of

young Christian men whom the Ottoman Turks conscripted from throughout their holdings, converted to Islam, and trained as soldiers.

E **Kastelli Hill** rises above the mosque; excavations at the top of the hill (closed but observable through the fence) reveal the remains of the Minoan city that early Greeks called Kydonia, for quince. The wharves along the harbor at the northern foot of the hill are lined with **F** **Venetian arsenali.** One has been converted to a dramatic exhibition space, and another houses a replica of a Minoan ship built for the 2004 Athens Olympics.

> *The Firkas, a waterside fortress, houses artifacts that trace Crete's millennia-long maritime history.*

> *Etz Hayyim Synagogue honors a Jewish communit that flourished on Crete for 2,500 years.*

drowned when the ship carrying them to Athens for transport to Auschwitz was torpedoed by the British. The Hania community was the last of the Jews who had lived on Crete for more than 2,500 years; they are mentioned in the Bible, and over the millennia they intermingled successfully with the various cultures that occupied the island. Under Venetian rule, many emigrated to Venice and from there to other parts of Europe. This rich legacy is captured in Hania's one remaining synagogue, formerly the Venetian Church of St. Catherine, beautifully restored and reopened in 2000 for the first time since it was destroyed during World War II. ⏱ 30 min. Parodos Kondylaki. ☎ 28210/96046. Free admission. Mon–Fri 10am–6pm (shorter hours on some winter days).

The Historical Museum is outside the old city center. From the Market, follow Andrea Papandreou a few blocks southeast to the public gardens. The museum is on Safkianaki, just south of the gardens.

⑨ ★ Historical Museum. A walk through the elegant turn-of-the-20th-century residential enclave south of the public gardens is in itself a pleasure, culminating in this once-grand town house filled with mementos of the island's 19th- and 20th-century history. These were not peaceful times in Crete, and you'll learn about freedom fighters who finally won independence from the Turks and, with the ai of some grisly photographs, the armed resistance against the German occupation during World War II. More peaceful times are evoke in charming rooms furnished with beautiful island textiles and domestic belongings. One room is devoted to Eleftherios Venizelos, who was born near Hania in 1864, was instrumental in gaining independence for Crete, and twice served as prime minister of Greece. His influence during the nation's formative years has earned him the moniker "maker of moder Greece." He and his son, Sophocles, prime minister in the early 1950s, are buried on a hilltop just east of the city. ⏱ 45 min. 20 Sfakianaki. ☎ 28210/52606. Admission 3€. Tues–Su 8:30am–3pm.

From Hania, follow the signs south and east out of the city to Souda. The port of Souda is 7km (4⅓ miles) east of Hania. Though buses serve these outlying sights, it is easiest to visi the following places by car. You can see all of them on an easygoing 1-day outing.

Aptera was a major settlement of ancient Greece and a thriving Roman trading post.

★ **Souda Bay.** The Akrotiri Peninsula juts o the Cretan Sea east of Hania. To the east d south, this broad headland encloses the ep waters of Souda Bay, one of the finest tural harbors in the Mediterranean. This ct was lost on neither the ancient Greek sidents of Aptera (see below), who built a rt on the shores of the bay as early as the h century B.C., nor on the waves of invaders d pirates who followed them. NATO now erates a large naval base on the peninsula. uda is also Hania's port, and the airport is the peninsula. While most travelers simply ss through Souda, many linger to visit the lied War Cemetery, where some 1,500 of e 2,000 Commonwealth soldiers who died the Battle of Crete are buried. ⏱ 30 min.

⓫ ★★ **Aptera.** Walking through the hilltop ruins of this ancient city, in the foothills of the mountains to the west of the Akrotiri Peninsula, is a head-spinning voyage through Crete's long history. Aptera was founded around 1200 B.C., at the end of the Minoan civilization. It became an important Cretan settlement for 7th- to 4th-century-B.C. Greeks; it's known that under them, Aptera had some 20,000 inhabitants and sent soldiers to aid the Spartans in their war against Athens. Aptera then became an important outpost for the Romans, for whom the city was a trading center that minted more than 75 different denominations of coins. The Romans built elaborate vaulted cisterns and a theater, and the Byzantines who followed them left a small chapel. Aptera fell into permanent ruin sometime after the 15th century, though the Turks built the 19th-century fortress of Izzedin on a promontory at

ptera is not on the Akrotiri Peninsula, but just 5km (3 miles) southeast of Souda on a ell-marked road.

12 ★ **Moni Agia Triada.** The lands at the northern tip of the Akrotiri Peninsula are the holdings of two adjacent monasteries. A cypress-lined drive leads through acres of olive groves to the beautiful Venetian Gate of Agia Triada, beyond which are flower-filled courtyards and cloisters, a church, and a small museum of icons. A shop sells the monastery's excellent olive oil, some of Crete's best. ⏱ 45 min. Daily 7:30am–2pm and 5–7pm.

13 ★★★ **Moni Gouverneto.** This Venetian Renaissance monastery at the northern tip of the Akrotiri Peninsula was built near the even more remarkable 11th-century Monastery of Katholiko, the oldest in Crete, founded by John the Hermit, one of the island's most popular saints. Tradition has it John fled Muslim persecution in Asia Minor by sailing across the Aegean on his cloak and came ashore on these lands, where he and 98 followers lived in the caves that riddle a wild, rocky ravine. These caves, accessible via a 30-minute walk on a path from the Gouverneto courtyard, have long been associated with worship. The **Cave of the Bear,** named for the ursine shape of a stalagmite in the cavern, is believed to have been a place of ritual for the Minoans and a sanctuary of Artemis for the ancient Greeks. John spent his last days in a cave-hermitage farther along the path, near the old Katholiko monastery he founded, partially cut out of the rock face and embellished with a Venetian facade. The steep path ends at the sea, where you can end your pilgrimage with a swim from the rocks surrounding a paradisiacal little cove. ⏱ 3 hr., with walk to and from sea. Daily 7:30am–noon and 3–7pm.

Stavros is 5km (3 miles) west of Gouverneto on a well-marked road.

14 ★ **Stavros.** The sandy beach at this scrappy little village is a pleasant place for a swim before heading back to Hania. The experience is all the more memorable because Stavros is famous as the setting for parts of the film *Zorba the Greek*; it is on this beach, backed by a barren promontory, that Zorba teaches the young intellectual, Basil, to dance.

From Stavros, follow the peninsula south into the eastern outskirts of Hania.

> *THIS PAGE* The beach at Stavros. *OPPOSITE PAGE Agia Triada Monastery.*

the far northeastern tip of the site. ⏱ 45 min. Free admission. Daily 9am–5pm.

From Aptera, return to Souda, where a well-marked road leads north across the Akrotiri Peninsula through Chordaki to the monasteries. Agia Triada is 10km (6¼ miles) north of Souda.

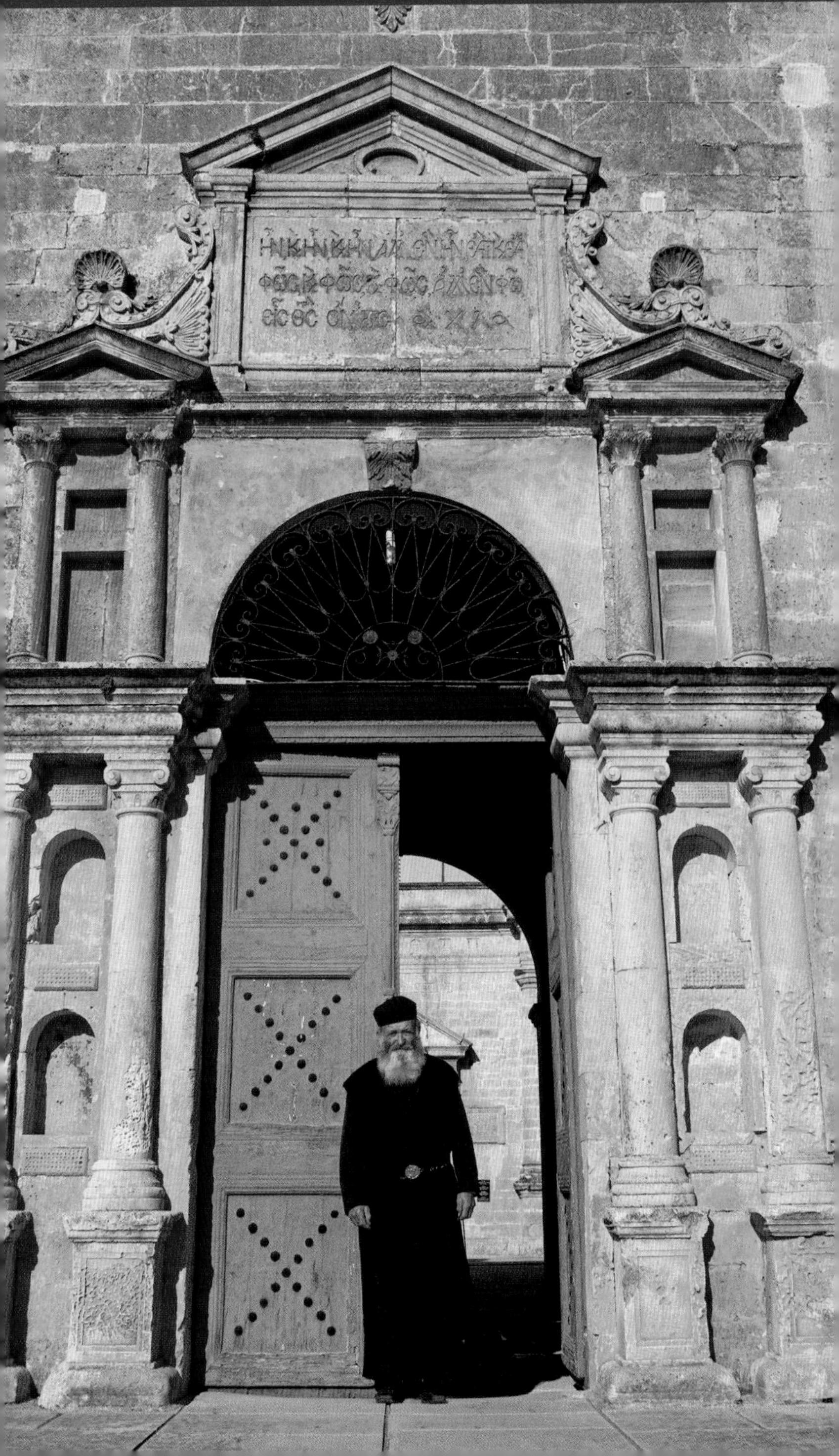

Where to Stay in Hania

> Spacious and stylish rooms at Casa Delfino surround the courtyard of a Venetian palazzo.

★★ Amphora VENETIAN HARBOR
Plenty of old-world ambience is on hand at this beautiful 14th-century Venetian mansion just above the outer harbor, along with remarkable views. The huge rooftop terrace and many of the rooms look across the water and the Old City to the mountains beyond. Many rooms have balconies, as well as kitchenettes, and guests receive a discount at the hotel restaurant, one of the best on the waterfront. Theotokopoulou. ☎ 28210/93224. www.amphora.gr. 20 units. Doubles 110€–130€ w/breakfast. MC, V.

★★★ Casa Delfino VENETIAN HARBOR
The engaging staff here works overtime to ensure guests feel at home, and quite a home it is! Owner Manthos Markantonakis has transformed his family's 17th-century Venetian palazzo into a remarkable place to stay. Rooms are enormous—many are two-level suites—and all are exquisitely and comfortably furnished. 9 Theofanous. ☎ 28210/87400 www.casadelfino.com. 20 units. Doubles 195€–210€ w/breakfast. AE, MC, V.

★★★ Doma SEAFRONT
One of the most distinctive hotels on Crete offers simple yet elegant accommodations in a seaside mansion. Antiques and a collection of Asian headdresses fill the top-floor breakfast rooms and other public spaces, and traditional Cretan furnishings decorate the handsome guest rooms. Some face the sea, but the quietest overlook the delightful garden; the airy penthouse may well be the choicest accommodation in Hania. 124 Venizelou. ☎ 28210/51772. www.hotel-doma.gr. 25 units. Doubles 110€–120€ w/breakfast. AE, MC, V.

★★ Porto Veneziano VENETIAN HARBOR
In these newer and extremely spiffy premises on the edge of the Old Town, most of the large and pleasantly decorated rooms face the sea and have airy balconies. Service is deft and personal, and a pleasant little garden is a quiet retreat in which to enjoy coffee or a drink from the hotel's own cafe/bar. ☎ 28210/27100. www.portoveneziano.gr. 57 units. Doubles 120€–140€ w/breakfast. AE, DC, MC, V.

★★ Villa Andromeda SEAFRONT
A seaside estate that housed the German High Command during World War II is now a luxurious enclave of eight suites surrounding a garden and swimming pool. Several spread over two levels, and some face the sea; all are comfortably and tastefully furnished. 150 Venizelou. ☎ 28210/28300. www.greekhotel.com/crete/chania/andromeda. 8 units. Doubles 200€–250€ w/breakfast. AE, MC, V.

Where to Dine in Hania

> At Tamam, Mediterranean specialties are served in a Turkish bathhouse and on the lane outside.

★★ **Apostolis** VENETIAN HARBOR *SEAFOOD*
Haniots have definite opinions about who serves the freshest fish in town, and this brightly lit place next to the harbor is inevitably near the top of the list (Karnagio on nearby Plateia Katehaki is another top choice). No need to consult the menu—the waiters will show you the fresh catch, displayed on a bed of ice. Akti Enoseos. ☎ 28210/43470. Entrees 7€–20€. MC, V. Lunch & dinner daily.

★★★ **Portes** VENETIAN HARBOR *GREEK*
Owner-chef Susanna Koutloulaki is Irish by birth, but her takes on such traditional staples as moussaka, shrimp saganaki, and grilled chops are excellent. The friendly environs spill onto a quiet backstreet along the walls in an out- of-the-way corner of the Old Town. 48 Portou. ☎ 28210/76261. Entrees 7€–13€. No credit cards. Lunch & dinner daily.

★★ **Psitopoleio** NEW TOWN *GREEK*
The butcher block and grill in the plain room make it clear that this is a meat-eater's paradise. Cretans make their way here for the renowned chops, ribs, organ meats, and other carnivorous offerings, all from local suppliers and deftly prepared. 48 Apokorono. ☎ 28210/91354. Entrees 6€–12€. No credit cards. Lunch & dinner daily.

★★ **Tamam** VENETIAN HARBOR *GREEK*
A former Turkish bath lends one of Hania's most popular restaurants its name, and the offerings are Mediterranean, from as far away as Turkey. Peppers grilled with feta, salads made with mountain greens, vegetable croquettes, and kebabs are served outdoors and in a room that once housed the cold pools of the bath. 49 Zambeliou. ☎ 28210/96080. Entrees 5€–14€. No credit cards. Lunch & dinner daily.

★★★ **The Well of the Turk** TURKISH QUARTER *MIDDLE EASTERN* You will find your way to this all-but-hidden restaurant south of the Venetian Harbor by keeping your eye on the minaret, and asking for directions along the way. An enticing selection of Greek and Middle Eastern appetizers, juicy lamb dishes, and other specialties are served on the ground floor of a Turkish house and in a lovely courtyard. 1–3 Kallinikou Sarpaki. ☎ 28210/54547. Entrees 7€–20€. No credit cards. Lunch & dinner Wed–Mon.

Top Shopping Experiences

Among Hania's endless parade of shops, two stand out, and they happen to be side by side. At **Carmela,** 7 Anghelou (☎ 28210/90487), owner-artist Carmela Iatropoulou shows the work of jewelers and sculptors from throughout Greece. The pieces are extraordinary, often inspired by ancient works and made according to traditional techniques. Carmela is often on hand to discuss her wares and Greek craftsmanship. **Cretan Rugs and Blankets,** 3 Anghelou (☎ 28210/98571), is enticingly filled with fine examples of top-quality local work, much of it antique and hand-woven.

Agios Nikolaos

Attractive and animated, this busy resort town climbs
steep hills above a natural curiosity—small but deep Lake Voulesmeni, linked
to the sea by a narrow channel. The Elounda Peninsula, the sleepy towns of Sitia
and Ipereta, and the palm-shaded beach at Vai, Crete's most famous patch of
sand, are within easy reach.

> Pretty Agios Nikolaos is built alongside the sea and around the shores of a deep lake.

START Near the port on the shores of Lake
Voulismeni. Agios Nikolaos is off the national
highway 70km (43 miles) east of Iraklion. You
will want to rent a car if you wish to use Agios
Nikolaos as a base for visiting eastern Crete.
TRIP LENGTH 3 days.

① ★★ **Lake Voulismeni.** Wedged between
the Gulf of Mirabello and the Sitia Mountains,
Agios Nikolaos picturesquely climbs the hills
that surround this lake in the center of town.
Legend has it that the lake was a favorite
bathing spot for the goddess Athena, and that
the waters are bottomless (indeed the depth
has been definitively measured at 65m/213
ft.). ⊙ 30 min.

② 🍽 **Chez Georges.** This airy perch high atop
a hillside above the lake provides a bird's-
eye view of the town and harbor—a perfect
spot for a snack or cocktail. 2 Kornarou.
☎ 28410/26130. $

③ ★ **Archaeological Museum.** These finds
from the early civilizations of eastern Crete
include one of the great masterpieces of early
Greek art, the so-called Goddess of Myrtos,
from around 2500 B.C. The playful and eerily
modern piece is a *rython,* a libation vessel, in
the shape of a long-necked woman cradling
a jug in her arms. Artifacts from the many
Minoan settlements on the southeast coast

1 Lake Voulismeni
2 Chez Georges
3 Archaeological Museum
4 Folklore Museum
5 Elounda
6 Spinalonga
7 Krista
8 Lato
9 Gournia
10 Ierapetra
11 Chryssi Island
12 Sitia
13 Moni Toplou
14 Vai

Where to Stay in Agios Nikolaos
Akti Olous 16
Elounda Beach 17
Elounda Mare 18
Hotel Astron 21
Hotel du Lac 25
St. Nicolas Bay 19
Sitia Bay 23

Where to Dine in Agios Nikolaos
The Balcony 22
Marilena 15
Pelagos 24
Sarris 26
Stavrakakis Rakadiko 20

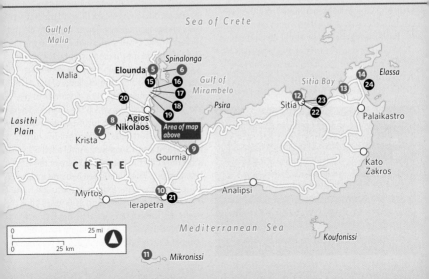

> *Embroidery and other textiles are a specialty in Krista.*

of the island include gold hairpins and a clay statue of a woman with a touchingly primitive face whose arms are folded in worship. The skull of a Greco-Roman athlete from the 1st century B.C. was unearthed intact, as prepared for burial, with a laurel wreath petrified on his skull; next to it is a coin that was placed in his teeth as payment to Charon for rowing him across the River Styx into the Underworld. ⏱ 1 hr. Admission 3€. Tues–Sun 8:30am–3pm.

Agios Nikolaos Essentials

Free parking is available along the sea, but observe parking signs carefully. Buses that connect Agios Nikolaos with Iraklion run about every half-hour throughout the day, and the fare is about 12€; buses also connect Agios Nikolaos with other towns throughout eastern Crete. The tourist office at 34 Kondogianni (☎ 28210/22357; Apr–Nov daily 8:30am–9:30pm) is extremely helpful.

④ ★ **Folklore Museum.** Colorful everyday items and local crafts pieces, from carved walking sticks to musical instruments, are displayed alongside Cretan textiles and embroidery. A re-creation of a typical village house, furnished with traditional wooden pieces and kitchen equipment, is especially appealing. ⏱ 45 min. 2 Kondalaki. ☎ 28410/25093. Admission 2€. Tues–Sun 10am–1pm.

From Agios Nikolaos, take the coast road north onto the Elounda Peninsula. Elounda village is 11km (7 miles) north of Agios Nikolaos.

⑤ ★★★ **Elounda.** A dramatic hillside road follows the Gulf of Mirabello along the flanks of the Elounda Peninsula to this once quiet fishing village. Some of Greece's most sybaritic resorts now surround Elounda and provide the world-weary with many luxuries, none of which can top the views of the crystal-clear waters of the gulf and the stark beauty of the landscape. Ancient Greeks established the city of Olus on these shores, though a noted temple to the mountain goddess Britomartis and other structures were submerged more than 2,000 years ago. Scant remains are now visible beneath the waves off a causeway just east of the village, and the waters above the ruins are popular with snorkelers. ⏱ 2 hr. to drive out to the peninsula (longer if you include a boat trip to Spinalonga).

⑥ ★★★ kids **Spinalonga.** When the ancient Greeks inhabited nearby Olus, this island in the Gulf of Mirabello was still a peninsula, and its seaward flanks were fortified to protect the busy shipping channels. These bastions did not thwart Arabic pirates who laid waste to the gulf shores around the 7th century, and the region was not inhabited again until the Venetians began to mine salt in the shallows of the gulf in the 15th century. They cut a channel to create an isolated island, which they named Spina Longa (Long Thorn) and fortified into a virtually impregnable fortress. The Turks didn't turn their attention to Spinalonga until a full 50 years after they overran the rest of Crete in the late 17th century. The island then became a place of refuge for Christians fearing persecution from the Ottoman occupiers, and 200 years later sheltered Turkish families after the Ottomans were overthrown in the revolution for Greek Independence in 1866. Refugees arrived again

Spinalonga has long been a place of refuge, most recently for lepers.

n 1903, this time under force, when Spinalonga
became a leper colony, used as such until 1952.
One of the entrances to the island, the one used
by arriving lepers, is known as **Dante's Gate,** so
fearsome was its reputation. Once there, the ill
received decent treatment, though they were
condemned to isolation on this barren outcropping. Today the island's spooky ruins and pebbly
beaches are popular with day-trippers, many of

whom arrive on tour boats. As boats approach
the island, they cruise slowly past the tiny, uninhabited nearby islet of **Agioi Pantes** to catch a
glimpse of the *agrimi*, also known as the *kri-kri*,
a species of long-horned wild goat endemic to
Crete and now endangered; this little island and
the Samaria Gorge (p. 253, ⑦) are among the
last refuges for the shy animals. ⊕1 hr. for visit of
ruins, longer with stop on beach.

Krista is 9km (5⅔ miles) southwest of Agios
Nikolaos on a well-marked road.

⑦ ★★ **Krista.** This mountain village is noted
for beautiful woven goods that are strung in
front of shops surrounding the beautiful *plateia.* More artistry fills the small, 14th-century
Panagia Kera, where some of the most accomplished Byzantine frescoes in Crete cover
the walls of the three naves. The scenes
depict the life of Christ, the Second Coming, some fearsome views of damnation, and
several lesser known biblical tales, including
the prayer of Saint Anna. The childless Anna
prayed fervently, promising to bring a child
up in God's ways, and she gave birth to Mary,
mother of Christ. Accordingly, the colorful
little church is popular with women seeking
to bear children. ⊕1 hr. North of town center
(1km/M mile). Admission 3€. Mon–Sat 9am–
3pm, Sun 9am–2pm.

Set Sail for Spinalonga

Boats sail across the Gulf of Mirabello to
Spinalonga from Agios Nikolaos, Elounda,
and Plaka, a little fishing village just north
of Elounda. The trip out from Agios Nikolaos takes about an hour and costs about
15€ a person, and from Elounda or Plaka
about 15 minutes for 7€ a person. Simply
walk along the docks in any of these towns
and you'll practically be pulled aboard one
of the excursion boats. Try to make the
trip early in the morning, leaving no later
than 10am, to avoid the midday sun and
the crowds that converge on the otherwise
deserted island. Back on shore, stop by a
newsstand to pick up a copy of *The Island,*
a novel by Victoria Hislop set in Plaka and
Spinalonga and usually on hand in Agios
Nikolaos and Elounda.

> *Crete's finest Byzantine frescoes adorn the walls inside Krista's Panagia Kera.*

Lato is about 4km (2½ miles) north of Krista on a well-marked road.

8 ★ **Lato.** Dorian Greeks, who occupied much of Crete from around 1100 B.C., built one of their most important cities in the cradle of two hills above Agios Nikolaos, which they settled as their port. Lato and nearby **Olus** (p. 286, **5**) were continually at war, and the sheltering hills and thick fortified walls and towers that now litter the site offered protection against frequent raids. Within the fortifications were a theater, acropolis, and agora, as well as an unusual arrangement of houses that even in their ruined state will remind you of the white-cube hillside villages you see today in the Cyclades (the roof of a lower house served as the court of the house above). You can still see the remains of cisterns that were cut into the rock faces to collect rainwater for city residents throughout the long, rainless summer. ◷1 hr. Admission 3€. Tues–Sun 8:30am–3pm.

Gournia is 19km (12 miles) east of Agios Nikolaos, off the coast road.

9 ★★ **Gournia.** This once-thriving Minoan community on the coast east of Agios Nikolaos is far more humble than Phaestos or Knossos—the fiefdom of overlords, not kings. Even so, the ruins of shops and dwellings provide a haunting look at what life may have been like 4,000 years ago. See p. 246, **8**.

Ierapetra is 17km (11 miles) south of Gournia and 36km (23 miles) southeast of Agios Nikolaos; a road heads south off the north coast just east of Gournia.

10 ★ **Ierapetra.** East of Agios Nikolaos, Crete narrows into a thin neck, barely 15km (9⅓ miles) across. A turn south just past the Minoan ruins at Gournia (p. 246, **8**) brings you to dusty, rambling Ierapetra, the southernmost city in Europe. You probably won't linger too long in Ierapetra; most visitors pass through town in search of the excellent beaches and coves that stretch from **Makriyialos,** 28km (17 miles) east, to the fishing and farming village of **Goudouras.** However, Ierapetra is amiable and well suited to some idle wandering through the jumbled **Old Quarter.** Because of its strategic position on the trade routes to Africa and the Middle East, the town has seen the passage of Minoans, early Greeks, Romans, Venetians, and even Napoleon. The emperor enjoyed a brief sojourn in the home of a prominent Ierapetra family during July 1798 after his victory at the Battle of the Pyramids in Egypt. Allegedly, the emperor came ashore with five crewmen to get fresh water. He was not recognized but fell into amiable conversation with a man who invited him to dine with his family and spend the night. The household awoke the next morning to find a thank-you note signed by their guest, who was then the most famous man in the world. The Romans built wharves that are still visible just below the blue waters of the port, and the Venetians constructed the **Fortress of Kales** in the 13th century to ward off pirate attacks. They fortified it extensively into its present appearance in 1626, as the threats of Ottoman attacks grew (daily 9am–sunset). Today Ierapetra has an end-of-the-world feel and basks in a hot, sunny climate, akin to that of nearby Africa, ensuring a very long growing season (much of Europe consumes tomatoes and cucumbers grown in and around Ierapetra). ◷1 hr.

> *Sheltering hills cradle ancient Lato and provide a vantage point over the sea below.*

⑪ ★★ **Chryssi Island.** Some of the best beaches in Crete ring this little island, also known as Gaidouronissi, a small volcanic outcropping in the Libyan Sea south of Ierapetra. Despite its isolation, Chryssi supported small Minoan and Roman settlements and was inhabited well into the Middle Ages by a few hearty souls who made their living panning for salt, until pirates took over the island as a base for plundering villages on the southern shores of Crete. The island has very few facilities, except for some primitive tavernas, and the only shade is to be found beneath a lovely copse of cedars. Many rare plants and marine animals thrive on the island, which has been designated by the E.U. as an Area of Outstanding Natural Beauty, and visitors are discouraged from disturbing the flora and fauna. In summer, boats for the island leave Ierapetra around 8 and 10am and return around 3 and 5pm. Purchase your tickets from one of the dozens of agencies in Ierapetra that organize excursions to the island; the round-trip fare is about 20€. ⏱1 day.

Sitia is 50km (31 miles) northeast of Ierapetra and 73km (45 miles) east of Agios Nikolaos.

⑫ ★★ **Sitia.** The easternmost city in Crete is a pleasant and lively farm town where sultanas and bananas are the important crops. Residents turn out in force on warm evenings for a leisurely amble along the promenade that follows the harbor and a sandy beach. A walk up the narrow, stepped lanes from the harbor, where fishing boats come and go past the palm-shaded Plateia Venizelou, brings you to the town's one monument, the **Karzama fortress,** built in the 13th century by the Venetians (daily 8am–sunset). In the 16th century, they fortified the walls, from which you can see semicircular cisterns, partially submerged in the shallows below, which the Romans used to hold fish until they were ready to eat them. Romans extensively fished the seas around Sitia, and a collection of their fishhooks are among the artifacts in the town's **Archaeological Museum,** in the southern outskirts on the Ierapetra Road (☎ 28430/23917; 2€; daily 9am–1pm and 2–5pm). Many of the holdings are finds from **Palaikastro** and **Kato Zakros,** at the far eastern end of the island (p. 247, ⑨ and ⑩), and include an ivory statue of a Minoan youth. The town's homey little **Folklore Museum** on Odos Therissou (2€; Tues–Sun 9am–1pm, but hours vary) is not often open,

> *Thick walls protected remote, windswept Moni Toplou from pirate raids.*

but if you happen to stop by when an attendant is present, you'll see some exquisitely woven rugs and blankets, displayed in rooms furnished in traditional Cretan style. ⏱ 2 hr.

From Sitia, take the coast road east for 13km (8 miles) to Moni Toplou.

⑬ ★★ **Moni Toplou.** A barren, windswept hillside at the northeastern tip of the island is the setting for this forbidding 15th-century monastery. The name means "armed with cannon," and the monastery is heavily fortified with walls 10m high (33 ft.) against centuries of plunder by pirates and other attackers. Monks at Toplou put up fierce resistance to the Turks, who slaughtered the community for their role in the 1821 revolution for independence, and to the Germans, who executed the abbot for his role in assisting the Allies and Cretan freedom fighters. Despite these harsh connections, Toplou is a delight, with a working windmill, shady courtyards paved with pebbles, a couple of chapels, and some remarkable icons, including one by acclaimed 18th-century artist Ioannis Koranos. His most famous work is the monastery's *Lord, Thou Art Great* icon; it depicts 61 miniature scenes from the Bible, encapsulating the scope of scripture, from Creation to the Last Judgment. ⏱ 1 hr. Off Sitia–Paleokastro road. Admission 3€. Daily 9am–1pm and 2–6pm.

Vai is 12km (7½ miles) northeast of Moni Toplou.

⑭ ★★ kids **Vai.** One of Europe's most celebrated beaches, a stretch of white sand backed by a grove of palms, stretches along the shores of a protected cove. Places of such remarkable beauty are bound to inspire legends, and fanciful stories attribute the palms to a band of Arab marauders who camped on the beach, enjoyed a meal of dates, and left the seeds to take root. In truth, these are not date palms but a species unique to Crete, and the presence of a palm grove at the eastern tip of the island was noted as early as Roman times. Vai is justifiably popular, so arrive early or late in the day to avoid the busloads of beachgoers who make the trip east from Iraklion and Agios Nikolaos. You will find quieter strands on the other side of the headlands immediately to the north and south of Vai. ⏱ 2 hr. At the far eastern end of island, 25km (15 miles) east of Sitia on a well-marked road.

> *Groves of palms shade a perfect crescent of sand at Vai.*

Byzantine Art on Crete

Byzantine art flourished in Crete in the 15th century, as artists fled to the island just before and after the fall of Constantinople in 1453. Crete became the center of the Byzantine art world, and hundreds of artists studied and worked in Iraklion (then known as Candia) and elsewhere around the island. As a Venetian possession, the island met Venice's demand for a steady stream of Byzantine-influenced icons and paintings, but Cretan art was shipped throughout Greece and other parts of Europe as well. Cretan artists also painted frescoes on the walls of churches and monasteries across the island, and it's estimated that more than 800 of these beautiful wall paintings remain in place. Some of the most elaborate and best-preserved are those in the **Panagia Kera** in the village of Krista (p. 287, **7**).

The art of icon painting is kept alive at **Petrakis Workshop for Icons** in Elounda (22 Papendreou; ☎ 28410/41669). The studio's artists supply churches throughout Europe and North America with beautifully painted icons, and pieces are available for sale in the shop.

Where to Stay in Agios Nikolaos

> St. Nicolas Bay, near Agios Nikolaos.

★★ **Akti Olous** ELOUNDA

A sandy beach and rooftop pool make this affordable alternative to the many luxurious resorts nearby especially pleasant. All of the small but bright and well-furnished rooms overlook the sea, and a restaurant and bar are perched just above the beach. **Waterfront.** ☎ 28410/41270. www.eloundaaktiolous.gr. 70 units. Doubles 75€–80€ w/breakfast. MC, V.

★★★ **Elounda Beach** ELOUNDA

The most famous and best of the large Greek resorts just keeps getting better and better. Accommodations come in dozens of variations, from villas with private pools to seaside bungalows with high-tech gadgetry that would make James Bond feel at home. The many amenities include water sports, spa treatments, and a variety of dining experiences, and the service is never less than top-notch. 3km (2 miles) south of Elounda village. ☎ 28410/63000. www.elounda beach.gr. 240 units. Doubles 400€–900€ w/ breakfast. AE, DC, MC, V.

★★★ **Elounda Mare** ELOUNDA

Most of the guests at this idyllic retreat, one of Europe's truly great resorts, come back year after year, and it is easy to see why. Bungalows are tucked into seaside gardens, rooms and suites furnished in traditional Cretan style afford expansive views over the Gulf of Elounda, and a sandy beach and several delightful restaurants are among the many amenities. 3km (2 miles) south of Elounda village. ☎ 28410/68200. www. eloundamare.com. 88 units. Doubles 400€–700€ w/breakfast. AE, DC, MC, V.

★ **Hotel Astron** IERAPETRA

The best budget option in town is not without drawbacks—some inexcusably brusque service and plain, dated decor chief among them—but the airy sea views, balconies, and proximity to the beach and center of town make this a decent choice for an overnight. 56 Kothri. ☎ 28420/25114. 70 units. Doubles 80€–90€ w/breakfast. MC, V.

★★ **Hotel du Lac** AGIOS NIKOLAOS

The dining room terrace overlooking the lake is a pleasant place for a meal, and you can enjoy the same views from one of the rooms upstairs. The best accommodations in the house are the newly renovated studios facing the lake. 17 28 Octobriou. ☎ 28410/22711. www. dulachotel.gr. 18 units. Doubles 60€–80€ w/ breakfast. AE, MC, V.

★★★ **St. Nicolas Bay** AGIOS NIKOLAOS

Within walking distance of Agios Nikolaos, this wonderful getaway offers many of the same amenities as the resorts farther out on the Elounda Peninsula—from a sandy beach to excellent dining. Once you settle into one of the attractive marble-floored rooms and suites, tucked away above the sea in verdant gardens, you may never want to leave the grounds. Thessi Nissi. ☎ 28410/25041. www. stnicolasbay.gr. 90 units. Doubles 450€–700€ w/breakfast. AE, DC, MC, V.

★★ **Sitia Bay** SITIA

All of these attractive studios and one-bedroom apartments have kitchens and face the sea, a sandy beach, and a large swimming pool. The center of town is just a short walk north along the seaside. 27 Patriarhou Vartholomeou. ☎ 28430/24800. www.sitiabay.com. 19 units. Doubles 118€–125€. No credit cards.

Where to Dine in Agios Nikolaos

★★ The Balcony SITIA GREEK/FUSION

The freshest local ingredients, from fish to lamb to mountain herbs, find their way into the dishes served with flair in this handsome old house on a back street. The dining experience here is memorable and a bit more exotic than you would expect to find in Sitia. 19 Founalidou. ☎ 28430/25084. Entrees 8€–18€. MC, V. Lunch & dinner Mon-Sat, dinner Sun.

★★★ Marilena ELOUNDA GREEK

The Elounda waterfront is a cluster of rather garish restaurants, but none match the excellent cuisine and attentive service on offer in this large room and garden. Grilled fish is a specialty, but you can dine very well on one of the house appetizer platters, a delicious array of spreads and small portions of meat and seafood selections. Harbor. ☎ 28410/41322. Entrees 6€–20€. MC, V. Lunch & dinner daily. Closed Nov-Feb.

★★★ Pelagos AGIOS NIKOLAOS SEAFOOD

What many locals consider to be the freshest fish in town is served in the handsome, simply furnished rooms and garden of this neoclassical mansion near the sea in the heart of town. The good selection of Cretan wines can lend another flourish to the reliably memorable meals served here. 10 Katehaki. ☎ 28410/25737. Entrees 8€–20€. MC, V. Lunch & dinner daily. Closed Nov-Mar.

★★ Sarris AGIOS NIKOLAOS GREEK

It's worth wandering through the back streets of town to find your way to this simple little taverna, where only a few dishes are prepared daily. These often include rich stews of game and seafood, served in warm months under a shady arbor overlooking a small church. 15 Kyprou. ☎ 28410/28059. Entrees 5€–8€. No credit cards. Lunch & dinner daily. Closed Nov-Mar.

★★★ Stavrakakis Rakadiko EXO LACONIA

GREEK   When visiting Krista and Lato (p. 287, ⑦; 288, ⑧), do yourself a favor and add this delightful little village taverna to the itinerary. Many of the ingredients that find their way into salads, dolmades, and other dishes are

> *A platter of appetizers is a meal in itself at Marilena in Elounda.*

homegrown, served in memorably friendly surroundings. Exo Laconia, 8km (5 miles) west of Agios Nikolaos. ☎ 28410/22478. Entrees 4€–8€. No credit cards. Lunch & dinner daily.

Beach Break

You don't have to venture far in Agios Nikolaos to find a beach. **Kliopatria,** albeit a bit crowded, is right in town, just over the hill from the harbor. The little eclipse of sand is sprinkled with shade trees and backed by cafes and bars. Umbrellas and lounges are available for rent, but you'll probably choose to do your beach-lingering on some of the more remote strands in this part of eastern Crete. However, Kliopatria is handy for a quick, refreshing dip.

Crete Fast Facts

Arriving

BY PLANE The major airports in Crete are in Iraklion and Hania, both served from Athens by **Olympic** (☎ 801/114-4444 reservations within Greece; ☎ 28102/44802 in Heraklion; ☎ 28210/57702 in Hania; ☎ 28430/24666 in Sitia) and **Aegean** (☎ 801/112-0000 reservations within Greece; ☎ 28210/63366 in Hania; ☎ 28103/30475 in Iraklion; www.aegeanair.com). In summer, both also handle charter flights from cities throughout Europe. Olympic also flies from Athens to Sitia, and **Sky Express** (☎ 2810/22350; www.skyexpress.gr) connects Iraklion with Rhodes, Kos, Mykonos, and other places throughout Greece. **BY BOAT** Iraklion and Hania are well served by daily ferries from Athens, and Agios Nikolaos and Sitia have limited service; Rethymnon is attempting to restore its ferry service, so stay tuned. Crete is also connected to other Greek islands by boat, especially the Cyclades and Dodecanese; popular routes are Hania and Iraklion to Santorini and Sitia to Rhodes. The two lines with the most frequent service are **Anek** (www.anek.gr) and **Minoan** (www.minoan.gr). All travel offices sell boat tickets. An excellent single stop for boat schedules and contacts is the website **Greek Travel Pages** (www.gtp.gr).

Dentists & Doctors

Crete has some excellent hospitals, such as the **University of Crete Medical Center,** outside Iraklion (☎ 2810/92111)—one of the best in southern Europe. Most hotels will be able to refer you to a local doctor or dentist who speaks English.

Emergencies

See p. 680, Fast Facts Greece.

Getting Around

BY CAR We recommend renting a car to access the more remote and most scenic parts of the island. Expect to pay about 30€ to 40€ a day, even in the busy August tourist season. Car rental is a big business on Crete, and you will find agencies in every town of any size. All agencies will provide a map, essential for navigating the many back roads of the island. Some major agencies are: **Avis** (Iraklion Airport; ☎ 28102/29402; www.avis.com), **Hertz** (Iraklion Airport; ☎ 28103/30452; www.hertz.com), and **Sixt** (Iraklion Airport; ☎ 28102/80915; www.sixt.com). **CreteTravel.com** (☎ 28250/32693; www.cretetravel.com) is a good source for car rentals from local agencies. **BY BUS** Crete is well served by an excellent bus network. Buses connect the major north coast cities and towns (Hania, Rethymnon, Iraklion, Agios Nikolaos, and Sitia) with great frequency and serve almost every other town at least once a day. Consult tourist information offices for schedules and other details.

Internet Access

See p. 681, Fast Facts Greece.

Pharmacies

See p. 682, Fast Facts Greece.

Police

See p. 682, Fast Facts Greece.

Post Office

See p. 682, Fast Facts Greece.

Safety

See p. 682, Fast Facts Greece.

Visitor Information

Crete has a fairly decent network of tourist information offices. The **Greek National Tourism Organization** runs offices in Iraklion, Hania, and Rethymnon. Other municipalities, including Agios Nikolaos, have municipally run tourist offices, which tend to be even more helpful. See individual towns in this chapter for locations and hours of tourist offices.

> Road signs in some spots on the island are in English, making navigation a little bit easier.

7
The
Cyclades

Favorite Moments in the Cyclades

Your head will start spinning the moment you sail into
Santorini's caldera or first glimpse the windmills of Mykonos or the mountains of Naxos from the sea. Whatever your first sightings of the Cyclades may be, the first impression will be favorable—and memorable experiences will keep on coming your way as you travel through the archipelago that for many travelers captures the essence of the Greek isles.

> PREVIOUS PAGE *The Golden Wellspring Monastery on Chrysopigi.* THIS PAGE *A path along the rim of the Santorini caldera.*

1 **Strolling along the Santorini caldera in the morning.** The cliffs glimmer in transcendent light, white villages look like a dusting of snow on the cliff tops, and boats sailing in and out of the caldera far below look almost Homeric. Few places on earth are more beautiful. See p. 324, **2**.

2 **Watching the sun go down on Santorini.** One of the world's most famous sunset spectacles is a reliable show on this island where the sky is cloudless on most days. Don't join the awestruck, gasping crowds in Ia. Instead, toast the event with a glass of the dry island white on your own terrace. Don't happen to have such a perch of your own? One of the swanky caldera-side bars in Fira will do nicely. See p. 322, **1**.

3 **Catching your first glimpse of Hora, Folegandros.** The white town high, high atop seaside cliffs seems to meet the sky, a vision of flat-roofed, cubical houses floating in air. Stepping into lanes and squares lined with flower-bedecked stairways and balconies does nothing to dispel the magic. See p. 320, **5**.

4 **Jumping into the sea off volcanic rocks, Milos.** You won't be able to resist diving into the turquoise coves etched out of white volcanic rock at Sarakiniko. The eerily shaped and colorless formations are so otherworldly you may feel you've swum into the Underworld. See p. 317, **2**.

5 **Climbing Profitis Elias o Pilos, Sifnos.** It's quite a trek up the 850m-tall (2,789-ft.) mountain, the highest on the island, to the isolated monastery at the summit. The views seem to extend across the entire Aegean Sea. See p. 353, **6**.

6 **Gazing at ancient marbles, Paros.** Parian marble has a way of catching your gaze and not letting go. After all, the most famous statue in the world, the *Venus de Milo,* is sculpted from

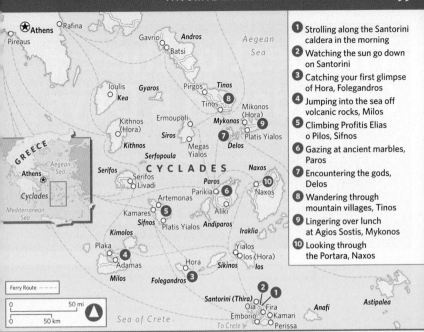

1 Strolling along the Santorini caldera in the morning

2 Watching the sun go down on Santorini

3 Catching your first glimpse of Hora, Folegandros

4 Jumping into the sea off volcanic rocks, Milos

5 Climbing Profitis Elias o Pilos, Sifnos

6 Gazing at ancient marbles, Paros

7 Encountering the gods, Delos

8 Wandering through mountain villages, Tinos

9 Lingering over lunch at Agios Sostis, Mykonos

10 Looking through the Portara, Naxos

---

he translucently white and luminescent stone. On Paros you will be intrigued by a much less formal display: Bits and pieces of columns and pediments, debris from ancient temples, are wedged willy-nilly into the walls of the 13th-century Venetian *kastro*, a head-spinning glimpse into civilizations past. See p. 336, 4.

7 Encountering the gods, Delos. One of the most sacred places for ancient Greeks still inspires, even in jumbled ruin. As you walk among temples and skirt the shores of the sacred lake, you'll get a sense of what a trip to this island might have meant to a pilgrim of long ago. See p. 308, 1.

8 Wandering through mountain villages, Tinos. Mazes of white cubical houses appear on stark hillsides, ruined castles cling to rocky spires, and boulders are strewn across green valleys. As you'll learn on your travels around this beautiful island, these enchanted landscapes have inspired the visions of saints and were once believed to be the domain of Boreas, god of the north wind. See p. 312, 3.

9 Lingering over lunch at Agios Sostis, Mykonos. Paradise and Super Paradise are the island's famous beaches, but Agios Sostis's crescent of sand is much more

> The Portara, gateway to the island of Naxos.

paradisiacal—and coming upon such a tranquil spot on an island as famously boisterous as Mykonos is all the more satisfying. The water is warm, the sands are soft, and a lunch of grilled fish or pork is served beneath a flowering vine at a simple beachside taverna. See p. 364.

10 Looking through the Portara, Naxos. The great unfinished doorway leads to nowhere but beautifully frames the blue sea and green Naxian hills. You almost want to believe the legend that the massive marble portal was meant to be the entrance to the palace that the god Dionysus built for his lover, Ariadne. See p. 342, 1.

The Best of the Cyclades in 5 Days

You can do a bit of island-hopping in the Cyclades even if you've only got 5 days, though the visual memories and colorful experiences may be a head-spinning jumble. You'll spend 2 days on each of the two most popular Cyclades, Santorini and Mykonos, and see why their reputations are well deserved. You'll also spend a day on Paros—not exactly a desert isle, and quieter than its two more-famous neighbors, it's a beautiful place to get in step with a slower Cycladic rhythm.

> Ia and other villages cling to the rim of Santorini's caldera.

START Santorini. **TRIP LENGTH** Total distance covered by boat on a round-trip circuit from Athens is about 500km (311 miles).

❶ **Santorini.** You will experience the beauty of Santorini from the moment you sail into the bay at the center of this volcanic archipelago.

From the deck of the ferry—and do arrive by boat rather than by plane, because sailing into Santorini is one of the great Greek experiences—you will be looking up at the 300m-high (1,000-ft.) cliffs that form the eastern flanks of the main island. The bay, some 10km (6¼

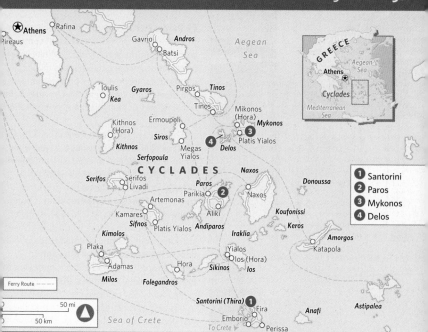

miles) long and as deep as 400m (1,312 ft.) in places, is the flooded caldera of a volcano whose eruptions, including a massive one around 1600 B.C., caused the center of a once-large island to collapse. Islets on the western side of the bay, Tharissa and Aspronissi, are other fragments of the rim.

As if this natural spectacle did not provide enough drama, from the sea the towns and villages that line the caldera look almost like apparitions. At first the clusters appear to be natural formations of white stone, until blue domes come into focus and you notice white cubical houses practically teetering on the sides of the cliffs.

The essential requirement for a stay in Santorini is lodging with a terrace overlooking the caldera. Top choices are **Imerovigli** (p. 325, **1**), a little village tucked onto the highest point on the caldera rim, and **Ia** (p. 325, **5**), the most picturesque village on Santorini, clinging to the northwestern tip of the caldera. In both, many traditional cave houses have been converted into hotels that are comfortable and full of character.

Your objective on Day 1 is to get an eyeful of the views. You may want to leave your terrace long enough to walk at least part of the way along the path that follows the caldera (p. 324, **2**) for 10km (6¼ miles), all the way from Fira, the busy island capital, to Ia. Be back on your terrace by sunset, though, to enjoy the view while sipping a glass of the island's famously crisp white wine.

On Day 2, venture away from the caldera to explore the rest of the island. (Buses run to most places of interest, but you'll make the most of your limited time on the island if you rent a car or motorbike; you can also join one of the many tours that make stops at the main attractions; see p. 371). Begin the day with a visit to three museums in **Fira** (p. 322, **1**), for a glimpse at the ancient wonders you'll encounter later in the day at Akrotiri and Ancient Thera: the **Museum of Prehistoric Thera,** the **Archae-ological Museum,** and the **Thera Foundation: The Wall Painting of Thera,** where beautiful Minoan frescoes are reproduced. From Fira, head south to **Pyrgos** (p. 327, **6**), the medieval capital of the island, where streets wind up to a ruined Venetian citadel. The monastery of **Prof-itis Elias** crowns a nearby peak, well worth the ascent for the airy views, and several **wineries** around Pyrgos offer tastings.

Akrotiri (p. 327, **8**) is one of the best-preserved ancient settlements in the Aegean.

> On Mykonos, the lanes of Hora were laid out as a
> maze to thwart invaders.

The so-called Minoan Pompeii was buried deep in ash during the eruption around 1600 B.C. and wasn't uncovered for another 3,300 years. The 40 stores, warehouses, and houses that line Akrotiri's main street are remarkably well preserved. **Ancient Thera** (p. 328, ⑨), dramatically crowning a rocky headland, has been shaped by Egyptians, Greeks, Romans, and Byzantines. Below the promontory is the best beach on Santorini, **Kamari**—a dramatic swath of silky black sand. ☺ 2 days.

The trip from Santorini to Paros takes 3 hours; an early-morning boat will reach Paros by midmorning.

Tips on Accommodations

True Greece (☎ 21061/20656; www. truegreece.com) specializes in personalized, distinctive tours and provides a fine selection of comfortable hotels with character throughout the Cyclades, with a focus on Mykonos, Santorini, and Naxos; they will also arrange complete itineraries.

❷ **Paros.** A one-day stopover on this attractive little island provides a pleasant contrast to worldly Santorini and Mykonos. While Paros is hardly undiscovered, the island is much quieter than its neighbors and provides at least a hint of what life was like in the Cyclades before Greek-island-hopping became an international passion.

The lanes of **Old Town Parikia** (p. 336, ❹) are typical of a Cycladic village, paved with white-etched stones, shaded with bougainvillea, and lined with pretty whitewashed houses. Parikia also claims two great treasures. The **Panagia Ekatontopylani** (Church of the Hundred Doors; p. 334, ❶), is one of the oldest churches in the world, an enclave grouped around lemon-scented gardens. Next door is the **Archaeological Museum** (p. 336, ❷), the repository of a sizable fragment of the Parian Chronicle, a marble slab that records events from 1581 to 299 B.C.

It is easy to explore the island on the buses that depart from a station next to the port. An afternoon's excursion takes you to **Lefkes** (p. 338, ❼), the medieval capital of Paros, where mazelike narrow lanes cascade down the mountainside. After a coffee on the beautiful *platela*, continue to **Naoussa** (p. 336, ❺), a fishing village that comes to life as a lively resort every summer. Some of the best beaches on the island surround Naoussa, and you may want to take a dip from one of them before enjoying a seafood dinner on the quay beside the submerged ruins of the Venetian *kastro*. ☺ 1 day.

The trip from Paros to Mykonos is less than 1 hour by fast boat. You will spend the next 2 nights on Mykonos.

❸ **Mykonos.** One of the world's favorite party islands is appealing to the rest of us too. The barren, wind-swept island is not a place of great natural beauty, but it has charm aplenty —as you will soon discover as you begin winding your way through the maze of little lanes that twist and turn through Mykonos Town (known to islanders as Hora) toward the breezy seaside Esplanade.

Hora (p. 356, ❶) is where you will want to spend at least a good part of your first day on the island, following the streets into the sea captains' quarter, **Little Venice** (p. 359, ❷), and stepping into the charmingly lopsided

You'll witness the sensual quality of local (Parian) marble at the Archaeological Museum on Paros.

Church of the Paraportiani (Our Lady of the Postern Gate) and the **Folklore Museum,** an atmospheric throwback to life the way it once was on Mykonos. Of course, many of the island's pleasures are more worldly, quite famously so, including the glittering shops along Metoyanni.

At some point in the day you will want to find yourself on a beach, and that is easy to do on a short bus or boat trip from Hora. The island's two most famous stretches of sand, **Paradise** and **Super Paradise** (p. 360, ❹), are far from paradisiacal, unless you're young, restless, and intemperate in your drinking habits. **Elia** and **Kalo Livadi** (p. 360, ❺), near the end of the north-coast bus and boat routes,

are prettier, cleaner, quieter, and much more pleasant; for the rundown on Mykonos beaches, see p. 361. Evening is the liveliest time in Hora, when Mykonites and their visitors stroll along the bougainvillea-scented lanes and drink in the sunset views from cafe terraces along the Esplanade and in Little Venice. ⏱ 1 day, 2 nights.

Boats for Delos depart from the eastern end of the Esplanade in Hora at 9am and return at 3pm. Most travel agencies on Mykonos advertise trips to Delos, as do many boat captains who dock along the Esplanade. The round-trip costs about 15€ (the crossing takes 30 min.), and 30€ if the trip includes a guide.

❹ **Delos.** Spend your final day on the island of **Delos** (p. 308, ❶), a sacred religious sanctuary and a flourishing center of trade in ancient Greece; one of the most important archaeological sites in the Aegean is littered with the remains of temples, baths, agoras, and villas. Boats leave in the morning and return in midafternoon—leaving time for one more swim from one of the legendary Mykonos beaches and another evening in Hora. ⏱ Half-day.

Cycladic Winds

Keep in mind that winds can wreak havoc on ferry schedules in the Cyclades. When the winds pick up, you may find that your boat is delayed or canceled. Santorini, Paros, Naxos, and Mykonos have airports, so you can fly off the island—or just sit back, relax, and consider it a surprise bonus to be stranded amid such beauty.

The Best of the Cyclades in 10 Days

It's not just that you'll experience five islands in 10 days; more than that, you'll see dozens of landscapes, enjoy a rich variety of experiences, and witness a lot of Greek island life swirling around you. You'll watch the sun set over the caldera in Santorini, find yourself amid ancient temples on Delos, and, if you're wise, take time to slow down long enough to sip coffee in a *plateia* in a Naxian mountain village and wander down a quiet lane on Sifnos.

> *Akrotiri, a Minoan settlement on Santorini, flourished 4,000 years ago.*

START Santorini. **TRIP LENGTH** Total distance covered by boat on a round-trip circuit from Athens is about 600km (373 miles). Keep in mind that winds can wreak havoc on ferry schedules in the Cyclades.

1 Santorini. On Day 1 you will not wander too far away from the rim of the caldera, taking in the sheer spectacle of this legendary island, which may have given rise to the Atlantis myth. If you are not staying in Ia, make your way to the most picturesque of all the villages on Santorini—the best route is the cliffside path that follows the caldera for 10km (6¼ miles) from **Fira** (p. 322, **1**). At sunset, take part in an island ritual and join the spectators who gaze to the west from the *kastro* and other high points in **Ia** (p. 325, **5**) for the natural color and light show at twilight Better yet, enjoy the spectacle from your own

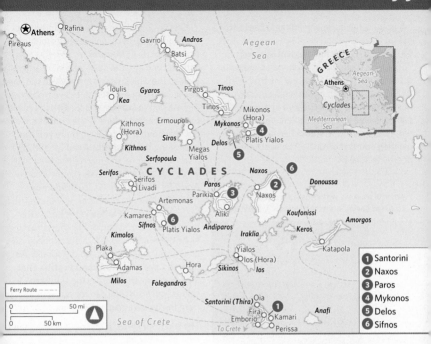

1 Santorini
2 Naxos
3 Paros
4 Mykonos
5 Delos
6 Sifnos

aldera-view terrace. Day 2 takes you away
from the caldera, to step into the island's me-
ieval past in **Pyrgos** (p. 327, 6), then even
arther back in time to **Ancient Thera** (p. 328,
an), home to everyone from Ptolemy's Egyp-
,an army to the Byzantines, and **Akrotiri** (p.
·27, 8), a remarkably well-preserved Minoan
ettlement. ⊙ 2 days.

`ake a morning boat for the 2-hour trip to
Naxos, arriving in midmorning.

2 Naxos. Naxos is the largest island in the Cy-
lades, and with rugged mountains and verdant
alleys, it's certainly one of the most beautiful.
pend Day 1 wandering around Naxos Town,
tarting with the **Portara** (p. 342, 1), a great
nfinished doorway from a 6th-century-B.C.
emple to Apollo at the end of the harbor. You'll
ome across other remains of ancient Naxos in
ne **Bourgo** (p. 344, 2), the lower section of
he Old Town, and palaces and churches from
Venetian rule in the narrow lanes of the **Kastro**
p. 344, 3), a time-defying medieval enclave
igh above the harbor.

On Day 2, drive into the interior. In the **Mel-
nes Valley** (p. 345, 4), you will encounter
kouros, a huge marble statue of a beauti-
ul youth lying in repose in the garden of a

Venetian estate at the **Pirgos Bellonia** (p. 346,
5), one of the many fortified tower houses
built by Venetian overlords. You will also explore the **Temple of Demeter** (p. 347, 7) in
Sangri and the lovely villages of the **Tragaea
Valley** (p. 347, 8). ⊙ 2 days.

**The crossing from Naxos to Paros takes less
than 1 hour.**

3 Paros. After the very short crossing from
Naxos, you will have almost two full days in
which to enjoy Paros, a small island with
plenty to keep you occupied. Spend the first
part of Day 1 in and around the port and
Old Town Parikia (p. 336, 4), a pleasantly
quiet quarter of Cycladic houses, little lanes,
and shady squares, with two remarkable

Getting There

To reach Santorini as early as you can on
Day 1, take the 7 or 7:30am fast boats from
Piraeus, which reach Santorini at 12:30 or
1pm; the midafternoon ferry, which arrives
in Santorini just after midnight, so you can
hit the ground running the next morning;
or the overnight boat, which docks in Santorini around 5am. See p. 370.

landmarks: the intriguing **Panagia Ekatonto-pylani** (Church of the Hundred Doors; p. 334, ❶), and, in the **Archaeological Museum** (p. 336, ❷), a fragment of the Parian Chronicle, a marble slab that records events from 1581 to 299 B.C. Make an afternoon's excursion by bus to **Naoussa** (p. 336, ❺), a character-filled fishing village and resort where you can wander along narrow, whitewashed lanes before planting yourself on one of the excellent nearby beaches.

> *Colorful shutters, whitewashed walls, and neatly trimmed paving stones distinguish Cycladic towns.*

On Day 2, make a leisurely exploration of the island, easy to do on the buses that leave from the port. At **Marathi** (p. 337, ❻), you can descend into the quarries that in antiquity yielded the white marble from which the *Venus de Milo* and other masterpieces were carved. Then it's on to **Lefkes** (p. 338, ❼), the island's medieval capital, where white houses cascade down a mountainside. From there you can walk along the **Byzantine Road** (p. 338, ❽), a section of stone and marble roadway that was the island's major artery in the Middle Ages, for 4km (2½ miles) to **Prodomos,** a mazelike little village of cubical whitewashed houses. Return to **Parikia** in the early afternoon and board a boat for the short crossing to **Antiparos** (p. 339, ⓫), a once-sleepy islet where you can descend into the spooky **Antiparos Cave** or climb **Mount Profitis Elias,** for sweeping views across the southern Cyclades—an effort you can reward with a swim from the beach at **Agios Giorgios.** ⊕ 2 days.

The trip from Paros to Mykonos is less than 1 hour by fast boat.

❹ **Mykonos.** Only a short boat ride away from Paros, worldly, sophisticated, much visited, and unabashedly hedonistic Mykonos seems as if it might be an ocean away from the quieter Cyclades. Even those who bemoan the fact that Mykonos is no longer a simple Greek isle—or for that matter, the favorite getaway of the jet set—are likely to fall under the island's spell. It's most beguiling in the mazelike lanes of **Hora** (p. 356, ❶), where you'll want to spend most of Day 1. You'll probably also want to get out of town for an afternoon swim, preferably at **Elia** or **Kalo Livadi** (p. 360, ❺), both easy to reach by bus, but return in time to enjoy the sunset from the **Esplanade** or **Little Venice** (p. 359, ❷). ⊕ 2 days.

❺ **Delos.** Day 2 should begin with a morning boat trip to the sacred island of **Delos** (p. 308 ❶), one of the most important archaeological sites in the Aegean, and end back in Hora, Mykonos. ⊕ Half-day.

Limited ferry service links Mykonos and Sifnos directly, though on some days you may have to change boats in Paros or another port; allow at least 3 hours for the trip.

Six welcoming villages cluster around Apollonia in the center of Sifnos.

9 Sifnos. End your 10 days of Cycladic island-hopping on what many aficionados consider one of the prettiest and most appealing islands in the Cyclades, if not all of Greece. These attributes are not a secret, especially to the many Athenians who have houses on Sifnos, but the island still seems like an out-of-the-way retreat. An excellent base is **Apollonia** (p. 350, **1**), a cluster of six villages on an inland hillside. From here it's easy to explore the rest of the island by bus. Begin Day 1 with a walk along the lanes that connect the Apollonia villages. Make the short excursion to **Chrysopigi** (p. 353, **7**), where you can visit the monastery of **Panagia Chrysopigi** (the Golden Wellspring) and enjoy a swim from the sandy beach at **Apokofto. Kastro** (p. 353, **5**), a medieval town crowning a seaside hilltop just east of Apollonia, is especially pleasant in the early evening, when you can catch a breeze on the seaside promenade, then wander through the narrow lanes. Have a hearty breakfast on Day 2, to prepare yourself for the climb up to **Profitis Elias o Pilos** (p. 353, **6**), a monastery atop the highest mountain on the island. Then end the day with a swim and a sunset view in **Vathy** (p. 354, **8**), a string of houses alongside a beach of fine sand on the southwestern tip of the island. ⏱ **2 days.**

Cycladic Architecture

On Santorini and other Cycladic Islands, houses were crowded together, one on top of another with common walls, to make optimal use of the land, provide protection, and save money and labor when materials often had to be transported on the backs of donkeys. Many houses on Santorini were built into the cliff face for extra economy. Walls were thick for warmth in the winter and for coolness in the summer, and windows were small. Often the only windows were in the front of the house, on either side of a windowed door, above which a clerestory window was placed to emit light and let hot air trapped near the ceiling escape. Local materials on Santorini were red and black volcanic stone and "Theran earth," a volcanic ash that served as mortar. Roofs were vaulted, an efficient way to bridge interior spaces without using support beams and to allow rain to run off into cisterns, where it was stored for drinking and irrigation. Even many flat-roofed houses are vaulted, with parapets built atop the vaults to serve as terraces or passageways to more houses.

Islands of Gods & Saints: Delos & Tinos

In antiquity, Delos was the most acclaimed of the Cyclades—in fact, the islands are so called because they form a circle (*kylos*) around this tiny and barren scrap of land, birthplace of the mythological twins Apollo and Artemis. A sanctuary to Apollo made Delos a sacred place of pilgrimage for ancient Greeks, and the island later shone in the secular realm as a great center of trade. Latter-day pilgrims set their sights on Tinos, seeking cures in the monumental Panagia Evangelistria tes Tenou (Our Lady of Tinos). With its soothing green landscapes and intriguing mountain villages, the island is indeed a cure-all for the world-weary.

> *The Church of Panagia Evangelistria tes Tenou (Our Lady of Tinos) surrounds cloisterlike courtyards.*

START Mykonos, departure point for most boats to Delos; boats from Mykonos also serve Tinos. **TRIP LENGTH** Allow a day on each of the islands.

SITE GUIDE
PAGE 310

1 ★★★ **Delos.** Delos was one of ancient Greece's most sacred religious sanctuaries and later a flourishing center of trade on the shipping routes between the Aegean world and the Middle East. For a few decades in the 5th

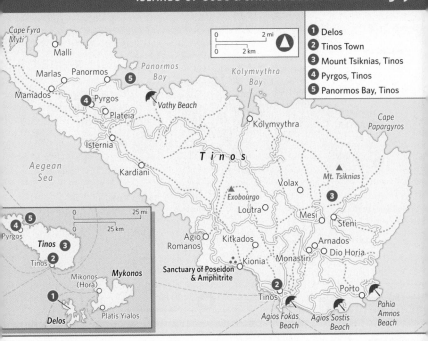

1 Delos
2 Tinos Town
3 Mount Tsiknias, Tinos
4 Pyrgos, Tinos
5 Panormos Bay, Tinos

entury, Delos was headquarters of the Delian eague, the confederation of Greek city-tates, and the repository for its treasury.

These days the island is uninhabited, but 's one of the most important archaeological ites in the Aegean. No one stays on Delos, ut day-trippers arrive by the boatload from Mykonos and the other Cyclades. The island vas removed from the rhythms of everyday fe even in antiquity, when no one was al-owed to be born, to die, or to be buried on Delos (the remains of locals were placed in a urification pit on Rhenea; see p. 358, **1**).

In myth, Delos is the birthplace of Apollo, od of music and light, begotten of Zeus and is lover Leto. When Zeus fell in love with Leto nd she became pregnant, Zeus's wife, Hera, vas furious and ordered the Python, the earth lragon, to pursue Leto. Poseidon took pity on eto and provided her a safe haven by anchor-ng Delos to the sea floor with four diamond olumns. She first stopped on nearby Rhenea to leliver Artemis; then she gave birth to Apollo n Delos, grasping a sacred palm tree on the lopes of Mount Kynthos, the highest hill on the sland, as Zeus watched from the summit.

The island became a center of an Apollo ult and hosted the annual Delian festival in

his honor. By 100 B.C., under Roman occupa-tion, a cosmopolitan population from through-out the Mediterranean world numbered 25,000, and a market was selling 10,000 slaves a day. Delos was gradually abandoned after most of the population was massacred in a wave of attacks in the first years of the new millennium. Besides occasional visitations by Venetians and crusaders, the temples, mosa-ics, and shrines were left to the elements.

A small **Archaeological Museum** on the island is the repository for some of these arti-facts, including statues of Apollo and Artemis, and pottery and other household objects that residents left behind. A snack bar on the

Getting There & Around

Most travelers visit Delos on day trips from Mykonos (see p. 356). Boats depart from the eastern end of the Esplanade at about 9am and return at 3pm or so. Expect to pay about 15€ for the roundtrip (the crossing takes 30 min.), or 30€ if the trip includes a guide. Pick up *Delos and Mykonos: A Guide to the His-tory and Archaeology* at the boat ticket kiosk on Mykonos. Tour operators on Paros and Naxos also run day trips to Delos.

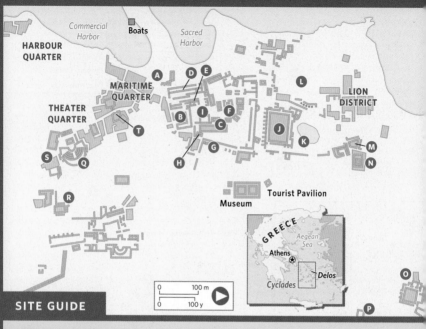

SITE GUIDE

1 Delos

Ⓐ The **Agora of the Competialists,** next to the harbor, was Roman, the domain of members of trade guilds known as Competialists. Just to the east is the **Ⓑ Delian Agora,** site of the slave market. Pilgrims once made their way from the harbor to the **Ⓒ Sanctuary of Apollo** along the **Ⓓ Sacred Way,** past two long, columned porticoes. After the 2nd century B.C., they would enter the sanctuary through the **Ⓔ Propytheria,** a triple-arched marble gateway that opens to a precinct of temples and shrines. Some of the oldest remains on Delos are here, including a shrine thought to be Mycenaean, from as early as 1300 B.C. Three great temples to Apollo were erected in the 6th and 5th centuries B.C. One of them, the **Ⓕ Porinos Naos,** housed the treasury of the Delian League from 477 to 454 B.C. Just beyond the eastern perimeters of Apollo's precinct are the ruins of the long **Ⓖ Sanctuary of the Bulls,** so called for a pair of carved bull heads over the entryway; two former headquarters of state business are next to the sanctuary, the **Ⓗ Bouleterion** (Council House) and the **Ⓘ Prytaneion** (Senate). The enormous **Ⓙ Agora of the Italians**

was once bordered by 112 columns, and the waters of the **Ⓚ Sacred Lake,** now dry, lapped against its edges. A 50m-long (164-ft.) promenade, the **Ⓛ Terrace of the Lions,** runs along the lake's western shores and is still lined with five of nine original marble lions. On the northern shore are the **Ⓜ House on the Lake,** an elegant residence, and the **Ⓝ Granite Palaestra,** a gymnasium and bath complex. Beyond the Palaestra is the **Ⓞ stadium,** where the Delian Games were first staged in the 5th century B.C. The nearby **Ⓟ synagogue** was built around 80 B.C. to serve Syrian and Lebanese Jews who came to Delos during the island's heyday as a trading center. The **Ⓠ theater,** carved into a hillside and surrounded by what was once the residential district of the island, could seat 5,000 spectators. Wealthy merchants and bankers commissioned elaborate villas, such as the **Ⓡ House of the Dolphins,** ★ **Ⓢ House of the Masks** (perhaps a boardinghouse for actors), and the lavish **Ⓣ House of Dionysus.** You can ascend **Ⓤ Mount Kynthos** on a stepped path for a stunning view of the sea and ancient city.

> *The Terrace of the Lions on Delos.*

> *The Church of Panagia Evangelistria tes Tenou.*

island sells beverages and light meals. ⏱ At least 5 hr. Site and museum: ☎ 22890/22259. www.culture.gr. Admission 5€ (included on most organized tours). Tues–Sun 8:30am–3pm.

Tinos is another easy day trip from Mykonos, and boat service between the two is frequent. You can also reach Tinos on regular service from Paros and Naxos, less than 1 hour away.

❷ ★★ **Tinos Town.** Green, mountainous Tinos is a religious island. This becomes evident even before you step foot ashore, when, sailing into the harbor, you see the domineering presence of the **Church of Panagia Evangelistria tes Tenou** (Our Lady of Tinos; open daily 8:30am–3pm; free admission) on a hill atop Tinos Town, the appealing capital and main port. More amazing is the appearance, as you linger over a coffee on Megalochais Avenue, of pilgrims crawling up the street on their hands and knees.

Their destination is the monumental marble church, built on the spot where a miracle-working icon of the Virgin Mary was unearthed in the 1820s. The location of the buried icon came in a dream to St. Pelagia, a

nun who was later canonized; since the icon appeared on the scene at the time of Greek Independence, Our Lady of Tinos became the patron saint of the new Greek nation. Pilgrims come from all over Greece to kiss the icon, which is said to grant miraculous cures. They leave behind ex-voto plaques, depictions in tin of arms, legs, hearts, and other afflicted parts that shine in the glow of thousands of offertory candles. ⏱ 1 hr.

❸ ★★★ **Mount Tsiknias, Tinos.** The highest summit on Tinos, Mount Tsiknias, rises some 670m (2,198 ft.) behind Tinos Town. The mountain was once believed to be the home of Borealis, god of the north wind, and Tinos has always been known and feared for its winds; ancient mariners used to make offerings to Borealis when they passed the island, and winds continue to thwart beachgoers and watersports enthusiasts.

Villages in the hills that unfold around the base of the mountain are some of the most beautiful and unspoiled in the Cyclades. A circuit begins in **Monastiri,** also known as Kechrouvni, 9km (5⅔ miles) north of Tinos Town. Sister Pelagia had her revelatory dream here in the convent of **Moni Kechrouvni,** and her head is kept in a wooden chest in a chapel devoted to her. **Arnados,** 1km (⅔ mile) east, and **Dio Horia** another 2km (1¼ mile) farther along, are magical little places, mazes of white Cycladic cubes where the narrow streets burrow beneath the houses and the roof of one house serves as the ntrance to the next. The landscape becomes vilder around **Xombourgo,** a rocky spire 5km 3 miles) to the north that the Venetians en-ircled with defensive walls. Aristocratic man-ions, barracks, and churches are now in ruin, ttering the green mountainside pastures with omantic-looking piles of stone. Villagers in **Volax,** in a boulder-strewn valley another 5km 3 miles) north, weave baskets that they sell rom their home workshops. ⏱ **3 hr.**

④ ★★ Pyrgos, Tinos. This lovely village at the orth end of the island is famous for marble, quarried just outside town. You'll notice mar-ole fanlights and lintels above the doorways of the stone houses as you follow the lanes that merge into a beautiful marble *plateia,* shaded y plane trees. A seven-spouted marble foun-ain splashes to one side of the square. In two ide-by-side village houses are the **Museum of Iannoulis Chalepas** (open Tues–Sun 11am–2pm and 6–8pm; admission 2€) and the **Museum of Tenos Artists** (open Tues–Sun 11am–2pm and 6–8pm; admission 2€), showcases or local craftspeople. The **Museum of Marble Crafts** (Wed–Mon 10am–6pm, till 5 in winter; ree admission), just outside the village, is a contemporary showplace for marble-working echniques that have been practiced on the sland since medieval times. ⏱ **2 hr.**

⑤ ★★ Panormos Bay, Tinos. The small port and the secluded coves that surround it are he most pleasant settings on the island for a swim and a seafood meal at one of the quay-side tavernas. ⏱ **2 hr.**

> *Moni Kechrouvni and other monasteries are tucked into the rugged mountainsides of Tinos.*

Where to Stay & Dine on Tinos

★★ Alonia Hotel
Along with the comfortable rooms and friendly service, gardens, a pool, and sea views make this one of the best choices for an overnight in Tinos. Amenities include a homey restaurant and bar, and Tinos Town is just 2km (1¼ mile) down the road. Outside Tinos Town on road to Agios Ioannis. ☎ 22830/23541. 30 units. Doubles 80€–125€ w/breakfast. MC, V. Closed Oct–Apr.

★★★ Metaxi Mas *GREEK*
The focus in this cozy restaurant just off the waterfront is on meze, from wonderful vege-table fritters to deep-fried little tomatoes. You

can easily make a meal of them, but heartier dishes are also on offer. Kontogiorgi alley. ☎ 22830/25945. Entrees 7€–20€. No credit cards. Lunch & dinner daily.

★★ To Koutouki tis Eleni *GREEK*
This is where the locals go for a meal, and they know what to expect—no fuss, excellent food, and good prices. You might be shown a fish or asked to step into the kitchen to see what's on the stove that day. Whatever you choose will be delicious. Off Evangelista. ☎ 22830/24857. Entrees 5€–10€. No credit cards. Lunch & dinner daily.

OUR TOWN

Life in the Ancient Greek City State

BY STEPHEN BREWER

LTHOUGH MANY OF THE GREAT CITIES of Ancient Greece now lie in rubble, their iscernible layouts still evoke a fairly civilized, orderly society that, by around 800 .c., was loosely organized into hundreds of independent city-states, or *polis,* that ontrolled their surrounding territories. The largest city-state, Sparta, held more 1an 3,000 square miles. Governed by free male citizens, the *polis* gave rise to West-rn notions of democracy, not to mention the word "politics." More than that, with 1eir shops, temples, residential streets, theaters, and stadiums, these early cities 1nd towns suggest the Greeks led a relatively comfortable daily existence.

Streetscape

Most cities were en-losed by ramparts, ften with massive for-fications. The stone valls at **Tiryns** were so ormidable they led to 1e belief that the city vas the birthplace of lercules (see p. 188).

THE ACROPOLIS, usually the highest oint in the city, was sacred precinct, ousing the most important temples. Valls, connected to 1e city fortifications, often enclosed the cropolis, providing place of refuge luring attacks. The **Acrocorinth,** 540m 1,700 ft.) above ncient Corinth, is ne of the world's nost remarkable ortresses and housed temple to Aphrodite, staffed with prosti-

tutes (see p. 186). **ENTRY** One gate served as the main entryway. **The Lion Gate** at Mycenae (see p. 189) is especially impressive.

THE AGORA was the downtown, or city center—where the populace came to socialize, shop in markets, and worship. Politicians convened in the agora to govern the city. **Delos,** once the major trading center of the Aegean, had several agoras to ac-commodate the many slave and commodity markets (see p. 308).

THE BOULEU-TERION, always in the agora, was the meet-ing hall of the town council. You can see the ruins of the *bouleuterion* in the **Athenian Agora** (see p. 42). The agora

had at least one **STOA,** a long, covered portico that provided shelter, housed market stalls and small businesses, and served as a meet-ing place. Two long, columned porticoes line the **Sacred Way on Delos** (see p. 310).

RESIDENTIAL DISTRICTS, often laid out along gridlike streets, surrounded the agora.

A THEATER was set beneath a slope to provide seating. Among many well

preserved examples in ancient Greek towns is the **Theater at Argos** (see p. 188).

THE GYMNASIUM AND STADION, outside the center of town, had a running track and athletic field; young men often lived on these premises

to receive physical training and education. You will come upon two gymnasiums at **Ancient Thera on Santorini** (see p. 328).

Home Sweet Home

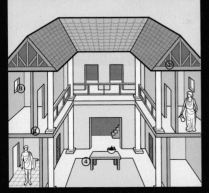

Houses were usually made of sun-dried brick on a foundation of stones. Burglars were called "wall piercers," because they could easily break through the walls.

① The **andron** was re-served for male guests and had a separate en-trance to the street so men would not have to encounter women of the house. This room was usually tiled, and the rest of the house had floors of packed mud. ② A **women's room.** ③ **Sleeping and storage rooms.** ④ The **courtyard,** where family life was

centered and meals were prepared. A **kitchen** had a hole in the ceiling for smoke from a brazier to escape. The **toilet** consisted of a chamber pot that was emptied into a gutter in the street outside. Gutters often drained into underground sewers that chan-neled waste water away from towns.

Off the Beaten Path on Milos

Small and rugged Milos, the westernmost island in the Cyclades, is best known for the most famous statue to come down to us from ancient Greece, the *Venus de Milo*. The artwork, of course, is no longer here, but in the Louvre in Paris, where it was shipped soon after a farmer unearthed it in his field in 1820. Travelers who explore Milos soon discover splendid, unspoiled beaches etched out of astonishing rock formations, some impossibly pictur-esque seaside villages, and a scattering of intriguing ruins. What's best about Folegandros is what is *not* there, so close is life to the way it's been for centuries. What *is* there also warrants the trouble it takes to get to the island—one of the most beautiful towns in the Cyclades, appealing landscapes, and good beaches.

> *Plaka sits high above the beautiful Gulf of Milos.*

START Milos. **TRIP LENGTH** Allow at least 4 days to see both islands.

❶ ★ Adamas, Milos. Milos's port sits to one side of the Gulf of Milos, a long, wide natural harbor that takes an enormous bite out of the center of the island. A tree-shaded **seafront promenade** is especially animated with stroll-ers and cafe loungers in the early evening, making for a scene about as cosmopolitan as you are going to stumble upon on Milos.

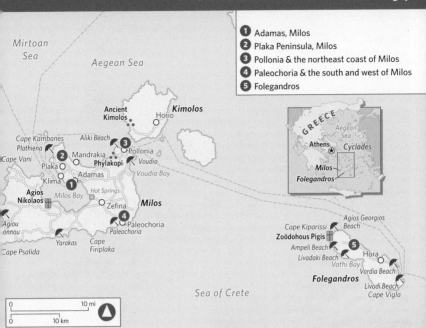

1 Adamas, Milos
2 Plaka Peninsula, Milos
3 Pollonia & the northeast coast of Milos
4 Paleochoria & the south and west of Milos
5 Folegandros

The **Mining Museum** (☎ 22870/22481; admission 3€; May–Sept daily 9am–2pm and –8pm, Oct–Apr Tues–Sat 8:30am–2pm) introduces you to the industry that has been active on the island since prehistoric times and still renders large tracts of the island off limits. Miners were unearthing obsidian—hard, black volcanic glass—to fashion arrowheads and razor-sharp blades as long as 13,000 years ago. Milos also supplied ancient Greeks with most of their fuller's earth, a household staple used for bleach, facial masks, and medicinal baths. ⏱ 2 hr.

2 ★★★ **Plaka Peninsula, Milos.** Plaka, the island capital high above Adamas, straddles the heights at the end of the peninsula that encloses the eastern side of the bay. White Cycladic houses tumble down the slopes, interspersed here and there with a Roman theater and other ruins of ancient Milos. Most intriguing are Greece's only **Christian catacombs** (Trypiti; ☎ 22870/21370; free admission; Tues–Sun 8:30am–1:30pm), a vast network of underground passages that burrow some 185m (607 ft.) into the soft earth. Some 2,000 early Christians were entombed in the tunnels in the 3rd and 4th centuries A.D.

> *Some of the best and least crowded beaches in the Cyclades ring Milos.*

Visitors walk through one of the damp, claustrophobia-inducing tunnels, past hundreds of burial vaults, into a large cavern once used for clandestine worship. One of the most riveting artifacts in Plaka's modest **Archaeological Museum** (admission 2€; July–Oct Tues–Sun 8:30am–3pm, Nov–Dec Tues–Sun 8am–2:30pm) is a terra cotta effigy of a vessel from

> *At Plathiena and elsewhere along the coast of Milos, turquoise coves are etched out of volcanic rock.*

about 3,000 B.C. that traders used to transport obsidian from Milos around the Aegean.

Klima, the port of ancient Milos, is an easy downhill stroll from the catacombs. Almost nothing remains of Klima's distant past, but the little collection of houses is charming. Klima and its seaside neighbors—Mandrakia, Firopotamos, Areti, and Fourkouvoni—are built around protective coves in a style unique to Milos. Whitewashed houses are dug

Getting There & Around

Milos is 4 to 6 hours by boat from Piraeus; service runs two or three times a day. You can also reach Milos by boat from other islands in the Cyclades, including Sifnos. A car is necessary to explore much of the island, and you can rent cars from the many agencies on the harbor in Adamas. Milos does not have an official tourist office, but these agencies also provide maps and other information about the island.

cavelike out of the hillsides, with waterside boathouses on the ground floor and living quarters above; their doors, shutters, and balconies are painted in bright shades of red, blue, and green that add even more luster to the blue seas that wash against them. Nearby **Sarakiniko,** 5km (3 miles) east of Plaka, is an astonishingly dramatic slice of the coast. A turquoise cove is etched out of white volcanic rock, creating an eerie moonscape that is an enticing spot for a swim. ☉ At least half-day.

❸ ★★ **Pollonia & the northeast coast of Milos.** Another dramatic volcanic seascape lies at the foot of the cliffs at Papafranga, where winds have shaped the white volcanic rock that lines the shores into strange formations. You can cross the folds and crevices on a well-worn path and descend to a deep fjord and, a little farther along the coast, three side-by-side sea caves. Just above the shore are the haunting remains of **Phylakopi** (free admission; June–Sept daily 8:30am–7pm, Oct–May daily 8:30am–3pm), a city that dates rom about 3,500 B.C. and was last inhabited around 1600 B.C., when refugees from the volcano on Santorini may have found sanctuary on Milos. Elements have worn away all but the faint remains of a large palace and a shrine.

Pollonia, a fishing village at the northeastern tip of the island, is the point of embarkation for boats to **Kimolos,** a quiet little place that will probably meet the expectations of even the most discerning traveler looking for an undiscovered Greek island. Car ferries from Pollonia make the 30-minute crossing about four times a day. Once on the island, take a look at scrappy little Hora, a jumble of whitewashed Cycladic houses where donkeys roam the streets. Then find your way to Aliki or Klima, the nicest of the island's excellent sand beaches. ⏱ 1 day with trip to Kimolos; 2 hr. without.

❹ ★★★ **Paleochoria & the south and west of Milos.** The best beaches on Milos are on the rugged south coast. One of the longest is **Paleochoria,** 10km (6¼ miles) south of Adamas, but all are beautiful, sandy, and nestled between rocky headlands. No road runs along the south coast, but with the aid of a good map, you can drop down from the north coast to Paleochoria and Provitas on paved roads and to Firiplaka and Tsigrado on dirt tracks.

The farther west you go, the wilder the landscape becomes. The scrub-covered terrain rises along the flanks of Mount Profitis Ilias and descends to the sea at Triades and a few other isolated beaches, reached only by dirt tracks or by the excursion boats that leave from Adamas (see below). Most of the southwest side of Milos is protected as a nature

> *Easygoing Pollonia is a fishing port on the northeast coast of Milos.*

Tour Milos by Boat

An excellent way to see the island's dramatic coastline is on a boat tour. Excursion boats usually hug the shore for close-up views of Sarakiniko and other volcanic seascapes, drop anchor for a swim from at least one of the island's sandy beaches, and stop at the island of Kimolos. Trips usually last all day, leaving the ports at Adamas or Pollonia at about 9am and returning at 4pm. Among the operators is **Milos Travel** in Adamas (☎ 22870/22000; www.milostravel.gr).

preserve, the domain of monk seals and other endangered species. Should you decide to trek across the countryside (any of the travel offices in Adamas will provide maps), be on the lookout for one of them, the Milos viper. ⏱ At least half-day.

Served just a few times a week from Piraeus, Folegandros is connected directly with Sifnos, Paros, and other islands in the Cyclades. You will not need a car on Folegandros; you can go anywhere by bus or on foot.

> *One of many narrow, mazelike streets in Hora, capital of Folegandros.*

5 ★★★ **Folegandros.** From the small harbor at Karovista, the road climbs 3km (2 miles) up the cliffs to Hora, an almost impossibly picturesque little place where narrow streets wind around three shady squares scented with lime trees. In the middle of the maze are the remains of the fort, or **kastro,** built by the Venetians when they took control of Folegandros and other Cyclades in the 13th century. The **Church of Kimisis tis Theotokou** (Mother of God) commands the highest spot in town, and the surrounding houses are flat-roofed cubes with whitewashed exterior staircases that climb to painted balconies; many are set onto the edge of the cliff, and all are bedecked with geraniums and bougainvillea.

A 5km (3-mile) walk along the cliffs brings you to **Ano Mera** (a bus also connects the two towns). The only other settlement on the island is surrounded by small farms parceled into plots by dry stone walls. The crops the stony earth yields and the catch the fishing fleet brings back from sea are still the mainstays of the island economy. Paths from Ano Mera lead to three of the island's most pleasant beaches, those at Livadaki, Ampeli, and, at the northern tip of the island, Agios Giorgios. Two other fine beaches, Agios Nikolaos and Angali, are tucked into coves midway between Hora and Ano Mera; the bus stops at the head of the steep paths leading down to both. Walks down to the coast follow the *monopathi,* rough stone paths that farmers used for centuries, flanked by stone walls and surrounded by countryside that is fragrant with the scent of wild herbs. ⏲ 2 days.

Where to Stay & Dine on Milos & Folegandros

> Tables at O Kritikos spill across one of Hora's tree-shaded squares.

★★ Anemomilos Apartments FOLEGANDROS

The most comfortable lodgings on Folegandros teeter at the edge of the cliffs and face the sea from terraces. A pool is set in the gardens, and the attractive apartments, with kitchenettes, are so appealing that you will want to settle in for a very long time. **Hora.** ☎ 22860/41309. 17 units. Doubles 80€–125€. MC, V. Closed Oct–Apr.

★★ Castro Hotel FOLEGANDROS

There's no shortage of atmosphere in this 13th-century Venetian castle on the edge of the cliffs. Rooms are small but most are filled with airy views, and some face the sea far below Hora from little balconies. **Hora.** ☎ 22860/41230. 12 units. Doubles 80€–125€. MC, V. Closed Oct–Apr.

★ Diporto MILOS GREEK

This old taverna where tables spill out into the alleyways of Plaka specializes in snails in tomato sauce, a hearty goat stew, and other traditional island dishes. Begin any meal as the locals who pack in here do, with a platter of appetizers—the zucchini balls with cheese and fried cheese pies are not to be missed. **Plaka.** ☎ 22870/23259. Entrees 6€–12€. No credit cards. Lunch & dinner daily.

★★ Melian Hotel MILOS

The waves crash right against the terrace of this stunning villa-like hotel outside Pollonia, and the large rooms and suites, all individually decorated in a comfortable traditional style, are the most deluxe lodgings on the island. Most of the terraces have hot tubs, a spa is on the premises, and the beach is just steps away. **Pollonia.** ☎ 22870/41150. 15 units. Doubles 100€–200€ w/breakfast. MC, V. Closed Oct–Apr.

★ O Kritikos FOLEGANDROS GREEK

Dining on Folegandros is basic, and most menus include *souroto* and other island cheeses and *matsada*, fresh pasta with rabbit or chicken. This simple taverna adds another twist—chicken, pork, and lamb grilled with herbs. **Hora.** ☎ 22860/41219. Entrees 6€–10€. No credit cards. Dinner daily.

★★ Villa Notos MILOS

These large, comfortable apartments at the edge of Adamas look over the bay and a small beach. All have sitting areas and large terraces and are equipped with small kitchens. The center of town is just a few steps away. **Adamas.** ☎ 22870/28200. 6 units. Doubles 80€–125€ w/breakfast. MC, V. Closed Oct–Apr.

Santorini

Little wonder that Santorini is the most visited of the Greek isles. You won't encounter too many vestiges of authentic Greece here or discover little-known terrain, but you will never tire of soaking in the natural beauty of one of the world's most spectacular islands. When you tear yourself away from the views of the volcanic caldera that sparkles far below the island's flanks, you can bask on black sand beaches and encounter the remains of prehistoric civilizations at Akrotiri and Ancient Thera.

> *You'll never tire of the views over Santorini's caldera.*

START Fira. **TRIP LENGTH** Allow at least 2 days to see the island.

❶ ★★★ Fira. The island capital surrendered its soul to tourism several decades ago, but the cliffside setting remains as intoxicatingly dramatic as ever. From Ypapantis, the walkway that follows the rim of the caldera, the view is never less than staggering. The blue sea sparkles some 300m (984 ft.) below, the cliffs take on multicolored hues in the sun, and white, cubical houses appear to tumble from the cliff tops. This extraordinary vista is especially dramatic from the stepped path that winds down the cliff face to the little harbor of Fira Skala, where you can board a cable car for the ascent. (Tour guides will try to cajole you into mounting a donkey for the ride up, but leave the poor swaybacked beasts in peace; the cable car makes the trip up in 2 min., runs every 15 min. from 7:30am to 9pm, and costs 3€).

It's a pleasure to take refuge from the crowds along shop-lined Erythron Stavron street in the nearby **Megaro Gyzi Cultural Centre** (next to cathedral; ☎ 22860/22244; www.megarogyzi.gr/en; admission 3€; Mon–Sat 10:30am–1pm and 5–8pm, Sun 10:30am–4:30pm), where fascinating photographs show Santorini as it looked before and just after the last catastrophic seismic event, the earthquake of 1956, which leveled much of the island. The handsome 17th-century mansion that houses the museum is one of the few historic homes in Fira that withstood the quake.

Archaeologists have unearthed two ancient sites on Santorini: **Ancient Thera** (p. 328, **❾**), from around the 9th century B.C., and **Akrotiri** (p. 327, **❽**), settled by Minoans from

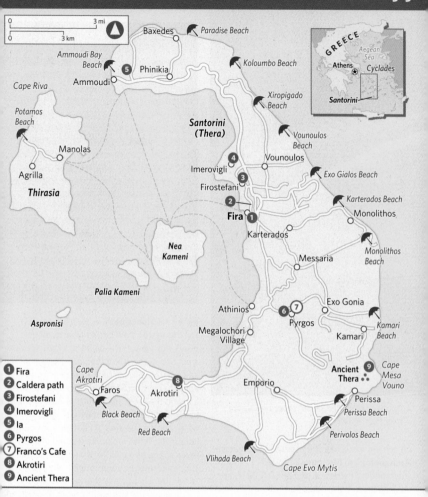

1 Fira
2 Caldera path
3 Firostefani
4 Imerovigli
5 Ia
6 Pyrgos
7 Franco's Cafe
8 Akrotiri
9 Ancient Thera

Crete around 3000 B.C. The island's greatest archaeological treasures are the stunning frescoes found virtually intact in Akrotiri. These have been carted off to the National Archaeological Museum in Athens, where they are star attractions. The island makes a good showing of the artifacts that remain in Fira's Museum of Prehistoric Thera, with some

Getting There & Around

Santorini is served by several flights a day from Athens, but one of the great Greek experiences is arriving by boat and sailing into the island's caldera. Ferries arrive from Piraeus in the early morning and late at night, and fast boats arrive in early afternoon. Santorini is also well connected by ferry and fast boat with Milos, Mykonos, Paros, and Naxos, and less frequently with Sifnos and Folegandros. Most boats arrive at the port of Athinios, connected to Fira by buses and taxis that meet the boats. Buses serve almost every corner of the island, though you may want to rent a car or motorbike for at least a day of your stay to zip around the island and visit Pyrgos, wineries, Akrotiri, Ancient Thera, and the island's famous volcanic beaches.

> *Paralia Kokkini (Red Beach) takes it namesake color from volcanic rocks.*

A Caldera Is Born

A caldera forms when molten rock, known as magma, is ejected from a volcanic crater during an eruption. Without the support of underlying magma, the land surrounding the crater collapses. A volcanic eruption several hundred thousand years ago created the caldera in Santorini, when the center of a circular island collapsed. The sea rushed in to fill the caldera, and volcanic debris from other eruptions has refilled the caldera many times over the millennia, only to collapse again. By the time of the eruption in 1600 B.C., the Santorini caldera was almost entirely ringed with land, except for one narrow channel. One of the largest eruptions on record, the 1600 B.C. explosion blew open additional channels, creating the present-day appearance of the caldera.

wonderful fresco fragments, and the adjacent **Archaeological Museum,** founded in 1902 (both behind cathedral; ☎ 22860/22217; admission 5€ to both; Tues–Sun 8:30am–3pm). The Akrotiri wall paintings are re-created in sophisticated three-dimensional photographs at the **Thera Foundation: The Wall Painting of Thera** (on caldera path past cable car; ☎ 22860/23016; www.therafoundation.org; admission 4€; May–Sept daily 10am–7pm). The paintings are among the largest and most intact artworks to come down from such a distant past, and the images of monkeys (indicating trade with North Africa), ships sailing past leaping dolphins, cows, and young women gathering saffron reveal much about this early society that disliked war and admired beauty. Even in reproduction, the paintings are stunning, as is the view over the caldera from the museum terrace. ⏱ 4 hr.

❷ ★★★ **Caldera path.** A path follows the top of the cliff from Fira to Ia, affording a bird's-eye view of the caldera. Walking even a portion of the 10km (6¼-mile) length of the cliff-top route is the best experience you are going to have on Santorini. Looking over the bay and the crescent of cliffs is like staring into the Grand Canyon—an ever changing scene in which the rock seems to change color before your eyes. What looks like a patch of snow takes shape as a cluster of houses; an islet suddenly catches your notice.

Santorini is actually the eastern rim of a volcano and the largest fragment of an island that was blown apart during a series of massive eruptions (a blast in 1600 B.C. is one of the largest volcanic eruptions ever recorded). Across the bay are other remnants of the rim, the isles of **Therasia** and **Aspronisi** (White Island), and in the center are two isles of blackened earth, **Nea** and **Palea Kaimeni** (New and Old Burnt Isles), the cones of volcanoes. This geology reveals itself slowly, and its unique beauty seems to intensify with every step you take along the caldera path. ⏱ At least 2 hr. to walk from Fira to Ia.

❸ ★★ **Firostefani.** This quiet outpost of Fira is a good place to appreciate the island's beautiful architecture. Fira, Firostefani, and many of

> *Santorini's caldera, capped by the village of Fira.*

the villages on Santorini were built atop the cliffs to protect them from pirates who once marauded around the Aegean. As you walk down any of the lanes that descend from the top of the cliff, you'll see the white cubical houses huddled together on narrow lanes, one on top of another, many dug into the side of the cliff—impossibly picturesque, though Cycladic architecture evolved from the harsh necessities of the sun-scorched barren landscape. ⏱ 30 min.

❹ ★★★ **Imerovigli.** At the edge of this enchanting little village, tucked into the highest point on the caldera rim, are more of the visual treats so common on Santorini—views of the caldera and **Skaros,** a rocky promontory just offshore. Skaros was once crowned with an ancient city and later the fortified town of Rocca, the seat of Venetian nobility and Turkish administrators. After descending the stepped, quiet streets of Imerovigli, then a precipitous drop down a cliff path, you'll reach the isthmus that connects Skaros to the rest of Santorini. Then it's uphill for 2km (1¼ mile) or so, along a cliff face of volcanic rock, to the ruins of the fortifications, toppled by earthquakes over the years, and a small chapel.

Your rewards for the excursion are the phenomenal views over the bay and up the walls of the caldera to the villages glistening on the cliff tops. ⏱ 4 hr., with walk up Skaros.

❺ ★★★ **Ia.** Santorini's most picturesque village clings to the northwestern tip of the caldera. Once populous and prosperous, home of many of the island's wealthy maritime families, Ia was all but leveled in the earthquake of 1956. Most of the residents fled, leaving behind a spooky yet beguiling ghost town of half-ruined houses overlooking the caldera. Recent years have been kind to Ia. Nikolaou Nomikou, the main pedestrian way, is lively once again, and the blue Aegean sparkles enticingly below the cave houses that have been reclaimed as comfortable hotels.

One of the town's neoclassical mansions, once home to sea captains, now houses the **Naval Maritime Museum** (☎ 22860/71156; admission 3€; Wed–Mon 10am–2pm and 5–8pm). The figureheads, ship models, and old photographs recall a time when, in the middle of the 19th century, Santorini launched one of the largest merchant fleets in the Aegean. By 1850, more than 200 Santorini vessels were shipping the island's wine to Russia,

> *In Pyrgos, white houses are built back-to-back and one atop the other beneath a Venetian citadel.*

transporting Russian wheat to ports of call around Europe, and sailing to Athens laden with volcanic pumice from the island used for the building craze then transforming Athens, the new nation's capital. Ship captains and sailors prospered, and the island still makes its living in small part from the sea. A small fishing fleet bobs in the sea far below the town in the little port of Ammoudi, reached by a flight of 300 stone stairs that wind down the cliff. A row of tavernas that serve fresh fish right off the boats line the quay, and a small pebble beach serves well for a quick swim.

Many visitors find their way to Ia to watch the sunset from the walls of the Kastro, at the western edge of town—a spectacular sight, but no more so here than anywhere

Fruits of the Vine

The eruption of 1,600 B.C. covered Santorini with ashy volcanic soil that is extremely hospitable to the Assyrtiko grape, a hardy variety that yields the island's distinctly dry whites and *vin santo,* a sweet dessert wine. Some 36 other varieties grow on Santorini, including the white Athyri and Aidani and the red Mantilaria and Mavrotagano. Growers twist the vines into low-lying basket shapes that hug the ground for protection against the wind, and nighttime mists off the sea provide just enough moisture. Several wineries offer tastings and tours; most of the larger operations cater to busloads of passengers from cruise ships, so don't expect a winery visit to be low-key. Some of the top wineries that offer tastings are **Boutari,** Megalochori (☎ 22860/81011); **Antoniou,** Megalochori (☎ 22860/23557); and **Santo,** Pyrgos (☎ 22860/22596). The enormous tasting rooms and terraces at Antoniou and Santo overlook the caldera, adding a bit of drama to enhance your tippling.

else on the caldera. ⏱ 4 hr., with walk down to
Ammoudi.

Pyrgos is 6km (3¾ miles) south of Fira and
easy to reach by bus.

6 ★★ **Pyrgos.** The longtime capital of the
island under the Venetians and Turks is inland,
far out of the way of harm that could arrive by
sea. Pyrgos makes a striking appearance as you
approach from the flat, arid landscapes of the
coastal plain: A cone of tiered houses rises on
the flanks of a hill beneath a Venetian citadel.
Built back-to-back and one on top of the other,
the cubical white houses provided a phalanx
against invaders, and the lanes that tunnel
beneath them could be blockaded to keep out
invaders. The once mighty castle at the top of
this medieval maze was indeed impenetrable
but not immune to earthquakes, one of which
toppled the walls and towers half a century ago.
The overgrown ruins afford views across the
island.

The monastery of **Profitis Elias** (p. 353, **6**)
crowns a nearby peak, the tallest on Santorini
at almost 1,000m (3,281 ft.). Islanders make
their way to these breezy heights not just for
the views but to pay tribute to the community
that provided a place of refuge and kept Greek
traditions alive at a secret school during Turkish rule in the 18th and 19th centuries. A shady
series of rooms off the courtyard houses some
of the rare books the monks safeguarded, as
well as icons. The enterprising monks also
produced excellent wine on their steep hillsides, shipping the output all over Europe on
their own merchant ship, which flew the monastery banner.

Vineyards still grow around Pyrgos and
nearby Megalochori. Their vintages, and those
of Santorini's other *canavas* (wineries), rank
among the top Greek wines. You may want to
stop at one or two in your travels around the
island (see box). ⏱ 2 hr.

---

⑦ 🍽 **Franco's Cafe.** A lookout at the top of
town serves snacks and drinks on a view-
filled terrace. You may want to come
back for a sunset cocktail or after-dinner
drink. Pyrgos. ☎ 22860/33957. $

Akrotiri is 6km (3¾ miles) west of Pyrgos and
can be reached by bus.

> *Profitis Elias Monastery is near Pyrgos.*

8 ★★★ **Akrotiri.** One of the best-preserved
ancient settlements in the Aegean, the
so-called Minoan Pompeii was settled by
Minoans who sailed over from Crete as early
as 3000 B.C. By 2000 B.C., Akrotiri was a

Is Santorini Atlantis?

That's the million-dollar question. What's
known is that earthquakes followed by
a massive volcanic eruption destroyed
much of Santorini some time around 1600
B.C. Plato tells us that Atlantis "disappeared into the sea depths" some 9,000
years before his time—but that's only one
zero off from 900 years (a mistake that's
come down through the ages, perhaps?).
Plato wrote in the 5th century B.C., so the
missing-zero theory places the destruction
of Atlantis tantalizingly close to the time of
the Santorini eruption.

> *Egyptians, Ancient Greeks, Romans, and Byzantines left their mark amid the ruins of Ancient Thera.*

flourishing urban center that grew olives and grain, created fanciful art, wove beautiful textiles, took peace so much for granted that residents saw no need to build defensive walls, and sent trade ships to ports as far away as Egypt.

Akrotiri was buried deep in ash during the eruption of 1600 B.C. and not uncovered for another 3,300 years, by workers mining ash and pumice in 1860. Human remains and valuables have never been found, suggesting that the inhabitants had enough warning to flee the city. What they could not take with them were the magnificent paintings that once covered the walls of their public buildings and homes, now in the National Archaeological Museum in Athens (and stunningly re-created in Fira; see p. 322, **①**).

The 40 stores, warehouses, and houses that line Akrotiri's main street are remarkably well preserved, as are many giant *pithoi* (earthenware jars) and their contents of oil, fish, and onions. More than two-thirds of the town still remains covered and may one day reveal more treasures and secrets of the past.

Akrotiri has been closed since a steel roof protecting the site collapsed in 2004. Reopening is scheduled for sometime in 2010 or 2011. One of the island's famously colored beaches, **Paralia Kokkini** (Red Beach), is next to Akrotiri; the small red volcanic pebble beach is at most times pleasantly uncrowded. ⏲ At least 2 hr. ☎ 22860/81366. www.culture.gr. Admission 6€. Tues–Sun 8:30am–3pm.

Ancient Thera is 6km (3¾ miles) east of Akrotiri and 6km (3¾ miles) south of Fira; the site can be reached by bus.

SITE GUIDE PAGE 329

⑨ ★★★ Ancient Thera. The most dramatic way to reach the ruins of this ancient city atop a rocky headland is on a steep path from the seaside town Kamari. A drive up the Mesa Vouna is almost as inspiring and reaffirms the notion that the ancients never underestimated the value of a good location. The town was settled in the 9th century B.C., and since then Egyptian palaces, Greek temples, Roman baths, and Byzantine walls have risen atop the seaside cliffs. The ruins are a jumble left behind by the different cultures that have swept across the island, but the views are so dizzying you probably won't mind a little confusion. Below the promontory is the most famous beach on Santorini: Kamari—a dramatic swath of silky black sand. ⏲ At least 2 hr. ☎ 22860/31366. www.culture.gr. Admission 4€. Tues–Sun 8am–3pm.

Close Encounters with a Volcano

The experience is not as dramatic as it seems. Excursions take you to **Nea Kaimeni** (New Burnt Isle), one of the cones of the volcano that still smolders in the caldera, and they often also stop for a swim in the hot springs that bubble up off **Palea Kaimeni** (Old Burnt Isle). Boats then continue to the quiet island of **Therasia,** a fragment of the rim across the caldera from Santorini, for lunch. All in all, this is a pleasant outing but not essential, especially if your time on Santorini is short. Excursions usually cost about 20€ and can be arranged with any of the legions of tour operators on the island; most boats leave from Armeni, below Ia.

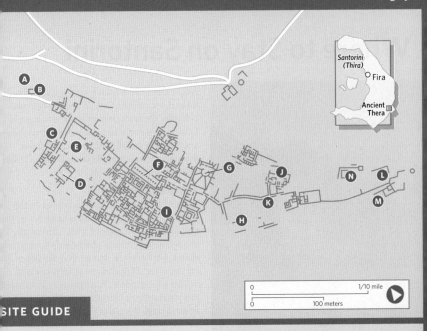

SITE GUIDE

9 Ancient Thera

The small **A Chapel of Agios Stefanos** stands on the foundations of the first Christian basilica on Santorini, from the 4th century. The Egyptian troops of Ptolemy, garrisoned on Santorini in the 3rd century B.C., dug the nearby **B Sanctuary of Artemidoros of Perge** out of rock. The **C Egyptian commandant's house** and a **D gymnasium** the soldiers used are a little farther along the main street. Just beyond is the **E agora,** the huge marketplace the Greeks established. The Egyptians added the monumental **F Stoa Basilike** (Royal Porch); the colonnade was 40m (131 ft.) long and 10m (33 ft.) wide. Just beyond is a **G Greek theater** (largely rebuilt by the Romans), a small **H Temple to Apollo** (refashioned in part as a Byzantine church), and a **I sanctuary to the Egyptian gods,** with niches for votives to Isis, Anubis, and Serapis. A larger **J Temple to Apollo Karneios,** the Ram, Protector of Flocks, is just down the street. The large **K Terrace of the Festivals** in front of the temple was the stage for the Karneia, a Greek festival in which young adolescents undergoing strict military training, *ephebes,* danced naked; it's been suggested

that the display inspired a large phallus carved onto a nearby wall and inscribed with the words "to my friends." Youths trained in the **L Gymnasium of the Ephebes** and bathed afterward in facilities that the Romans fashioned into elaborate **M baths.** Just below is a **N grotto** dedicated to the two patron deities of the *ephebes,* Hermes and Hercules.

Where to Stay on Santorini

> Caldera-side lodging makes the most of a stay in Santorini.

★★ Aressana Spa Hotel FIRA

Travelers put off by the steps that may make many caldera-view hotels impractical will find a welcome refuge in this stunning retreat set in a garden in the middle of Fira. Decor can be aggressively hip, but the stylish rooms are large and offer every comfort, and the pool is transcendent, as is the spa. ☎ 22860/23900. www.aressana.gr. 50 units. Doubles 210€–240€ w/breakfast. AE, MC, V.

★★★ Astra Apartments IMEROVIGLI

Dramatic eagle's-eye views over the caldera and the Skaros promontory set the scene for some of the most pleasant lodging in Santorini. Lovely suites and apartments surround a beautiful pool and cling to the side of the caldera, and the amazing setting and tasteful accommodations—with vaulted ceilings, beautiful tile work, and handsome wood and fabrics—are enhanced with service that focuses on every detail. ☎ 22860/23641. www. astra-apartments.com. 85 units. Doubles 250€– 380€ w/breakfast. AE, MC, V.

★★ Aura Marina AKROTIRI

Some of the nicest accommodations on the south end of Santorini face the sea from a hillside above the village of Akrotiri. These airy, handsomely furnished apartments have sitting rooms, kitchenettes, and bedrooms/sleeping lofts, and all open to large terraces with private plunge pools. You'll need a car to reach this pleasantly remote place, but that may be an advantage if you'd otherwise have trouble climbing up and down stairs to reach your lodging. ☎ 69760/14462. www.aura-marina. com. 9 units. Doubles 150€–200€. AE, MC, V.

★★★ Esperas IA

You'll feel like a cliff dweller at this welcoming enclave of traditional houses teetering on the edge of the caldera. The shops of Ia are just steps away, and a path leads to the stairs that descend to the beach at Ammoudi. Even so, you may not want to leave this enchanted perch. The views are stupendous from the private terraces (many with hot tubs) or the beautiful pool, and the comfortable accommodations, filled with traditional island furnishings, invite seclusion. ☎ 22860/71088. www. esperas.com. 17 units. Doubles 210€–280€ w/ breakfast. AE, MC, V. Closed Nov–Mar.

Watch Your Step

Many hotels along the caldera are accessible only via very long flights of steep steps. Staff members are usually on hand to carry your bags, but if you're not up to some fairly rigorous climbs, many of these places are not for you—and many are not suitable for young children. Ask about accessibility when booking and, if that's an issue, seek out lodgings on level ground.

★★ Hotel Keti FIRA

You don't have to take out a second mortgage to afford a caldera view. This delightful and reasonably priced inn clinging to the cliff face below the center of Fira is full of eye-catching scenery, enjoyed from a sunny communal terrace. Rooms are pleasantly vaulted, white-washed, and traditionally furnished. You'll do some climbing to get in and out of this hideaway, but your efforts are well rewarded. ☎ 22860/22324. www.hotelketi.gr. 7 units. Doubles 100€–120€ w/breakfast. No credit cards. Closed Nov to mid-Mar.

★★★ Ikies IA

On an island famous for dramatic settings, this aerie tucked away on the side of the caldera might just take the prize. All units are differ-ent, though each is a cliff house with a kitch-enette, a living area, and a bedroom or two, opening to a terrace with a private hot tub and eye-filling views. Attentive, low-key service accentuates the feeling that you are in a world of your own with the sparkling Aegean at your feet. ☎ 22860/71311. www.ikies.com. 11 units. Doubles 200€–250€ w/breakfast. MC, V.

★★ Paradise Hotel AKROTIRI

If you're willing to forgo the caldera views, you'll be lucky to find yourself in this delightful spot near the island's ancient sites and lava beaches. Pleasant rooms live up to the stan-dards of a Best Western affiliation and surround a flowery garden and enormous pool, and village life unfolds all around you. ☎ 22860/81277. www.hotelparadise.gr. 40 units. Doubles 85€–110€ w/breakfast. AE, MC, V. Closed Nov–Mar.

★★★ Zannos Melathron PYRGOS

The former capital of the island, an atmospheric medieval citadel, is the setting for a distinc-tive and luxurious hideaway, part of the Relais & Chateaux group, set in gardens behind high walls. Restrained old-world ambience fills the rooms and suites, all facing patios and a pool. Wine and food are first-rate, island views are extensive, and the welcoming lanes of Pyrgos are just outside the door. ☎ 22860/28220. www. zannos.gr. 12 units. Doubles 220€–250€ w/break-fast. AE, MC, V.

> *An 18th-century manor house in medieval Pyrgos is now the luxurious Zannos Melathron hotel.*

Your Big Fat Santorini Wedding

Where there's a setting as romantic as Santorini, there are bound to be wedding bells—along with wedding planners, hon-eymoon packages, newlywed spa treat-ments, and every other service under the Aegean sun. Just about every luxury hotel on the island offers a honeymoon suite and extra pampering for newlyweds, and couples who want to tie the knot with a caldera view can get all the help they need: the necessary licenses and documentation, translation, a choice of services (civil, Ro-man Catholic, Greek Orthodox), wedding dress and tuxedo rental, witnesses, and, of course, the perfect reception venue and honeymoon getaway. It's romantic as all get-out and great fun, but take the big event seriously—remember, the "I do's" you say on Santorini are legal back home, too. Check with hotels of your choice about their wedding and honeymoon packages, and go to www.weddingsantorini.com.

Where to Dine on Santorini

> *Restaurant-Bar 1800 occupies an 18th-century sea captain's mansion.*

★★ Kandouni IA *GREEK*

It's hard to pass by this 19th-century sea captain's house, where pork filets stuffed with apricots, pasta with salmon and caviar, and other innovative dishes are served in an enticing candlelit garden and in charming old rooms amid antiques and mementos of old Santorini. The Korkiantis family takes care of their guests with warmth and style, and will encourage you to linger over wine late into the evening. ☎ 22860/71616. Entrees 10€–25€. AE, MC, V. Lunch & dinner daily.

★★ Katina's AMMOUDI *SEAFOOD*

Fish tavernas line the quay at Ammoudi, the fishing port below Ia. All are good, and given the discerning taste of the islanders when it comes to seafood, none would stay in business for long if offerings were to fail the freshness test. Family-run Katina's stands out because it is one of the oldest and most revered places on the waterfront, yet it never lets down its high standards. At all these tavernas, the fresh fish, calamari, or octopus you choose from the iced display cases will be grilled and served with fresh salads and vegetables. Lapping waves and bobbing fishing boats provide a suitably nautical backdrop. **At bottom of steps from Ia.** ☎ 22860/71280. Entrees 10€–25€ or more, given that fish is sold by weight. No credit cards. Lunch & dinner daily.

★ Nikolas FIRA *GREEK*

An authentic Greek taverna seems almost out of place in Fira these days—but *that*, of course, is the appeal of the simple, whitewashed room that has been serving the old favorites, from a good moussaka to lamb in lemon sauce, for more than 50 years. Nikolas is usually on hand to make sure his guests are happy—and they are, especially in light of the down-to-earth prices. ☎ 22860/24550. Entrees 5€–10€. No credit cards. Lunch & dinner daily.

Santorini After Dark

Witnesses have been celebrating the quality of light in Santorini for centuries, probably even millennia: It's ethereal. It's transcendent. It's, to sum it up, romantic, especially at sunset. Many visitors traipse to Ia to watch the spectacle from there; those fortunate enough to be staying on the caldera witness the show from their own terraces; and many discerning viewers enjoy the fiery scene as a backdrop for a cocktail on the terrace of **Franco's** or **Palaia Kameni,** caldera-side bars in Fira. As the evening wears on, the young usually find their way to the string of ever-changing discos on the seaside in Kamari. Quieter venues in Fira include the stunning poolside bar at the **Aressana Hotel** and the very mellow **Art Café,** just off the caldera. The nearby **Kira Thira** is a serious, adult jazz bar with live music some nights and muted, conversation-inducing selections on others. In Ia, **Restaurant-Bar 1800** keeps the evening going with a lively bar scene well into the wee hours.

> Santorini's volcanic soil yields a bounty of local produce that appears in innovative creations.

★ **Restaurant-Bar 1800** IA *GREEK/CONTI-NENTAL* A 200-plus-year-old sea captain's house in the center of Ia is one of Santorini's favorite dining spots, and little wonder. Fresh fish, beautifully sauced with capers, and other inspired cuisine does justice to the exquisite decor—and, for that matter, to the views from the roof terrace. Main street, ☎ 22860/71485. Entrees 15€–30€. AE, MC, V. Dinner daily.

★ **Roka** IA *GREEK* A neoclassical house with a colorful garden in the back streets of Ia is a welcome retreat from the busy scene on the caldera rim. The traditional taverna fare sticks close to the basics, making the most of island ingredients. Peppers stuffed with rice and pine nuts, vegetable pies, and grilled meat and fish are unfailingly delicious. ☎ 22860/71896. Entrees 8€–15€. MC, V. Lunch & dinner daily.

★★ **Selene** FIRA *GREEK* Tucked onto a ledge in the cliff high above the caldera, this elegant retreat, which tops most best-in-Greece lists, works its magic from the moment you step through the gate into the candlelit, sea-facing garden. Dishes such as octopus with smoked eggplant, fava balls with capers, and herb-encrusted rabbit make creative use of local ingredients, ensuring that the spell lasts. Below cliff walk. ☎ 22860/22249. Entrees 20€–30€. AE, MC, V. Dinner daily. Closed Nov–Mar.

★ **Zafora** AKROTIRI *GREEK* From a seat on the terrace, you can take in the action of this pleasant little village (near the famous ancient site of the same name) while sampling tomato fritters, pasta with seafood, stuffed peppers, and other local favorites. This is an excellent spot for lunch if you're exploring the southern end of the island. ☎ 22860/83025. Entrees 5€–10€. No credit cards. Lunch & dinner daily.

Paros

Paros conceals enough quiet corners, including a beautiful Old Quarter behind the busy port in Parikia, to suit travelers looking for an island getaway; it has just enough of a scene, especially in seaside Naoussa, to satisfy those looking for a bit of sophistication; and, with cove-laced shores and terraced hillsides, it's pretty enough to please just about anyone. Within easy reach of Naxos, Mykonos, Santorini, Sifnos, and other Cyclades, Paros is an especially convenient stop on an island hop.

> Fishing boats in the port of Naoussa on Paros.

START Parikia, the island capital and port. **TRIP LENGTH** At least 2 full days to see the major island sights.

1 ★★★ **Panagia Ekatontopylani (Church of the Hundred Doors).** One of the oldest churches in the world is also one of the most alluring, is steeped in legend. Helen, mother of Constantine, the first Christian emperor of the Roman Empire, took shelter on Paros during a storm on her way to the Holy Land in 326. Here, it is said, she had a vision that she would find the True Cross during her voyage, and she vowed to build a church on Paros if she did. Her dream came to pass, and

Constantine completed the basilica upon his mother's death. The emperor Justinian rebuilt the church in the mid-6th century, and sent Isidoros, the architect of the Hagia Sofia in Constantinople, to Paros to build the dome. Isidoros handed the commission over to his apprentice, Ignatius, and was so filled with envy when he saw the splendid structure that he pushed the apprentice off the church roof. Ignatius grabbed Isidoros as he fell, and the two men plummeted to their deaths. A sculpture on the gate near the Chapel of St. Theodosia shows Isidoros rubbing his beard, a sign of apology, and Ignatius rubbing his head, perhaps plotting revenge. (More likely, the figure

1. Panagia Ekatontopylani
   (Church of the Hundred Doors)
2. Archaeological Museum
3. Gelato Sulla Luna
4. Old Town Parikia
5. Naoussa
6. Marathi Quarries
7. Lefkes
8. Byzantine Road
9. Valley of Petaloudes
   (Valley of the Butterflies)
10. Christos sto Daos
11. Antiparos
12. Scropios Museum

re satyrs who once adorned a temple of Dio-
ysus that stood on the spot.) Only 99 of the
ponymous 100 doors have been found, and
he last will not be located, legend has it, until
Constantinople is Greek once again. A thick
vall, embedded with monks' cells, surrounds
n entrance court shaded by lemon trees, and
vithin the cross-shaped church, frescoes,
cons, and a sea of columns of Parian marble
re bathed in soft light. The church is one of
Greece's most important shrines to the Virgin
Mary and is much visited on her feast days,
vhen pilgrims arrive from throughout Greece.
45 min. Near waterfront. ☎ 22840/21243.
ree admission. Daily 8am–8pm.

Getting There

The Paros airport runs several flights a
day to and from Athens. The island is also
served by 2 or 3 boats a day from Piraeus
in season, and it's well connected to Naxos,
Mykonos, Sifnos, Siros, Folegandros, and
other islands in the Cyclades. A tourist
information office on the waterfront is
sometimes open (June–Sept Mon–Sat
9am–1pm and 4–7pm), and the many
nearby travel agencies will also provide
information. A good bus network will take
you where you need to go on Paros, so a car
is not necessary.

> *Some of the world's most prized statuary was fashioned from marble quarried on Paros.*

❷ ★★★ **Archaeological Museum.** The **Parian Chronicle,** carved in marble quarried on the island, commands pride of place in these galleries and describes events between 1581 and 299 B.C., recording the invention of corn by the god Demeter, the fall of Troy, the voyage of the Argonauts, and the mix of fact and fiction that weave magically in and out of Greek history. The fragment here in the Paros museum tells only the tail end of the story, from 356 to 299 B.C., highlighting such benchmarks as the march of Alexander the Great and the birth of the poet Sosiphanes. If you wish to follow the entire chronicle, you need to travel to England, where the other slab has been on display at the Ashmolean Museum in Oxford since 1667.

Among the other intriguing remnants scattered about the museum is a marble frieze of the 7th-century-B.C. poet Archilochus, who was born on Paros and died on the island in a battle against the Naxians. The inventor of iambic pentameter is shown reclining on a couch, as if he is about to utter one of his famously ironic verses laden with such timeless insights as "for tis thy friends that make thee choke with rage." ⏱ 45 min. Near waterfront, behind church. ☎ 22840/21231. Admission 2€. Tues–Sun 8:30am–3pm.

③ 🍨 **Gelato Sulla Luna.** Delicious gelato, made on the premises from Italian recipes, makes an evening stroll along the waterfront all the more enjoyable. Waterfront, Parikia. $

❹ ★★★ **Old Town Parikia.** Old Parikia is a pretty cluster of whitewashed Cycladic houses. Lanes of paving stones etched with fresh white paint open into shady squares. Several are enlivened by marble fountains built under French-Ottoman rule in the late 18th century and inscribed with a jaunty verse that ends, "Come, good folk, every one, take drink but be sparing of me." A stepped street leads into the **Kastro,** the seaside fortress the Venetians cobbled together in the early 13th century from marble fragments of ancient temples. The pediments and pieces of columns are pieced randomly into the walls, presenting a jumbled glimpse into the days of classical Greece when Paros was famously wealthy from the marble quarried on the island by tens of thousands of slaves. The fortress provided the Venetians with little protection against pirates, and they were eventually chased off the island by the most famous medieval brigand of them all, Barbarossa. ⏱ 1 hr.

Naoussa is 10km (6¼ miles) east of Parikia.

❺ ★★★ **Naoussa.** Persian and Greek warships, Venetian galleons, Russian frigates taking on supplies during the Turko-Russian War of 1768–74, and the French pirate Hugue Crevelliers have all anchored in this ancient port on a broad gulf. Reminders of this storied past—a Venetian watchtower, the submerged ruins of the seaside *kastro*, and a medieval gateway—lend a colorful backdrop for the fishing boats bobbing in the harbor and the animated resort life that transforms the quiet village during the summer. Some of the best sands on the island flank Naoussa, including Santa Maria and Langeri to the east and Kolimbithres to the west, and beachgoers linger

> *Panagia Ekatontopylani was built by Constantine and rebuilt by Justinian in the 6th century.*

in town long enough to perch on the shady terraces of the seaside *ouzeries* and explore the shady, whitewashed lanes of the old town. The **Church of Agios Nikolaos Mostratou** reflects Naoussa's maritime traditions with the models and plaques of ships that mariners have left as offerings of thanks for salvation from drowning (daily 8am–6pm). ⏱ 4 hr., including a stop at the beach.

Marathi is 5km (3 miles) east of Parikia on the road that crosses the center of the island toward Kostos and Lefkes; the bus stop is just above the quarries.

⑥ ★★ **Marathi Quarries.** The white marble of Paros, dug out of three shafts in Marathi since antiquity, is translucently white and luminescent. Some of the greatest works of antiquity—among them *Hermes Carrying the Infant Dionysus* by Praxiteles, now in the Archaeological Museum in Ancient Olympia; the *Venus de Milo*; and temples on the sacred island of Delos—were crafted from highly prized Parian marble. Thousands of slaves worked the dank quarries night and day, wearing oil

> *Paros beaches are popular with windsurfers as well as sunbathers.*

> *The narrow lanes of medieval Lefkes wind down the flanks of a mountainside.*

> *Slaves with candles strapped to their foreheads quarried marble in Paros as early as the 3rd century B.C.*

lanterns strapped to their heads that gave the marble the name *lynchnites*, "won by lamplight." French engineers who came to Marathi in 1844 to mine marble for Napoleon's tomb at Les Invalides in Paris were the last to work the quarry. Visitors can now descend (bring a flashlight and wear shoes with a good grip) into the 91m-deep (300-ft.) tunnels to see the millennia-old marks of chisels and, in the middle quarry, a 3rd-century-B.C. relief of the gods. ⏱ 1 hr. Just off Parikia–Lefkes road; ask bus driver to get off. Free admission. Dawn to dusk (site is unattended).

Lefkes is 5km (3 miles) south of Marathi and 10km (6¼ miles) southeast of Parikia on a well-marked road across the center of the island.

⑦ ★★ **Lefkes.** The medieval capital Paros sits high atop an interior mountain, out of harm's way from the pirates who once raided the coast. Brigands who made their way this far inland were further thwarted by the town's mazelike arrangement of narrow lanes that cascade down the mountainside from the beautiful *plateia*. Rising high above the cluster of white houses are the impressive twin towers of the **Church of Agia Triada,** an enormous marble edifice from the 19th century (daily 8am–6pm). Windmills on an adjoining ridge are still used to grind grain, grown in a tidy patchwork of terraced fields interspersed with olive groves. ⏱ 2 hr.

You can access the Byzantine Road from the bottom of Lefkes; follow the signs.

⑧ ★★ **Byzantine Road.** A section of this stone and marble roadway, paved in the Middle Ages and once the main route across the island, descends from Lefkes through olive groves and grassy grazing land to Prodomos on the coastal plain below. The walk is easy— only about 4km (2½ miles), mostly downhill, from Lefkes. The road begins at the bottom of the village and is well marked. **Prodomos** is a vely little place, where cubical whitewashed ouses, gardens with bougainvillea spilling er the walls, and squat little chapels are onfusingly arranged in a bull's-eye pattern diating from a central *plateia*—a maze inten- d to thwart invaders and a delight in which wander today. Check schedules for buses om Prodomos back to Lefkes or Parikia, or ou could be stranded for hours. ⏱ 2 hr., for e walk to Prodomos and a look around.

taloudes is 5km (3 miles) south of Parikia f the road to the airport.

★ **Valley of Petaloudes (Valley of the But- rflies).** The grounds of a Venetian estate read across a small vale—a fresh, verdant ndscape watered by several springs and one the greenest patches on the dry island. The lley is especially enticing in the spring and rly summer, when flowers bloom in wild andon against a backdrop of cypress trees, d the air hums with the flapping wings of varms of butterflies—actually, a species of ger moth with spectacular brown and coral d wings. The best time to experience the ectacle is in the early evening, when moths the thousands awaken from their daytime umber and flutter upward toward the cool r. ⏱ 30 min. Petaloudes. Admission 3€. Mid- ay to mid-Sept daily 9am–8pm.

★ **Christos sto Daos.** The convent of Christ the Wood, on a hillside just above the Valley Petaloudes (reached by a path), is the final sting place of St. Arsenios, a 19th-century hoolteacher and abbot noted for his abil- y to conjure up rain in times of drought. In a mous exchange, he told a group of farmers ho sought out his divine services, "If you uly have faith, why have none of you brought nbrellas?" The nuns sometimes allow visi- rs to come into their walled compound to ew the tomb and take in the sweeping views the sea and the surrounding farmlands. 30 min.

ntiparos is 5km (3 miles) southwest of arikia. Boats run hourly throughout the day om Parikia (3€ each way, about 20 min.), d a ferry shuttles all day from Pounda (2€ ch way, about 10 mi.; easy to reach by bus om Parikia). A bus makes the rounds of lages and sights on Antiparos.

> *Butterflies flit along the shady paths through the Valley of Petaloudes (Valley of the Butterflies).*

⑪ ★★ **Antiparos.** This once-sleepy islet off the southwestern coast of Paros is most fa- mous for the **Antiparos Cave,** three spooky chambers, reached by a descent down 400 steps and filled with stalactites and sta- lagmites. Legions of visitors, including the 19th-century British poet Lord Byron, have scratched their names into the walls. The most noted visitation was on Christmas Eve, 1673, when a French nobleman arranged a candlelight mass for 500 celebrants in a

Wired Island

All of Paros has been wired for Wi-Fi, so you can go online from anywhere on the island—a nice perk that means you can be connected from even the simplest hotels.

> *The Scropios Museum re-creates whimsical Cycladic landmarks in miniature.*

Parian Sands

Some of the island's most popular beaches are on either side of the gulf of Naoussa— **Santa Maria,** popular with windsurfers, and **Kolimbithres,** interspersed with huge boulders. Both can be reached by boat or bus from Naoussa. The southeastern shores of the island are also lined with fine beaches, including the long strip of golden sands at **Chrissi Akti** (Golden Beach), where the annual World Cup windsurfing championships take place every August (offshore winds make it one of Europe's best windsurfing spots). The **F2 Windsurfing Center** offers rentals and instruction, and the **Aegean Diving College** offers scuba lessons and certification and excursions to shipwrecks and other submerged sites. The beach at nearby Glyfa is backed by the monastery of **Agios Ioannis Spiliotis** (St. John of the Cave), built around a grotto etched out of the hillside and the site of a miracle that occurred when St. John turned the doors to stone to protect residents who had taken refuge inside from marauding pirates.

40m-tall (131-ft.) cavern known as the Cathedral. An inscription on the base of a stalagmite 7m (23 ft.) tall and 6m (20 ft.) wide, known as the Altar, commemorates the event. The surroundings hardly seem solemn on a typical summer's day, when the cave and the rest of the once-idyllic island fill with visitors. A place to get away from it all is the summit of **Mount Profitis Elias,** 300m (984 ft.) high, affording sweeping views across the southern Cyclades. The hike from the tiny fishing village of Agios Giorgios is fairly easy, and a swim from the village's small beach awaits you on your descent. ⏱ 1 day with cave visit, hike, and swim. Cave: Admission 3€, summer only, 11am–3pm.

The museum is about 8km (5 miles) south of Parikia, off the road to Aliki.

⓬ ★ **Scropios Museum.** The Cyclades are magically re-created in a lovely garden, where carefully crafted models of the pigeon towers

of Tinos, the lighthouse of Andros, the Kastro in Parikia, and other monuments of the Cyclades stand side by side. All are the creation of **Benetos Skiadas,** who is often on hand to show off the model ships he builds and will make to order upon request. ⏱ 1 hr. Aliki road, near airport. ☎ 22840/91129. Admission 2€. May–Sept daily 10am–2pm and 6–8pm (hours vary).

Where to Stay & Dine on Paros

★★ Astir of Paros NAOUSSA

Swaying palm trees and lush gardens lend this lavish resort an exotic feel, though the views over Naoussa Bay are transporting in themselves. Rooms and suites are pleasant if not terribly exciting, and the many, many amenities include a huge swimming pool, tennis courts, spa treatments, and a shuttle bus into Naoussa. Outside Naoussa on Kolimbithres road. ☎ 22840/51976. 61 units. Doubles 200€–250€ w/breakfast. AE, DC, MC, V. Closed Oct–Easter.

★ Barbarossa NAOUSSA SEAFOOD

Sitting in an *ouzeri* on the waterfront is part of the Naoussa experience, and this is one of the oldest and best. You can linger for hours over meze, but if you want more, try the deftly prepared fish. Waterfront. ☎ 22840/51391. Entrees 10€–25€, snacks from 4€. No credit cards. Lunch & dinner daily.

★★★ Captain Manolis PARIKIA

Just steps from the harbor, this tidy little inn is an oasis of calm, with simple rooms that open to balconies and terraces overlooking a garden. The captain does not serve breakfast, but several cafes are just steps away. Market St. ☎ 22840/21244. 14 units. Doubles 60€–70€. No credit cards.

★★★ Hotel Dina PARIKIA

If you're not looking for luxury, you may find these simple rooms that open to plant-filled balconies and terraces to be your Parian paradise. The nicest is no. 8, at the back, with a balcony that faces a little chapel, which is so close you can almost reach out and touch the blue dome. Dina is a charming and helpful hostess and will tell you what you need to know about seeing the island. Market St. ☎ 22840/21345. 8 units. Doubles 50€–60€. No credit cards.

★★ Lefkes Village Hotel LEFKES

You'll glimpse this handsome, estatelike enclave on an adjacent hillside as you wander through Lefkes, and as a guest will enjoy similarly stunning views over the town and sea. The large, bright guest rooms surround a delightful

> You can linger over meze for hours in the many cafes on Paros.

swimming pool. ☎ 22840/41827. 25 units. Doubles 100€–200€ w/breakfast. MC, V. Closed Oct–Apr.

★★ Porphyra PARIKIA SEAFOOD

There's nothing fancy about this waterfront seafood house—in fact, the place looks like a big garage—but the seafood, especially the locally cultivated shellfish, is the best on the island. Mussels Saganaki, the house specialty, are a good start to any meal. Waterfront. ☎ 22840/22693. Entrees 7€–18€, varies since fish is sold by weight. AE, MC, V. Dinner daily. Closed Jan–Feb.

Naxos

Naxos can make many bold claims—beginning with its alluring sway over the god Dionysus, who descended to the island to sweep the jilted Ariadne off her feet. It's easy to see why he chose Naxos for his amorous pursuit. The island is the largest, greenest, and most scenic in the Cyclades, and it is topped with the archipelago's tallest peak. Naxos is also one of the lesser traveled of the major Cyclades, making the villages, valleys, mountainsides, and beaches all the more appealing for the visitors who do find their way here.

> *Much of the coast south of Naxos Town is one long stretch of sand.*

START Naxos Town. **TRIP LENGTH** Allow at least 2 full days to see the island.

❶ ★★★ Portara, Naxos Town. A great unfinished doorway stands on the islet of Palatia at the end of Naxos town harbor. According to myth, this is the entrance to the bridal palace that the god Dionysus built for Ariadne, daughter of King Minos of Crete. Ariadne helped the youth Theseus escape the maze of the Minotaur at Knossos (p. 241, **❷**), but Theseus abandoned her on Naxos. Dionysus took pity on the lovesick princess and swept down in a chariot borne by leopards to marry her. The story has inspired Titian's beautiful painting *Bacchus and Ariadne* and the

Getting There

The Naxos airport handles at least two flights a day to and from Athens. The island is also well connected by at least twice-daily boat service to and from Piraeus, with fairly frequent service to and from Paros, Santorini, Mykonos, Siros, and the other Cyclades. **Naxos Tourist Information** (☎ 22850/ 25201; daily 9am–8pm in season), next to the pier, is privately operated and a good source of information for what to see and do on the island as well as ferry and plane connections. The office also rents cars, as do many nearby agencies, and you'll want one to explore the inland villages.

1 Portara, Naxos Town
2 Bourgo, Naxos Town
3 Kastro, Naxos Town
4 Melanes
5 Pirgos Bellonia (Pirgos Tower)
6 Agios Mammas
7 Sangri
8 The Tragaea Villages
9 Apollonas

Aegean Sea

Naxos

Cape Stavros
Apollonas 9
Lionas
Mesi
Skadho
Ayiá
Koronos
Stavros Keramoti
Moutsouna
Koronida
Koronida
Mt. Fanari
Apiranthos
Psili Ammos
Hilia Vryssi
Kinidaros
Danakos
Kliedhos
Panermenis
Engares
Kouronohori
Moni
Filoti
Pyrgos Himarou
Galini
Melanes
Myli
Chalki
Mt. Zeus
Plafsari
Ayiou Ioannou
Khryssostomou
TRAGEA
Potamia
Kavalaris
Naxos Town
Galanado
Vivlos
Kato Sangri
Ano Sangri
Temple of Demeter
Cape Katomeri
Agios Prokopios
Agia Anná
Plaka Beach
Orkos
Pyrgaki
Kastraki Beach
Alyko Beach

Amyti Bay

Area of map at left

5 mi
5 km

Naxos Town

Aegean Sea

GROTTA
Mitropolis
Bus Station
Panayia Myrtidhiotissa
PARALIA
Palatia
Portara (Temple of Apollo) 1
Venetian Museum
KASTRO 3
Archaeological Museum
Bourgo 2
Paralia
PIGADHAKIA
Amyti Bay

1/10 mile
100 meters

Naxos Town

> *Arched passageways wind through the Kastro, the Venetian enclave at the top of Naxos Town.*

opera *Ariadne auf Naxos* by Richard Strauss. The more prosaic story is that the temple was begun by the tyrant Lygdamis in 530 B.C. in homage to Apollo and abandoned when he was overthrown in 506 B.C. A thousand years later the Venetians carted off much of the temple's marble to build their hilltop **Kastro** (below), but this door frame and lintel, constructed from slabs weighing 20 tons each, were too heavy to move. Along the

Naxos Noshes

Fortify your wanderings around Naxos with local cheeses and olives from **Tirokomika Proionda Naxou** (Papavasiliou; ☎ 22850/22230), a fragrant, old-fashioned food emporium. Accompany your choices with a selection of island wines from **Pamponas** (Paralia; ☎ 22850/22258), just down the way; the shop also stocks *kitro*, a lemon liqueur for which many Naxian households have a secret recipe. You will be offered a free tasting here—and you're likely to walk away with a bottle or two.

shore just to the north of the Portara are some of Greece's oldest antiquities—the submerged remains of houses and steps constructed by the Cycladic peoples who lived on the island as long as 5,000 years ago. ⏱ 30 min.

❷ ★ **Bourgo, Naxos Town.** From the busy port, the Kato Porto tou Yialou (Lower Shore Gate) leads into the narrow lanes of the Bourgo, the lower section of the Old Town. During Venetian rule, the Bourgo was home to the Greek citizens of Naxos and, long before that, Mycenaeans, classical Greeks, Romans, and early Christians, as extensive excavations of Ancient Naxos in front of the *mitripolis* (cathedral) reveal (free admission; Tues–Sun 8am–2pm). Bits and pieces of their churches, temples, and an agora are well marked. ⏱ 1 hr.

❸ ★★★ **Kastro, Naxos Town.** Narrow streets and arched passages wind uphill from the Bourgo into the Kastro, as the Venetian fortress and the neighborhood of tall houses that surround the walls are known. The coats of arms of noble medieval Venetian families appear above many of the doorways, and flowering vines trail over the walls surrounding

> *The Temple of Demeter outside Sangri.*

into the 18th century. The former French School, founded by Roman Catholic Jesuits during Ottoman Muslim rule in 1627, is another testimony to the permissiveness of the Turkish administrators. Nikos Kazantzakis, the famous Cretan author of *Zorba the Greek* and other modern classics, attended the school in 1896 but left abruptly when his father appeared at the door with a torch and demanded his son, shouting, "My boy, you papist dogs, or else it's fire and the ax!" The school now houses the **Archaeological Museum** (Kastro; ☎ 22850/22725; www. culture.gr; admission 3€; Tues–Sun 8:30am–3pm), a showplace for the sensuous, elongated, white marble Cycladic statuettes that date to 3,000 B.C. and resemble the work of 20th-century Italian sculptor Amedeo Modigliani. ⏲ 2 hr.

Melanes, one of four neighboring villages surrounded by olive groves and fruit orchards, is 7km (4⅓ miles) east of Naxos Town on the road toward Kinidharos.

④ ★★ Melanes. Melanes (also known as Flerio) is in one of the many lovely, verdant vales that carpet the interior of Naxos. In the garden of a Venetian estate nestled in a gorge at the end of the valley lies a *kouros,* a marble statue of a beautiful youth reclining on a pillow. The statue is some 6m (20 ft.) long and was carved in the 6th century B.C., probably intended for the **Sanctuary of Apollo** on Delos (p. 308, **①**). You can admire the boy's peaceful repose and enjoy the shady retreat as you sip a beverage at the cafe operated by the owner of the garden. ⏲ 30 min. Free admission.

Cycladic sculpture in the Archaeological Museum.

ell-kept gardens. Many residences are still ccupied by members of the families who built em, and the home of the Dellarocca-Barozzi an is open to the public as the **Domus Ve-etian Museum** (Kastro; ☎ 22850/22387; dmission 4€; June–Aug daily 10am–3pm and -10pm)**.** Salons are filled with the furnish-gs the family has collected during their 800 ears of residency, and the garden is the set-ng for summertime concerts.

Coats of arms of Venetian families also litter e marble floor of the cathedral, where Byz-ntine icons showing Western subjects reflect e influence of Eastern and Western traditions n the island. Naxos was both Venetian and urkish for many centuries, from 1210, when the enetian duke Marco Sanudo assumed the rule the Cyclades on behalf of Constantinople; enetian rule under lax Turkish oversight lasted

> *Ninth-century Agios Mammas Church is fittingly dedicated to the patron of shepherds.*

> *Venetians built Bellonia Tower House, a 17th-century mansion in the hills above Galando.*

Pirgos Bellonia is 5km (3 miles) south of Naxos Town on a well-marked road to the village of Galando.

5 ★ **Pirgos Bellonia (Pirgos Tower).** Venetian overlords built tall fortified towers across Naxos to provide refuge from pirate attacks and keep an eye on their estate workers from the upper stories. These formidable stone castles are a romantic, fairy-tale presence in the countryside, but they could be most unwelcoming when residents drew up drawbridges and poured boiling oil through the loopholes. When danger was imminent, residents lit fires on the flat roofs of their tower houses to warn their neighbors. The Bellonia tower is especially elaborate and was once the home of the Venetian archbishop of Naxos. An emblem of the Lion of St. Mark is embedded above the doorway, and on the grounds is a twin church, with a chapel for Roman Catholic celebrants and one for Orthodox Catholics. ⏱ 15 min; tower is a private residence, but churches are often open.

Agios Mammas is 3km (2 miles) south of Pirgos Bellonia on a well-marked lane off the road to Sangri.

Getting Wet on Naxos

The capes and promontories of the southwest coast shelter some of the island's finest beaches. The sandy strands closest to Naxos Town, especially Agios Yeoryios and Agios Prokopios, can be unpleasantly crowded, and it's well worth the small effort required to continue just a little way farther south. **Plaka,** backed by sand dunes and bamboo groves, and **Kastaraki,** etched with rock formations, both stretch for miles, leaving plenty of room for everyone. **Pyrgaki,** the southernmost beach on this stretch of coast but only 10km (6¼ miles) from Naxos Town, seems a world removed, with empty white sands and crystalline waters.

③ ★ Agios Mammas. One of the oldest churches of Naxos was built under the Byzantines in the 9th century as the island's cathedral and seat of the Greek Orthodox archbishops of the Cyclades. The stone church was abandoned through much of the Middle Ages but is still a commanding presence on the herb-scented hillside. Views extend far across the countryside where sheep and goats graze—an apt tribute to Mammas, the patron saint of shepherds. ⏱ 15 min; church is open only occasionally, but you can always enjoy the exterior.

Sangri is 3km (2 miles) south of Agios Mammas.

⑦ ★★ Sangri. Old tower houses and cypress trees rise from the end of a valley to mark the entrance to Sangri, a cluster of three small villages. **Mount Profitis Elias,** topped with a chapel and a ruined Byzantine fortress, overlooks Sangri, and at the foot of the mountain is a beautiful fortified monastery, **Timios Stavros** (the True Cross), now abandoned. In the 18th and early 19th century, before Naxos became part of a united Greece, monks here secretly taught Greek language and culture, which was so long neglected under the centuries of Venetian and Turkish rule. Sangri's most notable monument is the **Temple of Demeter,** about 5km (3 miles) outside Sangri on a well-marked dirt road (free admission). Dedicated to the goddess of grain, it's fittingly surrounded by fertile fields. Archaeologists have only recently re-erected the columns and pediments that had lain scattered about the site for centuries. ⏱ 1 hr.

Chalki, the first of the Tragaea villages, is 7km (4⅓ miles) northeast of Sangri on a well-marked road.

SITE GUIDE
PAGE 348

⑧ ★★★ The Tragaea Villages. The beautiful Tragaea Valley spreads across the center of Naxos. Olive groves and lemon orchards climb the slopes of mountainsides, and chapels, monasteries, and small villages overlook countryside that has changed very little from the days of the Byzantines. ⏱ Half-day.

Apollonas is about 10km (6¼ miles) north of Chalki and 12km (7½ miles) northeast of Naxos Town on well-marked roads to the northern tip of the island.

⑨ ★ Apollonas. This once-quiet fishing village is a popular, though undistinguished, summer resort. What attracts many travelers to the northern tip of the island are the good sandy beach and a huge *kouros,* 10m (33 ft.) tall. The statue was abandoned in the quarry where it was being carved in the 7th century B.C., probably because it cracked when it was shifted. ⏱ 1 hr.

> *This enormous kouros in the Apollonas quarry cracked during carving in the 7th century B.C.*

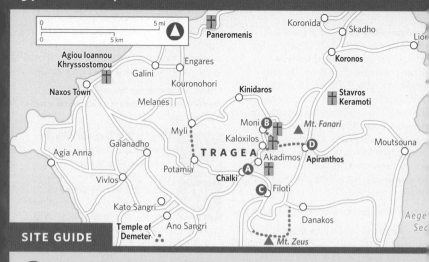

8 The Tragaea Villages

A **Chalki,** 7km (4⅓ miles) northeast of San-gri, surrounds a beautiful *plateia,* shaded by plane trees. In the 1,500-year-old, tile-roofed **Church of Panagia Protothrone** (Our Lady Before the Throne), layers of frescoes date to the 6th century, with the oldest depicting the Apostles. The 17th-century **Pirgis Frankopo-lous,** a Venetian tower house, is sometimes open to the public, and from the upper floors you can see a broad swath of the Tragaea Val-ley. **B** **Moni,** some 6km (3¾ miles) north, is a lovely mountain village known throughout Greece for the **Church of Panagia Drosiani** (Our Lady of Refreshment). Legend has it that during a drought in the 8th century, Naxians brought icons of the Virgin from churches across the island to the sea to pray for rain, and only the icon from this church, with a dome and walls of rough-hewn rock, yielded results. Some of the oldest frescoes on the walls of the three simple chapels date to the 7th century and are rich with imagery not always seen in Orthodox art (daily 8am–1pm and 4–6pm; hours vary). The white houses of **C** **Filoti,** 7km (4⅓ miles) south, sparkle on the flanks of Mount Zas, at a little more than 1,000m (3,281 ft.), the tallest peak in the Cyclades. The tower of the **Church of Kimisis tis Theotokou** (Assumption of the Mother of God) stands above the rooftops, a beacon to the revelers who come from all over Naxos in

mid-August for the island's biggest *paneyeri* (feast), in honor of the Virgin (daily 8am–1pm and 4–6pm; hours vary). From the village, a trail climbs the face of the mountain to the **Arghia Cave,** one of several caverns in Greece said to be the birthplace of Zeus. The cave is spectacular, entered through a natural arch, 10m (33 ft.) wide and 2.5m (8¼ ft.) high, that leads into a main chamber spanning more than 4,000 sq. m (43,056 sq. ft.) without sup-port. Tools found in the cave suggest human habitation more than 5,000 years ago. The streets of **D** **Apiranthos,** 12km (7½ miles) north of Filoti, are paved in marble, and the houses are made of rough, gray stone hewn from the mountain. The village is barely dis-tinguishable from the hillside out of which it is carved and seems to appear quite magically as you approach.

Where to Stay & Dine on Naxos

▸ *Harbor views are among the charms of the Chateau Zevgoli.*

★★ Apollon Hotel NAXOS TOWN

A former marble workshop provides airy quarters within walking distance of sights in town, but with room to park—handy for touring. The attractive guest rooms all have balconies. ☎ 22850/26801. 13 units. Doubles 120€–150€ w/breakfast. MC, V.

★★★ Chateau Zevgoli BOURGO

Just about everyone's favorite place to stay on Naxos is tucked next to the walls of the Kastro and overlooks the harbor. Lounges are filled with family heirlooms, and the guest rooms that surround a plant-filled courtyard are tastefully done with dark furnishings and a few antiques here and there. Owner Despini Kitini also rents apartments and studios around town. ☎ 22850/25201. 14 units. Doubles 90€–120€ w/breakfast. AE, MC, V.

★★★ Galaxy Hotel AGIOS GIORGIOS

The most luxurious lodgings on Naxos are these beautiful seaside studios that surround gardens and courtyards like a miniature Cycladic village. The accommodations are tastefully done with expanses of stone and stucco, and have welcome amenities such as kitchenettes and terraces. ☎ 22850/22422. www.hotel-galaxy.com. 54 units. Doubles 120€–150€. MC, V. Closed Oct–Apr.

★★ Old Inn NAXOS TOWN *GERMAN*

One of the most distinctive restaurants in the Cyclades specializes in German fare, prepared by former Berliner Dieter von Ranizewski. Homemade pâté, smoked pork, and sausages might be a welcome change from standard taverna fare. The surroundings, once a monastery, are as quirky as the menu. Near the harbor. ☎ 22850/26093. Entrees 8€–20€. No credit cards. Dinner daily.

★★★ Taverna Lefteris APRIANTHOS *GREEK*

The prettiest of the Tragaea Valley villages is the setting for one of the island's nicest dining spots, where excellent traditional meals are served in a marble-floored dining room and on a shady terrace. A drive through the valley and a meal here are the components of a perfect day on Naxos. ☎ 22850/61333. Entrees 5€–10€. No credit cards. Lunch & dinner daily.

★★★ Taverna to Kastro NAXOS TOWN *GREEK*

An animated square filled with restaurants and cafe tables below the walls of the Kastro is a pleasant place for a meal on a summer evening. The grilled meats and fish dishes are accompanied by local wines, and a meal comes with a view over the rooftops to the harbor. Plateia Braduna. ☎ 22850/22005. Entrees 7€–15€. No credit cards. Dinner daily.

Sifnos

Sifnos is the favorite getaway of too many people to be a well-kept secret, but it's still one of the most beautiful islands in the Cyclades. It's also the most serene at any time besides the month of August. Sifnos does not offer much in the way of nightlife and has no must-see sights, but the hillsides are green, the villages are dazzlingly white, and the coastline is etched with coves and lovely beaches.

> *Many of the island's plain white houses are getaways for Athenians.*

START Apollonia. TRIP LENGTH At least 2 days.

1 ★★★ **Apollonia.** The island's capital is a cluster of six villages (or five or seven, depending on whom you ask) that tumble across the inland hills in enchantingly haphazard fashion, a jumble of whitewashed houses and blue-domed churches interspersed with vineyards, orchards, and gardens. Flagstone footpaths delicately outlined in whitewash wind through the villages and converge on **Plateia Iroon** (Hero's Square). The **Popular and Folk Art Museum** (July to mid-Sept daily 10am–1pm and 6–10pm; 2€), to one side of the square, is a showplace for island embroidery and weaving, along with the earthenware pots and jars that Sifnians once loaded onto ships in exchange for staples. A short walk west up a path brings you to the **Panagia Ouranophora** (Church of Our Lady of the Heavenly Light), where a relief of St. George crowns the doorway and a marble column and a few other fragments of a temple to Apollo are scattered about the shady courtyard. ☺ 1 hr.

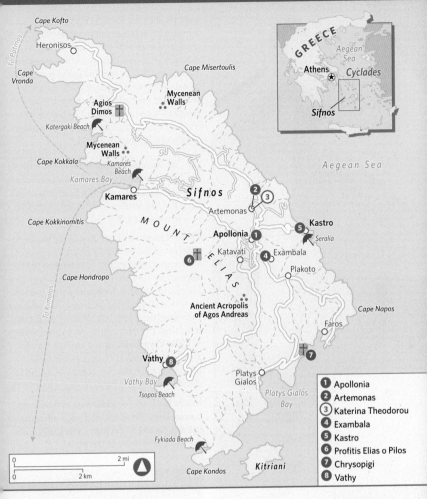

1 Apollonia
2 Artemonas
3 Katerina Theodorou
4 Exambala
5 Kastro
6 Profitis Elias o Pilos
7 Chrysopigi
8 Vathy

2 ★★★ **Artemonas.** The path from Plateia Iroon rises through the quiet little village of **Ano Petali,** drops down to a stone bridge across the Marinou River, then climbs into the most beautiful of the Apollonia villages. The remains of a temple to Artemis, sister of

Getting There

Sifnos is connected by daily boat service to and from Piraeus and Milos, and less frequent service runs to and from Paros, Santorini, Folegandros, and Mykonos. Boats arrive in Kamares, a waterside cluster of hotels and tavernas that is pleasant enough for a pit stop. From there, board one of the buses that travel every mile of road on Sifnos; there aren't many, so it's so easy to get around Sifnos by bus, foot, or taxi and forgo a rental car. From Kamares the road climbs through a narrow gorge, past olive groves and dovecotes clinging to the hillsides, and emerges at Apollonia. About 5km (3 miles) southeast, it's a good place to base yourself. The **municipal travel office** (Mon-Sat 10am–1pm and 4–7pm) on Plateia Iroon in Apollonia is very helpful, and sells a good map of walking routes on the island.

> *Neoclassic houses line the streets of Sifnos.*

Apollo and goddess of virginity and the hunt, are said to be buried beneath the Kochi, one of several churches that rise above the village rooftops. Worldly associations surround the **Panagia tou Barou** (Church of Our Lady of the Baron), named for one of the Italian nobles who ruled Sifnos from the 15th through early 17th centuries. The baron allegedly fell in love with a nun in a nearby monastery and turned his unrequited ardor toward local women; his offspring soon populated the quarter, known

ever since as the Barou in his honor. A bust of a more respectable resident, Nicholas Chrysogetos, stands near the village square. The surroundings have changed little since this hero of the 1821 War of Independence taught in Artemis before becoming Greece's first minister of education. This is a lovely spot in which to linger and sip a coffee before resuming your wanderings along any of the lanes that lead off the square. ⏱1 hr.

③ 🍽 **Katerina Theodorou.** At the island's favorite bakery, pastries and homemade candies, accompanied by excellent coffee, are on offer in a homey room. **Off main square. $**

❹ ★★ **Exambala.** The name of the southernmost of the Apollonia villages translates as "trouble in the night"—a reference to the days under Turkish rule when the village was famous for spirited, independence-oriented rhetoric and song that often got out of hand as the nights wore on. On a hillside just outside the village the large, whitewashed monastery of **Kyria Vryssiani** (Sacred Spring) stands among olive groves. The cool spring still bubbles forth in the courtyard and is said to supply the freshest water on the island. ⏱1 hr.

Kastro is 4km (2½ miles) east of Apollonia. Bus service is frequent, and you walk much of the way on one of the many *monopati* (mule tracks) that crisscross the island.

The Golden Years

Sifnians were among the wealthiest of the ancient Greeks, thanks to the silver and gold they mined. They flaunted their riches and made especially lavish offerings to Apollo on the sacred island of **Delos** (p. 308, ❶). One year the greedy Sifnians decided to substitute gilded lead for their offering of gold. Apollo, of course, detected the ruse and wreaked his revenge by conjuring an earthquake that caused the mines to flood. The mines did indeed stop yielding riches, but on account of natural causes. Many of the mines were dug beneath sea level and eventually filled with water, and others were simply depleted of their precious minerals over time.

5 ★★★ **Kastro.** While the villages of Apol-onia are light and airy, Kastro is somberly medieval, a fortress hugging a rocky promon-ory above the surf. The capital of Sifnos under Venetian rule was virtually unassailable, made so by a row of connected houses that form a solid defensive wall around the inner town. Tunnellike passages lead into a maze of little lanes and tiny squares lined with tall Vene-rian-era houses—and littered here and there with sarcophagi left behind by the Romans who occupied Sifnos. The two-room **Archaeo-logical Museum** (free admission; Tues–Sun 8:30am–3pm) is a repository for bits of pot-tery and friezes from the ancient city that occupied these heights 3,000 years ago. The **Church of the Eftamartyres** (Seven Martyrs) sits atop a sea-girt promontory far beneath a clifftop promenade that skirts the town's outer flanks. The scene of the white chapel practically floating on the waves is remarkably picturesque at any time, and almost impos-sibly so when wind-whipped waves buffet the sturdy white walls. ⏱ 2 hr.

From Katavati, a tiny hamlet just south of Exambala, a path plunges through a valley, then begins the ascent to Profitis Elias.

6 ★★ **Profitis Elias o Pilos.** The highest mountain on the island rises 850m (2,789 ft.) and is topped by an isolated monastery. O Pilos means "high one," a term that takes on special meaning as you make the 2-hour-long climb on a well-worn path and regard the panoramic views across what seems like most of the Aegean Sea. A monk is often on hand to show you around the thick-walled courtyard and chapel and offer a glass of cool water. The monastery celebrates the feast of Elias around July 20, when hundreds of celebrants make a nighttime pilgrimage up to the monastery carrying torches. ⏱ Half-day.

Chrysopigi is 8km (5 miles) southeast of Apollonia and well connected by bus. You can also walk on the *monopati* that cross the countryside from Apollonia to the coast.

7 ★★★ **Chrysopigi.** The **Monastery of Panagia Chrysopigi** (the Golden Wellspring) has been close to the heart of Sifnians since it was founded atop a rocky islet in 1650 to house an icon of the Virgin Mary that fishermen

> *Whitewashed, blue-domed churches and chapels are sprinkled across the hillsides.*

found washed up on the rocks. The image soon miraculously intervened to save the island from the plague—and came to the rescue again in 1928, when locusts descended upon the island. Yet another miracle occurred when two women fled to the monastery to escape pursuing pirates. They prayed to the Virgin, who interceded by creating a deep chasm in the rocks to separate Chrysopigi from the mainland (a bridge now crosses the rift above the churning sea). Fishermen bring their sons to the monastery to be baptized in a font on a

> In the hilltop Kastro, a maze of connected houses once provided a wall of defense.

rocky point at the very edge of the surf, and in so doing ensure that the boys will forever be safe from the perils of the seafaring life.

You can contemplate the beautiful monastery and its colorful associations from a sandy beach, **Apokofto,** nestled alongside an adjacent cove. A stone path leads around a headland to **Faros,** a small fishing village that takes its name from the lighthouse that guides the fleet past the rocky shoreline. ◷ 3 hr., with time on the beach and the walk to Faros.

Vathy is 5km (3 miles) west of Chrysopigi, directly across the island, connected by bus. A *monopati* also crosses the island from Chrysopigi to Vathy.

❽ ★★★ **Vathy.** Until a new road was laid a decade ago, the only way to reach Vathy was on

foot, donkey, or boat. (If you take the footpath that crosses the island here from Chrysopigi, you'll notice that as the path winds around the top of the peninsula above the Bay of Platos Yialos, it passes the Aspro Pirgos, or White Tower—a lookout post from around 500 b.c., when the mines of Sifnos still yielded gold and made the island an important outpost in the Aegean.) Even with this link to the rest of the island, Vathy remains a serene getaway, a small collection of houses alongside a beach of fine sand and backed by a verdant valley. This setting is made all the more beautiful by the presence of the **Monastery of the Taxiarchis Evangelistrias** (Archangel of the Annunciation), so close to the seaside that the whitewashed walls and a bell tower seem to rise out of the water. ◷ 1 hr.

Where to Stay & Dine on Sifnos

> Petali Hotel is a delightful aerie overlooking the island and surrounding sea.

★★ **Boulis Taverna** KAMARES *GREEK*
It's worth the trip down to the port just to enjoy a meal at this friendly taverna. Actually, many of the tavernas in town are good, but Boulis is the best, serving delicious salads and grilled meats that the family produces on its farm. Follow up a meal with a walk on the sandy beach. ☎ 22840/31648. Entrees 6€–12€. No credit cards. Lunch & dinner daily.

★★ **Chrysopigi** APOKOFTO *GREEK*
You can see the seaside monastery of the same name from the shady terrace of this *very* relaxed taverna on Apokofto Beach. Caper salad and other Sifnos specialties are made daily, and fresh fish from the fleet at Faros, just around the headland, is grilled to perfection. ☎ 22840/71295. Entrees 5€–15€. No credit cards. Lunch & dinner daily. Closed Oct–Apr.

★★★ **Elies Resort** VATHY
Sifnos has always been sophisticated, but quietly so, and this swank retreat on a hillside above Vathy brings a big dose of glossy glamour to the island. Whether this is a welcome change depends on your taste and budget, but rooms and suites are lavish, many with private pools; indoor/outdoor restaurants are excellent; and, best of all, the beautiful old seaside village of Vathy is just beyond the gates. ☎ 22840/34000. www.eliesresorts.com. 32 units. Doubles 240€–340€. AE, MC, V. Closed Oct–Apr.

★★ **Hotel Anthoussa** APOLLONIA
These rooms above the very popular Yerontopoulos Cafe are right in the center of town, yet they face a flowery garden or look out to the surrounding hills. Rooms are simple yet appealing, and the location is a handy base for exploring the rest of the island by bus. The open-air cafe downstairs is a great place to linger. ☎ 22840/31431. 15 units. Doubles 80€. MC, V. Closed Oct–Apr.

★★★ **Petali Hotel** APOLLONIA
This perch high above Apollonia is first-choice for a stay on Sifnos—comfortable, convenient, and commanding a view across the villages and the rolling interior hills to the sea. Rooms and suites are large and attractive and overlook the gardens from large terraces. All the village sights and services are an easy stroll away, but the pool and the summertime-only restaurant may tempt you not to leave the premises. ☎ 22840/32152. 25 units. Doubles 120€–200€ w/breakfast. MC, V. Closed Oct–Apr.

★★ **To Liotivi** ARTEMONAS *GREEK*
One of the oldest and best-known restaurants on Sifnos has introduced legions of travelers to caper salad, chickpea croquettes, and other island specialties. Service is not always first-rate, but a meal on the square out front or in a cozy dining room is still a memorable experience. ☎ 22840/31246. Entrees 8€–15€. No credit cards. Lunch & dinner daily.

Mykonos

Small, dry, and barren, Mykonos is one of the least
naturally attractive of the Cyclades—but it's a testament to the island's charms
that it is among the most famous of all the Greek islands. Attractions include
a beautiful main town, Hora, miles of sandy beaches, and boundless people-
watching. Ever since Jackie O. and other celebs started stepping ashore from
their yachts in the 1960s, Mykonos has been a place to see and be seen. You
may love the scene or want to flee from it, but Mykonos tends to work its spells
eventually on even the most resistant visitor.

> *Hora is one of Greece's most attractive and popular island towns.*

START Hora. **TRIP LENGTH** At least 2 days.

1 ★★★ **Hora.** No matter how crowded the
narrow streets may be, like legions of other international travelers, you will soon succumb to
the Cycladic charms of Mykonos Town (better
known as Hora). Wooden balconies hang from
white cubical houses, outdoor staircases are
lined with pots of geraniums, and oleander
and hibiscus scent the air. The experience is
made all the more pleasant by the absence
of motorized traffic, mostly prohibited beyond Plateia Mando Mavrogenous. This busy

square is named for the island heroine who
pushed back a fleet of invading Turks in the
War of Independence in 1822. Despite her
fame, the beautiful and aristocratic Mavrogenous died forgotten and in poverty on Paros,
but she is now honored with a marble bust.

Matoyanni Street, lined with expensive
boutiques, leads from the square into the Old
Quarter. The glittering wealth on this street
of paving stones etched with whitewash trim
belies the fact that until tourism transformed
the island in the 1960s, bleak, barren Mykonos

Aegean Sea

Cape Mavros

Cape Armenistis

Cape

Agios Sostis

Panormos

6 Panormos

Houlakia

Mersini

Mersini Bay

Fokos

Merchias Bay

Cape Evros

Agios Stafanos

Panormos Bay

Tourlos
Tourlos
Malaliamos

Marathi

Lake Marathi

Ftelia

Mykonos

Profitis Ilias Anomeritis

Area of map below

Hora

Moni Panagias Tourlianis

5 Ano Meara

To Delos

Vothanas

Megali Ammos

Airport

Lia

Cape Goni

Korfos

Vrissi

Kalafatis

Cape Kalafatis

Kapari

Kapari

Ornos

Kalo Livadi

Agios Ioannis

Psarou

Platys Gialos

Elia

Elia

Psarou

Platys Gialos

Agrari

Paradise

Super Paradise

Cape Mavrokefalas

Paraga

Nea Mykonos

Cape Alogomandra

| 0 | | 2 mi |
| 0 | | 2 km |

1 Hora
2 Little Venice
3 Kastro Bar
4 Paradise Beach
5 Ano Meara
6 Panormos & the north coast

WINDMILLS

3

Paraportianis

Alefkandras Square

2

BOATS TO DELOS

LITTLE VENICE

Karaoli Dimitriou Square

Fambrikas

Pippa

Dimostheni

Mitropoleos

Port

Sourmeli

Ipirou

Enoplon Dyanameon

Atki Kambani

Lakka

D. Koutsii

Matogianni
Fl. Zouganeli
Ag. Saranta

Manto Square

Agias Anna

Agias Stefanou

Agious Ioannou

Panachradou

Rochari

Agious Ioannou

| 0 | | 1/10 mile |
| 0 | | 100 meters |

Hora (Mykonos Town)

> *In Little Venice, houses built by wealthy sea captains hang over the Aegean.*

was the poorest island in the Cyclades. Humbler times on the island come to light in the **Aegean Maritime Museum** (Dinameon; ☎ 21081/25547; admission 3€; Apr–Oct Tues–Sat 10:30am–1pm and 6–9pm, Nov–Mar Tues–Sat 8:30am–3pm), filled with navigational bric-a-brac from the many centuries when Mykonos made its living from the sea. This was not always a respectable undertaking; the Mykonites were once corrupt corsairs, and by the 17th century the harbor at Mykonos was an infamous pirates' nest. Islanders later went to sea as merchants, earning the kind of middle-class respectability that is on display at **Lena's House** (☎ 22890/22591; free admission; Apr–Oct 6:30–9:30pm), the overstuffed home of a 19th-century sea captain. Around the corner is one of the island's favorite landmarks, the **Tria Pagadia** (Three Wells). Legend has it that a virgin who drinks from all three wells will soon find a husband, but the water is no longer potable— and virgins are few and far between on worldly Mykonos.

The esplanade that follows the harbor is especially pleasant in evening, when Mykonites and their visitors stroll and sit at cafe tables to catch a sea breeze. Just beyond the northern end is the **Archaeological Museum** (Agios Stefanos; ☎ 22890/2235; admission 3€;

Tues–Sun 8:30am–3pm), opened a century ago to exhibit funerary sculptures and vases that had just then been excavated from the purification pit on the island of Rhenea. The artifacts were originally buried with the dead on the sacred island of Delos; in the 5th century B.C., the oracle at Delphi advised the Athenians to cleanse Delos to reverse their defeats in the Peloponnesian War, so human

Getting There

Mykonos is very well connected to Athens by several flights daily. Frequent ferry service runs to and from Piraeus, and high-speed catamaran service goes to and from Rafina and Lavrio. Mykonos is also well connected by frequent boat service to and from Paros and Santorini. The island has two ports: the old port just at the edge of Hora and the new port 2km (1¼ mile) north in Tourlos. You can reach many beaches on the island by boat or bus, but you may want to rent a car or moped for a day to explore the otherwise inaccessible north coast. A **tourist office** just across from the old port on Enoplon Dhinameon (☎ 22890/23160) provides maps and info and will help you find a room.

Windmills on Alefkandra Ridge and elsewhere on the island once supplied the power to grind grain.

emains and funereal offerings were removed o the necropolis on Rhenea. From Mykonos omes a large *pythos* (vase) from the 7th cen- ury B.C. painted with vivid depictions of the all of Troy at the hands of soldiers emerging rom the wooden horse. ⊕ **Half-day.**

❷ ★★★ **Little Venice.** Many of the island's ea captains built homes at water's edge on he west side of Hora, so close to the sea that vaves wash against the lower floors—an ar- angement that is reminiscent of houses along he canals of Venice. Of course, those Italian vaterways are more placid than the Aegean, nd a drink on the seaside balconies of the ars in the captains' former dwellings often omes with a shower of sea spray.

Surrounding this atmospheric quarter re several remnants of old Mykonos. The **olklore Museum** (☎ 22890/22591; free

admission; Apr–Oct Mon–Fri 4:30–8:30pm) is a refreshing throwback to times past, evoked with household implements, costumes, and a re-created 19th-century kitchen. Stringed instruments reflect the island's long-standing musical traditions; even an islander who par- takes of the cosmopolitan nightlife for which Mykonos is famous probably also knows the ages-old laments sung during feasts at the island's more than 400 churches. The mu- seum is also the final resting place of Petros, a pelican who took shelter on Mykonos during a storm in the 1950s and soon became the is- land's mascot. Since the island began to pros- per from the arrival of well-heeled visitors not long afterward, Petros may well have brought good luck with him. Petros met his own bad fortune under the wheels of a car in 1985 and was stuffed for posterity.

> *Moni Panagias Tourlianis in Ano Meara.*

The **Church of the Paraportiani** (Our Lady of the Postern Gate) is actually four little churches that have been pieced together into a squat, rambling, lopsided assemblage that is both homely and utterly charming. In the absence of straight lines and any attempt at uniformity, the whitewashed walls look lumpy and rumpled, like a poorly iced cake, and they reflect the shadowy shades of the sea that crashes against the foundations.

The famous icons of Mykonos are the **windmills** that line the Alefkandra Ridge just across the water. Alefkandra means "whitening," and women used to wash their laundry in the surf and string it out on the ridge to take advantage of the same breezes that once propelled the giant blades—and still do, on special occasions. Other windmills line a barren ridge above Hora, and until a few decades ago 16 of these conical, thatch-roofed mills were in operation around Mykonos to grind grain. ⏲ 2 hr.

③ ☕ **Kastro Bar.** An island institution almost from the day it opened in 1976, Kastro Bar serves excellent cocktails, coffee, and other beverages but stakes its fame on the fantastic sea views, accompanied by classical music. Waterfront, Little Venice. ☎ 22890/23072. $

Paradise and Super Paradise beaches are about 6km (3¾ miles) southeast of Hora and can be reached by bus or by boat from Platos Yialos.

④ ★ **Paradise Beach.** The island's most famed stretches of sand, **Paradise** (Kalamopodi) and **Super Paradise** (Plintri) beaches, are the haunts of partiers and inebriates. Beachgoers uninterested in the scene will find these crowded, often dirty strands backed by beach bars to be far from paradisiacal—linger just long enough to plant your feet on the sands that put Mykonos on the map as a party island then move on. In the summer during a full moon, the midnight Full Moon Party would make Dionysus blush. ⏲ 1 hr.

Ano Meara is 8km (5 miles) east of Hora and connected by frequent bus service.

⑤ ★ **Ano Meara.** The only sizable settlement on Mykonos outside Hora is set amid stark, rolling hills in the center of the island. To one side of the shady *plateia* is the **Monastery of Moni Panagias Tourlianis,** where intricate carvings cover the marble bell tower, the screens near the altar, and the incense holders fashioned in the shape of dragons. Even a water spout in the courtyard is decorated with the carved figure of a woman wearing a crown and is accordingly known as the Queen. The monastery is the repository of an icon of the Virgin that has been working miracles since it was found in the countryside several centuries ago. Every August 15, the feast of the Virgin, the icon is carried in a procession across the island to the **Church of Agia Kyriaki** in Hora (main square; ☎ 0289/71249; open randomly).

Two of the island's finest stretches of sand, **Elia Beach** and **Kalo Livadi Beach,** are just outh of Ano Meara. The longest beach on Mykonos, Elia is protected from the north winds by steep hills; Kalo Livadi (Good Pasture) is at the end of a long, verdant valley and backed by a shady glen. You will not feel like a lone castaway at either, but you will have a good-sized patch of sand to yourself. ⏱ 1 hr.

A turnoff about 2km (1¼ mile) west of Ano Meara (follow sign for Panormos and Agios Sostis) leads onto a narrow road up to the northwestern end of the island to excellent beaches 5km (3 miles) north of the turnoff.

6 ★★★ **Panormos & the north coast.** The north of Mykonos seems a world removed from Hora and the south coast's beaches. Flat-roofed farmhouses look across olive groves and terraced fields toward sparkling **Panormos Bay,** a long and deep body of water that takes an enormous bite out of the northern side of the island. The shores are etched with sand-rimmed coves that are the reason most visitors venture north, especially to **Panormos** and **Agios Sostis** (below). ⏱ Half-day.

Mykonos Beaches

The beaches on Mykonos are not the best in Greece, but they are among the most popular. Offshore breezes, underwater scenery, and crystal-clear waters make the island one of the Aegean's favorite playgrounds for watersports enthusiasts. For diving and snorkeling excursions and instruction, try the **Mykonos Diving Center** on Paradise Beach (☎ 22890/24808; www.dive.gr) or the **Kalafati Dive Center** on Kalafati Beach (☎ 22890/71677). For windsurfing board rental and instruction, try **Mykonos Windsurfing Center** on Kalafati Beach (☎ 22890/72345). For jet-ski and water-ski rentals, try the **Water Sports Club Platos Yialos** on Platos Yialos Beach (☎ 22890/23160). For horseback riding on the beach, try **Mykonos Horse Riding** (☎ 22890/23160). If you're traveling with kids, you'll keep them smiling with a trip to **Watermania,** near Elia Beach (☎ 22890/71685).

South-Coast Beaches

In general, Mykonos's south-coast beaches are sandy and protected from the *meltemi* winds that blow in from the north. All the following south-coast beaches are accessible by bus and by summertime-only boats from Platos Yialos to nearby beaches:

• **Platos Yialos** & **Ornos,** popular with families

• **Psarou,** upscale party beach

• **Paranga,** on a quiet little cove

• **Paradise** & **Super Paradise,** party scenes

• **Kalafi,** best for watersports

• **Elia** & **Kalo Livadi,** among the least crowded and most pleasant of the south-coast beaches; both are partially nudist and one end of Elia is gay, but all beaches on Mykonos are gay-friendly.

North-Coast Beaches

The island's north-coast beaches are unspoiled and much less crowded. The exception is on those summer days when a hot wind sometimes blows in from the south, kicking up Sahara-like sandstorms on the south-coast beaches and chasing those craving the sun and surf up to the north coast. None of these north-coast beaches are accessible by public transportation:

• **Fokos,** excellent sand, popular with surfers

• **Ftelia,** at the end of Panormos Bay

• **Panormos** & **Agios Sostis,** without amenities but wild, windswept, beautiful, partially nudist, gay-friendly

Where to Stay on Mykonos

> *Chic and simple island style prevails at Belvedere hotel.*

★★ Apanema OUTSIDE HORA

A comfortable and casually elegant small re-treat surrounds a sea-facing terrace and pool. The large, airy rooms are simply but tastefully done and awash in white, and all have terraces or balconies. A casual poolside restaurant and bar will tempt you to stay put for the evening, but Hora is just a short walk away. **Tagoo, coast road to Tourlos.** ☎ 22890/28590. www.apanemaresort.com. 17 units. Doubles 200€–290€ w/breakfast. AE, MC, V.

★★★ Belvedere HORA

Should you have any doubt that Mykonos is the epitome of Euro-chic, you need only step into this super-cool retreat in the palm-shaded Fine Arts District of Hora. Rooms overlook the sea, gardens, and pool. A study in whitewashed sim-plicity, they're so stylish with handcrafted island furnishings and state-of-the-art audiovisual systems that you won't notice their small size. The in-house restaurant is the very hip open-air sushi emporium **Matsuhisa Mykonos** (yes, *that* Matsuhisa, aka Nobu), and a spa and lovely pool bar are among the amenities. ☎ 22890/25122. www.belvederehotel.com. 48 units. Doubles 220€–500€ w/breakfast. AE, MC, V. Closed Nov–Mar.

★★★ Cavo Tagoo OUTSIDE HORA

The island's most sophisticated getaway is just outside Hora above the new marina. Decor is golden stone and acres of soothing white with splashes of blues and greens. A sumptuous outdoor lounge surrounds the infinity pool. Huge rooms and suites are set amid beautiful gardens, with sea-facing terraces, many with private pools. All are filled with high-tech gadgetry, gorgeous furnishings, and soothing comforts. **Tagoo, coast road to Tourlos.** ☎ 22890/23692. www.cavotagoo.gr. 70 units. Doubles 200€–400€ w/breakfast. AE, MC, V.

★★ Elysium HORA

Mykonos is not quite the gay mecca it once was, but you would hardly know it from this hilltop retreat. It's a great place to stay even if you aren't a beautiful young male, though the poolside parties are definitely geared to those who are. Rooms are pleasant though unexcep-tional, but the pool, sauna, hillside views of Hora and the sea, and the friendly ambience are superlative. ☎ 22890/23952. www.elysium hotel.com. 42 units. Doubles 100€–180€ w/breakfast. AE, MC, V. Closed Oct–Apr.

★ Leto Hotel HORA

The location at the edge of Hora is the big plus, along with a seaside garden complete with pool, bar, and restaurant. Plain rooms maintain basic standards of comfort with not a hint of chic, but any shortcomings in style are offset by the hospitality and convenience to the harbor. The lovely Leto garden is a justifiably popular spot for weddings, so when booking, make sure an all-night party won't be interrupting your sleep. ☎ 22890/22207. www.letohotel.com. 25 units. Doubles 150€–200€. AE, MC, V.

★★ Mykonos Grand AGIOS IOANNIS

A sprawling complex above the sea at Agios Ioannis (where the film *Shirley Valentine* was shot) breaks the generic Greek resort mold with exceptional service and endless amenities that ensure guests feel pampered. Many of the sea-facing rooms are equipped with deep whirlpool tubs and steam rooms, and a beautiful pool sparkles above the private sandy beach. Given the spa, tennis courts, and nice choice of in-house bars and restaurants, you may be tempted never to leave the grounds. ☎ 22890/25555. www.mykonos grand.gr. 100 units. Doubles 250€–400€ w/ breakfast. AE, MC, V. Closed Nov–Mar.

★ Philippi Hotel HORA

It's hard to believe that Mykonos could still have a simple, family-run, Greek-style hotel, but here it is, right in the heart of Hora, with a pretty garden to boot. Rooms are simply furnished but spacious and many have balconies; those off the street are pleasantly quiet. Amenities are few, but the shops and restaurants of Hora are just outside the door. ☎ 22890/22294. 13 units. Doubles 90€. No credit cards.

★★ Semeli HORA

This lovely old home with rambling additions is on the outskirts of Hora. Each room is decorated differently, in styles ranging from chic contemporary to traditional. All are welcoming and comfortable, facing the pool and gardens from small balconies. Facilities include a spa, an indoor-outdoor restaurant, and even a bar in Little Venice to welcome you when you leave the premises. Ring road. ☎ 22890/27466. www.semelihotel.gr. 45 units. Doubles 250€–350€ w/breakfast. AE, MC, V.

★ Zorzis Hotel HORA

This 16th-century house-turned-inn captures Hora's old-world charm. It's filled with antiques and other stylish, homey furnishings. Balconies and a pretty little garden make it an oasis right in town. Kalogera St. ☎ 22890/22167. www.zorzishotel.com. 10 units. Doubles 95€–150€ w/breakfast. MC, V.

For Shoppers: A Tradition of Excellence

Fashion designers such as Christian Dior and Givenchy were chief among the international travelers who began to visit Mykonos in the 1950s. They discovered the island's distinctive textiles, often woven by hand in a striped pattern, and they incorporated the designs into their creations. Young Mykonites began designing their own fashions, and these were soon taken up by Jacqueline Onassis and other well-heeled visitors. The tradition continues. **Yiannis Galatis,** who applies island designs to thin, multicolored textiles, shows his famous gowns and other creations, including men's clothing, in his beautiful shop in Hora (Plateia Mando Mavrogenous; ☎ 22890/22255). **Dimitris Parthenis,** another innovative island designer, showcases his work and that of his daughter, Orsalia, in a shop near Little Venice (Plateia Alefkandra; ☎ 22890/23080). **Ioanna Zouganeli** carries on the family weaving craft and sells silk and mohair shawls, scarves, and other pieces from a delightful little shop facing Paraportiani (☎ 22890/22309). Mykonos is also known for jewelry, and the top of the line is **Ilias Lalaounis,** where stunning contemporary pieces based on classical designs are shown in a welcoming shop near Plateia Mando Mavrogenous (14 Polikandrioti; ☎ 22890/22444). **Efthimiou** sells almond sweets, a traditional Mykonos favorite, and Paraportiani wine made on the island (Zouganeli; ☎ 22890/22281).

Where to Dine on Mykonos

> La Maison de Catherine demonstrates the island's international flare with a fusion of Greek and French cuisine.

★ **Fish Taverna Kounelas** HORA *SEAFOOD*
This simple upstairs room with a cramped garden below is a Hora institution, living up to its reputation with simple preparations of the freshest catch available. Prices are fair but vary with weight. That said, you may have to negotiate with the surly staff to make sure they don't foist a lavish seafood feast on you. Near harbor and town hall. ☎ 22890/22890. Entrees 8€–20€. No credit cards. Dinner daily.

★★ **Kiki's** AGIOS SOSTIS *GREEK*
Few island experiences match a swim at beautiful Agios Sostis on the north shore followed by a lazy lunch beneath the flowering vine that shades Kiki's seaside terrace. Fish and meat are grilled outdoors, and you'll step into the kitchen to choose one of the delightfully fresh salads. The place has no electricity and shuts up at sundown. Entrees 6€–8€. No credit cards. Lunch daily. Closed Nov–Mar.

★★★ **La Maison de Catherine** HORA *GREEK/ FRENCH* One of the island's best restaurants was serving fusion cuisine long before that became a trend—wonderful seafood soufflés, French leg of lamb infused with island spices, and an apple tart with light Greek pastry. The candlelit room in the heart of old Hora is lovely and blessedly quiet. Near harbor. ☎ 22890/ 22890. Entrees 20€–35€. AE, MC, V. Dinner daily.

★★ **Matsuhisa Mykonos** HORA *JAPANESE*
The setting, in the poolside gardens of the Belvedere Hotel, is beautifully Greek, but the food, the inspiration of international celebrity chef Nobu Matsuhisa, transports you to Asia and South America—think sushi with a Latin influence. Quality and service are flawless, yet an elegantly informal aura prevails. Belvedere Hotel. ☎ 22890/22890. Set menus 70€–80€. AE, DC, MC, V. Dinner daily. Closed Nov–Mar.

★ **Niko's Taverna** HORA *GREEK*
This taverna that sprawls across a square in the heart of Hora really reels 'em in, but the moussaka, cabbage stuffed with feta, and other basic fare is reliably good. Avoid lunch and early evening, when the cruise-ship crowd packs in; by contrast, a late dinner beneath the trees is quite a nice experience. Near harbor. Entrees 6€–10€. MC, V. Lunch & dinner daily.

★★★ **To Maereo** HORA *GREEK*
Mykonos could use about a dozen more places like this one—simple and atmospheric, serving good traditional fare at reasonable prices. Most Mykonites feel the same way, so come early or late to avoid the crush, ask for a table on the little street, and tuck into country sausage, meatballs, zucchini fritters, and other delicious fare. 16 Kalogera. ☎ 22890/28825. Entrees 7€–10€. No credit cards. Dinner daily.

Mykonos After Dark

Many visitors to the island don't creep out of their lairs until sunset, and they have no lack of venues for their nighttime escapades when they do. Little Venice is the island's most popular spot at sunset, and four especially pleasant waterside bars—Kastro, Montparnasse, Katerina's, and Galeraki—serve up views from their balconies, along with refined music, sophisticated clientele, and decent cocktails (to be sipped slowly, at about 10€ a drink). Bars in the center of Hora are popular for after-dinner drinks and people-watching, and these pleasures go on well into the wee hours. **Aroma** and **Uno,** on Matoyanni Street, are the perennial favorites. **Pierro's,** also on Matoyanni, is the island's most popular gay club, and nearby **Icarus** and **Ramrod** hold their own with all-night music and drag shows. The late-night scene is liveliest at Paradise Beach, where **Cavo Paradise** and the **Paradise Club** get going at about 2am and charge hefty covers (at least 25€) for the privilege of dancing till dawn. The sobering morning swim is included. The Mykonos scene changes each season, so see what's new and hot once you get to the island.

Siros

One of the smallest Cycladic Islands is the capital of the archipelago; as you move around the islands, it's likely that you'll steam into Siros port for a short stop or to change ferries. Homer wrote of Siros being "good for cattle and good for sheep, full of vineyards, and wheat raising." What will persuade you to spend at least a day on Siros, though, are not rural pastimes, or for that matter, beaches, but the cosmopolitan pleasures of Ermoupolis, the beautiful city that was for many years the most important port in Greece.

> The neoclassical grandeur of Plateia Miaoulis reflects Siros's 19th-century wealth and prominence.

START Ermoupolis. **TRIP LENGTH** 1 day.

① ★★★ **Ermoupolis.** As you pull into the harbor, a multicolored jumble of domes, towers, neoclassic mansions, and Cycladic cubes spills down the hillside between two peaks, **Ano Siros** and **Vrontado.** The city's architectural riches, mostly from the 19th century, have earned Ermoupolis UNESCO World Heritage status.

Plateia Miaoulis, the heart of Ermoupolis, is paved in marble, ringed with palm trees, and flanked by many fine 19th-century buildings. The square and the neoclassical town hall are the work of German architect Ernst Ziller, commissioned in the 1860s to create landmarks worthy of the city's importance and wealth. You can step into the marbled and

Getting There

Boats steam into Siros from Piraeus and Rafina at least twice a day, and the island is well connected to Paros, Naxos, Mykonos, Tinos, and Santorini by boat. You can also get to some of the harder-to-reach islands in the Cyclades, such as Folegandros and Sifnos, from Siros. Among the many travel offices on the harbor is **Teamwork** (☎ 22860/83400; www.teamwork.gr), notable for a summertime bus tour of the island, about 20€, leaving from the office at 9am and returning around 4pm. The office also stores luggage, leaving you unencumbered to walk around Ermoupolis and head out to Galissas for a swim.

Cape Trimeson

Cape Diapori

Grammata Beach

Lia Beach

Syringas

Kambos

Kastri

Aegean Sea

Aetos Beach

Platos

Hartiana

Mytikas

Agios Georgios

Delfini Beach

Ano Siros

3

2 Vrontado

1

Kini Beach

Ermoupolis

Siros

Aegean Sea

To Paros & Naxos

Cape Katakefalos

Dhanakos

▲ **Mt. Volokos**

Lazareto

Galissas Bay

Armeos Beach

4

Galissas

Pagos

Ano Manno

Vissa

Hrousa

Azolimnos Beach

Finikas Beach

Finikas

Vari

Posidonia Beach

Posidonia

▲ **Mt. Axachas**

Vari Beach

Angathopes Beach

Megas Gialos

Megas Gialos Beach

Cape Viglostasi

GREECE

Aegean Sea

Athens ★

Cyclades

Siros

To Thessaloniki

To Tinos & Mykonos

| 0 | | 1 mi |
| 0 | | 1 km |

1 Ermoupolis
2 Vrontado
3 Ano Siros
4 Galissas

> *The Apollon Theatre, modeled after Milan's La Scala, hosts the summertime Festival of the Aegean.*

frescoed hallways to visit the **Archaeological Museum** (Plateia Miaoulis; ☎ 22860/86900; admission 3€; Tues–Sun 8:30am–2pm). The collections are not as inspiring as the sumptuous surroundings, but, as in any such museum in the Cyclades, the most moving works are the tall, elongated figures that early Cycladic artists fashioned some 5,000 years ago.

The square is almost always filled with patrons who seem to spend the entire day moving from one cafe to another. It's especially festive on weekend evenings, when a band plays in a band shell decorated with statues of the nine Muses. A *volta,* the evening stroll, usually proceeds from the square a block or so down Evangelou to Plateia Vardaki, then on to another 19th-century masterpiece, the **Apollon Theatre.** The theater was designed to resemble La Scala in Milan, and the first opera house in Greece (known as "la picola Scala") began welcoming the great performers of western Europe onto its stage in 1864. Siros was then an important stop on shipping routes from Venice to the Middle and Far East, and Italian merchants and travelers made the

theater a popular outpost of Italian culture. A recent renovation has restored the sparkle to the chandeliers and the many tiers of wood boxes, and a small gallery displays mementos from the great performances that once filled the hall (Plateia Miaouli; admission 2€; daily 10am–6pm). Productions continue during the Festival of the Aegean, when orchestras and performers come to Siros for two weeks in late July (p. 369).

Ship captains built fine neoclassical mansions on the streets around Plateia Miaoulis and Plateia Vardaki, lending the neighborhood its name, **Vaporia** (Greek for steamships). These houses were part of the great boom that transformed Ermoupolis during the mid-19th century, the first years of Greek Independence, when refugees came to Siros fleeing Turkish reprisals on other islands. Soon the harbor was the busiest in Greece, and Ermoupolis (appropriately named after Hermes, god of trade) was the commercial center of the new nation—and a contender for capital until that distinction went to Athens. The **Ermoupolis Industrial Museum** (off Plateia Iroon;

22810/86900; admission 3€; Tues–Sun
0am–2pm and 6–9pm), near the waterfront,
elebrates this heritage with displays evoking
the old shipyards, workshops, and neoclassi-
al building spree. ☉ 3 hr.

2 ★ **Vrontado.** Narrow streets and squares
ned with fine houses climb the Vrontado Hill.
his is the Greek Orthodox side of town, set-
ed by 19th-century refugees from other is-
ands; the city's Venetian enclave is across the
ity on the Ano Siros hill. Vrontado is topped
y the Church of the Anastasi (Resurrection),
nd the views from the church terrace extend
cross Ermoupolis to Tinos, Delos, and Mykonos. ☉ 1 hr.

3 ★★★ **Ano Siros.** Venetians settled this
ill in the 13th century, and their atmospheric
Old Quarter remains a world apart from Ermoupolis—an enticing maze of white Cycladic
ouses reached by streets of marble steps and
urrounding several churches and Jesuit and
Capuchin monasteries. Like Vrontado across
own, Anos Siros is also topped by a church—
he Roman Catholic **Basilica of San Giorgio,**

founded by the island's Venetian settlers in
the 13th century. Part of the hilltop is a city
of the dead, who lie beneath miniature Greek
temples and other ornate monuments in the
cemetery of **Agios Yeoryios.** Pherekides,
the 6th-century-B.C. Syrian who invented the
sundial and was the teacher of Pythagoras, is
honored with a bust in a pine-scented hilltop
park nearby. ☉ 1 hr.

Galissas is 8km (5 miles) west of Ermoupolis
and accessible in 15 min. on one of nine daily
buses that run from the dock to other parts
of the island between 8am and midnight in
summer (1.35€ each way).

4 ★ **Galissas.** While beaches alone won't
bring you to Siros, a dip in the sea puts a refreshing cap on a day exploring Ermoupolis.
Some of the most appealing beaches on Siros
are those on the western coast around Galissas, a small but rapidly growing seaside village. Sands at Galissas are backed by tamarisk
trees, and Armeos, a more remote beach, is a
short walk away. ☉ 2 hr.

Where to Stay & Dine on Siros

★★★ **Hotel Vourlis** ERMOUPOLIS
f you're over-nighting on Siros, do so in style
n this 19th-century mansion in the fashionable Vaporia district. Details and furnishings
are authentic, giving you a chance to experience the island's heyday. Some of the front
rooms have sea views. Mavrokordatou.
☎ 22810/88440. 8 units. 140€–180€. MC, V.

★★ **Taverna Lilis** ANO SIROS GREEK
A perch high on the Ano Siros hill ensures
magnificent views. One of the island's favorite
tavernas—the summertime terrace is especially popular—also serves excellent grilled
meat and fish. On some nights, Lilis offers
rembetika, the ballad-like music, extolling the
virtues of wandering, made popular by the late
Markos Vamvakaris, who was born on Siros.
☎ 22810/88087. Entrees 8€–20€. No credit
cards. Lunch & dinner daily.

★★ **To Kastri** ERMOUPOLIS *GREEK*
Make this simple place your midday stop
while exploring Ermoupolis. A local women's
union does the cooking, offering their daily
dishes cafeteria-style. You can be assured that
whatever is on offer is based on family recipes,
providing a tasty introduction to Greek home
cooking. Parou. ☎ 22810/83140. Entrees 5€–8€.
No credit cards. Lunch Mon–Fri.

Summer Music

Siros hosts two big festivals in summer.
The **Ermoupoleia** runs a program of concerts, plays, and other performances at
venues around town from June through
August. In July, the **Festival of the Aegean**
(www.festivaloftheaegean.com) hosts op-
eras and concerts on the stage of the Apollon Theatre, bringing many internationally
acclaimed performers to the island.

The Cyclades Fast Facts

Arriving

BY PLANE You can reach Mykonos, Santorini, Naxos, and Paros by air. Schedules vary by season, and operations are severely curtailed outside the busy July–August tourist season. In summer, **Olympic** (☎ 80111/44444 reservations within Greece; www.olympicair.com) has as many as six flights a day from Athens to Mykonos, six to Santorini, and two each to Naxos and Paros. **Aegean Airlines** (☎ 21062/ might just take the prize, an 61000; www. aegeanair.com) also runs daily flights to the same islands. **BY BOAT** By boat, you have many options, and service gets better and faster all the time. As a general rule, fast boats known as **hydrofoils** leave from Rafina (1 hr. northeast of Athens), and slower ferries leave from the port of Piraeus in the capital, but there are many, many exceptions to this rule. Many ferries to the Cyclades are operated by **Blue Star** (www.bluestarferries.com) and many fast boats by **Hellenic Seaways** (www.hellenic seaways.gr). The best single source for schedules is the excellent website of the **Greek Travel Pages** (www.gtp.gr). Other sources for information are offices of the Greek National Tourist Organization and the thousands of travel agencies around Greece that sell boat tickets; keep in mind, though, that an office may sell tickets for one line but not another and may not be forthcoming with competitors' schedules.

Dentists & Doctors

MYKONOS There's a small hospital in Mykonos Town (☎ 22890/23998). **SIROS** A large medical center is in Ermoupolis (☎ 22810/86666). All but the smallest islands have health clinics. Most hotels will be able to refer you to a local doctor or dentist who speaks English.

Emergencies

See p. 680, Fast Facts Greece.

Getting Around

BY BOAT All the Cycladic Islands have regular bus service, which is frequent in summer. Off-season, service slows, making it hard to island-hop. Year-round winds can wreak havoc on schedules. See the individual island coverage above for a brief rundown on boat service to and from each. Travel agencies on each of the islands can tell you how best to get from one to the other; if you're stuck, you can always backtrack to Athens to board a ferry back to the island you're trying to reach—just about all islands in the Cyclades can be reached on at least one boat a day from Athens. **BY BUS** All the islands will be served by bus. On most, buses meet the ferries, especially handy on cliff-fringed Santorini, Sifnos, and Folegandros, where ports are far below the main island towns. Bus networks reach even the most remote towns, though often only once or twice a day. On most islands, from small Sifnos to large Paros, you can get around quite easily by bus. Time permitting, you can also see all of Santorini by bus, and most of Mykonos with the exception of the north coast. Expect to pay about 1.40€ each way, and don't be shy about telling the driver where you want to get off; there are no designated stops on many rural routes. **BY CAR** A

> *A welcome sight for beachgoers on Naxos.*

ar will come in handy for exploring the inland
ountain villages of Tinos and Naxos; the
orth coast of Mykonos, which isn't served by
ublic transportation; and the ancient sites
nd beaches on the south coast of Santorini.
car is essential on Milos, to visit the many
atural attractions. Ports on all the islands are
hockablock with car-rental agencies; expect
o pay about 40€ a day in season, insurance
cluded. Forgo the temptation to rent a mo-
orbike; visitors who decide to get sporty keep
land clinics very busy.

nternet Access
aros now offers free islandwide Wi-Fi—a
end we hope may spread throughout the
yclades. Also see p. 681, Fast Facts Greece.

harmacies
ee p. 682, Fast Facts Greece.

olice
ee p. 682, Fast Facts Greece.

ost Office
ee p. 682, Fast Facts Greece.

afety
he picturesque villages on Santorini and
any other islands in the Cyclades are laced
ith steep steps, terraces without railings,
nd rough cobblestones. Keep a close eye on
hildren and watch your step. Also see p. 682,
ast Facts Greece.

isitor Information
he Cyclades have few official travel offices,
ut travel agencies on all the islands are forth-
oming. FOLEGANDROS You'll find especially
ood service on Hora through **Sottovento
ravel** (☎ 22860/41444; www.sottovento.
u). MILOS **Milos Travel,** Adamas, (☎ 22870/
2000; www.milostravel.gr). MYKONOS
ykonos Accommodations Center, next to
he port (☎ 22890/23160; www.mykonos-
ccommodation.com). NAXOS **Naxos Tourist**

> *Donkeys still make the climb up to Fira, but the
ascent is easier for man and beast via cable car.*

Information on the port (☎ 22850/25201).
PAROS **Parikia Tours** on the port (☎ 22840/
222470). SANTORINI In Fira at **Nomikos Travel**
(☎ 22860/23660; www.nomikosvillas.gr).
SIFNOS The **municipal travel office,** Plateia
Iroon, Apollonia, and **Aegean Thesaurus,** Kamares and Apollonia (☎ 22840/33151; www.
thesaurus.gr). SIROS **Teamwork Holidays,**
Plateia Miaoulis (☎ 22810/83400; www.
teamwork.gr). TINOS **Windmills Travel**
(☎ 22830/23398; www.windmillstravel.com).

Favorite Moments in the Dodecanese

The Dodecanese island group is the biggest in Greece and the farthest from the mainland. Rhodes is its pearl, known for its hedonistic atmosphere, secluded bays with some of Greece's finest shorelines, mountainous regions such as Mount Attavyros, which is sometimes snow-dusted at 1,215m (3,986 ft.), and hilltops capped by medieval castles and ancient temples. Rhodes also affords easy access—via ferry, *caique*, or cruise ship—to family-friendly Kos, postcard-perfect Symi, divine Patmos, and other more secluded Dodecanese Islands, not to mention Turkey.

> PREVIOUS PAGE *The Church of Our Lady, in Lindos.* THIS PAGE *At Lindos, a beach chair comes with a view of the acropolis.*

❶ Beholding the magnificent setting at Lindos. Even if you don't descend into the white-washed village or climb the hill to the acropolis for another amazing view, just take in the sight before you from the main road. You will not doubt that this land has been blessed by the gods. See p. 408.

❷ Eating alfresco on the beach, Agathi, Rhodes. There's nothing like sitting at a beachside taverna, such as in Agathi on Rhodes, and lunching on Greek salad and fish straight from the sea, served on paper table-cloths and washed down with ice-cold beer. See p. 403.

❸ Swimming in the super-buoyant, warm, shallow sea at Faliraki. You can easily make out the bottom and watch as cheeky fish nip at your ankles or dart away if you get too close. See p. 402.

❹ Stepping out for the night in Faliraki, Rhodes. After a day of fun on the beach, it's best to rest up for a meal at 10pm, the Greek dinner hour, followed by an hour of people-watching at an open-sided bar where a parade of revelers are charging up with great music before heading for the clubs. See p. 407.

❺ Spending an entire day wandering around Rhodes's Old Town. Ancient, medieval, Italian, Ottoman, and Rhodian cultures have all left their mark. It's a delight at every turn, from the bright pink flowers spilling over the walls,

❶ Beholding the magnificent setting at Lindos

❷ Eating alfresco on the beach, Agathi, Rhodes

❸ Swimming in the super-buoyant, warm, shallow sea at Faliraki

❹ Stepping out for the night in Faliraki, Rhodes

❺ Spending an entire day wandering around Rhodes's Old Town

❻ Sailing into Symi's harbor

❼ Riding a small boat on the open water around Symi

❽ Visiting the Asklepion ancient site in Kos

❾ Bathing au naturel in a hot spring at Bros Therma, Kos

❿ Examining a piece of foundation marble at the Western Excavation site in Kos

⓫ Exploring medieval landmarks such as the upper level of the ruined Castle of the Knights in Kos

⓬ Trodding centuries-old footpaths

⓭ Time traveling inside the Church of St. John the Divine in Patmos

⓮ Visiting the Monastery of St. John the Divine in Hora, Patmos

⓯ Standing in the Cave of the Apocalypse, Patmos

> *The Monastery of St. John the Divine commands a hilltop on Patmos.*

> *Your meal straight from the sea.*

to beautifully shaped mosques and fountains burbling quietly at the end of narrow lanes. See p. 390, ❷.

❻ **Sailing into Symi's harbor.** So what if the neoclassical mansions aren't all old? It's still one of the most photogenic sights in the world. Villas in warm brown shades reach from the hills to the sea. See p. 414, ❷.

❼ **Riding a small boat on the open water around Symi.** You'll realize how far from civilization you are as the scent of sage, thyme, and other hillside herbs permeates even the salty sea breeze. See p. 384, ❹.

❽ **Visiting the Asklepion ancient site in Kos.** In antiquity, Asklepion was the main place to go for water treatments, and it's still a site of pilgrimage for health practitioners and other devotees of hot springs, spas, and curative baths. See p. 420, ❾.

❾ **Bathing au naturel in a hot spring at Bros Therma, Kos.** This thermal spring bubbles up along a sandy shoreline and into the sea in its

Symi's appealing harbor in Yialos.

> *Medieval monks spared little expense in embellishing their Monastery of St. John on Patmos.*

atural state. The setting's a bit scrappy, but you love warm seas or hot springs, you'll be oo blissed out to notice. See p. 422.

Examining a piece of foundation marble t the Western Excavation site in Kos. You'll onder about how it fit into the whole, what art of a structure it formed, and how those c. stoneworkers built things to last. See p. 20, **5**.

Exploring medieval landmarks such as he upper level of the ruined Castle of the nights in Kos. You'll gain a palpable sense of he building's history and the way time has left s mark over hundreds of years. See p. 418, **3**.

Trodding centuries-old footpaths. These vere well worn by islanders before roads were uilt as little as a generation ago. They're rare-y used these days, but it's worth traversing he leg from Hora to the Cave of the Apoca-ypse in Patmos or the scenic path down the ali Strata steps from Horio to Yialos in Symi. ee p. 430, **4**; 415, **4**.

Time traveling inside the Church of St. ohn the Divine in Patmos. Although it was uilt in the late 10th century, the interior looks o different from the inside of a contemporary ireek Orthodox church, so you feel a connec-on to the medieval Christians who worshiped here. The saints were depicted in the same two-dimensional way, and biblical tales were told in pictures, to keep the congregants' thoughts on holy matters even when their attention drifted. See p. 431.

14 Visiting the Monastery of St. John the Divine in Hora, Patmos. Complete with black-robed monks, dark corridors that lead to restricted quarters, cells, and other unfamiliar, ascetic sights, it's otherworldly—until you get a whiff of the brothers' lunch: the familiar and tasty aroma of chickpea soup. See p. 429, **3**.

15 Standing in the Cave of the Apocalypse, Patmos. It was here where the Apostle John was said to have been cast down by the holy voice that relayed the Revelation of God. Many feel in awe even amid a crowd when they see the trinity of cracks in the overhanging rock, believed to be the actual site where John stood during the divine visitation. See p. 430, **5**.

The Island of Rhodes in 3 Days

Greece's fourth largest island (1,398 sq. km/540 sq. miles), Rhodes enjoys sunshine some 280 days of the year, low humidity, warm seas that lap the shores of numerous luxury resorts, an incomparable range of things to do, and a photogenic fortress town. Peacocks populate oases, and revelers descend on centuries-old monasteries in beautiful settings to celebrate the many saints' days, festivals, and weddings. The Rhodes Town tour, presented here, is likely to suit cruise ship passengers with just a few hours to sightsee. Travelers with a few days to spare can also visit a stunning beach and squeeze in a trip to Lindos.

> *A day at the beach in Rhodes is rarely a solitary experience.*

START Rhodes Town. TRIP LENGTH 3 days (about 100km/62 miles round-trip).

1 ★★★ kids **Rhodes Town.** Spend the first day sightseeing in **Rhodes Town** (p. 390). Start your morning with a coffee and cheese pie at the central **Thermai Cafe** (see p. 397), with the fountain at the entrance, or from one of the many cafe/pastry shops at the **New Market** (p. 390, ①) before walking along the harbor front into the **Old Town.** ⊕ 1 hr.

SITE GUIDE
PAGE 381

2 **Old Town.** The Old Town of Rhodes is a star attraction, and you can spend hours wandering its narrow streets, taking in the views and layers of history. ⊕ At least 6 hr.

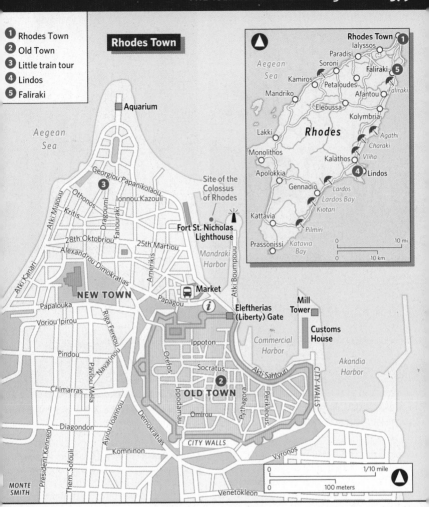

1 Rhodes Town
2 Old Town
3 Little train tour
4 Lindos
5 Faliraki

Rhodes Town

3 kids **Little train tour.** If you still have energy or want to see the sunset from a high vantage point, take a sightseeing tour of the town on the **little train tour** (p. 394, **13**) before returning to your hotel to crash and/or have dinner. After hours, you can choose among various **bars** in Rhodes Town (p. 397) or catch a bus or taxi (14km/8⅔ miles; service is frequent) to party in the beach resort of **Faliraki** (p. 407).

Take the Lindos road southwest 50km (31 miles), 1hr.

4 ★★★ **Lindos.** You can't leave the island without seeing its most spectacular sight, despite the crowds of visitors that flock here. Bus service from Rhodes is good, and the hour-long ride is only 4.50€ (compared to the 50€ one-way cab fare). The entrance to the village is closed to traffic, so leave your chosen mode of transport upon arrival, where you'll immediately be rewarded with jaw-dropping views from either entrance off the main road overlooking town. Wander the narrow alleys of whitewashed houses to get the feel of this kind of Greek village, with its mazelike,

> *In Rhodes Town, the Street of the Knights descends from the palace to the harbor.*

> *Lindos is known for fine textiles, carved wood, and other craftsmanship.*

meandering streets built high in the hills, obscured from the potentially rapacious view of passing pirate ships. Stop for a **refreshment or meal** (p. 411) before heading to the **acropolis** (p. 408, ❶), where medieval knights also created a fortress over the ancient citadel. You can climb the steps and walk amid the temple columns, overlooking expanses of sky and sea, a gorgeous and historic bay, a sandy crescent-shaped beach, and whitewashed houses. Back in town, you may want to shop for **souvenirs** (p. 408, ❸), or pop into the **Church of Our Lady** (p. 409, ❹) to have a look at the mosaics. If it's pre-dusk, make your way down to

For More Detailed Information

For detailed information on sights, hotels, and restaurants in Rhodes Old Town, see p. 390; Lindos see p. 408; Faliraki see p. 402.

Lindos Beach (p. 409, ❻) and go for a well-deserved swim and a typical Greek taverna meal beside the sea. Or return to your hotel to rest and freshen up before **dinner** (p. 411). ⏱1 day.

The resort of Faliraki is 14km (8⅔ miles) southwest of Rhodes Town on the Lindos road (20 min).

❺ **Faliraki.** Most people come to Greece to sample one of its superlative beach resorts. There are many, but Faliraki (p. 402) is the biggest and, therefore, your best bet for water-skiing, bungee jumping, or boating excursions. Find a beach chair amid the rows, or swim in that glorious, buoyant sea before heading out to party at night. Getting here from Rhodes Town is easy. For slightly less crowded alternatives, see p. 386, " The Best Dodecanese Beaches." ⏱1 day.

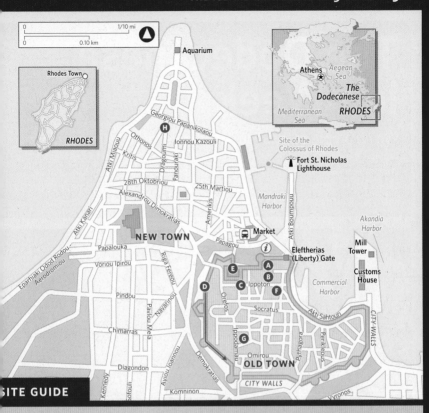

Aquarium

Athens
Aegean
Sea

**The
Dodecanese**

Mediterranean
Sea

RHODES

Rhodes Town

RHODES

Georgiou Papanikolaou

H

Ionnou Kazouli

Othonos

Atki Miaou

Kritis

Dragoumi

Panouraki

28th Oktobriou

25th Martiou

Alexandrou Dimokratias

Amerikis

Site of the
Colossus of Rhodes

Fort St. Nicholas
Lighthouse

Mandraki
Harbor

Akti Boumpoulou

Akandia
Harbor

NEW TOWN

Papalouka

Voriou Ipirou

Eparhiaki Odod Rodou
Aerodromiou

Atki Kanari

Riga Fereou

Navarinou

Pavlou Mela

Papagou

Market

i

Papagou

Eleftherias
(Liberty) Gate

Mill
Tower

Customs
House

E

A

B

C Ippoton

F

Commercial
Harbor

Akti Sahtoun

CITY WALLS

Pindou

Chimarras

Oreos

Ippodamou

Socratus

Pythagora

Perikleous

G

Diagondon

Aviou Ioannou

Demokratias

Omirou

OLD TOWN

CITY WALLS

Kennedy

Sofouli

Komninon

Vyronos

SITE GUIDE

2 Old Town

Pop into the A **Art Gallery Museum** (p. 391, 3) to see a temporary exhibition. Continue farther along, across the little square, and into the B **Decorative Arts Collection** (p. 391, 4) for a visual fix on household items of yesteryear. Continue and then turn right into the narrow, sign-bereft C **Street of the Knights** (p. 392, 5), where the Chevaliers of St. John once resided in their various quarters, based on their homelands. At the end is the gated entrance to the D **walls around the Old City** (p. 392, 6), protecting the marvelous E **Palace of the Grand Masters** (p. 392, 7) castle, a restoration, as is the Street of the Knights. Head back down Ippoton Street and turn right to get to the F **Archaeological Museum** (p. 393, 9), converted from the Knights' Hospital, with artifacts displayed ward by ward. Pass through the garden to see a re-created Turkish house, the Prehistoric Exhibit annex,

and the Epigraphical Museum. Take a break for lunch now, perhaps heading over to Greek food taverna G **Golden Olympiade** (8–10 Evdimou St.; ☎ 22410/20119; closed Nov–Mar; $) or to the no-name souvlaki restaurant opposite, in the small square on Apellou and Evdimou streets. If you have time, try a hamam and massage, exercised according to centuries-old tradition at the quaint H **Yeni Hamam** (p. 394, 10).

The Dodecanese in 1 Week

We recommend that you spend most of your time exploring the historic wealth and beauty of Rhodes before you move on to experience the charming beauty of Symi; pay homage to Hippocrates in nearby Kos, whose sandy shores attract families and cyclists; and then make a pilgrimage to pretty Patmos, where people flock to visit sites associated with biblical events.

> *Ruins of the ancient agora and harbor are littered evocatively around modern Kos Town.*

START Rhodes Town. TRIP LENGTH 150km (93 miles), 1 week (including 5½–7½ hr. sail time).

1 ★★★ **Rhodes Town.** Rhodes Town, and specifically its Old Town (p. 378, **2**), is the jewel of the Dodecanese Islands. Famous even in antiquity for its Colossus, one of the Seven Wonders of the Ancient World, it received preferential treatment when the Italians ruled the island group early last century and restored many sites and monuments. The island is reaping the benefits, as these sites, along with Rhodes's natural beauty, attract millions of visitors each year. You can easily spend a day wandering around the medieval city, walled off and complete with a moat

> A waterpark is among the many diversions at Faliraki on Rhodes.

(albeit a dry one). This is one of the most interesting and best-preserved sites in Europe. Don't miss the **Palace of the Grand Masters** (p. 329, **7**), which looks every inch the part of a swashbuckler's castle on the outside, though many rooms inside meticulously display antiquities found around the island. The scenes and scents here are heady, with climbing hibiscus and jasmine plants running riot over the Old Town walls. ⏱ 1½ days.

Faliraki is 14km (8⅔ miles) southwest of Rhodes Town, a 20-minute drive on the Lindos road.

2 ★★★ 🅺🅸🅳🆂 **Faliraki.** You certainly won't find peace and quiet at this popular resort, with a long stretch of sandy beach and sparkling blue waters, but it's the place to go if you love watersports and nightlife (read: if you're 18 to 30, or if you've got teenagers or even young children). Entertainments include a big **water slide park** (p. 403), bungee jumping, paragliding, glass-sided submarine rides, and chugging boat excursions that conclude with a beach BBQ. Here you can and should do something you wouldn't or couldn't do anywhere else. The nightlife is guaranteed to be memorable, too. See p. 402. ⏱ Half-day.

Take the Lindos road southwest for about 35km (22 miles), 40 minutes.

3 ★★★ **Lindos.** Stay another night at the beach resort of Faliraki, and from there take an excursion to the beautiful village of **Lindos** (p. 408). It's about 40km (25 miles) from Faliraki, and you can take an organized day trip through a travel agency, or catch one of the many buses that ply the main Rhodes-Lindos road, which runs right by this town. This stunning ancient Doric city is associated with the sea and also with the Apostle Paul, who disembarked at his eponymous bay. The other bay has one of the most inviting beaches, but in summer the town has a circuslike atmosphere, with tourists in droves. ⏱ 1 day.

Take the Lindos road northeast back to Rhodes Town 50km (31 miles, 1 hr). A boat from Rhodes to Symi takes 1½–2 hr.

4 ★★★ **Symi.** Rise very early, say goodbye to Rhodes, and take a boat to **Symi** (p. 412), 40km (25 miles) northwest of Rhodes. Boats of different speeds run on different days; try for a faster vessel that also makes a stop at **Panormitis** (p. 412, **1**), a sprawling 15th-century Greek Orthodox monastery, with a small museum on site, set in a lovely bay at the south of the island. Then continue on to **Yialo** (p. 414, **2**), Symi's postcard-perfect port, likely to be the Greece of your mind's eye. Spend some time wandering around, or hike up to the village of **Horio** (p. 415, **4**). Descend via the steps for more amazing views. Then wait for the next boat bound for Kos. ⏱ 1 day.

A boat from Symi to Kos takes 1½–3 hours.

5 ★ kids **Kos.** If you want to get your swims in between sightseeing, choose a hotel in the **Lambi** (p. 423) area of **Kos Town** (p. 418, **1**), on the beach but affording easy access to the compact town center. Kos Town's attractions aren't jaw-dropping, but they're abundant; the most interesting include the **Plane Tree of Hippocrates** (p. 418, **2**), the **Castle of the Knights** (p. 418, **3**), the small **Archaeological Museum** (p. 418, **4**), and **Asklepion** (p. 420, **9**), a sanctuary dedicated to healing, associated with **Hippocrates** (p. 420), the father of medicine, who was born on Kos. If you have time to visit only one sight, we recommend this one, amid a beautiful cypress grove. When hunger strikes, consider a trip to Zia, a village in the Mount Dikios foothills some 15km (9⅓ miles) from Kos Town. Dine on a balcony at **Avli Taverna** (p. 426) as the sun sets. If you're too worn out to leave Kos Town, watch the sun set over the water with the Turkish coast in silhouette from a **taverna** (p. 426) in the center of town. If you're a hot-spring aficionado, you might also want to make time for a pilgrimage to the curative hot spring **Bros Therma** (p. 422), with a natural seaside pool. If you're a nature lover, visit the salt marsh between **Marmari** (p. 424) and **Tigaki** (p. 425) beaches, where you may spot a migrating flamingo or hatching sea turtle. The next day, you're off to the holy island of Patmos. 🕐 1 day.

A boat from Kos to Patmos takes about 2½ hours.

6 ★★ kids **Patmos.** This small, 39 sq. km (15 sq. miles) island has topped *Forbes*'s list of the most idyllic places to live in Europe. It has a remarkably beautiful shape, with many coves and inlets; it's quiet; it has nice beaches, a UNESCO World Heritage Site (the traditional Greek village **Hora,** p. 429, **2**), and two pilgrimage meccas: the **Cave of the Apocalypse** (p. 430, **5**) and the **Monastery of St. John** (p. 429, **3**). If you have time, visit the old-fashioned way and take the steps down the rocky **footpath** (p. 430, **4**) from Hora to the Cave of the Apocalypse and possibly even farther, to the port of **Skala** (p. 428, **1**). If you have yet another hour to spare, consider an island tour and take in the scenery, scan the villages, and see which beach you like best for a photo op or possible return trip. It'll cost about 30€. 🕐 1 day.

> *Excursion boats ply the waters around the major islands in the Dodecanese.*

A boat from Patmos to Rhodes takes about 5 hours.

7 **Free day.** If you have spare time before returning to your cruise ship, port, or airport, this is mop-up day. Travel time to these islands is short, so you're likely to have time to check out attractions you may have missed during the week. If you want to experience another island en route, consider **Leros, Lipsi,** or **Kalymnos.** Just be sure you've checked the timetable and weather forecast with a travel agent or the port authorities before you set out. 🕐 1 day.

The Best Dodecanese Beaches

The Dodecanese Islands are graced with a wide variety of beaches. Here are a few pointers to help you find that perfect strip of sand and sea: Beaches along south-facing shores are less blasted by the *meltemi,* or Etesian winds, that blow from mid-July to mid-August. Rhodes's east-coast shores are lapped by the calmer and warmer Mediterranean Sea rather than the colder Aegean, and beaches with streams alongside them may be colder, but they're usually dry in summer. Beaches with cliffs behind them usually have steeper drops in the water as well; likewise, shorelines that back onto flatlands descend into the sea more gradually. Here are my favorites.

> *Agathi, one of many beaches on the coast south of Rhodes Town.*

★★★ kids **Agathi, Rhodes.** About a kilometer (½ mile) from Haraki Bay, this fine sandy beach has a shallow gradient, which makes it safe for children; watersports to keep older children entertained; and tavernas, beach chairs, and umbrellas for everyone. To reach the shore, you have to travel up and then down a gravel road just before you reach Haraki Bay. 40km (25 miles) southwest of Rhodes Town (p. 390).

Agathi, Rhodes	**8**
Agios Stefanos, Kos	**3**
Agrio Livadi, Patmos	**2**
Bros Therma, Kos	**4**
Faliraki, Rhodes	**6**
Kambos, Patmos	**1**
Kardamena, Kos	**5**
Lindos, Rhodes	**9**
Tsambica, Rhodes	**7**

★ kids **Agios Stefanos, Kos.** This nice stretch of sandy beach sits on a quiet bay beside the 5th-century ruins of the Basilica of St. Stephen, which juts into the sea. The islet visible in the distance is Kastri. Turn off the main road toward the coast, a fairly steep **descent.** 40km (25 miles) southwest of Kos Town (p. 418).

★★ kids **Agrio Livadi, Patmos.** This beach is my favorite in Patmos. It's in a bay, like all the beaches on this deeply indented island, and it's sandy. It has beach chairs and umbrellas, a few low-key watersports activities, a taverna that prepares great seaside meals, and, some

say, the warmest sea on the island. 2km (1¼ mile) north of Skala (p. 428, **1**).

★ **Bros Therma, Kos.** This hot spring may be hard to reach, and the natural pool locale may bear a resemblance to a gravel pit, but how many places on earth can claim a curative hot spring that empties into a little boulder-edged pool in the sea, so you can lie beside the ocean in warm water that's good for you? What's more, it's also on a beautiful island. **Toward Agios Fokas, 8km (5 miles) south of Kos Town** (see p. 418).

> *Crowded Faliraki on Rhodes gets high marks for cleanliness.*

> *Kambos and other beaches on Patmos are pleasantly uncrowded.*

★★★ Faliraki, Rhodes. Rhodes consistently earns the most Blue Flags for the cleanliness of its beaches; in 2009, 32 Rhodian beaches received the designation, and Faliraki took 12 of those. Arguably the most beautiful beach in the Dodecanese, the 4km (2½-mile) stretch is divided into zones. The beach has fine sand, a shallow gradient, and just about every imaginable type of watersport and excursion, making it popular with all age groups. Enormous hotel complexes appear one after another along the new road to Rhodes Town, and row upon row of beach chairs complete the lineup of amenities. 14km (8⅔ miles) south of Rhodes Town (see p. 390).

★★ kids Kambos, Patmos. This long stretch of sand and pebbles is set in a bay lined with shade trees. The island's oldest resort, with beach chairs and some watersports, it has a local feel. It's popular with families yet quiet, except during school vacations, when the kids can get a bit raucous. The excellent taverna opposite sets tables right in the sand, so you can dine literally on the beach. Now that's alfresco. 11km (7 miles) north of Skala, 600m (1,969 ft.) from Kambos village (p. 432).

★ Kardamena, Kos. This is Kos's main beach resort on the southeast side of the island, protected from the full blast of seasonal gales. With beach chairs and watersports, it's popular with package tourists who have a reputation for partying. The beach is 6km (3¾ miles) long, however, with a variety of hotels strung along it, so you don't have to join the fray if you prefer quiet. 29km (18 miles) southwest of Kos Town (p. 418).

★★★ kids Lindos, Rhodes. The beach in Lindos is long and fairly wide; it's got beach chairs, umbrellas, good tavernas, and a million-dollar setting beside the hill of Lindos Town and the walls of the acropolis. Your feet won't sink too far into the fine white sand, the sea is clear as can be, and schools of fish swim around the shallows. It's not too noisy with blaring music either. 55km (34 miles) southwest of Rhodes Town (p. 390).

★★ kids Tsambica, Rhodes. This beach is one of Rhodes's nicest, with a good taverna, canteens, watersports, fine sand, and a shallow gradient. For all of that, however, it gets very busy. You need your own transport, as the road to get here is very steep. It's named after a nearby church, known for answering the pleas of women who come and pray to conceive; thus its name is popular for Rhodian boys. For equipment rental, call **Seadoo Water Sports** (☎ 69773/43687). 30km (19 miles) south of Rhodes Town (p. 390).

Natural Kos

The island of Kos, 290 sq. km (112 sq. miles), is on the route of birds migrating from northern Europe to Africa. It's near the Asia Minor coast, south of Kalymnos and north of Nissyros. The island's remaining pine and cypress forest surrounds its highest mountain, Dikios 846m (2,776 ft.) high. A large area has been reforested, as other sections are quickly denuded by roaming sheep and goats.

It has a salt pan or marsh, Alkyes, that was once used for salt mining but now serves as a Natura 2000 wetland, along with a marsh in Psalidi and on Mount Dikios. Some 1,000 species of plants, common and uncommon, thrive here, including the *Phlomis lycia* (mint), *Jurinea consanguinea*, and rare *Silene urvillei*. At least 22 types of orchid have been found. It's also in the path of birds migrating in spring and autumn. Threatened and rare species, such as the bright yellow oriole (*Oriolus oriolus*), multihued European Bee-eater

(*Merops apiaster*), European Roller (*Coracias garrulous*), crested and stripy-winged hoopoe (*Upupa epops*), and various species of heron (*Ardea*), have all been spotted here.

Swallows and swifts come from Africa in spring and make their summer nests here, while on Mount Dikios you can find birds of prey such as Bonelli's Eagle (*Hieratus fasciatus*), the Long-legged Buzzard (*Buteo rufinus*), and the very rare Asian Blue-cheeked Bee-eater (*Merops superciliosus*), which is green with a red throat. On the salt-pan wetland at Tigaki beside the beach, or the marsh in Psalidi, rare birds such as the Greater Flamingo (*Pheonicopterus ruber*) and the Glossy Ibis (*Plegadis falcinellus*) can be seen, while threatened Loggerhead sea turtles (*Caretta caretta*) and Green turtles (*Chelonia mydas*) both lay their eggs in Tigaki. Northern European birds, such as ducks and swans, also come to the wetlands to pass the winter in a warm climate.

Rhodes Town

Rhodes Town's Old City is a UNESCO World Heritage Site, a living monument that's a delight to explore on foot. Coral and fuchsia-tinted hibiscus spill over fortification walls built by the Knights Hospitaller (Order of St. John of Jerusalem) in the 13th to 15th centuries. The walls and the buildings they enclose, many restored early in the last century, complement the eclectic mix of Ottoman mosques from the years of Turkish rule, ancient ruins, and modern-era shops that all pull at your gaze. You may have trouble prying yourself away, even if that means returning to a beach resort.

> The New Market on Mandraki Harbor is one of many elaborate 20th-century landmarks the Italians left behind on Rhodes.

START Mandraki Harbor. **TRIP LENGTH** 1 day.

① 🚏 **New Market.** You'll very likely enter Rhodes Town near the harbor-front bus terminal beside the New Market—a white, Italian-built, octagon-shaped arcade with Ottoman arches. Inside are restaurants and cafes as well as shops. Behind the New Market is Rimini Square and the entrance to the evening Sound and Light show, which may or may not be running. Outside facing the harbor is a row of cafes that vie with one another to display the most gorgeous and delectable cakes and pastries. Tables are set up opposite each shop. Choose one and watch the goings-on in the harbor and town as you collect yourself before starting your tour. ⏱ 20 min. Mandraki Harbor. $.

❷ ★★★ **Old Town.** To enter the Old Town from the New Market, walk alongside the harbor front and medieval wall, past the portrait artists and through **Eleftherias (Freedom/Liberty) Gate,** opened in the 1920s. Just inside is Symi (or Arsenal) Square. Relics

Where to Stay in Rhodes Town

Apollo Guest House **24**

Avalon Boutique Hotel **16**

Klimt Guest House **23**

Marco Polo Mansion **22**

Nikos Takis Fashion Hotel **17**

Spirit of the Knights **21**

Where to Dine in Rhodes Town

British Cafe and Bar **18**

Sarris Tavern **19**

Ta Kioupia **25**

Thermai Café **15**

Zizi Taverna **20**

1. New Market
2. Old Town
3. Art Gallery Museum
4. Decorative Arts Collection
5. Street of the Knights
6. City Walls
7. Palace of the Grand Masters
8. Pita Fan
9. Archaeological Museum
10. Yeni Hamam
11. Aktaion, Mandraki Harbour, New Town
12. Aquarium Museum
13. Little train tour
14. Monte Smith Hill

Site of the Colossus of Rhodes

Fort St. Nicholas Lighthouse

Mandraki Harbor

Akandia Harbor

Mill Tower

Customs House

Commercial Harbor

Eleftherias (Liberty) Gate

NEW TOWN

Papalouka

Voriou Ipirou

Pindou

Chimarras

Diagondon

Komninon

Ancient Stadium

MONTE SMITH

OLD TOWN

CITY WALLS

Vyronos

Socratus

Omirou

Ippoton

0   1/10 mi

0   0.10 km

of ancient Greek antiquities and Turkish mosques turn up everywhere in the Old City, including here, where the ruins of the 3rd-century-B.C. **Temple of Aphrodite** are just in front of the **Art Gallery Museum.** You could easily fill an entire day here. ⏱ At least 10 min.

3 Art Gallery Museum. This is one of three buildings that house the municipal art galleries. All hold exhibits of 20th-century and contemporary Greek artists; this one exhibits temporary work. (The **New Art Gallery** is near the aquarium at Haritou Sq.; ☎ 22410/43780;

Tues–Fri 8am–3pm, Sat 8am–2pm. The **Centre of Contemporary Art** is at 179 Socratous St., Old Town; ☎ 22410/77071; www.mga museum.gr; Tues–Sat 10am–2pm.) ⏱ 15 min. Symi Sq. ☎ 22410/23766. Admission 3€ for all 3 galleries. Tues–Fri 9am–2pm and 6–9pm, Sat 10am–2pm, in winter closed in the evening.

4 Decorative Arts Collection. Continue into the Old Town until you notice a fountain with a fish spout in a small square on your right. On the left is the entrance to this small museum of Dodecanese island folk art in the Knight's

> *In Old Town, narrow streets are lined with fine, old Turkish houses made from limestone quarried in Lindos.*

Arsenal building. The collection dates from the 11th century and includes some Italian and Turkish pieces amassed by an Italian ethnographer during Italy's occupation early last century. What's most striking is the detailed craftsmanship in the pieces here, from woodwork to pottery, costumes, and intricate embroidery, recalling an era when people took more time. All the exhibits are on the accessible ground floor. ⏲ 15 min. **Argyrokastrou Sq.** ☎ 22410/25500. www.culture.gr. Admission 2€. Tues–Sun 8:30am–2:40pm.

❺ ★ **Street of the Knights.** Continue on the road to Hospital Square, the rebuilt Inn of England on your left. On the right you will notice a narrow street devoid of awnings or signage, with massive walls on either side with arched lintels. Welcome to the 14th-century Rue des Chevaliers (Street of the Knights). The Palace of the Knights is at the end, but the way is lined by the inns of the various orders, organized into *langues*, or tongues, their coats of arms over the doorways. The Hospitallers of Provence, Auvergne, France (the largest),

Italy, Aragon, England, Germany, and Castile lived here before moving on to Malta after Rhodes fell to the Turks in 1522. On the left is the 15th-century restored *auberge* (meeting center) of the Spanish Inn, which holds conferences, exhibits, concerts, and a projection (Sun–Fri) of the Old Town's history. ⏲ 20 min. **Ippoton St.**

❻ **City walls.** At the end of the Street of the Knights, just in front of the palace, is the entrance to the walkway around the medieval walls. All the bastions are closed, but the views over the city and harbor are superb up here, and you can walk around to the exit. ⏲ 20 min. **In front of Palace of the Knights.** ☎ 22410/25500. www.culture.gr. Admission 2€. Tues–Sun 8:30am–1pm.

❼ ★★ **Palace of the Grand Masters.** If it weren't for the hordes of tourists, you might half expect an armored suit or a maiden in a cone-shaped hat to exit the 15th-century Palace of the Knights, with its massive walls, turrets, and crenellations. The Orders of the Knights assembled here, and the palace was

> *Various medieval coats of arms appear along the Street of the Knights.*

the Grand Master's residence in peacetime. The fortress was damaged by earthquakes and ruined after an explosion in 1856; before that, Turkish rulers had used it as a prison. The interior was rebuilt and modernized to serve as a summer palace for Italy's Victor Emmanuel III and Mussolini, who both failed to benefit, after losing World War II and the island territories shortly afterward. Relics dating back to antiquity—from medieval chests, ornate mirrors, and portrait paintings to mosaic floors and ancient pottery—are on display throughout the palace's many rooms and levels. In a fine display of historic continuity, young Greek women ogle gold jewelry that predates the Christian era; another room shows how the Colossus of Rhodes, one of the Seven Ancient Wonders, was imagined, often comically, through the centuries as it straddled the harbor. ◷ 1–2 hr. Ippoton St. ☎ 22410/25500. www.culture.gr. Admission 6€. April–Oct daily 8:30am–8pm, winter reduced hours. Closed Jan 1, Mar 25, Orthodox Easter Sun, May 1, Dec 25, 26.

⑧ 🍴 kids **Pita Fan.** Wander past houses with Turkish-style wooden balconies or the much-photographed seahorse fountain and 1577 synagogue (www.jewishrhodes.org) in **Martyr's Square,** in the old Jewish Quarter. Forgo the pricier, people-watching cafes on Ippokratous Square at the beginning of touristy Sokratous Street, the former Turkish bazaar, and find your way to this outlet on the corner. They make super gyros and other quick meals. You can buy souvlaki and a draft, to stay or to go, for all of 5€. Aeolou and Ermou sts. Old Town. ☎ 22410/73670. $.

⑨ ★ **Archaeological Museum.** Even if you're suffering terra cotta fatigue after seeing the palace pottery, the numerous display rooms in the converted Knights' Hospital are still worth a cursory look, if only for a glimpse of the kneeling *Aphrodite of Rhodes (Mikri Afroditi).* A garden courtyard shortcut leads to the fascinating **Prehistoric Exhibit, Turkish House**

> *The Turkish hamam still provides a soothing steam and massage.*

(open till 1pm), and **Epigraphical Museum.** The ancient road to the harbor is visible underfoot, and touching tombstones (steles) include that of Ploutos, aged just 3, who informs us that he died "loosening the support of a cart which had upon it a heavy load of stakes. I passed over the threshold of Hades; Antiochis was the name of my mother, who offered me patiently her breast, and Ploutos of my father, who made my grave." ⏱ 30 min. Museum Sq. ☎ 22410/31048 or 25500. www.culture.gr. Admission 3€. April–Oct Mon 1:30–8pm, Tues–Sun 8am–8pm; winter reduced hours. Closed Jan 1, Mar 25, Orthodox Easter Sun, May 1, Dec 25, 26.

⑩ ★★ **Yeni Hamam.** Get an authentic taste of what it was like to bathe before the era of private plumbing. Follow the signs to the *hamam* (*loutro* in Greek). At the entrance to this 16th-century restored public bathhouse run by the municipality, guests receive a pair of rubber sandals, a towel, and a locker key before bathing on a squat marble column under shafts of light that look like stars. The massage is definitely worth the time and money, providing an authentic "feel" of a bygone era. In winter, locals still come here to pass the time, much as they did in antiquity. Patrons are separated by gender. ⏱ 1 hr. Arionos Sq. ☎ 22410/27739. Admission 5€, massage 15€. Sun–Fri 10am–5pm Sat 8am–5pm; Sun closed in winter.

⑪ 🚊 kids **Aktaion, Mandraki Harbour, New Town.** There are a few landmark buildings built during Italian rule (1912–47) along the waterfront—the town hall, archdiocese, post office, National Theater buildings, and this one, with its signature Gothic arches. Prices are low at the old-fashioned pastry, coffee, and ice cream shop, which also serves breakfast, pizza, and snacks. A listed building owned by the city, it has a public playground in view and a play area inside. Eleftherias Sq. end of Plastira St. ☎ 22410/23431. $.

⑫ kids **Aquarium Museum.** The Hydrobiological Station (built in the 1930s) at the end of the island promontory is a quaint place for youngsters, but many of the tanks are at adult eye-level. Impressive and scary-looking specimens of very large fish will fascinate, including an odd-looking beached whale found in the 1970s. Go behind the museum to the tip of the island to see where the dark, choppy Aegean and calm Mediterranean seas meet. ⏱ At least 30 min. End of Kos St. ☎ 22410/27308. www.hcmr.gr. Admission 5€. Apr–Oct daily 9am–8:30pm, Nov–Mar daily 9am–4:30pm.

⑬ kids **Little train tour.** Take the little train for a round-trip tour of Rhodes Town. The train leaves every hour, takes about 45 minutes, and includes free water and juice. Take this tour in the morning or after the museums close; it's wonderful to catch the sunset from Monte Smith Hill. ⏱ 45 min. Departs from the Mall 2 (corner of Georgiou Papanikolaou and

> *Minarets of mosques dot the Old Town skyline.*

lona Dragoumi sts.), Rhodes Town. Admission 7€ adults, 3€ children 6 and over. Apr–Oct daily on the hour 9am–11pm.

⑭ Monte Smith Hill. This 100m (328-ft.) hill, also called **Agios Stefanos (St. Stephen),** was named after an adventurous British admiral who fought against Napoleon and in the American Revolution. The park houses the 3rd-century-B.C. **Temple of Apollo** (Acropolis of Rhodes; ☎ 22410/25500; www.culture.gr) and a restored marble theater and stadium where events still take place. Many come for a stroll at sunset to see the views of Rhodes Town and beyond. Buses depart from the Mandraki terminal, which is also a stop on the **little train tour.** ⏱ 1 hr. 3km (2 miles) southwest from the center of Rhodes Town. Free admission.

> *Medieval backdrops lend an exotic flair to even a casual meal in Old Town.*

Where to Stay in Rhodes Town

> At the Avalon, as in many other hotels in Rhodes Town, guests enjoy a terrace with a view.

★ Apollo Guest House

Like most Old Town hotels, this one occupies a 15th-century building. The rates are very good; the hotel is clean and comfortable; and the owners are helpful with travel info, transfers, and scooter rentals. Wi-Fi and an English breakfast, served in the courtyard, are included in the room rate. 28C Omirou St., 5 min. from Kokkini Porta (Red Gate). ☎ 22410/32003. www.apollo-touristhouse.com. 6 units. Doubles 45€–75€ w/breakfast. V. Mar–Nov, other dates by request.

★★ Avalon Boutique Hotel

Over a little bridge through the entrance to the Medieval Inn of Spain, off the Street of the Knights, this lovely all-suite hotel is set around a courtyard, with views to the city and harbor. Four suites have fireplaces. A daily cafe/bar serves drinks, snacks, and salads, and hosts special events. No elevator. Haritos St. ☎ 22410/

31438. www.avalonrhodes.gr. 6 units. Suites 130€–395€ w/breakfast. AE, DC, MC, V. Year-round.

Klimt Guest House

This hotel dates to around 1370. The top floor, which the French added in the 16th century, has three "hideaway" rooms; one snugly fits a family. A lounge, bar, and jewelry shop are open downstairs. 32–34 Agiou Fanouriou St. ☎ 22410/20745. www.klimt-guest-house.gr. 3 units. Doubles 70€–100€ w/breakfast. MC, V. Closed Feb.

★★★ Marco Polo Mansion OLD TOWN

A 15th-century Ottoman mansion is an exotic and comfortable retreat set in a lush garden. Each room is distinctive—one occupies a hammam—and all are beautifully decorated with deep hues and antiques. Non-guests are welcome at the excellent dinners served in the garden. Aghiou Fanouriou 40–42. ☎ 22410/25562. www.marcopolomansion.gr. 17 units. Doubles 120€–180€ with breakfast. Closed Nov–Apr.

★ Nikos Takis Fashion Hotel

Two Greek designers who claim to clothe celebrities opened a fanciful, oriental-themed hotel on the same street as Suleyman Mosque and opposite the St. John of the Collachio school building (ca. 1876). Everything is opulent, from the fruit, wine, and welcome drinks served upon arrival to sailboat rental and helicopter service. 26 Panaitiou Ave. ☎ 22410/70773. www.nikostakishotel.com. 7 units. Doubles 80€–150€ w/breakfast. AE, DC, MC, V. Year-round.

★★★ Spirit of the Knights OLD TOWN

Five luxurious suites and a cozily medieval chamber are tucked away in a beautifully restored Ottoman house in the quietest part of the Old Town. Hand-painted ceilings, marble baths, and other exquisite details are part of the surroundings, and a beautiful courtyard is cooled by a fountain. 14 Alexandridou. ☎ 22410/39765. www.rhodesluxuryhotel.com. 6 units. 200€–350€ with breakfast. AE, MC, V.

Where to Dine in Rhodes Town

A cool drink and good Greek food are a given at Thermai.

British Cafe and Bar BRITISH

Just opposite some ruins is the distinctive Union Jack sign for the British Cafe and Bar. It's a small, friendly place where you can get a full English breakfast, fish and chips, fries and gravy, tea and scones, ice cream and desserts, and, of course, a British beer. **Polydorou/Lagisandrou 34.** ☎ 22410/74185. Entrees 8€–9€. No credit cards. April–Oct daily breakfast & lunch, Mon–Sat dinner.

Sarris Tavern GREEK

Look for waiters wearing orange shirts and you've found this place. Locals and foreigners alike flock to Sarris for its very good Greek food, from oven-baked *yiouvetsi* (beef with orzo) to *kleftiko* (lamb and vegetables wrapped in paper and baked), meze, and seafood. **18 Evdimou St.** ☎ 22410/73707. www.sarristavern.com. Entrees 10€–12€. AE, DC, MC, V. Mar–Nov daily breakfast, lunch & dinner.

★ Ta Kioupia MODERN GREEK

Much lauded Ta Kioupia, in a rustic house just outside Rhodes Town, is so popular they've opened an outlet in Athens. The chef serves Rhodian fare in tantalizing variations. Choose a variety of meze, such as eggplant salad or chickpeas with pasta, or a choice of set menus for 45€ or 60€. Reservations are recommended. 12 Argonafton St. Tris-Ixia 85101, 9km (5⅔ miles) southwest of Rhodes Town. ☎ 22410/ 93448. www.takioupia.com. Entrees 10€–15€. AE, MC, V. Mon–Sat dinner.

kids Thermai Café INTERNATIONAL

If you've just gotten off a bus and want a break from the heat, this centrally located cafe with the fountain at the entrance, just past the public bathrooms, will certainly catch your eye. Couches and comfy chairs are grouped around coffee tables in a tree-shaded garden. The spinach pie is especially good. You'll also find long drinks, snacks, and appetizer plates, as well as coffee, pastries, and ice cream. An on-site play set will help keep the kids occupied. **Alex. Diakou and Dimokratias sts.** ☎ 22410/27262. Entrees 12€–15€. MC, V. Daily breakfast, lunch & dinner, reduced winter hours.

Zizi Taverna GREEK

For traditional taverna fare, served in a private courtyard in the Old Town, Zizi is easy to spot by the chef statue beckoning at the door on Agio Fanouriou Street, alongside the wide range of pictured menu items. Just off Socratous Street. **3 Menekleous St.** ☎ 22410/21724. www.restaurantzizi.com/en/home.html. Entrees 8€–8.50€. MC, V. Apr 10–Oct 31 daily breakfast, lunch & dinner.

Nightlife & High Rolling

Plenty of **cafes and bars** stay open late in both the Old Town (including Arionos Sq.) and the New Town (including Orfanidou St.). Risky revelers who want to up the ante flock to the **Casino Rodos,** a plush gaming space in the 1920s-era Grande Albergo Delle Rose Hotel. Table games include American roulette, blackjack, casino stud poker, and *punto banco*, plus video poker and slot machines. 4 G. Papanikolaou St. ☎ 22410/97500. www.casinorodos.gr. Admission (min. 23 yrs) 15€ valid for 24 hr. Open 24 hr. DC, MC, V.

MEZE
The Ultimate Greek Snacks BY TANIA KOLLIAS

THE EASTERN MEDITERRANEAN NAME MEZE (plural meze, mezes, or mezedes) derives from the Persian word for snack, *maze*, and refers to the starters, appetizers, hors d'oeuvres, tidbits, finger food, or tapas that are commonly prepared and eaten with a pre-dinner aperitif by those living around the sultry Mediterranean basin. These are late-evening mini buffets, prepared and served not as a focal point for the table but as fuel for socializing, sustaining dining companions as they drink and engage in lively conversation. Served in small dishes that everyone can dig into, they allow diners to sample a variety of flavors in one go. When a mixed plate of meze is served on a large tray for two, it's known as *pikilia*.

What Makes a Meze?

Just about any food can be pressed into service as a meze. Varieties from every food group, cooked in every way—from simple seasonal vegetables, to preserved olives and cheeses, to rare fare such as snails collected following a rain shower and fried with pungent herbs—are candidates. Innovations stem from the creativity of chefs, the season, the availability of certain ingredients in a region, and local culinary tradition.

Tomatoes, cucumbers, green peppers, and onions are chopped up and served as *horiatiki* (Greek salad), while other salads that are more like dips are created from legumes, potatoes, and vegetables.

LADERA Ladera arose from the dietary restrictions prescribed by Orthodox fasts. Many of the best *ladera* dishes— usually vegetables such as mountain greens, similar to spinach but boiled and served in olive oil (*lathi* in Greek), served with a lemon wedge—were perfected in monks' kitchens.

CHEESE Numerous soft white cheeses made from the milk of goats and sheep are served fried (*saganaki*) or as cheesy dips with salads. Regional variations include cheese-stuffed vegetables, such as mushrooms and long red peppers, or the Cretan Dakos, a wedge of cheese and tomato on a thick slice of crisp bread drizzled in olive oil. Even the complicated Greek classic *moussaka*—made with layers of eggplant, beef, and potato topped with béchamel sauce and baked—is often found on the meze menu.

SEAFOOD, MEATS & VEGETABLES Favorite meze from the fishermen's wharf include fresh salty fried fish eaten whole, kalamari, and sardines. Savory little phyllo-pastry pies, spicy sausages, meatballs, *dolmades* (ground beef and rice, wrapped in grapevine or cabbage leaves with lemon sauce), and croquettes of all kinds also make use of potatoes and other abundant, seasonal vegetables such as tomatoes or zucchini.

MOST COMMON MEZE Besides simple feta cheese and tangy black olives, the meze found on most menus, including taverna fare, are the dip-style salads such as *taramosalata* (pink cod roe dip); *tzatziki* made with creamy yogurt, cucumber, and garlic; and *fava*, a pureed bean dip; and *ladera* meze such as *horta* (boiled mountain greens); *loukaniko* (spicy sausage); and *ochtapodi* (grilled octopus).

Where to Find Meze & What to Drink with Them

In neighborhood tavernas, meze are called *orektika* (starters) and can be washed down with barrel wine such as a mountain-fresh rosé or the infamous retsina, a pine-resin- (some say turpentine-) flavored wine that pairs well with these savory snacks. Meze are also eaten at *mezedopoleia* (meze restaurants), *ouzeries*, or *tsipouradika*, combo restaurant-cafe-bars that serve meze with anise-flavored ouzo or grappalike *tsipouro* or *raki*. These fiery, high-alcohol liqueurs are brought to the table in a small bottle (*karafaki*), along with a bucket of ice. They must be drunk with food.

Excursions from Rhodes Town

Rhodes may be best known for its beach resorts, medieval Old Town, and ancient Lindos, but a number of other attractions around the island are worth a visit if you have a few hours or an extra day to spare. Here's a round-up of the best land-based excursions from Rhodes Town. Some sites are on the west coast and others are on the east, so you could potentially see all the places on either one coast or the other in one trip.

> *Clients have sought relief at Kalithea Spa since antiquity.*

★ **Ancient Kamiros.** Kamiros is an abandoned Dorian city that reached all the way to the coast, but excavations stopped on the hill. It was agricultural, producing figs, wine, oil, and ceramics for trade, and minting its own coins. By the 6th century B.C., the flourishing city had underfloor heating, oil was put on top of water to prevent evaporation, and a bathhouse was positioned at the city gates, as one had to be clean to enter the city. You can make out the ruins of a temple to Athena, a reservoir, and a stoa (portico), as well as dwellings. The stadium and amphitheater have not yet been found. The city was destroyed by earthquake and rebuilt in 226 B.C.

You can easily walk around the site. ⊕ 40 min. 35km (22 miles) southwest of Rhodes Town. ☎ 22410/ 40037. Admission 4€. Apr–Oct Tues–Sun 8am–7:30pm, Mon 1–7pm; Nov–Mar Tues–Sun 8:30am–2:40pm.

Filerimos & Ancient Ialyssos. At the summit of Mount Filerimos (267m/876 ft.), ancient Ialyssos is one of the island's three founding city-states. There's not much left but the ruins of the 3rd-century-B.C. Temple of Athena, a Byzantine church, an ancient cemetery, and the restored 15th-century church and monastery, **Panagia Filerimos.** Paths lead to a ruined castle and 4th-century-B.C. fountain. Climb the steps to

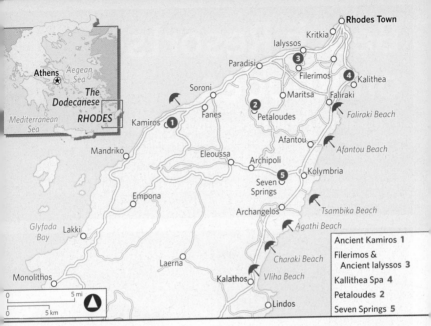

Ancient Kamiros 1

Filerimos &
  Ancient Ialyssos 3

Kallithea Spa 4

Petaloudes 2

Seven Springs 5

he large cross for a superb view. ☺ 1 hr. 15km (9⅓ miles) southwest of Rhodes Town, 6km (30 miles) from Ialyssos (Trianda). ☎ 22410/92202. Admission 3€. Apr–Oct Tues–Sun 8am–7:30pm, Mon 1–7:10pm; Nov–Mar Tues–Sun 8:30am–3pm. uses from Rhodes Town are infrequent, so take a axi or go as part of a tour.

Kallithea Spa. The curative springs at Thermi Kallithea have drawn patients since antiquity. he spa includes a semicircular atrium, rotun-das, cafes, and stone-paved walkways and rest reas along garden paths. When the spa re-pened in 1929, Italian architect Pietro Lom-ardi incorporated features from Doric, Roman, yzantine, and medieval times, with Arab, Otto-han, and local folk influences as well. Divers equent a cove here, and there's also a small, hallow, pebbly beach. ☺ At least 40 min. Off Kallithea Ave. (9km/5⅔ miles southeast of Rhodes Town; 5km/3 miles northeast of Faliraki n Kallithea Ave.). ☎ 22410/65691. www.kallithea prings.gr. Admission 2.50€. May–Oct 8am–8pm, Nov–Apr 8am–5pm.

Petaloudes. The Valley of the Butterflies is ne of the world's few natural habitats for the horax-resin-seeking Jersey Tiger moths (panaxia quadripunctaria). They are in decline, as tourists startle them, causing them to fly and expend the energy they need to survive until mating season. Down some steps from the en-trance is a small museum. It takes about an hour to walk the whole 1.5km (1 mile) circuit. If you're on a tour or the walkway is crowded, you can still get a feel for it by walking along paths be-side streams, pools, and waterfalls, and keeping an eye out for the orange-and-black butterflies, which are especially abundant from June to September. ☺ At least 30 min. 25km (15 miles) southwest of Rhodes Town. ☎ 22410/81801. Ad-mission 3€ (when no butterflies) or 5€. Apr–Oct daily 8am–7pm.

Seven Springs. Up a steep and winding dirt road is Epta Piges, or Seven Springs, a verdant little oasis with quite a few peacocks and a 1945 tav-erna with tables set up near the Loutanis River (**Epta Piges;** ☎ 22410/56259; www.eptapiges. com). The site also has a souvenir shop, play-ground, public toilets, and a 186m (610-ft.) tun-nel built by the Italians to take water to Kolymbia on the coast. Visitors can walk through the tun-nel, which ends at a small reservoir. ☺ 1 hr. 3km (2 miles) from the Rhodes-Lindos road, opposite (going inland) the turnoff for Kolymbia, 23km (14 miles) southeast of Rhodes Town.

Beach Resorts on Rhodes

The island of Rhodes has many beach resorts to choose from on both the west and east coasts, while Rhodes Town itself also has a slew of holiday hotels on its "nose." Some of these are towns in their own right; others are small and quiet. This selection includes one of the island's most popular, Faliraki, and one of the least touristed, Haraki Bay, plus two more popular resorts on the less windy east coast.

> *In easygoing Haraki, a promenade follows the curve of the shore beneath a medieval castle.*

★★★ **Faliraki.** The island's biggest resort has the most beautiful stretch of **beach** (some 4–5km/2½–3 miles), the island's best beach bars and clubs, and the most activities: beach-side bungee jumping, an enormous water park, a children's magic castle, and other indoor play areas, bowling, go-karts, minigolf, 3-hour cruises, glass-bottom boat and glass-sided submarine cruises, and various excursions. **Sotos Watersport Center** ☎ 69422/34598; www.deamaris-yachting.com) can also equip you to paraglide, jet-ski, ride banana boats, or charter a yacht. The main street is beach-resort kitsch, but the atmosphere is friendly, and luxury hotels reach for miles up the coast. The resort's reputation for hosting package tourists encouraged to drink till they dropped still lingers, and Faliraki

Fishing boats still take to the waters at Haraki and other seaside resorts.

...emains a place to party and meet people. ...he touts have largely gone, however, and the ...ids have grown up, returning here with their ...hildren, as the municipality busily rebrands ...allithea, the village to which the resort ad-...inistratively belongs. Faliraki's enormous ...★ kids **water park** (Kallithea Ave., 3 km/2 ...iles from Faliraki; ☎ 22410/84403; www. ...ater-park.gr; admission 20€ age 13 and over, ...5€ age 3–12. May, Sept–Oct 9:30am–6pm; ...une–Aug 9:30am–7pm) is on the excursion ...ircuit. It mostly attracts 18-to-30-year-olds, ...ut it's also popular with families, and toddlers ...ave a place too. Food and drink is available ...t snack bars. A free shuttle ferries visitors ...rom Rhodes Town and the group's six Faliraki ...otels. Faliraki is 14km (8⅔ miles) southeast of ...hodes Town.

...★ **Haraki Bay**. This low-key village resort has ...nice beach, a ruined medieval hilltop castle ...hat is stunning when lit up at night, and the ...ite of an old sugar factory that dates from the ...5th century, when there were only three oth-...rs in Europe (in the U.K., France, and Cyprus).

It has a pedestrian-only beachside promenade with tavernas, which get a bit noisy at night, interspersed with apartments, rooms to rent, and a few hotels. You can buy self-catering supplies at one of three supermarkets. Nearby ★★★ kids **Agathi Beach** is set in a bay on the other side of the promontory topped by ruined Feraklos castle. It has fine sand, a shallow gradient, watersports, three seaside tavernas with facilities (showers and toilets), beach chairs, and umbrellas (5€ per set). You can also free-camp on a ridge beside the beach. Named after the church grotto at the far end (note the odd graffiti in the rock face near here), Agathi would be a shorter walk around the castle from Haraki, but unfortunately it's fenced off. In any case, it's well worth the min-imal effort to get here. **Agathi Watersports** (☎ 69347/13830) charges 10€ for 10-minute rides on tires and whatnot, and 25€ for water-skiing. You can mail postcards at **George Su-permarket** (☎ 22440/51422), just left of the main road into town on the beach promenade. About a kilometer (⅔ mile) before Haraki and 500m (1,640 ft. mile along a gravel road. 14km

> *Pefkos and other once-quiet stretches of sand are now popular European getaways.*

(8⅔ miles) from Lindos, 41km (25 miles) south-east of Rhodes Town.

★ **Kolymbia**. Italians originally settled this resort, bringing water from Epta Piges (Seven Springs) across the main road 6km (3¾ miles) away. Now a full-fledged yet laid-back resort with a nice beach and a growing number of luxury hotels, it attracts mainly package and all-inclusive tourists from northern Europe. 3km (2 miles) from the main road, 23km (14 miles) southeast of Rhodes Town.

Pefkos. This once-sleepy fishing village just south of Lindos (4km/2½ miles) is a full-fledged resort with a nice beach lined with shady pine trees (pefkos means pine tree). It attracts mainly British package tourists, and travel agencies with offices in Rhodes Town and Lindos have closed up shop and relocated

here. The main street is lined with kebab shops, pizzerias, various Asian restaurants (Chinese, Thai, and Indian), and pool bars. The resort itself has some 50 restaurants and bars that also serve food. 59km (37 miles) southeast of Rhodes Town.

Hotels & Restaurants

Many beach resort towns in Greece operate only during the summer season, usually from April until October. After that, everything closes up, from the enormous hotel complexes to the restaurants and shops that cater exclusively to the tourism industry. For hotels and restaurants near Faliraki, see p. 405; Haraki Bay, see p. 406; Kolymbia, see p. 406; Pefkos, see p. 407.

Where to Stay & Dine in Rhodes Beach Resorts

> *The Esperides is one of the many huge resort hotels on Rhodes geared to seaside comfort.*

Faliraki

★ Apollo Beach FALIRAKI

Apollo Beach was the resort's first luxury hotel when it was built in 1975 at what was then the end of the coastal road. Now its location is very near the center of the action but not in it. It has a swimming pool, children's pool, restaurants, bars, a playground, tennis courts, and other amenities. Kallithea Ave. ☎ 22410/85513. www.apollobeach.gr. 312 units. Doubles 75€–158€ w/breakfast. AE, DC, MC, V. May–Oct.

kids Apollo Blue Palace FALIRAKI

This new five-star luxury property is under the same ownership as Apollo Beach next door. It has minimalist decor and a gorgeous swimming pool, restaurant, and bar for grown-ups, plus a children's pool and supervised club for kids up to 6. Kallithea Ave. ☎ 22410/85000. www.apollobluepalace.gr. 154 units. Doubles 150€–200€ half-board. AE, DC, MC, V. May–Oct.

kids Esperides Beach Hotel FALIRAKI

Esperides Beach is a family-oriented four-star hotel near the group's **Water Park** and **Magic Castle** (☎ 22410/84368; best for kids up to age 12), 3km (2 miles) from Faliraki along the coastal road. Bus service is frequent, and a little train makes the journey to this wonderland for kids with bumper cars, a carousel, a playground, pools for grown-ups and kids, entertainment, baby-sitting, aerobics, and a minimarket. Kallithea Ave. ☎ 22410-84200. www.esperia-hotels.gr. 575 units. Doubles 120€–200€ all-inclusive. AE, DC, MC, V. May–Oct.

★ Kastri Taverna FALIRAKI GREEK

For traditional taverna food as well as homemade, oven-baked pizza, fresh seafood, and grilled meat, it's worth the trip to Kastri. It's a little out of town, past the main junction on Kallithea Avenue, right on the beach toward Rhodes Town. Next to the Calypso Hotel. ☎ 22410/85381. Entrees 6€–11€. AE, DC, MC, V. April–Oct daily lunch & dinner.

★ Mythos Taverna FALIRAKI GREEK/INTERNATIONAL

This taverna serves everything from pizza and spaghetti to grilled meats, fresh seafood, and Greek specialties. It's easy to find on the main Rhodes–Lindos road. Opposite Ag. Nektarios Church. ☎ 22410/85791. Entrees 6€–20€. MC, V. Daily dinner.

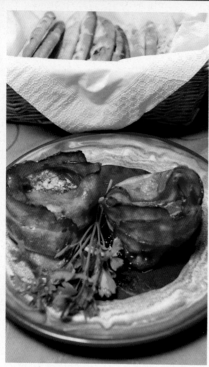

> You'll find everything from Greek fare to fast food on the beaches in Rhodes.

★ kids **Sun Palace Hotel** FALIRAKI
The Sun Palace Hotel is an all-inclusive, family-oriented resort with a pool, children's pool, playground, tennis court, playroom, and other services. With 253 rooms, bungalows, and family rooms, it's conveniently located on the coastal road, a short walk to town but near the beach. Kallithea Ave. ☎ 22410/85650. www.aquasolhotels.com. 253 units. Doubles 92€–168€ all-inclusive. MC, V. May–Oct.

Haraki Bay
★★ kids **Atrium Palace Thalasso Spa Resort and Villas** The area's main industry, this enormous complex attracts many Europeans with direct connections to the Rhodes airport. The location is out of the way, but some suites and villas have their own swimming pools, and the general property has a beautiful *thalasso* spa (seawater spa) and many other amenities, including children's activities, to keep guests relaxed and entertained. Kalathos Beach, 42km

(26 miles) southeast of Rhodes Town. ☎ 22440/31601. www.atrium.gr. 316 units. AE, DC, MC, V. Doubles 120€–207€ w/breakfast. May–Oct.

★★ kids **Haraki Bay Hotel and Restaurant**
GREEK You can stay, shop for your groceries and water toys, and eat like a king at this restaurant, which appears to be the only one in the area with an industrial kitchen. The owners are friendly, professional, and helpful yet discreet. If you need anything that's unavailable in Haraki, they are happy to get it for you, but for the most part they'll leave guests to do their own thing. Studios are also for rent here. End of the road toward the castle. ☎ 22440/51680/1. www.haraki-bay-hotel.com. 14 units. Doubles 55€–70€ w/breakfast. MC, V. May–Oct.

Kolymbia
★★★ **Atlantica Imperial Resort**
The Atlantica Imperial is one of this luxury hotel chain's three properties in Kolymbia, with others in Crete, Kos, and Cyprus. This one is right on the beach and offers half-board options. (The Aegean Blue at the other end of the bay is family-oriented and all-inclusive, and the third hotel is strictly for the Scandinavian market.) ☎ 22410/57000. www.atlantica hotels.com. 262 units. Doubles 94€ half-board (+ 20€ suppl. per person all-inclusive) to 254€ half-board (starting at 28€ suppl. per person all-inclusive). AE, DC, MC, V. Apr–Oct.

kids **Bonito Café** GREEK/ INTERNATIONAL/
ORGANIC This cafe, restaurant, and bar with studios for rent is a 3-minute walk from the beach. The studios are part of the main building, which also has an art gallery. Rooms have fridges, guests can use the kitchen in the cafe during off-peak times, and breakfast is included in the room rates. The restaurant serves Greek, international, and organic food, but the staff is happy to make special meals if necessary. It's a child-friendly place, with art classes

Alternative Lodging & Dining

In addition to the hotels listed here, Faliraki has an abundance of locally owned rental studios and small hotels (www.travel2 rodos.com). You can also find off-season steals on gorgeous villas, apartments, and studios through www.ownersdirect.co.uk.

or kids and plenty of books and games on hand. Adult programs include yoga classes and a spa menu, including massage treatments upon request. Airport pickup is a great deal at 15€. On the beach. ☎ 22410/56093. www.yogainrhodes.com. Doubles 35€–45€. Entrees 6.50€–17€. No credit cards. May–Oct Tues–Sun lunch, daily dinner.

Pefkos

★ kids **Flyer's Snack** *INTERNATIONAL* Just up from the beach, small and friendly Flyer's serves sandwiches, burgers, salads, baguettes, and mixed plates good for families. As suggested by the microlite plane on the roof, the owner is a microlite aficionado and will take customers up for 50€ for 15 minutes or 75€ for a half-hour. Children can fly too, accompanied by an adult. Main beach road. ☎ 22440/48177. flyers@rho.forthnet.gr. Entrees 2.50€–12€. No credit cards. May–Oct breakfast & lunch (till 7:30pm).

Lee's Beach Bar *INTERNATIONAL* At the end of the main road down to the beach on the left is Lee's, serving breakfast, snacks, and fast-food by day, including burgers, toasts (grilled ham and cheese), and souvlaki. After

> *Beach bars are a big part of the Rhodes scene.*

6pm, the menu changes, serving specialties such as chicken and pineapple, chicken in champagne sauce, or steak with strawberry sauce. Main beach road. ☎ 22440/48213. Entrees 2.20€–35€. MC, V. May–Oct daily 9:30am–11pm.

★★ kids **Summer Memories Aparthotel** This apartment hotel offers studios as well as one- or two- bedroom apartments with kitchenettes. A really good value, it's ideal for families and allows more freedom and space for couples and single travelers too. Built in 2000, the complex is in a great location, in a garden off the main road. It's close to the beach as well as restaurants and shops. The grounds encompass a pool and bar offering an extensive snack menu, karaoke and quiz nights, and a U.K.-based satellite sports channel. Main road. ☎ 22440/48401. www.summer-memories.gr. 37 units. Studios 25€–45€. MC, V. Open May–Oct.

Drink & Dance in Faliraki

At the ever-friendly **Jamaica Bar** (Ermou St.; ☎ 22410/85221), you can down a meal with your family during the day and a saucily named drink at night. Other well-known places for drinks and a snack are **Chaplin's** (☎ 22410/85662), on the beach, and **Champers** (☎ 22410/85989; www.champersbar.com), on Ermou Street (Bar St.). **Dance clubs**—including longtime favorites **Q** and **Bed** on Club Street (Kallithea Ave.) and **Liquid** off Bar Street (Ermou St.)—get going around midnight.

Lindos

Lindos has a spectacular setting on the southwestern coast of Rhodes. The acropolis towers above the village, also visible below the main road, and is flanked by two bays. One is the superb Lindos Beach; the other is romantic St. Paul's Bay, where the apostle is believed to have disembarked to preach Christianity. Now it serves as a marina, beach, and jaw-dropping backdrop for hundreds of weddings a year. From many vantage points, the views of the town, beach, and acropolis are amazing.

> *Whitewashed Lindos splays out from the base of its acropolis.*

START **Bus-stop square or Main Square town entrance.** TRIP LENGTH **1 day.**

① ★★★ **Lindos Town.** This delightful village has whitewashed houses, cobblestone alleys, and a stunning setting, but, unfortunately, it's also overrun with tourists and modern signs posted in prominent locations. Wander through the streets for new and old surprises all along the way to the acropolis. ⏱ At least 1 hour. 55km (34 miles) southwest of Rhodes Town.

SITE GUIDE
PAGE 410

② ★ **Acropolis of Lindos.** One of the three Doric city-states founded on the island, Lindos was renowned for its naval tradition. Going uphill to see the ruins and view is a must.

③ **Traditional Lindian House Souvenir Shop.** This old house set back from the road is a curious museum/art/souvenir shop run by the original owner's elderly granddaughter. Sections of the room are authentic, such as the living and sleeping areas, featured in the 1958

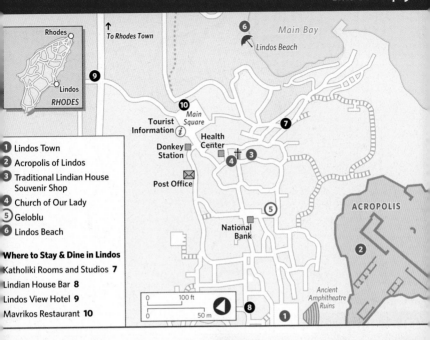

Map legend:

1 Lindos Town
2 Acropolis of Lindos
3 Traditional Lindian House Souvenir Shop
4 Church of Our Lady
5 Geloblu
6 Lindos Beach

Where to Stay & Dine in Lindos

Katholiki Rooms and Studios **7**
Lindian House Bar **8**
Lindos View Hotel **9**
Mavrikos Restaurant **10**

ssue of *National Geographic* on display. The owner may be preparing string beans for dinner as tourists wander in and out of this time warp. ⏱ 10 min. Acropoleos St. ☎ 22440/31251. No credit cards. Daily 9am–10pm.

4 ★ **Church of Our Lady.** The exterior belies a fantastically decorated interior (ca. 1799). The church likely dates from the 14th century, renovated by Grand Master d'Aubusson a century later, in 1489. He also erected the bell-tower showing his coat of arms. The pebble mosaic *chocklaki* floor is a technique that dates to Hellenistic times and reached its zenith in the Byzantine era. Still seen throughout the island, this example is a black-and-white zigzag. ⏱ 15 min. Acropoleos St. Mon–Sat 9am–3pm and 4:30–6pm, Sun 9am–3pm.

5 🍵 ★★ 🧒 **Geloblu.** From April through October, this exceptional cafe with an inner courtyard and roof garden serves properly made cakes such as blueberry cheesecake, trifle, *gâteau,* and chocolate-orange cake. From the Eastern oven, they do *ekmek* (Turkish bread pudding) and baklava pastries, and the ice cream is homemade and equally delicious too. Opposite Museum Bar, Lindos. ☎ 22440/31761. $.

> Shops line the way to the Acropolis.

6 ★★★ 🧒 **Lindos Beach.** With fine sand, a gentle slope, schools of fish, and a quiet air despite the surplus of beach chairs, this beach is divine. **Nefeli** (☎ 22440/31822) is one of a dozen or so tavernas along the beach, but it has a small play area and minirides. The main road and KTEL bus stop are just around the bend, about a 15-minute hike. The way is steep and may leave you breathless when the weather is hot, but there's a free shuttle service. Nearby is **Pallas (Skala) beach,** popular with young families. ⏱ At least 1 hr. Follow the signs down a path (steps at the end) from the village, or down a paved road from the main square, where there's a free shuttle service.

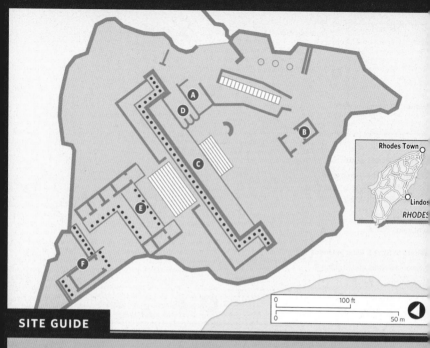

2 Acropolis of Lindos

When you first begin ascending the steps to the 15th-century Ⓐ **fortress,** built by Grand Master d'Aubusson, look for the unusual *trireme* relief, dated 170 B.C., carved into the stone wall. Left of the entrance at the top of the stairs are the remains of a Ⓑ **Roman temple** and the bases of some statues. Emperor Theodosius II ordered the destruction of idol remnants in A.D. 396 but took the marble-and-gold statue of Athena to Constantinople (modern-day Istanbul), along with treasures from other temples, where they were later destroyed. The stairway to the third level leads to a 3rd-century-B.C. Ⓒ *stoa* (portico), 87m (285 ft.) long and with 42 Doric columns, reconstructed during Italian rule in the 1920s and '30s. It contains the ruins of the Byzantine Ⓓ **Church of St. John.** From here you pass through the Ⓔ **Propylaea,** referred to as the "stairway to heaven," before reaching the 4th-century-B.C. Ⓕ **temple to the goddess Athena** at the highest point on the acropolis. An older temple stood here during the Archaic period, but it was destroyed, probably by fire. The interior measured 22m x 8m (72 x 26 ft.) and was built of local sandstone and plastered. Parts

of it were restored between 1936 and 1938 and again between 2000 and 2005. For 5€ each way, **donkey rides** are available near the main square in town and at the acropolis entrance, just in front of the **cafe.** Beyond there, you must walk, and it's rather steep and slippery on the flagstones, but only for 5 minutes or so. If you don't have mobility issues, you might as well walk. ⏲ 1 hour. ☎ 22440/31258. www.culture.gr. Admission 6€. Apr–Oct Tues–Sun 8am–7:40pm, Mon 1:30–7:40pm; Nov–Mar Tues–Sun 8am–2:40pm. Closed Jan 1, Mar 25, Orthodox Easter Sun, May 1, Dec 25, 26.

Where to Stay & Dine in Lindos

Katholiki Rooms and Studios OLD TOWN
This is one of a few places offering rooms for rent on the way to the beach and the acropolis. Four rooms (one large, one small, and two average-size) are available here. Inquire about vacancies at the corner supermarket with the large signs outside—one blue and white, one red and green. **Old Town.** ☎ 22440/31445. 4 units. Doubles 30€–40€. No credit cards. May–Oct.

★ **Lindian House Bar** GREEK/INTERNATIONAL
Eat in the courtyard, visit the roof garden, or drink inside a gorgeous 400-year-old captain's house with superb tiled floors, wood-engraved ceilings, and tall, Moorish-style windows. The establishment has been here some 20 years and serves Greek and international food with a wide variety of drinks from the enormous bar. The owners, who are Greek and English, are happy to arrange foreign wedding services, popular on this part of the island. ☎ 22440/31774. Entrees 4€–16€. AE, DC, MC, V. May–Oct daily breakfast, lunch & dinner.

★★ kids **Lindos View Hotel**
Just outside the village to the south of the island, this hotel is a short walking distance from the KTEL bus stop on the main route into town, after which point cars are prohibited. It has a panoramic view of the village and the acropolis; outdoor pools, including one for children; a playground; and a rooftop restaurant and bar. Accommodations range from standard doubles and suites to apartments. ☎ 22440/31477. www.lindosview.gr. 89 units. Doubles 50€. MC, V. May–Oct.

★★ **Mavrikos Restaurant**
Easy to find on the main square opposite the big tree at the entrance to town, this restaurant has been receiving rave reviews and chef awards for years. A step above the other restaurants and tavernas, it's where royalty and celebs come to dine. To try a selection of meze with wine, expect to spend double the usual 15€ per person, but it's worth it. **Main Square.** ☎ 22440/31232. Entrees 9.50€–26€. MC, V. Apr–Oct daily lunch & dinner.

> *Mavrikos is a Lindos landmark, known for casual elegance and straightforward, delicious cuisine.*

Lindos by Night

About 2 km (1¼ miles) out of Lindos is **Amphitheatre Club** (☎ 22440/44789; www. amphitheatreclublindos.com), a popular open-air nightspot in summer. You and a friend can take a free taxi there from midnight until 3:30am. Other popular clubs inside Lindos village are **Qupi** and **Arches** (http://archesclublindos.com).

Symi

Symi's port is horseshoe-shaped, below a picturesque hill with windmill-dotted ridges and neoclassical buildings cascading down its sides. Named after the seagod Glaucus's uncooperative love interest (a nymph also known as Scylla or Aegli), Symi is one of the few places where an industry—sponge-diving—endured from ancient times into the modern era, though diving has largely abated in recent years because of disease, cheap imports, and emigration, which lowered the local population. The number of residents on the small (58 sq. km /22 sq. mile) island has been rising again in recent years, as both native residents and immigrants from abroad are returning to cater to tourists, here mainly on day trips from neighboring Rhodes.

> In Yialos Harbor, an assemblage of handsome houses climbs the hillsides above sparkling waters.

START Panormitis. **TRIP LENGTH** At least half-day. Panormitis to Yialos sail time ½–1 hr. Yialos to Horio (3km/2 miles).

❶ **Panormitis Monastery.** Daily boats from Rhodes make a stop for about an hour at Taxi-archis Michalos Panormitis (Archangel Michael of Panormitis) en route to Symi's main port, Yialos. The monastery on the bay is dedicated to seafarer St. Michael who, as Symi's patron saint, attracts huge crowds for a week of festivities beginning November 1, as well as a regular contingent of summer tourists. The 15th-century monastery houses a revered icon of the archangel, an **Ecclesiastical Museum,** a **Byzantine and Folklore Museum,** a **library** with manuscripts, a **taverna,** and a **bakery.** Two- and three-story buildings face the waterfront with a bell-tower (ca. 1905) entrance.

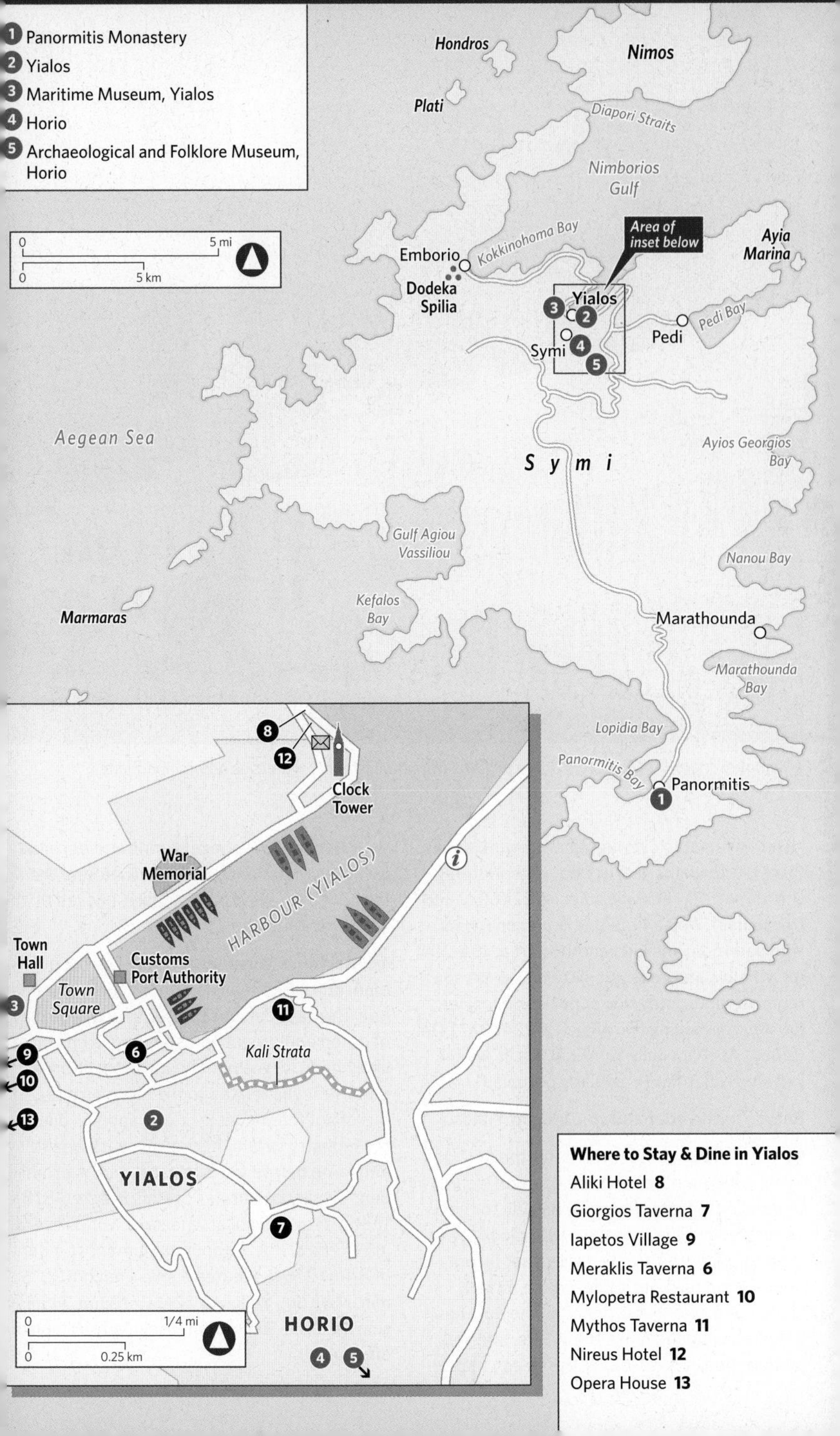

1 Panormitis Monastery
2 Yialos
3 Maritime Museum, Yialos
4 Horio
5 Archaeological and Folklore Museum, Horio

0   5 mi
0   5 km

Hondros

Nimos

Plati

Diapori Straits

Nimborios Gulf

Emborio   Kokkinohoma Bay

Dodeka Spilia

Area of inset below

Ayia Marina

Yialos
3 2

Symi
4

5

Pedi

Pedi Bay

S y m i

Aegean Sea

Ayios Georgios Bay

Gulf Agiou Vassiliou

Nanou Bay

Kefalos Bay

Marmaras

Marathounda

Marathounda Bay

Lopidia Bay

Panormitis Bay

Panormitis
1

8

12

Clock Tower

War Memorial

HARBOUR (YIALOS)

ⓘ

Town Hall

3

Town Square

Customs
Port Authority

9

10

6

11

Kali Strata

13

2

7

YIALOS

HORIO

0   1/4 mi
0   0.25 km

4 5

Where to Stay & Dine in Yialos

Aliki Hotel **8**

Giorgios Taverna **7**

Iapetos Village **9**

Meraklis Taverna **6**

Mylopetra Restaurant **10**

Mythos Taverna **11**

Nireus Hotel **12**

Opera House **13**

> *Remote Panormitis Monastery draws pilgrims with its cloisterlike, waterside accommodations.*

Visitors can stay overnight here, swim, and take nature walks year-round, except during the festival. ⏱ 1 hr. Panormitis. ☎ 22460/71581 (museums). 2-, 3-, 4-, 5- and 6-person rooms with bathroom and kitchenette start at 16€–20€ for a double and go to 25€–30€ for a 6-person room. In winter, stay free or pay a nominal fee for stays exceeding two nights. ☎ 22460/72414 (office) Apr–Oct daily 9am–2:30pm. In winter, just show up (office irregularly occupied).

Return to the boat and continue to Yialos.

❷ ★★★ **Yialos.** When you enter the port of Symi, villas painted in the palest pink, ochre, orange, or red spill down the hillside to the water's edge. The landmark 1881 clock tower is picturesque, as are the boats that tie up opposite on the south side, where a road leads up to the village, or *horio*. The port has been redeveloped since the 1990s. Still very picturesque, it is no longer the sleepy harbor with a couple of sponge stands and portside tavernas that it once was. Walk around the harbor either way to the square, backed by the Maritime Museum. ⏱ 1 hr.

❸ **Maritime Museum, Yialos.** The big ochre, blue, and white mansion on the main square is now the nautical museum, with dusty displays of dated equipment whose purpose has most likely been forgotten. The museum houses paraphernalia related to the fishing trade, merchant marine history, and sponge-diving—the industry to which Symi owed its wealth and fame before tourism escalated. A prominent display celebrates Stathis Hatzis (1878–1936), a revered local who set a world record in 1913 by diving without equipment to a depth of 84m (276 ft.) to free a ship's anchor. ⏱ 15 min. Main Sq., Yialos. ☎ 22460/72363. Admission 2€. Daily 10am–3pm (irregularly occupied off-season).

The several hundred steps of Kali Strata link Yialos and hilltop Horio.

The fastest way to Horio is to climb the steps of the Kali Strata. By car, the circuitous route is 3km (2 miles).

4 Horio. Horio is in many ways a typical Greek island village, with houses in various states of repair, a winding maze of alleys with views down to the sea glimpsed between tumbledown buildings, and, common in these parts, the ruins of a **castle of St. John** at its apex. Other than the views, there isn't much to see besides the **Archaeological and Folklore Museum** and perhaps the decrepit fortress, built with stones from the walls of an ancient acropolis and now the foundations for the **Panagia Church** and ruined **Athena**

Beach-Bereft

Beaches are not the draw on Symi, especially among visitors staying in nearby Rhodes. But if you have time to kill before your boat arrives, you may want to check out **NOS Beach.** It's small, narrow, and pebbly, but nearest the port, just below the main road beyond the clock tower. Boat taxis to east-coast beaches leave Yialos hourly until 1pm or 2pm, returning 4pm to 6pm in July and August; they're either "fast" or "slow," which is to say bigger or smaller. **Konstantinos-Irini** (☎ 69450/45068) is part of a reliable consortium. **Agia Marina** (15 min. away; 8.50€) is the closest beach beyond NOS; it's child-friendly in that it's sandy, but it's tiny with a few beach chairs and umbrellas set out on a concrete platform, and the bar/restaurant behind it is pricey. Next up are **Agios Nikolaos** (another small, sandy stretch 20 min. away; 8.50€), **Nanou Bay** (a long, pebble beach, 20–35 min. away; 10.50€), and **Marathounda** (rocky, 30 min. by fast boat; 12.50€).

Temple. People used to regularly climb the Kali Strata, the few hundred steps from Yialos to Horio, which was more populous two decades ago. Since then a road was paved, and homes along the way and many in the village were abandoned. The well-worn steps are mostly deserted now, collecting twigs in the corners, but they still provide the most direct way up. If you decide to travel by taxi (3€), try to descend via the stairs; the views make the 10-minute walk worthwhile. ⏱ 1 hour. 3km (2 miles) from Yialos by road, by taxi.

5 Archaeological and Folklore Museum, Horio. Follow the signs through the narrow streets and ruins of Horio to get to the Archaeological Museum. The director is a font of knowledge about the place, having worked there more than three decades. It occupies two neoclassical buildings, endowed by sponge merchants and Austria-Hungary's then-vice-consul in Symi. One contains a replica Symiot house, the other a hodge-podge of artifacts from the classical, Roman, early Christian, and Byzantine eras. ⏱ 30 min. ☎ 22460/71114. Admission 2€. Tues–Sun 8am–2:30pm.

Where to Stay & Dine in Yialos

> *Giorgios is the oldest taverna on the island and one of the best.*

★ Aliki Hotel

At one time Aliki was the only decent hotel on Symi. This 1895 neoclassical sea captain's villa on the waterfront, where the boats come in near the clock tower, has three floors, 12 double rooms, and three suites. All are decorated with antiques. You will pay for the privilege of staying here, and reservations are required. Akti G. Gennimata. ☎ 22460/71665. www.simi-hotel-aliki.gr. 15 units. AE, MC, V. 70€–130€ w/breakfast. Apr–Oct.

kids Giorgios Taverna GREEK

One of Symi's oldest tavernas looks the part, but it's still one of the best. It's also easy to find—beside Horio's main square, right at the top of the steps from Yialos. It doesn't look like much, with a plain signpost marked TAVERNA GIORGIO & MARIA and a wall inside plastered with old pictures. But the food is good and the menu is broad, from fresh fish and lobster to kebabs, chops, rabbit, lamb, and beef. Horio. ☎ 22460/71984. Entrees 7.50€–70€. MC, V. Daily lunch & dinner.

★★ kids Iapetos Village

This lovely complex of studios and two-floor apartments is set back from the port. Living areas are very spacious, and some units have full kitchens, including ovens and full-size fridges. The gorgeous, covered outdoor swimming pool has beach chairs and umbrellas, and a circular bar livens up the spacious, central flagstone courtyard with palm trees. Road beside Maritime Museum. ☎ 22460/72777. www.iapetos-village.gr. 29 units. AE, MC, V. 90€–135€ w/breakfast. Open Apr–Oct.

kids Meraklis Taverna GREEK

This taverna with a white awning, blue chairs, and blue-checkered tablecloths is just a block from the port at the end of Meniklidi Street. Meraklis means "connoisseur" in English, but the food is standard taverna fare delivered by quick and friendly servers. After your meal, try the homemade local goodies at **Stani,** the traditional bakery next door. ☎ 22460/71003. Entrees 7€–9€. AE, DC, MC, V. Mar–Dec daily breakfast, lunch & dinner.

Mylopetra Restaurant *MODERN GREEK*

If you want to splurge, head to this upscale restaurant with a full menu of seafood dishes fit for a gourmand. It's tucked away on a back street in an old stone building with arched doorways (check out the ancient tomb), and you can also dine in the courtyard. Entrees range from simple homemade ravioli with feta or fresh tomatoes and capers to full-on lobster feasts. ☎ 22460/72333. Entrees 23€–66€. V. May–Oct daily breakfast, lunch & dinner.

Mythos Taverna *GREEK*

On the far side of the port where the road goes up to the village, this taverna run by Chef Stavros serves a variety of dishes, including meat and fish selections. Two locations are right on the port, so you can sit and watch all the action from your roadside table. ☎ 22460/71488. Entrees 10€–22€. V. Apr–Oct daily dinner.

Nireus Hotel

Guests can sit and watch the bustling port from this waterside hotel just behind the landmark clock tower (*roloi*) and the statue of the fishing boy, *Michalaki* (by local sculptor Valsamis). Rooms on the ground or first floor have terraces or balconies overlooking either the port or the town. The popular on-site cafe, bar, and restaurant occupy a waterfront terrace. Nireus also has a hotel in the one-taverna-resort of Pedi. Akti G. Gennimata. ☎ 22460/72400. www.nireus-hotel.gr. 37 units. MC, V. 95€–135€ w/breakfast. Year-round.

kids Opera House

Owned by former residents of Sydney, the Opera House is a compound of Knossos blue, ochre, burnt orange, and brick-red painted apartments and suites built in a traditional style, and positioned around a central garden in a quiet hillside spot not far from the port. Suites are on the top floor of these two-suite, two-level buildings, and apartments are on the ground level. All are clean and spacious, some have bandylegged, upholstered chairs and other old-style furniture, and kitchen sinks have windows over them. Wedding and baptism receptions are held here, in either the 400-seat hall or the 500-seat roof garden. Signposted from road beside Maritime Museum. ☎ 22460/72034 or 71856. www.symiopera house.gr. 50 units. AE, MC, V. Suites 50€–90€; apts 90€–120€. Year-round.

> The charming Aliki Hotel occupies a sea captain's home at water's edge.

Kos

Pleasant and pastoral Kos is a bicycle-friendly island with low-lying plains that rise up to the mountains. Goats clamber over hillsides, the main town is the pedestrian-friendly port, and beach resorts to suit all tastes are situated along the coastline's long expanses of sandy beaches. Just 45km (28 miles) long and 11km (7 miles) across at its widest point, it's fairly small, and the prevailing feeling is slow-paced and provincial.

> *Pedal power is a popular mode of transport on Kos.*

START Finikon (near castle entrance). **TRIP LENGTH** 1 day. 8km (5 miles) round-trip (to Asklepion and back).

❶ Kos Town. A medieval fortress dominates the port of Kos, which didn't receive as many Italian-era (1912–47) restoration treatments as its more glamorous neighbor, Rhodes. You won't find a single head-spinning sight here; instead you'll stumble across numerous minor ones, both large and small but usually free. ⏱ At least 1 hr.

❷ ★ Plane tree of Hippocrates. The father of medicine is believed to have taught here in the 5th century B.C. The tree, propped up by cage-like bars, has been around a long time, but probably less than a thousand years. It's flanked by the boarded-up, Ottoman-era **Loggia Mosque of Hassan Pasha,** a beautiful three-story building with a corner minaret and shops on the ground floor. ⏱ 10 min. Finikon (palm-treed area in front of the castle entrance).

❸ ★ Castle of the Knights. Walk over the bridge of the old moat to the 15th-century fortress entrance. The inside is in ruins, but it's nonetheless charming. Masonry from ancient buildings is strewn or organized inside. A tilting staircase to the top level affords great views, but keep a firm hand on tots—the slat holes are near foot level and slant downward. ⏱ 30 min. Finikon (between Akti Miaouli and Akti Kountouriotou). ☎ 22420/27927. Admission 3€, under 18 and over 65 free. May–Aug Tues–Sun 8am–8pm, Mon 1:30–8pm; Sept until 7pm, Oct until 6:30pm; Nov–Mar Tues–Sun 8:30am–3pm.

❹ ★ Kos Archaeological Museum. This small museum built by the Italians houses some local gems. In one 2nd- or 3rd-century-A.D.

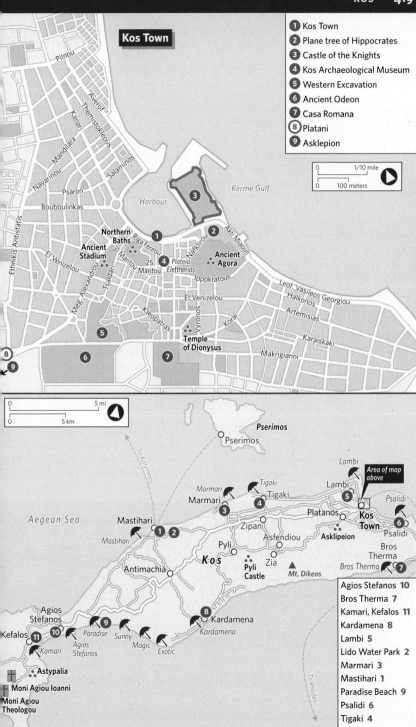

Kos Town

1. Kos Town
2. Plane tree of Hippocrates
3. Castle of the Knights
4. Kos Archaeological Museum
5. Western Excavation
6. Ancient Odeon
7. Casa Romana
8. Platani
9. Asklepion

0   1/10 mile
0   100 meters

Pilnou
Averof
Themistokleous
Kanari
Mandilara
Navarinnou
Salaminos
Psaron
Bouboulinkas
Ethnikis Antistatis
El Venizelou
Meg. Alexandrou
Tsaldari
31 Martiou
Riga Fereou
25 Maritou
Natklirou
Akti Miaouli

Kerme Gulf

Harbour

Northern Baths
Ancient Stadium
Plateia Eleftherias
Ancient Agora
Ippokratous
Leof. Vasileos Georgiou
El Venizelou
Halkonos
Kleopatras
Vyronos
Korai
Artemisias
Karaiskaki
Temple of Dionysus
Makrigianni

0   5 mi
0   5 km

Pserimos
○ Pserimos

Lambi

Area of map above

To Kalymnos

Marmari
Marmari
Tigaki
Tigaki
Lambi
Kos Town
Psalidi

Aegean Sea

Mastihari
Mastihari
Zipani
Platanos
Psalidi

Kos
Pyli
Asfendiou
Asklipeion
Zia
Pyli Castle
▲ *Mt. Dikeos*
Bros Therma
Bros Therma

Antimachia

Kardamena
Kardamena

Agios Stefanos
Paradise
Agios Stefanos
Sunny
Magic
Exotic
Kefalos
Kamari

Astypalia

✠ **Moni Agiou Ioanni**
✠ **Moni Agiou Theologou**

To Rhodes

Agios Stefanos **10**
Bros Therma **7**
Kamari, Kefalos **11**
Kardamena **8**
Lambi **5**
Lido Water Park **2**
Marmari **3**
Mastihari **1**
Paradise Beach **9**
Psalidi **6**
Tigaki **4**

mosaic bordered by beautifully sculpted statues, Hippocrates oversees the arrival of Asklepios; a 2nd-century-B.C. sculpture of a ram adores a seated Hermes with winged shoes; and a 4th-century-B.C. statue of Hippocrates is larger than life. **30 min. Eleftherias Sq. ☎ 22420/28326. Admission 3€. Apr–Oct Tues–Sun 8am–6:30pm, Nov–Feb 8:30am–3pm.**

5 **Western excavation.** This site is free; just enter wherever you see steps down into the dig. Covered areas indicate 3rd-century-A.D. mosaic floors or murals, including a depiction of the abduction of Europa by Zeus as a bull. The ancient road turns a corner and leads to the restored columns of a 2nd-century B.C, gymnasium. It's fun wandering around amid the ruins and trying to figure out how pieces fit together. **At least 30 min. Grigoriou E' St. Free admission.**

6 **Ancient Odeon.** The senate met here, and musicians and poets from Greece and Asia performed at this small 2nd-century-A.D. theater during the Asklepion festival. Roofed in antiquity, it has been restored twice, by the Italians and again recently. Facing the left side of it is a pretty mosaic. **15 min. Grigoriou E' St. May–Aug Tues–Sun 8am–8pm, reduced winter hours. Free admission.**

7 ★ **Casa Romana.** A 3rd-century-A.D. restored Roman house sits on the site of the ancient central public baths. Rooms and an inner courtyard have been rebuilt, and you can see part of the sub-floor heating system, mosaics, murals, and a well. There are plans to restore more of the site, including the hypocaust-heated baths. **30 min. Free admission. Grigoriou E' St. May–Aug Tues–Sun 8am–8pm, Mon 1:30–8pm; Sept Tues–Sun 8am–7pm, Mon 1:30–7pm; Oct Tues–Sun 8am–6:30pm, Mon 1:30–6:30pm; Nov–Mar Tues–Sun 8:30am–3pm.**

Head southwest out of Kos Town on the Kefalou road. Turn left (south) on the road to Asklepiou. 3km (2 miles).

8 **Platani.** Platani is a Muslim area famous for its kebabs and meze, and locals get their fix from an array of tavernas facing a roundabout. The most popular is **Asklipios "Ali" Restaurant** (☎ 22420/25264; $), which is packed on a Sunday afternoon. You might stop en route to the Asklepion.

Continue west on Asklepiou Rd. for 1 km (⅔ mile).

SITE GUIDE PAGE 421

9 ★★★ **Asklepion.** The Sanctuary of Asklepios is the island's most famous attraction, a pilgrimage site for the medically minded since antiquity. Built in the 3rd and 4th centuries B.C., after Hippocrates died in 357 B.C., it was a popular and opulent place to make offerings in the hope of receiving good health from the god of medicine. Destroyed by an earthquake in the 6th century A.D., the site was discovered in 1902. Restoration began in 1938 but stopped two years later.

Hippocrates, Father of Medicine

Hippocrates was born in Kos in 460 B.C., and died in Larissa, Thessaly, at the age of 104 (or 109). He was reputedly a descendant of Hercules on his mother's side and Asklepios on his father's side, and thus he was inducted into the cult or teachings of the Asclepiads (physicians). He also studied philosophy, rhetoric, and the sciences; learned the theories of Pythagoras; and traveled to Asia Minor, Egypt, Libya, Thrace, and Macedonia in pursuit of knowledge. Pericles called on Hippocrates to save Athens from a cholera outbreak, and rewarded him with knowledge of the Eleusian Mysteries (Hercules was the only other non-Athenian permitted that information) and perpetual free access to the city for him and his descendants. Hippocrates was tireless, enthusiastic, and uninterested in personal gain, forfeiting lucrative appointments in places such as Persia, an enemy of Greece. He passed on his knowledge to the young, wrote the Hippocratic oath—still a code of conduct for doctors today—and wrote prolifically, as evidenced by 57 surviving works. Many ancient authors cited him as an intellectual giant in his own time, as well as the first individual to classify medicine and treat patients in a methodical way.

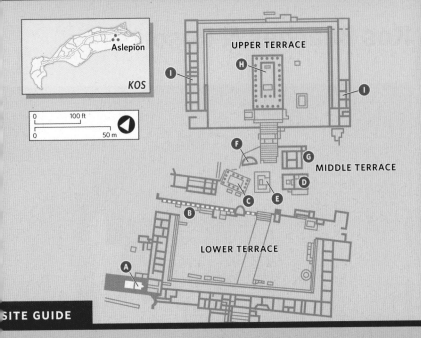

SITE GUIDE

9 Asklepion

The grove was the main seat for the Asklepi-ads, who guarded the secrets of medicine but practiced more hands-on, Hippocratic healing techniques than mainstream practitioners. Up a few steps is the Lower, or First, Terrace where, to the left, are the remains of **A Ro-man baths** from the 1st to 3rd century A.D. Di-rectly ahead on the left is a retaining wall with restored **B niches,** one of which issues spring water in winter that is still believed to be cura-tive. Up the steps to the Middle (Second) Ter-race are the remains of a **C temple to Apollo,** with reconstructed Corinthian columns; a **D temple to Asklepios;** an **E altar** with a central staircase; an **F exedra** (semicircle that contained a statue); and the **G priests' rooms.** On the Upper (Third) Terrace is the great 2nd-century B.C. **H Doric Temple of Asklepios** and the 13th-century chapel on the site dedicated to Panagia Tarsou (Panagia tou Alsous, Our Lady of the Grove). **I Patients' rooms** were built around the perimeter. The nearby **International Hippocratic Foundation** (☎ 22420/22131; www.ihfk.gr; Mon–Fri 10am–1pm) has a medicinal **herb garden;** open the

door into the front garden and follow the signs. There are some 158 labeled plants from the 254 species cited by Hippocrates. The garden is 700m (2,297 ft.) from the archaeo-logical site. A **cafe** at the entrance by the parking lot sells books and beverages. There's also a stop for a **small train** that in theory runs hourly (10am–6pm; 5€) but don't rely on it. There were no passengers on a mid-July after-noon. ⏰ At least 30 min. 4km (2½ miles) from Kos Town on Asklepiou Rd. ☎ 22420/28763. Admission 3€. Apr–Oct Tues–Sun 8am–6pm; Nov–Mar Tues–Sun 8am–3pm. Bus no. 8 runs hourly from Aktaion. An attendant can call a taxi (6€–8€) to take you back to Kos Town.

Kos Beaches & Resorts

> *Hot natural spring water bubbles onto the beach at Bros Therma.*

★ kids **Agios Stefanos** SOUTH (EAST) COAST
This nice stretch of beach sits beside the
5th-century-A.D. ruins of the Basilica of St.
Stephen, with columns restored by the Italians. Opposite is Kastri islet, with a chapel on
it. **Club Med** has a complex here, closed for
renovations at the time of this writing, but the
beach is not private; it's shallow, though, and
sandy only where the "village" is located. Turn
off the main road toward the coast, a pitched descent. 40km (25 miles) southwest of Kos Town.

★★ **Bros Therma** SOUTH (EAST) COAST
The road ends at this spring where hot, sulfu-
rous water bubbles to the surface of a natural,
boulder-enclosed pool on the beach. You can
soak up therapeutic benefits—treatment of
rheumatism and arthritis, among other ailments—by plunging in the hot pool or cooler
sea. The last section of road is steep, unpaved,
and gravelly, begging a question: If this site is

so important, why hasn't it been paved yet?
You can drive as far as the canteen providing
drinks, snacks, beach chairs, and umbrellas;
from there, it's 50m (164 ft.) to the pool. Past
Agios Fokas, 8km (5 miles) southeast of Kos
Town. Bus no. 1, 5 to Okeanis Hotel, no. 5 to
Therma hourly 10:15am–6:15pm from Aktaion
terminal. Bus: DEAS.

Kamari, Kefalos SOUTH (EAST) COAST
Kamari Beach is what visitors mean when
they say Kefalos, which also encompasses
the village and surrounding area. It attracts
mainly British package tourists on holiday for
one or two weeks; its charms include small
hotels, watersports, excursions to Nissyros,
Greek nights, a fishing BBQ, a 3-island cruise,
and a trip to Zia at sunset. It feels like Faliraki
on Rhodes in the 1980s. The sand is gray and
pebbly with a shallowish gradient and wide
beachfront. Overall, the landscape is a bit

> *Laid-back and low-key Kamari is on a pretty stretch of the south coast.*

more interesting than on the north coast, and the southern exposure also protects it more from the wind. Try **Hotel Ionikos** (☎ 22420/71166; www.ionikoshotel.gr), which has a public pool and restaurant. **Hotel Antonis** (☎ 22420/71533) also has a pool. You can rent scooters and buggies at **Katerina's** (☎ 22420/72036). 40km (25 miles) south-west of Kos Town. Bus: KTEL.

★ **Kardamena** SOUTH (EAST) COAST
The island's biggest resort faces the calmer south, with long stretches of organized beach with watersports (**Kardamena Watersports Center;** ☎ 22420/91444; www.koswater sports.gr) on either side of the port. It caters mainly to young British vacationers. There are no bicycles here, but a lot of precarious-looking buggies zip along the side roads. It's full of cafe-bars along the seafront and marina, where fishing boats line up. Try the

all-inclusive **Atlantica Porto Bello Royal** (☎ 22420/92101; www.atlanticahotels.com), or the **Cleopatra Classic** (☎ 22420/92257; www.cleopatrahotels.com), which also has studios, a little out of town (east) on Malibu Beach. Ten minutes away by bus is the family-oriented, all-inclusive **Akti Beach Club** (☎ 22420/92316; www.aktibeachclub.gr). 29km (18 miles) southwest of Kos Town. Bus: KTEL.

★ kids **Lambi** NORTH (WEST) COAST
Lambi's sand and pebble beach area starts right where the boats pull into the port and, farther along, becomes a proper family-friendly playground by the sea. The island's most established resort, it's lively—home to the **Tropical Island** and **Heaven** clubs—and frequented mostly by northern Europeans. Bicycle tracks and racks are everywhere. The bus line in this direction ends 2km (1¼ miles)

> Rugged mountains, palm trees, and proximity to Turkey lend an exotic flavor to Kos.

from Kos Town at the **Blue Lagoon Resort** (☎ 22420/54400; www.bluelagoonresort.gr). Lambi Beach, north of the port, Kos Town. Bus no. 2 from Iroon Polytechniou Sq. (at the port, end of Kanari St. with the dolphin fountain). Bus: DEAS.

Lido Water Park NORTH (WEST) COAST

Lido doesn't have a beach, but it has enough slides and pools to make it worth a day trip. Touted as 75,000 square meters (19 acres) of fun and water for "ages 5 to 55," it offers a range of amusements, including a giant slide, crazy river, and wave pool. Grown-ups may be relieved to know there's an adult-only pool and Jacuzzi, restaurant, bar, snack bar, and locker rooms. You'll need a bicycle or car to get here as it's in the middle of nowhere, on the way from Marmari to Mastihari, near the **Marmari Palace** (☎ 22420/59360; www.marmari palace.gr) and **Horizon Beach** (☎ 22420/58800; www.horizonbeachresort.gr). 2km (1¼ miles) east of Mastihari, 25km (15 miles) northeast of Kos Town. ☎ 22420/59241. www.lidowaterpark.com. 10am–7pm. Adults 17€, children ages 4–11 13€, children under 4 free.

★ Marmari NORTH (WEST) COAST

This wide expanse of fine white sand and pebble beach, across the salt marsh from Tigaki, has cheery umbrellas and painted pallet pathways along the beach area. It's shallow with some seaweed along the shoreline, which extends for some 2km/1¼ miles. **Christos Go-Carts** (☎ 22420/68184) is near here. For accommodations, try **Blue Jay Beach Hotel** (☎ 22420/41533 or 41637; www.bluejay beach.com) near the beach; **Captain's Rooms Studios** (☎ 22420/41431), just across the road; or **Palazzo Del Mare** (☎ 22420/42320; www.palazzodelmare.gr), a beautiful complex built in a hayfield with a pool and children's playground. 2km (1¼ miles) off the main road toward the coast, 16km (10 miles) northwest of Kos Town. Bus: KTEL.

kids Mastihari NORTH (WEST) COAST

Also spelled Mastichari, this smaller, older resort and fishing village is now home to massive, luxury hotel complexes. The wide expanse of long, sandy beach lined by shade trees has umbrellas and beach chairs, as well as tavernas and supermarkets behind the tree line. The gradient is shallow and thus good for children, but there's a fair bit of dried seaweed along the shoreline. A small ferry, **Anek** (☎ 22430/24144) plies a route to **Kalymnos** from here. Try the **Neptune** (☎ 22420/41480; www.neptune.gr), a convention center that also has a glorious spa; the all-inclusive **Princess of Kos Hotel** (☎ 22420/41524; www.princessofkos.com); kid-friendly **Gaia Royal** (☎ 22420/42231; www.gaia-hotels.com); or **Andreas Studios** (☎ 22420/59050; www.kosrooms.com). 27km (17 miles) northwest of Kos Town. Bus: KTEL.

Paradise Beach SOUTH (EAST) COAST

Many say this beach, also known as Bubble Beach, is the best on the island, but that's debatable. The sand is fine, but there are some rocks just under the water; the strip is narrow; the beach chairs are practically hinged together, and they're a foot away from water's edge (so no walking hand in hand along the shoreline here); and the facilities are portable toilets within whiffing distance. **Paradise Beach Restaurant and Café/Bar** (☎ 22420/71263; July–Aug daily 9am–6pm) affords a more civilized environment. Kefalos Bay has

> *Shade trees are a welcome amenity on the wide sands at Mastihari.*

better **beaches** farther east of here. Try **Golden** or **Magic Beach** (turn off the main road at the Thyme honey shop). 33km (21 miles) southwest of Kos Town.

Psalidi EAST (NORTH) COAST
This established resort southeast of Kos Town has many big hotel complexes and not much else around or between them. It begins after **Theodorou Beach** ends, past the marina in Kos Town. You'll know it by the plane trees that line the road. The beach itself is sandy, rocky, and wind-swept. Note the beach chairs face away from the sea. Try the **Sun Palace Hotel & Spa** (☎ 22420/24530; www.sun palace-kos.com). 4km (2½ miles) southeast of Kos Town. Bus: DEAS.

kids Tigaki NORTH (WEST) COAST
Also spelled Tingaki, this area is rural, and a lot of families cycle along the quiet coastal road. There are signs for horseback riding

near the salt marsh (Alkyes), which attracts migrating flamingos and other birds. Rocky in some places and deep sand in others, the beach stretches for some 10km (6¼ miles). While it slants into the water, it's still shallow, with some seaweed. Look out for nesting (or hatching) loggerheads or green turtles. It's narrow and rocky with pine trees near the beachside **Byron Apartments** (☎ 22420/69494); then it widens out farther west, and there's no cover there. Beach chairs and umbrellas are 6€. The resort is spread out; a central square has tavernas, supermarkets, and other amenities. Try the **Iberostar Astir Odysseus** (☎ 22420/49900; www.iberostar.com), or the all-inclusive, family-oriented **Aquis Marine Resort and Waterpark** (☎ 22420/68860; www.aquisresorts.com). 11km (7 miles) northwest of Kos Town, 2km (1¼ miles) off the main road toward the coast. Bus: KTEL.

Where to Stay & Dine on Kos

> *Gaia Garden is a cheerful, family-oriented retreat in Lambi.*

★ **Americana Hotel** KOS TOWN
This updated hotel is set back from the road near the waterfront. Rooms are small with many amenities and plentiful comfy throw pillows. Front-facing rooms are blindingly sunny, but the curtains and shutters in tandem effectively shade the room. The knowledgeable American owner can arrange airport transfer and a lot more. 14 Karaiskaki St. & Papatheofanous sts., Agia Marina. ☎ 22420/22947. www.hotel-americana.com. 15 units. MC, V. 50€–65€ w/breakfast. Year-round.

★ **Avli Taverna** ZIA *GREEK*
On the ridge in **Zia,** in the foothills of Mt. Dikios, this taverna affords views of Zia's renowned sunsets from either a roof garden or a balcony. If you're lucky, you may be treated to the cinnamon-flavored drink Mama makes.

End of the main road on the cliff side. ☎ 22420/69185. Entrees 5.50€–9€. MC, V. Daily dinner.

★ kids **Gaia Garden Hotel** LAMBI
Accessible via shuttle from Kos Town, the popular Gaia Garden in Lambi has bungalows, as well as family rooms, a children's pool and playground, a pool, a restaurant and bar, tennis, beach volleyball, a gym, an Internet corner, and free Wi-Fi. The beach is about a 5-minute walk away. You can book through www.booking.com. ☎ 22420/25804 or 26055. www.gaia-garden.com. 95 units. AE, DC, MC, V. 40€–80€ w/breakfast. May–Oct.

★ kids **Jumbo Style Restaurant** KOS TOWN
GREEK/INTERNATIONAL In a plaza that's great for people-watching, this restaurant is run by a Greek-Australian who serves everything

from pizza to seafood. The turnover is high, the food is fresh, and the portions are large. The Greek platter and mixed grill for two are popular. Takeout is available. **Agias Paraskevis Sq.** ☎ 22420/24780. Entrees 6.50€–15€. Cash only. Apr–Oct daily breakfast, lunch & dinner.

★★ Kos Aktis Art Hotel KOS TOWN
This hotel right by the harbor lives up to its origins as a 1960s-era Xenia hotel—state hotels erected in the best locations throughout Greece. It has been updated, of course, affording all the modern amenities, including a gym, cafe/bar/restaurant, and Wi-Fi. **7 Vas. Georgiou St.** ☎ 22420/47200. www.kosaktis.gr. 42 units. AE, DC, MC, V. 100€–230€ w/breakfast.

★ Olympiada Restaurant KOS TOWN *GREEK*
This restaurant across from a green area makes great homemade *moussaka* and other Greek specialties. They offer a twist on the ubiquitous Greek salad (*horiatiki*), with yellow and red peppers and the mandatory slab of feta, plus soup and plenty of other options as well. **2 Kleopatras & Vas. Pavlou sts.** ☎ 22420/23031. Entrees 5€–9€. MC, V. Open Feb–Nov daily lunch & dinner.

kids **Pizza Con** KOS TOWN *PIZZA/GREEK/AMERICAN* In addition to pizza, extensive menu items here include Tex-Mex dishes, burgers, and even sweet pizzas (such as chocolate), which makes it popular with kids. Near archaeological sites and a taxi station, it's great for a break or snack. Free Internet. **1 Makrygianni St.** ☎ 22420/22055, ☎ 69079/20515 (for

> Kos Town is well supplied with family-style, outdoor restaurants such as Olympiada.

deliveries). www.pizzacon.gr. Entrees 4€–7€. Cash only. Daily dinner.

kids **Sol Kipriotis Village** PSALIDI
In Psalidi, past the marina and Theodorou Beach, this hotel complex is one of many in an established resort that has pools, bars, restaurants, children's entertainment, water slides, and the like. The beach is rather stony, but if you prefer to sit poolside, it's a good choice. **Psalidi, 3km (2 miles) south of Kos Town.** ☎ 22420/27640. www.kipriotis.gr. 650 units. AE, DC, MC, V. All-inclusive. 100€–240€. Apr–Oct.

Kos Nightlife

Kos Town's **bar street** (Blessa St.) starts at the harbor front, and there are cafes at the **ancient agora entrance** (Nafklirou St.). For live music and dancing in a former Turkish bath, try **Hamam Club** (1 Nafklirou St.; ☎ 22420/24938), next to the taxi station. Happy hour runs nightly from 9pm until midnight.

Patmos

The silent, sacred isle of Patmos is where St. John the Divine (or Theologian) wrote the Book of Revelation in the Cave of the Apocalypse. The fortress-like Monastery of St. John, surrounded by the traditional village, Hora, towers above the port, Skala. The island is only 12km (7½ miles) north to south, and excursion boats visit nearby islands. Its natural beauty and many deep bays make it a popular stop among cruise-ship passengers as well as religious pilgrims.

> *The whitewashed houses of Hora surround the Monastery of St. John.*

START Skala Port. 8km (5 miles) round-trip (to Hora and back to Skala). **TRIP LENGTH** Half-day.

1 Skala. Skala is where most Patmos residents live. It bisects the island at its throat, making it accessible to beaches here and off the shore of its friendly harbor. The main amenities are concentrated around the quay at the main square. Shops, hotels, and restaurants are strung along the harbor front and down a few connecting streets. Orient yourself here,

then make your way via bus, taxi, scooter, or car to Hora. You can glean much information about the holy sites from the **Orthodox Culture and Information Center** (Main Sq.; ☎ 22470/33316; Apr–Oct daily 9am–1pm and 6–9pm), Patriarchal Exarchate of Patmos. You can sit and listen to 8-minute or 40-minute documentaries done by an English-language religion channel, arrange to meet with the local clergy, or read up and learn about Orthodoxy here. They also keep current bus schedules. ⏱ At least 1 hr.

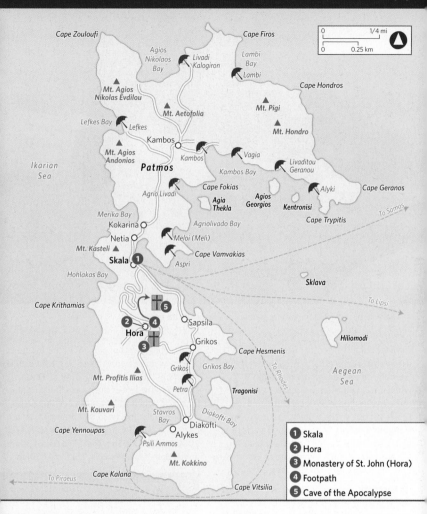

Map Legend

1 Skala
2 Hora
3 Monastery of St. John (Hora)
4 Footpath
5 Cave of the Apocalypse

Hora is 4km (2½ miles) south of Skala. The bus or taxi to Hora (5€) will drop you off at a hairpin curve, and from there you walk into town, following signs through a maze of flagstone alleys and past souvenir merchants to the monastery.

2 ★ **Hora.** The town in itself is a beautiful example of a traditional, whitewashed village with its maze of streets, lintel engravings, chapels, and beautiful views. Hora is now mainly residential, with little sign of commercial activity once you get lost in its streets. It's better to wander them after you've seen the monastery though. ⊕ At least 30 min.

SITE GUIDE
PAGE 431

3 ★★ **Monastery of St. John, Hora.** The Monastery of St. John the Theologian (aka John the Divine, Apostle John, John of Patmos) was founded in 1088 by an ascetic from Bithynia, Hosios (Blessed) Christodoulos. Like other hilltop fortresses, it had to withstand raids on its many sheltered bays by pirates and, eventually, Turks, who prevailed. They let the monks live a quiet life, however, as did the Normans, Franks, Venetians, Vatican, and Knights of St. John before them, since Byzantine Emperor Alexis I ceded the island to

> *A network of old footpaths provides pleasant ambles across the island.*

Christodoulos. (Like other islands in the group, in the 20th century, Patmos fell under Italian, German, and Allied occupation until 1947, when it was returned to Greece.) With a terrace affording views over the island and tables set out on the *plateia* (square) as well, **Vangelis Taverna** (Agias Levias Sq., Hora; ☎ 22470/31967) is the best place to savor the aura of the Hora. What's more, it's easy to find, open May through October.

4 Footpath. Footpaths crisscross Patmos. If you want to walk as people did for centuries, breathe fresh island air fragrant with herbs, and admire the scenery after you've wandered out of Hora, you can do so here. It's a pleasant downhill walk to the Cave of the Apocalypse. The stones are unhewn, so wear thick-soled shoes. ⏱ 30 min. Hora-Cave of the Apocalypse path, 2km (1¼ miles) from Hora or Skala.

5 ★★ Cave of the Apocalypse. The cave where St. John lived in exile and received the Revelation is in a zealously guarded monastery, with tour groups angling past one another in this holy place. The flagstone thresholds are well worn, and steep steps take you past the 18th-century **Chapel of St. Artemios** before you reach the cave, divided by a bulging, overhanging rock cleft in three places, where St. John heard "a great voice like a trumpet" (Rev. 1:10). You enter St. Anna's Chapel on the left of the cave. On the right is where St. John lived. You can see the niches he used to rest his head and prop himself up. ⏱ 20 min. 2km (1Nmiles) from Skala. ☎ 22470/20800 or 231234. Sun, Tues, Thu 8am–1:30pm and 4–6pm; Mon, Wed, Fri, Sat 8am–1:30pm.

St. John in Exile

Patmos didn't rate high in antiquity. In the 6th to 4th centuries B.C., a town of some 12,000 to 15,000 residents flourished on Kasteli Hill, behind present-day Skala, but it was rarely mentioned in literature. The Romans used it to exile transgressors, such as John the Apostle, who was reputedly sent here in A.D. 95 after running afoul of Emperor Domitian for preaching Christianity in nearby Ephesus. He lived in a cave (now known as the Cave of the Apocalypse), where the Book of Revelation was revealed to him, and he dictated it to his disciple, Prochoros. A year later, Domitian was assassinated, and St. John returned to Ephesus, where he died at age 99, in A.D. 104.

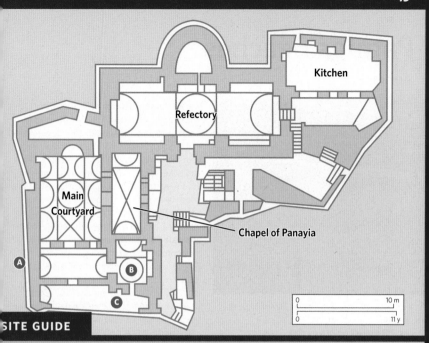

Kitchen

Refectory

Main Courtyard

Chapel of Panayia

A

B

C

0	10 m
0	11 y

SITE GUIDE

③ Monastery of St. John

You'll pass the photogenic **A** **Chapel of the Saints Apostles,** with its glorious view at the monastery entrance. The **B** **main Church of St. John the Divine** is built on an early Christian basilica, which in turn was the site of an ancient temple to Artemis. St. Christodoulos founded the community in 1088; his skull is encased in a silver sarcophagus. It is a living church that mixes old with new: A robe hangs over a chair, there are candles to light, buildings are still whitewashed, and burnt marble columns support plants set near the door. The monastery houses a library, a bindery, calligraphy workshop, and restoration center for manuscripts and parchments; the monastery collection of early Christian documents is second only to the collection on Mount Athos.

A **C** **small museum** includes 17th- and 18th-century Benediction crosses with miniature scenes in wooden filigree set in jeweled silver and gilt. Vestments include a 19th-century Russian one fit for St. Nick, with gold embroidered red velvet. A medieval epigonation —a pillow-like piece of material that hangs from the priest's waist—depicts a scene of

the Last Supper. Upstairs are many more icons rich with symbolism and early Christian marble fragments, including a moving though headless sculpture of the Virgin and Child. The designs from the 4th to 11th centuries look decidedly Celtic. A **shop** here sells mainly to Orthodox clergy. ⏰ At least 1 hr. ☎ 22470/20800 or 31234. www.patmosmonastery.gr. Sun, Tues, Thu 8am–1:30pm and 4–6pm; Mon, Wed, Fri, Sat 8am–1:30pm. Museum admission 6€, 3€ on Sunday. No photos allowed.

Patmos Beaches

> *Kambos and other beaches are backed by pines.*

★★ kids Agrio Livadi NORTH COAST

This beautiful, organized sandy and pebbly beach is set in a bay, with beach chairs, umbrellas, and watersports gear for rent from **Hellen's Place** (☎ 69721/92175). It's a good bet for families. It's also said to have the warmest water on the island. There's no place to stay overnight, but there's a taverna nearby called **O Glaros** (☎ 22470/31475) and a kiosk that sells beach toys. ⏱ 5 min. by taxi. 2km (1N mile) north of Skala.

Grikos SOUTH COAST

This quiet bedroom community offers new holiday homes, apartments, and villas for rent or for sale up the side of a hill from the beach. It has a few tavernas and a narrow, pebbly, tree-shaded stretch of shoreline with a few thatched umbrellas and small craft tied up. The draw here is another picturesque beach, **Petra**, or **Kalikatsou**, about a 10- to 15-minute walk away, with umbrellas and a canteen. If you want to stay right at the water's edge, try the refurbished **Silver Beach** (☎ 22470/32652; http://silverbeach-patmos.focusgreece.gr), or a little farther back, the swank **Pico Bello Hotel** (☎ 22410/23282, ☎ 69769/53646 mobile; picobellohotel@yahoo.gr), which has beautifully decorated, spacious apartments, suitable for families with children. ⏱ 10 min. by taxi. 11km (7 miles) south of Skala.

★★ kids Kambos (Kato) NORTH COAST

The longest stretch of beach on the island, Kambos has an old summer seaside resort feel to it. Some 600m (1,969 ft.) from the village with the same name, it has the most facilities and watersports, which draw the island's greatest concentration of young families. At a table under trees right on the beach, you can have seaside taverna fare. If you want to stay overnight, you can do so at the restaurant, **Ta Kavourakia Restaurant and Rooms to Rent,** which has rooms with balconies upstairs (☎ 22470/31745). Up the hill overlooking the bay is the more luxurious **Patmos Paradise Hotel** (☎ 22470/32624, Athens ☎ 21042/24112; www.patmosparadise.com), with its own pool, tennis, and sauna. ⏱ 10 min. by taxi. 5.5km (3½ miles) north of Skala, 600m (1,969 ft.) from Kambos.

kids Meloi (Meli) NORTH COAST

This narrow stretch of tree-shaded beach runs along a bay near Skala. Its approach is shallow and safe for kids. It has a seafood taverna, **To Melloi** (☎ 22470/31888) and a campsite, **Stefanos Camping** (☎ 69450/67206; www.patmosweb.gr/camping.htm), but no umbrellas or beach chairs. Bungalows at **Porto Scoutari Romantic Hotel & Suites** (☎ 22470/33123; www.portoscoutari.com) are some 250m (820 ft.) away, with a pool and spa. ⏱ 5 min. by taxi. 1.5km (1 mile) north of Skala.

Psili Ammos SOUTH COAST

This wide swath of fine sand beach has shade trees, but it's accessible only via an **excursion boat** from Skala, such as the *Aphrodite* (☎ 69770/35231; also to other destinations), which leaves you on the beach all day. Otherwise it's a half-hour slog up, down, and through the countryside from Diakofti village. There are no facilities here. It may also get quite windy, and if the gales whip up, the boat won't be coming back. Check the forecasts before setting out. ⏱ 1 hr. by boat. 10km (6¼ miles) south of Skala.

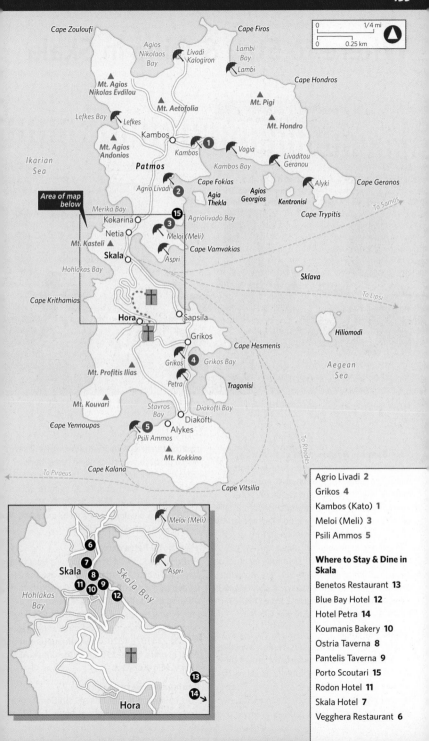

Agrio Livadi **2**

Grikos **4**

Kambos (Kato) **1**

Meloi (Meli) **3**

Psili Ammos **5**

Where to Stay & Dine in Skala

Benetos Restaurant **13**

Blue Bay Hotel **12**

Hotel Petra **14**

Koumanis Bakery **10**

Ostria Taverna **8**

Pantelis Taverna **9**

Porto Scoutari **15**

Rodon Hotel **11**

Skala Hotel **7**

Vegghera Restaurant **6**

Where to Stay & Dine in Skala

> *Fish soup is the house specialty at Pantelis Taverna.*

★★★ **Benetos Restaurant** SAPSILA *MODERN GREEK* Chef- proprietor Benetos Matthaiou has a formidable reputation, with impressive reviews in glossy magazines and numerous guidebooks. Once he's returned to Patmos, after wintering in Miami, he puts a spicy twist on classic dishes such as shrimp in saffron sauce, filet mignon in peppercorn sauce, and whole lobster. Patrons dine on the veranda overlooking Skala. You'll need wheels to get here. Road to Grikos 3km (2 miles) from Skala. ☎ 22470/33089. www.benetosrestaurant.com. Entrees 10€–23€. MC, V. June–Oct Tues–Sun dinner.

★ **Blue Bay Hotel**
The big draw here is the cliffside view over the bay entrance to the port where the cruise ships drop anchor, and the absolute silence at night; sounds of nature don't even stir the air. The hotel is just around a bluff from the town. Rooms are nothing special, but a couple have their own rooftop terraces with panoramic views. There's also a place to swim just down some steps from the road, as the narrow town beach is on the far side of town, about a 10-minute walk. 100m (328 ft.) from Skala. ☎ 22470/31165 or 34065. www.bluebaypatmos.gr. 27 units. MC, V. 90€–116€ w/breakfast. Apr–Nov.

★★★ **Hotel Petra** GRIKOS
At this luxurious hideaway above a beautiful bay and beach, accommodations are suites awash in comfortable style. A sumptuous breakfast and other meals are served on a welcoming terrace. The many amenities include a swimming pool and outstanding service. ☎ 22470/34020. www.petrahotel-patmos. com. 13 units. 185€–296€ with breakfast. AE, MC, V. Mid-Apr–Oct.

Koumanis Bakery *BAKERY*
This bakery sells all kinds of traditional cakes and cookies as well as cheese pies and breads

ou'll be glad to know about it if you want a
te lunch and all the restaurants are closed
r the afternoon (2 or 3pm to 5 or 6pm). **Main**
q. ☎ 22470/32894.

stria Taverna *GREEK*

his restaurant has an extensive menu, good
od, and a great, well-signed location near
he main square right in front of the port,
ith outdoor tables under an awning. It fully
elivers on the standard island lunch of Greek
alad, fries, grilled octopus, and beer. Por-
ons are generous, and the price is right too.
22473/00501. Entrees 7.50€–10€. Cash only.
aily lunch & dinner.

Pantelis Taverna *GREEK*

ery near Ostria right on the street just back
om the waterfront, Pantelis gets lots of rec-
mmendations for its fresh, traditional Greek
od. It's known especially for its *kakkavia* (fish
oup), and its lamb or beef *stifado* (stew with
nions). ☎ 22470/31922. Entrees 5€–12€. Cash
nly. Mar–Oct. Daily lunch & dinner.

★★ Porto Scoutari

ovely rooms, with sitting and sleeping areas
rnished with antiques, face the sea and a
een garden. A bistro, spa, and beautiful pool
re among the many amenities, which include
he gracious hospitality of owner Elina Scout-
ri. Outside Skala center. ☎ 22470/33123.
ww.portoscoutari.com. 30 units. 140€–240€.
C, V. Closed Nov–Apr.

Rodon Hotel

his typical old-style, three-story Everyman's
otel draws families and budget travelers on
oliday. On a road back from the port, it's
uiet even by Patmos standards. Rooms are
mall and sparsely furnished but clean, and
he terrace out front is lovely. Most clients
ese days are Italian vacationers, which is
tting, given that Italy once ruled the island
roup and one of the owners speaks Italian.
69779/44978 or 22470/31371. www.skala
otel.gr. 16 units. No credit cards. 30€–75€.
ay–Oct.

> *A Greek staple tops off any meal.*

★ kids Skala Hotel

The bougainvillea-covered Skala Hotel is just
off the main road but set back through an
arbor and across a central courtyard. It's got a
welcoming swimming pool, and all the rooms
in the three-story building have balconies and
free Wi-Fi, though they're a bit cramped. An
on-site conference room accommodates 400
people. 50m (164 ft.) from the sea. ☎ 22470/
31343. www.skalahotel.gr. 78 units. MC, V.
75€–140€ w/breakfast. Easter–Oct.

Vegghera Restaurant *MODERN GREEK*

If you want to splurge in Skala, walk north
to the new marina to this upscale restaurant
decorated in traditional style with rock and
wood. Specialties include lobster pasta as well
as shrimp and eggplant semolina with orange
and ginger. The chocolate soufflé with vanilla
ice cream makes for a perfect ending. New
Marina. ☎ 22470/32988 or 69773/94598.
www.patmosweb.gr/vegghera.htm. Entrees
18€–28€. DC, MC, V. Apr–Sept daily dinner.

Rhodes & the Dodecanese Fast Facts

Arriving

BY AIR On **Rhodes,** Diagoras International Airport (RHO) (☎ 22410/88700 or 83200 for info) is served by **Aegean Air** (☎ 21062/61000; www.aegeanair.com) and **Olympic Airlines** (☎ 21096/66666; (www.olympicair.com) from Athens and islands; it also serves direct overseas scheduled and charter flights from Europe and the Middle East. To fly into **Symi,** transfer from Rhodes or Kos. On **Kos,** flights operate from Hippocrates International Airport (KGS) (tel] 22420/56000). To reach **Patmos** by air, transfer from Samos International Airport (SMI) (☎ 22730/87800) or Leros Airport (LRS) (☎ 22470/22275), connected to Athens and Rhodes. **BY SEA** Various boats provide service between **Rhodes** and Athens, other islands, and Turkey. Various boats serve **Symi** from other islands. Various services sail to **Kos** from Athens, other islands, and Turkey. **Anem Ferries** (☎ 22420/59124 or 22430/51630; www.anemferries.gr) connects Kalymnos to Mastihari. Various boats connect **Patmos** to Athens and other islands. Buy tickets from booths at the ports or at travel agencies. Check the websites **www.openseas.gr** for domestic and international destinations and **www.gtp.gr** for domestic routes. Check with each island's **Port Authority** for sailing bans: on **Rhodes** ☎ 22410/27695, 28666, or 23693; on **Symi** ☎ 22460/71205; on **Kos** ☎ 22420/26594; on **Patmos** ☎ 22470/31231 or 34131.

Currency Exchange
See p. 681, Fast Facts Greece.

Doctors & Dentists
RHODES **Krito Medical Centre,** 3 Ioannou Metaxa Street (☎ 22410/38008 or 30020), staffs reliable specialists and dentists, open 7 days a week in summer; **Bardos Clinic,** 15 Ethnikis Antistaseos Street (☎ 22410/21222), provides 24-hour emergency and dental service. **LINDOS** Try **Polydinamo Iatriou Lindou** (☎ 22440/31224; Mon–Fri 9am–10pm). **SYMI** For medical assistance, we recommend

Health Centre in Yialos (☎ 22460/71290) and **Health Centre** in Horio (☎ 22460/71316; for a dentist, try ☎ 22460/72050. **KOS** Try **Kos Hospital** (☎ 22420/22300 or 54200). **PATMOS** Try the 24-hour **Health Center** on Skala–Hora road (☎ 22470/31211). For dental treatments, we recommend **Dr. Kokkinos** (☎ 22470/33075) or **Dr. Maka** (☎ 22470/33147), both in Skala.

Emergencies
RHODES Try **First Aid/General Hospital,** Agii Apostoli Street, Megavli (☎ 22410/80000) or **Euromedica Clinic,** Koskinou (☎ 22410/45000; www.euromedica.gr). For other emergency numbers, see p. 680, Fast Facts Greece.

Getting Around
BY BOAT See "Arriving," above. **BY BUS** On **Rhodes,** KTEL buses (☎ 22410/75134, 27706 or 27775) run to and from Rhodes Town to Faliraki and the east coast. RODA (city) buses (☎ 22410/26300) run to and from Rhodes Town to Faliraki, the west coast, Valley of the Butterflies, Filerimos, and Ancient Kamiros. In Lindos, free shuttles run to the beach and the KTEL bus stop. On **Symi,** there's a bus stop on the port's south side; for schedules to Yialos, Horio, or Pedi, dial ☎ 69453/16248; for Panomitis call ☎ 22460/71311. On **Kos,** DEAS (☎ 22420/26276) makes connections between Kos Town and environs. KTEL provides island-wide service from 7 Kleopatras Street, Kos Town (☎ 22420/22292). On **Patmos,** a bus runs infrequently between Skala, Hora, Grikos, and Kambos. **BY TAXI** On **Rhodes,** cab prices, listed at taxi stands, are relatively expensive. The ride from the airport to Rhodes Town or Faliraki is about 20€; to Lindos about 50€. For Radio (demand) taxi in Rhodes Town, dial ☎ 22410/69800 or 69600 outside Rhodes Town); for special-needs taxis, dial ☎ 22410/69390. In **Rhodes Town,** there's a taxi rank at Mandraki Harbor (☎ 22410/69800 or 69600). In **Faliraki,** cabs line up at the end of Ermou (Bar) Street by the beach (☎ 22410/85444). In **Lindos,** they're on the

main square. From **Haraki,** taxis are about 50€ to Rhodes Town. **Savaidis Travel** (Pefkos; 22440/48130; www.savaidis-travel.gr) or tour operators such as **Olympic Holidays** ☎ 22410/60749; www.olympicholidays.com) offer day tours once or twice a week for about 20€ return. In **Symi,** the taxi stand is on the port's south side. In **Kos,** taxis line up at the port and opposite the roadside Altar of Dionysus archaeological site, on Grigoriou E' Street ☎ 22420/22777 or 23333). On **Patmos,** taxis line up at the port (☎ 22470/31225).

Internet Access
See p. 681, Fast Facts Greece.

Pharmacies
See p. 682, Fast Facts Greece.

Police
RHODES For the tourist police, dial ☎ 22410/27423 or 23329; for traffic police, call ☎ 22410/44131. In **Faliraki,** call ☎ 22410/34700. On **Symi,** the police are in Yialos beside the clock tower (☎ 22460/71111). KOS For police, dial ☎ 22420/22222; for the tourist police, call ☎ 22420/26129. PATMOS The police and tourist police are on the main square in Skala (☎ 22470/31303).

Post Office
RHODES The post office in Rhodes Town is on Eleftherias Square (☎ 22410/35560). SYMI In Yialos at the clock tower (☎ 22460/71315). KOS In Kos Town (☎ 22420/22250). PATMOS In Skala on the main square (☎ 22470/31316). Also see p. 682, Fast Facts Greece.

Safety
See p. 682, Fast Facts Greece.

Telephones
See p. 683, Fast Facts Greece.

Toilets
Restaurants and cafes are lenient; buy a soft drink in courtesy. Usually a wc sign indicates public restrooms. Also see p. 684, Fast Facts Greece.

Visitor Information
RHODES On Rhodes, the **GNTO** (EOT) tourist information office is on the corner of Papagou and Makariou sts. (☎ 22410/44333 or 44335; www.ando.gr/eot). The **Rhodes Town** tourist information office is on Rimini Square (☎ 22410/35945 or 22413/61200; www.rhodes.gr). The **Dodecanese Tourism Organization** is on 1 Eleftherias Square (☎ 22413/60515 or 60608). **Olympic Holidays** (☎ 22410/60749; www.olympicholidays.com) provides well-located hotels and studios in the Dodecanese, including Symi; they also run excursions. In **Lindos,** the tourism office is on Lindos Square, Plateia Eleftherias (☎ 22440/31900 or 31227; www.lindos.gov.gr). SYMI In Yialos, try **Kalodoukas Holidays** (☎ 22460/71077; www.kalodoukas.gr) or Symi Tours (☎ 22460-71307; www.symitours.com). KOS On Kos, the municipal tourist office is on 7 Akti Kountourioti (☎ 22420/24460; Mon–Fri 7:30am–3pm). In **Kefalos,** Asklipios Tours is on the waterfront (☎ 22420/72143; www.asklipiostours.com). PATMOS In **Skala,** the municipal tourist office is on the main square (☎ 22473/60300, off-season info ☎ 22470/33320; Apr–Sept Mon–Fri 8am–2:30pm). **Apollon Travel** provides bus timetables and other information (☎ 22470/34105 or 31324; daily 9am–10pm). We also recommend **Astoria Travel** (☎ 22470/31205) and **GA Ferries** (☎ 22470/31217).

Favorite Moments in the Northeastern Aegean

Hugging the Turkish coast, the islands of the Northeastern Aegean share little besides proximity and topography, with forested mountainsides, valleys carpeted with orchards and olive groves, and dramatic coastlines. Samos, Chios, and Lesbos can each claim its own distinct pleasures—classical ruins on Samos, fascinating medieval villages on Chios, and hot springs and splendid beaches on Lesbos. On all three islands, however, you can still easily wander away from popular coastal towns into untrammeled hinterlands for unspoiled natural beauty.

> PREVIOUS PAGE Elaborately stenciled houses in Pyrgi. THIS PAGE Dazzling mosaics cover the interior of Nea Moni.

❶ **Hiking through forests filled with birdsong, Samos.** Set your sights on the hills above Kokkari, where forests carpet mountain slopes, and deep valleys and streams dart through copses of cypress and pine. Take a break now and then to enjoy a glass of the local wine in the mountain villages. See p. 459, ❸.

❷ **Gazing up at the largest free-standing statue to come down to us from ancient Greece, Samos.** The prize of the Archaeological Museum in Vathy, a *kouros*—a marble statue of a naked youth—towers more than 5m (16 ft.) high. See p. 458, ❶.

❸ **Stepping into the darkness of the Efpalinio Orygma (Tunnel), Samos.** It's eerily fascinating to experience the legacy of Polycrates, a 6th-century B.C. tyrant with a penchant for murder and pillaging, an ear for lyric poetry, and an eye for fluted columns. You can also feel the fate of the thousands of slaves who chipped away with hammers and chisels for a decade or more to bore 1,035m (3,396 ft.) through Mount Kastro. See p. 462, ❺.

❹ **Walking down a lane hemmed in by golden stone in Kambos, Chios.** One of the pleasures of exploring this coastal plain—a patchwork of orange and lemon groves and ornate, Turko-Greco-style estates—is to be a voyeur: A look

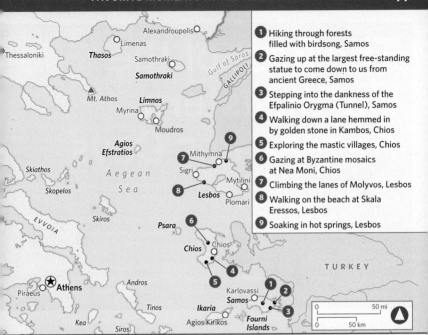

1 Hiking through forests filled with birdsong, Samos

2 Gazing up at the largest free-standing statue to come down to us from ancient Greece, Samos

3 Stepping into the dankness of the Efpalinio Orygma (Tunnel), Samos

4 Walking down a lane hemmed in by golden stone in Kambos, Chios

5 Exploring the mastic villages, Chios

6 Gazing at Byzantine mosaics at Nea Moni, Chios

7 Climbing the lanes of Molyvos, Lesbos

8 Walking on the beach at Skala Eressos, Lesbos

9 Soaking in hot springs, Lesbos

through wrought-iron gates reveals jasmine-scented gardens, pebbled courtyards, and arched verandas that have been the domains of Genoese aristocrats, Turkish pashas, and shipping magnates. See p. 469, 3.

5 **Exploring the mastic villages, Chios.** With their solid rows of houses forming fortress-like walls, arcaded streets, and elaborately patterned exteriors, the 20 or so *mastihari* are some of the most beautiful medieval villages in Greece. They are surrounded by the island's most welcoming landscapes, where olive groves and mastic orchards rise and fall across gently rolling hills. See p. 469, 4.

6 **Gazing at Byzantine mosaics at Nea Moni, Chios.** The naves, the dome, and eight supporting niches of the octagonal *katholikon* are decorated with dazzling Byzantine mosaics depicting saints and sinners—the latter being devoured by fish. Ongoing preservation efforts are restoring these long-neglected treasures to their onetime glory. See p. 469, 5.

7 **Climbing the lanes of Molyvos, Lesbos.** The narrow streets and alleys that wind up the hillside from Molyvos's pebbly beach emerge into shady squares cooled by fountains and come

to a Genoese castle. For a whiff of exotica, step into a mural-bedecked Ottoman mansion; then retrace your steps down the hillside to enjoy a coffee on the animated quay. See p. 478, 6.

8 **Walking on the beach at Skala Eressos, Lesbos.** The golden sands stretch for 3km (2 miles)—leaving plenty of room for a swim and a long trek. Think of yourself as following in the sandy footprints of Ancient Erossos natives Sappho, who may have composed her poetry while feeling these sands beneath her feet, and Theophrastus, a student of Plato, who may have lain on the beach while musing on botany, metaphysics, and ethics. See p. 479, 8.

9 **Soaking in hot springs, Lesbos.** You can take your pick of venues, from a rustic bathhouse beside a steaming, bubbling stream at Polychnitou to the modern facilities at Paralia Thermis. Best of all is soaking in a pool at Eftalou then finding one of the hot spots where the springs empty into the sea. See p. 476, 4.

The Best of the Northeastern Aegean in 5 Days

You'll soon discover how much the three main islands of the Northeastern Aegean differ in appearance and in spirit. Samos is lush and verdant, Chios is craggy (just as Homer described it) and forested in fragrant pine and cedar, and Lesbos is carpeted in olive groves in parts and a barren moonscape in others. All three islands go about their affairs independently of one another, despite their relative proximity. Even getting from one to another can be tricky, but it's worth mastering the logistics for a glimpse into three distinctive ways of Greek island life.

> Kokkari is one of many attractive seaside towns on Samos.

START Samos. **TRIP LENGTH** Sailing from Samos to Chios to Lesbos you'll cover about 110km (68 miles).

❶ Samos. On verdant Samos, you will come upon ancient ruins, polished resort life, and rugged, unspoiled scenery. Your first encounter with the ancient past, when Samos was the

wealthiest island in the Aegean, will be in the **Archaeology Museum** in Vathy (also known as Samos Town), the busy capital and port. You will find yourself staring up at the largest free-standing statue to come down to us from ancient Greece—a towering *kouros*, 5m (16 ft.) tall. This marble image of a young man once stood alongside the Holy Road that led from the city of Ancient Samos to the monumental **Heraion** (p. 463, ❻), the largest temple in the Greek world, devoted to the goddess Hera, wife of Zeus.

You will probably not find much else to keep you in Vathy, so follow the north coast west just 10km (6¼ miles) and settle in for the night in **Kokkari** (p. 459, ❷), one of the island's most attractive seaside towns. Kokkari is no longer the quiet fishing port it once was, but pretty beaches rim nearby coves, and forested, village-laced mountains rise just beyond the coast. After a swim, follow the road inland through orchards and fields into the cool, shady forests of the **Platanakia** region, where unspoiled villages are tucked into the hillsides (p. 459, ❸).

If you take an evening boat for Chios on Day 2, you will have almost a full day to see the rest of Samos, including the ancient sites you merely glimpsed in the Archaeological Museum on Day 1. The coast is especially scenic around **Potami,** about 25km (15 miles) west of Kokkari, where you can walk along a stream from the sand and pebble beach to the Potami **waterfall** (p. 460, ❹) or follow a seaside path to the pine-backed sands of **Megalo Seitani** (p. 460, ❹). From there, drop some 30km (18 miles) across the island to Pythagorio, built atop the city of **Ancient Samos** (p. 450, ❶). From 538 to 522 B.C., the tyrant Polycrates constructed some of the great wonders of the ancient world in and around the town. You can see all of them in various states of ruin: a 6km (3¾-mile) circuit of massive walls, a 370m (1,214-ft.) jetty and sea wall, and, to ensure

Getting There & Around

If you're traveling by boat, plan a morning arrival from Piraeus in Vathy at 4am or, preferably, 7am. To make the most of your short time on the island, rent a car when you get off the boat. You can also fly to Samos from Athens and other airports around Greece.

> A kouros *in the Archaeological Museum on Samos.*

a steady supply of fresh water, a 1,036m (3,399-ft.) tunnel dug by thousands of slaves. Polycrates commissioned the **Heraion** (p. 463, **6**), just outside Ancient Samos. ⏱ **2 days.**

On the evening of Day 2, take a boat from Samos to Chios (3–4 hr.). Rent a car when you disembark, or take a taxi to your hotel and rent a car the next morning.

2 Chios. After an evening arrival from Samos, settle into **Kambos** (p. 469, **3**) for two nights. In this seaside retreat just south of Chios Town, jasmine-scented lanes are lined with aristocratic mansions, some of which now accommodate guests. Spend Day 3 exploring the island, beginning with a 30km (19-mile) drive south to tour some of the most beautiful medieval villages in Greece—the so-called *mastihari* (mastic villages), named for the resin of the mastic tree that once brought the island great wealth (p. 469, **4**). Spend the morning wandering down the narrow lanes of Pyrgi, Mesta, and any of the other villages that appeal to you; the circuit should end on the black pebble beaches at **Mavra Volia** and **Foki.**

Head north again for a stop in **Chios Town** (p. 466, **1**). Most of what you will want to see is on and around **Vounakiou,** the main *plateia:* the shops and stalls of the bazaar; the Byzantine museum in the Medjitie Djami Mosque; 12th-century frescoes in the Giustiniani mansion and the atmospheric lanes of the old Genoese *kastro* that surround it; and, finally, the Maritime Museum and the Argenti Museum, filled with artifacts from across the island. In late afternoon, continue north about 15km (9⅓ miles) to **Nea Moni,** a Byzantine-era monastery that houses a miraculous icon amid a sea of dazzling mosaics (p. 469, **5**). ⏱ **1 day.**

Take a morning boat from Chios to Lesbos (3 ½ hr.); depending on the time of year, this can mean departing before 4am, though on some days you can find a boat at a more reasonable hour. You can also fly from Chios to Lesbos on one of several weekly flights (see p. 445 for more about travel between the islands). Rent a car when you get off the boat to make the most of your short time on the island.

3 Lesbos. If you take a morning boat from Chios, you'll arrive on the island early in the afternoon of Day 4, allowing time to drive the north coast of the island as far as **Molyvos** (p. 478, **6**), about 60km (36 miles) west of the port at Mytilini. Beautiful Molyvos, on a hillside above the sea (still also known on the island by its old name, Mythimna), is a convenient place to stay while exploring the island. On the way, stop at **Mandamadhos** (p. 477, **5**), famous for its Church of the Taxiarchis (Archangel Michael) and a miraculous icon of the archangel, the island's patron saint.

Once you've settled into Molyvos, wander down to the harbor along narrow lanes overhung with balconies weighted down with geraniums and occasionally opening onto shady

Tips on Accommodations

Masticulture (☎ 22710/76084; www. masticulture.com) specializes in Chios, arranging accommodation in traditional houses and locally run hotels. For accommodations on Lesbos, contact **Petra Tours** (☎ 22530/41390); on Samos, contact **Samina Tours** (☎ 22730/87000).

squares. In the late afternoon, make the 30km (18-mile) drive southwest to **Skala Eressos** (p. 479, ⑧), home of the ancient poet Sappho. The 3km (2-mile) expanse of brown sand is one of Greece's finest beaches and a good spot from which to watch the sun set.

Begin Day 5 with a drive from Molyvos to **Petra,** just 5km (3 miles) south, for a swim off the long, sandy beach (p. 479, ⑦). Then retrace your steps to **Mytilini** (p. 474, ①). Take a walk up Ermou, a boisterous market street filled with stalls, little shops, and a bazaar, and step into the Archaeological Museum, where several rooms of a Roman villa have been reconstructed to show off beautiful mosaics. In outlying **Varia,** a leafy suburb 4km (2½ miles) southeast, the home of native painter Theophilos Hatzimihail is now filled with his colorful paintings of island scenes and other subjects. A bit of a surprise awaits you at the nearby **Theriade Museum**—drawings, lithographs, and paintings by Matisse, Picasso, Giacometti, and many others collected by

Northeastern Aegean Island Hopping

Unlike the Dodecanese and Cyclades, with their frequent connections between islands, the Northeastern Aegean Islands are not terrifically well linked: The islands tend to go about their business independently of one another, so residents don't find many reasons to travel from one to another. Travelers who want to visit the three major islands—Samos, Chios, and Lesbos—in one fell swoop may be frustrated by the lack of frequent connections. Visiting the trio requires some planning if you have limited time and need to move efficiently from one island to the next. For some advance strategizing, check out the excellent ferry schedules on the **Greek Travel Pages** website (www.gtp.gr), run by a private firm that services the Greek travel industry. Once you hit the ground in Greece, check schedules with offices of the **Greek National Tourist Organization** (GNTO; see p. 668). Also check with travel agencies as soon as you arrive on an island to make sure you can move on to the next one as planned. **Note:** Schedules change frequently.

> In Mytilini, on Lesbos, you'll experience the liveliness of a workaday Greek town.

Stratis Eleftheriades, a native of Lesbos who became a prominent publisher of Parisian art journals.

Drive 30km (19 miles) south to **Agiassos,** a mountain town surrounded by orchards and vineyards (p. 476, ③). Thousands of pilgrims from all over Greece follow the cobblestone streets to the church of the Panagia Vrefokratousa (Madonna Holding the Infant) to pay homage to an icon of the virgin supposedly painted by St. Luke the Evangelist. End Day 5 with a swim off the long, sandy beach at nearby **Vatera** (p. 476, ④) and a soothing soak at **Polychnitou,** a valley where hot springs bubble from the richly colored earth (p. 476, ④). ⏱1½ day.

The Northeastern Aegean in 7 Days

You'll pack a lot of sights and experiences into a week.
These include ruins such as the remains of the Heraion, the largest temple built in the ancient Greek world; medieval towns and villages, most remarkably the fortified *mastihari* (mastic villages) of Chios; and beaches, including the one at Skala Eressos on Lesbos, which comes with quite a provenance: The poet Sappho ran her academy for young women on a nearby hillside. Your travels will be enriched with wine, olive oil, ouzo, *mastika* (a potent liqueur made from mastic), and the *filoxenia* (hospitality) for which the islands are noted.

> Samos's Archaeological Museum houses statues from the Heraion, ancient Greece's largest temple.

START Samos. **TRIP LENGTH** 110km (66 miles) sailing from Samos to Chios to Lesbos.

❶ **Samos.** Spend Day 1 on the north coast, settling into Kokkari, 10km (6¼ miles) west of Vathy, and relaxing on one of the beaches that line a string of surrounding coves (p. 459, ❷). On Day 2, get a sense of the island's rural pleasures on a circuit of the mountain villages (p. 459, ❸) above Kokkari; then head about 25km (15 miles) west of Kokkari to hike into the idyllically remote beaches at **Mikro Seitani** and **Megalo Seitani** (p. 460, ❹). Day 3 takes you back to civilization—ancient civilization, that is. You'll step back 2,500 years to see the monuments left behind by the tyrant Polycrates in and around **Pythagorio**—the

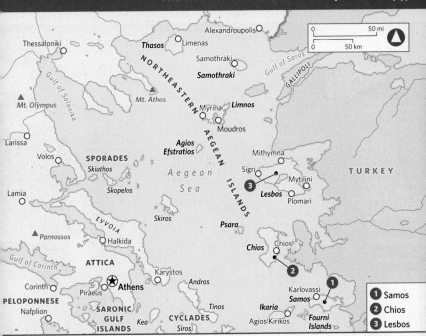

current name for Ancient Samos (p. 450, ❶), 4km (8⅔ miles) southwest of Vathy. These include a jetty visible beneath the clear waters of the harbor, a circuit of massive walls, a remarkable tunnel, and the Heraion, the largest temple in the ancient Greek world. The final stop is the **Archaeological Museum** in Vathy (p. 458, ❶), where you can stare up at a towering *kouros*, a statue of a male youth, one of many that once lined the Holy Road that led from Ancient Samos to the Heraion. ⏱ 2 days.

On the evening of Day 2, take a boat from Samos to Chios (3–4 hr.). Rent a car when you get off the boat, or take a taxi to your hotel and rent a car the next morning.

❷ **Chios.** After an evening arrival from Samos, settle into your hotel; **Kambos** (p. 469, ❸), just south of Chios Town, is an especially appealing and convenient place to stay. Spend the morning of Day 3 exploring this seaside enclave, where sun-dappled lanes are lined with exotic mansions owned by the island's wealthy families (many of whom made their fortunes in shipping) as well as the foreign aristocrats who once ruled the island. Then head 30km (19 miles) south to explore the *mastihari*, the villages that once made their

fortunes harvesting mastic (p. 469, ❹). Pyrgi, Mesta, and some 20 other villages are fortresslike, with arcaded lanes and defensive towers. In Pyrgi, houses are ornately decorated with etched designs. After making a circuit of the villages, swim on one of the exotic black pebble beaches at Mavra Volia and Foki.

Begin Day 4 in **Chios Town** (p. 466, ❶). Try to arrive midmorning, when the shops and stalls around the Vounakiou, the main *plateia*, are bustling with shoppers. Explore the courtyard of the Medjitie Djami Mosque; then wander through the Portara Maggiora into the seaside Kastro, just north of the square, and step into the Giustiniani mansion to see 12th-century frescoes from an island church. Two other old mansions south of the *plateia* are filled with mementos of old Chios: the Maritime Museum and the Argenti Museum.

Getting There & Around

If you're traveling by boat, you can plan a morning arrival from Piraeus in Vathy. To make the most of your time, rent a car when you get off the boat. You can also fly to Samos from Athens and other airports around Greece.

> *Skulls at Nea Moni on Chios are grim remnants of a Turkish massacre in 1822.*

After lunch, continue north. First stop is **Vrontados** (p. 468, ❷), a seaside suburb of Chios Town where Homer lived and taught from the so-called Daskalopetra (Teacher's Rock), according to some accounts. The next stop is **Nea Moni** (p. 469, ❺), an 11th-century monastery in the forested mountains 16km (10 miles) north of Chios Town that is slowly being restored to reveal some of the world's finest examples of Byzantine mosaics. The landscape becomes starker and craggier north of the monastery. **Anavatos,** 10km (6¼ miles) north of Nea Moni, is an eerie but remarkable place—an all but deserted village that teeters atop a 300m (984-ft.) bluff (p. 470, ❻). **Volissos** (p. 470, ❻), another 10km (6¼ miles) along a road that skirts the isolated northwest coast, climbs an arid hillside beneath a Byzantine fort—a world removed from busy Chios Town and sophisticated Kambos. ⏲ 2 days.

Plan to take a morning boat from Chios to Lesbos (3½ hr.) on Day 5. You can also fly from Chios to Lesbos on one of several weekly flights. Rent a car when you get off the boat.

❸ **Lesbos.** After a midday arrival from Chios, make the 60km (37-mile) drive west from the port at Mytilini to Molyvos. This picturesque town meanders up a hillside to a Genoese castle and is within driving distance of most places on the island (p. 478, ❻). After settling in, spend the rest of Day 5 wandering the narrow lanes and shady squares and step into the early-19th-century **Komninaki Kralli** mansion, home of a wealthy Ottoman merchant, to see the delightful murals depicting dancers and the urbane and spiritual wonders of Constantinople.

Spend Day 6 exploring the western end of the island. First stop is Petra, just 5km (3 miles) south, where a long stretch of sandy beach is backed by a massive rock monolith; atop the 114 rough-hewn steps is the **Glykfylousa Panagia** (Our Lady of the Sweet Kiss), built in the 17th century to house an icon of the Virgin Mary (p. 479, **7**). **Skala Eressos,** 30km (19 miles) southwest, is backed by a beautiful, fertile coastal plain and skirts one of the finest beaches in Greece (p. 479, **8**). The town is also popular, especially with women, for its associations with the poet Sappho, who lived here from 615 to 562 B.C. The road comes to the southwestern tip of the island at **Sigri,** 10km (6¼ miles) west. The landscape is so arid it will come as little surprise when you stumble upon the **Petrified Forest**—a collection of fallen and standing tree stumps turned to stone over the past 20 million years (p. 479, **9**).

Day 7 takes you first to **Mandamadhos,** a little town atop an inland plateau where the Church of the Taxiarchis (Archangel Michael) houses a miraculous icon of the archangel, patron saint of the island (p. 477, **5**). From there, continue to **Mytilini** (p. 474, **1**) for a walk up the busy shopping street Ermou and a visit to the Archaeological Museum for a look at the Roman rooms from a Roman villa. Outlying **Varia** is home to an intriguing duet of museums: the Theophilos Museum shows off the work of Lesbos-born painter Theophilos Hatzimihail, whose primitive and colorful art captures scenes of island life, and the Theriade Museum, an unlikely showcase of drawings, lithographs, and paintings by Matisse, Picasso, Giacometti, and many others.

Now head to the south of the island, to **Agiassos,** a beautiful mountain village where the church of the Panagia Vrefokratousa (Madonna Holding the Infant) houses an icon of the Virgin (p. 476, **3**). End the day with a swim at **Vatera** (p. 476, **4**), where golden sands stretch for 7km (4⅓ miles). A final indulgence is a soak in the thermal pools at **Polychnitou** (p. 476, **4**). Or, for a little more luxury, at **Paralia Thermis, Loutra Yeras,** or one of the other hot springs around Mytilini (for more on thermal baths on Lesbos, see p. 477). ⊙ 2½ days.

> Sappho trod the sands at Skala Eressos more than 2,500 years ago.

More Ancient Wonders

You may want to add a day or three to the "Best of the Northeastern Aegean in 5 Days" or the "Best of the Northeastern Aegean in 7 Days" tours to include two ancient sites in Turkey. **Ephesus** and **Pergamon,** two of the greatest cities in the Greek and Roman worlds. Ephesus is just a short boat trip away from Samos (p. 463) and Pergamon is within tempting reach of Lesbos (p. 478). Back in Greece, you may also want to venture north to **Samothraki** to see the Sanctuary of the Great Gods, one of the most important and least visited of Greece's many ancient ruins. Philip II of Macedonia, the Spartan leader Lysander, and the historian Herodotus were among the many initiates sworn into a mystery cult in this beautiful sanctuary in the shadows of Mount Fengari (p. 453, **3**).

In the Footsteps of the Ancients

The Northeastern Aegean encompasses some of the most fascinating sites of antiquity. On Samos, you will discover a great temple to the goddess Hera and the ruins of a city that ruled the Aegean a full century before Athens entered its Golden Age. On Samothraki, you will climb through the Sanctuary of the Great Gods, where warriors, poets, ordinary citizens, and slaves were initiated into a mysterious cult.

> *Islanders rallied in 1824 to build a seaside castle at Pythagorio to repel a Turkish attack.*

START Samos. TRIP LENGTH Allow at least 3 days for travel and seeing the sights, more if you wish to hop over to Turkey to visit Ephesus and Pergamon. The distance from Samos to Samothraki is about 200km (124 miles).

❶ ★★★ **Pythagorio, Samos.** Just as Pericles built many of the wonders we associate with ancient Athens, the tyrant Polycrates left his mark on Ancient Samos, on a slightly smaller but nonetheless impressive scale. During the

1 Pythagorio, Samos
2 Heraion, Samos
3 Sanctuary of the Great Gods, Samothraki

12 years of his rule, from 538 to 522 B.C., the enlightened despot created one of the most famous and cultured cities in the ancient Aegean—a magnate for poets, artists, musicians, philosophers, and mathematicians. Polycrates also built some of ancient Greece's great engineering and architectural marvels. Although a few of them no longer survive, such as his elaborate palace, you can view traces of four masterworks in and around Pythagorio (as the city of Ancient Samos has come to be called): a massive jetty, a circuit of walls, a highly sophisticated water tunnel, and the Heraion, a temple in honor of the goddess Hera.

Polycrates controlled trade throughout the eastern Mediterranean, and Samos is only a short row away from the coast of Asia Minor and its once-powerful city states—realities that necessitated a circuit of **massive walls,** 6km (3¾ miles) long, which in large part still climb the slopes of Mount Castro to enclose the city and harbor. To protect the harbor

Travel Tip

You may want to cover this tour in stages, seeing the archaeological sites on Samos, then picking up the tour again after visiting Chios and Lesbos, continuing to Samothraki from Lesbos.

where he anchored his 40 *triremes* (warships) and the various craft with which he and his marauders plundered islands across the eastern Aegean, Polycrates commissioned the engineer Eupalinos to build a massive **jetty and seawall,** 370m (1,214 ft.) in length. Much of the stone structure is still visible just beneath the waves and creates a pattern that, when viewed from the hillsides above, is shaped like a *tigani* (frying pan)—the Samians' nickname for the town. Pythagorio himself, in fact, was known as Tigani until the 1960s.

Polycrates then commissioned Eupalinos to provide the city with a steady supply of fresh water from springs in a fertile valley behind Mount Castro. One solution was an aqueduct, but that could have been blocked off or contaminated in a siege. A far more secure method was to build a tunnel beneath the mountain. Without the aid of compasses, surveying equipment, or sophisticated mathematics, Eupalinos designed a channel 1,036m (3,399 ft.) long. Hundreds of slaves worked

Ephesus & Pergamon

Two of the greatest cities in the Greek and Roman worlds, Ephesus and Pergamon are not in Greece but on the Turkish mainland. Any traveler keen on seeing remnants of ancient Greece should venture out of the way to include these two magnificent landmarks on the classical itinerary. You can reach both easily on day trips from Samos and Lesbos: Ephesus is just a short boat trip away from Samos (p. 463), and Pergamon is within tempting reach of Lesbos (p. 478).

from each end, using picks and chisels to dig along a remarkably level line, until they met in the middle after an estimated 10 to 15 years. The engineering is ingenious. An underground, 850m-long (2,805-ft.) conduit carried water from the spring to the tunnel entrance on the north side of the mountain. A walkway through the tunnel is 2m (6½ ft.) high, allowing workers access to clear debris and make repairs. Water flows through a neatly cut channel to one side of this passageway. At the southern exit, the water again entered an underground channel that carried it into the ancient city.

The tunnel supplied water for more than a thousand years. Long after that, it provided a safe refuge during attacks on the city. Archaeologists rediscovered the tunnel in 1882, clued in to its existence by the Greek historian Herodotus, who lived on Samos in the 5th century B.C. and wrote about a passage "dug through a mountain . . . through which water is conducted and comes by pipes to the city, brought from an abundant spring." Today's visitors clamber down a steep staircase into a narrow passageway that emerges into a 300m-long (990-ft.) segment of the tunnel. The experience could induce claustrophobia in even a veteran spelunker, and seeing the straight lines of the shaft and the ancient chisel marks in the stone walls is likely to bring chills to the spine of even the most blasé observer. ⏱ Half-day to see the town and tunnel.

The Heraion is 5km (3 miles) southwest of Pythagorio, just beyond the airport off the road to Myli.

❷ ★★ Heraion, Samos. Polycrates also turned his attentions to a temple honoring the goddess Hera, wife of Zeus. A temple stood near the swampy banks of the Imbrasos River, 6km (3¾ miles) southwest of Pythagorio, as early as the 9th century B.C. Hera was allegedly born alongside the river, and she consummated her relationship with Zeus on the banks. By the 6th century B.C., the architects Roikos and Theodoros had built a much larger temple on the site, in which an altar to the goddess was surrounded by a sea of 168 columns. An earthquake leveled the temple soon after it was completed; in turn, Polycrates, not to be outdone, created the largest temple ever

> *Statuary lines the road that linked Ancient Samos to the Heraion, a temple devoted to Hera.*

built in Greece. Polycrates met his end at the hands of the Persians before the massive temple was complete, but even by the time of his death it was four times larger than the Parthenon.

Sailing to Samothraki

Getting to Samothraki can be difficult. One way is to cross from Samos, Chios, or Lesbos to Turkey, where you can catch a bus that runs up the coast to Alexandroupoli, where connections to Samothraki are regular and reliable (allow at least a day for the trip). Far easier is to take a boat from Samos, Chios, or Lesbos (the trip from Lesbos to Samothraki takes 5 hours), but these ferries are not always in service. Tour operators on any of the islands can help arrange your journey.

A roadway called the **Iera Odos** (Holy Road) linked the temple to Ancient Samos. Some of the thousands of statues that once lined the stone avenue, including a huge *kouros,* are in the **Archaeological Museum** in Vathy, a mandatory stop before leaving the island (p. 458, **1**). The temple was quarried for marble over the centuries, and today only one column remains standing, a lone emblem of former might. For details on visiting the archaeological sites in and around Pythagorio, see p. 450, **1**. ⏱ 1 hr.

3 ★★★ **Sanctuary of the Great Gods, Samothraki.** One of the most magical, and least visited, of Greece's many ancient ruins lies in a wooded valley in the shadows of Mount Fengari on the island of Samothraki. The craggy island, rising imperiously from the sea, is a dramatic

SITE GUIDE PAGE 455

> *Ancient followers of a Mystery religion worshipped in the Sanctuary of the Great Gods on Samothraki.*

setting for such a sacred place. Little wonder that Poseidon is said to have watched the goings-on of the Trojan War from the island's rugged mountaintops.

From 1000 B.C. to the 4th century A.D., the sanctuary was the ceremonial center of a cult that practiced a Mystery religion that remains inscrutable to this day: Initiates, who included Philip II of Macedonia, the Spartan leader Ly-sander, and the historian Herodotus, swore on penalty of death not to speak of the rituals that transpired in the sanctuary. What is known is that initiation was a two-stage process: The first stage invoked a spiritual rebirth with re-enactments of the birth, death, and rebirth cycle and a feast; the second absolved the initiate of transgressions with a confession and baptism in bull's blood. Anyone, including women, slaves, and non-Greeks, could be initiated, though only a few initiates moved on to the second stage—probably because these candidates were forced to meet strict moral criteria.

The central deity was the Great Mother, the mistress of the natural world, whose male subordinates were Kadmilos, the virile god of the phallus, and the Kabeiroi, twin demons on whose good graces mariners relied, since they could brew up a storm on whim. As colonists arrived from other parts of Greece, the deities were merged with the Olympian pantheon. The Great Mother was melded into Demeter, Aphrodite, and Hecate; Kadmilos was inte-grated with Hermes; and the Kabeiroi became Kastor and Pollux.

The most spectacular remnant of the Sanctuary is the *Winged Victory of Samothrace*, a marble statue of the goddess Nike that Poliorcetes, king of Macedonia, presented to the Kabeiroi in the late 4th century B.C. in thanks for their help in defeating the armies of Egyptian King Ptolemy II. The sensual marble statue, of course, is not here but in the Louvre in Paris, so you will have to settle for a cast in the Archaeological Museum. Even so, what re-mains at Samothraki, spread over three large terraces bounded by streams and ravines, is impressive and intriguing. ☉ 4 hr. ☎ 25510/41474. www.culture.gr. Admission 3€. Apr-Oct daily 8am-7pm, Nov-Mar 8:30am-3pm.

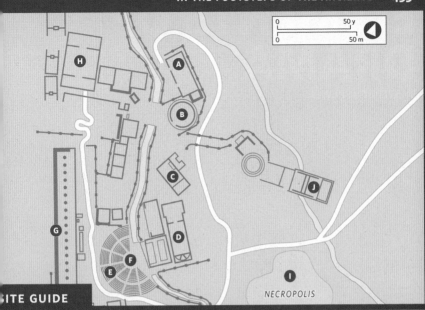

SITE GUIDE

❸ Sanctuary of the Great Gods

Candidates for initiation were dressed in white gowns and given a lamp in the sacristy of the **Ⓐ Anaktoron** (literally, House of the Lords). They then proceeded into the main hall for a ceremony that entailed a ritual cleansing, a libation to the gods, and dancing. Later they entered the priestly quarters for a lecture on the meaning of the initiation. The **Ⓑ Arsinoeion** was the largest circular building in ancient Greece, a gift from Egyptian Queen Arsinoe. It was used as a welcoming hall for ambassadors sent from city-states to attend ceremonies. A rock altar may have at one time been used for sacrifices. The **Ⓒ Temenos,** the largest building on the site, was an open-air banquet hall where post-initiation feasts were held. The most impressive ruins are those of the **Ⓓ Hieron,** the temple where candidates underwent their second initiation, accompanied by ritual cleansing and sacrifice; five columns have been re-erected, and stone benches for spectators and the sacred stones where initiates gave their confessions are still in place. The many votive offerings found near here include elaborate vases and statues, as well as fishhooks and seashells presented by fishermen and mariners for protection at sea.

Just beyond the scant remains of the **Ⓔ theater** is the **Ⓕ Nymphaeum of Nike,** where the *Winged Victory* stood until removed by French archaeologists in 1863. The long **Ⓖ Stoa** was an open-air portico where initiates stayed, and many inscribed their names on the walls. The **Ⓗ Ruinenviereck,** a medieval fortress, rises at the south end of the Stoa. A **Ⓘ necropolis** on the east side of the site was used for more than a thousand years, until the end of the Roman era; many of the interred wear iron rings, as naturally occurring iron was a sign of the power of the Great Mother. The **Ⓙ Propylon,** north of the necropolis, was an elaborate entrance portico that bridged a stream. It was a gift from King Ptolemy II of Egypt.

ELEMENTS OF DRAMA

BY STEPHEN BREWER

WHETHER WE'RE WATCHING a Shakespearean drama or *30 Rock,* weeping over a three-hanky melodrama or rooting for an action hero, we owe a lot to the Ancient Greeks. For them, the inventors of drama and comedy, theater provided a way to give vent to their ever-present fears of enemy armies and the wrath of the gods, to laugh uproariously at human and divine foibles, to feel the satisfaction of a happy ending, and to cry and tremble as they witnessed murder, incest, and other manifestations of the darker side of the human psyche. While production methods and special effects have become unfathomably more complex, the cornerstones of the dramatic arts haven't changed much since they were laid down, along with the stone slabs of the first theaters, during the Golden Age of Greece.

Enduring Classics

Passion, love, vengeance, incest, heroic deeds—the twists and turns of the great Greek dramas still grab our attention.

SOPHOCLES'S *ANTIGONE* (442 B.C.), *Oedipus the King* (429 B.C.), and *Oedipus at Colonus* (406 B.C.) dramatize the mythological tale of Oedipus, who kills his father and marries his mother.

IN *MEDEA* (431 B.C.), Euripides unleashes his wrathful title character on her unfaithful husband, Jason, his fiancée, and even her own children.

THE ORESTEIA TRILOGY (458 B.C.), by Aeschylus, recounts adultery, matricide, and other dastardly deeds that confront King Agamemnon of Argos when he returns from the Trojan War.

THE CLOUDS (423 B.C.), a spoof on Socrates and other intellectuals of the day, is one of the most enduring works of Aristophanes.

Modern Revivals

▶ Aeschylus might be flipping in his tumulus, but his *Persians* provides some good background material for the film *300* (2007).

▶ French actress Isabelle Huppert has famously portrayed Euripides's vengeful Medea on stage and in the film *Medea Miracle* (2007), set in modern-day Paris.

▶ Euripides's *Trojan Women* hit the silver screen in 1971, starring Katharine Hepburn (Hecuba), Vanessa Redgrave (Andromache), and Irene Papas (Helen). *Troy* (2004), with Brad Pitt and Orlando Bloom, puts another spin on the same event.

▶ Greek-American diva Maria Callas (at left) portrayed the genocidal Medea in 1961.

▶ In *Morning Becomes Electra* (1931), Eugene O'Neill's stage version of Aeschylus's *Oresteia* trilogy, the Trojan War hero Agamemnon becomes Civil War General Ezra Mannon, and townsfolk of a small New England seaport stand in for the chorus.

The Building Blocks

CA. 800 B.C.
Homeric **epics,** oral narrations of the Trojan War, are a popular form of entertainment and the origins of drama.

CA. 600 B.C.
A **chorus** sings narratives at the Dionysia festival in Athens, honoring the god Dionysus.

CA. 550 B.C.
The poet Thespis adds a single **actor,** who assumes different characters by changing masks; plays are **tragedies,** based on the woes of mythological heroes and gods.

CA. 500 B.C.
Satyr plays, burlesque versions of mythological tales, full of pranks, gags, and overt sexual overtones, are first performed.

499 B.C.
Stone slabs are set into a slope of the Acropolis to create the **Theater of Dionysos,** the first permanent theater (enlarged in 325 B.C.).

486 B.C.
Comedy, in which ordinary people are blessed with good fortune, is introduced.

472 B.C.
Aeschylus produces the world's **oldest surviving play,** *The Persians*—a report on the Athenian victory over Xerxes at the Battle of Salamis.

471 B.C.
Aeschylus introduces a second actor, creating **dialogue.**

468 B.C.
Sophocles introduces a third actor, creating **complex interactions.**

465 B.C.
A *skene* (backdrop) is added to productions; *skene* is the origin of the word scene.

335 B.C.
Aristotle defines the six **Elements of Drama,** still fundamental to theater today: plot, theme, character, dialogue, music, and spectacle.

Samos

Excellent beaches are among Samos' many assets, and these have not gone unnoticed. Much of the coastline becomes a holiday haven in the summer, but it's easy to retreat to verdant, vineyard-clad hillsides, quiet mountain villages, and the rugged, cove-lined northwest coast. Polycrates, the 6th-century B.C. tyrant of Samos, left temples and other remarkable engineering feats behind at Pythagorio. Ephesus, one of the greatest cities of classical Greece, is temptingly close, just across the narrow straits that separate Samos from Turkey.

> *Tsabou and other beautiful beaches line the coast west of Kokkari.*

START Vathy, where your boat from Piraeus or other islands will likely arrive; you'll probably want to pass through town and settle into Kokkari, Pythagorio, or another resort. **TRIP LENGTH** Allow at least 2 full days to see the island.

❶ ★★ Archaeological Museum, Vathy. Just beyond Vathy's waterside municipal gardens is one of Greece's largest archaeological collections.

Samos was a major power in the Aegean as early as the 7th century B.C. Early Samarians traded with Egypt and cities on the Black Sea, dug elaborate tunnels and built magnificent sanctuaries to the gods, and cultivated the wines for which Samos is still noted. You will encounter much of this past as you tour the island (see the "In the Footsteps of the Ancients" tour, p. 450), and many of the most treasured finds are here in Vathy. From the Heraion, a sanctuary devoted to the goddess Hera, wife of Zeus (p. 463, ❻), comes one of six monumental *kouroi*, statues of naked youths that flanked the roadway leading to an enormous temple. Towering

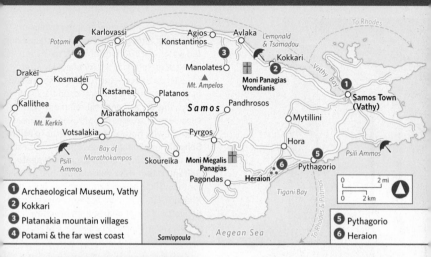

1 Archaeological Museum, Vathy
2 Kokkari
3 Platanakia mountain villages
4 Potami & the far west coast
5 Pythagorio
6 Heraion

> *The fortified Monastery of Moni Vronta.*

more than 5m (16 ft.), the gray-and-white marble *kouros* is the largest free-standing statue from ancient Greece to survive intact.

Other statuary from the Heraion includes the **Genolos Group,** named for the sculptor who inscribed his name on the bases of his pieces. The marbles depict a family—a reclining patriarch, his seated wife, a boy playing the pipes, and three girls poised to sing. The family seems

to be showing its devotion and eagerness to pay tribute to the goddess, but the marbles may also be a bit of ostentation—ancient one-upmanship flaunting the wealth required to commission such an elaborate offering. ⏱ 1 hr.

Kokkari is 10km (6¼ miles) west of Vathy on the north coast road.

2 ★★ **Kokkari.** One of the island's most attractive seaside towns stretches along a sandy beach between two headlands known as the Didymi, the twins. As popular as Kokkari is these days, the rocky summits seem to close the village neatly off from the modern world. You'll get a few glimpses of what life here was like until fairly recently, when the quay was piled high with fishing nets rather than cafe tables. A small fleet still sets out from the docks, and fields of *kokkari,* the small onions from which the village takes its name, stretch toward the alluring, forested hills above the coast. Just to the west of Kokkari, the tree-lined coast road passes a string of coves fringed with pebbly beaches at Lemonakia, Tsamadou, Aviakia, and, the prettiest of them all, Tsabou. ⏱ 2 hr.

3 ★★★ **Platanakia mountain villages.** From Aviakia, about 3km (2 miles) west of Kokkari, a road heads south through orchards and cool, shady forests that carpet the foothills of the Platanakia region. The terrain here is some of the most scenic on Samos, and the villages are the most beautiful. Exploring the Platanakia

SITE GUIDE PAGE 461

> *The seaside village of Kokkari.*

climbing dozens of steep, slippery steps or swimming through bone-chillingly cold spring fed waters for 100m (328 ft.) or so.

West of Potami is the most scenic stretch of coast on Samos—the roadless, isolated domain of clambering goats and, on the offshore rocks, the shy and endangered monk seal. A seaside path crosses olive groves and hillsides fragrant with the scent of wild herbs to **Mikro Seitani,** a rockbound cove with a small beach, and then the pine-backed sands of **Megalo Seitani** farther west. Allow about half an hour for the walk to Mikro Seitani and an hour to Megalo Seitani, and bring plenty of water; a bathing suit is optional at both beaches.
🕐 **Half-day with hikes to waterfall and beaches.**

requires a car, a little backtracking, and, if you wish, a few hikes through mountain valleys along streams that dart through copses of cypress and pine. 🕐 **Half-day.**

Karlovassi is about 25km (15 miles) west of Kokkari on the north coast road.

4 ★★★ Potami & the far west coast. You'll probably want to pass right through Karlovassi—an old-fashioned workaday town and the island's second port—and set your sights instead on the sand and pebble beach **Potami,** 2km (1¼ mile) farther west. Another place to cool off is the Potami waterfall, in a shady river gorge about a 20-minute hike inland from the beach. The path skirts the 11th-century **Church of Metamorphosis,** with some faded frescoes, then reaches a string of little pools. You can reach the foot of the cascades by

Fruits of the Vine

Samos is famous for its wines, produced from grapes grown mostly in the north of the island on terraced hillsides. Many are sweet, amber-colored dessert wines yielded from the white muscat grape, though some dry whites and a rosé are also produced. Very few vineyards have tasting rooms, though you can sample a variety of the island's output at the otherwise underwhelming **Samos Wine Museum** in Malagari, a suburb of Vathy (off Yimnasiar-hou Kateveni; ☎ 22730/87511; admission 2€; Mon–Sat 8am–8pm). You'll enjoy a more atmosphere-packed introduction in the village tavernas on Mount Ampelos (p. 461, **3**), where farmers and their donkeys trek up and down the hillsides tending to their vineyards.

As you travel around the island, you'll likely be offered many glasses of Samos-made ouzo; this island's rendition of the milky and potent elixir of pressed grapes, berries, and herbs is said to be the most flavorful in Greece. *Souma,* firewater concocted from the stems of grapes gathered from the bottom of the crushing vats, is often drunk at the end of a meal, inducing sound sleep much more effectively than sheep-counting.

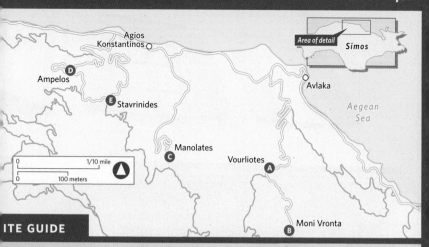

Agios
Konstantinos

Ampelos **D**

E Stavrinides

Manolates **C**

Vourliotes **A**

Area of detail   *Simos*

Avlaka

*Aegean
Sea*

0 ——— 1/10 mile
0 ——— 100 meters

B Moni Vronta

ITE GUIDE

3 Platanakia Mountain Villages

Vourliotes, about 3km (2 miles) above Aviakia, is a lovely little collection of tile-roofed houses with brightly colored shutters. The vineyards that surround the village yield some of the island's best wine, on offer in any of the tavernas on the *plateia*. **B Moni Vronta,** a fortified monastery, commands a hilltop high above Vourliotes. A decade ago, fires inflicted considerable damage on the 16th-century monastery, the oldest on Samos, and burned the double row of cypress that once shaded the approach. Repairs are slowly restoring the walls and the many nooks and crannies, among them a little cavelike chapel dug out of the outer walls of the compound. You can walk to the monastery from Vourliotes on a steep dirt track that zigzags up the slope, a climb of about 7km (4⅓ miles), or make the much shorter drive, about 2km (1¼ mile) on a steep road past terraced vineyards.

You can also make an uphill hike through a beautiful river canyon for about 5km (3 miles) to **C Manolates,** another delightful mountain village of steep cobblestone lanes. By car, you need to return to Aviakia, follow the coast west for about 2km (1¼ mile) to Platanakia, then head inland for another 5km (3 miles) up the slopes of Mount Ampelos to Manolates. Village houses are whitewashed and decorated with elaborate floral designs, and the surrounding hills and valleys attract many birds,

especially nightingales; one particularly lush and birdsong-filled glen has been designated the **Valley of the Nightingales.** Ambitious hikers can follow a path from Manolates up the summit of Mount Ampelos, the second-tallest peak on the island at 1,153m (3,783 ft.); allow at least half a day for the trek to the top and back. By car, you can visit two more pretty villages in the coastal foothills, **D Ampelos** and **E Stavrinides;** reaching them requires another return to the coast and a turn inland for about 2km (1¼ mile) from Agios Konstantinos. All these villages are watered by springs, said to be the sweetest in Greece, bubbling up in their *plateias* and the surrounding countryside.

> *Proud houses crowd the narrow lanes of the Old Quarter of Vathy (Samos Town).*

Pythagorio is about 25km (15 miles) southeast of Karlovassi on a well-marked road that crosses the island.

5 ★★★ **Pythagorio.** This very popular resort town is named for Pythagoras, the 6th-century-B.C. mathematician and philosopher who was born on Samos. Pythagorio is more accurately associated with the tyrannical Polycrates, whose capital, the ancient settlement of Samos, lies beneath the cobbled streets of Pythagorio. The fierce warrior grasped control of the island by killing one brother and exiling another, and he became enormously wealthy through his piratical attacks on islands throughout the Aegean. He was eventually crucified by the Persians, but not before funding a building spree that created some of the greatest wonders of the ancient world. Beneath the modern dock you can see the submerged traces of the 500m (1,640-ft.) jetty that Polycrates built to provide safe anchorage for his fleet of 40 *triremes* (warships), the first to be used in ancient Greece. To ensure water for the city in times of siege, he marshaled engineers and a vast force of slave labor to dig the **Efpalinio Orygma** (north of town; ☎ 22730/61400; admission 4€; Tues–Sun 8:45am–2:45pm), an aqueduct that bores 1,035m (3,396 ft.) through Mount Kastro. You can squeeze into the tunnel through a narrow channel, once used to drain overflow, and then walk along a 650m (2,133-ft.) section of the shaft (see also the "In the Footsteps of the Ancients" tour, p. 450, **1**).

The orange-tree-scented hillsides above the harbor are outlined here and there with portions of the 6km (3¾-mile) circuit of walls and gates that Polycrates erected to thwart the many enemies he made as far afield as Egypt and Sparta. The **Moni Panagias Spillanis** (Monastery of the Virgin of the Grotto) (free admission; 9am–6pm), tucked into a glade above the tunnel, takes its name from a cave behind the courtyard, where the Virgin is honored in a humble little shrine within a dank cave that in the time of Polycrates was the domain of oracles.

A Side Trip to Ephesus

Ephesus—one of the ancient Greeks' great cities—is not in Greece, but in Turkey. Yet Kusadasi, the port just outside Ephesus, is a short, 1½ hour hop away from Vathy on Samos. The Temple of Artemis at Ephesus was, like the Heraion in Samos, one of the Seven Wonders of the World; in fact, the Ephesian temple was modeled on the Samian one. The city's most famous monument is the **Library of Celsus,** completed in 135 A.D., when Ephesus was the second-largest city in the Roman Empire. You can easily visit Ephesus on a day trip from Samos, whether you travel on your own via one of the twice-daily ferries (35€ round-trip) or join one of the many organized Ephesus tours that operate out of Vathy and Pythagorio (about 100€, travel included). For a one-day visit, you won't need a visa, whether you travel on your own or with a group.

> *A lone column is all that remains of the Heraion, one of ancient Greece's greatest achievements.*

The stone walls of the **castle** that belonged to Lykourgos Logothetis, a local lord, rises above the red tile roofs of the Old Town. Islanders took up tools to help build the fortress in 1824 to defend themselves against the Turkish fleet. Under the leadership of Logothetis, Greek ships routed the Turks just offshore on August 6, 1824 (Transfiguration Day), and the victory is commemorated in the Church of the Transfiguration, which now shares the hilltop with the castle. In nearby Mytilini, fossilized remains of the *samotherium* (an extinct short-necked, three-toed giraffe) and other animals who roamed Samos millions of years before the arrival of humankind make up the fascinating collections of the **Museum of Natural History** (Mytilini village, 3km/2 miles northeast of Pythagorio; ☎ 22730/52055; admission 3€; Mon-Sat 9am-3pm, Sun 10am-3pm). ⏱ 5 hr. to see Pythagorio and museum in Mytilini.

The Heraion is 5km (3 miles) southwest of Pythagorio just beyond the airport off the road to Myli.

6 ★★ **Heraion.** Polycrates's greatest achievement was his temple honoring the goddess Hera, wife of Zeus, 6km (3¾ miles) southwest of Pythagorio. The massive complex—the largest temple ever built in Greece and one of the Seven Wonders of the Ancient World—was four times larger than the Parthenon and surrounded by 155 rows of columns. Only one column and very little else of the grandiose monuments remain standing, but the foundations alone convey the enormous scale of the temple and the sacred precinct that surrounded it. The Imbrasos stream flows through fields next to the site and meets the sea nearby; Hera was allegedly born on the swampy banks, and she had her trysts with Zeus alongside the slow-moving waters (see also the "In the Footsteps of the Ancients" tour, p. 452, **2**). ⏱ 1 hr. Near coastal village of Potokaki. ☎ 22730/95277.www.culture.gr. Admission 3€. June-Sept Tues-Sun 8am-7:30pm, Oct-May Tues-Sun 8:30am-3pm.

Where to Stay on Samos

> *The pool and beach at Doryssa.*

and soothingly contemporary. There's even a **Museum of Folk Art,** showing what life on the island was like before places like this arrived on the scene. ☎ 22730/88300. www.doryssa. gr. 307 units. Doubles 170€–300€. AE, MC, V. Closed Nov to mid-Apr.

★ **Hotel Samos** VATHY

For a one- or two-night stay in Vathy, it's hard to beat this waterfront hotel with sea views, a roof garden, and a rooftop pool. Rooms are plain but clean and functional, though the waterfront noise makes air-conditioning a necessity. Shops and the Archaeological Museum are a short walk away. 11 Safouli. ☎ 22730/28377. www.samoshotel.gr. 96 units. Doubles 60€–75€. MC, V.

★★ **Olympia Apartments/Olympia Beach**

KOKKARI Some of the most pleasant accommodations in town offer a choice of options. The apartments, scattered throughout six houses in the village, surround flower-filled courtyards and have living/sleeping areas and kitchens. Basic rooms at the beach hotel are directly on the water. ☎ 22730/92324. www. olympiabeach.gr. 34 units. Doubles 60€–80€ w/breakfast, apartments 90€–140€. MC, V. Closed Nov–Mar.

★ **Sama Hotel** PYTHAGORIO

What these plain, simple rooms right in the center of Pythagorio lack in luxury they make up for with location. The waterfront and archaeological sites are within an easy stroll, and the shady lanes of the Old Town provide a surprisingly tranquil setting. ☎ 22730/61123. www.sama.gr. 14 units. Doubles 40€–60€. MC, V. Closed Nov to mid-Apr.

★★ **Tsamadou** KOKKARI

A simple, whitewashed inn near the beach ensures a comfortable stay with air-conditioning, fridges, a garden room, and balconies off all the large, airy rooms. A snack bar serves throughout the day. ☎ 22730/92314. www.tsamadou. com. 11 units. Doubles 80€–100€ w/breakfast. AE, MC, V.

★★ **Arion Hotel** KOKKARI

One of the island's nicest places to stay is a world apart, set on a hillside above Kokkari. Rooms are scattered among lawns and gardens, and most have panoramic views across the sea and coastal hills. The beaches are an easy trek down the hill, and a beautiful pool suffices nicely when you want to stay put. ☎ 22730/92020. www.arion-hotel.com. 112 units. Doubles 150€–180€ w/ breakfast. AE, MC, V. Closed Nov–Mar.

★★★ kids **Doryssa Seaside Resort** OUTSIDE

PYTHAGORIO The island's largest hotel complex offers all the standard resort amenities, including a choice of restaurants and bars, watersports, a beach, a spa, and a wide choice of accommodations, in a hotel section or in bungalows meant to create a village atmosphere; rooms throughout are extremely comfortable

Where to Dine on Samos

★ **Ammos Plaz** KOKKARI *GREEK*
This longtime Kokkari favorite is right on the beach serving traditional stews and mousaka, along with fresh fish the family brings in themselves. West end of beach. ☎ 27310/2463. Entrees 5€–8€. MC, V. Lunch & dinner daily. Closed Nov–Mar.

★ **El Greco** VATHY *GREEK*
The Pachymanolis family restaurant, on a side street off the harbor, is as popular with locals as it is with visitors. Grilled meats, fish, traditional starters, and a wide range of other fare are served in attractive surroundings. Pindarou t. ☎ 22730/24042. Entrees 6.50€–9€. MC, V. Lunch & dinner daily.

★ **Galazio Pigadi** VOURLIOTES *GREEK*
One of the top stops for lunch around the mountain villages above Kokkari is this simple taverna, where in good weather meals are served under a sprawling vine in front. Hearty stews and other traditional dishes are served with pitchers of excellent wine from the vineyards that climb the surrounding hills. ☎ 22730/93480. Entrees 6.50€–9€. MC, V. Lunch & dinner daily. Closed Oct–Mar.

★ **Tarsanas** KOKKARI *GREEK*
A quiet lane in the Old Town is the setting for a friendly, family-run pizzeria/taverna that also serves excellent Greek home cooking. Step into the kitchen to see what's fresh that day, and wash it down with the house wine. Old Town. Entrees 6€–9€. MC, V. Lunch & dinner daily.

★ **Taverna Artemis** VATHY *GREEK*
Just off the waterfront, one of Vathy's most popular restaurants is often crowded with locals. Seating is in a large, noisy room or on the more pleasant terrace. Well-prepared standards include excellent meze that are meals in themselves. 4 Kefalopoulou. ☎ 22730/23639. Entrees 6.50€–9€. Cash only. Lunch & dinner daily.

Samos at Night

The nightlife season on Samos, through July and August, is short but fairly rollicking. Venues come and go each year, though they tend to cluster in the same general areas—around Kefalopoulou, near the waterfront in Vathy; around the base of the jetty in Pythagorio; and on the beachfront promenade in Kokkari. In general you will find clubs with indoor dance floors playing international pop and waterside terraces set up like cocktail lounges. Top choices for cocktails are the cafes along the cozy harbor in Pythagorio.

Chios

The harvesting and shipment of mastic—the fragrant sap of local evergreen trees—brought this craggy island a good share of the prosperity evident in the jasmine-scented lanes of Kambos as well as in the so-called mastic villages. Chios is one of the least-visited of the major Greek island and goes about its business independent of outsiders, thanks to the wealth and means generated by mastic. You'll come upon Greek life the way it really is in the bazaar of Chios Town and elsewhere. As an added bonus, in Vrontados and Volissos, you can walk in the footsteps of Homer, who was allegedly born on the island, though the timing and even fact of his birth are highly disputed.

> Some scholars claim that Homer was born, or at least resided in, Volissos, on the stark north of the island.

START Chios Town, where your boat from Piraeus or other islands will probably arrive.
TRIP LENGTH Allow at least 2 days to see the island.

❶ ★★ Chios Town. The island capital has lost its looks over the years to invasions, earthquakes, and ill-conceived building sprees. But what the city, also known as Chora, lacks in beauty it makes up for with bustle, especially in the bazaar around Vounakiou, the main *plateia*. The jumble of stalls and small shops evokes the proximity of Asia Minor, just 9km (5⅔ miles) across the Strait of Chios, as does the minaret of the **Medjitie Djami.** The timbered porch and courtyard of the former mosque are littered with Muslim tombstones, carved marble lintels from churches on the island, cannons that once defended the *kastro,* and other bits and pieces that make up the rather scattershot **Byzantine Museum** (Plateia Vounakiou; ☎ 22710/26866; admission 2€; Nov–Mar Tues–Sat 10am–1pm, Sun 8:30am–3pm, Apr–Oct Tues–Sat 8:30am–3pm).

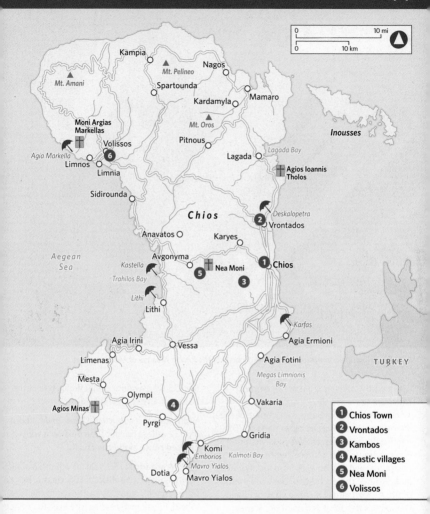

①	Chios Town
②	Vrontados
③	Kambos
④	Mastic villages
⑤	Nea Moni
⑥	Volissos

The Byzantines built the walled, seaside castle just north of the square in the 10th century. Venetian traders enlarged the compound when they were granted the island in the 14th century, and the Turks took Chios from them in 1566 and added fountains, *hamams*, and mosques. Within the **Portara Maggiora,** the main gate, are the wood and plaster houses of the Ottoman Turks who banished Greeks to precincts outside the Kastro walls. Among the few residences that don't look as if they might soon topple over is the medieval **Giustiniani mansion** (inside Kastro; ☎ 22710/22819; admission 3€; Tues–Sun 9am–2:30pm), the

home of the powerful Genoese family that once oversaw the island. It's now loaded with 12th-century frescoes of the prophets from the Church of Panagia Krina, on the Kambos plain south of Chios Town.

Two collections south of Vounakiou near the cathedral provide engaging glimpses into island life. The neoclassical mansion of the Peteras clan—one of many Chios families that made a fortune in shipping—is now the **Maritime Museum** (Stefanou Tsouri; ☎ 22710/44139; free admission; Mon–Sat 10am–2pm), showing off ship models, paintings, instruments, and other nautical knickknacks.

> *In Chios Town, old tombstones litter the grounds of the former Mosque of Medjitie Djami.*

A nearby mansion houses the **Argenti Museum** (2 Korais; ☎ 22710/28256; admission 1.50€; Mon–Fri 8am–2pm), home of the charmingly idiosyncratic collections of 20th-century Chian aristocrat and local historian Philip Argenti, who gathered embroideries, costumes, and folk objects from around the island. Among the portraits of past generations of the Argenti family hangs a copy of Eugène Delacroix's despair-filled painting, *Scenes from the Massacre at Chios.* The original, in the Louvre in Paris, was inspired by the events of 1822, when Turks savagely quashed the Greek struggle for independence on Chios by killing 20,000 men, enslaving 50,000 women and children, and exiling another 20,000; only 2,000 Greeks remained on Chios after the attacks. News of the slaughter did much to rally western Europe behind the Greek Independence movement—fueled in large part by this painting and a wildly popular poem by Victor Hugo, "L'Enfant de Chios." Most of the rare volumes in the adjoining Korais Library are from wealthy islanders; it's a testimony to the fortunes made in Chios from shipping that the 135,000-volume collection is one of the largest in Greece. ⏱ Half-day.

Vrontados is a suburb of Chios Town, about 3km (2 miles) north of the port on a well-marked route along the coast.

❷ ★ **Vrontados.** This seaside suburb of Chios Town makes two extraordinary claims. Before Christopher Columbus journeyed to the New World, he allegedly set ashore here for advice on routes and navigational tactics from local seafarers (who still make up a good part of the population); while on the island, he discovered the pleasures of mastic (see "Stuck on Mastic," p. 473). What's more, Homer allegedly lived here and taught from a boulder conveniently topped with a lectern-like outcropping. The rock was probably an ancient altar to Cybele, the nature goddess, but with the sea glistening below and birdsong coming from the lemon and olive trees, the so-called **Daskalopetra (Teacher's Rock)** would certainly have been a delightful place to listen to the greatest of all orators. ⏱ 1 hr.

3 ★★ **Kambos.** This plain that stretches along the coast just south of Chios Town—a patchwork of orange and lemon groves and ornate, Turko-Greco-style estates—has long been the realm of the foreign elite who've ruled the island and local aristocracy. High walls of golden stone hem in the narrow lanes, but a peer through the wrought-iron gates often reveals jasmine-scented gardens, pebbled courtyards, and arched verandas and balconies. Many of the estates are derelict, and have been since the massacres of 1822 and an earthquake that leveled much of the island in 1881. Many, though, retain their splendor, and a few offer accommodations; with an air of exotic sophistication, Kambos is one of the most inviting places to stay on the island (p. 472). ☺ 2 hr.

Pyrgi, the first of the mastic villages you'll come to when approaching from the north, is 20km (12 miles) south of Chios Town on a well-marked road down the center of the island.

4 ★★★ **Mastic villages.** The soil of Chios is especially well suited to mastic, a tree that produces an aromatic and useful resin. Hippocrates prescribed mastic for everything from snake bites to boils, Romans used it to clean their teeth, and Turkish harems chewed mastic to sweeten their breath. Mastic is still made into gum, toothpaste, mouthwash, cosmetics, and a digestion-abetting liqueur; some medical researchers claim that mastic can also lower blood pressure and boost the immune system. The Genoese established 20 or so *mastihari* (mastic villages) to ensure a steady supply of the pleasantly smoky-tasting little mastic pellets—so valuable at one time that the Turks spared these villages when they depopulated the island in 1822. With their solid rows of houses forming fortresslike walls, arcaded streets, and elaborately patterned exteriors, the *mastihari* are some of the most beautiful medieval villages in Greece. They are surrounded by the island's most welcoming landscapes, where olive groves and mastic orchards rise and fall across gently rolling hills. ☺ Half-day.

SITE GUIDE PAGE 471

Nea Moni is 25km (15 miles) north of Pyrgi on a road up the center of the island, passing through Agios Yeoryios Sikousis.

> *Megas Taxiarchis, in Mesta, is one of the largest churches in Greece.*

5 ★★★ **Nea Moni.** As is the case with many monasteries in Greece, the story of Nea Moni begins with the mysterious appearance of an icon. In 1066, three shepherds saw a strange light in the undergrowth and found, surrounded by flames, a beautiful icon of the Virgin Mary. The icon announced that Constantine would become emperor of Byzantium. When this portent came to pass, Constantine and his wife, the Empress Zoe, built a beautiful monastery to house the icon. The blackened image hangs near the altar beneath the dome of the octagonal *katholikon* (main church). The naves, dome, and eight supporting niches are decorated with dazzling Byzantine mosaics depicting saints, Christ washing the disciples' feet, sinners being devoured by fish, and myriad other scenes. The icon is believed to work miraculous cures for the faithful; in recent years it's been credited with sparing

> *The Monastery of Nea Moni.*

glory. A chapel on the grounds is filled with skulls, some showing ax marks, of the 600 monks and 3,500 islanders who sought refuge during the Turkish massacres of 1822 and were slaughtered when Ottoman troops broke through the gates. ⏱ 2 hr. ☎ 22710/44139. Donations welcome. Apr–Oct Tues–Sun 8am–1pm and 4–7pm, Nov–Mar Tues–Sun 8:30am–3pm.

Anavatos is about 10km (6¼ miles) northwest of Nea Moni, off the road through Avgonyma.

6 ★★ **Volissos.** The farther north you travel on Chios, the stark, craggy landscape becomes more unrelenting and the villages starker. **Anavatos** teeters atop a 300m (990-ft.) bluff; the village is a virtual ghost town, more or less abandoned since the slaughter of 1822, when 400 residents threw themselves off the precipice rather than meet their fate at the hands of the Turks. In **Volissos,** about 12km (7½ miles) farther north, stone houses are scattered on the flanks of an arid hillside beneath a Byzantine fort. Homer, some legends have it, was born here; according to others, he came to Volissos when he learned that a local poet was plagiarizing his work, sorted the matter out, and settled in. ⏱ 2 hr.

An Island of Shipping Magnates

Chios has fostered an unlikely number of shipowners, in part because the pine forests that once carpeted the island supplied timber for shipbuilding, and largely because the rocky islands provided few livelihoods other than seafaring. Even under Ottoman rule, Greek shipowners from Chios made fortunes trading throughout the Aegean and Black seas. In a nation of mariners—4,000 Greek ships account for 8% of world shipping—Chians still man the helm, operating more than half the Greek ships on the world seas. Chios and its tiny neighbor, Oinousses, are home to such shipping dynasties as Lemos, Kulukundis, Pateras, Carras, and Papalios. In August, when members of these clans return to their villas on the island, Chios is one of the wealthiest places on the planet. The maritime tradition continues among Chians who start out with one boat and slowly assemble a fleet.

the monastery when it stood in the path of fires that engulfed the surrounding forests. No such intervention delivered the monastery from an 1881 earthquake, however, which sent the dome and many of the beautiful mosaics crashing to the ground. Since the monastery was declared a UNESCO World Heritage Site, they are slowly being restored to their onetime

4 Mastic Villages

Pyrgi is named for its now-ruined defensive tower, but it is best known for its houses elaborately decorated with *xysta;* with this technique, a layer of gray-black volcanic sand is coated with white lime and then etched with circles, diamonds, stars, other elaborate geometric patterns, and floral motifs to reveal the dark layer beneath. The design craze also shows up in the 12th-century **Church of Agii Apostoli,** on the *plateia,* where the exterior is banded with brick and the interior walls are awash in colorful frescoes of biblical scenes and St. Paul's visit to Chios in the 1st century A.D. At **B Olimbi,** a tall and well-maintained defensive tower, common to most of the villages, rises from the *plateia.* These towers provided a lookout, a strategic redoubt for launching weapons, and a place of refuge where residents could gather on the top floors in time of siege and pull up a drawbridge behind them. The most strikingly defended of the mastic villages is **C Mesta,** with an outermost perimeter of houses that create solid, fortresslike walls; none of these exterior walls are pierced with doors or windows, presenting a solid stone wall to the world beyond the village. Only a few gates lead into the maze of narrow lanes and tunnels that burrow between and beneath the houses. These architectural hurdles were meant to deter pirates, for whom the mastic-rich villages were a prime target.

Mesta has two churches named for the Archangel Michael; **Megas Taxiarchis,** on the *plateia,* is especially aptly named—it's the larger of the two and one of the largest churches in Greece. Marauders who arrived by sea and set their sights on the inland villages did not have far to travel; Mesta is only 5km (3 miles) east of the sand beach at **D Apothika.** More dramatic are the strands of smooth black pebbles at **E Mavra Volia and Foki;** backtrack through Pyrgi and continue 5km (3 miles) to coastal Emorio and walk to these exotic beaches from there.

Where to Stay on Chios

> *Pipidis Traditional Houses provide atmospheric, medieval quarters in Mesta.*

★★★ Argentikon Luxury Suites KAMBOS

Pampered luxury prevails at the 16th-century estate of the island's aristocratic Argenti family, recently renovated with no end of 21st-century refinements. Extensive gardens, a spa, romantic indoor/outdoor dining room, and eight exquisite suites with period furnishings and frescoed ceilings provide the ultimate getaway. ☎ 22710/33111. www.argentikon.gr. 8 units. Doubles from 450€ w/breakfast. MC, V. Closed Nov–Mar.

★★ Grecian Castle CHIOS TOWN

A castle it's not, but this handsome stone complex recently converted from an old factory is certainly comfortable. The sea is nearby, and the appealing, traditionally furnished, marble-floored rooms surround a large garden and swimming pool. The larger rooms in the rear of the garden are the best choice. ☎ 22710/44740. www.greciancastle.gr. 55 units. Doubles 120€–140€ w/breakfast. AE, MC, V.

★★ kids Mavrokordatiko KAMBOS

This stone manor house from 1736 offers enormous guest rooms, some of which open directly onto the grounds. A lovely courtyard serves as an outdoor restaurant, and the grounds are well suited to energetic children, who are extended a warm welcome. ☎ 22710/32900. www.mavrokordatiko.com. 9 units. Doubles 80€–90€ w/breakfast. MC, V. Closed Nov–Mar.

★★★ Perleas KAMBOS

A stone mansion and two outbuildings set amid fragrant citrus orchards are the setting for distinctive and delightful accommodations, filled with antiques and carefully chosen artwork. Breakfast and dinner on request feature fresh produce from the estate. Guests are welcome to wander the grounds and take in the views from the delightful terraces and patios. ☎ 22710/32217. www.perleas.gr. 7 units. Doubles 350€ w/breakfast.

★★ Pipidis Traditional Houses MESTA

A stay in a mastic village is all the more memorable in these medieval surroundings. Several houses on the narrow lanes have been outfitted as apartments, with kitchens, exposed stonework, vaulted ceilings, and other comforts. ☎ 22710/76029. 4 units. Doubles 60€–70€. No credit cards. Closed Nov–Apr.

★★ Volissos Traditional Houses VOLISSOS

These finely renovated houses, converted to comfortable apartments, provide a distinctive getaway. Volissos is at the north of the island, about 40km (25 miles) from Chios Town, but the remote location is a plus given the nearby beaches, the views over the sea and craggy mountains, and the chance to experience village life. ☎ 22710/21421. 16 units. Doubles 50€–90€. No credit cards. Closed Nov–Apr.

Where to Dine on Chios

> *You can settle into island life at Volissos Traditional Houses.*

★★ **Hotzas** CHIOS TOWN *GREEK*
The oldest taverna in Chios Town is not easy to find, but that's not a problem—just about anyone you ask has enjoyed a meal in the jasmine-scented garden at one time or another. The menu changes daily to utilize the freshest fish and vegetables, but count on squid, mussels, and the house ouzo. 3 Yioryiou Kondili. ☎ 22710/42787. Entrees 6€–18€. No credit cards. Dinner Mon–Sat.

★ **Taverna Mesaionas** MESTA *GREEK*
The main plateia of Mesta is a lively setting for a meal. The *tiropitakia* (cheese balls) and other meze, served at one of the outdoor tables, round out a memorable experience. ☎ 22710/76050. Entrees 6€–14€. No credit cards. Lunch & dinner daily.

★★ **Theodosiou** MESTA *GREEK*
This old-fashioned waterfront *ouzeri* under an arcaded portico specializes in grilled meat and fish; the simple fare is delicious. Nerorion 33. ☎ 22710/24250. Entrees 6€–14€. No credit cards. Dinner Mon–Sat.

★★ **Yiorgo Passa's Taverna** LANGADA *SEAFOOD* This fishing village about 10km (6¼ miles) north of the center of Chios Town is where islanders go for a seafood dinner. The quay is lined with excellent fish tavernas. Prices are reasonable across the board, and the fish is fresh; Yiorgo Passa's stands out for its excellent service and deft preparations. Here as elsewhere, fish is priced per kilo, but you can order any size portion you wish. Quay. ☎ 22710/74218. Entrees 6€–25€; fish is sold by weight. No credit cards. Lunch & dinner daily.

Stuck on Mastic

You won't have to look far to find the local resinous product served up in dozens of concoctions—chewing gum, cosmetics, toothpaste, candy, soap, and a delicious and potent liqueur called *mastika.* The narrow lanes of the mastic villages are lined with shops selling these products. You can watch as harvesters extract resin from the bark of mastic trees or try your own hand at the technique on tours with **Masticulture** (www.masticulture.com).

Lesbos

Greece's third-largest island, known to most Greeks as Mytilini (also the name of the island capital), is famous as the ancient birthplace of the female lyric poet Sappho, but the appeal far surpasses that claim to fame. Lesbos also produces what many connoisseurs consider the best olive oil in Greece, and the island introduces visitors to some little-known gems of 20th-century art, the healing effects of hot springs, lovely seaside villages, and some of the finest beaches on the Aegean.

> *Mytilini sprawls across a promontory, surrounded by the sea.*

START Mytilini, where your boat from Piraeus or other islands will probably arrive. **TRIP LENGTH** Allow at least 2 days to see the island.

❶ ★★ **Mytilini.** Old Mytilini, laid out by Byzantines and Ottoman Turks, sprawls across a hilly promontory between harbors on the south and north. A largely Turkish fortress, tucked into a fragrant pine forest, takes up the eastern flank of the promontory. **Ermou**—a boisterous market street filled with stalls, little shops, and a bazaar—bisects the center of town, providing a color-filled foray into a workaday Greek town. Exotic flourishes include neoclassical mansions lining narrow lanes off Ermou and beautiful Turkish baths about halfway up the street from the main (south) harbor.

The **Archaeological Museum** (8 Noviembrou; ☎ 22510/28032; admission 3€; Jan–Oct Tues–Sun 8:30am–3pm, Nov–Dec Tues–Sun 8am–2:30pm) is the repository of remnants left behind by the many cultures that have thrived on Lesbos. Three rooms from a Roman villa are especially engaging, with their glittering mosaic floors. Many of the floor panels depict scenes from plays by Meander, with actors wearing masks and costumes; others portray Socrates, the Muses, and lyric poets. They were no doubt meant to reflect the literary tastes of the villa owner and perhaps set the scene for dramatic readings and performances. ⏱ At least 2 hr.

Varia is about 5km (3 miles) south of Mytilini on a well-marked road south along the coast.

② ★★ Varia. A pair of museums in this quiet, outlying quarter introduces you to the island's little- known but nonetheless remarkable presence on the 20th-century art scene. The painter Theophilos Hatzimihail was born in a pink stone house surrounded by olive groves in 1873, and his birthplace is now the **Theophilos Museum** (Varia; ☎ 22510/41644; admission 2€; Tues–Sun 8:30am–3pm). Theophilos was better known as an eccentric than as an artist and often walked the streets of Mytilini dressed as a Greek god or Alexander the Great. Lesbos-born art critic and publisher Tériade discovered the ill and impoverished artist in 1919 and supported him until his death from food poisoning in 1936, safeguarding his works. Unfortunately, Theophilos painted much of his work on the walls of cafes and houses that have long since been destroyed or covered with whitewash. The 86 canvases in the four rooms here are delightful—primitive and colorful, depicting island folk as well as gods, goddesses, and saints.

Tériade, whose given name was Stratis Eleftheriades, left Lesbos for Paris in 1915, westernized his name, and established himself

> *Mosaic floors from a Roman villa, now in the Mytilini Archaeological Museum.*

as the publisher of the avant-garde art journals *Minotaure* and *Verve*. Tériade published and collected works by many of the great artists of the early 20th century. Through these associations the **Tériade Museum** (Varia; ☎ 22510/23372; admission 2€; Apr–Oct

> *Shady lanes wind through the mountain village of Agiassos.*

Tues–Sun 8:30am–3pm and 5–8pm, Nov–Mar Tues–Sun 8:30am–3pm) is hung with drawings, lithographs, and paintings by Matisse, Picasso, Giacometti, and many, many others. ⏱ 2 hr.

Agiassos is about 25km (15 miles) southwest of Mytilini off a well-marked road toward Polychnitou.

❸ ★★ **Agiassos.** Among the many travelers finding their way to this beautiful mountain village are pilgrims who follow the winding cobblestone streets to the **Church of the Panagia Vrefokratousa** (Madonna Holding the Infant; open daily 8am–1pm and 5:30–8:30pm). An icon of the Virgin, supposedly painted by St. Luke the Evangelist and brought to the church from Jerusalem in 803, is said to have worked a miraculous cure upon an 18th-century Turkish administrator of the island. Just as

miraculously, the grateful Turks excused the village from taxation. This event is celebrated August 15, on the Feast of the Virgin, when the icon is paraded through the street. Workshops built into the walls of the church and surrounding the nearby bazaar sell pottery and handcrafted wooden furniture, much of which transcends tackiness and is very well wrought. Orchards and olive groves climb the surrounding slopes of Mount Olympus—one of 19 so-named peaks in Greece whose craggy summit stands sentinel over the town's old tile rooftops. ⏱ 1 hr.

Vatera is about 20km (12 miles) southwest of Agiassos on the well-marked road to the south coast, in the direction of Polychnitou.

❹ ★ **Vatera.** A winding road skirts the flanks of Mount Olympus, then drops down to the southern coast at the spectacular beach at Vatera, where golden sands stretch for 7km (4⅓ miles). More hedonistic indulgence awaits at **Polychnitou,** a valley where hot springs bubble and boiling streams flow through richly colored beds of minerals. Since antiquity, these waters have been channeled into thermal pools and stone bathhouses. Most stand in eerie ruin amid the steaming

Suggested Detour

About 5km/3 miles) west of Mandamadhos, follow the winding road down to Skala Sikaminias, a picturesque port at the northernmost point of the island where a tiny chapel teeters on a rock above the waves.

> *Lovely Molyvos winds up a hillside from a pebbly beach and busy fishing port.*

waterscape, but one, marked the Polychnitou Baths, still operates in July and August (daily 7am–noon and 3–8pm), and at very limited times the rest of the year. ⏲ 2 hr.

Mandamadhos is about 30km (19 miles) north of Vatera. Follow the road north across Mount Olympus, then northwest around the Gulf of Kalloni, then north to Mandamadhos.

❺ ★★ **Mandamadhos.** This little town atop an inland plateau is close to the heart of islanders. The **Church of the Taxiarchis** (Archangel Michael) houses a miraculous icon of the archangel who is believed to be the leader of the army of God and patron saint of the island. Legend has it that pirates attacked the monastery in the Middle Ages, slaughtering all but 1 of the 40 monks in residence. The survivor, a young novice, came out of hiding, found the corpses of his brothers, and fashioned the blood-soaked earth into an image of Michael. The earthen likeness was miraculously transformed into a beautiful wooden icon that the religious kiss while offering prayers for health and success. They also leave behind many pairs of small tin shoes, to be worn by the archangel as he rushes about the island on his nightly rounds to ensure the well-being of the faithful. ⏲ 1 hr.

Soaking in Sappho Territory

The thermal springs of Lesbos have been popular gathering spots since antiquity, offering relief from rheumatism, digestive complaints, and unspecified world-weariness. Two particularly scenic spots are **Polychnitou,** where springs bubble up along a rocky valley (p. 476, ❹), and **Eftalou,** outside Molyvos (p. 478, ❻), where you can take a soak in the bathhouse pools or find one of the hot spots where the springs empty into the sea. **Loutropolis Thermis,** outside Mytilini, was a popular gathering place for ancient Greeks and Romans, who combined a soak with a visit to a temple to Aphrodite (Venus), goddess of love; early-20th-century patrons stayed in a grand hotel, now abandoned, on the grounds. Two other establishments near Mytilini are **Paralia Thermis,** where modern facilities adjoin the ruined Roman/Byzantine baths, and **Loutra Yeras,** where the hot waters are channeled into two vaulted chambers, one for men and one for women. Most thermal establishments are open from about 9am to 1pm and 4 to 8pm, and charge 3€, towel included.

> *Stone steps lead to the Glykophilousa Panagia (Our Lady of the Sweet Kiss) in Petra.*

From Mandamadhos, the road cuts across the northern tip of Lesbos to Molyvos (25km/15 miles).

6 ★★★ **Molyvos (Mithymna).** Though this picturesque hillside town of stone houses that hang above the sea has reverted to its ancient name, islanders still use Molyvos as well, from

Hilltop Pergamon

One of the most important cities of the Greek world sits atop a wooded hillside just inland from the Turkish coast. Magnificent artifacts from the site fill the Pergamon Museum in Berlin, but what remains, especially on the acropolis, is stunning. Ruins include sanctuaries to Trajan and Athena, royal palaces, and a library (Marc Antony presented the 200,000 scrolls to Cleopatra as a wedding gift). You can reach Pergamon on your own from Lesbos, on the regular ferries that make the short crossing to Cesme, Turkey, where you can catch a bus to the site. Many of the travel agencies near the port in Mytilini offer day tours to Pergamon for about 60€. A visa is not required for a day visit.

the days of Byzantine rule. (By the time you get this far in Greece, you will have realized that many places have two or more names.) During the Trojan War, Achilles besieged the town, but his armies were unable to penetrate the walls. The daughter of the king could not resist the charms of the handsome warrior and opened the gates for him; most unchivalrously, Achilles promptly slew the young woman once he was inside the walls. Molyvos is these days besieged with visitors, but on the streets and alleys that wind up the hillside from the pebbly beach you will stumble upon many quiet, shady squares and nooks and crannies graced with splashing fountains. A 14th-century Genoese castle crowns the hilltop, and from the ramparts another woman—this one the wife of the medieval governor—again played a hand in the town's fate when she repulsed a Turkish attack by putting on her husband's armor and leading the citizenry in a counter-charge. The Turks eventually took the town, and you can step into one of their houses, the early-19th-century **Komninaki Kralli mansion** (follow signs to the School of Fine Arts; free admission; daily 9am–5pm), to see the murals depicting dancers and the urbane and spiritual wonders of Constantinople. ⏲ Half-day.

Petra is 3km (2 miles) south of Molyvos on the well-marked coast road.

⑦ ★ Petra. A long stretch of sandy beach is Petra's most popular asset, but you may be tempted away from the forest of sun umbrellas by the alluring prospect of climbing a massive rock monolith that rises from the midst of the tile-roofed Old Quarter. At the top of 114 rough-hewn steps is the **Glykophilousa Panagia** (Our Lady of the Sweet Kiss), built in the 17th century to house an icon of the Virgin Mary. One day, so the story goes, a fisherman accidentally dropped the icon from his boat. That night he saw a strange light burning atop the rock. He came ashore, climbed to the top, and found his icon, lit by a candle. He took the icon back to his boat, but the next day it went missing again and then re-appeared atop the rock—obviously, the place the Virgin wished to be. The **Vareltzidhena Mansion** (free admission; Tues–Sun 8am–2:30pm) is one of many beautiful houses from the days of Ottoman rule that line the shady streets behind the beach; as in the Komninaki Kralli mansion in nearby Molyvos, the rooms are decorated with charming murals, here with circus bears, sailing ships, and courting couples. ⏲ 2 hr.

Skala Eressos is 35km (22 miles) southwest of Petra. Follow a route to the southwestern end of the island through Skaohori, Vatoussa, and Andissa.

⑧ ★★ Skala Eressos. Even if Skala Eressos's exquisite, 3km (2-mile) expanse of brown sand weren't among the finest in Greece, this seaside town would have many admirers. Ancient Erossos was home to the poet Sappho, whose lyrical praise of young women has lent the island's name to desire between women, drawing many female visitors to the animated port and fishing village—making little Skala Eressos one of the world's leading resorts for gay women (p. 680). The scant ruins of the city where Sappho wrote and ran a small academy for young women litters a nearby hillside. While there, you can also pay tribute to another Erossos native, Theophrastus, a student of Plato, successor of Aristotle at the Lyceum, and a prolific writer on botany, metaphysics, and ethics. You should also take time to behold the views across the fertile coastal

> *Sunsets are spectacular at Skala Eressos, where the golden sands stretch for 3km (2 miles).*

plain from medieval Erossos, perched on the hillside above Skala Eressos. ⏲ 2 hr.

From Skala Eressos, travel north again toward Andissa, then west to Sigri on a well-marked road, a trip of about 20km (12 miles).

⑨ ★ Sigri. The road west meets the sea at this windswept little town, built around a massive but derelict Turkish castle. The bleak, rocky landscape that surrounds Sigri is nowhere more desolate than it is in the **Petrified Forest,** a collection of fallen and standing tree stumps turned to stone over the past 20 million years. Should you be intrigued, check out **Sigri's Natural History Museum of the Lesbos Petrified Forest** (forest and museum: admission 5€); July to mid-Sept daily 9am–8pm, mid-Sept to late Sept daily 8:30am–7pm, Oct–June Tues–Sun 9am–5pm) explores the local geology in depth. ⏲ 2 hr.

Where to Stay on Lesbos

> *The coast around Molyvos is backed by pleasant hotels.*

★ **Blue Sea Hotel** MYTILINI

Balconies off all the comfortable, airy rooms overlook the ferry docks and waterfront to provide a bird's-eye view of the port's busy comings and goings. Ermou, with its colorful bazaar, is just a short stroll away. 49 Venizelou. ☎ 22510/23994. 58 units. Doubles 55€–75€ w/ breakfast. MC, V.

★★★ **Loriet** VARIA

A 19th-century estate on the beach just outside Mytilini provides atmospheric lodgings in a character-filled mansion and a 1970s-era modern wing. Suites in the mansion are huge and elaborately appointed, beamed attic rooms and a cottage are cozy, and the newer hotel rooms and small apartments are pleasantly contemporary. All accommodations share a beautiful garden, saltwater pool, and a beach near the end of the property. The Varia museums are nearby. ☎ 22510/43111. www.loriet-hotel.com. 35 units. Doubles 85€–350€ w/breakfast. AE, MC, V.

★★ **Olive Press Hotel** MOLYVOS

The waves lap against the stone walls of this converted factory, where handsomely contemporary rooms face the sea and surround a flower-filled garden and swimming pool. Many of the balconies hang right over the water, and a pebble beach and jetty make it easy to jump right in. ☎ 22510/71205. www.olivepress-hotel.com. 50 units. Doubles 95€ w/breakfast. MC, V. Closed Nov–Mar.

★★ **Pyrgos of Mytilene** MYTILINI

An ornate, early-20th-century mansion in the Old Quarter has been lovingly restored. Some of the rooms are in the eponymous tower, others are lavishly decorated in Empire style, and most have balconies. An elaborate breakfast is served in a sunny conservatory and in the rear garden. 49 Venizelou. ☎ 22510/25069. www.pyrgoshotel.gr. 12 units. Doubles 120€–150€ w/breakfast. AE, MC, V.

★★ **Sea Horse Hotel** MOLYVOS

Most of the rooms hang right over the harbor, an easy stroll from the quiet lanes of the Old Town. Comforts include air-conditioning and double-pane windows, which are handy when you want to shut out the lively scene on the quay below in favor of some shut-eye. 49 Venizelou. ☎ 22510/71320. 16 units. Doubles 65€ w/breakfast. MC, V. Closed mid-Oct to mid-Apr.

Where to Dine on Lesbos

★ **Averoff 1841** MYTILINI *GREEK*
This old-fashioned favorite on the port never falls from favor, serving *patsa* (tripe), roasted lamb, and other home-style dishes in a welcoming room. Port. ☎ 22510/22180. Entrees 5€–15€. No credit cards. Lunch & dinner daily.

★ **Captain's Table** MOLYVOS *GREEK/SEAFOOD*
A view of the sea, fresh fish caught by the owners' family, friendly service, and *bouzoukia* music some nights all contribute to a memorable meal, but the cooking alone sets this harbor-front institution apart. Mussels and fresh anchovies are renowned, as are the spicy eggplant and other vegetarian dishes. Harbor. ☎ 22530/71241. Entrees 6€–20€. V. Lunch & dinner daily.

★ **Kafeneon O Ermes** MYTILINI *GREEK*
This 100-year-old *ouzeri* is resplendent with Belle Epoque charm, with big mirrors and paintings by local artists. Most of the patrons come to drink and nibble on the dozens of small plates available. Homey main courses are delicious, too. Epano Skala. Entrees 6€–10€. No credit cards. Lunch & dinner daily.

★ **O Stratos** MYTILINI *SEAFOOD*
This top contender for the best seafood on the island is right on the quay. Forgoing any attempt at posh surroundings, its focus is the freshness of the fish displayed on ice near the entrance. Waterside tables are at a premium on warm summer nights. Fanari Quay. ☎ 22510/21739. Entrees 8€–20€. MC, V. Lunch & dinner daily.

★ **Soulatso** SKALA ERESSOS *GREEK/SEAFOOD*
One of Greece's most beautiful beaches creates a backdrop for a meal at this simple seaside taverna, where you may be tempted to try such local favorites as *sardeles pastes* (fresh sardines, skinned and seasoned); the house specialty is octopus, grilled to tender perfection, and accompanied by local ouzo. Beachfront. ☎ 22530/52078. Entrees 6€–20€. No credit cards. Lunch & dinner daily.

> The daily catch is superlatively fresh at the Captain's Table in Molyvos.

Festive Lesbos

In July and August, Molyvos stages a highly touted **Theater Festival,** when plays and concerts are presented on an outdoor stage in the hilltop castle. The **Eressos Women's Festival,** in Skala Eressos in September, stages two weeks of poetry readings, concerts, dances, and other events geared, of course, to women.

Northeastern Aegean Fast Facts

> *Frequent flights to all three islands spare you a 12- to 16-hour ferry crossing from Piraeus.*

Arriving

BY PLANE In summer, **Olympic Airways** (☎ 80111/44444 for reservations within Greece; www.olympicair.com) runs several year-round flights a day from Athens to all three islands; regular service shuttles between Lesbos and Chios and, less frequently, from Samos to the other islands. Schedules vary with the season, and operations are curtailed outside the busy July–August tourist season. **Aegean Air** (☎ 21062/61000; www.aegean air.com) also flies to the three islands. **BY BOAT** You have many options, but remember, the trip from the port of Piraeus in Athens to these far-flung islands is long (about 12 hr.), and boats often arrive in the wee hours; hotels in the Northeastern Aegean are accustomed to guests arriving at 4am. Samos is served at least once a day from Piraeus, with boats calling at Vathy and/or Karlovassi; Chios is served several times a week from Piraeus; and Lesbos is served daily from Piraeus; you can also reach Lesbos several times a week on service from Rafina to Sigri. The best single source for schedules is the excellent website of the **Greek Travel Pages** (www.gtp.gr). Other sources for information include the **Greek National Tourist Organization (GNTO)** and the thousands of travel agencies around Greece that sell boat tickets; keep in mind, though, that an office may sell tickets for one line but not another and neglect to mention competitors' schedules. Port Authority offices at ferry docks have current schedules, but personnel may not speak English.

Dentists & Doctors

SAMOS There are hospitals on Samos, in Vathy (☎ 22730/83100). **CHIOS** Outside Chios Town (☎ 22710/44301). **LESBOS** On Lesbos, outside Mytilini (☎ 22510/43777). Most hotels will be able to refer you to a local doctor or dentist who speaks English.

Emergencies

See p. 680, Fast Facts Greece.

Getting Around

BY BOAT Travel agencies on each of the islands can tell you how best to get from one to the other, but service can be infrequent. In general, expect a boat a day from Samos to Chios (less frequently outside summer), and at least one a day from Chios to Lesbos. For details see www.gtp.gr. **BY BUS** All the islands are well-served by bus, though buses are geared to the schedules of islanders rather than sightseers, running early in the morning and evening but infrequently during the day. **BY CAR** On all three islands, you will want to rent a car for touring, especially if your time is short. Ports on all the islands are chockablock with car-rental agencies; expect to pay about 40€ a day in season, insurance included. Forgo the temptation to rent a motorbike—visitors who decide to get sporty keep island doctors very busy.

Internet Access

See p. 681, Fast Facts Greece.

Pharmacies

See p. 682, Fast Facts Greece.

Police

Local police will be able to deal with most emergencies. You will be most likely to find English-speaking assistance through the Tourist Police, who have offices in major towns; you can reach them through the central operator at ☎ 171.

Post Office

See p. 682, Fast Facts Greece.

Safety

In the mountainous forests of Samos, be

> *Personal motorized transport is handy for touring the islands.*

careful of steep drops and poorly tended tracks. Likewise, steps and cobblestone streets in some villages, such as the mastic villages on Chios and hilly Molyvos on Lesbos, may be hard to negotiate for travelers with limited mobility. Also see p. 682, Fast Facts Greece.

Visitor Information

SAMOS You'll find a municipal tourist office at 4 Ikosipemptis Martiou, Vathy (☎ 22730/81031; www.samos.gr). **Samina Tours**, Soufilis 67, Vathy (☎ 22730/87000; www.samina.gr) offers advice and excursions to Ephesus. **CHIOS** The municipal tourist office is at 18 Kanari, Chios Town (☎ 22710/44389; www.chios.gr). **Masticulture** (☎ 22710/76084; www.masticulture.com) arranges tours of the mastic orchards and villages and other ecotourism adventures. **LESBOS** The tourist office is on the harbor, Mytilini (☎ 22510/44165; www.lesvos.gr). **Petra Tours** (☎ 22530/41390; www.petratours-lesvos.com) offers car rentals, tours, walks, and other outdoor adventures.

Favorite Moments in the Sporades

Persian armies, pirates, weekending Athenians, and sun-seeking Northern Europeans are among the legions who have admired the coves, forested islands, and secluded islets of the Sporades—one of the most beautiful archipelagos in the Aegean. Skiathos, Skopelos, Alonnisos, and Skyros reveal their charms easily, especially at moments like these.

> PREVIOUS PAGE *Sea cliffs and white marble stones distinguish the sands of Lalaria Beach on Skiathos.*
> THIS PAGE *Skiathos Town rises and falls over two seaside promontories.*

❶ Squeezing into Spilia Skotini (Dark Cave), Skiathos. Even in the company of a boatload of camera-clicking fellow explorers, you may feel an exhilarating sense of discovery as you float into this spectacular sea grotto. The splash of waves, the shimmer of the sea, and the luster of the light all conspire to transport you into a watery revelry. See p. 504, ❸.

❷ Getting into the rhythms of Lalaria Beach, Skiathos. At first you won't quite know what that murmur is. Then you slowly become accustomed to the soft, incessant rumble of white marble stones rolling back and forth in the surf, amplified by sea cliffs that enclose one of Greece's most beautiful beaches, dappled by the play of sun and turquoise water. See p. 504, ❸.

❸ Feeling the golden sands between your toes on Koukounaries Beach, Skiathos. The perfect crescent backed by pines is a Greek

1 Squeezing into Spilia Skotini (Dark Cave), Skiathos
2 Getting into the rhythms of Lalaria Beach, Skiathos
3 Feeling the golden sands between your toes on Koukounaries Beach, Skiathos
4 Setting your sights on Agios Ioannis, Skopelos
5 Counting church domes from the Kastro in Skopelos Town, Skopelos
6 Walking up to Hora, Alonnisos
7 Sailing through the National Marine Park of Alonnisos Northern Sporades
8 Catching the first glimpse of Skyros Town, Skyros

isle fantasy. Your surfside stroll will not be a solitary experience, but a short walk through shady, sandy-floored groves will deliver you to a string of quieter sands on the Mandraki Peninsula. See p. 503, 2.

4 Setting your sights on Agios Ioannis, Skopelos. The little white chapel on a rocky outcropping above the surf has appeared in films, postcards, and who knows how many photos and home videos. Celebrity aside, the humble landmark is a touching testimony to the power of faith—and the builder's eye for a great location. See p 511, 6.

5 Counting church domes from the Kastro in Skopelos Town, Skopelos. In the island's enchanting capital, one of the most appealing towns in Greece, 123 churches punctuate the lanes that climb the hillside. It's been said that islanders count churches, not sheep, to induce sleep, but the sight of so many blue domes will probably inspire you to get to your feet and start exploring. See p. 508, 1.

6 Walking up to Hora, Alonnisos. The time-honored way to make the ascent to Old Town—along the path that winds from the

port through orchards—is still the most satisfying. The view from the top of the sparkling sea and scattered islets is stupendous, as is the experience of jumping into the waters of a forest-clad cove on your descent. See p. 496, 1.

7 Sailing through the National Marine Park of Alonnisos Northern Sporades. Dolphins will escort your cruise through pristine waters off an archipelago that is home to creatures as diverse as the shy Mediterranean monk seal and the mythical Cyclops. (The cave where the one-eyed monster was blinded by Odysseus, according to Homer, is in the park.) A swim in a secluded cove tops off the experience. See p. 498, 2.

8 Catching the first glimpse of Skyros Town, Skyros. This hilltop *hora* appears to defy gravity, and at first sight the white houses clinging to a rocky mount high above the coastal plain look like a mirage. Make the ascent to the upper town, where a walk along the steep, narrow lanes only heightens the illusion. See p. 514, 1.

The Sporades in 6 Days

In 6 days, you can savor a strong taste of the Sporades. On Skiathos, you can partake of spectacular beaches and rocking nightlife; on Skopelos, you will encounter one of the most beautiful towns in Greece, along with rolling countryside carpeted with pines and orchards; and on quiet Alonnisos, you will be surrounded by the natural beauty of a national marine park.

> The pine-clad coast around Skiathos Town is fringed with spectacular beaches.

START Skiathos Town. TRIP LENGTH Expect to spend about half a day at sea, as you travel to Skiathos and from there to Skopelos and Alonnisos, then a full day traveling through the National Marine Park of Alonnisos Northern Sporades by boat.

① **Skiathos.** If you manage to be both a sun worshiper and night owl, you will have a full schedule on Skiathos. You can stay busy round

the clock with at least 50 beaches to choose from by day and as many dance-club options by night.

Most visitors spend at least some time on the island's beaches, and you'll probably want to head to one as soon as you settle in on Day 1. Beachgoers usually set their sights on the **south coast** west of Skiathos Town. If you harbor hopes of a quiet strand, you'll be disappointed at first, but to find a little isolation,

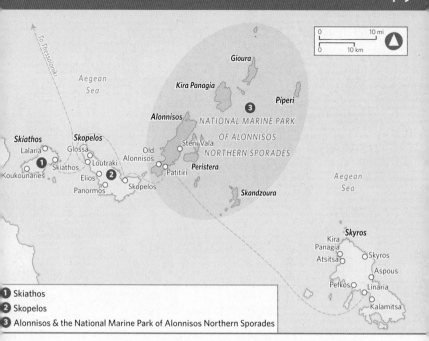

1 Skiathos

2 Skopelos

3 Alonnisos & the National Marine Park of Alonnisos Northern Sporades

keep heading west, to the **Mandraki Peninsula** and the sands that line its shores.

By early evening, islanders and their visitors, who far outnumber year-round residents in summer, congregate for a *volta* along the quays of Skiathos Town, taking time out to watch the sun set and to ogle one another from the terraces of a long string of waterfront cafes and *ouzeries* (p. 502, 1).

On Day 2, venture up to the north coast. The best way to see this rugged side of the island is on an excursion boat from the port in Skiathos Town. You'll pull ashore first at **Lalaria,** a spectacularly beautiful beach surrounded

Getting There

The fastest and easiest way to reach Skiathos is by a short flight from Athens. By boat, the options are ferry (3 hr.) or hydrofoil (1½ hr.) from Volos or Agios Konstantinos (respectively a 4-hr. and 3-hr. bus ride from Athens), or by hydrofoil (1 hr.) from Kymi, on the island of Evvia (a 2½-hr. bus ride from Athens). Skiathos is connected with Skopelos and Alonnisos by frequent ferry and hydrofoil service.

by natural arches and sea grottoes, and then sail on to a pebbly strand below Kastro, the island's onetime capital. Kastro long ago tumbled into the sea, and the ruins tottering on a seaside cliff are eerie and intriguing. If the rugged, brush-covered landscapes on the north coast appeal to you, return on foot or by taxi that afternoon to the **Moni Evangelistrias monastery,** surrounded by pines and cypress atop a deep ravine (p. 504, 4). On Day 3, move on to Skopelos. ⏱ 2 days.

In summer, 8 hydrofoils run daily between Skiathos and Skopelos (45 min.; additional daily ferries make the trip in 90 min.). The easiest way to see the island is by rental car, though buses run to many beaches and some towns, including Klima and Glossa.

2 **Skopelos.** Plan to arrive on Skopelos late in the morning of Day 3, so you can spend a few hours wandering through the lanes of **Skopelos Town**—one of Greece's most appealing towns and the best base for your stay on the island. An uphill climb brings you to the 13th-century **Kastro.** As you take in the view, you'll notice an astonishing number of churches —123 in Skopelos Town and 360 on the entire

> *Whitewashed houses and trim little churches vie for space on the hillside lanes of Skopelos Town.*

island (p. 508, **1**). In the afternoon, head down to one of the beaches southeast of town, and dive into the sea (p. 510, **3**).

Spend Day 4 exploring the rest of the island. First tour some monasteries perched on

Tips on Accommodations

To book hotels, villas, and private rooms on Skiathos, contact **Mare Nostrum Holidays,** 21 Papadiamantis, Skiathos Town (☎ 24270/21463); on Skopelos, **Madro Travel,** waterfront Skopelos Town (☎ 24240/22145; www.madrotravel.gr); on Alonnisos, **Albedo Travel,** waterfront, Patitiri (☎ 24240/65804; www.albedotravel.com), and **Alonnisos Travel,** waterfront, Patitiri (☎ 24240/000; www.alonnisostravel.com); on Skyros, **Skyros Travel,** waterfront, Skyros Town (☎ 22220/91600; www.skyrostravel.com). Also check out the Skiathos Association of Hoteliers (www.skiathoshotels.gr) and Skopelos Association of Hoteliers (www.skopelos.net).

the slopes of **Mount Poulouki.** You'll encounter some beautiful frescoes and icons in **Agia Barbara** and the other churches and chapels, but most impressive are the settings amid olive groves, fruit orchards, and pine forests. You can reach some of the monasteries on a morning's hike from Skopelos Town, and they are also accessible via a network of narrow roads (p. 509, **2**). In the afternoon, head down the island to **Klima,** abandoned by the earthquake of 1965 and slowly coming back to life (p. 510, **5**). After a stop at **Hovolo,** one of the island's most scenic beaches, continue to **Glossa,** almost as beautiful as Skopelos Town and much quieter. The most popular landmark these days is just to the east of town, **Agios Ioannis Church.** Above the sea on a rocky outcropping, the little chapel is so incredibly picturesque that it steals the show in the film *Mamma Mia!*. See p. 508. ☉ 2 days.

Several hydrofoils and ferries run daily between Skopelos and Alonnisos (under 1 hr.). You won't need a car on Alonnisos if you

tay in or near Patitiri; you can reach Hora and
ome beaches by bus, taxi, and/or on foot, and
ou'll tour the park via excursion boat.

**3 Alonnisos & the National Marine Park
of Alonnisos Northern Sporades.** So far,
ou've moved from worldly Skiathos to quieter
Skopelos. As you travel even farther east into
the Aegean, you'll encounter beautiful natural
settings on Alonnisos, surrounded by the
National Marine Park of Alonnisos Northern
Sporades. The 2,200 sq. km (849 sq. miles)
park encompasses eight islands, 22 rocky
outcroppings, and the surrounding seas—all
protected as one of the last remaining habitats
for the highly endangered monk seal, as well
as falcons, dolphins, wild goats, and many
other aquatic and terrestrial species of flora
and fauna (p. 496, **2**).

You can sail through the park by boat on
Day 6, but spend the remainder of Day 5 on
land exploring this delightfully green island
covered in pine, oaks, and scrub in the north
and olive groves and fruit orchards in the
south. Climb to hilltop **Hora,** the former capital abandoned after the 1965 earthquake, and
then travel up the east coast to the beaches
around **Kokkinokastro,** about 3km (2 miles)
north of Patitiri and served by the island bus
(p. 496, **1**).

Spend Day 6 exploring the park on a tour
boat. In season, many offices on the waterfront in Patitiri run excursions; most last a
full day, include lunch, and pull ashore now
and then on deserted islands for swimming,
snorkeling, and the chance to catch a glimpse
of wild goats and rare seabirds. Expect to pay
about 40€ a person. ⏲ **2 days.**

> *Cruises show off the natural wonders of the National Marine Park of Alonnisos Northern Sporades.*

The Sporades in 9 Days

Nine days in the Sporades will provide a bounty of experiences. You can lie on countless beaches and dance till dawn in Skiathos, wander through beautiful towns and villages and take in endless sweeps of forested mountainsides on Skopelos, and cruise through the pristine waters and islets that surround unspoiled Alonnisos. A sail to the east brings you to Skyros, a unique outpost of Greek island life the way it once was, topped by a beautiful *hora* that seems to float in the clouds.

> The Tripia Petra, arches sculpted by the wind out of marble headlands, frame the beach at Lalaria.

START Skiathos. **TRIP LENGTH** You'll spend about a day traveling to and among four islands, but that too will be an experience, plus a day touring the National Marine Park of Alonnisos Northern Sporades by boat.

❶ Skiathos. Two days on Skiathos will allow for beach-hopping on the south coast, an excursion to the north coast, and squandering as many pre-dawn hours as you wish in the bars and clubs that draw hordes of summertime revelers to this island from Athens and northern Europe. However you reach Skiathos, plan to arrive on the island by the early afternoon of Day 1. Your lodgings will most likely be in Skiathos Town or in one of the many resorts on the south coast. Settle in, and then hop on the bus that runs up and down the coast, making stops at beaches and hotels. First, set your sights on **Koukounaries,** 12km (7 miles) west of Skiathos Town. The golden sands skirting a sparkling bay fringed with pines are some of the most beautiful in Greece. If you're in search of a little more solitude than Koukounaries provides, stroll through sandy-floored pine groves to **Limonki Xerxes** and **Elias,** two lovely beaches on the Mandraki Peninsula at the far western tip of the island (p. 503, ❷). Return to Skiathos Town in time for a cocktail at one of the many bars along the quays, and while you're there (p. 502, ❶), check with one of the travel offices near the port to plan an excursion by boat the next day to Lalaria and Kastro.

You'll set sail on the morning of Day 2. First stop is **Lalaria,** a scenic beach backed by cliffs

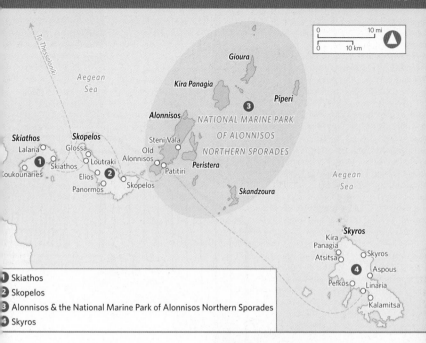

1 Skiathos

2 Skopelos

3 Alonnisos & the National Marine Park of Alonnisos Northern Sporades

4 Skyros

aced with spectacular sea grottoes. Most
boats squeeze into the largest, **Spilia Skotini,**
shimmering in beautifully ethereal light (p.
504, 3). The next stop is usually the pebbly
strand below Kastro, the island's onetime capital. Take another swim, and then scramble up
to the ruins of this once heavily fortified town,
abandoned in the early 19th century when the
demise of piracy made it safe to settle next to
the sea (p. 505, 5). Boats usually return to
Skiathos Town by midafternoon, leaving time
to board the beach bus and plop down on your
favorite stretch of sand. ⏲ **2 days.**

2 **Skopelos.** The morning of Day 3, move on
to Skopelos. Settle in and spend the rest of the
day exploring Skopelos Town (p. 508, 1). You
won't come upon many landmarks, though the
steep, mazelike lanes of balconied houses covered with flowering vines are enchanting. Try

Getting There

See p. 488, "The Sporades in 6 Days," for
tips on getting to Skiathos, Skopelos, and
Alonnisos. For continuing to Skyros, see
p. 515.

> An upward glance on Skiathos usually takes in a
belfry or church dome.

> *Skopelos has so many churches it's said that islanders count steeples rather than sheep to fall asleep.*

to make the uphill climb to the 13th-century Kastro and step into the **Folk Museum,** filled with artifacts from the island. Devote Day 4 to exploring the rest of the island. In the morning, make the rounds of the monasteries on **Mount Poulouki** and in the afternoon travel north to **Klima** (p. 510, ⑤), a deserted town slowly being resurrected, and then move on to **Glossa,** another beautiful town set amid orchards next to the sea at the northern tip of the island (p. 511, ⑥). ⏱ 2 days.

③ **Alonnisos & the National Marine Park of Alonnisos Northern Sporades.** Day 5 takes you farther east, to **Alonnisos** (p. 496, ①). Plan to arrive by early afternoon, so you'll have time to climb up to **Hora,** the old capital, and take a bus to one of the beaches around **Kokkinokastro.** A swim here comes with the chance to glimpse the remnants of the ancient

sunken city of **Ikos** on the seabed. Day 6 takes you out to sea, on an excursion into the **National Marine Park of Alonnisos Northern Sporades,** a refuge for the highly endangered Mediterranean monk seal (p. 496, ②). You are not likely to see the elusive animal, but you will see dolphins and seabirds and enjoy stops on deserted beaches on some of the eight islands within the park's boundaries. ⏱ 2 days

On Day 7, move on to Skyros. The trip takes 1–4 hr. (In high season, 1 hour if the Alonnisos Skyros ferry is running. In the off season, at least 4 hr., when the trip requires a transfer at Kyma on the island of Evia for a Skyros-bound boat.)

④ **Skyros.** Skyros is set off by itself in the middle of the Aegean, quite distant from the other Sporades, and you'll soon discover how

Pirates of the Aegean

Greece has a long tradition of piracy that dates back to ancient times. Hundreds of islands, most of them uninhabited, once provided hidden anchorages from which to launch attacks on merchandise-laden ships crisscrossing the Aegean on the way to and from the Near East, North Africa, and Western Europe. The Sporades, floating in the lucrative sea routes to and from Thessaloniki, were pirate lairs well into the 19th century. An infamous female pirate, Adrina, operated out of Sporades until islanders slaughtered her marauders and she plunged to her death from a rock above the bay at Panormos—but not, or so the story goes, before burying a horde of gold somewhere along the shoreline. Soon enough, islanders wised up and grew wealthy by alerting pirates to merchant ships that were especially ripe for plunder and receiving a cut of the profits in return. Skyrian workshops still turn out ceramics and handcarved chests and chairs based on exotic designs that pirates brought to the island from afar.

> A virile statue of British poet Rupert Brooke raised eyebrows on Skyros in the 1930s.

he small island is in every aspect a land apart. The only real settlement, Skyros Town, seems to float in midair atop its craggy bluff. Many islanders still wear traditional garb—baggy trousers for the men, head scarves for the women—and houses are proudly decorated with distinctive ceramics and carved furniture. You can get a close look at these traditions at the **Manos Faltaits Museum,** just off the square and presided over by a statue commemorating the British poet Rupert Brooke, who died on a hospital ship anchored off Skyros in 1915 (p. 514, ❶). You can visit the poet's grave on the south of the island, but first, spend the remainder of Day 8 exploring the north end, starting with the beaches just below Skyros Town, Magazia, and Molos. At Palamari, on the northern tip, the beach is backed by the ruins of a 4,000-year-old settlement. Some of Skyros's best beaches are around **Atsitsa,** where expanses of white pebbles are shaded by pines and cedars (p. 516, ❷).

On Day 9, head south through landscapes that are much more rugged than those in the north. Several fine beaches line the coast around **Kalamitsa** and **Kolymbada,** and the road ends at **Tris Boukes,** a beautiful bay surrounded by pine groves and olive groves that are the final resting place of Rupert Brooke (p. 518, ❸). ⏱ 2½ days.

The National Marine Park of Alonnisos Northern Sporades

Founded in 1992, the National Marine Park of Alonnisos Northern Sporades protects the waters and islands of the eastern Sporades and the myriad creatures who thrive there—including falcons, seabirds, and, most notably, the highly endangered monk seal. Alonnisos is the only inhabited island within the park boundaries; cloaked in green and decidedly low-key, the little island is an especially pleasant place from which to explore the park's pristine waters.

> Desert-island beaches are among the protected wonders of the National Marine Park.

START Alonnisos. TRIP LENGTH At least 2 days.

❶ ★★★ **Alonnisos.** Even if Alonnisos weren't within the boundaries of the National Marine Park, the island would be nirvana for nature enthusiasts, with its rugged landscapes of pine and cedar forests, rockbound coasts, and

an ambience that is far more low-key than tha of Skiathos or Skopelos.

The long, narrow island, 23km (14 miles) from north to south and 3km (2 miles) at its widest point, is covered with pine, oak, and scrub in the north and olive groves and fruit

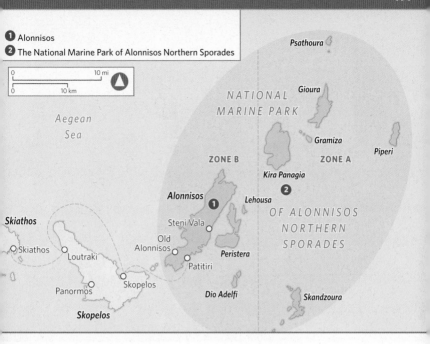

1 Alonnisos
2 The National Marine Park of Alonnisos Northern Sporades

orchards in the south. Beaches are pebbly and less spectacular than those on Skiathos and Skopelos, but the waters, protected as they are by the national park, are some of the purest in the Mediterranean. These seas also harbor a number of ancient shipwrecks as well as some sunken vessels from the days of Byzantine and Venetian occupation; diving is restricted but available through **Alonnisos Diving School,** Patitiri (☎ 24240/66360).

The island's only two sizable settlements are in the south. Beautiful hilltop Hora, or Old Town Alonnisos, was largely toppled by an earthquake in 1965 and abandoned. Residents were relocated to the hastily expanded port town, **Patitiri**—which takes its name from the dockside wine presses that were much in demand until the 1950s, when phylloxera laid waste to the island's vines.

Now populated mostly by Northern Europeans, Hora is slowly being restored and is more pretty than authentic. On a clear day, the views extend all the way to Mount Athos on the northern mainland. A road, with bus service, connects the two towns, as does an old, stepped mule track on which you can make the ascent in less than an hour. Most beaches

are on the east coast, accessible off the island's only north–south road; several cluster around **Kokkinokastro,** about 3km (2 miles) north of Patitiri, and can be reached by bus. The walls of the ancient city of **Ikos** are visible beneath the waves.

Alonnisos is laced with a network of 14 trails that traverse the length of the island, crossing olive groves, pine forests, and rocky gorges and dropping down to secluded coves. Walking tours and route maps are available from the **Alonnisos Walking Club** (www. alonnisoswalks.co.uk); you can contact the club via the website or through **Albedo Travel** in Patitiri, ☎ 24240/65804. If you plan to do some serious walking on Alonnisos, pick up

Getting There

Alonnisos is about 10km (6¼ miles) east of Skopelos and is connected by several hydrofoils and ferries a day in season. You will not need a car for this tour; you can navigate Alonnisos on foot or by bus, and you'll be touring the marine park by boat. Plan to arrive in the morning for a full day on the island.

> *Old town Alonnisos is known to locals as Hora.*

a copy of *Alonnisos Through the Souls of Your Feet*, available at Albedo and elsewhere on the island, or in advance through the walking club's website. ⏲ 1 day.

In summer, you can tour the park on excursion boats from Alonnisos; you'll see signs advertising trips along the dock in Patitiri, where the park also runs an information booth (summer only, hours vary). Alonnisos Travel offers tours on a beautiful sailboat, the *Planitis* (waterfront, Patitiri; ☎ 24240/000).

2 **kids** ★★★ **The National Marine Park of Alonnisos Northern Sporades.** The marine park was established in 1992 to protect the endangered Mediterranean monk seal, whose numbers in Greek seas are now estimated to be less than 200. The park covers 2,200 sq. km (849 sq. miles), making it the largest marine protected area in the Mediterranean. Within the park are eight islands, of which only Alonnisos is inhabited, 22 rocky outcroppings, and the marine habitats that surround them. In addition to the shy seals, who rarely

Rooms with a View

Two excellent hotels, open from mid-May through September, are a good value in convenient locations for park guests. On a hilltop above Patitiri, ★★ **Atrium Hotel** (☎ 24240/65750; www.atriumalonnissos. gr; doubles 120€–130€ w/breakfast) offers some of the most luxurious accommodations on the island. Rooms are stylish and very comfortable; views are spectacular; and amenities include a swimming pool, bar, and excellent service. ★★★ **Paradise Hotel** (☎ 24240/65160; www.paradise-hotel.gr; doubles 60€–80€ w/breakfast) is a pleasant little retreat above the sea on one of the pine-clad hillsides surrounding Alonnisos. Rooms are simple but comfortable, and most overlook the pool and terraced gardens to the sea; first floor units are especially nice, with terraces surrounded by greenery. Swimming in a beautiful cove just beneath the hotel may prove to be the height of your visit to the park.

...ake an appearance, falcons, dolphins, and ...ild goats also call the island home, along ...ith many less showy but nonetheless invalu-...ble species of sponges, algae, and land-...ubbing flora, including the wild olive.

Tour boats, often escorted by dolphins, ...hug past the scattered island refuges, though ...sighting of the seals and wild goats they ...rotect is almost as rare as a glimpse of the ...yclops who inhabited a cave on one of the ...lands, cliff-ringed Gioura, in Homer's *Odys-*...*ey.* Boats keep a safe distance from **Piperi,** ...ne major habitat for the monk seal and rare ...leonora's falcon. Stops often include **Kyra** ...**anagia,** for swimming, snorkeling, and a walk

to the island's one outpost of civilization, the all-but-abandoned **Megistis Lavras** monas-tery; **Psathoura,** where the tallest lighthouse in the Aegean rises above a white-sand beach and the remains of an ancient city is visible on the seabed; and **Peristera,** opposite Alonnisos and alluring for its remote beaches.

Conservationists applaud the park's pres-ervation efforts, while many locals claim the park impinges on resort development, fishing, and other economic opportunities. Make it a point to let restaurateurs and hoteliers know that you have come to the Sporades in part to enjoy the park—that the park enhances tour-ism rather than hindering it. ⏱ **1 day.**

The Mediterranean Monk Seal

The Mediterranean monk seal is one of the world's most endangered marine mam-mals—only an estimated 600 exist world-wide. Hunting probably pushed the num-bers close to extinction as early as Roman and medieval times, and even until recently fishermen routinely killed off the seals to cut down on competition—2.5m long (more than 8 ft.) and weighing up to 300kg (661 pounds), the seals devour 3kg (7 pounds) of fish, octopus, squid, and other sea creatures a day. Since development has sullied once pristine shorelines, the seals no longer lounge and whelp on open beaches and instead seek out sea caves with submerged entrances far from human intrusion. Bat-tered by waves, the caves are less than ideal nurseries, and infant mortality is high. For ancient Greeks, sighting a monk seal was an omen of good fortune. The creature's survival would bode equally well for the Sporades.

NATION OF ISLANDS

BY TANIA KOLLIAS

GREECE HAS AN ESTIMATED 6,000 TO 9,000 ISLANDS AND ISLETS. Only about 200 are populated. They account for 20% of the landmass of this England-sized country but only 12.5% of the population. Many fishermen, sponge divers, boat-builders, and merchant seamen who lived off the sea left after WWII, but some of their children have returned to cater to tourism, the country's second largest earner after shipping. Some 27 islands have airports, and ferry routes to remoter ones are subsidized. Services wind down in winter, when villagers often move to second homes in mainland cities.

Island Sampler

Whether lush and mountainous, barren and flat, or, like Kefalonia, graced by gorgeous beaches such as Myrtos (left), each island has a history and culture as unique as its landscape.

CORFU
Location: Ionian Islands
Area: 591 sq. km (228 sq. miles)
Population: 10,000
On this island opposite Italy and historically tied with Venetian, French, and British rule, the locals think of themselves as descendants of a more sophisticated West European tradition.

CRETE
Location: Southern Greece
Area: 8,336 sq. km (3,218 sq. miles)
Population: 600,000
Greece's largest island is famous for its longevity-promoting Cretan Diet: olive oil, whole grains, and unlimited local fresh fruits and vegetables; limited fish and dairy; and a glass of red wine with dinner. Crete ships surplus produce to the rest of Greece.

EVIA
Location: Central Greece
Area: 3,580 sq. km (1,382 sq. miles)
Population: 220,000
Greece's second largest island is connected to the mainland by two bridges, making it seem part of the mainland. It's also one of the least visited and least expensive islands, with natural spas such as Gialtra, attractive villages such as Ano Potamia, and beautiful beaches such as Chiliadou.

GAVDOS
Location: Southern Greece
Area: 27 sq. km (10 sq. miles)
Population: 80
At the southernmost tip of Europe, in the Libyan Sea some 24 nautical miles south of Crete (1½–3½ hours away by boat), Europe's southernmost territory is a place to literally get away from it all, with about 40 inhabitants and villages abandoned when Gavdos became a pirate hideaway during Venetian rule.

SANTORINI
Location: Southern Cyclades
Area: 73 sq. km (28 sq. miles)
Population: 13,670
The volcanic eruption that covered Akrotiri in the 17th century B.C., forming Santorini's stunning caldera, pre-dated the eruption of Vesuvius that covered Pompeii in 79 A.D. by nearly two millennia.

SKOPELOS
Location: Sporades
Area: 101 sq. km (39 sq. miles)
Population: 5,000
Interest in holding weddings, honeymoons, and anniversaries in lush and little-visited Skopelos has spiked since *Mamma Mia!*, with Meryl Streep, was filmed here in 2008.

Flora & Fauna

Greece supports some 5,500 species of flora, including rare and endemic species. Oak, fir, fig, and olive trees, plus juniper, oleander, and prickly pear cactuses are common in Greece's temperate climate, as are wildflowers and herbs, including mintlike dittany, a medicinal specialtyon Crete.

Greece's 900 animal species include Crete's endemic Kri-kri wild goat and rare Cretan wildcat.

The loggerhead sea turtle, most associated with the island of Zakynthos, and the monk seal are protected; Aegean dolphins and porpoises are also endangered.

Fish are hardy and lean, due to a paucity of nutrients in the sea, but they have been over-fished, and the effect of sea pollution is a concern.

How They Formed

The Greek Islands are a continuation of Europe's Alpine range, which reaches through the Aegean Sea to Crete, created some 60 million years ago during the Alpine Orogeny. Erosion at Gibraltar caused the Atlantic Ocean flooding of the Mediterranean basin some 6 million years ago (thought to be the basis for the biblical flood). The islands are the mountain summits penetrating the surface.

Greece is earthquake-prone, as its small Aegean Sea tectonic plate is jostled by the larger Eurasian, African, and Arabian plates. It has volcanoes, too: The South Aegean Volcanic Arc includes Nisyros and Santorini, which are active, and Milos and the Methana peninsula, which are dormant.

Skiathos

Philip of Macedonia, Persian king Xerxes, and many occupiers over the centuries probably made less of an impact on this island than travelers have made in the past 30 years or so. Yet Skiathos doesn't entirely lose its identity in the presence of 50,000 visitors a year. Outside Skiathos Town and the resort-and-sand-lined south coast, the small island retains much of its rugged, pine-clad beauty.

> In Skiathos Town, day-to-day life centers on the busy waterfront.

START Skiathos Town. **TRIP LENGTH** 2 days will allow you time to lie on a beach and see the sights.

❶ ★ Skiathos Town. Outdoor cafes, postcard stands, and souvenir shops are as profuse as the bougainvillea that climbs whitewashed houses clustered on two low-lying hills above the harbor. Among the picturesque remnants of old Skiathos are the fort that knights of Venice erected on a pine-clad peninsula known as **Bourtzi**. It's now a cultural center connected to the mainland by a causeway. An old quarter of cobblestone and stepped

lanes surround the **Church of Trion Ierarchon** (Three Archbishops) to the west of the port, and the **Papadiamantis Museum** (off Papadiamantis St.; ☎ 24270/23843; admission 2€; Tues–Sun 9:30am–1pm and 5–8pm), just off the harbor, is the humble, simply furnished home of islander Alexandros Papadiamantis, one of Greece's finest writers of fiction. Far more popular than these relics of erstwhile island life are the modern bars, clubs, and *ouzeries* stretching cheek-by-jowl along the waterfront all the way to the yacht harbor, confirming that most visitors come to Skiathos in search of sun and fun.

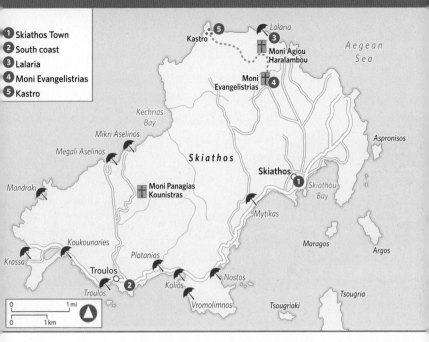

1 Skiathos Town
2 South coast
3 Lalaria
4 Moni Evangelistrias
5 Kastro

No matter where you stay on the island, you'll spend some time in Skiathos Town; all roads converge there, and the port is the departure point not only for ferries but also for excursion boats to the relatively remote north coast and islets just offshore. ☺ Half-day.

A shuttle bus plies the south coast as often as every 15 minutes in the summer, making 25 stops between Skiathos Town and Koukounaries.

2 ★★★ **South coast.** Most of the island's famed beaches ring the coves and bays that etch the south coast. All are sandy and protected from the northerly *meltemi* winds, just as a welcome barrier of pine trees shields them from an almost unbroken line of resorts, shops, and restaurants. **Koukounaries,** 12km (7 miles) west of Skiathos Town, is widely touted as the most beautiful strand on the island. No one can deny the loveliness of this golden crescent, stretching for 1km (½ mile) with crystalline waters backed by fragrant pine groves, but you'll be sharing your appreciation with thousands of other beachgoers.

Those in search of relative quiet can stroll from Koukounaries for about 2km (1 mile) through shady groves to **Limonki Xerxes** and **Elias,** two lovely beaches on the Mandraki Peninsula at the far western tip of the island. Limonki Xerxes is named for the Persian king who moored his fleet here before his ill-fated attempt to conquer the Greek mainland during the Persian wars in the 5th century B.C. A few piles of stones on the peninsula are believed to be some of the world's first lighthouses, erected by the Persians to guide their *triremes* safely across the reefs at night. Nudists usually find their way to **Little Banana** (a

Getting There

The fastest and easiest way to reach Skiathos is on a short flight from Athens. By boat, the options are ferry (3 hr.) or hydrofoil (1½ hr.) from the mainland ports of Volos or Agios Konstantinos (respectively 4 hr. and 3 hr. from Athens by bus), or by hydrofoil (1 hr.) from Kymi, on the island of Evvia (2½ hr. by bus from Athens). You won't need a car while visiting the island—you can reach the south coast beaches by shuttle bus and sites on the north of the island by excursion boat. A municipal tourist office on the harbor is open daily 9am–8pm in season.

> *Koukounaries is widely regarded as the most beautiful beach on Skiathos.*

non-anatomical reference to the shape and color of the beach). ⏱ Half-day.

Lalaria and the grottoes can be reached only by boat; excursions leave from the port in Skiathos Town about 10am every day. You can also hire a water taxi, but it's costly and you'll share the beach and grottoes with excursion boat tours anyway.

❸ ★★★ kids **Lalaria.** The top contender for the island's most scenic spot is this beach of marble pebbles nestled beneath limestone cliffs. The **Tripia Petra,** natural arches sculpted from the rock by wind and waves, frame the beach, and the marble seabed imbues the turquoise waters with a nearly supernatural translucence. Caves are etched into the base of the cliffs, and just to the east are three spectacular sea grottoes—**Spilia Skotini** (Dark Cave), **Spilia Galazia** (Azure Cave), and **Spilia Halkini** (Copper Cave). Boats squeeze through the narrow channel into Spilia Skotini and shine a light to transform the 6m-high (20-ft.) cavern into a neon blue water world. ⏱ Half-day.

Moni Evangelistrias is 5km (3 miles) north of Skiathos Town, accessible on foot via a well-

marked path through the brush (ask at the Tourist Information Office). If you are driving or taking a taxi to the monastery, don't miss the pretty and remote beach at Megas Yialos on the way.

❹ ★ **Moni Evangelistrias.** A setting atop a deep ravine amid pines and cypresses lends this large monastery of golden stone an especially ethereal quality. It was founded by monks who left Mount Athos after a dispute in 1794. Like many monasteries around Greece, the compound was soon sheltering revolutionaries fighting for freedom from the Turkish occupation. It's claimed that the first Greek flag was woven here and raised above the high walls in 1807. The icon-filled church has been restored, and monks' cells, a kitchen, and a refectory surround the shady courtyard (open daily; free admission). ⏱ 2 hr.

Boat excursions to Lalaria usually include a stop on the beach beneath Kastro, from which a steep trail climbs the cliffs to the ruins. Overland, Kastro is 10km (6¼ miles) northeast of Skiathos Town; by car from Moni Evangelistrias, take a narrow road west, then

The Church of Trion Ierarchon rises from the heart of the Old Quarter of Skiathos Town.

orth up to Kastro (3km/2 miles). From the oad, a short steep path leads to the ruins.

5 ★★ **Kastro.** By the 16th century, repeated irate raids forced islanders to take refuge in fortified compound on high ground. A drawridge, moat, and high, thick walls deterred nvaders approaching by land, and steep cliffs lropping into the water thwarted any approach y sea. Over the years a thriving village of 300 ouses and 22 churches took shape within the valls. Kastro was abandoned for Skiathos Town n the 1820s, when piracy dried up with the reation of the new Greek state, making seaside ettlement safe once again. The elements have aken their toll on the wind-swept headland, nd all but a few houses and churches have rumbled into the Aegean. You can walk around he ruins and peer in at the faded frescoes in he church of **Yeni Nisi tou Khristou,** but most mpressive are the views across the sea to the slet of **Kastronisia.** ⏱ 2 hr. including beach time you'll have about an hour at Kastro on a boat our).

Sand & Surf

More than 50 beaches ring Skiathos, and 50,000 summertime visitors set their sights on them. In July and August, you'll be hard pressed to find an unoccupied patch of sand anywhere on the island, but if you don't mind company, you'll enjoy some of Greece's most beautiful shores. You'll be able to rent beach chairs and umbrellas on most beaches, even on the more remote strands on the north coast accessible only by boat. You'll also find plenty of ways to stay active, especially on the south coast beaches. Activities abound on Kanapitsa Beach, where the **Kanapitsa Water Sports Center** (☎ 24270/21298) will equip you to water-ski, jet-ski, and windsurf, and the **Dolphin Diving Center** (☎ 24270/21599), organizes dives and offers certification. On Vassilias Beach, **Stefanos Ski School** (☎ 24270/21487), rents boats and runs water-skiing and wakeboard lessons.

Where to Stay on Skiathos

> *The ocean side pool at Atrium.*

★★★ **Aegean Suites** MEGALI AMMOS, NEAR SKIATHOS TOWN Luxury defines these beautiful seaside suites where guests feel like they are staying in a private villa. Handsome and comfortable accommodations are complemented by beautiful gardens, a nearby beach, and intimate lounges and restaurants. Skiathos Town is just a walk or short taxi ride away. ☎ 24270/24069. www.santikoshotels.com. Suites 350€–600€ w/breakfast. AE, MC, V. Closed late Oct to mid-Apr.

★★★ **Atrium** PLATANIAS, SOUTH COAST One of the island's nicest beach hotels is attractive and intimate, commanding endless sea views from a pine-clad hillside on the south coast, some 8km (5 miles) outside Skiathos Town. Wood and warm stone add a great deal of character to all the accommodations, which range from doubles to lavish maisonettes. The beach is a short walk down the road, and a restaurant, cocktail lounge, and beautiful pool and terrace help make Atrium an ideal refuge. Agia Paraskevi. ☎ 24270/49345. www.atriumhotel.gr. 75 units. Doubles 120€–160€ w/breakfast. AE, MC, V. Closed Oct to mid-May.

★★ **Bourtzi** SKIATHOS TOWN It stands to reason that sophisticated Skiathos should have accommodations as chic as these contemporary and comfortable rooms in the center of Skiathos Town. The pool will tide you over between trips to the beach, and the cocktail lounge may provide all the nightlife you need. 8 Moraitou. ☎ 24270/21304. www.hotelbourtzi.gr. 24 units. Doubles 135€–150€ w/breakfast. MC, V.

★★ kids **Skiathos Princess** PLATANIAS, SOUTH COAST This huge south coast resort complex, the largest on the island, may not provide an authentic sense of Greece, but the rooms and suites are extremely comfortable and attractive, and the beautiful pool, spa, choice of restaurants, and sandy beach heighten the draw. Agia Paraskevi. ☎ 24270/49731. www.skiathosprincess.com. 131 units. Doubles 150€–220€ w/breakfast. AE, MC, V. Closed late Oct to mid-Apr.

★★ kids **Troulos Bay** TROULOS, SOUTH COAST This lovely, low-key beachfront hotel, on the south coast about 10km (6¼ miles) west of Skiathos Town, manages to capture the easygoing ambience of the island with beautifully landscaped grounds, a pretty beach, and attentive service. Rooms are plain but attractive, and all have seaview balconies. ☎ 24270/49390. www.troulosbayhotel.gr. 43 units. Doubles 90€–100€ w/breakfast. Closed Nov–Apr.

Where to Dine on Skiathos

★ **Maria's** SKIATHOS TOWN *ITALIAN*
If you're willing, or eager, to forgo traditional Greek taverna fare for a night, look no farther than this excellent, casual trattoria that would hold its own in Italy. Thin-crusted pizzas are superb and can be accompanied with huge, excellent salads and the house wine. **Near harbor. Entrees 6€–12€. No credit cards. Dinner daily.**

★★ **Taverna Alexandros** SKIATHOS TOWN
GREEK This Skiathos institution serves traditional taverna fare on a tree-shaded terrace and in a stone-walled room just off the harbor. Best bets are the standards—meats grilled over an open fire and the daily special, varying according to the freshest market offerings. Live music adds a festive note to dinners during the summer season. **Behind the old port. ☎ 24270/22431. Entrees 6€–8€. MC, V. Lunch & dinner daily.**

★★ **Taverna Amenos** SKIATHOS TOWN *GREEK*
The self-proclaimed oldest taverna on the island is also, in the minds of many regulars, the best. Grilled meat and simply prepared fish from the market on the quay below is served on a balcony overlooking the bay. Friendly service

> *Skiathos may draw chic visitors, but* stifado *and other traditional fare are still local favorites.*

enhances one of the most pleasant dining experiences on Skiathos. **Atop the stairs at the far end of the old port. ☎ 24270/021003. Entrees 7€–14€. MC, V. Lunch & dinner daily.**

★★ **Taverna Selini** SKIATHOS TOWN *GREEK*
Many visitors eat here almost every night, to take in the sweeping views of the harbor while dining on traditional favorites such as *kelftiko,* feta-stuffed roast lamb, and *stifado,* beef cooked in red wine and vegetables. **Above the old port. ☎ 24270/24460. Entrees 6€–12€. MC, V. Lunch & dinner daily.**

★★★ **Windmill** SKIATHOS TOWN *GREEK/MEDI-TERRANEAN* A converted mill is the setting for the most memorable dining experience on Skiathos. The rambling terraces are romantic, the food is international and deftly prepared, and service is polished and warm. **Above Papadiamantis St. ☎ 24270/24550. Entrees 12€–20€. No credit cards. Dinner daily. Closed mid-Oct to May.**

Skiathos After Dark

You can count on Skiathos Town for a lively nightclub scene, just as you can be assured of finding a bar or club to your taste on the narrow lanes off Papadiamantis Street in the center of town and on the quays of the old port. What you can't rely on is a club surviving much longer than a season or two. A reliable year-in, year-out island institution is the **Aegean Festival,** staged from late June through early October in the outdoor theater of the Bourtzi, the pine-clad fortress that Venetians erected in the harbor in the 13th century. Events range from classical Greek drama to modern dance and experimental music; most begin at 9:30pm and cost 15€.

Skopelos

This near neighbor just to the east of Skiathos is larger, greener, and, for the most part, carpeted by pine groves and orchards rather than by resorts. Not that Skopelos shuns visitors—it's just that here you'll still encounter relatively undisturbed island life in the spectacular countryside, on the cove-etched coast, and in two of the most beautiful small towns in Greece, SkopelosTown and Glossa.

> An amble up and down the lanes of Skopelos Town is one of the island's greatest pleasures.

START Skopelos Town. **TRIP LENGTH** Allow at least 2 days to explore the island, with a bit of time for relaxing on a beach and wandering around Skopelos Town. You won't cover more than 100km (60 miles) in your explorations.

1 ★★★ **Skopelos Town.** The island capital and the administrative center for the Sporades, Skopelos Town remains one of the most appealing island towns in Greece, holding its own against an onslaught of visitors. (The most recent surge in popularity was inspired by the film *Mamma Mia!*, shot in

large part on the island.) White houses and blue-domed churches climb a hillside above the bay, and brightly painted shutters and balconies complement a colorful array of climbing vines. The hilly quarters above the waterfront reward casual strollers with views back to the sea over rooftops of rough-hewn slate and the pine-clad hills that ring the port. Provided you walk up, you'll eventually reach the 13th-century Kastro. The Venetian lords who were awarded the Sporades after the sack of Constantinople in the 13th century erected this stronghold on the foundations

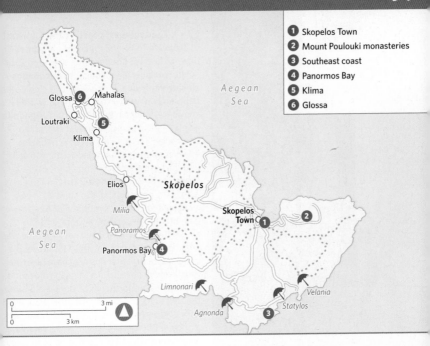

1 Skopelos Town
2 Mount Poulouki monasteries
3 Southeast coast
4 Panormos Bay
5 Klima
6 Glossa

of an ancient acropolis from the 5th century B.C. Amid the ancient masonry are the ruins of fortress walls built by Philip of Macedonia when he took the island in 340 B.C.

The highest and oldest of the town's 123 churches, 11th-century **Agios Athanasios,** rises from within the Kastro walls. All in all, Skopelos has 360 churches, many built by grateful islanders who survived the mass slaughter of Barbarossa, the Ottoman pirate. The sight of so many white churches glistening on the hillsides inspired the novelist Lawrence Durrell to remark that islanders count churches not sheep when they can't sleep. Back down the hill, the **Folklore Museum,** Hatzistamatis St. (☎ 24240 23494; admission 3€; open May–Sept daily 10am–10pm), focuses on domestic furnishings and embroidery for which island women are known throughout Greece; just as interesting is the old mansion in which the costumes, ceramics, and other handiwork are arranged. ◷ Half-day.

With a map from the tourist office, you can explore these monasteries on foot along a well-marked path in less than a day. You can also reach some of them on rough roads by car.

2 ★ **The Mount Poulouki monasteries.** The slopes of Mount Poulouki, topping a peninsula to the east of Skopelos Town, cradle a clutch of the island's 40 monasteries amid olive groves and prune and almond orchards that give way to deeply green pine forests. **Moni Evangelismou,** about 4km (2½ miles) east of Skopelos Town, was founded in 1712 by a Skopelitan noble who imported monks from Mount Athos to establish a center of learning. Today the all-but-deserted compound is best appreciated for its remote location and

Getting There

From Skiathos, about eight hydrofoils make the 45-minute crossing to Skopelos Town daily; others serve Glossa. Most boats from the mainland ports of Agios Konstantinos and Volos first stop at Skiathos, where you often have to change boats. You can get around Skopelos by bus, but for a short stay a rental car is best. The municipal tourist office is on the pier in Skopelos Town (☎ 24240/23231; daily 9:30am–10pm in season).

> *Revelers masquerade as brides as part of Skopelos Town's carnival celebrations.*

spectacular views toward Skopelos Town and the sea, as well as a beautiful *iconostasis* containing an 11th-century icon of the Virgin Mary (daily 8am–1pm and 4–7pm). **Agia Barbara,** about 6km (4 miles) east of Skopelos Town, is heavily fortified, surrounded by a high wall, and the church is decorated with frescoes that colorfully depict the main feasts in the Orthodox calendar. **St. John the Baptist** (also known as Prodromos, or Forerunner) is only 300m (984 ft.) away, housing some especially beautiful icons. Just beyond the pair is **Metamorphosis,** the oldest monastery on the island, founded in the 16th century (hours for the last three vary considerably). ⏲ Half-day. Follow signs toward Moni Evangelismou from Skopelos Town.

❸ ★★ **The southeast coast.** To the southeast of Skopelos Town, the rugged terrain drops down to seaside promontories surrounded by small, sparkling bays along the **Drachondos-chisma Peninsula.** This is where St. Reginos is believed to have slain a dragon that was devouring islanders in the 4th century. **Agnonda,** a small fishing port on the west side of the peninsula 5km (3 miles) south of Skopelos Town, is named for an island youth who sailed into the cove after his victory in the 546 B.C. Olympic games. **Stafylos,** 2 km (1 mile) east across the peninsula, is also steeped in ancient legend, named for the son of Ariadne, daughter of Minos, king of Crete, and Dionysos, the god who rescued her when she was abandoned on Naxos (p. 342). Whatever the real parentage of Stafylos may have been, he is believed to have been a Minoan who found his way this far north. A 3,500-year-old tomb thought to be his was unearthed in 1935, filled with gold and weapons. Stafylos is these days a popular but low-key beach, while **Velania,** a short trek across a headland, is more isolated and quieter; bathing suits are optional. ⏲ 2 hr.

Panormos Bay is due west of Skopelos Town, about 7km (4 miles), via a road that drops south and then follows the coast toward Glossa.

❹ ★★ **Panormos Bay.** Beach life on Skopelos centers on **Milia, Adrina,** and other strands lining this broad, sheltered bay, once a lair for pirates (see p. 495). A few stony remnants of an 8th-century B.C. settlement are hidden amid the pine woods above the sparkling waters. Inland are the orchards where farmers grow plums and apricots, for which Skopelos is famous throughout Greece—plums and prunes appear frequently in stews and other dishes served on the island. ⏲ 1 hr.

Klima is 13km (10 miles) north of Panormos Bay and 20km (12 miles) west of Skopelos Town, off the road that runs up the west coast of the island.

❺ ★ **Klima.** An earthquake dislodged all the residents of one of the island's most prosperous towns in 1965, but Klima is slowly being reclaimed. Some trim houses, newly whitewashed and roofed with red tiles, are taking shape amid the rubble in **Ano Klima,** the

> *Agios Athanasios is the oldest and highest of the 123 churches in Skopelos Town.*

upper town, and **Kato Klima,** the lower town. Even so, the place still has the feel of a ghost town, and looking through paneless windows and open doorways you'll catch glimpses of abandoned bakery ovens and *kalliagres,* hand-operated olive presses, remnants of life the way it was when the village came to a standstill. **Elios,** just 3km (2 miles) south, hurriedly assembled in the wake of the 1960s earthquake, is far less colorful than Klima, whose residents were resettled here. Next to town, though, is cliff-backed **Hovolo,** one of the island's most scenic beaches. **Kastani,** about 2km (1 mile) south of Elios, is one of the few sandy beaches on the island. ⏱1 hr.

Glossa is 3km (2 miles) north of Klima on the coast road.

6 ★★★ **Glossa.** The island's second settlement after Skiathos Town is much more bucolic and also beautiful, rising from the sea on terraced hillsides. Steep streets wind past gardens where residents grow prunes and almonds, just as they do in the surrounding orchards, and most of the houses have sturdy balconies looking out to sea. The most popular landmark these days is just to the east of town, **Agios Ioannis Church.** On a rocky outcropping above the sea, the little chapel is so incredibly picturesque, it steals the show in the film *Mamma Mia!* ⏱1 hr.

Where to Stay & Dine on Skopelos

> *Kitchens on Skopelos turn out memorable preparations of seafood and island-grown produce.*

★★ kids **Adrina Beach** PANORMOS

With a romantic namesake (the female pirate Adrina) and a perch above a beautiful cove, this pleasant little resort is a true island get-away. Large rooms, sea-view terraces and verandah, and a wonderful pool and beach are among the many amenities. The nicest accommodations are the large, simply furnished two-floor maisonettes, ideal for families. ☎ 24240/23371. www.adrina.gr. 52 units. Doubles 150€ w/breakfast. AE, MC, V. Closed Oct–late May.

★★ **Englezos** SKOPELOS TOWN *GREEK*

Served in an attractive portside setting, the innovative menu here ranges from souvlaki and other Greek classics to superb pasta dishes and delicious starters. Eggplant with island-grown apricots, a fish stew with prunes, and many other dishes put fresh island produce to memorable use. Waterfront. ☎ 24240/22230. Entrees 8€–16€. MC, V. Lunch & dinner daily.

No Room at the Inn

While Skiathos and Skopelos are well endowed with comfortable hotels, if you arrive in high season without a reservation, your only option may be to rent one of the many rooms available in private homes. The municipal tourist office in Skiathos Town can help you find a room there, and homeowners with ROOMS TO LET signs usually meet the boats. You'll find ROOMS TO LET signs all over Skopelos, especially in Skopelos Town and Glossa (in Glossa, shops and tavernas often advertise rooms).

★ **Hotel Denise** SKOPELOS TOWN
One of the most pleasant lodgings in town sits on a hillside just above the port, affording views of the town, sea, and surrounding mountains. All the large, bright rooms open to balconies. The pool is a perfect retreat after a day spent on the beach or sightseeing. ☎ 24240/22678. www.denise.gr. 25 units. Doubles 100€ w/breakfast. No credit cards.

★★ **Ionia Hotel** SKOPELOS TOWN
A wonderful location in the center of town, with views of the hillside and sea, ensures a memorable stay here. The large rooms are simply but comfortably furnished, and all have terraces and surround a lovely garden and pool. ☎ 24240/22568. www.ionia.gr. 45 units. Doubles 60€ –95€ w/breakfast. MC, V. Closed Nov–Apr.

★★ **Molos** SKOPELOS TOWN *GREEK*
The top choice for a meal on the harbor is this simple, old-fashioned taverna. Salads, lamb and pork dishes, and the house wine are all excellent. You may be taken into the kitchen to view the offerings. Waterfront. ☎ 24240/22551. Entrees 7€–10€. No credit cards. Lunch & dinner daily.

★★ kids **Skopelos Village** NEAR SKOPELOS TOWN This pleasant retreat is just a short walk from the port, yet it seems to be in a world of its own. Extremely spacious, bungalow-like accommodations, with crisp, attractive furnishings and fully equipped kitchens, are scattered amid fragrant gardens and around two sparkling swimming pools. A beach is just beyond the entrance, and the center of Skopelos Town is a short walk away. The hotel's **Agioli** restaurant serves dinner and light meals throughout the day. ☎ 24240/22517. www.skopelosvillage.gr. 36 units. Doubles 175€–195€ w/breakfast. MC, V. Closed Nov–Apr.

★★★ **Taverna Agnanti** SKOPELOS TOWN *GREEK* The island's finest restaurant has been serving for more than 50 years and seems to get better all the time. Grilled pork with wild fennel, chicken breast with sun-dried

Carnival Madness

The 12 days of pre-Lenten Carnival celebrations are especially festive on Skopelos, with two idiosyncratic traditions. The **Trata** is a raucous celebration of seagoing life—the islanders were master shipbuilders until well into the early 20th century. Men gather in the morning to construct makeshift boats, then put on masks and costumes and carry the craft through the streets, singing, dancing, and goading onlookers as they go. Once at the seaside, they burn and sink the boats in a final burst of revelry. **Valch's Wedding** is a women-only event, in which costumed bridal parties dance their way through the streets and squares of Skopelos Town to the accompaniment of folk music, stopping along the way for sweets and wine. Valch's Wedding isn't the only time women call the shots; Skopelos is a matrilineal society, and property is passed to women and held in a woman's name even after marriage.

tomatoes, and smoked cheese in grape leaves do justice to the handsome dining room and romantic terrace. Next to town hall, Glossa. ☎ 24240/33606. Entrees 8€–20€. No credit cards. Lunch & dinner daily.

★ **Taverna Alexander** SKOPELOS TOWN *GREEK* Islanders tend to call this place Alexander's Garden, and an al fresco meal in the courtyard behind a stone wall in the center of town is an ever-popular occasion. The taverna fare is traditional, with some excellent fish and pork dishes. Off waterfront, near OTE. ☎ 24240/22324. Entrees 7€–15€. MC, V. Dinner daily.

Skyros

Adrift by itself in the Aegean, 50km (31 miles) east of the mainland and at least that far from the other major Sporades, Skyros is a land apart. You will discover that there is something different about this island as soon as you set eyes on Skyros Town, a cliff-hugging, white mirage that seems to float above the surrounding plain. The impression won't wane as you explore the rest of this most distinctive Greek island.

> It's no accident that the steep main street of hilltop Skyros Town is known as Sisyphus.

START Skyros Town. TRIP LENGTH At least 2 days, with many hours wandering through Skyros Town and about a day exploring the rest of the island.

❶ ★★★ **Skyros Town.** The island's only sizable town and home to most of the 3,000 Skyrians inspires many flattering comparisons—to a mirage, a magical kingdom, or,

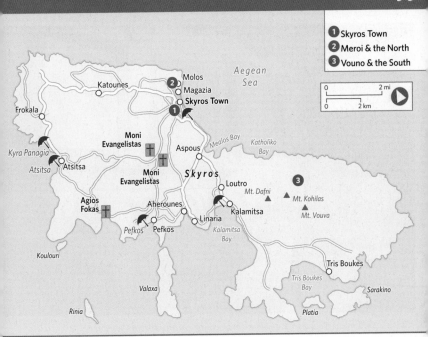

1 Skyros Town
2 Meroi & the North
3 Vouno & the South

Aegean Sea

Molos
Katounes
Magazia
Skyros Town
Frokala
Moni Evangelistas
Aspous *Mealos Bay* *Katholiko Bay*
Kyra Panagia
Atsitsa Atsitsa
Moni Evangelistas
S k y r o s
Loutro *Mt. Dafni* *Mt. Kohilas* 3
Agios Fokas
Aherounes Kalamitsa *Mt. Vouva*
Pefkos Pefkos Linaria
Kalamitsa Bay
Koulouri
Valaxa
Tris Boukes
Tris Boukes Bay *Sarakino*
Rinia
Platia

0   2 mi
0   2 km

most accurately and prosaically, to a village on one of the islands in the Cyclades. It's only fitting that this stunning collection of white, flat-roofed houses clinging to a high rocky bluff has figured in myth since ancient times. The sea nymph Thetis sent her son, Achilles, to the island disguised as a young woman to outwit the oracle's prediction that he would die in the Trojan War; the ruse worked until Odysseus unmasked the boy's true identity and sent him off to battle on a Skyrian pony. Theseus, founder-king of Athens and son of Poseidon and Aegeus, fled to Skyros when he fell out of favor; but Lycomedes, king of the island, pushed him over a cliff. Even the town's main street is known as Sisyphus, and the reason soon becomes abundantly clear once you start hiking up the steep incline. At the top is the **Venetian Kastro** and, within the walls, the monastery of **Agios Yeoryios.** Farther down the slope on **Plateia Rupert Brooke** is a statue memorializing the British poet, who in 1915 died on a hospital ship just off Skyros and is buried on the southern end of the island (p. 518, 3). The flatteringly virile bronze nude is not a likeness but an immortalization of poetry that caused a public outcry when it was unveiled in the 1930s.

The **Manos Faltaits Historical and Folklore Museum** (Plateia Rupert Brooke; ☎ 22220/92158; admission 2€; May–Oct Tues–Sun 8:30am–3pm; hours vary at other times), just off the square, brings together traditional pottery, household items, costumes, and furniture gathered from around the island. Seeing the fascinating collection is all the more satisfying

Getting There

The challenge of getting to Skyros can deter even the most determined traveler. In summer, sometimes, you can travel directly to Skyros from the other Sporades; otherwise, you will need to take a boat to Kymi on the island of Evvia for a Skyros-bound boat; total travel time with connection can be at least 4 hr. If you are bypassing the other Sporades and traveling directly to Skyros, fly or take one of the twice-a-day boats from Kymi; the crossing takes about 2 hours; Kymi is about 2 ½ hours from Athens by bus.

> *Bric-a-brac from local homes at the Manos Faltaits Historical and Folklore Museum.*

once you begin to witness how many of these collectibles are still part of everyday island life. Many Skyrian homes are museum-like repositories for colorful plates, embroidery, copperware, and carved furniture—a point of pride and a throwback to the days of Byzantine occupation when families made fortunes by trading with pirates, who brought back loot from the lucrative Near East sea lanes. Some older men on the island still wear baggy trousers and black caps, and as you wander along the steep lanes of Skyros Town you'll come upon women in long scarves sitting in doorways bent over embroidery noted for vibrant colors and fanciful flower and bird designs. The **Archaeological Museum** (Plateia Rupert Brooke; ☎ 22220/91327; admission 2€; Tues–Sun 8:30am–3pm), also near the square, displays small stone vessels and other primitive finds from Palamari. ⏲ Half-day.

You can drive around the north of the island in a counterclockwise circuit from Skyros Town; from Agios Fokas, head west then north again to Skyros Town. The entire circuit on a well-marked road is less than 30km (19 miles) and can be completed in half a day.

❷ ★★ **Meroi & the North.** Skyros is cinch-waisted, and the fertile, forested north varies so much from the arid, rugged south that it has been conjectured, wrongly, that the island was at one time two separate land masses. Two seaside villages are side by side, just below Skyros Town. **Magazia,** at the bottom of a stairway from Plateia Rupert Brooke, fronts a sandy beach that extends 1km (½ mile) into Molos, a fishing village. **Pouria,** just to the north, is surrounded by weirdly shaped rock formations that were shaped not by wind and waves but by Romans, who quarried the stone. **Palamari,** at the tip of the island 13km (8 miles) north of Skyros Town, was settled around 2,000 B.C. by traders and sailors for whom, judging by the trenches and thick stone walls, life on the island must have been a tenuous business. A sandy beach skirts the harbor where the inhabitants once beached their vessels. **Atsitsa,** 14km (9 miles) west of Molos on the Bay of Petros, is surrounded by several beaches along the pine- and cedar-clad northwest coast; one of the most appealing, **Kyra Panagia,** is a 15-minute walk north of Atsitsa. **Agios Fokas,** 5km (3 miles), south of Atsitsa, is usually touted as one of the island's

Ponies & Pagan Processions

Large herds of the diminutive Skyrian pony once scampered across the rocky interior of Skyros, though now they number less than 150. It's believed that these beautiful little beasts are the horses that frolic on the Parthenon frieze, and Achilles allegedly rode one into battle during the Trojan War. Since the ponies have been isolated on Skyros, their bloodlines have changed little over the millennia. Time was, Skyros farmers put the ponies to work for the harvest, then released them to graze on upland plateaus in the winter. Farm machinery has curtailed the ponies' careers as beasts of burden, and they vie for terrain with sheep and goats. The ponies are now protected, and efforts are afoot to preserve and restore the remaining herds. While you are unlikely to catch a glimpse of a Skyrian pony in the wild, at the **Skyrian Horse Project** in Molos (☎ 22220/92918; donations accepted; daily 11am–1pm and 6:30–8pm), you can get as close as you wish—and, if you are under the age of 15, climb onto one.

Another age-old tradition in Skyros is the pre-Lenten (*apokriatika*) festival, famous throughout Greece. On each of the four Sundays before Clean Monday (the first Monday of Lent), men and a few large women don goat hair jackets and goat masks and drape themselves in goat bells. Other men, dressed in traditional wedding garb, and women and children, in their Sunday Western-style dress, surround them. The ensembles proceed through the streets of Skyros Town, singing, brandishing shepherds' crooks, and reciting bawdy verses. When two groups meet, they try to outdo each other with bell clanking, ribald gestures, and shouting. Scholars love the event, tracing the tradition to pagan Dionysian revels and Achilles-style cross-dressing (p. 514, ❶), as do the many spectators who make it a point to visit the island for the goings-on. If you plan to attend, book a room months in advance.

most beautiful beaches, though it's actually a triplet of little bays edged with white pebbles. ⊕ Half-day.

From Aspous, about 3km (2 miles) south of Skyros Town, a single road leads south through a desolate, rocky landscape. A trip down the south coast, with a stop or two to swim, takes a couple of hours.

❸ ★★ **Vouno & the South.** As you head south, the rocky coast gives way to beaches at Kalamitsa, about 3km (2 miles) south of Aspous, and Kolymbada, another 2km (1 mile) south. The scrappy collection of houses that surround both are some of the few signs of human habitation on this end of the island. The road ends on the shores of **Tris Boukes Bay,** 7km (4 miles) south of Kolymbada and 15km (9 miles) south of Skyros Town. Rupert Brooke is buried here, amid an olive grove, in a simple grave inscribed with words from his own poem "The Soldier": "If I should die think only this of me/ That there's some corner of a foreign field/ That is forever England." Brooke spent only a few days on the island in 1915—long enough to incur a mosquito bite that led to blood poisoning. He died on a hospital ship in Tris Boukes Bay. ⊕ Half-day.

Where to Stay & Dine on Skyros

> *The pool at Hotel Nefeli is quite a luxury on rugged and remote Skyros.*

★ **Hotel Angela** MOLOS
This lovely little whitewashed compound surrounding a swimming pool is just below Skyros Town, steps from the beach at Molos. Rooms are simple but perfectly kept and comfortable. All have balconies with glimpses of the sea and the white town on the bluff above.

☎ 22220/91764. 14 units. Doubles 90€–100€ w/breakfast. No credit cards.

★★★ **Hotel Nefeli** SKYROS TOWN
Suites, apartments, and hotel-style rooms at this stylish small inn spread through three buildings, and all are distinctly decorated. The center

f Skyros Town and the beach are a short walk
way, but you may want to stay put to enjoy
he pool, terrace, and excellent restaurant.
☎ 22220/91964. www.skyros-nefeli.gr. 16 units.
Doubles 100€–120€ w/breakfast. MC, V.

★★ **Kristina's at Pegasus** SKYROS TOWN
GREEK/INTERNATIONAL A neoclassical build-
ng is the setting for one of the island's most
popular restaurants, run by an Australian
proprietor and chef. While the food is not
raditionally Greek, the cooking relies on local
ish, meat, and produce, and the salads and
imply prepared eggplant and other vegetar-
an choices are some of the best offerings on
he menu. ☎ 22220/91123. Entrees 6€–16€. No
redit cards. Lunch & dinner Mon–Sat.

★★ **Maryetes** SKYROS TOWN GREEK
This longtime favorite is known for fish and
grilled meats, served in a simple but always
crowded dining room in the center of Skyros
Town. Scenes spied from the warm-weather
errace, on the town's main street, add a great
deal of entertainment value to a meal. You
can eat very well during your stay on Skyros
by alternating meals between Maryetes and
O Pappous ki Ego (below), just up the street.
Main street. ☎ 22220/91311. Entrees 6€–10€.
No credit cards. Lunch & dinner daily.

★★ **O Pappous ki Ego** SKYROS TOWN GREEK
The name translates as "My grandfather and
I," and the appealing room, a former pharmacy, is now under the watchful eye of the
grandson. The dolmades and other meze are

delicious, as are some of the meat and fish
dishes; cuttlefish in anise sauce is a specialty.
Live music is sometimes performed on weekend evenings. Main street. ☎ 22220/93200.
Entrees 6€–10€. No credit cards. Lunch & dinner
daily.

Skyros Centre ATSITSA & SKYROS TOWN
Not a hotel, this well-established "holistic"
vacation resort has beachside units near
Atsitsa and accommodations in traditional
houses in Skyros Town. You will need to book
well in advance for programs that last a week
or two and include sessions in dance, yoga,
handicrafts, sailing, meditation, writing, and
more. All are a very nice way to experience the
island. For more information, check out the
center at www.skyros.com.

★★ **Skiros Palace** OUTSIDE SKYROS TOWN
One of the few resorts on the island is low-key
and comfortably simple. You will not find much
in the way of luxury, but furnishings are comfortable, and terraces and balconies face a large
pool and a long, sandy beach. Skyros Town is
3km (2 miles) away, but a minibus makes the
run several times a day. Girismata Kampos.
☎ 22220/91994. www.skiros-palace.gr. 80 units.
Doubles 110€ w/breakfast. AE, DC, MC, V.

Rooms to Let

Skyros has relatively few hotels, but finding
a room is generally very easy—an eager
throng, mostly women, meets passengers
disembarking from boats with signs and
cries of ROOM TO LET. You will also encounter room-letters near the main bus stop in
Skyros Town. These accommodations are
in private homes and immaculately kept.
You'll save yourself and a potential host
time and trouble if you arrive with some
idea of where you want to stay on the island. Set your sights on the upper part of
Skyros Town—the narrow lanes are delightful, the views are sweeping, and the beach
is a walk away.

Shopping on Skyros

If you develop a penchant for the island's
colorful weaving, woodworking, and ceramics while peering through the doorways
of houses or visiting the Faltaits Historical
and Folklore Museum (p. 514, ❶), you're in
luck, because you can take a bit of Skyrian
handiwork home with you. The museum
has a workshop where artisans create
many of the traditional handiworks, and
these are for sale in the museum shop,
Argo, on the main street in Skyros, near
Plateia Rupert Brooke (☎ 22220/92158).
You will find beautiful ceramics at **Yiannis
Nicolau,** whose shop/studio is in Magazia,
next to the Xenia Hotel, and masterfully
handcarved wood chairs and chests in the
studio of **Lefteris Avgoklouris,** near the
post office in Skyros Town (☎ 22220/
91106). **Ergastiri,** in the marketplace, also
sells beautiful ceramics.

The Sporades Fast Facts

> *Internet cafes allow you to stay connected even on the most far-flung islands.*

Arriving

BY PLANE You can fly to Skiathos and Skyros on **Olympic Airlines** (☎ 801/114444 reservations within Greece; flight time from Athens is about 30 min.). Skiathos is well served by year-round daily service and twice-daily service in the summer; Skyros is served by two or three flights a week. From Skiathos, it is easy to reach Skopelos and Alonnisos by sea. **BY BOAT** You cannot reach the Sporades by boat from the ports near Athens. Ferries and hydrofoils sail to Skiathos, Skopelos, and Alonnisos from Agios Konstandinos and Volos on the mainland north of Athens; ferries and hydrofoils also run from Kymi, on the island of Evvia (connected to the mainland by bridge), though service is much less frequent. Boats will often stop at Skiathos first and continue from there to Skopelos, where you may have to change to

a boat for Alonnisos. Travel time by ferry from Agios Konstandinos or Volos to Skiathos is 3 hours, by hydrofoil 1½ hours. **BY BUS** Buses connect Athens and Agios Konstandinos, Volos, and Kymi; allow at least 3 hours for the trip. For more information, contact **Hellenic Seaways** (☎ 210/419-90000; www.hellenic seaways.gr). Book ahead in summer.

An excellent source for schedules, which change constantly, is the website of the **Greek Travel Pages** (www.gtp.gr). Ticket offices throughout Greece will sell tickets, including the bus connection, to the Sporades except for Skyros. The only way to reach Skyros by sea is on ferries run by **Skyros Shipping Company** (www.sne.gr); boats sail from Kymi to Skyros once or twice daily, depending on the season. You will need to buy the Skyros-bound ticket at the dock in Kymi.

Dentists & Doctors

You will find clinics on all the islands. SKIA-THOS **Skiathos Medical Centre,** ☎ 24270/22222. SKOPELOS **Skopelos Medical Centre,** ☎ 24240/22222. ALONNISOS **Alonnisos Regional Clinic of Patitiri,** ☎ 24240/65208. SKYROS **Skyros Medical Clinic,** ☎ 22220/92222. In addition, most hotels will be able to refer you to a local doctor or dentist who speaks English.

Emergencies

See p. 680, Fast Facts Greece.

Getting Around

BY BUS You can get around the islands by bus. Skiathos is especially well served, with a shuttle bus that runs up and down the south coast stopping at beaches. BY CAR You can get by without a car on all the islands, though a short rental will be handy for a day of touring on Skopelos and Skyros. You will find car rental agencies on every island. BY BOAT On all the islands you can reach remote beaches by caique from the main ports. Excursion boats are the most convenient way to tour the main north coast sights on Skiathos and the only way (besides renting a private boat) to tour the Marine National Park of Alonnisos Northern Sporades. It is easy to travel between Skiathos, Skopelos, and Alonnisos on frequent boats and ferries. Reaching Skyros from the other Sporades islands is quite difficult. A summertime-only boat sometimes connects the other islands and Skyros; at other times it is necessary to connect in Kymi.

Internet Access

SKIATHOS TOWN **Internet Zone Cafe,** 28 Evangelistrias. SKOPELOS **Click & Surf,** just up from the police station—ask for Platanos Square, then proceed up past the supermarket.

Pharmacies

See p. 682, Fast Facts Greece.

Police

SKIATHOS TOWN The **police station** (☎ **24270/21-111**) is about 250m (820 ft.) from the harbor on Papadiamandis, on the left; the **tourist police** booth is about 15m (49 ft.) farther along on the right. SKOPELOS The **police station** (☎ **24240/22-235**) is up the narrow road (Parados 1) to the right of the National Bank, along the harbor. SKYROS The **police station** (☎ **22220/91-274**) is on the street behind the Skyros Travel Center.

Post Office

SKIATHOS TOWN The **post office** (☎ **24270/22-011**) is on Papadiamandis, away from the harbor about 160m (525 ft.) and on the right; it's open Monday through Friday from 7:30am to 2pm. SKOPELOS The **post office,** on the port's far east end (take the stepped road leading away from the last kiosk, opposite the bus/taxi station), is open Monday through Friday from 8am to 2:30pm. SKYROS The **post office** is near the bus square in Skyros town; it's open Monday through Friday from 8am to 2pm.

Safety

See p. 682, Fast Facts Greece.

Visitor Information

SKIATHOS TOWN You'll find municipal tourist office on Papadiamantis. You can also contact the tourist police in Skiathos (☎ 24270/23172). SKOPELOS You'll also find municipal tourist offices on Skopelos (waterfront, Skopelos Town; ☎ 24240/22205). The many travel agencies located on all the islands are excellent sources of information; the companies mentioned in "Tips on Accommodations," p. 490, are especially helpful.

Favorite Moments in Northern Greece

Greece's northern city, Thessaloniki, is the cosmopolitan capital of the Macedonian region and has been a crossroads for trade from the east, west, north, and south since antiquity. Hellenistic, Roman, Byzantine, Ottoman, and Jewish civilizations all left their mark. The city is well-placed for trips to ancient sites such as Pella, Vergina, and Dion, just a couple of hours away. You can also spend a day climbing or hiking in the foothills of majestic Mount Olympus, home of the mythical Greek gods. Then you can either head for the nearby beach or visit Mount Athos, a peninsula with virgin forests, enormous centuries-old monasteries, and priceless Byzantine treasures.

> PREVIOUS PAGE *The view from the summit of Mount Olympus.* THIS PAGE *Monks on Mount Athos may invite you for a meal.*

❶ **Wandering around the Pella Archaeological Museum.** The guards are friendly and may point out their own favorite pieces, such as the statuette of Eros sleeping. See p. 530, ❶.

❷ **Exploring the treasures at the tumulus of Philip II at Vergina.** The ancient mural

depicting Persephone's abduction still resonates in this nation of beach resorts that shut down in winter: Each fall, everything dies from the sorrow of Dimitra (Demeter), Persephone's mother, aggrieved by her daughter's return to the Underworld; then in spring, everything comes back to life, when Persephone

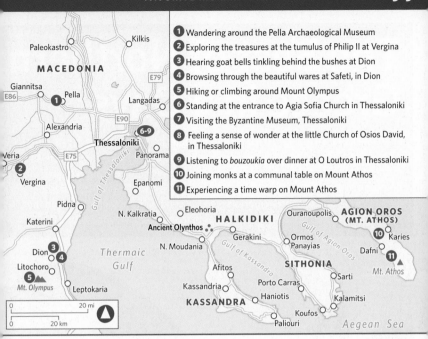

1 Wandering around the Pella Archaeological Museum
2 Exploring the treasures at the tumulus of Philip II at Vergina
3 Hearing goat bells tinkling behind the bushes at Dion
4 Browsing through the beautiful wares at Safeti, in Dion
5 Hiking or climbing around Mount Olympus
6 Standing at the entrance to Agia Sofia Church in Thessaloniki
7 Visiting the Byzantine Museum, Thessaloniki
8 Feeling a sense of wonder at the little Church of Osios David, in Thessaloniki
9 Listening to *bouzoukia* over dinner at O Loutros in Thessaloniki
10 Joining monks at a communal table on Mount Athos
11 Experiencing a time warp on Mount Athos

...eturns to the land of the living and her mother ...ejoices. See p. 531, 2.

3 Hearing goat bells tinkling behind the ...ushes at Dion and imagining Pan playing ...is flute on a knoll. In the foothills of Mount ...lympus, it's easy to understand how Greeks ...ame up with myths to explain the world ...around them. See p. 532, 3.

4 Browsing through the beautiful wares ...made by the innkeepers at Safeti, in Dion. ...Whether you're watching the weavers at work, ...shopping for gifts to bring home, or sampling ...he edibles for sale, you'll feel inspired by this ...ndustrious family. Their inn is a beautiful ...lace to stay in this enchanting town dedi-...ated to Zeus. See p. 533.

5 Hiking or climbing around Mount Olym-...us. Exhilarating nature trails lead up the ...nythical mountain home of the gods. See p. ...41, 2.

6 Standing at the entrance to Agia Sofia ...Church in the center of Thessaloniki. At the ...threshold of this centuries-old house of wor-...ship, it's hard not to ponder the historic events ...he city has seen. See p. 550, 4.

7 Visiting the Byzantine Museum, Thessa-loniki. You'll be amazed by the craftsmanship in this collection. See p. 551, 9.

8 Feeling a sense of wonder at the little Church of Osios David, in Thessaloniki. It's astonishing to hear how this church's mosaic of Jesus and the prophets survived centuries under plaster during Turkish rule and, before that, iconoclastic rampages in the 8th and 9th centuries. See p. 553, 18.

9 Listening to *bouzoukia* over dinner at O Loutros in Thessaloniki. On a sultry evening, nothing beats hearing live Greek music while dining at one of the tables beside the old Turkish baths. See p. 559.

10 Joining monks at a communal table on Mount Athos. You'll help prepare a meal and then share it at a local monastery or one of its dependencies. See p. 537, 2.

11 Experiencing a time warp on Mount Athos. Nature is still virginal on Mount Athos. The only modern intrusions are the occasional ring of cellphones and the trail of jets over-head. See p. 537, 2.

The Best of Northern Greece in 3 Days

If you have only 72 hours in the north, spend the first day sightseeing in Thessaloniki, an ancient melting pot of Greek, Roman, Jewish, and Ottoman cultures. On the second day, take an easy tour to Pella and Vergina, the old stomping grounds of King Philip II of Macedonia and his son, Alexander the Great. From the land of great mortals, you'll ascend to the home of Zeus and the Greek gods on your last day, on the slopes of magnificent Mount Olympus.

> *The ages unfold as you walk past the 4th-century Rotunda, with its 16th-century minaret, and other landmarks of old Thessaloniki.*

START Thessaloniki TRIP LENGTH 3 days (210km/ 130 miles total).

1 Thessaloniki. Your first day will be busy, so warm up at a leisurely pace on Thessaloniki's waterfront promenade. Then set off to see the ★★ **White Tower** (p. 551, **7**)—all that remains of the city's 15th-century ramparts—en route to the ★★★ **Archaeological Museum** (p. 551, **8**), housing treasures from prehistoric times to the Roman era, and the

award-winning ★★★ **Museum of Byzantine Culture** (p. 551, ❾) next door. From there, a convenient lunch stop is **Navarinou Square; Omorfi Thessaloniki** (6 Navarinou Sq.; ☎ 2310/270714) has a good selection of meze, such as baked shrimp with cheese, salads, kalamari, and grilled steaks. After lunch, continue north on Gounari Street past the cool shops and ruins of the **Galerian Complex** (p. 550, ❻) to **Egnatia Street** (p. 552, ⓬)— the ancient route from Rome to modern-day Istanbul—and the ancient **Arch of Galerius** (p. 551, ⓫). Continue to the ★ **Rotunda** (p. 552, ⓭) for a peek at the mosaics inside St. George's Church, one of Thessaloniki's oldest. Behind the Rotunda, walk along legendary Apostolou Pavlou Street, where the apostle Paul walked to address the ancient Thessalonians. Continue heading north to the 19th-century Old Turkish Quarter in **Ano Polis** (p. 552, ⓱). The main drag, Agia Sofia Street, is

a fair hike uphill, but you'll be rewarded with beautiful views from a historic area. Stop for coffee in the Tsinari district (D. Poliorkitou St. and vicinity) after you've visited the little Church of Osios David, from A.D. 500—the main reward for climbing all the way here. For dinner, head to the Ladadika district for an evening meal at ★ **Kioupia** (p. 558), followed by a nightcap at one of the cafe-bars there, before you bed down in Thessaloniki. Before heading out to Vergina in the morning, pick up some picnic supplies from ★★ **Modiano Market** (p. 548, ❷) for the road trip. ⏱ 1 day.

From Thessaloniki to Pella, head westbound on Egnatia St./Monastiriou St. through Konstantine Karamanlis Ave. to Rte. 2/E86 on the Thessaloniki-Edessa road till you reach Pella (40km/25 miles, 40 min.).

❷ **Pella.** Birthplace of Alexander the Great, Pella was the "new" capital of Macedonia after it moved from ancient Aigai in the 5th century B.C. Highlights include the ancient agora, which has been partially restored, and the houses with mosaic floors still intact. The museum contains more mosaics and treasures from the site and surrounding area. The

Hotels & Restaurants

For details on sights, hotels, and restaurants in Thessaloniki, see p. 548; in Vergina, see p. 533; in Litochoro, see p. 542.

> *Alexander the Great was born in Pella, where wealthy residents embellished their villas with mosaic floors.*

> *The ruins at Dion are wonderfully evocative of the ancient city dedicated to Zeus.*

museum is in the modern village of Pella, 2km (1¼ miles) away. **See p. 530,** ❶. ⏱ At least 1 hr.

To reach Vergina from Pella, head southeast to Rte. 2/E86 on the Thessaloniki-Edessa road and follow signs for the road to Veria (Beroia) turning southwest. Head south at the town of Alexandria for the road to the Egnatia Odos (E90). Take it southwest, turning off at Exit 14 at Rte. 4 southeast bound for Vergina. 63km/39 miles, 1 hr.

❸ ★★★ **Vergina.** This is the region's main attraction, so if you have limited time, this should be your main stop. The tumulus of King Philip II of Macedonia's tomb has been turned into a museum, and the structure and finds within are unique. Highlights are the royal tombs of King Philip and his grandson,

Alexander IV. The solid gold box that contains Philip's bones is engraved with the 16-point Vergina sun. **See p. 531,** ❷. ⏱ 1 hr.

From Vergina to Dion, backtrack onto Rte. 4 to the Egnatia Odos/E90/A2 and the national road (Rte. 1) south toward Athens. Then take the exit for Dion (or Diou), following the B-road signs, heading right on the Diou-Karitsas road. 100km/62 miles, 1 hr. 10 min.

❹ ★★ **Dion.** Take some time to wander around this abandoned ancient city named in honor of Zeus. Legend says that the women who killed Orpheus washed their hands of the sin in the cleansing springs that remain here. The overall atmosphere is more compelling

Litochoro is set amid verdant forests in the foothills of Mount Olympus.

than any single find, though the swampy **sanctuary of Isis** heightens the allure. Spend the night in Dion if you have your own vehicle, or continue to Litochoro and find a room there for an early start up the trails of Mount Olympus the next morning. **See p. 532, ③.** ⏱ At least hr.

From Dion to Litochoro, head southeast on the Diou-Karitsas road and continue to the turnoff south (right) for Litochoro. 7km/4⅓ miles, 15 min.

⑤ ★ **Litochoro.** This typical touristic mountain village caters to the many visitors who come to the area to hike the beautiful trails and see the unique flora around the slopes of **Mount Olympus** (p. 541, ②), a national park. In the foothills, Litochoro has a large army base at the entrance and accommodates many trekkers throughout the hiking season. Children on school trips and from boys' and girls' clubs are frequent visitors. You can buy all your supplies here for a day out on the hill. The town also makes a convenient base for an excursion to ancient Dion just 7km (4⅓ miles)

away. **See p. 540, ①.** ⏱ At least half-day, with Mount Olympus.

⑥ **Mount Olympus.** Take a nature walk in the foothills of Greece's most famous mountain, as home of the ancient gods and the highest peak in Greece, at 2,919m (9,577 ft.). **See p. 541, ②.** ⏱ At least half-day, with Litochoro.

⑦ ★★ **Plaka Beach.** Unique for a mountain town, Mount Olympus is also near some pretty nice beaches, just a few miles away on the Pieria region's long coast. Take a taxi or bus to popular Plaka Beach, equipped with umbrellas, lounge chairs, and other amenities. The bus here leaves hourly in summer from the Litochoro KTEL station, on the main road. Or go to **Gritsa Beach,** also organized, on the main Litochoro-Katerini bus route. Buses leave hourly in summer. For Gritsa, disembark at **Camping Mitikas** (☎ 23520/61275, winter ☎ 23520/81595; www.campingmitikas.com) and walk straight through the campsite to reach the sand. 5km (3 miles) east of Litochoro. ⏱ At least 1 hr.

In the Footsteps of Philip II & Alexander

This tour leads you through the ancient territory of the great Macedonian kings, Philip II and his son, Alexander the Great. Ancient Aigai, near Vergina, was the old capital of the Dorian Makedni tribe (aka the Macedonians) when they moved out of the Pindus Mountains in the 7th century B.C. It was in Vergina where Philip II's spectacular tomb was discovered undisturbed. Ancient Pella was also a capital of the Macedonians, and lovely Dion was the holy city where Alexander the Great amassed his troops.

> *Elaborate frescoes adorn the Vergina tomb of Philip II, father of Alexander the Great.*

START Ancient Pella, 40km (25 miles) west of Thessaloniki on the E86 to Edessa. **TRIP LENGTH** 1 day (163km/101 miles).

❶ Pella. In 356 B.C., Alexander the Great was born in Ancient Pella, the "new" capital of the Kingdom of Macedonia, after it relocated here

...from ancient Aigai in the 5th century B.C. The site is isolated, so you'd likely come only as a stop on a day tour from Thessaloniki, but it's famed for its beautiful pebble floor mosaics. A museum houses some of them as well as unique artifacts such as the horned Athena and a darling statue of sleeping Eros. The museum is in the modern village of Pella, which was relocated a couple of kilometers away in 1914, when archaeologists began excavations on the ancient site. Significant finds include a large agora (market), which has been partially reconstructed; a cemetery; sanctuaries of Aphrodite, Demeter, and Cybele; large houses where some mosaic floors are still *in situ*, and a palace that's closed to the public. ⏱ At least 1 hr. Off E86, Thessaloniki–Edessa road. Site: ☎ 23820/31160. Museum: ☎ 23820/32963. www.culture.gr. Site and museum admission 6€. Apr–Oct Tues–Sun 8am–8pm (or sunset), Nov–Mar Tues–Sun 8:30am–3pm.

Head southeast to Rte. 2/E86 on the Thessaloniki–Edessa road, follow signs for the road to Veria (Beroia), and turn southwest. Head south at the town of Alexandria for the road to the Egnatia Odos (E90). Take it southwest, turning off at Exit 14 at Rte. 4 southeast for Vergina. 63km/39 miles, 1 hr.

② ★★★ **Vergina.** Philip II of Macedon (382–332 B.C.) was the father of Alexander the Great. These Macedonian kings ruled much of the ancient world, starting from here. The stunning tombs of King Philip II were discovered in 1977 and opened to the public in 1993. Thanks to some deliberately placed red herrings, they were unplundered. From the tumulus entrance, you descend underground and see a rare ancient fresco depicting the abduction of Persephone and a frieze of a hunting scene. The tomb of Alexander the Great's 14-year-old son, Alexander IV, is here (he was poisoned along with his mother Roxana after Alexander the Great's death). Philip II was entombed here after he was assassinated in a nearby theater, where Alexander the Great was crowned. Philip's wine-washed bones were placed in a solid gold casket depicting a 12-point Vergina sun. Philip's crown is also here among other beautifully displayed finds. ⏱ 1 hr. Off E90, near Veria, Vergina. ☎ 23310/92347. www.culture.gr. Admission 8€. Nov–March Tues–Sun 8:30am–3pm (2:30pm last admission); Apr–Oct Tues–Sun 8am–8pm (7:30pm last admission), Mon 1:30–8pm (7:30pm).

> *In northern villages, social life centers on tavernas such as Dionysos.*

Backtrack onto the Egnatia Odos/E90/A2 and the national road heading south toward Athens. Take the exit for Dion (or Diou) following the B-road signs (heading right on the Diou-Karitsas road). 100km/62 miles, 1 hr. 10 min.

SITE GUIDE
PAGE 535

③ ★★ Dion. In the foothills of Mount Olympus, the ancient city of Dion holds its own against better-known and better-placed ancient sites. It's spread out and there's perhaps less to see, but the bucolic atmosphere, with ground springs and copses, is appealing. Dedicated to Zeus, the city was the source of the spring where female followers of Dionysus cleansed their hands after killing Orpheus, the mesmerizing lyre player of myth who also lived on the mountain. The Macedonian king Archelaos (413–399 B.C.) built a temple to Zeus and other buildings in Dion, including a stadium for the Olympic Games. In 334 B.C., Alexander the Great (356–323 B.C.) used the area to gather troops, holding court in an enormous 100-couch tent, before setting off on his decade-long campaign to Persia. The remains you see now date mainly from Roman and early Christian times. Spend at least half a

> *The entrance to the royal tombs at Vergina was not discovered until 1977.*

day here so you can explore at a leisurely pace. When you're finished, we recommend grabbing a bite at ★ **Dionysos,** opposite the museum (☎ 23510/53276; entrees 8€–20€; no credit cards; breakfast, lunch, and dinner daily). It opens early, closes late, serves great Greek food, and sells souvenirs. Try the locally produced house wine, and you might be treated to the local firewater, *tsipouro* (grappa), too.

Where to Stay & Dine in Vergina

Moussaka and other hearty dishes of the north make the most of fresh local ingredients.

Dimitra House VERGINA

ach suite in this two-story hotel on a quiet, esidential street is elegant and has unique menities such as a kitchenette or minibar, fire-lace, or piano. There's a BBQ outside, and the wners will arrange babysitters for guests. It's bout 100m (328 ft.) from the site. Discounts re available for extended stays. 5 Athinas St. 23310/92900. zisseka@yahoo.com. 10 units. tudio 80€–120€ w/breakfast. No credit cards.

ilippion VERGINA GREEK

he Greek food here is excellent—made from resh and simple local ingredients combined to reate homemade specialties such as mous-aka. The fresh pasta and frozen yogurt are lso worthwhile. Just up the road (50m/164 ft.) rom the site. ☎ 23310/92892. Entrees 8€–10€. MC, V. Daily breakfast, lunch & early dinner.

Vergina Pension VERGINA

This is Greece's answer to a motel—a typical, wo-story hotel decked out in pine furniture,

just outside the village. Balconies wrap around the building, and the ground floor has a big breakfast room and snack bar. 55 Aristotelous St. ☎ 23310/92510. 10 units. Doubles 45€–60€ w/breakfast. No credit cards.

Shopping Then Dropping in Dion

Opposite the museum, the distinctive, mauve-painted ★★ **Safeti** (☎ 23510/ 46272; www.safetis.gr) offers beauti-ful handmade crafts and foods as well as four beautifully appointed comfortable suites (year-round; about 85€). One has a hot tub, another has a fireplace, and all have great furnishings, air-conditioning, dataports, and kitchenettes with micro-waves. The industrious and talented family that owns the place also runs two shops downstairs; one sells organic preserves, liqueurs, and sweets, and the other sells rugs, bags, dolls, and copper ware.

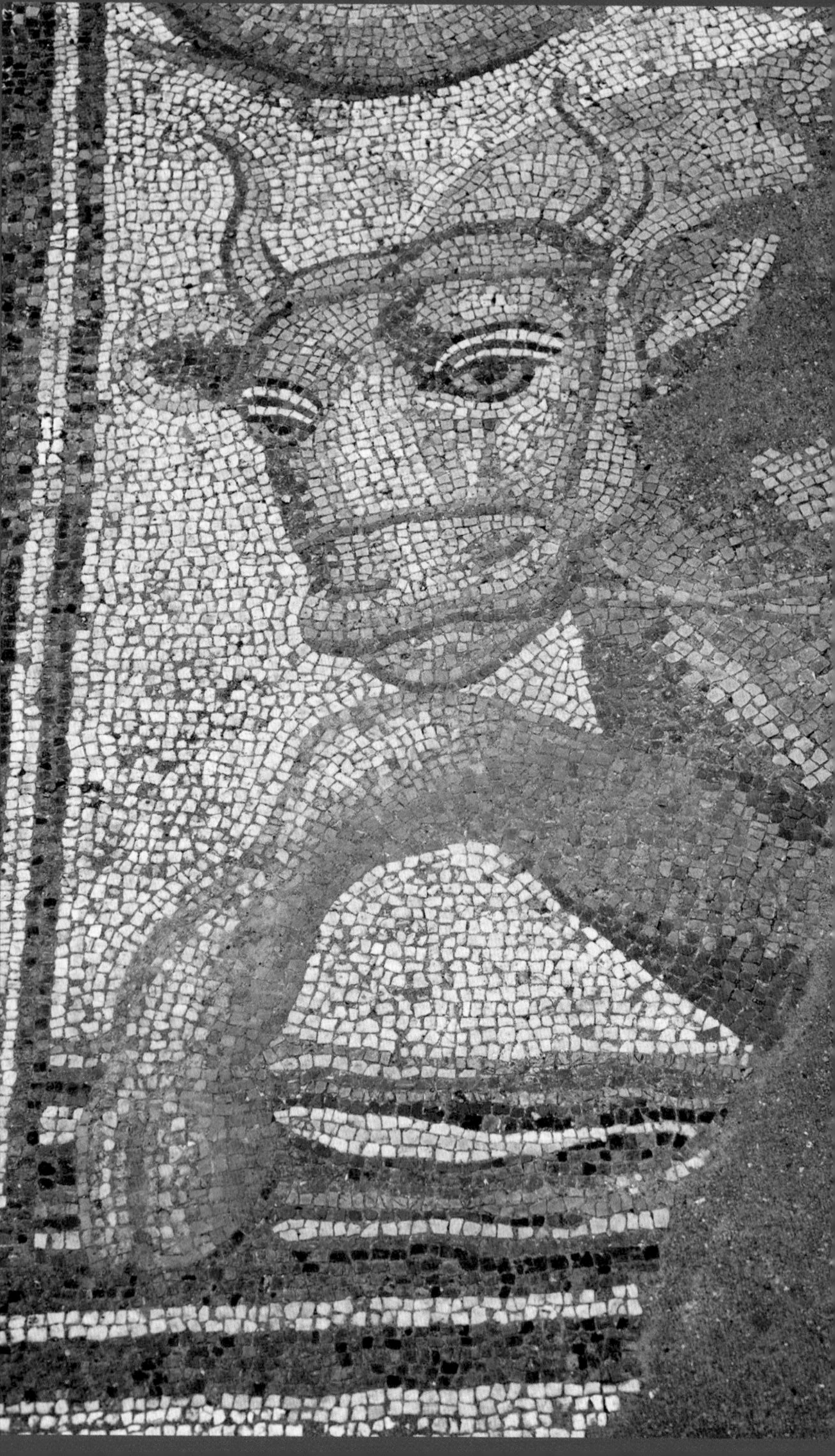

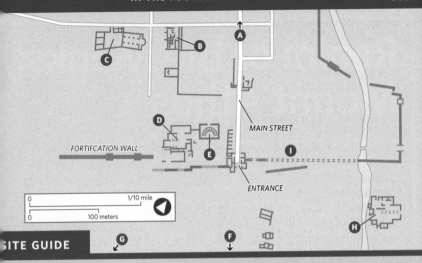

SITE GUIDE

❸ Dion

The site is divided by the modern road. On the east side, note the enormous Roman-era ⒶVilla of Dionysos, which has a striking mosaic floor. ⒷShops and houses were found on the west side, where you'll see the foundations of an early ⒸChristian basilica, as Dion was also an early bishopric. ⒹCentral baths are discernible by the pipes for the under-floor heating system. The small Ⓔodeion was thought to be connected with the therapeutic cult of Asklepios. Statues found here are in the site museum. You might hear goat bells tinkling behind the bushes here, or near the small ⒻRoman theater, and it's not hard to imagine an appearance by Orpheus himself, or at least Pan. You'll also see the big ⒼHellenistic-era theater, but the happiest site is the swampy ⒽSanctuary of Isis, furnished with copies of the original statues that stood here. The ⒾMuseum (☎ 23510/53206; www.culture.gr; admission 3€; Tues–Sun 8:30am–3pm). has some interesting artifacts related to military innovations, an ancient shock absorber, and an early pipe organ, known as a *hydraulis*, from the 1st century B.C. The basement features a mosaic of Alexander, and a good video presentation describes the area, the finds, and the context. ⏱ At least 1 hr. Off E75/1A, Thessaloniki-Athens national road. Site: ☎ 23510/53484. www.culture.gr. Admission 4€. Reduced admission for site and museum 6€.

Nov–Mar daily 8am–4pm, Apr–Oct daily 8am–5pm. 90km (56 miles) south of Vergina, 87km (54 miles) southwest of Thessaloniki, 7km (4⅓ miles) north of Litochoro. Bus or train: transfer to local bus at Katerini, 16km/10 miles north of Dion.

Realm of the Monks: Mount Athos

On the third "finger" of the Halkidiki Peninsula, farthest east, is a semiautonomous territory known as Mount Athos, or Agion Oros (Holy Mountain). The 50km by 12km (31-mile by 7½-mile) peninsula is covered in dense forestland, with a mountain to the south that rises 2,033m (6,670 ft.). Women are forbidden entry, though the peninsula is dedicated to the Virgin Mary (see "Of Monks & Men," p. 539). The area is divided among 20 monasteries and their dependent cloisters and hermitages, which together hold the largest collection of early Christian books, relics, and other treasures. It's also a naturalist's delight, as most of it hasn't been disturbed for centuries, except by the 2,000-odd resident Orthodox monks and visitors. Before you reach the territory, you'll spend at least some time in the "border town" of Ouranoupolis, a summer resort.

> *Monastic decor on Mount Athos is not necessarily Spartan.*

START Ouranoupolis. Ouranoupolis to Dafni on Mount Athos is 50km (31 miles) to the southeast. **TRIP LENGTH** Sailing time is 1½–2 hr.

1 kids Ouranoupolis. Many northern European families spend their holiday here. The sea is aquamarine and the beach is narrow but sandy. There are more hotels on nearby

Map legend:
1 Ouranoupolis
2 Mount Athos

Trypiti

Hilandari (Serb)   Esfigmenos
Ouranoupolis
AGION OROS (MT. ATHOS)
Ammoliani
Zografou (Bulgarian)   Vatopedi
Konstamonitis   Pantokratoros
Gulf of Agion Oros   Dochariou   Karies   Stavronikitas
Xenofontos   Koutloumousiou
Agios Pavlos   Iviron
Panteleimon   Filotheou
Xiropotamou   Karakalou
Dafni
Simon Petras
Grigoriou
Dionysiou
Agios Pavlos   Megisti (Great) Lavra

Thracian Sea

MACEDONIA   Nigrita
Thessaloniki   Stavros   Strymonic Gulf
HALKIDIKI   Thracian Sea
Ouranoupolis
Katerini   Mt. Athos
Thermaic Gulf   Gulf of Kassandra
Mt. Olympus   Gulf of Agion Oros   Area of map above

—mouliani islet, with boat service from here or —om the Trypiti dock a couple of miles away. The area was called Prosforion before 1922, when it was expropriated from Vatopedi Monastery, renamed "Heaven's City," and used to accommodate an influx of refugees from Asia Minor. The **Tower of Prosforion** (☎ 23770/1389 or 71651; admission €2; Jun–Oct daily 9am–5pm) is the town landmark, on the main square at the waterfront. It's a much-altered Byzantine structure, dating to the 12th century but inhabited as recently as the 20th by an American couple who helped resettle Asia Minor refugees after their arrival in 1922. The interiors afford many nice views of the surrounding area and sea.

On the main road in town beside the pharmacy, ★ **Athos Sea Cruises** (☎ 23770/71370; tickets €17; May–Oct.) runs 3-hour excursions around the peninsula from May to October at 10:30am; a second boat departs at 1:30pm from June to September. Recorded commentary provides detailed information on the peninsula and the eight monasteries you'll pass. Grilled-cheese sandwiches, pizza, chips, and other snacks are served onboard along with soft drinks and alcoholic beverages. Try to make a reservation the day before.

Ouranoupolis to Dafni on Mount Athos is 50km (31 miles) to the southeast. Sailing time is 1½–2 hr.

2 ★ **Mount Athos.** This semiautonomous region is self-governed within the Greek state, subject politically to the Ministry of Foreign Affairs and religiously to the Ecumenical Patriarch of Constantinople (Istanbul). It's divided into 20 territories, each with a cardinal monastery and dependent monastic establishments (cloisters, hermitages, cells). The monasteries are communal, and each has a superior who is a member of the Holy Assembly, elected for life by the monks. A representative to the Holy Community (administrative authority) is elected yearly.

Tip for Female Travelers

Ouranoupolis is a low-key beach resort on the border of Mount Athos, so if families or partners want to tag along while men are on the Holy Mountain, where women are prohibited, they can stay here, enjoy the sand and sea, and take a cruise around the peninsula. In winter, however, accompanying females and family are better off staying in Thessaloniki.

> *Many of the 20 monasteries hug the coast, where the Virgin Mary allegedly came ashore when her ship was blown off course.*

A four-member Holy Supervision holds executive authority and is elected by the five monasteries that hierarchically precede them.

The 20 monasteries in order of hierarchy are Megisti (Great) Lavra, Vatopedi, Iviron, Hilandari (Serb), Dionysiou, Koutloumousiou, Pantokratoros, Xiropotamou, Zografou (Bulgarian), Dochiariou, Karakalou, Filotheou, Simon Petras, Agios Pavlos, Stavronikitas, Xenofontos, Grigoriou, Esfigmenos, Panteleimon (aka Rossiko), and Konstamonitis.

Men who want to visit a monastery need written permission from the **Holy Mount Athos Pilgrim's Bureau** in Thessaloniki (109 Egnatia St.; ☎ 2310/252578; piligrimsbureau@c-lab.gr; year-round Mon–Fri 9am–4pm, Sat 9am–2pm), which issues about 10 passes a day for non-Orthodox guests, and about 100 a day for Greek Orthodox visitors. You don't need to go in person, but you must contact the monastery directly and make a reservation through the Pilgrim's Bureau at least 6 months in advance. Send a copy of your passport, and tell them which monastery

Eats & Sleeps in Ouranoupolis

In a peaceful setting on a bluff, just beyond the main town, ★ kids **Skites** (1 km/⅔ mile south of Ouranoupolis; ☎ 23770/71140, 23770-71141; www.skites.gr. 25 units. Doubles €100–160 w/breakfast. MC, V. May–Oct) is a small complex of garden bungalows steps from a beach. There are no TVs on site, but the bar and outdoor pool are entertaining enough, not to mention the beach and live cultural events—such as classical music concerts, poetry readings, or theater presentations—which often take place in the evenings. The restaurant serves a variety of dishes, including vegetarian options. Another dining option in town is ★★ **Kritikos** (☎ 23770/71222; entrées €10–15; MC, V; year-round daily noon–midnight), which has ranked among the top ten restaurants worldwide. Macedonian dishes are made from local ingredients, typically washed down with homemade spirits.

ou plan to visit. Photos may be allowed, but
videos and films are prohibited.

Visitor's permits to enter the area (*dia-
monitirios*) are dispersed at the bureau's **Ouranoupolis branch office** (main road, behind the
bus station; ☎ 23770/71422; year-round daily
9am–1:30pm). The permit is for 3 nights/4
days, and costs €25 for Greek Orthodox and
€30 for other denominations. Visits can be
extended by the authorities in the administrative town of Karyes. You need to be in Ouranoupolis by 9am to get the permit and the
boat to Dafni on the peninsula, which departs
at 9:45am (sail time 1½–2 hr.). Local transport
takes visitors to Karyes (13km/8 miles inland)
and onward to the monasteries. ⏱ 1 day. 50km
(31 miles) southeast of Ouranoupolis, 120km (75
miles) southeast of Thessaloniki.

> *Megisti Lavra was the first monastery on Mount
Athos, founded in 963.*

Of Monks & Men

Tradition holds that the Virgin Mary was
blown off course from Ephesus and landed
on Mount Athos, decreeing it her special
place. The peninsula is dedicated to her, but
women haven't been allowed here for 1,050
years. Monks first settled here in the 10th
century, and by the 14th there were hundreds of monasteries. When the territory
came under Greek jurisdiction, the state
limited the number to 20 and their dependencies in 1924. Women are banned from
within 500m (1,640 ft.) of the peninsula or
face a mandatory jail term—the harshest

penalty for breaking a 1954 law enacted 2
years before women could vote—despite
European Parliament objections that the
ban blatantly violates equality. The monks
argue that tradition and their religious
freedom are of a higher order, and that the
monasteries are private property. Whether
Europe's women agree or are even aware,
taxpayer funds from the E.U. and Greece
have been used to maintain the historic
complexes and upgrade the standard of living for the 2,000-odd monks living there.

Mount Olympus & Litochoro

Like Mount Fuji or Kilimanjaro, Mount Olympus is an irresistible challenge for many climbers, however difficult and dangerous the last 30 minutes of the climb to Mytikas, the highest peak (2,919m/9,577 ft.). For the fit, however, it's a once-in-a-lifetime experience to ascend the country's highest mountain range, legendary home of the 12 principal gods in Greek mythology. Trekkers free of the desire to mount the summit will find nature walks and beaches to explore; the seashore is just a couple of miles away from the foothill town of Litochoro, where most hikes up and around the mountain begin.

> Pretty Litochoro is the starting point for the three walking routes to the summit of Mount Olympus.

START Litochoro **TRIP LENGTH** About 6 hr. from Athens and 1½ hr. from Thessaloniki.

❶ ★ **Litochoro.** At 300m (984 ft.), this resort village in the foothills of Mount Olympus is the main starting point for treks up the mountain. Given its unique position only 5km (3 miles) from the sea, it's a popular holiday spot.

Beside the Enipea River, it's believed to be the successor of flooded ancient Pibleia, home of the Muses. It also grew from a monastery, St. Dionysus, established here in 1540. By the 19th century it had a well-known seafaring tradition, as it was settled by islanders sent by antipagan zealot Emperor Theodosius, who came to convert the inhabitants living on the

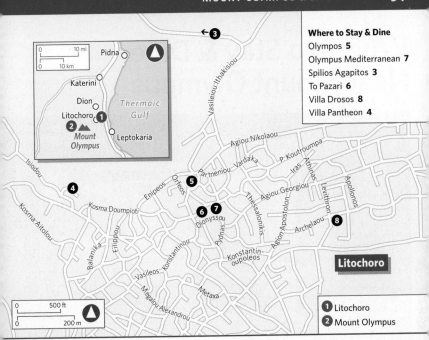

Where to Stay & Dine
Olympos **5**
Olympus Mediterranean **7**
Spilios Agapitos **3**
To Pazari **6**
Villa Drosos **8**
Villa Pantheon **4**

1 Litochoro
2 Mount Olympus

pantheon's holy mountain. The area was a base for resistance and bandits until the early 20th century, when it became part of Greece in 1912, and again during World War II. 7km (4⅓ miles) southwest of Dion, 100km (62 miles) southwest of Thessaloniki. By bus or train: 1½ hr. from Thessaloniki, transfer at Katerini for Litochoro.

2 ★★ **Mount Olympus.** Mount Olympus is Greece's biggest mountain—easily visible from Thessaloniki across the gulf. The highest of the multipeak range is **Mytikas** or the **Throne of Zeus,** at 2,919m (9,577 ft.). It's a national park that draws thousands each year to walk the nature trails amid the mountain's rich flora and fauna, much of which is endemic. The next highest peak is **Skolio** at 2,911m (9,550 ft.). Most people stop their ascent here, because the last stretch to Mytikas is a rock scramble that can be fatal. The peaks get a regular dusting of snow from November to April. We recommend a detailed map, such as the excellent one published by **Anavasi** (www.mountains.gr), sold in Litochoro and the Refuge for 7.50€. ⏱ 1 day.

> *It's easy to imagine the gods residing on the cloud-shrouded, snow-capped heights of Olympus.*

Where to Stay & Dine Near Mount Olympus

> Zeus himself might feel at home amid the templelike marble opulence of the Olympus Mediterranean.

Olympos LITOCHORO *GREEK GRILL*
For simple souvlaki or slow-cooked food delivered to the table fast, go to the main square. Olympos is just beside the National Bank. They also serve burgers, spaghetti, omelets, steaks, and schnitzel. You can eat here or take out your order. Kentriki Platia (Central Sq.). ☎ 23520/84282. Entrees 5€–10€. No credit cards. Daily breakfast, lunch & dinner.

Olympus Mediterranean LITOCHORO
In a great location in town beside a good taverna (To Pazari), this spa hotel has an indoor pool and sauna, and offers massage treatments. Each room is decorated uniquely and tastefully in contemporary decor; some have hot tubs and fireplaces. The lounge has a cafe-bar. 5 Dionyssou St. ☎ 23520/81831. www.olympus.mediterraneanhotels.gr. 23 units. 90€–120€ w/breakfast. AE, DC, MC, V.

Spilios Agapitos MOUNT OLYMPUS
This well-known refuge **(Refuge A)** and restaurant serving hearty, home-cooked food on the mountainside (at 2,100m/6,890 ft.), is about a 6km (3¾-mile), 3-hour walk from the end of the road at **Prionia** (1,100m/3,609 ft.), where there's another restaurant. From Litochoro, it's 24km (15 miles) and 5 hours. Stop here, eat lunch, and return to Litochoro, or stay on. From here, it's another 5km (3 miles) or another 2½ to 3 hours, most of which is easy going (to Skala at 2,882m/9,455 ft. and on to the Skolio summit at 2,911m/9,551 ft.). The last bit up Mytikas is a scramble. Blankets are supplied, but bring your own sheets, towels, soap, flashlight, map, and indoor shoes. Refuge A. ☎ 23520/81800. www.mountolympus.gr. Bunk 12€, 10€ for mountaineer association members (any nationality). 110 beds. No credit cards. Last check-in 8pm, lights out 10pm. Restaurant serves daily breakfast, lunch & early dinner. Entrees 4€–7€. Mid-May to Oct.

> *Meaty Greek staples, such as souvlaki, are welcome after a hike in the mountains.*

To Pazari LITOCHORO *GREEK*

This taverna is just beside the Olympus Mediterranean hotel, so you don't have to go far for great seafood and meat dishes. Their spicy appetizers are good too, and so are the prices. The food is locally sourced and served with village wine. If you like soup, try the fish soup here. Just up and past the central square, and around the corner to the left. **25th Martiou St.** ☎ 23520/82540. Entrees 6€–12€. No credit cards. Daily lunch & dinner.

kids Villa Drosos LITOCHORO

This hotel in a quiet spot opposite a church (St. George) looks like a big house with balustrades across arched openings. The rooms are typical, but it's also got a seasonal outdoor pool and fireplace in the lounge-bar-cafe. The garden is gated, and it's across the street from a park. Free Wi-Fi. Opposite the park on Agiou Nikolaou Street, turn into Athinas Street at the kiosk. **20 Archelaou St.** ☎ 23520/84561 or 84562. www.villadrosos.gr. Doubles 40€–55€, breakfast add 5€ per person. 13 units. MC, V.

kids Villa Pantheon LITOCHORO

This hotel is about a 10-minute walk out of Litochoro town. (There are video directions on their site.) It's really a treat to stay here; guests return year after year for its beautiful views of the mountains and the sea, its comfortable three- to four-bed suites, and good

> *Olympos specializes in souvlaki and other hearty comfort foods.*

value. There's also a game room, and breakfast is a la carte. Reserve ahead on weekends and holidays. **End of Agiou Dimitriou St.** ☎ 23520/83931. www.villapantheon.gr. 12 units. Doubles 50€–60€. AE, DC, MC, V.

THE PANTHEON
The Gods & Goddesses of Mount Olympus
BY STEPHEN BREWER

	THE GOD	REALM OF THE GOD	FAVORITE ACCESSORY
	APOLLO	God of light, order, reason, and poetry ▶	Lyre
	ARES	God of war	Bronze-tipped spear
	ARTEMIS	Virgin goddess of the hunt	Quiver of arrows
	ATHENA ▶	Goddess of wisdom and human endeavor	Shield and spear
	DEMETER	Goddess of fertility and agriculture	Sheaves of wheat
	DIONYSUS	God of wine, pleasure, and the theater	Drinking cup

FOURTEEN GODS AND GODDESSES RULED the ancient Greeks' universe from Mount Olympus (p. 541), influencing everything from the weather to the whims of the human heart. For all their divine powers, the gods were amazingly humanlike in appearance and spirit, with strengths and weaknesses, passions and vanities. All in all, they were fairly compassionate. Only 12 gods resided on Mount Olympus at any one time; depending on the period in Greek history and the individual doing the accounting, Hestia, Demeter, Dionysus, and Hades were at times dislodged from the Olympian heights.

ROMAN COUNTERPART	CLAIM TO FAME	PERSONAL STYLE
Apollo	Patron of Delphi, home of the famous oracle; won many musical contests among the other gods	Perennially youthful and handsome, with long, golden hair
Mars	Fought many battles and indulged in many affairs; like his mother, Hera, he was difficult and headstrong and often quarreled with the other gods and goddesses	◀ Fierce, beardless, proud, often wore a helmet and nothing else
Diana	Loved to hunt but was a protector of all creatures; she helped her mother, Leto, give birth to her twin brother, Apollo	Usually carried a bow and arrow and wore a knee-length gown
Minerva	Sprang fully grown from the head of Zeus; she was patron of Athens, and the Parthenon was built in her honor	Sophisticated, full of advice on such matters as weaving, sewing, and metallurgy
Ceres	Introduced wheat to humanity and provided all nutrition on earth	Peace loving and benign, with golden hair and slender feet
Bacchus ▶	Traveled around the world in the company of satyrs, always having a good time	Lighthearted and good natured, noted for his long, shoulder-length hair

	THE GOD	REALM OF THE GOD	FAVORITE ACCESSORY
	HADES	God of the Underworld	Three-headed hound, Cerberus
	HEPHAESTUS	God of fire and metalworking	Hammer and tongs
	HERA	Queen of the Gods, wife/sister of Zeus, goddess of marriage and women	Crown
	APHRODITE	Goddess of love and beauty	Mirror
	HERMES	God of travel, commerce, and thieves ▶	Winged sandals and cap
	HESTIA	Virgin goddess of hearth and home	Veil
	POSEIDON	God of the sea ▼	Trident
	ZEUS	King of the gods	Thunderbolt

ROMAN COUNTERPART	CLAIM TO FAME	PERSONAL STYLE
Pluto	Remained in the Underworld, surrounded by darkness and silence	Gloomy, with dark locks that fell over his brow
Vulcan	Accepting husband of the adulterous Aphrodite; blacksmith to the gods	Elderly, bearded, kind hearted, and disabled from birth; when his mother, Hera, saw how unattractive he was, she threw him from Mount Olympus
Juno	Rather than succor Hercules, whom Zeus fathered with a mortal, Hera dropped her milk into the universe, creating the Milky Way; she was worshipped in June, still the month when many couples wed	A steely beauty, she was not above taking revenge on those with whom her husband had trysts
Venus	Married to Hephaestus, but carried on a long and passionate affair with Ares, god of war; gave birth to Eros, cupid of love, who accompanied her everywhere	Sensual, lovely, always smiling, liked to wear jewelry
Mercury	Messenger of the gods, escorted the dead to Hades; had a penchant for thievery and cheating since infancy	Speedy and cunning, handsome and athletic
Vesta	Forever pure, she rejected the advances of Apollo and Poseidon	Bashful and modest, kind and forgiving
Neptune	Preferred mode of transport was giant sea shell pulled by sea horses	Sturdy, with long, blue hair and a dark beard; moody, would cause earthquakes, tempests, and floods when displeased
Jupiter	Wildly promiscuous, he was the father of many children on earth; responsible for the weather, which changed with his moods	Commanded respect; had a good sense of humor, was just but rather unpredictable

Thessaloniki

Known as Greece's second city, the port town of Thessaloniki (also known as Salonica) has functioned as a crossroads of cultures and goods for much longer than Athens, and it shows. It was on the ancient route from Rome to Constantinople—the Via Egnatia, a road that exists today. Greeks, Romans, Jews, and Turks have all left their mark on the landscape and cuisine, and Balkan citizens still use the city and Halkidiki Peninsula as a holiday playground. Thessalonicans are comfortable in their cosmopolitan skin, even if they now appear a little frayed around the edges. The sites are also less glamorous than the capital's, but there are many to see. Most are spread out north and south of Egnatia Street (or Road, or Odos in Greek), from Eleftheriou Venizelou Street until HANTH Square (XAN is the YMCA, TH is for Thessaloniki). We start from the west, venturing east and then north to Ano Polis.

> *The Arch of Galerius was erected in honor of the co-emperor in A.D. 305.*

START Dikastirion Sq. **TRIP LENGTH** 1–2 days.

① **Panagia Chalkeon.** This is one of the oldest standing domed cruciform churches anywhere, from 1028. Dedicated to the Virgin of the Copper (smiths), it's located in the traditional copper-working area, where many shops still sell copper wares at low prices. If the church is open, take a look at the mosaics inside. ◷ 10 min. Egnatia and 2 Chalkeon St., Dikastirion Sq.

② **★★ Modiano Market.** Every town should have one—a public market with a variety of sellers and their produce all under one roof. This glass-roofed building is named after its architect, Eli Modiano, and sells all kinds of food, as well as flowers and spices. ◷ 20 min.

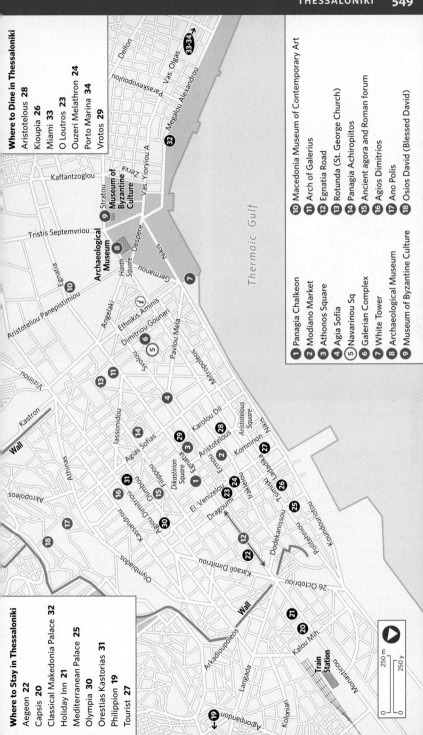

Where to Dine in Thessaloniki

Aristotelous **28**
Kioupia **26**
Miami **33**
O Loutros **23**
Ouzeri Melathron **24**
Porto Marina **34**
Vrotos **29**

1. Panagia Chalkeon
2. Modiano Market
3. Athonos Square
4. Agia Sofia
5. Navarinou Sq
6. Galerian Complex
7. White Tower
8. Archaeological Museum
9. Museum of Byzantine Culture
10. Macedonia Museum of Contemporary Art
11. Arch of Galerius
12. Egnatia Road
13. Rotunda (St. George Church)
14. Panagia Achiropiitos
15. Ancient agora and Roman forum
16. Agios Dimitrios
17. Ano Polis
18. Osios David (Blessed David)

Where to Stay in Thessaloniki

Aegeon **22**
Capsis **20**
Classical Makedonia Palace **32**
Holiday Inn **21**
Mediterranean Palace **25**
Olympia **30**
Orestias Kastorias **31**
Philippion **19**
Tourist **27**

> Like the Rotunda, many of Thessaloniki's Byzantine landmarks (the largest such concentration in Greece) are being restored.

> Markets and parks soften the city's edges.

Bounded by Aristotelous, Ermou, Vas. Irakleiou, and Komninon sts. Mon–Sat 7am–3pm.

3 ★★ **Athonos Square.** The maze of lanes leading from pedestrian **Aristotelous Street,** with its open square near the waterfront, is unmarked on maps, but it's fun to wander aimlessly past the area's many copper sellers and boisterous tavernas. ⏱ 30 min. Bounded by Egnatia, Karolou Dil, Ermou, and Aristotelous sts.

4 ★ **Agia Sofia.** This church is part of the Paleochristian and Byzantine Monuments of Thessaloniki, a World Heritage Site. Its front entrance is a popular meeting spot. Its founding is disputed, but the church is believed to date from the 8th century, when Orthodox churches were beginning to adopt their now-familiar cruciform style, in transition from the basilica form. Noteworthy are two mosaics: One depicts the Ascension, and the other shows Mary holding Jesus in her arms. In the 8th and 9th centuries, iconoclasts replaced her image with a cross, but the Panagia was later put back. ⏱ 15 min. Agias Sofias and Ermou sts. ☎ 2310/270253. May–Oct daily 7am–1pm and 6–7pm, Nov–Apr daily 7am–1pm and 5–6:30pm.

5 🍴 **Navarinou Square.** Gounari Street leads to this tree-filled square with its own "Manneken Pis" fountain—a bronze boy peeing. Lined with the awnings of restaurants and cafes, it's a favorite haunt of students and youth. **Omorfi Thessaloniki** has great food; try the seafood meze. 6 Navarinou Sq. ☎ 2310/270714. $

6 **Galerian Complex.** During his reign in the 4th century A.D. as Rome's co-emperor of the provinces, Galerius did some serious town building. Gounari Street—a student-friendly pedestrian street with book and record shops, boutiques, and restaurants—runs along the ruins of his palace. The Octagon building is thought to be his throne room. The ancient Hippodrome racetrack is on the other side of the street. ⏲ 10 min. Gounari St.

7 ★★ **White Tower.** The last medieval tower left standing is the postcard of Thessaloniki. The cylinder-shaped, 29m (95-ft.) stone structure was built by the Ottoman Turks in the 16th century as part of the city's walls, but was later used as a place of execution. Restored in the 1980s for the 2,300th anniversary of Thessaloniki's founding, it's now the city's museum. A steep, winding staircase ascends five levels, offering a great view of the city and harbor. ⏲ 1 hr. Nikis and Pavlou Mela sts. ☎ 2310/267832. www.culture.gr. Admission 3€, free for ages 19 & under. Tues–Sun 8:30am–3pm.

8 ★★★ **Archaeological Museum.** This museum contains artifacts excavated near an archaic temple at nearby Thermi, tombs at Sindos, the Egnatia highway (the ancient road from Rome to Constantinople), the Thessaloniki-Skopje road, and a railway line. The collection includes gold jewelry from the 6th to the 2nd century B.C., and exhibitions explore the history of Thessaloniki and the region, from prehistoric times to the Roman era. ⏲ 1 hr. 6 Manoli Andronikou St. ☎ 2310/830538. www.culture.gr. Admission 6€; combined ticket with Byzantine Museum 8€. Nov–Mar Tues–Sun 8:30am–3pm, Mon 10:30am–5pm; Apr–Oct daily 8am–8pm.

9 ★★★ kids **Museum of Byzantine Culture.** Right next to the archaeological museum is this cultural gem, awarded the Council of Europe's museum prize in 2005. It beautifully presents collections of Byzantine art, from icons to jewelry and embroidery, including a standout 9th-century enamel-and-gold filigree bracelet. A room upstairs shows how pottery was made. The **gift shop** sells books on Byzantine culture, museum reproductions, and postcards. ⏲ At least 30 min. 2 Stratou Ave. ☎ 2310/868570. www.mbp.gr. Admission 4€; combined ticket with Archaeological Museum 8€. Nov–Mar Tues–Sun 8:30am–3pm, Mon 10:30am–5pm; Apr–Oct 8am–7:30pm, Mon 1–7:30pm.

> *The White Tower, one of many such defenses that encircled the medieval city, was whitewashed in the 19th century.*

10 **Macedonia Museum of Contemporary Art.** This noteworthy museum has a growing permanent collection of installation art, videos, sculpture, painting, photography, and holograms by contemporary Greek and foreign artists, including work by Dennis Oppenheim and an Andy Warhol screen-print of Alexander the Great. Temporary exhibitions are also worth a look. ⏲ 30 min. 154 Egnatia St., Helexpo. ☎ 2310/240002 or 281212. www.mmca.org.gr. Admission 4€. Tues, Thurs, Sat 10am–6pm; Wed 10am–10pm; Fri 10am–7pm; Sun 11am–3pm.

11 **Arch of Galerius.** This roadside landmark was built in A.D. 305 to commemorate the Roman co-emperor's victory over the Persians a few years earlier. Eroded bas-reliefs depict his battles in this restored part of the original structure that spanned the ancient Roman road and a passageway leading to the Rotunda. ⏲ 5 min. Egnatia St. at Gounari St., Sintrivaniou Sq.

> *Agios Dimitrios rose above the Roman city in the early years of Christianity.*

⑫ Egnatia Road. The main thoroughfare through Thessaloniki is Egnatia Street, which follows the same path as the ancient Via Egnatia from Rome (save the trip across the Adriatic) to Constantinople. Thessaloniki was a commercial crossroad, as it still is today, with close ties to the Balkans and to Turkey. Walk along a section in the center of town, perhaps to **Aristotelous Square** on the waterfront, the center of town. ⏱ At least 5 min.

⑬ ★ Rotunda (St. George Church). Built in A.D. 306 as a temple or mausoleum for Emperor Galerius, who met his end elsewhere, this rotunda was converted to a church later in the 4th century by the Byzantine emperor Theodosius the Great. It contains fragments of beautiful mosaics. In 1590, the Ottoman Turks turned it into a mosque and built the minaret still standing today. The structure has been undergoing restoration since 1999 (it was closed until then after a 1978 earthquake). Services, exhibitions, and concerts take place here. ⏱ 10 min. Dimitriou Gounari St. ☎ 2310/968860. Free admission. Nov–Mar Tues–Sun 8:30am–3pm, Apr–Oct Tues–Sun 8:30am–7pm.

⑭ Panagia Achiropiitos. This early basilica-style church, built in the 5th century and dedicated to the Virgin, is one of the world's oldest churches in continuous use. Achiropiitos means "not by (human) hand" and refers to an icon of Mary that miraculously appeared in the church in the 12th century. The church has elaborate column capitals and pretty mosaics under the arches. ⏱ 10 min. 56 Agias Sofias St.

⑮ ★ Ancient agora and Roman forum. The Roman forum was built on the site of the Greek agora, or marketplace, discovered by accident in the 1960s during construction of the foundations for the city's courts. The most discernible ruin is the 2nd-century-A.D. odeion, a theater where Romans watched athletic events, music performances, and gladiator contests. ⏱ 15 min. Behind (north of) Dikastirion Sq., btw. Filippou and Olimbou sts. ☎ 2310/221266. Free admission. Tues–Sun 8:30am–3pm.

⑯ Agios Dimitrios. This five-aisle basilica is the main church for the city's patron saint, Dimitrios. The church (ca. 5th c.), which replaced an older structure on the site of **Roman baths,** was rebuilt following the Great Fire in 1917. A few original mosaics from the 5th to the 7th century survived; the rest are restorations. Downstairs in the **crypt** you can see what's left of a holy water font and the baths, where Dimitrios is believed to have been martyred. ⏱ At least 10 min. Corner of Agiou Dimitriou and Agiou Nikolaou sts. (1 block north of the Roman forum, at the base of the Upper City). ☎ 2310/270591 (crypt). Free admission. Crypt Mon 12:30–7pm, Tues–Fri 8am–4:30pm, Sat 8:30am–3pm, Sun 11am–3pm.

⑰ ★ Ano Polis. The "Upper City" is an area of town that includes the **Old Turkish Quarter** and a notable church, both worth the effort

Places to Take the Kids

If you're traveling with children, consider taking them to the **Thessaloniki Science Centre and Technology Museum.** The building itself looks out of this world. Inside, it features a large-format theater, a planetarium, a virtual reality simulator that takes passengers on journeys underwater and through outer space, and a museum with three permanent exhibitions: an amusing interactive exhibition (Technopark) that focuses on physics and chemistry, and displays on ancient Greek technology and classic cars. The simulator is suitable for children 7 years and older, and headphone translations aren't required. Headphones with English translations are available for theater presentations, and the shows are suitable for children age 5 years and up. There's also an on-site **library** with

Internet access, a conference room that seats 200, a **coffee shop** and **snack bar** for light meals, and a **gift shop.** 6th km Thessaloniki-Thermi road. ☎ 2310/483000. www.noesis. edu.gr. Admission Cosmotheater 2D 8€, 6€ for kids/students 5–18; Cosmotheater 3D 10€, 8€ kids; simulator 6€, 4€ kids; museum 7€, 5€ kids; planetarium 8€, 6€ kids. Tues–Fri 9am–2pm, Fri 5–8pm, Sat 3–9pm, Sun 11am–9pm.

★ **Magic Park** is an enormous, deluxe amusement park with rides for all ages—from baby carts to bumping boats and a minicarousel in Babyland, plus rides for bigger kids. 12th km Thessaloniki–Airport road. ☎ 2310/476770. www.magicpark.gr. Admission 11€, 7€ kids, free if they're under 1m (39 in.) tall.

required to hike up here. Nineteenth-century Thessaloniki lives on, with its wood-framed houses and balconies protruding over narrow, cobblestone streets. It also has fantastic views over the city and the Thermaic Gulf. Taxis may be reluctant to navigate the streets, but you can take bus no. 23 from Eleftherias Square (2 blocks west of Aristotelous Sq.), on the waterfront side, which leaves every 10 to 15 minutes and follows an interesting route through the narrow streets. It takes about 30 minutes on foot, heading north from the White Tower, along Ethnikis Aminis Street. ⏱1 hr.

⑱ ★★ **Osios David (Blessed David).** I'd come up here just to see this 6th-century church with its lovely mosaic and view over the city.

The original entrance has been bricked up, but the highlight is the rare beardless Jesus, with symbols of the evangelists Matthew, Mark, Luke, and John (depicted as an angel, eagle, lion, and ox, respectively), flanked by the prophets Ezekiel and Habakkuk. It was hidden from iconoclastic rampages in the 8th and 9th centuries, then plastered over by the Turks when the church was turned into a mosque. Tradition holds that it was rediscovered in 1921 by an Egyptian monk who had received a vision of the work. During his visit, an earthquake struck and revealed the mosaic, and then he died. No photos allowed. 7 Timotheou St., near intersection of Dimitriou Poliorkitou and Agia Sofia sts., Ano Polis. No phone. ⏱20 min.

The Jews of Salonica

The story of the Jews of Thessaloniki would be a long and happy one were it not for the atrocities of World War II.

Alexandrian Jews were among the first to settle here in 140 B.C. More arrived during the Roman and Byzantine eras, when the Jews also spoke Greek, the lingua franca at the time, and the Apostle Paul is said to have preached at their synagogue. Eastern European Jews arrived through the 14th and 15th centuries, and from 1492, a massive wave of Jews expelled from Spain and Portugal during the Spanish Inquisition arrived, attracted by the Ottoman Empire's favorable policies following their conquest of the Christian Byzantine Empire. Others came from Italy, France, and North Africa, so that by 1553, Thessaloniki became the Jewish center of Europe with some 20,000 co-religionists, according to Jewish sources. Thessaloniki was also attractive for its position as a trading center between East and West, and it was renowned for its silk and wool.

Following the Great Fire of 1917, 90,000 of the city's 170,000 citizens were Jews. Zionist leaders David Ben-Gurion and Yitzak Ben-Zvi called Thessaloniki a model city, with its many Judeo-Spanish street names, 100 synagogues, 17 Jewish quarters, and some 20 Zionist organizations. The Jewish population began dwindling between the wars, however, when Jews emigrated to France, the U.S., and Palestine. But the Nazis dealt the deadliest blow between March and August 1943, when they deported 43,850 people (95% of the city's Jewish population) to concentration camps in Poland. Some 2,000 survived the war, but many left for the U.S. and Palestine. Only about 1,200 remain. A memorial is held each year at a Holocaust monument in Eleftherias Square.

- The **Jewish Community of Thessaloniki** is on the first floor of the **Yad Lezicaron Synagogue** (26 Vas. Iraklio St.; ☎ 2310/275701 or 223231; www.jct.gr; open Mon-Fri 9am-3pm), built on the site of the Bourla Synagogue used by Jews working in the nearby marketplace.

- Few Jewish buildings survived the 1917 fire and World War II, but this one houses the **Jewish Museum of Thessaloniki** (13 Agiou Mina St.; ☎ 2310/250406; www.jmth.gr; 3€; Tues, Fri, Sun 11am-2pm, Wed-Thurs 11am-2pm and 5-8pm). Jewish life is presented through photographs, video, and artifacts. There's also a **library.**

- The **Monastirioton Synagogue** (ca. 1925; 35 Syngrou St.) was used as a Red Cross warehouse during World War II and thus survived. It's open only for special occasions and for group visits. Contact the Jewish Community well in advance to go in.

Where to Stay in Thessaloniki

> *Capsis is a comfortable, conveniently located hotel popular with business travelers.*

Aegeon

Among the accommodations clustered east of Dimokratias Square convenient to the center, train station, port, and nightlife districts, this six-story hotel is one of the nicest. Renovated rooms are small but nicely decorated with attractive art and rustic ceramic tiling. Windows are soundproofed, and Wi-Fi is free throughout. The owners run two more hotels in the area and one near the airport. **19 Egnatia Rd.** ☎ **2310/522921. www.aegeon-hotel.gr. 59 units. Doubles 60€–90€ w/breakfast. AE, DC, MC, V.**

Capsis

This big hotel is near the train station on the main road into town. Many business travelers stay here during Thessaloniki's major international trade fair in September. Rooms are nothing special, but big beds, thick carpets, and plenty of heat in winter ensure that your stay will be comfortable. They're wheelchair accessible, and there's also a rooftop pool, gym, sauna, free Wi-Fi throughout the hotel, and free use of a business center with computers and Internet access. For an extra 10€, guests can stay until 8pm. Parking is 10€. **18**

Monastiriou St. ☎ **2310/596800. www. capsishotel.gr. 412 units. Doubles 102€–142€ w/breakfast. AE, DC, MC, V.**

★ Classical Makedonia Palace

Thessaloniki's landmark hotel is on the waterfront, affording great views across the city and the gulf, including Mount Olympus. It's part of the luxury Classical Hotels chain and offers amenities such as down comforters and pillows, marble bathrooms, stereo/CD players, and i-Pod docks in some rooms. It has an outdoor pool, a health club, a hair salon, two restaurants, a bar and pool bar, babysitting, and free outdoor parking. Indoor parking is 17€. Low season is July and August. **2 Meg. Alexandrou St., Faliro.** ☎ **2310/897197. www.classicalhotels.com. 284 units. Doubles 210€–500€. AE, DC, MC, V.**

kids Holiday Inn

This well-known chain hotel is near the train station, so it's convenient for early departures. The rooms feel luxurious with classic decor and "sleep-well" mattresses, and the windows have blackout curtains and soundproofing to block

> *The Tourist Hotel provides lots of character at a good price in a handy location.*

noise from this busy arterial road. All the necessities for both business and family travel are provided, including connecting rooms and babysitting. One room is wheelchair accessible. The on-site gym is free. 8 Monastiriou St. ☎ 2310/563100. www.hithessaloniki.gr. 177 units. Doubles 130€–280€ w/breakfast. AE, DC, MC, V.

★ Mediterranean Palace

This elegant, six-story hotel on the edge of Ladadika near the port is popular with business travelers. It's luxurious with chandeliers, marble-top furniture, and richly upholstered chairs. Rooms have broadband Internet, and free Wi-Fi is available in common areas. They can arrange hair appointments in room or at a salon, babysitting, business services, and car rental. Parking is 11€. 3 Salaminos at Karatasou sts., Ladadika. ☎ 2310/552554. www.mediterranean-palace.gr. 119 units. Doubles 175€–350€ w/breakfast. AE, DC, MC, V.

Olympia

This old-style, seven-floor hotel was built in 1965 on the site of public baths dating to 1931. It's well-maintained, the room decor is modern (some units have Jacuzzis), and the location is quiet and convenient, close to the ancient agora/Roman forum and Agios Dimitrios Church. The bar-restaurant is open 24 hours.

A full American breakfast is served. Outdoor parking is free; a spot in the closed garage is 16€. Free Wi-Fi in the lobby. 65 Olimbou and Papageorgiou sts. ☎ 2310/235421. www.hotelolympia.gr. 111 units. Doubles 88€–100€ w/breakfast. AE, DC, MC, V.

kids Orestias Kastorias

Although it's a bit spartan, this hotel is a good buy for families and budget travelers. The 1920s three-story walk-up is on a quiet street leading from the ancient agora (forum) to Agios Dimitrios Church. Rooms are spacious if plainly decorated, and prices include tea, coffee, and cookies all day. Rooms have free Wi-Fi. Group and company discounts are available. 14 Agnostou Stratiotou St. ☎ 2310/276517. www.okhotel.gr. 37 units. Doubles 52€–65€. MC, V.

Philippion

This modern-style destination hotel is on a secluded hilltop in Seih-Sou Forest. A free shuttle bus goes to central Agia Sofia Square (5–30 min., depending on traffic) in town, from 7:45am to 12:15am. The airport is also about 15 minutes away. The comfy rooms, which all have balconies and views of the forest or the sea, are unusually spacious with minibars, and there's a bar-restaurant, sports cafe, and outdoor pool. Parking is free. **Dasos Seih-Sou,** 5km/3 miles northeast of the center, Agios Pavlos. ☎ 2310/203320. www.philippion.gr. 92 units. 75€–95€ w/breakfast. AE, DC, MC, V.

★ Tourist

This is a good budget choice in a prime spot off Aristotelous Square, the heart of town. A historic, three-story building with large rooms and high, decorative ceilings, it's very popular

with both business and pleasure travelers. Rooms feel elegant and have Wi-Fi and a minibar. Discounts are available for extended stays and groups. Book well in advance. **21 Mitropoleos and Komninon sts.** ☎ 2310/270501. www. touristhotel.gr. 37 units. Doubles 75€–100€ w/ breakfast. AE, MC, V.

Thessaloniki by Night

Like the city itself, Thessaloniki's best nightlife neighborhoods are spread out. There are cafe-bars along **Nikis Avenue** on the waterfront (the Paralia) and near the White Tower. Some intimate bars are located along **Proxenou Koromila Street,** parallel to Nikis, east of Aristotelous Square. **Ladadika** is another nightlife area, with cafe-bars along Katouni Street. **Odos Oneiron** (3 Vaiou St., Ladadika; ☎ 2310/555036) is a taverna with live *rembetika* (1920s urban blues) that relocates to Halkidiki in summer. There are clubs in **Sfageia,** south of the train station along 28th Octovriou Street near the waterfront. For example, **Mylos** (56 Andreadou Georgiou St., Sfageia; ☎ 2310/551836; www.mylos.gr), a well-known entertainment complex converted from a mill, features art and music entertainment. Check their website to see who's playing. **Vilka** (58, 26th Oktovriou St., Sfageia; ☎ 2310/ 522940) is an industrial space turned into

a "recreation center" with an art gallery, cafe-bar, small theater, and two nightclubs: the **Vilka Club** for concerts, special club nights, foreign DJ nights, and live sets; and **Mamounia,** the Greek music club. An art and music festival (www.reworks.gr) is also held here. The cafe-bar area in the courtyard is open year-round, daily from noon to 1am. More *bouzoukia* and Greek music clubs are located on the **Thessaloniki-Airport road.** Highbrow entertainment can be found from September to June at the **Thessaloniki Concert Hall,** aka Megaron Mousikis (25th Martiou and Paralia sts.; ☎ 2310/ 895800; www.tch.gr). The **Regency Casino Thessaloniki** (12th km Thessaloniki-Airport road, Aerodromio; ☎ 2310/491234; www. regency.gr; Sun–Thurs free admission 7am–8pm, 6€ after 8pm; open daily 24 hr.) is one of Europe's biggest, located near the airport. The minimum age is 23 with valid identification.

Where to Dine in Thessaloniki

> *A lively dining scene includes such atmospheric landmarks as Aristotelous Ouzeri.*

★ **Aristotelous Ouzeri** GREEK/MEZE

To try appetizers, a Thessaloniki-style meal, or even a cup of coffee, pop in here. It's centrally located on Aristotelous Street, behind the iron-gate entrance. The stuffed squid is a specialty, or try the crispy sardines. Desserts are an adventure, with traditional spoon sweets in summer and things like semolina halva in winter. 8 Aristotelous St. (btw. Iraklio and Tsimiski—numbers repeat on the square farther down). ☎ 2310/230762. Entrees 7€–15€. AE, DC, MC, V. Mon–Sun lunch & dinner.

★ **Kioupia** POLITIKI/GREEK

This classy restaurant is on a small square across from a fountain in the Ladadika district. It's popular (reservations recommended) for Politiki cuisine—Greek food from Istanbul or Smyrna (the movie *Touch of Spice* pays homage)—and other regional specialties. 3-5 Morichovou Sq., Ladadika. ☎ 2310/553239. www.kioupia.gr. Entrees 8€–16€. AE, DC, MC, V. Daily lunch (Sun till 5pm), Mon–Sat dinner. Closed Dec 25 and Jan 1.

★ **Miami** GREEK/SEAFOOD

This elegant seafood restaurant on the waterfront has more of an island feel than its American namesake suggests. Around since 1945, it serves wonderful fish and more than 300 types of wines, mainly regional varieties. It's well worth traveling the 15 minutes or so from the town center, especially for a special occasion. Book ahead on weekends. Take bus no. 5 from Meg. Alexandrou Street, Faliro. 18

> *Fresh fish is a staple in this city on the sea.*

Thetidos St., Nea Krini. ☎ 2310/447996. www.miami.gr. Entrees 10€–25€. AE, DC, MC, V. Daily lunch & dinner.

★★★ O Loutros GREEK/MEZE

This meze restaurant, on a quiet street beside a medieval **Turkish bathhouse**, serves Politiki specialties such as baked tuna and cuttlefish in wine sauce. Men sit at a table outside in summer and play the bouzouki on weekends. Dishes are unusual and tasty; so is the barrel retsina (pine resin) wine—give it a try, along with an Eastern-style dessert. 5 M. Kountoura St., Bezesteni. ☎ 2310/228895. Entrees 6.50€–12€. AE, DC, MC, V. Daily lunch & dinner (Mon–Sat till 1am, Sun til 6pm). Live bouzoukia Fri–Sat.

Ouzeri Melathron MEDITERRANEAN

Chefs are trained in Mediterranean cuisine here at the "Ouzo Mansion," where meze and, you guessed it, ouzo are the main attractions. Portions seem a little measured if you're used to a Greek-style dollop, but you probably won't notice if you're not a native

Greek. Stoa Ermeion, 23 Venizelou St. at Ermou St. ☎ 2310/220043. www.ouzoumelathron.gr. Entrees 5.70€–11€. AE, DC, MC, V. Daily lunch & dinner. Closed Dec 25 and half-day Easter.

Porto Marina GREEK/SEAFOOD

When you want seafood right off the boat, head to Nea Krini. The area, and the strip of restaurants along the road, is known for its seafood blowouts. Prices are a bit higher here, but try this taverna, which serves everything from grilled fish to lobster. 79 Plastiras St., Aretsou, Nea Krini, Kalamaria. ☎ 2310/451333. Entrees 8€–20€. AE, DC, MC, V. Daily lunch.

Vrotos GREEK/MEZE

This place on the edge of Athonos Square is known for its unique Thessaloniki meze. Choose from specialties such as baked feta, leek pie, dolmades (vine leaves stuffed with rice), and other treats. 6 Mitropolitou Gennadiou St., Athonos Sq. ☎ 2310/223958. Entrees 9€–17€. No credit cards. Daily lunch (Sun till 5pm), Mon–Sat dinner. Closed 3 weeks in Aug.

Northern Greece Fast Facts

> *The airport in Thessaloniki is one of Greece's major hubs.*

Arriving

BY AIR **Thessaloniki Macedonia International Airport** (SKG), 4th km Thessaloniki–Perea national road, Mikras (☎ 2310/473212; www.thessalonikiairport.gr), runs flights from European cities and these domestic carriers: **Aegean Air** (☎ 2310/239225; www.aegeanair.com) and **Olympic Airlines** (☎ 801/801-0101 or 210/355-0500; www.olympicairlines.com). BY SEA Ferry service from Thessaloniki varies every year but boats usually run to the islands of Limnos, Lesvos, and Chios. **Aegean Thalassic Agency,** 21 Kountourioti and 1 I. Dragoumi sts., portside (☎ 2310/500800), is the main ticket agent for **Hellenic Seaways** (www.hellenicseaways.gr) and **Minoan** (www.minoan.gr), but also sells tickets for the company currently sailing, Anek and Nel Lines. **Karacharisis Travel and Shipping Agency,** 8 Kountourioti Street, portside (☎ 2310/522716), is the main agent for Nel Lines (www.nel.gr). **Polaris Travel Agency,** 81 Egnatia Street (☎ 2310/276051, 278613, or 232078; polarisk@otenet.gr), sells all kinds of tickets. **Zorpidis Travel,** 4 Salaminos and Kountourioti sts., portside (☎ 2310/555995; www.zorpidis.gr), also sells air and train tickets, and excursions outside Greece. BY BUS In Thessaloniki, KTEL is at 194 Giannitson Street, Menemeni (☎ 2310/595408; www.ktel.gr).

Urban bus no. 1 goes from the train station to the KTEL terminal. Bus no. 78 goes from the KTEL bus terminal to the train station and airport. **BY CAR** Rental cars are 45€ to 60€ a day from **Hertz** (www.hertz.gr) at the Thessaloniki airport (☎ 2310/473952) or at 39 Polyechniou Street in the city center (☎ 2310/224906). Outside Thessaloniki, driving is easy on improved roads. In Thessaloniki, traffic jams are common, and parking is difficult. Buses are convenient, and taxis are cheap and easy to flag. **BY TRAIN** About 10 trains run per day from Athens to Thessaloniki; a few are express (4½ hr.). Ask there about limited train service to Litochoro, Vergina, or Pella.

Doctors & Dentists
See Emergencies, below.

Emergencies
THESSALONIKI Contact **Ahepa Hospital,** 1 Kyriakidi St. (☎ 2310/993111), or **Ippokration Hospital,** 49 Konstantinoupoleos St. (☎ 2310/892000). **KATERINI** Contact **Katerini General Hospital** (☎ 23510/57200). Also see p. 680, Fast Facts Greece.

Getting Around
BY TAXI In Thessaloniki, call **Lefkos Pyrgos** (White Tower; ☎ 2310/214900), **Makedonia** (☎ 2310/550500), or **Euro** (☎ 2310/866866 or 551525). In Litochoro, you can reach a private driver at ☎ 6977/320853 (8.50€ to Litohoro station; 12€ to Dion). **BY PLANE, TRAIN & BUS** For boat, plane, train, and long-distance bus schedules, call ☎ 1448. For general information, contact **Thessaloniki Public Transport,** 90 Papanastasiou St., Botsari (☎ 2310/981250; www.oasth.gr).

Internet
See p. 681, Fast Facts Greece.

Pharmacies
See p. 682, Fast Facts Greece.

Police & Tourist Police
THESSALONIKI Tourist Police: 3rd Floor, 4 Dodekanissou Street, Dimokratias Square (☎ 2310/554871). **LITOCHORO** ☎ 23520/81111.

> *Mere mortals have been finding their way to the residence of the gods for millennia.*

Port Authority
Thessaloniki Port Authority (☎ 2310/531504; www.thpa.gr).

Post office
THESSALONIKI 26 Aristotelous and Vatikiotou sts. (☎ 2310/277434). **LITOCHORO** ☎ 23520/84222.

Telephones
See p. 683, Fast Facts Greece.

Toilets
Look for standard restroom icons or WC; there's usually a public one at the port. You can also buy a drink at a cafe and use the facilities there or at archaeological sites.

Visitor Information
THESSALONIKI The **Greek National Tourism Organization** is at 136 Tsimiski at Dagli streets (☎ 2310/221100 or 252170), or at the airport (☎ 2310/471170; www.gnto.gr; Mon–Fri 8am–3pm, Sat 8:30am–2pm).

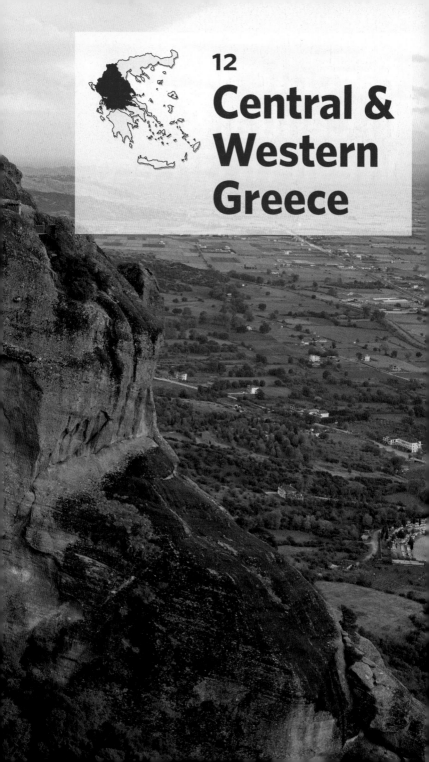

12
Central & Western Greece

Favorite Moments in Central & Western Greece

The central and western regions contain some of Greece's most beautiful natural scenery. The Pindus Mountain range runs through rugged Epirus in the northwest, famed for its remote villages, stone bridges, and the Vikos Gorge. The Pelion Peninsula, midway between Thessaloniki and Athens, has a ski resort, pretty villages, nature trails, and beaches. Delphi is a popular day trip with its poster-perfect ancient site, and Meteora's monastery-topped mountains are among the most spectacular sites in the world. Here are my favorite experiences in the region.

> PREVIOUS PAGE *Agios Stephanos Monastery in the Meteora.* THIS PAGE *The 5th-century-B.C. bronze* Charioteer *at the Delphi Museum.*

❶ **Seeing the eyes of** *The Charioteer,* **Delphi Museum.** It's rare to see an ancient statue with the paint still on it, and looking into the eyes of one from the 5th century B.C. is a thrill. See p. 576, ❸.

❷ **Taking in the surrounding mountains and valley from the magnificent theater at the Sanctuary of Apollo in Delphi.** From the center of the ancient world, the view is beautiful. See p. 577, ❹.

❸ **Crossing 19th-century bridges specially made for Smudgy (Moutsouris) the Steam Train.** This narrow-gauge train plies a 16km (10-mile) route to the village of Milies in Pelion. See p. 575.

❹ **Appreciating all things great and small in Meteora.** As you walk along the path from Kalambaka, wildflowers and intricately patterned lichen compete for your attention against the massive rock backdrop. See p. 581, ❷.

❺ **Seeing the rock face of the Meteora lit up at night.** From the balcony of the hotel in Kalambaka, these twisted peaks topped by monasteries look literally out of this world. See p. 581, ❸.

❻ **Wandering through the cobbled streets of Metsovo.** You'll find plenty to admire in Metsovo, from the beautiful mountain setting with panoramic views to the lucky children kicking around a ball on the grass at an elevated park nearby. See p. 586, ❶.

❼ **Walking across 18th-century stone bridges in Zagori.** This mountainous region is known for its beautiful bridges spanning meandering rivers. See p. 590.

1. Seeing the eyes of *The Charioteer*, Delphi Museum
2. Taking in the surrounding mountains and valley from the magnificent theater at the Sanctuary of Apollo in Delphi
3. Crossing 19th-century bridges specially made for Smudgy (Moutsouris) the Steam Train

4. Appreciating all things great and small in Meteora
5. Seeing the rock face of the Meteora lit up at night
6. Wandering through the cobbled streets of Metsovo
7. Walking across 18th-century stone bridges in Zagori
8. Hiking through the world's deepest gorge
9. Experiencing awe at the ancient sanctuary at Dodona
10. Marveling at the industrial arts in the Foti Rapakousi Museum
11. Admiring the craftsmanship of artifacts in the Silver Hall (Treasury)
12. Peering at the tomb of Ali Pasha, near the Fetiye Mosque

8 Hiking through the world's deepest gorge. At the Vikos Gorge in Zagori, you'll be awed by the rock walls soaring overhead and charmed by the quaint mountain villages along the way. See p. 589, ⑤.

9 Experiencing awe at the ancient sanctuary at Dodona. This is where the will of Zeus and his consort, Dione, were interpreted through the rustling of an oak tree. By all means, try to get permission to climb to the top tier of the enormous theater. See p. 595, ⑬.

10 Marveling at the industrial arts in the Foti Rapakousi Museum. The collection includes everything from weapons to music boxes.

Outdoors beside the building, the overgrown garden, with its carpet of wild poppies and long grass, is a nice break from the museum sites. See p. 594, ⑤.

11 Admiring the craftsmanship of artifacts in the Silver Hall (Treasury). The only disappointment is that photos are prohibited. See p. 595, ⑪.

12 Peering at the tomb of Ali Pasha, near the Fetiye Mosque. Here lie the remains of a man whose name is practically a household word. He was both feared for his cruelty and admired for his accomplishments, which had a lasting effect on the region. See p. 595, ⑨.

The Best of Central & Western Greece in 3 Days

On this 3-day tour from Athens, you'll visit the center of the ancient world in Delphi, the uncanny peaks of the Meteora monasteries, and the premier mountain village of Metsovo for some famous cheese. Then you'll cross 200-year-old stone bridges in the beautiful Zagori region en route to the spectacular Vikos Gorge before heading to Ioannina, the capital of the northwest, with its intriguing medieval town.

> *Delphi is nestled in rugged mountains at what ancients believed was the center of the world.*

START Arachova is 171km (106 miles) from Athens, a 2-hr. 20-min. drive on the national road (Rte. 1) northbound, exiting at Kastro (Rte. 48) westbound for Amfissa. **TRIP LENGTH** 3 days, 427km/265 miles (excluding return trip to Athens).

1 ★ **Arachova.** Admire the scenery as you pass through this ski village on the way to Delphi, one of the country's major archaeological sites. If you're peckish, grab a coffee, cheese pie, and perhaps a souvenir, such as pompon slippers or honey. See p. 576, **1**. ⏱ 20 min.

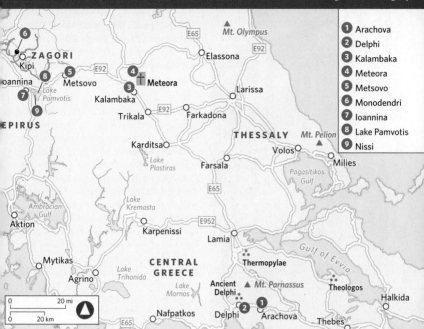

❶	Arachova
❷	Delphi
❸	Kalambaka
❹	Meteora
❺	Metsovo
❻	Monodendri
❼	Ioannina
❽	Lake Pamvotis
❾	Nissi

ontinue on Rte. 48 west to Delphi. 12km (7½ iles), 15 min.

❷ **Delphi.** Congratulations, you've reached ne center of the ancient world! Take a look round the ★★ **museum** (p. 576, ❸). For-unately, you can't miss the beautiful face, vith eyes intact, of the prominently displayed ronze *Charioteer of Delphi*. Then explore the ★★ **archaeological site** (p. 577, ❹), encoun-ering the rebuilt Athenian Treasury (some riginal friezes are in the museum); the Sacred Vay (Iera Odos); an ancient *omphalos* (navel tone), which marked the center of the earth t the **Sanctuary of Apollo;** and the theater, vhere you'll have a commanding view over the ills of Mount Parnassus and down the valley ɔ the sea on a clear day. Have lunch in the illage at **Taverna Vakhos** (p. 576, ❷) before eading out again. See p. 576. ◷ 2½ hr.

ake Rte. 48 west and north. Exit to Rte. 27 ɔr Lamia; then take the national road (Rte. 1) orth and exit at Lamia bound for Trikala and .alambaka (Rte. 30). 227km (141 miles), 4½ hr.

❸ ★ **Kalambaka.** The spectacular scenery, ne view of the lit-up Meteora rock faces t night, and the monasteries are the main

attractions here. After your long journey, rest up in your hotel before heading out to the square in Kalambaka for dinner at a taverna (p. 580, ❶) and an early night. ◷ **Evening and overnight.**

❹ ★★★ **Meteora.** In the morning, choose from one of the medieval **monasteries** (p. 582) and head up the hill to see it—prefer-ably via the ★ kids **footpath** (p. 581, ❷), though you can make the trip by car or bus (3km/2 miles) as well. The biggest and most popular is Grand Meteoro, which has the most to see. You might also spot climbers scaling these fabulous, otherworldly rock formations. After you've been inside a monastery, admired the religious Byzantine art, and pondered what the monks' existences might have been like atop the summits before the road and bridges were built, head out toward Metsovo. See p. 581, ❸. ◷ 2 hr.

Head north on Rte. 6 to Egnatia Odos Panagia I/C (interchange), then west to Metsovo. 70km (43 miles), 40 min.

❺ ★ kids **Metsovo.** This is another ski village, but you're not hemmed in by a rock face; the vantage is high, overlooking the mountaintops

> *The main street in Arachova, which clings to the slopes of Mount Parnassus.*

Take the Egnatia Odos west, bound for Monodendri, Zagori. Exit to Rte. 6 for Ioannina. Take Rte. 20 north for Krya and exit at Metamorfosi northeast for Central Zagori (Karyes, Asprageli, Monodendri). 82km (51 miles), 1 hr. 45 min.

6 ★ **Monodendri.** You're in the famed Zagorohoria mountain village region now. This one is famed for being the main entrance to the ★★ **Vikos Gorge** (p. 589, **5**)—the deepest in the world, proportional to its width. It's a remarkable valley that shows Greece is much more than islands and the sea. Walk down the well-marked path from the upper square on the main road to the lower one, where you can have a coffee or lunch. Or walk right past to the start of the Vikos Gorge, at the entrance of Agia Paraskevi Monastery, for photo ops. Head out and detour to ★ **Kipi** (p. 588, **3**) to see the picturesque, 18th-century stone bridges, or start making your way to Ioannina, where you'll spend the next couple of nights. See p. 589, **4**. ⏱ At least 1 hr.

Head southwest out of Zagori to Rte. 20 south to Ioannina. 36km (22 miles), 45 min.

7 ★ **Ioannina.** Find your hotel, rest up, and head out for dinner. Then stroll along the waterfront of Lake Pamvotis to get into the atmosphere. If you're in a group, you can take a 40-minute lake **cruise** (try Kostas, ☎ 6944/470280; 5€ or 6€, including an island stop) to relax, admire the view, and learn some local history before heading back to your hotel (p. 596).

The northwest regional capital has a few spots you shouldn't miss, so the following morning make sure you explore the Old Town, known as the ★★ **Kastro.** Walk through the gate and make your way through the narrow streets to ★★ kids **Its Kale** (p. 594, **6**), the Inner Citadel. Walk around the open space and examine the **Fetiye Mosque** (p. 595, **8**) and **Ali Pasha's Tomb** (p. 595, **9**), and then have a look inside the **Byzantine Museum** (p. 595, **10**), especially if you like religious art. The former Royal Pavilion building (1958) housing the museum is just one on the site of the famed *seraglio*, or palace, which saw the likes of Lord Byron when he paid Ali Pasha a visit in the early 19th century. Go inside the ★★ **Silver Hall** (Treasury; p. 595, **11**) and admire the

and valleys in a panoramic sweep. The roofs are pitched, made of slate to ease the snow's falloff. The narrow streets are cobbled for easier traction, it's very green, and there are plenty of grills and a cafe. If little ones need to run off some energy, climb to the grassy park, also on the square. Don't forget to buy a wedge or wheel of cheese from here. Try **Tositsa Cheese Products** (☎ 26560/41723) on the square; the village is renowned for it. You can also grab a light lunch or takeout from bakeries along the main road. Explore the square and then wander through the central Agia Paraskevi church or the **art gallery** (p. 648). See p. 586. ⏱ 40 min.

ilver, have a coffee and snack at the **cafe,** and hen head back through the gates for a little rip across the lake to Nissi. ◷ Evening and vernight.

❸ Lake Pamvotis. Ioannina is on the edge of his lake, which is some 7.5km (4⅔ miles) long nd as wide as 5km (3 miles) in places, with n average depth of 4m to 5m (13–16½ ft.). Its reshwater bounty—eels, crayfish, and other lelicacies—is a specialty of the island, Nissi. A own legend involves the 1801 drowning of the eautiful Lady Frossyni and her 17 attendants, fter Ali Pasha's son had an affair with her vhile her husband was in Venice. One version ays the son's jealous wife appealed to Ali Pa-ha, who shut the mistress and her attendants way in a church. Two nights later, they were acked and drowned. If you love silver and lon't have time to browse in town, the **Tradi-ional Handicraft Center,** at 11 Arch. Makariou t. (☎ 26510-27660; www.kepavi.gr; Mon–ri 9:30am–2:30pm & 5:30–8:30pm, Sat):30am–8:30pm, Sun 10am–6pm) is the place or you. Ioannina has been crafting the metal ere since the 17th century. All handmade, it's old new or in antique shops in town, including nany shops along Averoff St., in the old Turk-sh bazaar parallel to Averoff (to the west), ind at this lakeside center, where some 40 vorkshops sell and make their wares on site. ◷ 30 min.

Ali Pasha

Ali Pasha was born to a powerful clan in Tepelena, Albania, in 1741. After angling for a title with the ruling sultan in Istanbul, he finally was appointed pasha of Ioannina in 1788, when the city was at its economic peak and still part of the Ottoman Empire. He built his palace and a cavalry school in the Kastro, rebuilt the Fetiye Mosque and the town walls in 1815, and became even more powerful, extending his control and consolidating power throughout the region. He had connections in the courts of Europe, but he drew the ire of the sultan, who finally acted against him: In 1822, the Sublime Porte's forces killed him while he was hiding in the Panteleimon Monastery with his wife, Vassiliki, on Nissi.

> *Inside Grand Meteoro, the highest and richest of the Meteora monasteries.*

⑨ 🖥 ★ kids **Nissi.** Cross the lake on one of the **boats** that pass every half-hour (.80€ one-way) to this small islet, just 500m–800m (⅓ mile–½ mile). Wander through the narrow streets of the town, and visit one of the monasteries built after the Franks' conquest of Constantinople in 1204 through the 17th century. Then browse for **specialty sweets** (try Nifi Glyka-Pappas; ☎ 26510/86276) or souvenirs from one of the many shops lining the road to the boats. It's also worth stopping to visit the spot where Ali Pasha was found and executed in 1822. It's now a **museum** (Panteleimon Monastery; ☎ 26510/81791). To stock up before leaving the island, try **Kyra Vasiliki,** which sells fresh meat and lake delicacies such as frog's legs (☎ 26510/81081; daily 8am until the last boat at 9:45pm). ◷ At least 1 hr.

Return to Athens via the Rio-Antirio bridge heading south on Rte. 5 (E951, E55) and west on Rte. 8A (E65) through Corinth (Rte. 8, 8A, E94), to Athens. 432km (268 miles), 7 hr.

The Best of Central & Western Greece in 1 Week

You don't have to tear around through the lush mountains and valleys that are the highlights of the Greek mainland on this tour. Here you get a rare chance to compare the sites of two ancient oracles, at Delphi and at Dodona, before heading to majestic Meteora, where medieval monasteries cap unique rock formations, and possibly detouring to the Pelion Peninsula. Then it's on to the remote mountains and deep canyons at Metsovo and Zagori and, finally, into Ioannina, a unique town on the shores of Lake Pamvotis—a good base for exploring the region's most interesting features.

> *Kalogeriko Bridge near Kipi was on the trade routes that reached as far as Vienna and Odessa.*

START Delphi is 183km (114 miles), 2 hr. 35 min. from Athens on the national road northbound, exiting westbound at Kastro (Rte. 48) for Amfissa. TRIP LENGTH 1 week, 456km (283 miles; excluding return to Athens).

❶ **Delphi.** The first stop is the oracle of Delphi. Take a look around the ★★ **museum** (p. 576, ❸), with its unique finds from this site, where city-states tried to outdo each other in their offerings to Apollo. Then visit

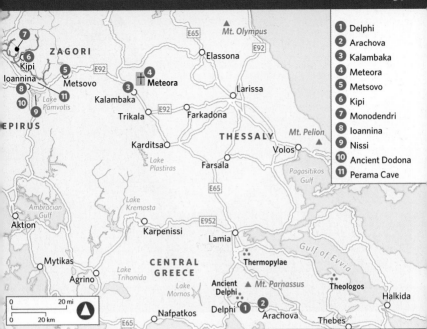

1 Delphi
2 Arachova
3 Kalambaka
4 Meteora
5 Metsovo
6 Kipi
7 Monodendri
8 Ioannina
9 Nissi
10 Ancient Dodona
11 Perama Cave

...he ★★★ **archaeological site** (p. 577, 4)
...nd walk along the **Sacred Way** (Iera Odos)
...ast the ruins of the treasuries (the restored
...thenian Treasury conveys a good sense of
...ow the original looked). You'll see another
...mphalos (navel stone), older than the one in
...he museum, meant to signify the center of the
...ncient world. See the view from the theater
...nd continue to the stadium, where games
...ook place every 4 years. See p. 576. ⊕ 2 hr.

... backtrack on Rte. 48 east to Arachova. 12km
...7½ miles), 15 min.

2 ★ **Arachova.** Spend the night in this lively
...ski village at the base of Mount Parnassus,
...ome of the Muses, and namesake of Paris's
...istoric cafe district (Montparnasse). It sees
...a lot of day-trippers in summer and Athenian
...skiers in winter. Have a leisurely dinner or
...enjoy an evening in at your hotel, perhaps co-
...zying up to a fire. If you love trains and you like
...driving, spend the following afternoon on the
...beautiful mountain peninsula **Pelion** (p. 575),
...where the little steam train will take you on a
...memorably scenic journey. Otherwise, head
...northwest, to Meteora. See p. 576. ⊕ Evening
...and overnight.

On the morning of Day 2, take the Arachova-
Polydrossou road north toward Gravias, then
Rte. 27 north toward Lamia, national road,
Rte. 1 to Trikala exit, heading northwest on
Rte. 30 to Trikala. Then take Rte. 6 north to
Kalambaka. 218km (135 miles), 4 hr.

3 ★ **Kalambaka.** As you approach Meteora,
the rock formation looms ahead—an otherworldly extrusion erupting out of the plains
like Australia's famed Uluru. Like most geo-
logical wonders, it's even more impressive up
close. Spend the night here and rest after the
journey, getting your bearings in the town, or
driving the circuit around the monasteries a
couple of miles away, taking advantage of the
late-afternoon light. See p. 580. ⊕ Evening and
overnight.

4 ★★★ **Meteora.** Learn which medieval **monasteries** (p. 582) are open, decide which ones
you want to visit, and then go see two
or three of them on your third day. The trip
by road is 3km (2 miles), or you can take the
★ 🄺🄸🄳🅂 **footpath** (p. 581, 2) from Kalambaka.
When you've had your fill, leave the religious
and natural wonders and make for Metsovo.
⊕ At least 2 hr.

> *The Vidomati River has carved out the deep, narrow Vikos Gorge.*

> *Wildflowers carpet the green valleys at the base of the Meteora pinnacles.*

Head north on Rte. 6 to Egnatia Odos Panagia I/C, then west to Metsovo. 70km (43 miles), 40 min.

5 ★ kids **Metsovo.** It doesn't take long at all now to reach this village on the new Egnatia Odos. The trade-off is the spectacular mountaintop scenery on the old winding road. The village, with its cobblestone streets, is known for its cheese and its hospitality toward skiers traversing the slopes on Black Mountain (Mavrovouni). At 1,150m (3,773 ft.) above sea level, it has a beautiful slopeside setting, with a panoramic view of the surrounding mountains. The air feels crisp, and you can bask in it with a hot chocolate at a cafe on the main square, such as the Galaxy Hotel and Restaurant (p. 591), or have lunch at one of the local grill restaurants. Your next stop is the remote Zagori region, so be sure to withdraw cash from here first. See p. 586. ⏱ At least 1 hr.

Take the Egnatia Odos west to Kipi, Zagori. Exit to Rte. 6 for Ioannina; then take Rte. 20 north bound for Krya-bound. Exit at Metamorfosi and head northeast for Central Zagori (Karyes, Asprageli, Kipi). 82km (51 miles), 1 hr. 45 min.

⑥ kids Kipi. Tour the villages of Kipi and Kouk-uli to see just two examples of the beautiful 8th- to 19th-century stone bridges of the famed Zagori region: the triple-arched Kalog-riko Bridge and the lovely Kontodimos Bridge, both by the side of the road. You'll have time to stroll across them before heading out to Monodendri, where you can spend the night before walking the famed Vikos Gorge the next morning.

Head back on the Asprageli road west and turn off north for Vitsa and Monodendri. 16km (10 miles), 20 min.

⑦ ★ Monodendri. This pretty village is the "main entrance" to the **Vikos Gorge** (p. 589, ⑤)—the world's deepest in proportion to its width, according to the *Guinness Book of World Records*. A path through the village is well-marked to the main trail head, through Agia Paraskevi Monastery. Then make your way to Ioannina, where you'll spend the next couple of nights. See p. 589. ☽ Evening and overnight.

On Day 4, head southwest out of Zagori to Rte. 20 south to Ioannina, where you will base yourself for the rest of the itinerary. 36km (22 miles), 45 min.

⑧ ★ Ioannina. Spend Day 4 on an adventure trip in Zagori (p. 590); then retire to your hotel in Ioannina for a rest before heading out for dinner and a stroll along the lakeside. On Day 5, see the sights of the northwest region's capital first, by visiting the ★★ **Kastro** (p. 592, ①). Spend a few hours wandering through the Old Town exploring the museums inside the ★ **Northeast** (p. 594, ③) and Southeast cita-dels. ★★ kids **Its Kale** (p. 594, ⑥) is the Inner Citadel or Acropolis, which is an open space with a few buildings still standing. One is the 18th-century **Fetiye Mosque** (p. 595, ⑧) near **Ali Pasha's Tomb** (p. 595, ⑨). The **Byzantine Museum** (p. 595, ⑩) is also located in the citadel; the modern-era building contains religious art. Silver and other artifacts are in the nearby ★★ **Silver Hall** (Treasury; p. 595, ⑪), which houses more varied medieval craft works. Back outside the Kastro walls, you can shop for handcrafted silver and other souve-nirs at the **Traditional Handicraft Center** on the lakeshore. ☽ 3 nights.

> *Stalagmites and stalactites create fantastic shapes in Perama Cave.*

⑨ ★ kids Nissi. Take one of the frequent boats over the short crossing of **Lake Pamvotis** (p. 568, ⑦) to the town on the islet **Nissi** (Nissi means "island" in Greek; p. 595, ⑫). The main attractions here are the medieval monasteries; if you have time to see one, walk through the woods and try to enter (visiting hours are not regular). Most visitors make their way to **Agios Panteleimon Monastery,** part of which has been turned into a **museum,** as the site where Ali Pasha was caught and killed by Turkish forces in 1822. The entrance fee is nominal, and it's nearly always open. The streets en route are good places to pick up souvenir baklavas or other local bakery specialties. If you want to sample the bounty of the lake, for either lunch or dinner, try **Kyra Vasiliki,** which serves fresh eel, crayfish, and frog's legs, as well as more pedestrian regional dishes (☎ 26510/81081; daily 8am until the

> *Zeus spoke through the oracle at Dodona, where one of the largest ancient theaters in Greece stands out among the ruins.*

last boat at 9:45pm). Return to the mainland for an evening stroll around **modern Ioannina.** Wander through the old Turkish bazaar district west of Averoff St., go down Averoff and window-shop, and, at night, after dinner (p. 596), walk along the lakeshore promenade and stop at a café for a nightcap. Begin Day 6 by exploring the **Archaeological Museum** for an hour or so, before heading to Ancient Dodona. ⏱ 1–2 hr.

Take Dodonis Ave./Rte. 5 southwest to Egnatia Hwy. and exit at Dodoni (for Zoodochos Pigi). 22km (14 miles), 30 min.

❿ ★★ Ancient Dodona. This ancient, open-air sanctuary of the most powerful god of sky and thunder, Zeus, and his consort, Dione, goddess of the earth, is in the most majestic location, where the gods' power is palpable. The Early or Middle Bronze Age (2600–1500 B.C.) oracle was considered ancient even in antiquity, with evidence of an earlier cult dedicated to a Great Goddess, connected with doves and the sacred oak tree. Herodotus writes of the legend of two black birds that flew out of Egypt, settling in Libya (Zeus Ammon) and in Dodona, where it proclaimed the place for the oracle. Aristotle refers to it as the "site of the great flood," and Odysseus (Ulysses) asked here if he should return to Ithaca openly or in secret. It's the region's most important and fascinating site. See p. 595, ⓭. ⏱ 2 hr.

Return to Ioannina for the night.

⓫ kids Perama Cave. Spend your final day just outside Ioannina at this impressive stalactite and stalagmite cave in Perama, found in 1940 by villagers looking for bombing cover in World War II. It's Greece's biggest in area, at 14,800 sq. m (159,306 sq. ft.), and the path through the caverns stretches more than a kilometer, but it's well lit and well traveled. Locals worshiped ancient gods here, and animals used it for shelter. The 45- to 60-minute tour climbs 1,100m (3,609 ft.). Five hundred steps wind downhill and uphill through the site; 163 of them are phill at the exit. You can take a shorter 20- to 30-minute tour of the first 400m (1,312 ft.) to the second chamber (aka Great Chamber, Chamber of Royal Palaces), which is the biggest and most impressive, with mercifully few steps. Spilaou St., Perama. ☎ 26510/81521. www.spilaio-perama.gr. Admission 7€, 3€ students, 5€ seniors

65 and over. Sept–May daily 9am–5pm, Jun–Aug daily 9am–7pm. 3km (2 miles) northeast of Ioannina (Rte. 6.). Turn into the village and follow the road about 400m (1,312 ft.). Entrance is on the left-hand side.

Return to Athens.

Smudgy the Pelion Steam Train

A peculiar aspect of this small country is the dramatic changes in the landscape over short distances. That topographical variety is on bold display on the lush and mountainous Pelion Peninsula—the land of centaurs and birthplace of Achilles, where Jason and the Argonauts first set off to find the Golden Fleece. Hamlets on the peninsula host skiers in winter, who come to ski Agriolefkes, at 1,350m (4,429 ft.); beachgoers in summer; and nature lovers in spring and fall. Many northern Europeans live here year-round. You can sample the region's beauty by taking a unique little train on a tour through the countryside from Ano Lehonia to Milies.

The rare 60cm (2-ft.) narrow-gauge railway, built by Evaristo de Chirico (father of surrealist painter Giorgio), served the region's commuter-transport train from the countryside into Volos, the region's main town, for more than 70 years, until 1971. In 1996, the train, known affectionately as "Moutsouris" (Smudgy), restarted as a tourist attraction, with new steam engines run on diesel and restored wooden cars. Once

again it passes spectacular views of the Pagasitic Gulf, the mountains, and old stone and iron bridges. It departs for the 80-minute, 16km (10-mile) journey at 11am from Ano Lehonia, 13km (8 miles) southeast of Volos, to Milies, a hamlet with nature trails, a historic library, and a church, the 1741 Taxiarches. The train returns at 4pm. Check the latest schedules at the **Volos train station** (☎ 24210/24056) or at the **OSE travel agency** (☎ 24210/28555) inside the station. Tickets are 17€ round-trip. Open July to August daily, April to June and September to October on weekends and holidays.

Good food and drink are to be had 300m (984 ft.) from the station in Milies at **Dryalos** (☎ 24230/86690; www.dryalos.com; 75€–85€ w/breakfast). Traditional stone-house accommodations cater to winter visitors with in-room fireplaces and to summer visitors with a beach just 8km (5 miles) away. For nourishment, try **Symposio Taverna** (☎ 24230/86120), easy to find in the town center by the church, and known for its *spetsofai* (sausage), a Pelion specialty.

Delphi & Arachova

The Sanctuary of Apollo was a major place of pilgrimage in antiquity. Devout visitors came from all over the Hellenic world and beyond to curry favor and seek advice from the Pythia priestess, the earthly oracle of Apollo, god of the sun, poetry, history, music, dance, healing, and more (p. 544). Nearby is the skiing and tourist village of Arachova, where you can enjoy lunch and the vibrant social scene, which is especially lively on winter weekends.

> A tholos (round temple) dedicated to Athena is one of many sacred shrines at Delphi.

START Arachova.

❶ ★ **Arachova.** You'll probably stop in Arachova on the way to or from Delphi. This picturesque mountain village is a base for skiing 2,457-m (8,061-ft.) **Mount Parnassus** (☎ 22340/22700), home of Pegasus and the Muses. Many souvenirs are for sale along the main road, including rugs, wool slippers, homemade pasta, and honey. For lodgings, consider the **Generalis Guesthouse** (☎ 22670/31529; www.generalis.gr), with an indoor pool, or the luxe **Hotel Santa Marina** (☎ 22670/31230; www.santa-marina.gr), with an elegant **restaurant** (Vrachos) and children's playground. Hwy. 48, 160km (99 miles) northwest of Athens, 8km (5 miles) east of Delphi.

Continue on Hwy. 48 west 8km (5 miles) to Delphi.

❷ **Delphi.** Most people see Delphi on a day trip from Athens, but you can also stay the night in the village, which is within walking distance to the site. **Hotel Varonos,** at 25 Pavlou and Frederikis streets (☎ 22650/82345; www.hotel-varonos.gr), offers Frommer's readers 30% off its high-season rate. **Taverna Vakhos,** at 31 Apollonos Street (☎ 22650/83186), has a view and serves delicious house specials such as rabbit and homemade wine. Hwy. 48, 168km (104 miles) northwest of Athens, 8km (5 miles) west of Arachova.

❸ ★★ **Delphi Archaeological Museum.** The museum houses finds from the site, including a sphinx from the 6th century B.C. and a bronze charioteer from 474 B.C. The collection also features a Roman-era *omphalos,* or "navel stone," marking the spot the ancient Greeks believed to be the center (navel) of the world. According to mythology, Zeus released two eagles at opposite ends of the earth (which was considered to be

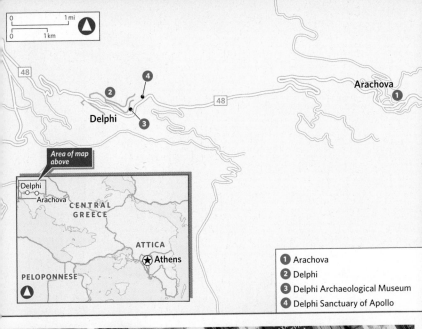

Area of map above

Delphi
Arachova
CENTRAL GREECE

ATTICA
★ Athens

PELOPONNESE

1 Arachova
2 Delphi
3 Delphi Archaeological Museum
4 Delphi Sanctuary of Apollo

> *The road to Delphi passes through Arachova, where villagers tempt travelers with all sorts of worldly goods.*

flat at that time), and the point where they crashed into each other and fell to the ground marked the center. ☎ 22650/82312. www. culture.gr. Admission 6€ museum, 9€ museum and site. May–Oct Tues–Sun 8am–7:15pm, Mon 1:30–8:45pm; Nov–April daily 8:30am–2:45pm. Closed Dec 25–26, Jan 1, Mar 25, Orthodox Easter Sunday, and May 1.

SITE GUIDE
PAGE 579

4 ★★★ **Delphi Sanctuary of Apollo.** If you visit just this one ancient site in Greece, you won't leave disappointed. The sanctuary lies on the lower slopes of Mount Parnassus, with a view through a valley of olive trees down to the Gulf of Corinth.

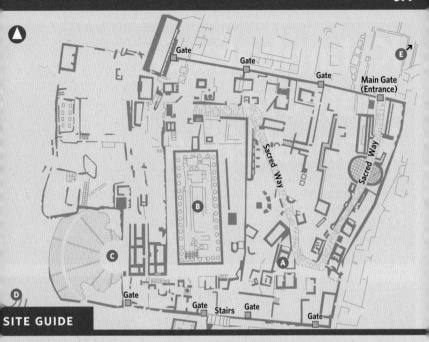

SITE GUIDE

④ Delphi Sanctuary of Apollo

From the main entrance, follow the Sacred Way, a reconstructed marble path lined with the ruined treasuries of Greek city-states that tried to outdo each other in their efforts to offer gifts to the god Apollo. The Ⓐ **Athenian Treasury** was rebuilt in 1906 with most of the original pieces but with casts of the metopes depicting scenes such as Hercules' labors and the battle of the Amazons. Some of the original friezes are in the museum. **Iera Odos** (Sacred Way) hits a plateau at what was once the inner sanctum of the Ⓑ **Temple of Apollo.** Pilgrims from all over the Western world came here to seek advice or have their fortunes told by a seer, the oracle of Delphi, a priestess over 50 who spoke the wisdom of Apollo. The priestess delivered her auguries on a tripod inside a chamber. It's believed she was intoxicated by vapors emanating from cracks deep in the rocks. Her prophecies were interpreted by priests, prophets, and holy men. Earthquakes, looting, and landslides have damaged the temple's partially underground chambers. The 4th-century-B.C. Ⓒ **theater** at the top of the sanctuary is the best preserved of its kind in Greece—owing no small thanks to

the Romans, who rebuilt it some 2,000 years ago. Musicians and performers competed here in the Pythian Games, which eschewed Olympic athletic competition in favor of cultural pursuits in honor of Apollo. The view of the whole site is fantastic from the theater, but you can climb up even farther to the long, tree-lined, 6th-century-B.C. Ⓓ **stadium,** where the Pythian Games' athletic contests took place. After you leave the sanctuary, if you keep walking down the main road, you see Delphi's most-photographed ruins below you. These are located in the Marmaria area, so named because it was later used as a marble quarry. The most striking sight is the remains of the small, round Ⓔ **Temple of Athena Pronaia (Tholos),** built in 380 B.C. In the 1930s, 3 of the original 20 outer columns were re-erected, and a section of the lintel was replaced on top. The temple is at its most beautiful when the sun sets behind it. ☎ 22650-82312 or 82346. www.culture.gr. Admission 6€, 9€ site and museum. May–Oct Tues–Sun 8am–7:15pm; Mon 1:30–8:45pm; Nov–April 8:30am–2:45pm. Closed Dec 25–26, Jan 1, Mar 25, Orthodox Easter Sunday, and May 1.

Kalambaka & Meteora Monasteries

The Greek mainland has its fair share of eye-catching places, but the plains of Thessaly—the breadbasket of Greece—are especially rich in beauty and history. Surrounded by mountain ranges, the standout destination in this most spectacular region is Meteora—a UNESCO World Heritage Site that's also protected by church and state.

> *It's easy to see how the cloud-scraping Meteora monasteries made medieval hermit monks feel closer to God.*

START Kalambaka is 350km (217 miles) northwest of Athens on the national road (E75/Hwy. 1). Turn off to E65/Rte. 3 at Lamia, then at Neo Monastiri to Rte. 30, then from Trikala to Kalambaka on E92/Rte. 6. **TRIP LENGTH** 2 days.

1 ★ **Kalambaka.** This is the main village at the foot of the rock face, where you can spend the night and admire the view, which is especially dramatic when spot-lit from below after dark. Many visitors come to Kalambaka on excursions. A cheery hotel at the base of the trail leading to the monasteries is **Alsos House,** at 5 Kanari Street (☎ 24320/24097; www.alsoshouse.gr), which also provides insider information on rock climbing in the area. A luxe option is **Divani Meteora**

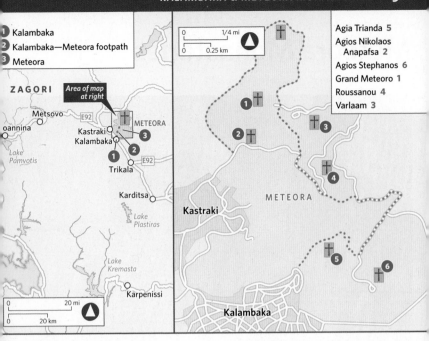

1. Kalambaka
2. Kalambaka—Meteora footpath
3. Meteora

ZAGORI

Area of map at right

Metsovo
oannina
Lake Pamvotis
Kastraki
Kalambaka
Trikala
Karditsa
Lake Plastiras
Lake Kremasta
Karpenissi

METEORA

E92

Agia Trianda 5
Agios Nikolaos Anapafsa 2
Agios Stephanos 6
Grand Meteoro 1
Roussanou 4
Varlaam 3

METEORA

Kastraki

Kalambaka

☎ 24320/23330; www.divani.com), just outside the village on the national road. There are several small tavernas to choose from around the squares on the main street, Trikalon. A few more bed-down options are in Kastraki, a hamlet 1km (⅔ mile) farther along the road toward the monasteries.

2 ★ kids Kalambaka–Meteora footpath. If you can manage the easy, hour-long hike, take the Kalambaka trail at least one way, especially during the fall, winter, or spring. The wildflowers are gorgeous, interspersed with colorful lichen. Go up Vlahava Street through the Old Town to reach it, and exit the path at Agia Trianda Monastery. Note that it's an hour-long 4km (2½-mile) walk along a shadeless road from here to the bus stop at Grand Meteoro. If you're into rock climbing, you'll be scraping heaven here. Groups of six or more can visit Varlaam and Grand Meteoro, then rappel 20m (66 ft.) down one of the rocks with **Trekking Hellas,** at 10 Rethymnou Street in Athens (☎ 210/331-0323; www.trekking.gr). Equipment and an English-speaking guide are included in the fee of 20€ per person.

Take the Meteoron road to Meteora. 3km (2 miles).

3 ★★★ Meteora. One of the most spectacular, spiritually uplifting places in the world has got to be Meteora (from *meteoros,* which means suspended). Hoodoo-shaped mountains emerge from the plains, and their formation remains a mystery. Some of the pinnacles are topped by Byzantine-era monasteries. For protection, proximity to the heavens, and isolation from worldly diversions, hermit monks constructed them here in the 9th century, when the only way up was by net and winch or rope ladder. Over the centuries, they diminished the perils of dwelling here by carving steps into the rocks, building bridges, and installing electric hoist systems. For 60 years, the large, red-roofed structures have been connected by road. Of the 24 monasteries established between the 1400s and 1600s, 6 are inhabited, and 2 more were recently restored. Many treasures were stolen during World War II. While the monasteries still house some bright frescoes, illuminated manuscripts, paraphernalia, and holy relics of interest, the main draw for the layperson is the setting. The ban against female visitors was lifted in 1948, so anyone can visit in conservative dress. Timing will usually determine which monastery you visit.

Meteora Monasteries

> *Lavish 16th-century frescoes embellish Grand Meteoro, a 400-step climb from the valley floor.*

Agia Trianda (Holy Trinity)

This 15th-century monastery was featured in the Bond film *For Your Eyes Only*. It once had the most monks; now it has four. Nearly everything was looted in World War II, including the bell. **St. John the Baptist Chapel** is hewn into the rock here, and it contains an icon of Christ dressed in local costume. ☎ 24320/22220. Admission 2€. Nov–Apr Fri–Tues 10am–3pm, May–Oct Fri–Wed 9am–5pm.

Agios Nikolaos Anapafsa

Founded in the 14th century on a very small surface area, this tall monastery has 16th-century frescoes by celebrated painter Theophanes the Cretan—including a depiction of Jonah in the mouth of a fish. The monastery was abandoned in 1900, restored in 1960, closed in 1982, and opened only for summer tourists. In 1997, it began operating again, and two monks live there today. Access is via steps carved in the rock and electric hoists.

☎ 24320/22375. Admission 2€. May to mid-Nov Sat–Thurs 9am–3:30pm, mid-Nov to Dec 6 Sat–Thurs 9am–3pm, Dec 7–Apr Sat–Thurs 9am–1pm.

Agios Stephanos

This monastery was founded in the 12th century, its chapel was rebuilt in the 15th, and the basilica chapel with its 16th-century frescoes and other buildings have been restored. St. Stephen's enjoyed protection from Byzantine noblemen, Danube principalities, and the leader of Orthodoxy himself, but help eventually deserted it, and most of the property and its holdings were expropriated or looted by 1949. It became a convent in 1961, and the nuns ran it as an orphanage and primary school at one time. Now about 30 nuns live here and look after a collection of books and manuscripts from this site and other monasteries, on display in the **museum.** ☎ 24320/22279. Admission 2€. Nov–Apr

Tues–Sun 9:30am–1pm and 3–5pm, May–Oct
Tues–Sun 9am–1:30pm and 3:30–5:30pm.

★★ Grand Meteoro

This monastery dedicated to the Transfiguration of Christ was founded by St. Athanasios Meteorites in the 1300s and endowed by a Serbian king. Formerly the richest, biggest, and most important monastery, it is now also the most accessible and popular. A **museum** shows how the monks lived and contains various artifacts, including a rack of skulls. You can wander through chapels where ecclesiastical treasures are on display and peek at the 16th-century frescoes in the narthex—the area in front of the screen (iconostasis). An on-site **library** contains Byzantine and post-Byzantine manuscripts, many of them illuminated. A gift shop sells books and trinkets. ☎ 24320/22278. Admission 2€. Apr–Oct Wed–Mon 9am–5pm, Nov–Mar Thurs–Mon 9am–4pm.

Roussanou

Founded in the 14th century, the convent dedicated to Agia Varvara was a place of refuge during clashes with the ruling Turks in the 18th and 19th centuries. It was plundered during World War II and restored in the 1980s. Since 1988, it has functioned as a convent. Sixteenth-century frescoes adorn the north-facing church, whose unusual orientation owes to the rock formation. In the past, residents ascended via rope ladders and a winch. Today visitors and the 16 nuns in residence simply cross a bridge to get here. ☎ 24320/22649. Admission 2€. Nov–Apr Thurs–Tues 9am–2pm, May–Oct Thurs–Tues 9am–6pm.

Varlaam

The second-largest monastery, next to Grand Meteoro, Varlaam was founded by an ascetic in the 14th century and built 200 years later. Its main chapel is eastern European in style, and the monastery was known for creating manuscripts, embroidery, and ceremonial biers. It contains relics and valuable icons, painted in the 14th and 16th centuries, that were stolen twice from a church in Kalambaka. It has a 12-ton tank that was once used to collect rainwater but is now a museum piece. Today it's home to seven monks. ☎ 24320/22277. Admission 2€. Nov–Apr Sat–Wed 9am–3pm, May–Oct Fri–Wed 9am–4pm.

> *Everyday items show the practical side of life in a medieval mountaintop monastery.*

The Deserted Ones

Deserted ruins remain at inaccessible **Prodromos,** which was abandoned in 1745; the precariously located **Agia Moni,** built in 1614 and ruined in an 1858 earthquake; **Hyselotera,** the highest monastery dedicated to the Highest in the Heavens, founded in 1390 and forsaken in the 17th century, likely because of its perilous location; **Ypapanti** built into a cave in 1366 but restored to preserve its bright frescoes and a gilt iconostasis (attached to Grand Meteoro); and inaccessible **Agios Dimitrios,** an outlaw headquarters destroyed by Turkish gunfire in 1809. **Agios Antonios** and restored **Agios Nikolaos Padova** (ca. 1400), a dependency of Agia Trianda, are closed to the public.

MONASTIC LIFE

BY TANIA KOLLIAS

SINCE THE GREAT SCHISM IN 1054, when Rome split from the four other centers of Christianity—Antioch, Constantinople, Jerusalem, and Alexandria—Greece has been the spiritual home of Eastern Orthodoxy, with 300 million adherents in Greece as well as in the Middle East, Eastern Europe, and Russia. Even in Orthodox nations that were part of the Ottoman Empire and missed the West's Reformation and Enlightenment, the Church managed to keep its ancient rites and traditions, especially at monasteries. In isolated monastic communities like those on Mount Athos and in Meteora, monks and nuns devote their days to prayer, fasting, service, and obedience.

GRAND METEORO, METEORA

(p. 583)
Originally endowed by a Serbian king in the 14th century, Grand Meteora is the richest and biggest monastery of the five that are still operational in the Meteora area. Typical of the region's original 24 monasteries, Grand Meteora seems to defy gravity atop a pinnacle of sandstone. This spectacularly inconvenient location required the use of a pulley system to import provisions, but it ensured seclusion and protected the settlements during the Middle Ages and Turkish occupation. Now Grand Meteora is accessible to outsiders; an onsite museum, gift shop, and library with medieval manuscripts provide opportunities to meet the monks.

MEGISTI LAVRA, MOUNT ATHOS
(p. 537, **2**)
Founded by Athanasios the Athonite in 963, Megisti Lavra is the largest, oldest,

and most respected monastery on the peninsula of Mount Athos (p. 536)—a male-only, semi-autonomous settlement of some 2,000 monks, also under UNESCO protection. Megisti Lavra is encircled by ramparts

and structured like a medieval town, inhabited by more than 300 monks. Megisti Lavra and the 19 other monasteries of Mount Athos are the biggest repository of early Christian art in the world, with beautifully crafted icons and other religious artworks by 14th-century painter Theophanes the Greek, 16th-century Theophanes the Cretan, and others.

MEGA SPILEO, PELOPONNESE
(p. 207, **1**)
This large, once-rich monastery on the side of a cliff was established in a cave where a 4th-century shepherd girl found an icon of the Virgin thought to be crafted by St. Luke. The icon survived fires

and other ravages. The mythical River Styx (modern Mavroneri), a link to the Underworld in whose magical waters Achilles was dipped by his heel, is nearby.

MONASTERY OF ST. JOHN THE THEOLOGIAN, PATMOS, DODECANESE
(p. 429, **3**)
The apostle John reputedly received the Book of Revelation and wrote his gospel in a cave near this hilltop

fortress founded 1,000 years ago in dedication to him. UNESCO inscribed it a World Heritage Site in 1999 as "one of the few places in the world where religious practices that date back to early Christian times are being practiced unchanged." Even so, it has been affected

by the demands of modern life, including cruise ships, visible in the harbor, unloading religious pilgrims.

Eastern Orthodox Christianity 101

▸ Led by head bishop, who is "first among equals" but not infallible like the pope

▸ Greek not Latin is the defining language

▸ Priests allowed to marry

▸ Mary was virtuous but not born without "original sin"

▸ Eucharist leavened and always taken with wine

▸ Follows Julian calendar

▸ Saints depicted in icons rather than statues

▸ Priests and monks bearded

Mountains & Valleys: Metsovo & Zagori

Zagori is a mountainous region in northwest Greece celebrated for its breathtaking scenery. Together with its charming villages (Zagorohoria), the area is known for its diverse flora and fauna, unique stone houses, arched bridges over meandering rivers, and the Vikos Gorge—a main attraction. The region suffered depopulation as many of the Greeks, Vlachs (a Romanian-origin minority), and the previously nomadic Sarakatsani left for even greener pastures. Many houses are abandoned, but some are getting new life as tourist accommodations. The most famous product—apart from carpets and other crafts associated with colder climes—is the regional cheese, which is especially abundant in Metsovo, the biggest town in the area.

> Monodendri is a starting point for hikes through the Vikos Gorge.

START Metsovo is 370km (230 miles) northwest of Athens (via Trikala) on the national road (E75/Hwy. 1). Turn off to E65/Rte. 3 at Lamia, then at Neo Monastiri to Rte. 30, then from Trikala to Metsovo on E92/Rte. 6.

1 ★ kids **Metsovo.** Metsovo is a beautiful town of 6,000 in the Pindos Mountains at 1,150m (3,773 ft.) above sea level. It's also the bedroom for nearby **ski centers** at Mavrovouni (Black Mountain), with its stone, slate-roofed houses and steep, cobblestone streets. You used to get here from Kalambaka on a winding mountaintop road with gorgeous panoramic vistas. Now you're spared the long drive and switchbacks thanks to the Egnatia Odos. All the streets are cobblestone here, and the **central square** is beside a pretty churchyard, a shop selling artisanal cheeses that the minority Vlach town is renowned for (try the smoked Metsovone), and a few grill tavernas. Nearby is the local grassy park where kids kick around a ball, and down the road is a modern art gallery, **E. Averoff** (☎ 26560/41210; www.averoffmuseum.gr; admission 3€; Sept 15–July 14 10am–4pm, July 15–Sept 14 Wed–Mon 10am–6:30pm), with pieces by well-known Greek artists.

Take Egnatia Odos west for 40km (25 miles) to Ioannina I/C. Take Rte. 20 northwest to Kalpaki for 32km/20 miles. 70km (43 miles).

1 Metsovo
2 Kalpaki 1940–41 War Museum
3 Kipi
4 Monodendri
5 Vikos Gorge

> *Stepped lanes wind through mountainside Metsovo.*

② **Kalpaki 1940–41 War Museum.** Outside the village of Kalpaki on the western edge of Zagori is a site commemorated for its morale-boosting role in World War II. The outnumbered Greeks pushed back the Italians invading from Albania in the November 1940 Battle of Kalpaki (Elaias), thus handing the Allies their first major land victory. (A book and film on Greece's war efforts, *Sword of Zeus*, are scheduled for release in 2011.) A statue of a caped soldier stands on a hilltop, and the museum is at the village's south entrance by the roadside. The word "oxi" (meaning "no") is written on a monument across the street, commemorating the locals' reply to Italy's ultimatum on October 28, 1940, to occupy Greece. Memorabilia includes posters, weapons, clothing articles, photos depicting Italian soldiers relaxing with a sheep mascot and local women helping to build a bridge, and a

> *Medieval Kipi on the banks of the Vagiotikos River.*

British sketch referring to that other famous battle at Thermopylae, wherein Spartans in armor lean out of a "Greek Heroes" pediment to give a hand to their modern-day counterparts. May–Sept and holidays year-round, daily 9:30am–6pm; Oct–Apr daily 9:30am–1pm. 30km (19 miles) northwest of Ioannina.

Take Rte. 20 southeast to Asprageli road; then turn northeast to Kipi. 33km (21 miles).

③ ★ kids **Kipi.** This village is the capital of central Zagori, said to take its name from the numerous gardens (*kipi*) cultivated along the Vagiotikos River, which flows nearby. Also known as Vagia, it has a history dating back to the 1400s, and it's also renowned for the

The war museum in Kalpaki commemorates a 1940 Greek victory over invading Italian troops.

beautiful 18th-century arched stone bridges in the area. The Vikakis (Little Vikos) River begins at the Kontodimos Bridge and runs toward the village of Tsepelovo. A small **folk museum** (☎ 26530/71826) on the main road displays some local artifacts, costumes, and domestic items. There are a few places to stay and eat here. 38km (24 miles) from Ioannina.

Take the Asprageli-Koukouli road southwest and turn north to Monodendri. 16km (10 miles).

4 ★ **Monodendri.** This typical Zagori village sees a lot of tourism on day trips through the region, and it's the main starting point for hikes, weather permitting, through the Vikos Gorge. Other places of interest are the ancient **Molossi site,** from the 9th to the 4th century B.C., found between the villages of Monodendri and Vitsa and believed to be the first settlement in the ancient state of Epirus. (If you have a mastiff, or Molosser, breed of dog, you can pay homage here.) You'll see a few things with the name Rizarios, the village's main benefactors, including an ecclesiastical school and a handicraft school; the latter has a **gift shop** (☎ 26530/71119; daily 10am–5pm) at the lower square. While here, check out what's on display in the **Rizarios Exhibition Center** (☎ 26530/71573; admission 2€; Wed–Mon 10am–5pm), also en route to the lower square. It usually holds temporary photo exhibits. In summer, theatrical performances and other events sometimes take place at the **outdoor theater.**

5 ★★ **Vikos Gorge.** The Vikos Gorge is a tourist-poster canyon carved by the Vidomati River. At 12km (7½ miles) long, it's in the *Guinness Book of World Records* as the deepest canyon proportional to its width—900m (2,950 ft.) deep and 1,100m (3,600 ft.) rim to rim, though it can extend farther than that in places. You can access it from three trails out of Monodendri: the upper square and through the Petrodasos (stone forest); Grounia, starting behind Agios Athanasios Church; and via Agia Paraskevi Monastery, the most traveled. Many nature walks run through this area and between the villages.

Zagori Stone Roads & Bridges

Some 60 stone bridges in Zagori date from the 18th and 19th centuries, spanning rivers whose waters run in summer, which is unusual in Greece. The bridges and steps were needed to connect the 46 villages to the outside world and to trade. They're generally named after the people who paid to build them. Artisans started on either end and met in the middle. The biggest of these is the elegant, three-arched **Kalogeriko (Plakidas) Bridge** (1814) in Koukouli, near Kipi, initially built by a monk and reconstructed in 1865. The 1753 **Kontodimos (Lazarides) Bridge** near Kipi is also much-photographed and is the start of a trek up the Vikakis River to Rogovo Monastery through a narrow, sometimes flooded gorge.

Also famous are the stone steps that linked the villages before a road was built. The best known are the 18th-century **Vradeto Steps** to the eponymous village, the highest in Zagori, which didn't have road access until 1973 (to Kapesovo). A shorter walk is on a path from Koukouli to Kipi, but many others are in good condition. People living in these depopulated villages still get their supplies from traveling bakers and grocers, now by car along paved roads. Get more info at the **Northern Pindus National Park Information Center** in Asprageli (☎ 26530/22241; daily 10am–3:30pm).

Where to Stay & Dine in Metsovo & Zagori

Adonis Hotel METSOVO
A newer addition to the central square area, just across from pretty Agia Paraskevi Church, this large hotel caters to the numerous visitors on ski holidays, with fireplaces in rooms as well as in the lobby. It also has a cafe-bar, parking, and Internet access. **Central Sq.** ☎ 26560/42300. 12 units. Doubles 75€–125€ w/breakfast. MC, V.

Galaxy Hotel and Restaurant METSOVO
GREEK This homey restaurant and hotel (aka Galaxias) is right on the main square. A few rooms have fireplaces, and all are decorated in cheery and distinctive Metsovite textiles. The restaurant serves hearty local specialties, traditional pastas, and spit roasts. You can also stop by to warm up with a hot chocolate on the terrace. Free Wi-Fi. **Central Sq.** ☎ 26560/41202. www.hotel-galaxias-metsovo.gr. 10 units. Doubles 45€–70€ or 60€–85€ w/breakfast. Entrees 7€–11€. AE, MC, V. Restaurant daily lunch & dinner.

kids Machalas Hotel KIPI
This new stone hotel consists of a series of stand-alone one- and two-bedroom apartments in a .8-hectare (2-acre) garden, grouped around a large central courtyard that also has a playground. It's perfect for families. Ceilings are considered fair game for artistic endeavors in these parts, and the traditional overhead decoration here warms the space. All rooms have fireplaces and some have hydro-jet massage. It's also wheelchair (and stroller) accessible. ☎ 26530/71630. www.machalas.gr. 11 units. Doubles 70€–150€ w/breakfast. MC, V.

★ Monodendri Hotel and Restaurant MONODENDRI *GREEK* This guesthouse is built in the traditional style, with stones and wood-patterned ceilings. There's a bar, and you can eat at the **restaurant** (Katerina's) on site, which serves homemade specialties, including many kinds of savory pies filled with cheese, chicken, and lamb. They also make a packed lunch for trekkers. ☎ 26530/71300 or 69441/55488.

> *Stou Michali in Kipi is the place to feast before or after a hike through the Vikos Gorge.*

www.monodendrihotel.com. 8 units, 15 units next door. Doubles 50€–80€ w/breakfast. Cash only. Entrees 5€–9€. Restaurant daily breakfast, lunch & dinner.

★ Stou Michali Restaurant KIPI *GREEK*
You can grab coffee and a cheese pie or a full meal from this casual spot in town under the same ownership as the Machalas Hotel. Various salads, dips, and wines are on offer, but the meat menu is the draw, ranging from lamb, goat, and rooster to sausages and steaks, beef, and pork. Their homemade savory pies are great to pack for a trip through the gorge. **Upper Sq.** ☎ 26530/71976 or 71630, or 69444/35100. www.stoumixali.gr. Entrees 8€–18€. MC, V. Daily breakfast, lunch & dinner.

Ioannina

Ioannina, the capital of the northeast, is in a remote, mountainous region. Its ancient peoples—the Pelasgians, Thesprotians, and Molossians—came from different stock than the better-known Macedonians and Mycenaeans. The town on the shores of Lake Pamvotis is young by Greek standards, with records dating from the 9th to the 10th century, when it was a provincial township with an unusually nice castle. By the 18th century, it was a prosperous, multireligious town. Its famous despot, the cruel but industrious Ali Pasha, still looms large.

> Quiet squares and old houses in the Old Quarter evoke the city's Balkan, Ottoman, and Byzantine heritage.

START Ioannina is 431km (268 miles) northwest of Athens on Rte. 8A toward Patras, then Rte. 5 via Arta, over the Rio–Antirio bridge.

① ★ **Kastro.** The Kastro, or Outer Citadel, forms a small area with shops and houses hugging the fortification walls of the Its Kale (Inner Citadel), with its ruins and restored buildings. The Kastro is built on a promontory in the lake and has wonderful views of the islet, Nissi, from the inner citadels. Most of the older houses here date from the 20th century.

② **Old Synagogue.** The late-18th-to early-19th-century synagogue (aka Inner Synagogue, Kahal Kadosh Yashan) is on the site of an earlier one and served the Greek-speaking Romaniote community that was 2,000

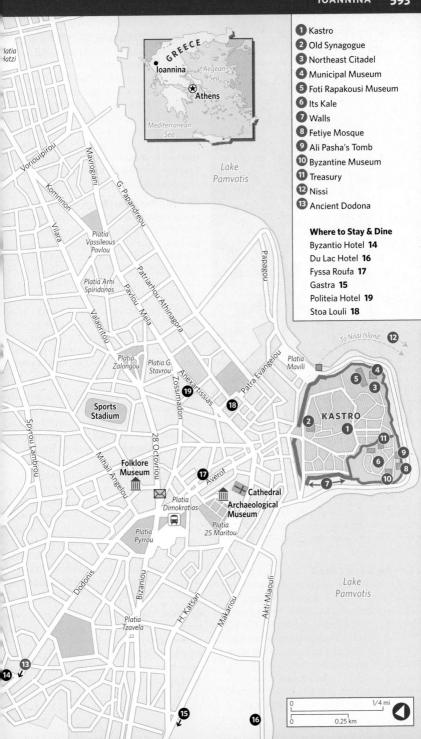

1. Kastro
2. Old Synagogue
3. Northeast Citadel
4. Municipal Museum
5. Foti Rapakousi Museum
6. Its Kale
7. Walls
8. Fetiye Mosque
9. Ali Pasha's Tomb
10. Byzantine Museum
11. Treasury
12. Nissi
13. Ancient Dodona

Where to Stay & Dine
Byzantio Hotel 14
Du Lac Hotel 16
Fyssa Roufa 17
Gastra 15
Politeia Hotel 19
Stoa Louli 18

GREECE

Aegean Sea

Ioannina

Athens

Mediterranean Sea

Lake Pamvotis

To Nissi Island

Platia Mavili

KASTRO

Sports Stadium

Folklore Museum

Platia Dimokratias

Cathedral

Archaeological Museum

Platia 25 Martiou

Platia Pyrrou

Lake Pamvotis

Platia Tzavela

0   1/4 mi
0   0.25 km

> Tyrant Ali Pasha ruled from a splendid court within the gates of the Its Kale.

members strong before World War II but now has dwindled down to 50. It's believed to be one of the largest and nicest Jewish buildings in Greece. Open on Jewish holidays and by appointment. Ioustinianou St., Kastro. ☎ 26510/25195 or 28541.

❸ ★ **Northeast Citadel.** Outside the ramped gate is the **library,** a rare example of Islamic urban architecture, and the only *hamam* (Turkish bathhouse) in Epirus, dating from the 16th to 17th century but in disrepair. Opposite the *hamam* is the **Soufari-seraglio** that was turned into Ali Pasha's cavalry school. In the courtyard, now built over by a primary school, are the remains of a **bathhouse,** the only urban Byzantine building found in the Kastro, which was itself built on Hellenistic walls.

❹ **Municipal Museum.** The 1618 Aslan Pasha Mosque dominates this enclosed area that feels like an overgrown garden. You enter from a ramp near the kitchen of an Ottoman *madrassa* (or *medresse,* Islamic school). The mosque has been restored, and there are artifacts from the Muslim, Christian, and Jewish communities in the front entrance, while the worship area has been left as is. 18 Alex Noutsou St. ☎ 26510/26356. Admission 2.50. Sept–Apr daily 8am–5:30pm, May–Aug daily 8am–7:30pm. Closed Dec 25 and Jan 1.

❺ ★ **Foti Rapakousi Museum.** The 17th-century *madrassa* holds artifacts from the 17th to the 19th century. Most of the items are weapons, but there are also vases and everyday items, such as a standout rosewood pipe, donated by a collector who also restored the pieces under expert direction. The concept of industrial art is vivid in the beautifully crafted weaponry. At least if you were staring down the barrel of a gun it was a pretty one. Instruments and books are also on display. 20 Alex. Noutsou St. ☎ 6972/904666. Free admission. Sept–June daily 9am–3pm, July–Aug daily 9am–6pm.

❻ ★★ kids **Its Kale.** Also called the Inner Citadel, Inner Acropolis, and Southeast Citadel, this is Ioannina's crown attraction. There's a **cafe** near the entrance of the sprawling open area surrounded by walls and the lake. It wasn't always this empty—the Byzantine-era buildings were destroyed by Ali Pasha, who built a large **palace** (*seraglio*) and its attendant service buildings and alleyways after bringing in earth to level the summit. The *seraglio* had women's and men's apartments and reception rooms, based on European and Muslim models. It was very impressive to European visitors and took up much of the Its Kale, but it was destroyed, along with most of the buildings, in an 1870 fire. Free admission. Daily 8am–10pm.

❼ **Walls.** The enclosing inner and outer walls were built by Ali Pasha between 1795 and 1815 and employed European engineers. There were guardhouses and other buildings along and within them, as well as a bathhouse, three main gates, and two secondary ones.

Fetiye Mosque. It was built by Ali Pasha around 1795 as the *seraglio* mosque, on the site of an older one that was likely on the site of the Byzantine Taxiarches church. It's never been open to the public, but the *tzami* (mosque) was last restored in 1990, after being altered for use as a Greek Army building.

Ali Pasha's Tomb. The iron-caged tomb of Ali Pasha (1741–1822) was surrounded by a more ornate cover until 1940. The current one dates to 1999. The tomb contains the remains of him, a wife (d. 1809), and a son. His head was taken to Istanbul after he was hunted down by the Sultan's forces and killed on the islet Nissi.

Byzantine Museum. A fire in 1870 destroyed buildings in the citadel, including the *seraglio*. A military hospital was built in its place and then demolished to build the 1958 Royal Pavilion based on plans of local mansions. The pavilion was restored for a museum in 1995 and contains icons, paintings, and frescoes, including an icon of *Christ in Judgment* surrounded by all the saints, and a fresco of the *Judas Kiss*. Kastro Ioannina. ☎ 26510/39580. Admission (includes Treasury) 3€, 2€ seniors 65 and over, free for E.U. students and Sun and holidays Nov 1–Mar 31, 4€ ticket for both Archaeological and Byzantine museums. Tues–Sun 8am–5pm.

★★ Treasury. This early-19th-century building survives, likely used as a reception area for visiting dignitaries. A part was turned into Agii Anargyri Church in the 20th century. The **Silver Hall (Treasury)** now houses items of the Byzantine Museum mainly made of silver, for which Ioannina is renowned. The artists incorporated elements from the Byzantine tradition as well as western European, Venetian, and Russian styles in their work. The filigree is impressive, as are the large, decorative belt buckles. **Same tickets and hours as the Byzantine Museum.**

★ kids Nissi. A cruise on the lake is fun, but you can take a quick journey over to the island, called both Nissi or Nissaki, on one of the **boats** that run every 30 minutes. Have a look around the narrow streets, buy a souvenir or specialty sweet, or head to the main attraction, the quarters, now a **museum** (attached

> Boats cruise the waters of Lake Pamvotis and call at Nissi Island, where Ali Pasha met his end.

to Panteleimon Monastery; ☎ 26510/81791), where Ali Pasha was found hiding and was killed by the Sultan's forces in 1822. See p. 569, ⑨.

SITE GUIDE PAGE 597

⑬ **★★ Ancient Dodona.** The oracle of the divine couple, Zeus and Dione, lived in the sacred oak tree in this inspiring location near Ioannina. From the 8th to the 4th century B.C., their will was made known by the rustling leaves. Prophets also interpreted the sound made from striking one of the copper cauldrons mounted on tripods in a circle around the tree, connected so that when one was struck they would all reverberate. *Selli* (the prophets) didn't wash their feet so as to remain in contact with the earth, the tree, and the will of the gods. The tree was cut and its roots dug out in the 4th century A.D. The site was deserted, likely after Slav incursions in the 5th century. Excavations first began in 1875 and continued again from 1950.

Where to Stay & Dine in Ioannina

> *Traditional elegance at the Politeia Hotel.*

Byzantio Hotel
This big, spacious, old-fashioned hotel is about a 20-minute walk to town. It's a well-run, average hotel that offers parking, Wi-Fi, a bar, a restaurant, and a good buffet breakfast. Vimoundou St. ☎ 26510/40453. www.byzantio-hotel.gr. 104 units. Doubles 62€–75€ w/breakfast. AE, DC, MC, V.

★ kids Du Lac Hotel and Congress Center
This large deluxe hotel complex on the lake-shore is just a few minutes' walk south of the Kastro. There's a pool and children's pool, a snack bar, a restaurant, and a bar overlooking the lake. They host conferences and can arrange adventure excursions in Zagori. Akti Miaouli and Ikkou sts. ☎ 26510/59100. www.hoteldulac.gr. 129 units. Doubles 165€ w/breakfast. AE, DC, MC, V.

Fyssa Roufa GREEK
You can eat anytime at this restaurant on the main road in Ioannina, as it's open 24 hours. They don't deliver but you can take away, especially if you're up and no one else is. Specialties include lamb fricassee, chicken soup, and baked octopus. 55 Averoff St. ☎ 26510/26262 Entrees 6€–10€. No credit cards. Daily 24 hr.

Gastra GREEK
This popular restaurant is a culinary adventure and destination, especially on Sunday afternoons. The name refers to the old-fashioned way the food is cooked—in a casserole dish (*gastra*) inside a wood-burning oven. Regional and chef specialties, such as *keftedes* (meat patties) in red sauce or goat with potatoes, are lowered into the fire on pulleys. Get to the restaurant through a garden; you can dine in the spacious indoor area, or outdoors under the vines. 16A Kostaki St. ☎ 26510/61530. Entrees 8.50€–13€. AE, DC, MC, V. Tues–Sun lunch & dinner.

★ kids Politeia Hotel
This beautiful, traditional hotel complex is grouped around a courtyard in the historic center of town. It has a coffee room open till 11pm and does great breakfasts. They're very helpful and can provide info, make reservations, and do laundry. 109 Anexartisias St. ☎ 26510/22235. www.etip.gr. Doubles 85€–100€ w/breakfast and parking. MC, V.

★ Stoa Louli GREEK
Get into the atmosphere of historic Ioannina at this restaurant in the old agora, in an arcade covered with a glass roof. They serve beef and traditional specialties, including *soutzouki politiko* (sausages in tomato sauce), chicken kebabs, filet steaks, and many other dishes found on Greek menus (such as zucchini patties or rocket salad). 78 Anexartisias St. ☎ 26510/71322. Entrees 6.90€–11€. No credit cards. Daily lunch & dinner.

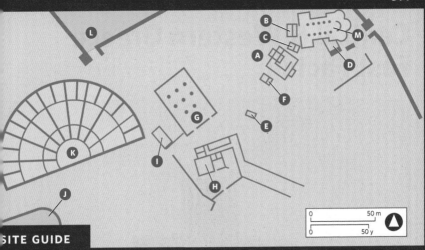

SITE GUIDE

13 Ancient Dodona

Many ruins are scattered around the sprawling site, and layers of buildings have accrued over time, from the Bronze Age to Roman times and the Christian era, often incorporating parts from earlier structures. Foremost was the **A Iera Oikia** (Sacred House), the temple of Zeus erected in the 4th century B.C. beside the oak tree. Another tree has been planted on the site. The ruins comprise the **B old** and **C new temples of Dione;** the later one, built after 219 B.C., has a stone base and local *breccia* (stone) columns that were veneered with marble. The only Doric temple is the 3rd-century-B.C. temple for hero-ancestor **D Heracles (Hercules),** built during the reign of King Pyrrhus. A **E temple to Aphrodite,** Zeus's daughter, was also built during his reign. The goddess **F Themis's Ionic temple** made a worship trinity with Zeus and Dione. You can also see the outside walls and reinforcing Ionic columns for the buttress-roofed, Doric colonnade-fronted **G Bouleuterion (council chamber).** More buildings include the **H Prytaneion,** where the eternal flame burned, officials dined, and the Epirote Alliance and League met. A small building, the **I House of Priests,** juts into a corner of the site-dominating theater, built in the early 3rd century B.C. for the Naia festivals held every 4 years, together with a **J stadium** to hold the games. The **K theater** is one of the largest

in Greece and can seat 17,000. It's built on a slope and dramatically faces a valley and mountains to the south. The large site of the **L acropolis,** dated to the 4th century B.C., was where the inhabitants took refuge in times of attack. It has a cistern hewn into the rock. A three-aisled basilica-type **M church** was built in the 5th century A.D. using materials from the site. It was rebuilt in the 6th century, likely after an earthquake. Archaeologists also found the remains of huts where sanctuary attendants lived and an ancient kiln used to fire pots and cooking, from around 1900 B.C. Dodona, Epirus. ☎ 26510/82287. Admission 3€, 1€ seniors 65 and over, free for E.U. students. Nov–Apr daily 8:30am–3pm, May–Oct daily 8:30am–8pm. 22km (14 miles) southwest of Ioannina. Dodonis Ave./Rte. 5 to Egnatia Hwy., then the Dodoni exit (for Zoodochos Pigi).

Central & Western Greece Fast Facts

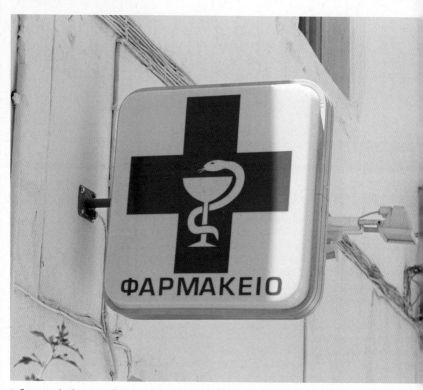

> Green marks the spot—pharmacy signs are a common and welcome sight in Greek towns.

Arriving

BY AIR Ioannina National Airport (IOA) (☎ 26510/83600) is served domestically by **Aegean Air** (☎ 210/626-1000; www.aegean air.com) and **Olympic Airlines** (☎ 210/966-6666; www.olympicair.com), which fly from Athens. **BY BUS (KTEL) Urban bus no. 024** to/from Syntagma Square (Amalias Ave.) goes to Terminal B Station, 260 Liossion Street, Athens, for buses to Arachova, Delphi, Kalambaka, or Volos (Pelion). Call 210/831-7186 or ☎ 210/832-9585 for Volos. **Urban bus no. 051** to/from Omonia Square (Menandrou St.) goes to Terminal A Station, 100 Kifissou Street, Athens, for buses to Ioannina or Metsovo (via Ioannina). Call ☎ 210/512-9363. Regional **KTEL** bus stations are as follows. **Delphi:** ☎ 22650/82317. **Kalambaka:** ☎ 24320/22432. A Kalambaka to Meteora bus makes a round trip to Grand Meteoro Monastery twice a day from Dimarchiou Square May to August. Departs Mon–Fri 9am, 1pm; Saturday and Sunday 8:30am, 12:30pm. Returns 1pm. 1.40€ one-way, 10 minutes. **Ioannina (transfer here for Metsovo):** ☎ 26510/26286. **Volos (Pelion):** ☎ 24210/33253 or 25527. **BY CAR** Highways are generally new and in good condition; secondary roads might not be. Turn-offs are often not well signposted. ***Caution:*** Drivers are aggressive. Speed limits are up to

20kph/75 mph. Vehicles use the shoulders s a slow lane. **Greek Automobile Touring Club** (ELPA), 395 Messogion Avenue, Agia Paraskevi, Athens (☎ 210/606-8800, road assistance ☎ 10400; www.elpa.gr). **BY TRAIN** OSE ☎ 1110. **OSE Athens** Larissis Station (Theodorou Deliyanni St., Athens) Call ☎ 1110, or ☎ 1440 for departures recording (www. ose.gr or www.trainose.gr). **Kalambaka:** Call ☎ 24320/22451. Two trains a day from Athens (4 hr. 40 min.). Tickets 21.40€ first class, 14.60€ second class. **Volos (Pelion):** Call ☎ 24210/24056. OSE travel agency (train tickets only), inside the station (☎ 24210/28555). One direct train a day from Athens (4 hr. 40 min.), or change at Larissa (five more from there). Tickets 40.20€ first class, 28.20€ second class.

Doctors & Dentists

ARACHOVA Health Center ☎ 22670/31300. Monday to Friday 9am to 1pm. **DELPHI** Health Center (☎ 22650/82307). Monday to Friday 8:30am to 1:30pm. Outside those hours for emergencies: Amfissa General Hospital ☎ 22650/22222). **IOANNINA** Ioannina General Hospital, Makriyanni Avenue. (☎ 26510/80111). Ioannina University Hospital ☎ 26510/99111). **KALAMBAKA** Health Center ☎ 24320/22222). Monday to Friday 9am to pm, emergencies 24 hours. **METSOVO** Health Center (☎ 26560-41111-2). Open 24 hours. **VOLOS** General Hospital (☎ 24210/94200; www.volos-hospital.gr).

Emergencies

See p. 680, Fast Facts Greece.

Getting Around

BY BUS For bus company numbers, see "Arriving," above. **BY TAXI Arachova:** ☎ 22670/31566. **Delphi:** ☎ 22650/82000. **Ioannina:** ☎ 26510/46777. **Kalambaka:** ☎ 24320/22310 (to Meteora one-way is 8€). **Metsovo:** ☎ 6945/742607.

Internet

See p. 681, Fast Facts Greece.

Pharmacies

See p. 682, Fast Facts Greece.

Police & Tourist Police

DELPHI Tourist police. 3 Ang. Sikelianou Street (☎ 22650/82220). **ARACHOVA** ☎ 22670/31333. **IOANNINA** Tourist police ☎ 26510/65934 or ☎ 26510/65922. **KALAMBAKA** Tourist police ☎ 24320/78000. **METSOVO** ☎ 26560/41233.

Post Office

ARACHOVA Xenia Square (☎ 22670/31253). **DELPHI** 25 Pavlou and Fred streets (☎ 22650/82376). **KALAMBAKA** 46 Trikalon Street (☎ 24320/22466). **IOANNINA** 1 28th Octovriou and Botsari streets (☎ 26510/26437) and 14 G. Papandreou Street (☎ 26510/71440). **METSOVO** 3 Tositsa Street (☎ 26560/41245).

Telephones

See p. 683, Fast Facts Greece.

Toilets

See p. 684, Fast Facts Greece.

Visitor Information

ARACHOVA Old School, Roloi, Arachova (☎ 22670/31630 or 31262; open daily 9am-9pm, Sat-Sun and holidays closed 2-5pm). **DELPHI** Town Hall Tourist Info, 11 Apollonos and 12 Vas, Pavlou and Frederikis streets (☎ 22653/51300; Mon-Fri 7:30am-2:30pm). **IOANNINA** EOT/GNTO 39 Dodonis Avenue (☎ 26510/41868; Mon-Fri 7:30am-3pm). **KALAMBAKA** Town Hall tourist info, Dimarchiou ground floor, Dimarchiou Square (☎ 24320/77734; Nov-Apr Mon-Fri 8:30am-2:30pm; May-Oct Mon-Fri 8am-9pm, Sat-Sun 10am-4pm). **METSOVO** Town Hall, 2 Averoff Street (☎ 26560/42825). **ZAGORI** Northern Pindus National Park Information Center, Asprageli (☎ 26530/22241; daily 9 or 10am-3:30pm).

13
Corfu & the
Ionian Islands

Favorite Moments in the Ionian Islands

Much more verdant than the Aegean Islands, Corfu and its neighbors adrift in the Ionian Sea seem a world apart from the rest of Greece. Corfu, especially, is awash in the flavor of other cultures—a strong essence of Italy and France with an overlay of British formality. This is not to say, though, that you'll leave Greece behind when you set sail for these islands—the pleasure of being on Kefalonia is to be surrounded by unspoiled Greek life, and Ithaca is the legendary homeland of Homer, the most famous Greek of all.

> PREVIOUS PAGE *The white sands at Myrtos, Kefalonia.* THIS PAGE *Spili Melissani is an eerie, watery realm on Kefalonia.*

❶ **Wandering through the narrow lanes of Corfu Town, Corfu.** You'll get lost more than once, and you won't mind a bit as you travel through the centuries, across cultures, past Venetian loggias, Greek churches, and British palaces. See p. 619, ❸.

❷ **Coming across the ruins of Greek temples at Mon Repos, Corfu.** It's satisfying enough to walk through beautiful gardens into a neoclassical palace where the Greek royal family summered and Prince Phillip of England was born.

Then, on a short stroll along the seaside, you'll come upon an ancient city, the extent of which has yet to be unearthed. See p. 626, ❶.

❸ **Looking down at Paleokastritsa from the Angelokastro, Corfu.** The island has many overlooks but none can top this aerie—a ruined castle some 300m (984 ft.) above the waves. The coves of Paleokastritsa etch the shoreline at your feet, and forests of cedar and cypress are spread like a soft carpet far below. See p. 630, ❺.

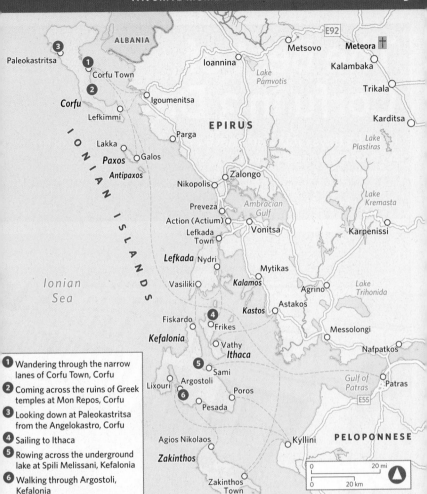

1. Wandering through the narrow lanes of Corfu Town, Corfu
2. Coming across the ruins of Greek temples at Mon Repos, Corfu
3. Looking down at Paleokastritsa from the Angelokastro, Corfu
4. Sailing to Ithaca
5. Rowing across the underground lake at Spili Melissani, Kefalonia
6. Walking through Argostoli, Kefalonia

4 Sailing to Ithaca. The craggy, mountainous profile is stunning, as befits an island associated with a myth that has captivated audiences for almost 3,000 years. True romantics will think of Odysseus, and Penelope awaiting his return, and maybe the poem by that great modern Greek man of letters, C. P. Cavafy: "When you set out on the voyage to Ithaca / Pray that your journey may be long / Full of adventures, full of knowledge." See p. 617, 6.

5 Rowing across the underground lake at Spili Melissani, Kefalonia. The play of light on water creates an unearthly realm, and the mystery is heightened by knowing that the cave is part of an underworld that extends for miles across the island. For a sunny tonic, find your way to Myrtos and lie on some of Greece's most beautiful sands. See p. 616, 4.

6 Walking through Argostoli, Kefalonia. You won't find landmarks, monuments, ruins, or history-rich lanes and squares. In fact, you won't come upon much that predates the 1950s, when an earthquake destroyed much of the island and its capital city. Instead, you will be immersed in a swirl of Greek life and experience the pleasure of blending into the everyday scenes. See p. 614, 1.

The Best of Corfu in 3 Days

In just 3 days, you won't have time to venture off Corfu. But there's much to see on one of Greece's most beautiful islands, where mountainsides are carpeted with olive groves and evergreens, the coast is ringed with sandy beaches, and a fascinating, centuries-old city, Corfu Town, remains remarkably intact.

> The Palace of St. Michael and St. George is a remnant of the longtime British presence in Corfu Town.

START Corfu Town **TRIP LENGTH** Corfu is relatively small, and good roads make exploring easy; depending on where you stay, you can see much of the island without logging much more than 100km (62 miles) on your rental car.

❶ Corfu Town. The island's many occupiers all left their marks here, resulting in a gracious medley of French-style arcades, British palaces and gardens, and Venetian fortresses, all imbued with a Greek sensibility. Spend the better part of Day 1 exploring this remarkable city, recently designated a UNESCO World Heritage Site.

The place to begin is the **Spianada (Esplanade),** one of Europe's largest squares (p. 618, ❶). As enticing as the expanse of greenery is, the cafes at one side, under the arcades

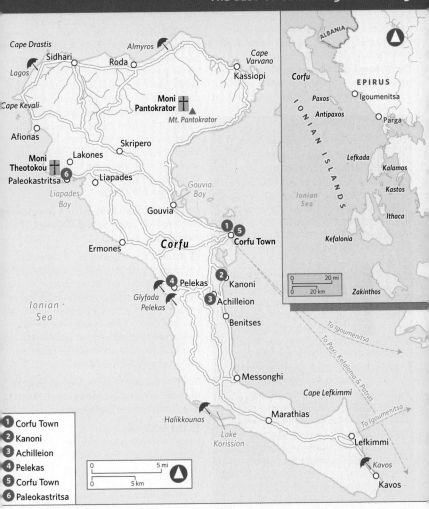

1 Corfu Town
2 Kanoni
3 Achilleion
4 Pelekas
5 Corfu Town
6 Paleokastritsa

known as **the Liston,** are even more so. Any-one would need a very good excuse to walk by the long line of tables without sitting down for a spell, as many Corfiots do. You'll want to return to the Spianada later to venture into some of the landmarks that surround it—cer-tainly the **Paleo Frourio,** with its hilltop views, and the **Palace of St. Michael and St. George,** for a look at a collection of Asian art and an amble through the seaside gardens. First, though, you'll want to experience the amazing old quarter just beyond the Liston.

There's no better way to get a sense of Corfu than to wander through the narrow

lanes (kantounia) of **Old Town,** past churches, shops, and tall Venetian houses (p. 619, 3). You're bound to get lost, but sooner or later the tall campanile of the **Cathedral of Agios Spyridon** will come into view, or you will come to the stony flanks of the **Neo Frourio** (the new fortress) or some other landmark. The tall, shuttered houses are evocative of Italy and France, while the street life is decidedly Greek. Shops sell everything from expensive jewelry to olive oil, the island's sweet kumquat liqueur, and household staples. No small part of Old Town's appeal is the bustle of activity that takes place here daily.

When you've had your fill, retrace your steps to the Liston and continue south along the waterfront. Follow the promenade first to the **Archaeological Museum,** where Medusa holds court from the island's prized antiquity, a pediment frieze from a temple to Artemis (p. 623, ❽). If you're willing to continue walking, follow the waterfront about 2km (1¼ miles) to **Mon Repos,** the former palace of the island's British governors and later the Greek royal family (you can also reach the palace by bus; see p. 626, ❶). At this lovely seaside estate, you can walk through beautiful gardens, inspect the ruins of ancient temples and Byzantine chapels, and swim from a beach where Greek royalty once lounged. In the evening, return to the Liston, where all of Corfu seems to turn out for a *volta* (stroll). For more on Corfu Town, see p. 618. ⏱ 1 day.

On Day 2, head south from Corfu Town toward the Achilleion, stopping first at Kanoni. 5km (3 miles) south.

❷ **Kanoni.** The next morning, it's time to venture just a bit farther afield, outside Corfu Town. Ever since the 19th century, the view from Kanoni (named for the cannon installed by the French)—across a sweep of sparkling sea, verdant coastline, and two islets—has been among the most-touted stops on the Greek isle tour. The vista is no less dazzling today. See p. 627, ❷ . ⏱ 30 min.

Continue another 14 km (8.5 miles) south to the Achilleion, just outside Gastouri, 19km (12 miles) southwest of Corfu Town.

❸ **The Achilleion.** Built in 1890 by Elisabeth, Empress of Bavaria and queen of the Austro-Hungarian empire, the Achilleion was meant to evoke the grandeur of ancient Greece. The salons decorated in pseudoantique style, the immense statues, and the frescoes depicting mythological scenes miss the mark but are memorable nonetheless—if nothing else as a window into the strange ways of royals. The palace is an ostentatious oddity, but the views over the sea are beautiful. See p. 629, ❸ . ⏱ 1 hr.

From the Achilleion, drive west across the island to Pelekas, 11km (7 miles) northwest of Gastouri.

Cast of Characters

Corfiots, both natives and transplants, have proven to be as colorful and character-filled as the landscapes.

St. Spyridon, a 3rd- to 4th-century Cypriot shepherd-turned-bishop, arrived on the island posthumously, when a Corfiot monk brought his remains to Corfu from Constantinople. Spyridon has allegedly saved the island from famine, the plague, and an attempted Turkish invasion in 1716, when he helped repel 33,000 Ottoman troops by making a fearsome appearance brandishing a cross and a torch. He is also reputed to have intervened to save the church named after him in Corfu Town when it survived a direct hit by a German bomb in 1944. The saint's role in the Turkish defeat is celebrated on August 11, when islanders say special prayers and parade Spyridon's icon through the streets.

On the more worldly end of the spectrum is Sisi, more formally known as **Elisabeth,** the Bavarian duchess-turned-empress of the Austro-Hungarian Empire. The beautiful fashion plate spent her life traveling, writing poetry, carrying on love affairs, and reading ancient Greek texts. She was especially fond of Corfu, where she eventually settled in the Achilleion, a villa that evokes her favorite Greek, Achilles, the handsome hero of the Trojan War.

Brothers **Gerald and Lawrence Durrell** lived on Corfu in the idyllic years just before World War II. Gerald was enamored of the island's flora and fauna, which influenced his later work as a naturalist and zookeeper. He recounts the Corfu years in *My Family and Other Animals.* Lawrence, a noted novelist and travel writer, evokes the island's beautiful landscapes in his account of Corfu, *Prospero's Cell.* Their writings helped make the island popular with British travelers.

Where's Kerkyra?

Corfu is also known as Kerkyra; you'll often see this name used on schedules and maps.

> *The streets of Corfu's Old Town bear the architectural stamp of the island's French and Venetian conquerors.*

④ Pelekas. The most popular viewpoint from hilltop Pelekas is **Kaiser's Throne,** a rocky summit favored by Kaiser Wilhelm, who inhabited the Achilleion in the early 20th century, after the murder of the Empress Elisabeth. The outlook extends up and down the forested coast, and the inland view takes in the **Ropa Valley,** a patchwork of fertile fields, vineyards, olive groves, and orchards. You have several choices for an afternoon swim, but best of all is **Myrtiotissa,** just north of Pelekas. See p. 629, ④. ⏲ 2 hr.

Backtrack to Corfu Town, 13km (8½ miles) east.

⑤ Corfu Town. Begin the morning of Day 3 in Corfu Town, with another stroll in Old Town and a stop in a museum or two. The **Museum of Asian Art** (p. 622, ⑤), in the Palace of St. Michael and St. George, is a delight to come upon in Corfu. A collection of Samurai swords, Noh masks, and Chinese porcelains are as beautiful as the seaside gardens. Corfu was once a center of icon painting, and the Byzantine Museum reveals the East-West complexity of the art. ⏲ Half-day.

On the afternoon of Day 3, drive northwest about 15km (9⅓ miles) to Paleokastritsa.

⑥ Paleokastritsa. In the afternoon on Day 3, head west again, this time to Paleokastritsa, about 15km (9⅓ miles) from Corfu Town. Popularity has not yet overtaken the beauty of these coves backed by cliffs and forests.

> *A seaside monastery is among the charms of Paleokastritsa.*

When you tire of sitting on a beach, make the ascent to Angelokastro, a ruined medieval castle 300m (984 ft.) above the sea. See p. 630, ⑤. ⏲ 2 hr.

Return to Corfu Town in the evening for one last stroll through Old Town and a drink on the Liston.

The Best of Corfu & the Ionians in 6 Days

Six days will allow just enough time to get a taste of the Ionians. You'll spend the first 3 days on Corfu, exploring fortresses, palaces, and other remnants of a long past, as well the forested interior landscapes and the beach-fringed coast. By Day 4 you will be on Kefalonia, where a very different atmosphere prevails—whereas Corfu is cosmopolitan, Kefalonia is quintessentially Greek. The trip ends, appropriately enough, on Ithaca, the island where the 20-year-long voyage of Homer's Odysseus drew to a close.

> *The 18th-century houses on the port In Fiskardo are among few structures that survived a 1953 earthquake.*

START Corfu Town. **TRIP LENGTH** On driving tours of the three islands you won't cover more than 200km (124 miles) by car; to reach Kefalonia from Corfu, a distance of about 150km (93 miles), you'll be at sea most of a day, depending on schedules and the route you decide to take.

① Corfu Town, Corfu. During your 3 days on Corfu, you will want to return to explore Corfu Town several times. Wherever else you stay on the island, you'll never be too far from the island capital, and the town rewards visit after visit. Some travelers join the many Corfiots who begin and end each day on the Liston,

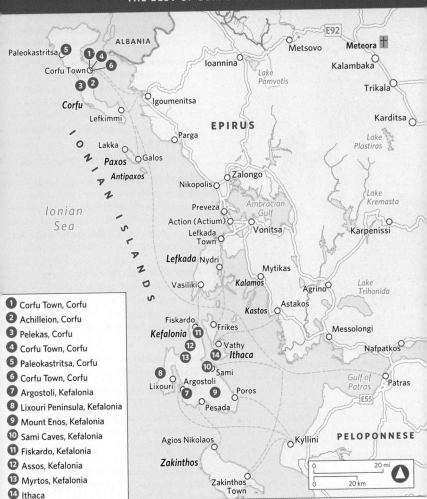

1 Corfu Town, Corfu
2 Achilleion, Corfu
3 Pelekas, Corfu
4 Corfu Town, Corfu
5 Paleokastritsa, Corfu
6 Corfu Town, Corfu
7 Argostoli, Kefalonia
8 Lixouri Peninsula, Kefalonia
9 Mount Enos, Kefalonia
10 Sami Caves, Kefalonia
11 Fiskardo, Kefalonia
12 Assos, Kefalonia
13 Myrtos, Kefalonia
14 Ithaca

the beautiful arcade that faces **the Spianada** (Esplanade; p. 618, 1), sipping coffee in the morning, wine or ouzo at night, and watching life transpire on this beautiful expanse of greenery. The experience is especially memorable on summer weekend evenings when one of the island's many bands performs in the ornate music pavilion on the Spianada.

The only way to experience **Old Town** is to wander aimlessly in what seems to be an endless maze of lanes that open onto small squares (p. 619, 3). You'll get lost again and again, but the compact quarter is wedged between hard-to-miss landmarks that you'll stumble upon sooner or later—the **Neo Frourio** (New

Fortress) on the west, the Old Harbor on the north, and the Spianada on the west.

You'll want to interrupt idle wanderings from time to time to strike out for Corfu Town's considerable museums and attractions. Save the Museum of Asian Art, the Museum of Byzantine Art, and the fortresses for tomorrow, and on your first day immerse yourself in Old Town before heading to the city's southern outskirts. This way you will get a sense of the island scenery and enjoy some time on a beach without really leaving town. Follow the pleasant seaside promenade south from the Spianada to the **Archaeological Museum** (p. 623, 8). Most of the artifacts here,

> *Empress Elisabeth flaunted her obsession with Achilles at the Achilleion, her garish palace outside Corfu Town.*

including a remarkable temple pediment depicting Medusa, are from **Paleopolis** (p. 626, ❶), the ancient city that is scattered in ruin across the grounds of Mon Repos estate. Less than 2km (1¼ miles) south, Mon Repos is the former summer residence of the British lord high commissioners and later the Greek royal family; a walk across the wooded grounds brings you to **temples to Hera and Poseidon** from the 7th and 6th century B.C., **Roman baths,** and an early Christian chapel from the 5th century. A beach below the estate is the best place for a swim close to Corfu Town. See p. 618. ⏲ 1 day.

The Achilleion is in Gastouri, 19km (12 miles) southwest of Corfu Town.

❷ **Achilleion, Corfu.** On Day 2, venture south of Corfu Town to another remnant of royalty, the **Achilleion.** The palace that Empress Elisabeth of the Austro-Hungarian Empire built in 1890 is a monument both to Achilles and to bad taste, but it's a sight you won't soon forget. See p. 629, ❸. ⏲ 1 hr.

From the Achilleion, drive west across the island to Pelekas, 11km (7 miles) northwest.

❸ **Pelekas, Corfu.** From there, venture across the island to **Pelekas,** for stunning views of the coast and the fertile interior from Kaiser's Throne, and then descend to some of the island's finest beaches, including the best of them all, the beautiful sands at **Myrtiotissa.** See p. 629, ❹. ⏲ 2 hr.

Return to Corfu Town, 13km (8 miles) east.

❹ **Corfu Town, Corfu.** Return to Corfu Town for the evening *volta,* when it seems that everyone on the island congregates around the Spianada. Plan to arrive in time to visit one of the museums—at the **Museum of Asian Art** you can top off a tour of the galleries with a walk in the adjoining seaside gardens of the **Palace of St. Michael and St. George** (p. 622, ❺). The lanes and squares of Old Town are most engaging in the evening, when they are crowded with strollers and late shoppers, and the old stones are lit by the glow of lamplight. ⏲ 1 day.

Drive northwest across the island about 15km (9⅓ miles) to Paleokastritsa

❺ **Paleokastritsa, Corfu.** Day 3 takes you back to the west coast of the island, this time a bit farther north, to **Paleokastritsa,** a string of forest-backed coves about 15km (9⅓ miles) from Corfu Town. You'll want to spend the better part of the day here, enjoying your pick of a string of beaches, taking time to sit in the shady courtyard of **Theotokou Monastery,** and making the ascent through the cliffside villages of Lakones and Krini to **Angelokastro,** a ruined medieval castle 300m (984 ft.) above the sea. See p. 630, ❺. ⏲ 1 day.

Drive the 15km (9⅓ miles) back to Corfu Town.

❻ **Corfu Town, Corfu.** End the day again in Corfu Town. If you have not already done so, step into the **Byzantine Museum** to lose yourself amid the saints depicted on hundreds of lavish icons (p. 623, ❻). Then enter the gates of the **Paleo Frourio** (Old Fortress) and climb to the summit of the citadel for views of the town and the sea lanes surrounding it (p. 622, ❹). ⏲ 1 day.

Reaching the island of Kefalonia from Corfu can be as easy as taking one of the direct boats that run between the two islands a couple of times a week in the summer (the trip takes about 5 hr.). Alternatives are to take the boat to Patras and continue by sea from there, or to fly on AirSea Lines (p. 632).

7 Argostoli, Kefalonia. You will arrive in the workaday port town Sami, but move on and base yourself in **Argostoli,** the capital, from which you can easily tour the island. You'll discover, as you settle in on the evening of Day 3, that Argostoli has few historic monuments or, for that matter, much that predates the 1950s, when the town and most of the rest of the island was rebuilt after a devastating earthquake in 1953. Spend part of the morning on Day 4 strolling along the waterfront's thumblike inner bay and from Plateia Valianona along pedestrian Lithostroto through the heart of town. For a look at the island's past, which isn't evident on the modern streets of Argostoli, step into the **Korgialenio History and Folklore Museum.** For more on Argostoli, see p. 614, **1**. ⏲ 2 hr.

Nearly nonstop ferries ply the waters of the bay that separates Argostoli and Lixouri; the crossing (much shorter than the long drive around the bay) takes about 15 min.

8 Lixouri Peninsula, Kefalonia. Later on Day 4, board a ferry for the short trip across the bay to the **Lixouri Peninsula,** to end the day on one of a string of sandy beaches. See p. 615, **2**. ⏲ Half-day.

Take the ferry back to Argostoli. The road up Mount Enos is off the Argostoli–Sami road; the turnoff is about 7km (4⅓ miles) east of Argostoli.

9 Mount Enos, Kefalonia. On Day 5, tour the rest of the island. The best route takes you west to the slopes of **Mount Enos,** the Ionians' tallest summit, carpeted with a shaggy species of fir unique to the mountain. See p. 616, **3**. ⏲ 1 hr.

The island's famous caverns are near Sami, the main port, about 15km (9⅓ miles) east of Argostoli. On the Argostoli-Sami Road, you'll come first to Drogarati, 4km (2½ miles) southwest of Sami.

10 Sami Caves, Kefalonia. Next stops are the two caves of Sami: the stalagmite-filled chamber at **Drogarati,** and **Spili Melissani,** where an underground lake is lit by ethereal light. See p. 616, **4**. ⏲ 2 hr.

Fiskardo is about 25km (16 miles) north of Sami. Follow the road through Agia Efimia up the east coast of the northern peninsula.

11 Fiskardo, Kefalonia. At the end of the road north is this beautiful fishing port. With 18th-century houses lining the harbor, it was the only town on the island left intact after the 1953 earthquake. See p. 615, **5**. ⏲ 2 hr.

When returning from Fiskardo to Argostoli, about 35km (22 miles), follow the west coast and make short detours to Assos, about 10km (6¼ miles) south of Fiskardo, and Myrtos.

12 Assos, Kefalonia. Two other stops are worth a detour as you make your way south back to Argostoli. The first is **Assos** (p. 616, **5**), where a ruined castle stands above another pretty fishing port. ⏲ 1 hr.

Drive south 5km (3 miles).

13 Myrtos, Kefalonia. Just south of Assos, this sumptuous stretch of white sand is a standout even among the many splendorous beaches in Greece. ⏲ 1 hr.

Boats frequently make the short crossing between Kefalonia and Ithaca, from Sami to Pisaetos or Vathy (sail time about 40 min.). Boats also depart from Fiskardo to Frikes (sail time about 1 hr.).

14 Ithaca. You can easily visit the legendary island of Ithaca on a daylong excursion from the island of Kefalonia. On Day 6, set out from Sami to make the short crossing. The island is famously associated with Homer, as the home Odysseus seeks for 20 years in the aftermath of the Trojan War. The **Cave of the Nymphs, the Fountain of Arethusa,** and a few other sites have a tenuous connection with Homer's tale, but the real pleasure of the island is the rugged, forested landscapes and two especially appealing seaside villages, **Frikes** and **Kioni.** See p. 617, **6**. ⏲ 1 day.

Greek by Definition

FETA

BY TANIA KOLLIAS

GREEKS ARE BIG CHEESE EATERS and apparently have been since antiquity. Cheese was known to be a staple of early Olympian athletes' diets. In Homer's *Odyssey*, Odysseus observes the man-eating, one-eyed Cyclops Polyphemus milking ewes amid racks of cheese. Contemporary Greeks consume some 27 kilos (59 pounds) a year—the most per capita in the world—and about 40% is feta. Tangy, pure white, and firm but crumbly, it's best known in raw form as the cheese that lends a sharp, salty bite to *horiatiki*—the classic Greek salad. Because it doesn't melt, it's great cooked as well, most commonly in filo-pastry pies such as *tiropita* (cheese pie) and *spanakopita* (spinach pie).

National Treasure

In 2002, after a 16-year court battle with Denmark and Germany, Greece won the exclusive right to produce authentic feta cheese. The European Commission ruled that feta is Greek by definition and granted the cheese Protected Designation of Origin (PDO) status. Bulgaria, Romania, Albania, Turkey, Russia, France, and Denmark produce similar cheeses—including cow's milk varieties whitened to reverse the natural yellowing of bovine cheese. Only Greek feta made by traditional means, however, can be called feta within the E.U. Even within Greece, production is restricted to traditional Greek herding communities in Macedonia, Thrace, Epiros, Sterea Hellas, Peloponnese, and the island of Lesbos.

Facts on Feta

HISTORY
The ancients believed the process of making feta was passed on from the gods of Mount Olympus.

NAME In Modern Greek *tiri feta* means cheese slice. *Fetta* also means slice in Italian.

PROCESS Feta can be made with pasteurized or unpasteurized sheep and goat's milk.

FAT Fat content is high, ranging from 45 to 60%.

STORE Feta doesn't last long after it has been opened, and so it's essential to keep it bathed in brine.

How Feta Is Made

SHEEP'S MILK (and up to 30% goat's milk) is curdled with rennet at a temperature of 24° to 36°C (75°–97°F).

WHEY IS removed, and curds are cut into large pieces and then set in molds to drain.

ONCE DRAINED, the slices are salted and left to sit in low temperatures.

CURDS ARE then barreled with brine and left to mature for a few weeks to a few months.

Kefalonia & Ithaca

If you have a few extra days, expand your horizons beyond cosmopolitan Corfu and visit these other islands—known to locals as the real Ionians. A cruise south takes you into a different world—to mountainous Kefalonia, where everyday Greek life will swirl around you as you explore caves, fishing villages, and sandy beaches, and rugged and wild Ithaca, steeped in Homeric legend.

> Beautiful bays etch the coastline of mountainous Kefalonia.

START **Argostoli, capital of Kefalonia** TRIP LENGTH Allow 3 days to tour Kefalonia and Ithaca. You'll cover a little more than 100km (62 miles) by car; the sea crossing between Kefalonia and Ithaca is about 1 hr. each way.

1 ★★ **Argostoli.** The capital of Kefalonia is new, largely built after a 1953 earthquake that destroyed just about every building on the island. After the quake, an estimated 100,000 of the 120,000 residents left the island, and Argostoli was all but deserted. While such a provenance is not promising, Argostoli is

lively and appealing, stretching along the shores of an inner bay. The main attraction is being someplace so thoroughly Greek, with few concessions to tourism. Stroll around **Plateia Vallianou;** then follow **Lithostroto,** the pedestrian-only main street, through the heart of town. Among the few landmarks is the **Korgialenio History and Folklore Museum,** filled with furniture, tools, and other artifacts of old Kefalonia, along with fascinating photographs of the island before the quake (Ilia Zervou; ☎ 26710/28835; admission 3€; Apr–Oct Mon–Sat 9am–2pm). Peratata, 8km

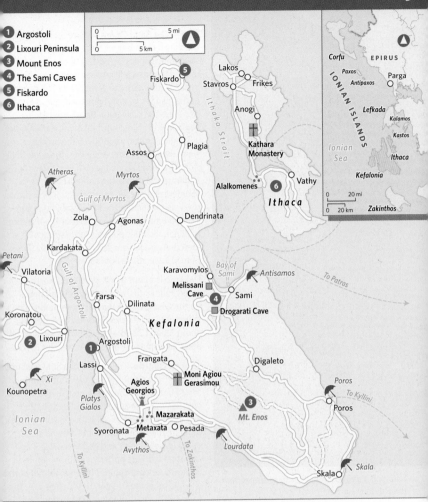

1. Argostoli
2. Lixouri Peninsula
3. Mount Enos
4. The Sami Caves
5. Fiskardo
6. Ithaca

(5 miles) east of Argostoli, is home to **Agios Andreas Bay,** lined with gorgeous beaches. ⏱ Half-day.

Nearly nonstop ferries ply the waters of the bay that separates Argostoli and Lixouri; the crossing (much shorter than the long drive around the bay) takes about 15 min.

2 ★★★ **Lixouri Peninsula.** Lixouri, the island's second-largest town, is fairly unremarkable, but the **beaches to the south** are spectacular. You'll encounter these sands as soon as you head south from Lixouri: At **Lepeda,** just 2km (1¼ miles) south, strange rock formations rise from a long stretch of red sand. Just beyond,

on the southern tip of the peninsula, other stretches of red sand are backed by cliffs at **Xi** and **Megas Lakkos. Kounopetra** (Rocking Stone), 2km (1¼ miles) west, has lost its main attraction—a rock that moved rhythmically every 20 minutes but ceased to do so after the 1953 earthquake—but the golden sands are enticing even without the rocking rock, as are those at remote **Agios Nikolaos,** another 2km (1¼ miles) farther west. ⏱ Half-day.

Take the ferry back to Argostoli. The road up Mount Enos is off the Argostoli–Sami road; the turnoff is about 7km (4⅓ miles) east of Argostoli.

> *Vathy, on Ithaca, is linked with many scenes from the Odyssey.*

❸ ★ **Mount Enos.** The tallest summit in the Ionians rises 1,600m (5,250 ft.) in the center of Kefalonia. A unique species of fir, *Abies cephalonica,* flourishes in the ecosystem the mountain creates and carpets the shaggy slopes, designated a national park for the trees' protection. A road rounds the mountain's flanks to the summit, from which the views over the Ionians, the Peloponnese, and the central mainland are phenomenal. ⏱ 2 hr.

The island's famous caverns are near Sami, the main port, about 15km (9⅓ miles) east of Argostoli. On the Argostoli-Sami Road, you'll come first to Drogarati, 4km (2½ miles) southwest of Sami.

❹ ★★ **The Sami Caves.** Nature endowed the **Drogarati chamber** with a forest of fantastic stalagmites and near-perfect acoustics—so refined that concerts are sometimes performed in the cave, where the great Maria Callas once performed (Argostoli–Sami road; admission 4€; May–Oct daily 9am–6pm). **Spili Melissani,** 5km (3 miles) north of Sami, is even more dramatic. It's also eerie, given the presence of a weird hydrologic phenomenon—the water that sloshes around inside the roofless cavern flows underground across the entire island from a submerged sea cave near Argostoli. A boatman rows visitors across the little lake, where sunlight pouring through the collapsed roof creates multicolored hues on rock and water (coast road to Agia Efimia; admission 6€; daily 9am–6pm). ⏱ 2 hr. to see both caves.

Fiskardo is about 25km (16 miles) north of Sami. Follow the road through Agia Efimia up the east coast of the northern peninsula. When returning from Fiskardo to Argostoli, about 35km (22 miles), follow the west coast and make short detours to Assos and Myrtos.

❺ ★★ **Fiskardo.** This colorful fishing port on the northern tip of the island would win the "most beautiful" contest even if it weren't the only town on the island spared by the 1953 quake. The cluster of tall 18th-century houses that line the harbor are backed by hillsides richly forested in fir and cedar. In 2006, construction workers added even more allure to the town when they unearthed a Roman burial site and adjacent theater, untouched over the past 2,000 years. Behind a stone door that still swings on two stone hinges were a wealth of gold jewelry, bronze votive offerings, and pottery. In the small theater, stone backrests are still perfectly in place on the four rows of seats. Excavations are ongoing, and the site is not yet open to the public.

A ruined Venetian castle overlooks **Assos,** another pretty fishing port, about 10km (6¼ miles) south of Fiskardo. **Myrtos,** about 3km (2 miles) south of Assos, stands out as one of the most beautiful beaches in Greece. Of the many beaches making that claim, this one is a bona fide top contender, with white sands that follow a turquoise inlet backed by white cliffs and forests. ⏱ 4 hr. with stops at Assos and Myrtos.

It is easy to continue to Ithaca from Kefalonia, though your timing will determine whether you take the ferry from Fiskardo to Frikes, or Sami to Pisaetos or Vathy. All these crossings are less than an hour. Any travel agent can provide current schedules and sell tickets.

6 ★★ **Ithaca.** The fabled home of Odysseus, where Penelope patiently awaited the hero's return for 20 years, will provide classicists with only faint evidence of any association with the greatest myth of all time. But rocky, mountainous, and cliff-edged Ithaca should quench anyone's thirst for an unspoiled Greek isle. Homerphiles who come in search of sites from the *Odyssey* needn't stray too far from **Vathy,** the attractive port and island capital. The **Cave of the Nymphs,** about 3km (2 miles) outside of Vathy and accessible by road, is where Odysseus hid gold and copper given to him by the Phaeacians, who delivered the hero to **Dexia Beach** below; you can peer into the colorfully lit cavern, then walk on the soft sands, now littered with supine sunbathers, where the hero was gently placed in deep sleep. The **Fountain of Arethusa,** where Odysseus, dressed as a beggar, went to meet his loyal swineherd, is a bit harder to reach; it's underwhelming once you make the 3km (2-mile) drive south on a marked road then follow a path for another 3km (2 miles).

> *The collapsed roof of Spili Melissani allows sunlight to pour onto underground waters.*

Travelers who wish to take in a bit of scenery should head north for about 16km (10 miles) from Vathy to **Moni Katheron,** a 17th-century monastery that commands sweeping views across the island. **Frikes,** a fishing village on the north about 5km (3 miles) beyond the monastery, surrounds a beautiful harbor, as does picturesque **Kioni,** 4km (2½ miles) southeast. ⏱ 1 day.

Where to Stay & Dine on Kefalonia

★★ **Captain's Table** ARGOSTOLI *SEAFOOD*
This old-fashioned favorite just around the corner from the main square, with an iced piscine display out front, is where islanders come for a fine meal. The cuisine and appealing decor certainly do not disappoint. A delicious fish soup is the house specialty, and some excellent meat dishes are on offer as well. Plateia Vallianou. ☎ 26710/23896. Entrees 6€–20€. MC, V. Dinner daily.

★ **Cephalonia Star** ARGOSTOLI, KEFALONIA
No one's going to rave about the simple, basic rooms, but the bay views and prime location more than compensate. Service is friendly, and

the premises are spotless. Metaxa (waterfront near Port Authority). ☎ 26710/23181. 43 units. Doubles 90€ w/breakfast. MC, V.

★★★ **Hotel Ionian Plaza** ARGOSTOLI, KEFALONIA The island's nicest hotel is in the center of the action on Plateia Vallianou, but the pedestrian-only surroundings ensure a measure of quiet. Terraces surround the ground-floor lounges, and the large guest rooms upstairs are bright and colorful—many overlook the town from balconies. Plateia Vallianou. ☎ 26710/25581. www.ionianplaza.gr. 43 units. Doubles 130€ w/breakfast. AE, MC, V.

Corfu Town

One of Greece's most attractive towns is an intoxicating and at times overwhelming blend of the cultures that have claimed Corfu as their own. A Venetian flavor, with a touch of southern Mediterranean ocher and pastels, wins out on the narrow lanes lined with tall, shuttered houses. Byzantine churches and French arcades add to the mix, made all the more salubrious by the English gardens and palaces next to shimmering Greek seas.

> *The British added a church to the Paleo Frourio (Old Fortress), fashioning the facade after a Doric temple.*

START The Spianada **TRIP LENGTH** Allow the better part of 2 days to appreciate the town and its many sights. If you have at least 3 days, intersperse your explorations of Corfu Town with excursions to other sights on the island.

❶ ★★★ The Spianada (Esplanade). An expanse of greenery at the eastern edge of the Old Town is one of Europe's largest squares and the stagelike setting for much of the island's social life. The Paleo Frourio is on the seaward flanks of the square, and Corfiots come and go amid many landmarks of the cosmopolitan mix of cultures that have left their mark on the island. Cricketers compete on the pitch adjacent to a monument honoring Sir Thomas Maitland, the first British governor of the island, who is more favorably remembered for his romantic liaison with a Portuguese-Celanese dancer than for his autocratic rule. The island's orchestra plays from an ornate pavilion on warm summer nights, within earshot of the Liston, a beautiful arcade modeled after the Rue de Rivoli in Paris and filled with the patrons of sophisticated cafes. The name derives from the word "list"—a sort of social registry of the island's elite residents, for whose pleasure the Liston was built. The writer Gerald Durrell, who was raised on Corfu, wrote that "you would sit beneath a little table under the arcades or

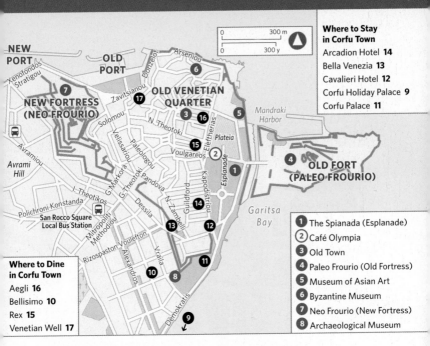

**Where to Stay
in Corfu Town**

Arcadion Hotel **14**
Bella Venezia **13**
Cavalieri Hotel **12**
Corfu Holiday Palace **9**
Corfu Palace **11**

NEW
PORT

OLD
PORT

Arseniou

Xenofondos
Stratigou

Dionziou

NEW FORTRESS
(NEO FROURIO)

Zavitsianou

Avramiou

Solomou

OLD VENETIAN
QUARTER

N. Theotoki

Mandraki
Harbor

Avrami
Hill

Velissariou
Paleologou

G. Markora
G. Theotoki

I. Theotikos

Pandova

Polichroni Konstanda

San Rocco Square
Local Bus Station

Mitropoliti
Methodiou

N. Zambeli

Dessila

Rizospaston Voulefton

Alexandros

Vraila

Demokratis

Eleftherias
Plateia

Voulgareos

Kapodistriou

Guilfordou

Esplanade

OLD FORT
(PALEO FROURIO)

Garitsa
Bay

**Where to Dine
in Corfu Town**

Aegli **16**
Bellisimo **10**
Rex **15**
Venetian Well **17**

① The Spianada (Esplanade)
② Café Olympia
③ Old Town
④ Paleo Frourio (Old Fortress)
⑤ Museum of Asian Art
⑥ Byzantine Museum
⑦ Neo Frourio (New Fortress)
⑧ Archaeological Museum

beneath the shimmering trees and, sooner or later, you would see everyone on the island and hear every facet of every scandal." We visitors might miss some of the social nuances unfolding around us, but it's easy to imagine that for Corfiots the observation still holds true. ① 1 hr.

② 🍽 **Café Olympia.** These tables are some of the most pleasant spots under the Liston arcades for a coffee, cocktail, or snack, served well into the wee hours. Liston. ☎ 26610/39097. Daily 9am–2am. $.

③ ★★★ **Old Town.** Old Corfu, one of Greece's most attractive and appealing island capitals, is wedged onto the end of a squat peninsula, between the old port and the sea to the north, the Neo Frourio to the west, and the Paleo Frourio to the east. Narrow lanes, *kantounia*, and stepped streets twist and turn past Venetian loggias, Greek churches, British palaces, and French arcades, rising and falling through the medieval Campiello, Jewish ghetto, and other old districts. This mazelike terrain is well suited to an aimless stroll; when looking for

SITE GUIDE PAGE 621

an address or a landmark in the Old Town, be prepared to ask your way several times; when you become disoriented, look for the campanile of **Agios Spyridon,** the tallest structure in town. ① 4 hr.

> *Town Hall served as an opera house for 200 years.*

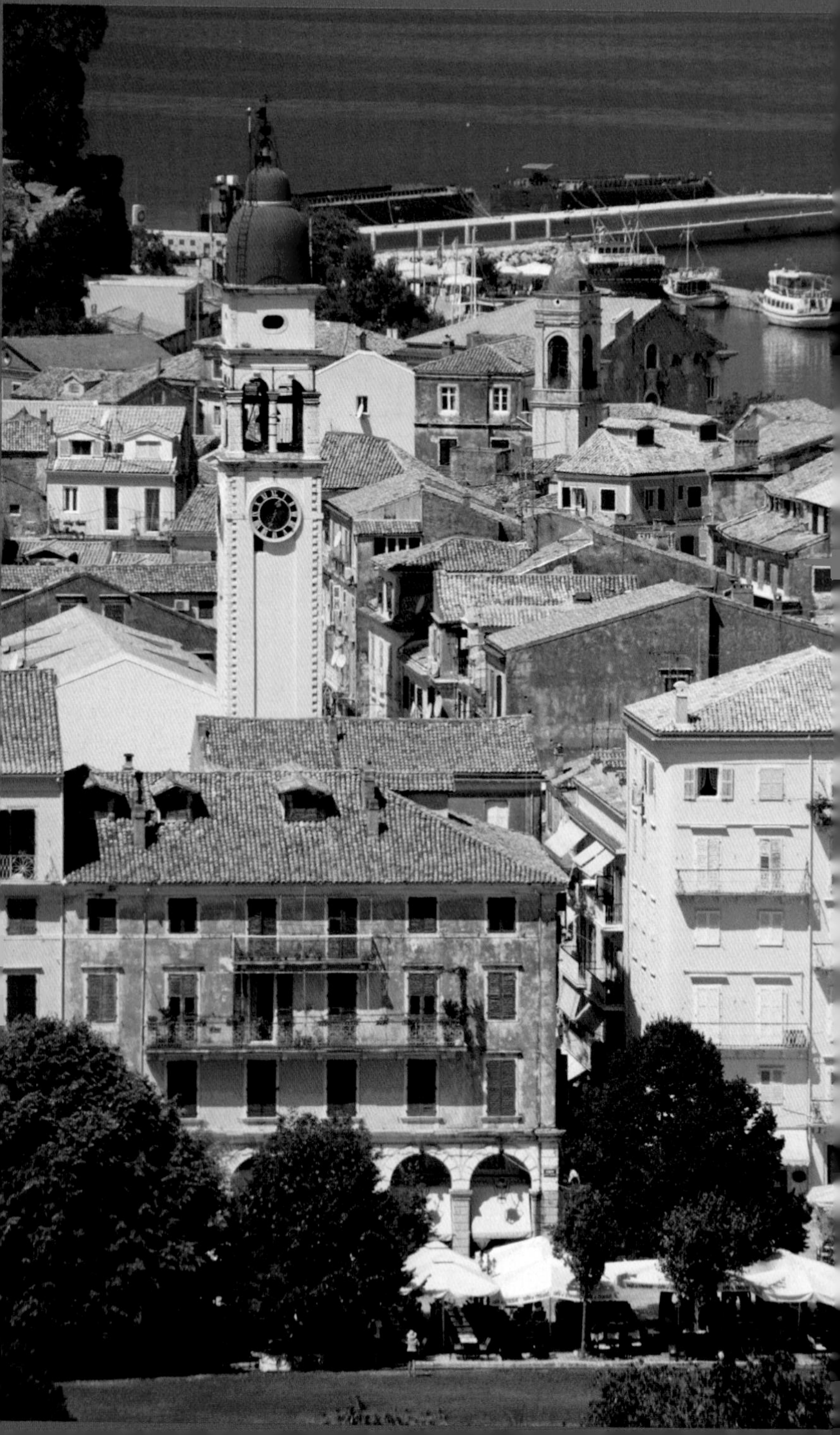

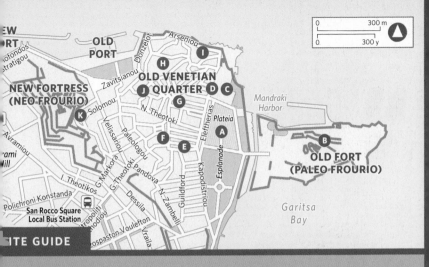

3 Old Town

Begin on the south end of the Ⓐ **Spianada** (Esplanade), beneath a statue of Ioannis Kapodistrias, a Corfiot who became the first president of a united Greece in 1829 and was shot and stabbed to death by political opponents 2 years later. The enticing expanse of greenery is usually populated with children playing ball and young couples escaping watchful eyes. The Ⓑ **Paleo Frourio** (Old Fortress) looms to the east (p. 622, ❹) and the Ⓒ **Palace of St. Michael and St. George** are visible to the south (p. 622, ❺); return to explore these fascinating landmarks later, but now cross the Spianada to the arcaded Ⓓ **Liston,** built during the brief French occupation after Napoleon was granted the island in 1807 and reminiscent of the Rue de Rivoli in Paris, on which it is modeled. Even if you're not ready for a coffee, a walk along the line of cafes is pleasantly sociable and brings you to the Catholic Ⓔ **Cathedral of Agios Iakavos,** best known as San Giacomo, built in 1588 to serve the Venetian and French inhabitants of the island. Across Dimarchiou Square is the Ⓕ **Town Hall,** which was Corfu's opera house for almost 200 years and, before that, a Venetian loggia. In addition to the Italian repertoire, many Greek works were performed here for the first time. Follow Nikiforio Theotaki, the town's stylish main avenue, to the Ⓖ **Cathedral of Agios Spyridon;** the tallest church on the island, with a domed bell tower, is dedicated to Corfu's patron saint, a 4th-century Cypriot who performed several miracles in service to Corfu—not the least of which was saving his church from destruction when a Nazi bomb fell on it in 1944. The saint is entombed in a silver casket that is paraded through the streets four times a year. Just beyond are the winding lanes of the Ⓗ **Campiello,** the medieval quarter. It's best to leave any sense of purpose behind and simply wander through the narrow lanes, darkened by the balconies of tall Venetian houses and lined with small shops. Some landmarks to seek out are the Ⓘ **Byzantine Museum** (p. 623, ❻), near the waterfront in the Church of the Panayia Andivoumniotissa, and the Ⓙ **Mitropolis,** the Greek Orthodox cathedral, near the Old Port. Just beyond is the Ⓚ **Jewish Quarter,** a once-thriving community that was decimated in June 1944, when Germans rounded up some 2,000 Jewish residents and shipped them to Auschwitz, where most perished; only 200 escaped imprisonment and were hidden by non-Jewish Corfiots. A 300-year-old synagogue (Sat 9am–6pm; at other times call the Jewish Community Center for special entry, ☎ 26610/38802) has been restored and houses a collection of torah crowns.

> *The domed bell tower of the Cathedral of Agios Spyridon will help you navigate the maze of Old Town.*

④ ★★ Paleo Frourio (Old Fortress). Corfu was defended by two fortresses, the old and the new, though the Old Fortress predates the New Fortress by only a century; it was begun by the Byzantines on a hilly seaside promontory in the 12th century. Corfu Town was once entirely confined within the walls of the Paleo Frourio, beneath two castles crowning twin peaks. Venetians dug the moat that separates the fortress from the Spianada and thwarted several Turkish onslaughts. The British tore down most of the other Byzantine and Venetian remnants and erected, facing the sea at the base of one of the summits, an Anglican church in the style of a Greek temple, fronted by six Doric columns. Views from the heights sweep across the town and sea to the forested coast of Albania. A statue on the Spianada next to the entrance to the fortress commemorates Count Schulenburg, the hero of the siege of 1716, an Austrian general who went into service for the Venetians. With a force of 5,000 Venetians and 3,000 Corfiots, the count repelled a 22-day-long siege by 33,000 Turkish forces. The thick, unassailable walls of the Paleo Frourio were no doubt a factor in the successful outcome, as was an alleged appearance of a ghostlike St. Spyridon brandishing a torch and a cross (p. 606). ⏱1 hr. East side of Spianada. Admission 4€. Tues–Fri 8am–8pm, Sat–Sun 8:30am–3pm.

⑤ ★★ Museum of Asian Art. The Palace of St. Michael and St. George was built for the British Lord High Commissioner in 1819 and, when British rule ended with the unification of the Ionian Islands with Greece in 1864, became a residence of the Greek Royal family. Staterooms now house one of Europe's finest collections of Asian art, an unexpected delight to come upon in Corfu. Samurai swords, Noh masks, and Chinese porcelains were amassed by Corfiot diplomats and merchants in the late 19th and 20th centuries. Exotic trees bloom in the palace gardens that overlook the bay and the sea lanes into the harbor, and a cafe shows works by contemporary artists. The royal family, whose members included England's Prince Philip, used to slip down the iron staircase at the end of the garden to take a dip in the waters below. ⏱2 hr. North end of Esplanade. ☎ 26610/30443. Admission 3€. Tues–Sun 8:30am–3pm.

> The grounds of the Mon Repos are littered with ancient temple ruins.

> Icons painted on Corfu, on display in the Byzantine Museum, show the distinctive influence of the Italian Renaissance.

6 ★ **Byzantine Museum.** Corfu sustained a long tradition of icon painting and, with Crete (another Venetian posession), was one of Greece's major centers for the art form. Of note, amid the many Corfiot pieces on display on an upper floor of the Church of the Panagia Andivoumniotissa, is the distinct influence of Western artistic traditions on highly stylized Byzantine forms. No doubt due to the island's close ties with Venice and proximity to the West, shades of the Renaissance creep into the naturalistic depictions of the various saints and sinners, often set against distinctly Italian-looking backgrounds. A wonderful swath of mosaic flooring is from an early Christian church in the ancient city of Paleopolis, the ruins of which litter the grounds of Mon Repos, south of town (p. 626, **1**). ⏲ 1 hr. Church of the Panagia Andivoumniotissa. Arseniou Mourayio. ☎ 26610/38313. Admission 2€. Tues–Sun 8:30am–3pm.

7 ★★ **Neo Frourio (New Fortress).** New is a relative term for this massive fortification the Venetians erected when they took control of the island in the 13th century. These days the high walls, adorned here and there with the Venetian winged lion of St. Mark, still serve as a barrier, dividing the modern city and new port to the south and west from the narrow lanes of the old town. Stalls of the fish market fill the former moat. Within the walls are a maze of medieval tunnels and battlements that you can explore on excellent guided tours, included in the admission price. ⏲ 1 hr. West side of Old Town, next to harbor. Admission 4€. May–Oct daily 9am–9pm.

8 ★★ **Archaeological Museum.** Medusa, the Gorgon with hair of venomous snakes and a stare that could turn anyone who beheld her to stone, is the star of this collection from a Temple of Artemis that once stood nearby on the grounds of **Mon Repos** (p. 626, **1**). The Medusa relief, from about 590 B.C., adorned the temple pediment and is the finest example of archaic Greek art to survive the millennia. Artisans took a bit of liberty with mythical storytelling. Legend has it that Medusa gave birth to her sons Pegasus and Chrysaor the moment Perseus beheaded her, but she is shown here with both her head and her offspring. You'll want to compare this touchingly naive rendering with the reliefs you see from the Parthenon in Athens or the Temple of Zeus in Olympia—those only slightly later works are much more refined and sophisticated. A magnificent marble lion that now crouches near the Medusa Gorgon is from the Tomb of Menekrates, where a 7th-century-B.C. Corinthian colonizer of the island was interred (the tomb is in a necropolis just south of the museum, off the beautiful seaside promenade). ⏲ 1 hr. 1 Vraila. ☎ 26610/30680. Admission 3€. Tues–Sun 8:30am–3pm.

Where to Stay in Corfu Town

> *A year-round pool is one of the amenities at the lovely Corfu Palace, the island's first resort-style hotel.*

★★ Arcadion Hotel CORFU TOWN
An old-world hostelry near the center of town is filled with Corfiot charm—wrought-iron bedsteads, bright fabrics, and views over the Spianada and the sea from many of the rooms and the roof garden. Amenities include a health club. 21 Kapodistriou. ☎ 26610/37670. www.arcadionhotel.com. 33 units. Doubles 95€ w/breakfast. AE, MC, V.

★★ Bella Venezia CORFU TOWN
You may well feel you've been whisked across the Adriatic to Italy in this pleasant Venetian mansion, full of polished wood and brass and set in a pretty garden. Rooms are handsomely done in a contemporary classic style, and amenities include a welcoming bar. 4 Zambelli. ☎ 26610/20707. www.bellaveneziahotel.com. 30 units. Doubles 110€–140€ w/breakfast. AE, DC, MC, V.

★★ Cavalieri Hotel CORFU TOWN
The location could not be better—on the Spianada, overlooking the Old Fortress and, from rooms on the higher floors, the sea. You can also take in the views from the roof garden. The velvet-walled lobby and lounges are decidedly old-world, though rooms are done in bright traditional style. 4 Kapodistriou. ☎ 26610/39041. www.cavalieri-hotel.com. 50 units. Doubles 110€–140€ w/breakfast. AE, DC, MC, V.

★ Corfu Holiday Palace SOUTH OF CORFU TOWN
This former Hilton, one of several big resort complexes on the island, has the advantages of the stunning Kanoni views along with the proximity of Corfu Town. Rooms are comfortable though fairly standard, and those overlooking the airport are definitely to be avoided; villas and suites are more lavish. The gardens and pools are lovely, and the hotel is home to Corfu's only casino. A shuttle bus makes the run to and from town. Nausicas, Kanoni, 5km (3 miles) south of Corfu Town. ☎ 26610/36540. www.corfuholidaypalace.gr. 256 units. Doubles 110€–220€ w/breakfast. AE, DC, MC, V.

★★ Corfu Palace EDGE OF CORFU TOWN
The island's one-time glamour spot is a bit faded, but it hasn't lost its edge. Rooms are comfortable with balconies that face the sea, though some units are in need of refurbishment. Luxuriant gardens, indoor/outdoor pools, and excellent service provide a relaxed resort experience, though Old Town is just a short walk away. Leoforos Demokratis. ☎ 26610/39485. www.corfupalace.com. 115 units. Doubles 175€–300€ w/breakfast. AE, DC, MC, V.

Where to Dine in Corfu Town

Aegli CORFU TOWN *GREEK*
The Liston arcades are the perfect setting for this elegant old-timer, where bacala (salted codfish) and other Corfiot specialties are on offer. Snacks and drinks are served on the terrace throughout the day—the fruit salad is an island favorite. 23 Kapodistriou. ☎ 26610/39949. Entrees 10€–20€. AE, DC, MC, V. Lunch & dinner daily.

Bellisimo CORFU TOWN *GREEK/INTERNATIONAL* The menu is traditionally Greek, with a few concessions, including excellent hamburgers, to the Stergiou family's longtime residency in Canada. The Greek meze plate, loaded with keftedes and other favorites, is a meal in itself. Plateia Lemonia. ☎ 26610/41112. Entrees 5€–15€. No credit cards. Lunch & dinner daily.

Rex CORFU TOWN *GREEK*
An island institution, serving in a townhouse just off the Spianada for more than a century, sticks to the moussaka-and-pastitsada basics, but it does them very well. The terrace is an excellent spot for coffee or a drink and people-watching at its best. 66 Kapodistriou. ☎ 26610/39649. Entrees 10€–20€. AE, V. Lunch & dinner daily.

Venetian Well CORFU TOWN *GREEK/INTERNATIONAL* You'll have to ask your way a couple of times before finding this charming square in

> *A coffee on the Liston is a ritual for many Corfiots.*

the depths of Old Town, but your efforts will be rewarded with a romantic setting either on the square ringed by tall old houses or in the candlelit dining room. Deft and creative pastas and other dishes are based on market-fresh ingredients. Plateia Kremasti. ☎ 26610/44761. Entrees 10€–25€. MC, V. Lunch & dinner daily.

Seafood Village

A west-coast hamlet strung out along a white pebble beach backed by cypress trees, Agni is blessed with three seafood restaurants. Corfiots have their particular favorites, but all are excellent and serve freshly caught fish. You may well want to come back a few times to try all three: Taverna Nicholas (☎ 26630/91243), Toula's (☎ 26630/91350), and Taverna Agni (☎ 26630/91142). All are open May through October and serve lunch and dinner daily. Agni is about 15km (9⅓ miles) north of Corfu Town.

Corfu at Night

To sample the island's nightlife you don't need to venture farther than the Spianada. Cafes under the Liston arches serve well into the early morning, and many of the island's clubs are at the north end of the square. On summer evenings, bands and orchestras often perform in the pavilion in the center of the square.

Around Corfu

It only stands to reason that an island with a capital as captivating as Corfu Town should be remarkable in its own right. And Corfu is remarkable, with cliff-backed sandy shores and the mountainsides carpeted with forests and silvery olive groves that have inspired the myths of Homer, the theater of Shakespeare (Prospero and Miranda are exiled here in *The Tempest*), and more than a few postcards.

> *The beautifully wooded grounds of Mon Repos descend to a little beach where royals used to swim.*

START Mon Repos, just 2km (1¼ miles) south of Corfu Town. **TRIP LENGTH** About 1½ days; visits to sights around the island can be nicely interspersed with time in Corfu Town over the course of at least 3 days.

From Corfu Town, it is an easy and pleasant walk of about 2km (1¼ miles) to Mon Repos, along the waterfront south of the Old Town.

1 ★★★ **Mon Repos.** This neoclassical villa, set amid English-style gardens next to the sea, was once the summer residence of the British lord high commissioners. Like the Palace of St. Michael and St. George in Corfu Town, Mon Repos went to the Greek royal family when

Corfu was unified with Greece in 1864. Prince Philip, Duke of Edinburgh and husband of England's Queen Elisabeth II, was born at Mon Repos in 1921, though he and his family were exiled from Greece soon thereafter in the aftermath of the Greco-Turkish war. The Greek government took over the estate in the early 1990s, and several of the staterooms have been restored to show off artifacts from Paleopolis, the ancient city of Corfu that appears in scattered ruin on the grounds of the estate. A walk across the wooded grounds leads to temples to Hera and Poseidon from the 7th and 6th centuries B.C., and nearby are Roman baths, an early Christian chapel from the 5th

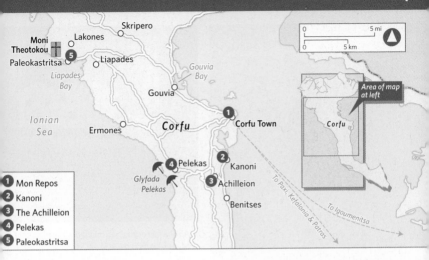

1 Mon Repos
2 Kanoni
3 The Achilleion
4 Pelekas
5 Paleokastritsa

entury, and a Byzantine church. A lovely little each below the temple ruins is popular with Corfiots wishing to get away from the more crowded strands closer to town. ⏱ **2 hr.** Seaside, 2km (1¼ miles) south of Corfu Town. ☎ 26610/41369. Admission 3€, no admission fee or gardens and ruins. Tues–Sun 8:30am–7pm.

The classic Kanoni viewpoint is a hillside terrace, crowded with souvenir stands and onlookers, about 3km (2 miles) south of Corfu Town and very well marked on the road eading south.

2 ★ **Kanoni.** The view from the verdant hillsides of Kanoni, a residential enclave just south of Corfu Town, was once among the requisite stops on the Grand Tour. The sweep of sparkling sea and verdant coastline, from a hillside where the French installed cannons (kanoni) to keep the Russians at a distance, is captured on millions of postcards and takes in two islets floating in the bay. On **Vlaherna**, a lone cypress sways above the white-washed convent. **Pontikonisi,** or **Mouse Island,** is so picturesque, with its chapel set amid a grove

▸ The Monastery of Theotokou now houses a famous icon of the Virgin.

> *After a few ouzos, you might buy the myth that Mouse Island is the ship of Odysseus, turned to stone.*

of pines, that you want to believe the legend that the island is really the ship on which Odysseus sailed home to Ithaca, turned to stone by Poseidon in revenge for the death of his son, Polyphemus. You can walk out to Vlaherna on a causeway and take a boat (3€, all day) to Pontikonisi, as thousands of Corfiots do on August 6 to celebrate the feast of the Transfiguration. We advise you to save yourself the trouble, as the outlook from the shoreline is much more magical than the views toward the overbuilt coast and airport from the island. ⏱1 hr.

> *Columns from the Temple of Artemis still stand at Mon Repos.*

Hitting the Corfu Trail

Hikers can traverse the entire island on the Corfu Trail, 220km (137 miles) in length, from Cape Asprokovas in the south to Cape Agias Ekaterinis in the north. The trail crosses the island's most scenic landscapes, including the **west coast, Ropa Valley,** and **Mount Pantokrator,** Corfu's highest summit. Some of the most magical scenery is around the base of the mountain, where centuries-old olive groves have been allowed to go wild, creating primordial-looking forests mixed with oak and chestnut. There's no need to bring camping gear, because you can find rooms and tavernas along the way. For information on walking packages, check out **www.travelling.gr/ corfutrail.** For maps and itineraries, get a copy of *The Companion Guide to the Corfu Trail,* by Hilary Whitton Paipeti; order online at www.corfutrailguide.com.

You will find watersports concessions at just about any beach on the island. The **Achilleion Diving Center,** in Paleokastritsa and Ermones, offers dives and instruction (☎ 6932/729011; www.diving-corfu.com). **Next Holidays** arranges parasailing, windsurfing, snorkeling, water-skiing, and other watersports around the island (☎ 6945/ 265048; www.corfunext.com). **The Corfu Golf Club** course is one of the best in Greece and ranges across beautiful terrain in the Ropa Valley (fees are 55€ for 18 holes, much less with many special offers available; ☎ 26610/94220).

Kaiser Wilhelm found the Achilleion's excesses so appealing that he bought the palace in 1907.

he Achilleion is outside Gastouri, 8km (5 niles) south of Corfu Town; from Kanoni, acktrack 2km (1¼ miles) to the outskirts and ollow the well-marked road to Gastouri and he Achilleion.

❸ ★ The Achilleion. Few palaces are more eautifully situated—on a verdant, flowery illside above the sea—or linked with a more omantic figure, Elisabeth of Bavaria (aka isi), empress of the Austro-Hungarian em-ire. That said, in few other places will you ncounter such exuberant excess or better roof that money alone cannot buy taste. Sisi ailed around the Mediterranean on the royal acht almost constantly to escape court life Vienna. She built the palace after the death f her only son, Crown Prince Rudolf, and his istress, in a famous murder-suicide known the Mayerling Affair. The estate is filled the seudoclassical staterooms and gardens with tatues and frescoes of the gods and god-esses. Sisi showed a distinct preference for chilles, whose tragic death in the Trojan War an early age she associated with her son's; e god is depicted riding a chariot across a esco on the ceiling of the entrance hall and in everal statues, one of which towers 5m (16½

ft.). The Emperor Kaiser Wilhelm of Germany bought the palace in 1907, soon after Sisi was stabbed to death by a terrorist in Geneva. The Kaiser left many imperial imprints on the pal-ace, including a stone walkway and overpass to the beach below the gardens, known as the Kaiser's Bridge (designed so his highness would not have to come into contact with ordi-nary Corfiots), and an inscription on the base of one of the Achilles statues, TO THE GREATEST GREEK FROM THE GREATEST GERMAN. When the ostentation gets to be overwhelming, turn your back on the statuary to take in the spec-tacular sea views. ⏱ 1 hr. Gastouri. ☎ 26610/ 56245. Admission 6€. Apr–Oct daily 8am–7pm, Nov–Mar daily 8:30am–3:30pm.

From Gastouri, follow a network of well-marked roads northwest across the narrow neck of the island for about 7km (4⅓ miles) to Pelekas.

❹ ★★★ Pelekas. Hilltop Pelekas is best known for its views over the island interior and up and down the coast, where sumptuous folds of forested mountains drop into the sea. The most noted viewpoint is Kaiser's Throne, a rocky summit outside of town where Kaiser Wilhelm used to ride to enjoy the vistas. Just

> *Paleokastritsa and other west coast beaches fringe bays beneath tall cliffs.*

The coast near Pelekas is lined with some of Corfu's most beautiful beaches. Pelekas Beach, below town, is a long stretch of sand backed by cliffs and, more noticeably, an enormous resort complex. The popular resort of Ermones is just to the north of Pelekas, and two beautiful sandy beaches stretch between the two: very popular Glifida, and best of all, Myrtiotissa, described by the British writer Lawrence Durrell as "perhaps the loveliest beach in the world." ⏱ **Half-day.**

Paleokastritsa is 15km (9⅓ miles) north of Pelekas.

⑤ ★★★ Paleokastritsa. The ancient city of Scheria allegedly stood on these shores, and it's claimed that shipwrecked Odysseus washed onto the beach on a raft and was found by Nausicca, who escorted him to the palace of her father, Alkinoos, king of the Phaeacians. Alkinoos welcomed Odysseus into his palace, with its walls of bronze and gates of gold, and dispatched ships that were steered by thought alone to take the wanderer home to Ithaca. No physical evidence has ever emerged to place the roots of such a story here on the west coast of Corfu. But by virtue of beauty alone, this string of sparkling coves backed by cliffs and forests certainly seems like a setting where a myth like this could unfold. In some places, civilization encroaches rather unattractively on the spectacular scenery, but the farther you walk from the village, the more appealing the beaches are. Theotokou, a monastery atop a seaside bluff, is a tranquil retreat, with spectacular sea views and a shady courtyard filled with cats and exotic plantings. A small museum houses a 12th-century icon of the Virgin (daily 8am–1pm and 3–8pm; free admission). Two villages, Lakones and Krini, overlook Paleokastritsa from the heights of an adjacent mountainside. The views are even more spectacular from Angelokastro, a ruined medieval castle 300m (984 ft.) above the sea. You can reach the castle, about 5km (3 miles) north of Paleokastritsa, on a steep, cliff-hugging road that ascends through Lakones and Krini to a short path that crosses the top of the cliffs to the castle ruins. ⏱ **Half-day.**

From Paleokastritsa, return to Corfu Town on a well-marked route that crosses the island and then drops down the east coast (25km/1⑥ miles).

below the summit stretches the Ropa Valley, Corfu's agricultural heartland, a patchwork of fertile fields, vineyards, olive groves, and orchards. The island is famous in Greece for its wine and oil, as well as kumquats, introduced by the British and made into a sweet, orange-colored liqueur, candies, jams, and other tasty comestibles. Not so bucolic is nearby Aqualand Water Park, on the plains below the town, with slides, tunnels, and pools that are immensely popular with young travelers (Ethniki, Pelekas; ☎ 26610/58583; www.aqualand-corfu.com; admission 23€; May–June and Sept–Oct daily 10am–6pm, July–Aug daily 10am–7pm).

Where to Stay & Dine Around Corfu

★★★ Casa Lucia CENTRAL ISLAND
Corfu Town and the east- and west-coast beaches are within an easy drive of this charming compound of cozy bungalows and small villas set amid rolling olive groves in the center of the island. But you may not want to venture away from the lush gardens and pretty pool; each unit has a nice terrace and kitchen, and many are well-suited to families who want to settle in for a while. Corfu-Paleokastritsa road, 13km (8 miles) northwest of Corfu town. ☎ 26610/1419. www.casa-lucia-corfu.com. 9 units. Doubles 70€–95€. AE, DC, MC, V. Closed Nov–Mar.

★ Etrusco KATO KORAKIANA *GREEK/ITALIAN*
Corfiots travel from all over to enjoy some of the island's best cuisine, served on a terrace and in a handsome dining room in a small village near the east coast. Delicious homemade pastas make use of local fish and seafood, and tasty lamb and other dishes are prepared to traditional recipes. Kato Korakiana, about 15km (9⅓ miles) north of Corfu Town. ☎ 26610/3342. Set menu 40€. MC, V. Dinner daily. Closed Nov–Apr.

★ Kontokali Bay Resort & Spa NORTH OF CORFU TOWN   This big resort north of Corfu Town is a standout for its beautiful seaside gardens and attractive, large rooms. The most pleasant are the bungalows tucked among the pines and cedars. Two swimming pools, a beautiful beach, an enormous spa complex, and a variety of restaurants are among the many amenities. Kontalaki Bay, 6km (3¾ miles) north of Corfu Town. ☎ 26610/90500. www.kontokalibay.com. 250 units. Doubles 170€–260€ w/breakfast. AE, DC, MC, V.

★ Levant Hotel PELEKAS
An airy perch on a mountaintop next to Kaiser's Throne ensures magnificent views up and down the coast. Rooms are simply and pleasantly traditional in their decor. A swimming pool is surrounded by the large and luxuriant gardens, and the terrace of the

> At Casa Lucia, attractive bungalows and small villas surround a beautiful garden.

bar-lounge is a delightful spot to enjoy the sunset. Pelekas. ☎ 26610/94230. 26 units. Doubles 70€–95€ w/breakfast. MC, V.

★ Taverna Limeri KATO KORAKIANA *GREEK*
At this informal village taverna, make a meal of the meze, made fresh that day. Offerings often include a surprise or two, such as pork in cranberry sauce or homemade lamb sausages. Salads, from fresh village produce, are excellent, too. Kato Korakiana, about 15km (9⅓ miles) north of Corfu Town. ☎ 26610/97576. Entrees 8€–18€. MC, V. Dinner daily.

Accommodations Tip

Corfu Holidays (☎ 69744/16629; www.corfutoday.com) arranges hotels, villas, and apartments all over the island.

Corfu & the Ionian Islands Fast Facts

> *The crime rate is low in Corfu, but police are on hand to help with directions.*

Arriving

BY AIR The easiest way to get to Corfu from Athens is by air, via twice-daily flights on **Olympic Airlines** (☎ 801/114-4444) or **Aegean** (☎ 801/112-0000 within Greece). Flights take a little more than an hour. EasyJet and other companies fly directly to Corfu from London, Manchester, and many other European cities. The Corfu airport is just 3km (2 miles) southeast of Corfu Town. You can

also fly to Corfu from Patras on **AirSea Lines,** with limited schedules (☎ 801/118-0060; www.airsealines.com). You can fly directly to Kefalonia on several daily Olympic Airlines flights. **BY SEA** In the absence of ferry service from Piraeus to Corfu, it is difficult to reach the island by sea from Athens. Options are to drive or take the bus to Igoumenitsou on the mainland and make the short (1-hr.) crossing from there (the bus trip from Athens takes bout 6 hr.) or take the train or bus to Patras nd a ferry from there (usually overnight, bout 8 hr.). A hydrofoil operates between goumenitsou and Corfu in high season, cutng the trip to about half an hour. For detailed chedules for crossings within Greece, go to /ww.gtp.gr. A daily ferry sails between Patras nd Kefalonia (about 2 hr.).

You can also reach Corfu from several ports 1 Italy, including Ancona, Brindisi, and Venice. chedules vary, with severely curtailed service utside of high season; the crossing from Brinisi and Bari takes about 10 hours, longer to nd from other ports. For information on inernational ferries, visit www.ferries.gr. Boats ock at Corfu's New Port, just north of the Jld Town and within walking distance of most Corfu Town hotels and businesses.

Dentists & Doctors

Most hotels will be able to refer you to a local octor or dentist who speaks English. Corfu own has a good-sized hospital, **Julius Andritti** (☎ 26610/882239).

Emergencies

See p. 680, Fast Facts Greece.

Getting Around

BY CAR You can get to major towns and resorts n the island's decent bus network, but you'll robably want to rent a car to tour Corfu, to ee the more remote parts of the island. Exect to pay about 30€ to 40€ a day, even in he busy August tourist season. Car rental is a ig business on Corfu, and you will find agenies in every town of any size. **Corfu Holidays** ☎ 69744/16629; www.corfutoday.com) is ne of many tour operators and travel agenies that will arrange car rental in advance. **BY BOAT** You can reach Kefalonia from Corfu

via direct boat service; the trip takes about 6 hours but runs only a few times a week, even in high season, and often less frequently. An alternative is to travel to Patras and take the more-frequent several-times-daily boats from there. **BY AIR AirSea Lines** (☎ 801/118-0060; www.airsealines.com) flies from Corfu to Kefalonia, with limited schedules, and to Patras.

Internet Access

See p. 681, Fast Facts Greece.

Pharmacies

See p. 682, Fast Facts Greece.

Police

The main police station in Corfu Town is near the post office in the New Town at 19 Leoforos Alexandros (☎ 26610/39575). Also see p. 682, Fast Facts Greece.

Post Office

The main post office in Corfu Town is at 26 Leoforos Alexandros in the New Town (☎ 26610/25544; Mon–Fri 7:30am–8pm). Stamps (*grammatossima*) can be purchased at most newsstands.

Safety

Corfu is by and large safe, with very little crime, especially against tourists.

Visitor Information

The **Ionian Islands Tourism Directorate,** at Rizospaston and Polila, New Town, Corfu (☎ 26610/37520; Mon–Fri 8:30am–1pm, sometimes later and on weekends in summer), is well stocked with maps and brochures. On Kefalonia, you'll find the tourist information office in Argostoli, near the Port Authority on Metaxa (☎ 26710/22248; summer daily 7:30am–2:30pm and 5–10pm, winter Mon–Fri 8am–3pm).

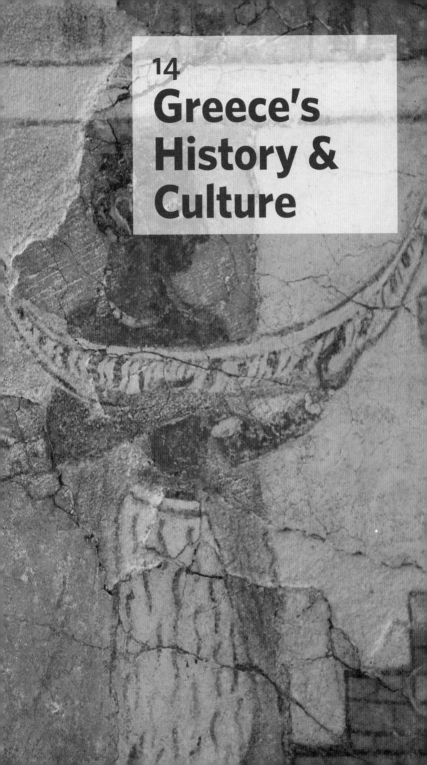

Greece: A Brief History

> PREVIOUS PAGE *A Minoan fresco at the Archaeological Museum in Iraklion, Crete.* THIS PAGE *Sculptures by Phidias adorn the frieze of the Parthenon.*

Ancient History

The history of Greece and its willful people is longer and more absorbing than a cursory look can convey. The earliest continuously occupied site was discovered at the **Franchthi Cave** in southeast Argolid, Peloponnese; evidence suggests the site was inhabited from 20,000 B.C. until 3,000 B.C.

Evidence of simple pastoral and agricultural settlements and mountain tribes have also been found elsewhere on the mainland, including **Dimini,** near Volos in Thessaly, which dates from the Late Neolithic period, 4800–4500 B.C.

The Ancient Greeks existed all around the Mediterranean and Black Sea coasts, but the oldest and most important civilization in Europe is considered to be that of the **Minoan** people (3000–1400 B.C.) of Crete. This Bronze Age culture worshiped an earth goddess and traded around the Mediterranean, selling timber, building ships, and possibly sailing through France to reach England for its metal. They were the regional strongmen in seafaring and trade, with bases on islands such as Cyprus and Thira (Santorini). Thira's volcano erupted around 1627 B.C., perhaps triggering a tsunami that contributed to the civilization's decline. Outstanding displays of Minoan culture can be viewed at the palace of **Knossos** near Iraklion, Crete, with its famous frescoes; the **Heraklion Archaeological Museum** (www.culture.gr), with its outstanding Minoan collection; and the Naval Museum (www.marmuseum.tuc. gr) at the Old Harbor in Hania, Crete, with its reconstruction of a circa-1500 B.C. boat, the *Minoa.*

The next major civilization was the **Mycenaean** (1600–1100 B.C.), on the southern mainland, known to us through archaeological finds but also through stories such as Homer's *Iliad,* which tells of kingdoms at Knossos (King Minos, for whom the ivilization is named), Mycenae (King Agamemnon), ·parta (King Menelaus), the varrior Achilles, and the siege •f King Priam's Troy (Ilium). Around 900 B.C., the Greek alphabet replaced Linear A, he ancient Minoan script, and Linear B, created by the Mycenaeans. During this ime, the pantheon of gods eplaced the earth goddess.

Greece emerged from its **Dark Ages** (ca. 1100–750 ›.c.) of Dorian invasions, and Greek civilization began o center on city-states in maritime regions including southern Italy, Egypt, and Asia Minor/Anatolia, now modern-day Turkey. It made advances in the arts, sciences, philosophy, and politics, and much knowledge of the world stems from his time. Five of the seven Ancient Wonders were built during the **Classical era** (ca. 500–300 B.C.): the **statue of Zeus** in Olympia (destroyed); he **Colossus of Rhodes** destroyed); the **Mausoleum at Halicarnassus,** now Bodrum, Turkey (dismantled, some bas reliefs in the U.K.); he **Temple of Artemis** at Ephesus (destroyed); and the onetime tallest building, the **Lighthouse in Alexandria** destroyed).

With trade came wars, and here were many between the city-states. People fled and founded colonies elsewhere, including in Marseille (Massalia, by the Ionian Phocaeans n 600 B.C.) and Emporion

(Empuries) in Spain in 575 B.C., now in ruins.

The Spartans were known for their austere and militaristic form of governance, while Athens took a different course with democracy. These city-states fought each other in the **Peloponnesian War** (431–404 B.C.), but soon thereafter they united against the massive invading force of the Persians. First the Greeks won, at the **Battle of Marathon** in 490 B.C. Ten years later, at **Thermopylae,** the Persians won against a small army led by King Leonidas of Sparta. Finally the Athenians defeated the Persians in 480 B.C. at the **Battle of Salamis,** led by Themistocles, who fought and won the battle decisively at sea.

Later, under the rule of the **Macedonians,** led first by Philip II of Pella and then by Alexander the Great from 338 B.C., inroads were made as far east as India.

Following the Roman conquest in the 2nd century B.C., more Greeks moved to new towns around the Mediterranean coast founded by Alexander and run by generals after his death in 323 B.C. The last leader of the Hellenic empire, Cleopatra of the Ptolemies, ruled in Alexandria, Egypt, until she and Marc Anthony were defeated by Rome's Octavian in 30 B.C. They both committed suicide.

With the advent of Christianity, the Eastern Orthodox Church centered

on **Byzantium,** or **Constantinople,** the main city of the Eastern Roman Empire, from A.D. 330. Byzantium was the center of the early church and held many treasures and artifacts of Christianity until the city was ransacked by crusaders en route to Jerusalem in 1204. After more than 1,000 years, Constantinople finally fell on Black Tuesday, May 29, 1453, to the Ottoman Turks. This occurrence remains a defining moment. Greeks still refer to Istanbul, the core of their religious world, as The City. Steven Runciman's account of the siege in *The Fall of Constantinople* is a riveting read.

The rest of Greece fell to the **Ottomans** from 1456 to 1821, after more than three centuries of rule by Venetians, Franks, and Catalans. Under the Ottomans, many Greeks left for western Europe and brought ancient Greek texts with them, influencing the Renaissance. Those who remained became a subject people, and the phrase "under the Turkish yolk for 400 years" became a common refrain—and excuse.

Modern History
Greece's modern era follows its **War of Independence,** which began in 1821, when the bishop at the Monastery of Agia Lavra, Peloponnese, raised the flag of revolt and called for freedom or death. The ideals of Greece had captured the imagination of

> *The Changing of the Guard at the Tomb of the Unknown Soldier in front of Parliament is an hourly celebration of Greek Independence.*

the Romantics in western Europe, some of whom traveled to the exotic Levant, which Greece was considered part of at the time, to take up the fight. Among them was Lord George Gordon Byron (1788–1824).

In 1827, Britain, France, and Russia crushed the Ottoman and Egyptian naval forces at the **Battle of Navarino** in the Peloponnese. Greece was finally granted autonomy by its guarantors, who decided it should have a monarchy, though one chosen from outside their dominion. The 17-year-old son of King Ludwig of Bavaria, the Catholic Otto, arrived with an entourage in 1833, but he wasn't very popular, especially after refusing to deliver a **constitution.** It was granted 10 years

later following demonstrations at the square in front of his Athens palace, now Parliament, renamed Syntagma (Constitution) Square.

From the beginning of the modern republic, **employment** in the public sector has been of paramount importance and bloated because of a paucity of private-sector work opportunities in the impoverished and politically fractured state. This situation persists today.

In 1862, uprisings occurred in Athens after the unpopular King Otto and Queen Amalia left on a tour of the Peloponnese. They went back to Bavaria. The Greeks requested Britain's Prince Alfred but got Prince Christian William Ferdinand Adolphos George (George I) of Holstein-

Sonderburg-Glucksburg, whose father became king of Denmark.

The new state sought to expand its territory to Greek-speaking areas still under Ottoman rule—the **Megali Idea** (Great Idea). Meanwhile the countryside was plagued by brigands, whose notoriety intensified after the Dilessi murders in 1870, when English aristocrats were slain while touring Marathon.

Greece expanded its small territory through the 1800s, incorporating concessions from the guarantor powers, who controlled bordering areas, such as the Ionian Islands.

Italy wrested the Dodecanese Islands from the Ottomans in 1911 as that empire further weakened. Greece nd its allies Bulgaria and Ser-ia declared war on the Otto-hans a year later, with Greece aking more territory in the **irst Balkan War.** In 1913, King George I was assassinated in hessaloniki. Three months ater, Greece took Thrace in he **second Balkan War,** after Greece and Serbia were at-acked by former ally Bulgaria.

With the outbreak of World War I, Greece was divided along royalist and republican nes in what became a schism hat persisted for decades. King Constantine I, son of George I and husband of So-hia (Kaiser Willhelm's sis-er), wanted neutrality, while ro-republican Prime Minister leftherios Venizelos was an Anglo-French supporter. Con-tantine was expelled.

Following the war, the Al-es agreed to help Greece's xpansion into Smyrna on he Turkish coast, as Italy had lready moved into Antalya. The Young Turk movement tirred nationalism in Turkey oo, however, and, under Mustafa Kemal Ataturk, they ought off the Greeks in the **Greco-Turkish War of 1919–2.** Thousands of Christians lied in a massacre in Smyrna fter Ataturk insisted on their otal evacuation rather than protection, which resulted n what Greeks call the **Asia Minor Catastrophe.** By 1922, nost Orthodox Christians n Turkish territory had been expelled, and Turkey received Muslims from Greece in a nass population exchange: 2 million Christians for 350,000 o 500,000 Muslims. Chris-ian refugees in Greece took p wherever they could, ncluding the palace, now

Parliament. The population of Athens doubled between 1920 and 1928, and Greece's population rose to 6.2 million. In 1933, Greece defaulted on international payments.

Through most of its modern history, Greece has suffered political instability, with frequent coups and countercoups. In World War II, with the monarchy restored in a rigged plebiscite, the appointed dictator, General Ioannis Metaxas, replied "No" ("Oxi") to Italy's request to surrender on October 28, 1940, now a national holiday. Greece was under German, Bulgarian, and Italian occupation from 1941 to 1945, and the Greek Jewish population was almost completely wiped out.

In 1944, Stalin and Churchill made a percentages agreement, stating that London's interest in Greece was 90% to Moscow's 10%, the exact reverse for Romania. Just after the war, Greece was divided along nationalist and leftist lines in a bitter civil war that lasted until 1949. Eventually government forces, supported by Britain and the United States, prevailed over the left, which had emerged from the World War II guerrilla movement. At the end of the war, 80,000 were dead and hundreds of thousands of refugees had fled the country.

Following years of political turmoil, in 1967, a group of ultra-nationalist colonels seized power in a brutal coup. King Constantine quit the country after turning on the coup leaders whom he had initially endorsed. He was stripped of his property and title before Greece officially

ended the monarchy in a 1974 referendum that restored democracy.

The colonels' regime collapsed after a bloody crackdown on a student revolt on November 17, 1973, and then a failed coup in Cyprus that led to the island's division.

With the fall of communism in the early 1990s, the Former Yugoslav Republic of Macedonia was at odds with Greece over its name and use of Greek symbols, since **Macedonia** also forms a region in Greece.

NATO allies Greece and Turkey came to the brink of war in 1987 and again in 1996, in a volatile dispute that persists to this day over boundaries in the Aegean Sea.

In 1999, Greece and Turkey both suffered devastating earthquakes and came to each other's aid, helping a historic thaw in relations.

Greece entered the **Eurozone** in 2001 and, along with 11 other members, dropped its national currency (the 2,500-year-old drachma), for the euro in 2002.

In 2004, the **Olympic Games** returned to their homeland after 108 years, but Greeks will be paying for it for years to come.

In 2009, despite economic advances, the country's massive national debt finally brought years of high growth to a halt. As most of Europe was recovering from the worst of the international financial crisis, Greece's problems were only just beginning. In an attempt to avoid defaulting on its debts, the socialist government imposed widespread cuts in public spending.

A Timeline of Greek History

B.C.

1627–1600 B.C. Eruption of volcano on Thira (Santorini); Akrotiri destroyed; the voyage of the Argonauts; exploits of Hercules.

1300–1200 B.C. Mycenaean palace built atop Acropolis in Athinai (Athens)—a cultural, administrative, and military center.

800 B.C. Formation of the Greek alphabet (left).

776 B.C. First Olympic Games take place in Olympia.

600 B.C. Coins first used as currency (Aegina's silver drachma).

508–507 B.C. First Athenian democracy established.

480 B.C. The Battle of Thermopylae. Greeks led by Sparta's King Leonidas fall to the Persians in the famous last stand.

478 B.C. Athens League forms and rules over Greek cities.

461 B.C. First Peloponnesian War between Athens and Sparta.

447–438 B.C. Parthenon built during Pericles's "Golden Age of Greece.

431 B.C. Second Peloponnesian War.

336 B.C. Alexander the Great succeeds Philip II and conquers Persia.

58 B.C. Rome conquers Greece and adopts its gods.

A.D.

A.D. 50 Apostle Paul preaches in Athens.

300s–400s Athens is a philosophical and educational mecca; Hadrian's Library (left) is rebuilt.

582 Slaves and Avars attack Athens.

1054 The Great Schism divides the east (Orthodox) and west (Roman) churches.

1100s–1400s Greece conquered by Franks, Catalans, Venetians, and Ottomans.

1204 Frank Crusaders sack Constantinople.

1453 Constantinople is overrun by Turks (5,000 v. 80,000).

1600s–1700s Ottoman rule.

1749–1800 Turks force Greeks to sell antiquities to foreigners.

1800

1801-03 Lord Elgin ships Parthenon sculptures to England.

1805 The British Consul forbids further pillaging.

1821 The War of Independence begins, lasting 9 years.

1827 In Battle of Navarino, Western powers crush Ottoman/ Egyptian forces.

1829-33 Greece becomes a monarchy under 17-year-old Catholic Prince Frederick Otto of Wittelsbach, son of Bavaria's King Ludwig.

1834 Capital moved from Nafplion to Athens.

1843 Constitution demanded of King Otto (left) in front of the palace (now Parliament, on Syntagma (Constitution) Square).

1896 First modern Olympic Games.

1900

1922-1923 Greece receives 1.1 million refugees from Asia Minor (Turkey); Athens's population doubles between 1920 and 1928.

1940-1941 Italy and Germany occupy Greece in World War II.

1944 Churchill and Stalin agree on respective spheres of influence over Greece and Romania.

1946-1949 Cold War hostilities fuel civil war.

1967 Martial law issues in a brutal 7-year dictatorship.

1973 Tanks invade Polytechnic campus (left), killing 34 students.

1981 Greece joins EEC (European Economic Community).

1996 Greece and Turkey come to brink of war over islet of Imia.

1999 Earthquakes in Turkey and Greece thaw relations with Turkey.

2000

2000 *Express Samina* ferry sinks near Paros, killing 80.

2001 John Paul II becomes first pope to visit Greece since 1054.

2002 Greece enters Eurozone.

2004 Greece soccer team wins European Championship; Olympic Games (left) held in Athens.

2008 Youth riots in Athens follow the fatal police shooting of a teenage boy.

2009 Triggered by massive debts, Greece is thrown into a serious financial crisis that shakes confidence in the euro and rattles world markets.

Greece's Art & Architecture

> The kouros, *in the Archaeological Museum in Vathy, Samos.*

Ancient Art
Ancient Greek art and sculpture have been major influences in the West and the East, shaping what is still considered **the ideal.**

From 2000 B.C., the Cretan **Minoans** (p. 248), with their beautiful frescoes and pottery, inspired the **Mycenaeans** (p. 248), who took up the banner of civilization from 1400 B.C. The lionesses facing each other over the gate at the palace in Mycenae are the oldest stone sculpture in Greece. Finds including engraved silver and gold cups and *rhytons* (vessels used to pour libations), with Minoan- and Mycenaean-inspired themes are also remarkable.

After the Mycenean age, art didn't flourish for another 700 years or so until the **Archaic period** (750–500 B.C.). This era saw the formation of city-states and the establishment of trade with lands as far away as Egypt. Egyptian influence is unmistakable in the rigid depiction of young men and women in Archaic *kouroi* and *kourai*—thought to represent people or servants of the gods.

Some 300 years later, the gods themselves took on perfect human form in the marble sculptures created during the **classical era,** when Hellenic art reached its apex. Artists began carving and painting scenes on pediments and friezes as well.

Athletic performance was exalted then as now, and perfection of the human form in motion was achieved in sculpture with Myron's *Discus Thrower* (surviving in copies). Polyclitus wrote a book (*Kanon*) on symmetry in sculpture and also created marble masterpieces, but the greatest sculptor of classical Greece is said to be **Phidias,** who designed the Parthenon friezes—battles, legends, and processions, including serene-faced gods, representing order triumphing over chaos (p. 196). *A Winged Victory* by Paionios is a symbol for Greece; a more famous Hellenistic statue, *The Winged Victory of Samothrace,* is in the Louvre.

In the 4th century B.C., **Praxiteles** carved beautiful young men and women (p. 177); Scopas of Paros endowed his sculptures with open-mouthed pathos, as seen on friezes on the Mausoleum at Halicarnassus and on the Ludovisi Ares, which is also attributed to his contemporary, Lysippus. Lysippus sculpted Alexander the Great's head and the widely copied, circa-330 B.C. Apoxyomenos statue, originally in bronze.

Sculpture flourished in Hellenic areas around the Mediterranean; distinct styles emerged in Pergamum, Syria, and Rhodes. Examples are *The Winged Victory of Samothrace,* carved from the best Parian (from Paros) marble; the *Venus de Milo* (Aphrodite of Milos, the island); and Chares of Lindos's Colossus of Rhodes. Fellow Rhodians Agesander, Athenodorus, and Polydorus are credited with carving the much-studied Laocoon group now at the Vatican Museum.

No paintings exist from antiquity, but **Apelles,** the court painter of Philip II and Alexander the Great, is believed to have been the best artist. Pottery painting followed fine-art painting, however, and a plethora of examples of this art form survive, especially on vases.

Archaic pottery replaced geometric patterns with Eastern-influenced real and mythical animals, flowers, and the now-typical *anthemion* (palmette), most commonly seen on roof tiles. Rhodes, Corinth, and Athens all had their own styles: plants and animals, fantastical creatures, and humans, respectively. Black-figure pottery first appeared in the 7th century B.C. with humans as the subject, and Athens produced most of it. At the top of this form was said to be the painter (or potter) **Amasis** in the 6th century B.C. With the 530-B.C. invention of the red-figure technique (black background, red clay), attributed to an Andokides workshop vase painter, artists were able to paint in finer detail. Athens became a center of ceramic exports by the 4th century B.C., and quality suffered with mass-production, much as it has today. Pottery is still a top seller at souvenir shops all over the country, with much shelf space given to ancient reproductions.

> *Pottery painting, often depicting gods and heroes, flourished in ancient Greece for seven centuries.*

Pre-Classical Architecture

NEOLITHIC AGE (6800–3200 B.C.)

Evidence of early human habitation has been found all over Greece, and the city of Athens has been continuously inhabited for some 7,000 years. In addition to the ancient ruins standing beside apartment blocks, the capital has a wealth of Byzantine churches (p. 200), 19th-century neoclassical buildings and parks, and a 21st-century cobblestone walkway on which to view them. In Crete, some houses are built just as they were in Neolithic times, with rectangular flat roofs supported by posts and beams. These features remain, or have been modified using stone arches.

> At the height of Greece's Golden Age, Pericles built the Parthenon to assert the supreme power of Athens.

AEGEAN BRONZE AGE (2800–1100 B.C.)

Mycenaean palaces, such as the one at ancient Mycenae in the Peloponnese (p. 188, **6**), evince the Middle Eastern tradition of treating buildings as works of art. They featured colorful frescoes in the Minoan tradition, contrasted with massive stone blocks. A palace also existed on the acropolis. No remains survived, but Mycenaean artifacts displayed at the **National Archaeological Museum** (p. 46, **8**) convey a sense of the style.

Classical Architecture

HELLENIC & HELLENISTIC AGES (8TH C. B.C.–2ND C. A.D.)

All the principal temples and monuments of Athens were built during this period in the much-celebrated Doric order. Rectangular temples were made of limestone, tufa, and the grandest ones of crystalline marble, with tapered columns and unadorned capitals. Beautiful, strong Mount Pendeli marble (called Pentelic marble) was used for the Parthenon, built between 447 and 438 B.C., a perfection of classical style

(see p. 44, **4**). In the late 5th century B.C., Doric elements were combined with a more restrained version of the east Aegean's Ionic order, recognizable by their volute (spiral-shape or scrolled) capitals. This can be seen in the **Erechtheion,** with its distinctive caryatid-supported porch, and the perfectly proportioned **Temple of Athena Nike,** both on the Acropolis in Athens. Also around the 5th century B.C., Corinthian-order acanthus capitals appeared. These columns feature a leaf design, but in Athens few examples have been found, including those on the **Temple of Olympian Zeus** (started in 174 B.C. and completed by Hadrian in A.D. 132), and on the 334-B.C. Lysicrates monument.

Byzantine-, Venetian- & Ottoman-era Architecure

BYZANTINE PERIOD (4TH–15TH C.)

Following Theodosius's ban of ancient cults in 437, Christianity quickly filled the vacuum. The Christians did not build temples on the scale of ancient Greek monuments but rather constructed either cross-shaped domed churches or basilicas with sculpted capitals, cornices, and a screen separating the *naos* (church proper) from the sanctuary. Floors and lower walls were marble, while the upper walls had mosaics. Few early basilicas have survived. A great number of churches from the Byzantine era have survived, however, especially in Athens (p. 76) and in Thessaloniki (p. 548). Typically, these

> *Agios Dimitrios in Thessaloniki is a fine example of a Byzantine basilica.*

are small, narrowly proportioned, domed, cross-shaped churches with inner frescoes and fine outer tilework and brick masonry. Two examples are the **Kapnikarea** (p. 78, **4**) and **Agii Theodori** churches (p. 78, **5**) in Athens.

POST-BYZANTINE PERIOD (16TH–19TH C.)

Architecture from this time is difficult to date, because of fragmentary remains of Frankish, Venetian, and Turkish monuments, which were constructed using a combination of older, pre-existing materials. One such example is the **Daphni Monastery** (p. 79, **10**) in Athens. It was originally constructed in the 6th century and underwent many changes after Byzantine rule: Gothic pointed arches,

for instance, were added by Catholic monks.

Around the country in rural areas, houses were built using the materials at hand, usually stone with wood decoration (in Epirus and Thessaly). Construction centered around the market and church square.

The **Zagorohoria** region of Epirus and Pelion are home to beautiful examples of two-story, slate-roofed houses, with stone ground floors and plastered upper stories. The top floor typically has a living room with sofas built into the walls, and the ceilings are usually made of elaborately carved wood. Stones tend to be the same size throughout a structure, but the rock color differs from village to village, depending on available materials.

On the islands and in coastal areas, pirate raids affected the architecture, with houses built close together along mazelike narrow streets (difficult to find your way around), and sometimes within castle or city walls. The most beautiful buildings were the churches and village fountains; the most striking and best-known folk architecture of this type is on the Cycladic Islands, with their iconic cubic, flat-roofed design; small, draft-resistant windows; and sun-deflecting whitewash. Variations include the ornate dovecote features on **Tinos** houses (p. 312, **2**), medieval architecture in Catholic-inspired **Siros** (p. 366), the 18th-century houses on **Mykonos** Harbor's waterfront (Little Venice, p. 359, **2**), and the

> *The neoclassical Zappeion in Athens hosted events during the first revival of the Olympic Games in 1896.*

vaulted houses dug into the cliff on **Santorini.**

In the Dodecanese, the beautiful town of **Lindos** on the island of Rhodes has sea captains' houses dating from the 17th century with pebble-mosaic floors in the courtyards.

During the Cretan Renaissance, under Venetian rule, houses—whose walls were attached so that residents could get around across rooftops rather than on the street in times of attack— were built with ornamented arched gates and corniced double-windows.

Neoclassical Period
(19TH–20TH C.)
After 1850 and with the arrival of the Bavarian king and his entourage, neoclassical elements appeared in mansions and housing in towns such as Athens (chapter 3), Nafplion (p. 214), Siros (p. 366), and Symi

(p. 412), together with ornate, wrought-iron railings around balconies. Athens was an idyllic city of 200,000 and was distinguished at the turn of the 19th century by a renewed interest in neoclassicism—a Romantic, Victorian-era attachment to the ancient Greek traditions. Homes, courtyard gardens, and beautiful public buildings erected by wealthy Diaspora patrons all adhered to this style brought from the German school, epitomized in the Academy of Athens, the University of Athens, and the National Library, all designed by the Hansen brothers. Many of these buildings, some with antique elements incorporated into their facades, are protected under a 1978 presidential decree, showing some conservationist foresight amid rampant development. The 20th century marked a shift, though: The population greatly

increased in a very short period of time, and new, modern, multistory office and apartment buildings went up, as was the fashion in other western European capitals.

In the countryside, houses in the Peloponnese (chapter 5) are often two-story, with the ground floor used as a storehouse and barn, and an outside staircase leading to the top floor with a living room, bedroom, and fireplace. In the Mani region of the Peloponnese, families built their houses around a square-shaped tower. The tower houses are famous and can reach four floors. They have "scalding holes" over the main entrance from which to throw hot water on invaders. Mainland houses are usually two-story, with storage on the ground floor and an internal staircase to the upper floor, which has a balcony

> *A spectacular walkway now skirts the base of Athens's Acropolis and links many of the city's major archaeological sites.*

overlooking the street. The oven is in the backyard. The architecture in the mountain town **Arachova** (p. 576) is well known, with its gray limestone and red-tiled roofs.

Houses in the Saronic islands (chapter 4) are similar, except on **Hydra** (p. 156), where the island's unique architecture is protected by the government. Two- and three-story stone houses with red tile roofs are built into the hillsides. Inside they're distinguished by marble floors and ceiling murals.

The **Ionian Islands** (chapter 13) are marked more by European and particularly Venetian architecture, with two-story country houses enclosed behind tall walls, with the storeroom, kitchen, and sometimes an oil press on the ground floor.

Modern Architecture

INTERWAR & POSTWAR PERIODS (20TH C.)

Greece absorbed more than 2 million refugees from Asia Minor between 1919 and 1922 and relocated them all over the country. Athens grew to more than a million inhabitants by the 1930s, and mass migration from the countryside into the city occurred in the late 1940s and early 1950s, during and just after the civil war. The state turned a blind eye to illegal construction for much-needed housing. Meanwhile, transportation had improved, and British villas and garden suburbs sprang up in the north, in the **Psychiko** and **Filothei** neighborhoods, and the south, in **Paleo Faliro**—areas that had been used by Athenians as summer resorts.

The population of Athens continued to swell in the following decades. An urban renewal project based on a 170-year-old plan to reclaim the chaotically overdeveloped and polluted city began in the 1990s. Light industry was moved out and car emissions regulated. The historic center was transformed with a hugely successful pedestrian zone under the **Unification of the Archaeological Sites of Athens** plan, with listed, restored buildings and a pedestrian walkway lined with cafes connecting ancient sites.

Modern Art & Design

ART

Greece's artistic legacy didn't wither after the classical era. In medieval times, artists such as **Theophanes the Cretan** (died 1559) painted icons and frescoes, and a number of good ones are in monasteries in Mount Athos and Meteora. **El Greco** (Kyriakos

> *Sophia Kokosalaki and other Greek designers are gaining a foothold in the European fashion world.*

Theotokopoulos, 1541–1614), a student of Titian, was born in Crete,though he lived and died in Toledo, Spain. **Nikiforos Lytras** was a 19th-century painter who used light and shade to beautiful effect. **Yiannoulis Halepas** from Tinos was the 19th-century sculptor who tapped out his most celebrated piece, *The Sleeping Lady,* for the tomb of an industrialist's daughter in Athens's First Cemetery. **Nikolaos Gyzis,** another 19th-century artist from Tinos, painted charming domestic scenes, and **Nikos Hadjikyriakos-Ghikas** is another big name from the early 20th century (though his name is spelled so many different ways that you might not find all his oeuvre in the same virtual place).

The clarity of the light in Greece is famous, perfect buildings stand alongside crumbling wrecks, and most settings are on the water surrounded by hills, or up in the mountains. Athens's street graffiti isn't half-bad either. In fact, the city thrives on chaos, and so do the artists, so, not surprisingly, there's a lively art scene. You can learn to paint at ateliers in Psyrri, and numerous private galleries are located throughout town as well as on islands such as Rhodes, Andros, and Hydra.

ART GALLERIES

The main 19th-century Greek artists are represented in galleries in Athens and at the **Averoff Museum** (modern-art gallery) in Metsovo (☎ 26560/41210; www.averoffmuseum.gr).

One private contemporary gallery devoted to the human form (rotating more than 3,000 works of local and European artists) is the **Frissiras Museum** in Plaka, housed in a gorgeous neoclassical building at 3 Monis Asteriou Street (☎ 21032/34678; www.frissirasmuseum.com).

The **Municipal Art Gallery** on Koumoundourou Square holds some outstanding temporary exhibits, and on permanent display are works by 20th-century Greek artists, plus Ernst Ziller, an architect who helped shape 19th-century Athens, at 51 Piraeos Street (☎ 210/324-3023).

The main art gallery in Athens is the **National Art Gallery & Alexandros Soutzos Museum,** with Greek and foreign 19th- and 20th-century paintings, but it also curates broad-appeal temporary exhibitions, at 60 Vas. Konstantinou Street (☎ 210/723-5937; www.nationalgallery.gr)

See what's currently on at Dakis Joannou's **Deste Foundation for Contemporary Art,** at 11 Filellinon

> *Lalaounis Jewelry Museum shows off the bold designs of Greece's leading modern jewelry designer.*

and Emmanuel Papa streets, Nea Ionia (☎ 210/275-8490; www.deste.gr) or at the **Ileana Tounta Contemporary Art Centre,** at 48 Armatolon and Klefton (literally, Cops and Robbers) streets, Ambelokipi (☎ 210/643-9466, www.art-tounta.gr), another big-name gallery in Athens. If you want to hang out with an artistic crowd, try **Bios,** at 84 Piraeos Street, Kerameikos (☎ 210/342-5335; www.bios.gr).

FASHION

Most visitors consider people here generally well dressed—a little flashier than in Paris and London, perhaps a bit more like Italy next door. Athens is an international city of 4 million and a hub of southeastern Europe, but its location off the beaten western European track has meant that it's also been off the fashion map. Although it's not known for its fashion anymore, it was in antiquity,

when the Greeks' gowns were coveted. During Byzantine and Ottoman rule, Greece was considered part of the Levant, and exotic, Eastern-influenced costumes and regional dress were the norm for both men and women.

Over the past few years, since borders have become more porous and movement across the world has become easier and cheaper, Greek fashionistas have looked westward for their wardrobes. Homegrown designers with international success include **Sophia Kokosalaki** (www.sophiakokosalaki.com), whose collections have appeared on the catwalks of London, Paris, and Milan, and the edgier **Angelos Frentzos.**

Another name that may be familiar outside the country is **Michalis Aslanis** (www.aslanishome.gr), who designed for Jacqueline Onassis and has shown in France, Italy, and Germany. **Makis**

Tselios (www.makistselios.gr) and **Nikos-Takis** (www.nikos-takis.com) have also been around for decades.

Athens has lately made inroads in the industry by holding international fashion weeks that also help showcase designers' work domestically as well as to the foreign market. One outlet with selected designers, **nine below** (www.ninebelow.gr), has some nice original clothes and great prices. More names to look for while here are **Deux Hommes** (www.deuxhommes.gr), **Mi-Ro** (www.mi-ro.gr), **Celia Kritharioti** (www.celiakritharioti.gr), and **Erotokritos** (www.erotokritos.com). Some of these labels can be found at **Attica Department Store** (see p. 96).

JEWELRY

It seems there's gold and silver jewelry wherever you turn, with standouts in Athens and Rhodes. Greek jewelry, whether modern works of art or museum copies, is beautifully crafted and well priced. If you want to delve a little deeper, head to the **Lalaounis Jewelry Museum** (p. 59), near the Acropolis Museum in Makriyianni. You'll view the gamut of that jeweler's bold designs and experiments through the years in big-window displays. There are Lalaounis shops where you can purchase his designs in town, too.

Another famous jeweler, **Elena Votsi** (p. 101), designs striking outsize rings, bracelets, and necklaces. She had the honor of redesigning the "heads" side on Olympic medals.

Music, Literature & Cinema

> The theme Mikis Theodorakis composed for the film Never on Sunday (1960) is a modern classic.

Music

Greece has a long musical tradition, the word for "song" being related to ancient plays. The progression of Greek music took a different monophonic, rhythmic course than Western music, best represented in Byzantine chant, while folk and popular music has an Eastern character common to the Balkans and the former Ottoman Empire.

Musical entertainment is a major cultural industry with an enormous output and numerous singers for such a small country.

Greeks consume a lot of music, both recorded and live, and Greece produces and listens to much more of its own music than countries with much bigger populations. According to a 2002 Eurobarometer survey, 63% of the population listened to Greek music, while only 25% listened to international pop

music. Anecdotal evidence suggests the ratio today is not far off.

Greek artists tend to perform hundreds of concerts a year in small, clublike venues, so they have plenty of opportunity to hone their stage skills. They also regularly play in the wider Mediterranean region in various genres that have broad appeal, from pop to folk and everything in between. There's a lot of blending, so young and popular artists singing in a traditional style are just as likely to make the charts as the latest pop diva.

Popular music exploded in the cities after 1922, with musicians arriving from Asia Minor following the mass, religion-based population exchange. The hard-luck music of the refugees is called *rembetika* and has been likened to the blues, with a bouzouki player and usually a female vocalist in the ensemble, all

seated in a row playing to small audiences.

Greek folk music is played during feasts on instruments such as the bouzouki, *oud, baglama, tambouras,* and *daouli.* Dancing is a big part of the event. There's even a type of rap (*mantinada*) on the islands of Crete and Amorgos in which performers make up the words as they sing. In towns, you might see and hear roaming street musicians, usually Gypsies, playing popular tunes on the accordion, guitar, violin, and sometimes a clarinet.

A sample of well-known pop singers includes the glitzy **Anna Vissi,** who has topped the charts for years. A diva of dance tunes is **Despina Vandi** who is married to an ex-soccer star (Demis Nikolaidis). The torch anthem of the 2004 Athens Games, "Pass the Flame," was sung by the unpretentious songster **Yiannis Kotsiras.** Greece won the Eurovision competition in 2005 with "My Number One," sung by **Helena Paparizou.**

Tolis Voskopoulos and **George Dalaras** have sold millions of albums, the latter having collaborated with the likes of Sting and Emma Shapplin (though he's much better on his own). Composers **Manos Hatzidakis** (*Never on Sunday*) and **Mikis Theodorakis** of *Zorba the Greek* fame are musical giants.

Marinella's singing career has spanned decades, while

> *Bouzouki music and dancing are mainstays of popular entertainment.*

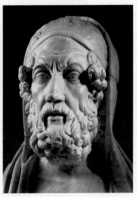

> *Homer laid the foundations of Western literature and drama.*

Eleftheria Arvanitaki is considered the biggest ethnic singer today. Her music is popular outside Greece, and she has collaborated with Philip Glass. Another popular singer, **Nana Mouskouri,** is famous for her eyeglasses as well as her voice.

Nightstalker is an English-speaking rock band with a devoted following. The best songstress for club-closing, end-of-the-night (read drunk and emotional) music is **Haris Alexiou,** who sings popular (*laika*) and art song (*entechno*) music for the masses, also selling millions.

Literature

The earliest known Greek writings are in **Linear B,** a Mycenaean script dating from 1500 to 1200 B.C. found on clay tablets, and refer to trade. The earliest literary works found are 8th- or 9th-century-B.C. epic poems by **Homer:** the *Iliad,* on the Trojan War; and the ***Odyssey,*** on the journeys of Odysseus (Ulysses). Both were written in ancient Greek, the oldest language in continuous use and the one on which the Latin alphabet is based. **Hesiod** (ca. 700 B.C.) wrote about his difficult rural life and a history of mankind, including the gods. Lyric poetry was poetry sung in a chorus and accompanied by a lyre, also dating to about 700 B.C.

The ancient Greeks also invented **drama,** which told the stories of past heroes and legends in both tragedy and comedy. These performances were attended as religious festivals in honor of Dionysus. At the theater dedicated to him below the Acropolis, awards for best plays were bestowed and displayed on Tripodon Street in Plaka. **Aristophanes** wrote bold comedies that sometimes poked fun at democracy.

Herodotus first wrote literary prose, while **Thucydides** meticulously researched his account of the Peloponnesian War, influencing the scholarship of later historians. **Xenophon** carried on the work in *Hellenica*, written between 411 and 362 B.C., while he also wrote about Socrates (*Apology, Symposium,* and *Memorabilia*).

In the 4th century B.C., **Socrates, Plato,** and **Aristotle** (a student at Plato's Academy who wrote treatises on logic, science, politics, ethics, government, and dramatic interpretation) were philosophy heavyweights who all left a huge legacy of learning. The 5th-century-B.C. philosopher and agnostic **Protagoras** caused a stir with his maxim that man is the measure of all things.

In the 3rd century B.C., Alexandria displaced Athens as the center of the Hellenic

> *Theo Angelopoulos, director of* Ulysses' Gaze.

world, with King Ptolemy I founding the Alexandrian Library as a repository of the great Greek works.

Theocritus (310–250 B.C.) created pastoral poetry that was perfected by **Virgil,** and his contemporary **Apollonius** wrote *The Argonautica* about Jason and the quest for the Golden Fleece. Greek writing continued under Roman rule, with novels, literary criticism, and the books of the New Testament. History books that have survived include accounts about the Olympics by **Timaeus** (3rd c. B.C.) and 2nd-century-B.C. **Polybius's** account of Rome's rise to power.

Siculus (1st c. B.C.) wrote the *Bibliotheca Historica*, and **Plutarch** (2nd c. A.D.) has been read for centuries. *The Enneads* by Plotinus influenced western Europe well into the 17th century.

Strabo (d. A.D. 23) wrote about all the peoples and geographies known by the Greeks and Romans up to that time, and **Pausanias** (2nd c. A.D.) wrote on what he witnessed in his travels. His contemporary **Ptolemy** wrote about astronomy and the earth-centered world, works that endured until the time of Copernicus and Galileo, some 15 centuries later.

Men of letters from the 1800s onward include **Kostis Palamas** (1859–1943), who wrote the lyrics to "The Olympic Hymn" (music by Spyros Samaras), considered Europe's greatest poet of the time and twice nominated for a Nobel Prize. His contemporary, lyric poet and playwright **Angelos Sikelianos** (1884–1951), has also been nominated. **George Seferis** (1900–71) was a diplomat who wrote poetry about the human condition, life's long journey, and the burden of a glorious past and the paucity and disasters of the present, including having to flee his native Smyrna. He won the Nobel Prize for Literature in 1963, while **Odysseas Elytis** (1911–96), a contemporary of avant-garde painters and poets in Paris, became a Nobel laureate in 1979. Crete-born **Nikos Kazantzakis** (1883–1957) is one of the best known Greek writers of the 20th century, in part because of the success of his novel *Zorba the Greek.* Most Greeks on tours of Alexandria, Egypt, stop at the museum-house of **Constantine Cavafy** (1863–1933), who wrote sparsely worded, unconventional poems on personal themes with a universal resonance.

Cinema

If you're in Greece for any length of time and watch TV, you're likely to find a black-and-white movie playing on at least one channel. Greece churned out scores of films a year in the 1950s and 1960s, and going to the movies was popular entertainment. You can still enjoy the legacy at old-fashioned, glitzy playhouses and outdoor theaters as well as at multiscreen complexes. Greek-born filmmaker **Costa-Gavras** captured the oppression of the time with his political thriller *Z* (1969). Actress and political activist **Melina Mercouri** won international acclaim for *Never on Sunday* (1960), a hard-hitting celebration of Greek life and culture; she later became the first female Minister of Culture for Greece. The industry petered out when the 1967–74 junta was in power, but it has enjoyed a small-scale revival with help from the state, beginning with films such as **Olga Malea's *The Cow's Orgasm*** in 1997. Internationally, a much-awarded Greek filmmaker is **Theo Angelopoulos,** director of ***Ulysses Gaze,*** starring Harvey Keitel. And, last but not least, **Elia Kazan** was born in Istanbul to Greek parents. Kazan, who became an American citizen, won two Academy Awards for Best Director, for *On the Waterfront* and *Gentleman's Agreement.*

Greek Food & Drink

> Octopus grilled on a wood fire is a taverna favorite.

What & When to Eat

Greeks are more concerned with the quality and freshness of their food than they are with the place where it's served, which could literally be falling apart without anyone's minding if the meal is good. But that's all part of the charm. Fruits and vegetables taste strong and fresh (you will likely remember the taste of a tomato long after returning home), and portions are generous. Other hallmarks of good Greek food are the generous use of pungent herbs for both flavoring food and making teas, and the generous use of olive oil.

For breakfast and as a snack, various savory pies are sold at countless holes-in-the-wall. **Tiropita** (cheese), **spanakopita** (spinach), and **bougasta** (cream/semolina) are the most common. **Koulouri** (round bread "sticks"), roasted chestnuts, and corn on the cob are sold on the street. The midday meal is the biggest of the day, eaten at home around 2 or 3pm after being cooked in the morning by Mama or Grandma. Students are dismissed from school around 1pm, and shops and businesses close between 1:30 and 3pm. In the summer, when the heat of the day is unbearable, the midday meal is followed by a siesta. Then, depending on the day, it's back to work, out for the evening stroll, and then out for dinner at 10pm. Kids and all.

If you want to eat where the locals do, look for restaurants that are full at 10pm—the Greek dinner hour. Dining in Greece is not a staid affair, and it'll be boisterous. Tavernas (typical Greek restaurants that serve barrel wine) that cater to tourists are open all day or at least earlier than

Opening Hours

"Open for breakfast" means open in the morning, but hours vary. Lunch is usually served from noon until 2 or 3pm (but sometimes until 6 or 7pm). Dinner is usually served from 7pm until midnight or later. The Greek dinner hour is usually 10pm.

> A meal often starts with meze, a selection of spreads, salads, and other small dishes.

the usual 7pm, and you'll find these in tourist centers such as Plaka in Athens, and at beach and mountain resorts, where dinner is served earlier for early-rising skiers.

There are many kinds of restaurants, including **ouzeries** that specialize in starters, traditionally washed down with ouzo. Countless neighborhood **tavernas** (square tables, paper tablecloths, woven-seat chairs) serve simple Greek food in big portions with barrel wine. There are also **psistaria** (grill restaurants) that serve up steaks and souvlaki (kebabs), and the **mageiria,** or cookhouses, serving buffet-style stews with rice, pasta, meat sauce, and fish. Generally, the *mageireia* is the Greek equivalent of the fast-food joint, except the food is slow-cooked and kept warm, and ready to serve when you walk in—the kind of place where you can sit down for lunch and eat by yourself. Dessert is uncommon except in more touristy areas and at the many upmarket restaurants

that serve variations on traditional Greek fare, such as fusion cuisine, but you may get a plate of watermelon on the house, particularly after a large order or if there are a lot of people.

Meze

Greeks eat a lot of starters or appetizers, mezedes or **meze** (see p. 398), which include dips and salads, before the main course or on their own. There's always a bowl of salad, usually Greek **horiatiki,** or village salad, but also cabbage, spring, and more commonly, **roka** (rocket, arugula), often with sun-dried tomatoes and walnuts.

A taverna meal usually starts with meze, whereas they're the the main course at *ouzeries,* late-evening joints where you wash down the snacks with ouzo, an anise-flavored liqueur. Of the dips, **tzatziki** with yogurt, garlic, and cucumber is popular, as is **fava,** a bean purée. Sample a selection of **kroketes** (croquettes) made with potato, cheese, zucchini, or tomato if they're on the menu, or seafood dishes such as marinated or grilled **ochtapodi** (octopus) or **melitzanosalata** (eggplant salad).

Meat

Greeks say "Get to the roast" when they mean "Get to the point." Meat is now the main event with few exceptions, whether it's a **brizola** (plain cut steak) or chop, **stifado** (rabbit stew), or **lemonato** (lemon-flavored roast).

Kebabs—better known here as **souvlaki** (small spit) or **gyro** (meat shaved off a vertical rotisserie)—need

> *Sweets from the Stani Bakery on Symi.*

little introduction, though some outlets now offer different kinds of pitas and sauces to slather and wrap around the pieces of chicken or pork.

Moschari yiouvetsi is chunks of beef baked with orzo pasta, onion, tomato, and wine in individual clay pots. Another baked dish is *arni kleftiko:* lamb usually cooked with cheese and herbs in a packet of wax paper. More lamb dishes are *arni psito* or *arni tou fournou,* roasted with garlic and herbs. *Katsika* (goat) is cooked in a similar way.

You can also get **beef stifado,** a stew made with copious amounts of wine, rosemary, tomato, and baby onions. You've likely never seen a slab of *brizola hirini* (pork) like those you'll get here, which have no resemblance to the small North American chops. Get it as a cheaper but filling and tasty substitute for *brizola moscharisia* (beef

steak). **Avgolemono** (egg-and-lemon sauce) also goes with pork, lamb ar **pastitsio,** a lasagna made with ground beef and macaroni. Layered with potatoes, eggplant, and béchamel, it's **moussaka.**

Ground beef is also the main ingredient for **keftedes,** a meat patty that can stand alone, "beefed up" with egg, grated onion, bread crumbs, and spices, then coated in flour before being fried. Mixed with rice and dropped in water with an *avgolemono* sauce, it becomes **giouvarlakia. Biftekia** is a meat patty, not beef steak. You can also find **gemista** (ground beef mixed with rice and stuffed in large tomatoes or green peppers), cabbage, vine leaves, **kolokithakia gemista** (zucchini/courgettes), and **papoutsakia** (eggplant/aubergines, meaning little shoes).

Seafood

If you want to try the (somewhat depleted) bounty of the sea, here is a glossary to help you find your fish on the menu:

cod	*bakaliaros*
crab	*kavouri*
herring	*regga*
lobster	*astakos*
mackerel	*skoubri*
mussels	*midia*
octopus	*ochtapodi*
red mulle	*barbounia*
salmon	*solomos*
shrimp	*garides*
smelt	*marides*
sole	*glossa*
squid	*kalamari*
swordfish	*xifias*
trout	*pestrofa*

Pasta

Like most things handed down from antiquity, pasta is thought to have been first used by ancient Greeks, and then adapted and improved or made bigger by the conquering Romans or Turks. It

> *Home cooking—informed by recipes handed down from generation to generation—is still the mainstay of Greek cuisine.*

was called **itrion,** a mixture of wheat and flour that was boiled rather than baked or fried. This is probably what is now referred to as **trachana,** a soup "noodle" made by boiling rolled bits of grain-size dough akin to couscous.

Cheese

Worldwide, Greece consumes the most cheese per person—some 27 kilos (60 lb.) a year—beating out even the French. Tangy **feta** (goat's cheese, see p. 612) is the best-known, but there are many more types, including an unusually high number of whites. You can also order it fried **(saganaki).** Popular soft white cheeses are **mizithra** (the hard, aged version is excellent on pasta), **manouri,** and **anthotyro,** a mild and creamy cheese. There's also **graviera** (Gruyère), **kasseri, kefalotyri,** smoked **Metsovone,** and **haloumi,** a widely available Cypriot cheese that squeaks when you eat it.

Dessert

Greek yogurt (yiaourti) is famous, best when served from a traditional clay container. It's thick and wonderful drizzled with honey (*meli*). A wine-related dessert specialty is **mustalevra:** grape must and flour, which is dark, wobbly, and sweet, often found in bakeries. Asia Minor–influenced sweets—found all over Thessaloniki and other parts nearer to Turkey where many Greeks lived before the mass population exchange in 1922—are getting easier to find in Athens as well, so you can more easily sample some of these unique pastries and puddings. **Baklava** is flaky, thin phyllo pastry layered with walnuts and pistachios and soaked in honey syrup; variations include a candied fruit or chocolate center.

Dandourma is an ice cream concoction mixed with milk and cherry syrup, and **kaimaki** is a uniquely flavored ice cream (literally frozen cream). In Thessaloniki, Eastern-style pastries and puddings are a fine art. Well-known bakeries are **Agapitos,** 53 Tsimiski Street (☎ 231/023-5935; www.agapitos.gr), and **Hatzi,** also in Athens, 5 Mitropoleos Street, Syntagma (☎ 210/322-2647; www.chatzis.gr), where you can try the unique **tauk giouksu** or some other cream dessert you'll probably never get a chance to taste again. Some say **Terkenlis,** 30 Tsimiski Street (☎ 231/027-1148; www.terkenlis.gr) is the best, while **Averoff,** 11 Vas. Georgiou Street (☎ 231/081-4284; www.averof.gr) caters to special dietary requirements with its sugar-free sweets.

Wine

Harsh-tasting **retsina,** the strong pine-resin wine that actually accompanies some Greek foods quite nicely, is a small part of the story of Greek wine, which extends back some 6,500 years and involves Dionysus, the god of wine. In antiquity, it's believed that Greeks didn't drink wine with their dinner but paired it with fruit, nuts, and desserts. It was also watered down by the host, as it still is in some restaurants, especially at the height of summer. Greek wines, all labeled with a vintage year, can have a higher alcohol content than wines from elsewhere.

In tavernas, you may or may not shun **barrel wine**

krasi), ordered by the kilo (not liter), and brought to the table in distinctive tin jugs. The better grapes are normally reserved for bottles, but if you can lower your nose, so to speak, this is all part of the taverna experience. About 70% of the time, it'll still be pretty good.

Rosés also shouldn't be ignored, as these are produced mainly in the mountainous regions and go well with a mix of dishes such as meze. In rural areas and on the islands, wine is produced (and if not bottled, then barreled) on the family plot, alongside the cans of olive oil and jars of honey. It may not be great, but families have had the opportunity to perfect their techniques over the years, and some have turned into well-respected wine estates.

There's also a huge selection to choose from, from regions and *domaines* all over the country. We have our favorites (**Amethystos** is consistently good), but we aren't above buying the local *hima*—barrel wine sold at the corner store in 1.5-liter water bottles. Some wines can be excellent one year and less good the next, so ask at the neighborhood *cava* (wine shop/off-license/liquor store) for a recommendation.

Ouzo

Although most Greeks now prefer whiskey, the national distilled drink is still ouzo, a clear, licorice-flavored liqueur that turns cloudy when you add water, though you can also drink it neat. Said to be called "uso" from the phrase

> *Ouzo, consumed with appetizers, is the national drink.*

"Anis Uso Per Marsilia" stamped on sacks of anise imported from Sicily but meant for Marseilles, ouzo is made from fermented grape skins, mixed with star anise and other herbs, boiled in a still, and stored for a few months before being diluted to 80 proof/40% alcohol. Drink too much and you'll get a killer headache; one or two glasses is enough. It's usually consumed with appetizers and seafood (hence *ouzeries*), on islands and by the seaside. It was traditionally the drink of fishermen and at *kafenia* (coffee shops), where you still find older men sitting around talking and playing cards or backgammon. There are thousands of licensed

stills all over the country, but the best-known ouzo comes from the east Aegean island Lesbos.

The big-name brands (Mini, Ouzo 12, Plomari) are controlled by international conglomerates, and most exports go to Germany with the nostalgic vacationer or expat Greek in mind. Crete's version, **raki** (lion's milk), also Turkey's national drink, isn't flavored with anise and is more like Italian grappa. It's called **tsipouro** in other regions of the country, such as Ioannina, which has *tsipouradika* restaurants to accompany their particularly fine version. You can get smooth **rako-melo** (raki and honey) on the island of Amorgos, too.

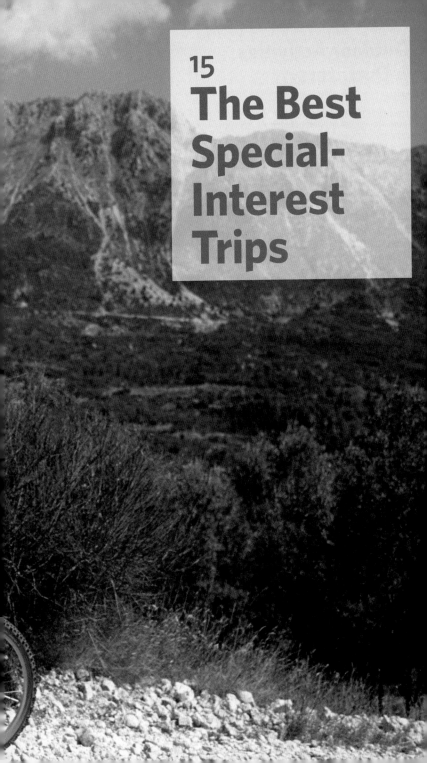

15
The Best Special-Interest Trips

Outdoor Activities & Outfitters

Biking

You can take self-guided or scheduled bicycle tours around islands and mainland areas with Athens- and New York-based **Cycle Greece,** 45 Aristotelous Street, Omonia Square, Athens (☎ 210/921-8160 or ☎ 800/867-1753 in the U.S.; www.cyclegreece.gr). Cycling is ideal for families (youngsters from age 9 are best, but ask about younger ones, as support vehicles offering snacks, water, and emergency rides are also an option). There are also sail-and-cycle combo tours, and multi-activity, special-interest, and customized tours that combine cycling and walking or cycling and vineyard walks.

Amsterdam-based **Cycletours Holland** (☎ 31/2052-18490; www.cycletours.com) runs a Greece-based bicycle village in Kalavarda, on the west side of Rhodes. They use hybrid bikes for easy 25km to 70km (15–43-mile) trips to sites such as ancient Kamiros and Petaloudes (Valley of the Butterflies), as well as a strenuous trip to the summit of Mount Profitis Elias.

Diving

With its thousands of islands and atolls, Greece has a very long coastline—some 18,400km (11,433 miles), including the mainland. Divers are free to go just about anywhere except inside wrecks (which are considered gravesites, but may also be archaeological sites), nature parks, and research areas. The **Aegean Dive Center,** at 53 Zamanou and Pandoras streets, Glyfada (a suburb of Athens; ☎ 210/894-5409; www.adc.gr), visits 24 dive sites in Attica, plus the islands in summer.

The biggest diving school on the island of Rhodes is **Dive Med College,** at 33 Lissavonas Street, Rhodes Town (☎ 22410/61115 or 69323/19040; www.divemedcollege.com), which offers a 1-day Discover Scuba course (and films the dive), so you can get your feet wet and start exploring right away. They also conduct snorkeling lessons for children 10 years or older.

Beginners, including kids age 8 and older, can start diving in Kallithea Bay through Rhodes's **Trident Diving School,** at 2 Skevou Zervou and Kapodistriou streets, Rhodes Town (☎ 22410/29160 or 69443/68444; www.

> PREVIOUS PAGE Cycling in the Ionian islands. THIS PAGE Paros and other islands are world-renowned for windsurfing.

tridentdivingschool.com). They dive in- and offshore, at depths from 2m to 30m (6⅔–98 ft.), also at five more locations around the island.

Waterhoppers, at 45 Kritika Street, Rhodes Town (☎ 22410/38146 or 69725/00971 or 69444/27308; www.waterhoppers.com), also offers a 1-day course, as well as mapping, fish identification, and regular PADI certification. The minimum age is 10.

Hiking

In western Greece, **No Limits** (☎ 26550/23777; www.nolimits.com.gr) organizes rafting, trekking, horseback riding, climbing, 4WD trips, and many more activities through the Zagori region (near Grevena), Konitsa, Prespes (Lakes), and Meteora.

You can take a 2-hour excursion or an overnight camping trip through Rhodes's natural forests, mountains, rivers, and seaside regions by 4WD or on all-terrain bikes with **Off Rhodes Extreme Adventures** (☎ 69555/82362; www.offrhodes-adventures.com). They'll organize anything from off-road safaris to trekking and cave-rappelling, and, depending on your budget and needs, you can camp or live it up in hotels. They also organize family adventures.

In central Greece, groups of six or more rock climbers can visit the Varlaam and Grand Meteoro monasteries at Meteora, then rappel 20m (66 ft.) down one of the rocks with **Trekking**

ellas, at 10 Rethymnou Street in Athens ☎ 210/331-0323; www.trekking.gr). Equipment and an English-speaking guide are included in the 20€ per-person fee.

For around 35€ per day (45€ with transport), Lindos-based **Village Holidays** (☎ 22440/31100; www.walking-rhodes.com) runs **Walking Rhodes**—guided walks along the coast or up in the mountains (Oct–May) Boots, poles, rucksacks, and lunch can be included.

Horseback Riding

Wyoming-based **Equitours** (☎ 800/545-0019 toll-free in the U.S. or 307/455-3363; www.ridingtours.com) operates riding holidays in Crete and on the Pelion Peninsula.

Through **Odysseia Stables** in Crete ☎ 28970/51079 or 51080, or 69428/36083; www.horseriding.gr), you can relax by the pool at the Equestrian Country Hotel, go on trips, and take lessons.

Sailing

Greece is a maritime country with a major sailing tradition, so if you know how to sail (or want to hire a skipper), and have a group of friends or a family, sailing holidays are a great way to see the country's islands and coastlines. Bare boats are popular and increasingly included in package holidays booked abroad as well as within Greece. It's a pleasant and economical way to travel, as it combines the transport, accommodation, and destination all in one. Other options include catamarans and motor yachts. Contact the **Hellenic Shipbrokers Association,** at 2 Dragatsi Street, Piraeus (☎ 210/422-0055; www.hsa.gr) for more information and help in finding the right yacht for you. **Vernicos Yachts,** at 11 Poseidonos Avenue, Alimos ☎ 210/989-6000; www.vernicos.gr), and **Easy Sailing,** at 10 Poseidonos Avenue, Alimos ☎ 210/985-9363; www.easysailing.gr), are just two companies that organize these kinds of trips and hire out skippers, cooks, and mega-yachts.

Tennis

Tennis courts are widely available at Greece's main hotels and resort complexes, and most towns have clubs. If tennis is the focus of your travels, try the **Mark Warner Lakitira Beach Resort** (☎ 0871/703-3887; www.markwarner.co.uk) on Kos—cited as one of the top 10 European tennis resorts.

Germany-based **Sunball Tennis** (☎ 49/221/794-09030; www.sunball-tennis.com) organizes lessons at resort complexes in Crete, Halkidiki, Corfu, and Kos.

Windsurfing

You can practically set your clock by the annual *meltemi* **(Etesian)** winds that revisit Greece each summer, which is good news for windsurfers. Paros, Naxos, and Crete are great windsurfing meccas, as is Vassiliki Bay in Lefkada (Lefkes), in the Ionian Sea. **Neilson,** a U.K.-based outfitter (☎ 084/4879-8155 toll-free in the U.K.; www.neilson.co.uk) can help you arrange a tour.

Educational Travel

Archaeology

You can't go on digs in Greece unless you're with the Archaeological Service or a foreign archaeological school, but New York-based **Archaeological Tours** (☎ 866/740-5130 toll-free in the U.S., ☎ 212/986-3054; www.archaeologicaltrs.com) runs a trip to the main sites of antiquity, including Mycenaean, Hellenic, Macedonian, and Byzantine sites.

Art

Learn how to tap out a marble sculpture the way the ancients did on a 5-day trip to the Cycladic island Tinos. The tour, which includes three 5-hour workshops, is run by well-known Greek outfitter **Trekking Hellas,** 10 Rethymno Street, Athens (☎ 210/331-0323. www.trekking.gr).

Greece affords plenty of inspiration for painters, with its famously clear natural light, varied subject matter, and color contrasts. **Sunvil** (☎ 44-20/8758-4758; http://greece-holidays.sunvil.co.uk), a U.K. tour operator, runs painting tours based on the islands Alonissos, Amorgos, Ikaria, and Samos.

The U.S.-based **Island Center for the Arts** (☎ 617/623-6538; www.islandcenter.org) conducts classes in painting, photography, and Greek culture on Skopelos between June and September. As it is affiliated with the Massachusetts College of Art, some educational institutions grant credits for its courses.

Cooking

Learn the delights of cooking healthy Mediterranean cuisine on the Saronic island Poros at the Odyssey Center in Askeli, through

Greek Island Activities (☎ 22980/23687 or 69766/86099; in the U.K. ☎ 44-1546/603-852; www.greekislandactivities.com; Apr–Nov). You can also go for walks, relax by the pool, and give the Greek language a try.

Through **Glorious Greek Kitchen** (☎ 210/689-8877; www.dianekochilas.com), Diane Kochilas, a Greek-American expert on Greek food, offers a variety of cooking classes and culinary tours in Athens and on Ikaria.

Seminars and tours on Crete combine travel with cooking lessons and investigations of the healthy Mediterranean **Cretan diet** at **Crete's Culinary Sanctuaries** (www.cookingincrete.com).

Greek Language Schools

One of the best-known schools for learning modern Greek is the **Athens Centre**, at 48 Archimidou Street, Mets, Athens (☎ 210/701-2268 or 5242; www.athenscentre.gr), which offers immersion, conversation, and literature courses throughout the year and a summer language school, poetry classes, and an art workshop on Spetses.

The **Hellenic American Union,** at 15 Didotou Street in Athens (☎ 210/368-0900; www.hau.gr), offers language courses, including conversation and exam preparation.

The **Lexis Centre of Greek Language and Culture,** at 48 Daskalogianni Street, in Hania, Crete (☎ 28210/55673; www.lexis.edu.gr) also runs language courses.

Through U.S.-based **Lingua Service Worldwide** in Connecticut (☎ 800/394-5327 in the U.S. or 203/938-7406; www.linguaserviceworldwide.com), students stay with host families while learning Greek (modern, ancient, or business) in Athens or Crete.

Wine Tours

Wine Roads of Northern Greece (☎ 23102/81617 or 81632; www.wineroads.gr) promotes self-guided routes and winery visits in Crete, Rhodes, Santorini, and the Peloponnese. They provide itineraries for 3- to 5-day trips, suggest hotels in each town, and dispense general information about Greek wine.

Athens-based **Wine Tours Greece**, at 60–62 Kallifrona Street (☎ 210/361-3509; www.winetoursgreece.com) conducts guided and DIY tours through the Peloponnese.

Multi-Activity Adventures & Outfitters

Cretan Adventures, at 10 Evans Street in Iraklion, Crete (☎ 28103/32772; www.cretanadventures.gr) organizes treks of all kinds in Crete, Santorini, Meteora, and the Zagori in western Greece. Hiking, walking, canyoneering, bicycling, horseback riding, and family outings include meals, accommodation, and transportation.

With many years of sailing experience , **Neilson** (☎ 44-844/879 -8155 in the U.K.; www.neilson.co.uk), part of the Thomas Cook group of companies in the U.K., offers a range of mostly **water-based activities** for beginners, families, couples, groups, or solo travelers. Participants can play tennis or go dinghy sailing, windsurfing, scuba diving, water-skiing, wakeboarding, or mountain-biking at their resorts in northern Greece.

Through Adventure Tourism Services in the U.K., **Odyssey Activities** (☎ 22980/23687 or 69766/86099; 44-15/4660-3852 in the U.K.) www.greekislandactivities.com) organizes multi-activity stays on the Saronic island Poros. Participants can sea-kayak, cycle, snorkel, sail, or take guided walks or language and cooking classes.

In Athens, **Trekking Hellas**, 10 Rethymnon Street (☎ 210/331-0323; www.trekking.gr), organizes adventure excursions and multi-day tours, from rafting and climbing expeditions to kayaking and horseback-riding all over Greece. They also run tours that explore Greek history, the Mediterranean diet, and wine tasting.

Sustainable & Holistic Travel

Agritourism

Agrotouristiki, at 8 Kolokotroni Street in Athens (☎ 210/331-4117; www.agrotravel.gr) is a governmental body set up to promote alternative tourism, with a focus on cultural or nature-oriented activities as a way to educate visitors about traditional life in Greece and to stimulate rural economies.

A member of the European Federation of Farm and Village Tourism (eurogites.com),

Wine tours make stops at Sigelakis Estates on Santorini and other noted vineyards.

Guest Inn, at 34 Kefallinias Street in Glyfada (☎ 210/960-7100; www.guestinn.com) is a network for finding traditional and rural accommodations, including organic farm stays in the countryside of Greece. Trips are organized by region, accommodation type, and themes, including bird-watching, mountain retreats, wine tours, seaside vacations, and river sports.

Crete and the Pindos mountain range in the north of Greece are the stomping grounds of U.K.-based **Sherpa Walking Holidays** (☎ 44208/577-2717; www.sherpa-walking-holidays.co.uk/countries/greece.asp). They organize walking tours through the Zagori villages, Mount Olympus, and Crete.

Take your family on a back-to-the-land holiday and stay on a farm, go on nature walks, and join in olive gathering and pressing through **Village Holidays/Walking Rhodes** (☎ 22440/ 31100 or 31402. www.walking-rhodes.com), which organizes agritourism stays near Lindos on Rhodes.

The **Amfikaia** (☎ 22340/48860 or 69775/ 76196; www.amfikaia.gr) is located between Tithorea and Amfiklia villages behind Mount Parnassus, some 160km (99 miles) north of Athens. One of the nicest farm stays is in these beautiful, stone-built, self-contained bungalows, complete with fireplaces. Guests can return to the land by gardening; baking bread; caring for and feeding the animals, including chickens and ducks; and, most specially, tending to the rare Thessalian and Skyros ponies. Guests can ride the ponies, mountain bike, or go for mountain walks.

Conservation

U.K.-based **Responsibletravel.com** (www.responsibletravel.com) is a great resource for all kinds of special-interest trips as well as volunteering opportunities. Their Greek options include dolphin conservation, two sailing and conservation holidays, and volunteering trips to help save Caretta sea turtles. Tours range from 6 days to 12 weeks.

GVI (Global Vision International; ☎ 888/ 653-6028 toll-free in the U.S.; www.gviusa.com), a nonpolitical, nonreligious organization with offices in the U.S., U.K., Ireland, and Australia, also provides opportunities to volunteer for conservation projects, such as turtle and dolphin conservation.

Retreats

You can go on more active (or relaxed) and intimate trips with U.S.-based **Astragreece**'s Thordis Simonsen (☎ 303/321-5403; www.astragreece.com), an American writer and teacher of biology and cultural anthropology, based in Elika, Peloponnese. She conducts walking- and writing-focused tours in her home region, as well as in the Cycladic Islands, Crete, and Zagori. Tours run from 10 days to 2 weeks for up to 8 people.

In the dramatic Mani region of the Peloponnese, the **Spirit of Life Center** (☎ 27210/78240; www.thespiritoflife.co.uk), near the fishing village Agios Nikolaos, offers a variety of yoga and holistic courses (including beekeeping), for all levels from March through October. Participants and/or their nonparticipating partners can go on walks and take a classical tour to Messini, Gythio, Olympia, Mystras, and Kardamyli.

Created by Greek and American co-founders and authors of books such as *The Joy of Burnout,* the U.K.-based **Skyros Center** (☎ 44-1983/865566; www.skyros.com), famous for its indigenous ponies, runs courses in yoga, life coaching, writing, music, and art, and sponsors singles holidays on Skyros east of Evia.

The **Osho Afroz Meditation Center** (☎ 22530/53666 or 69372/45038; www.oshoafroz.com) is a back-to-basics, meditation-based center with summer courses in primal work, tantra, reiki, and ayurvedic massage as well as pottery, jewelry making, painting, gardening, and caring for livestock. Eressos is in southwest Lesbos (Mytilene) about 88km (55 miles) from Mytilene town, and the beach is 2km (1¼ miles) from the center. Food is vegetarian, and accommodations are provided in twin rooms, wooden huts, or tents.

At **Villa Eva** (☎ 22730/30020; www.villaeva-samos.gr), near Karlovasi at Agios Nikolaos in north Samos, rooms have kitchenettes and views to the sea and garden. Guests follow a daily energizing program of light morning exercise, soft body work, and evening meditation, plus seminars on yoga and craniosacral therapy. Guests explore the nearby cove beaches, take nature walks, or hop over to Patmos, Ephesus in Turkey, or Samos to explore historic sites. Classes are held in Greek, German, Danish, or English.

Dutchwoman Oona Giesen teaches a soft version of hatha yoga at the **Yoga Center**

Wedding & Honeymoon Trips

Rhodes—especially Lindos, with its amazing backdrop of St. Paul's Bay—is the setting for hundreds of weddings a year. **Exclusively Lindos** (☎ 084/56/527127; www.exclusivelylindos.com) serves as a matchmaker between couples and selected wedding planners, and they offer a champagne cruise on their glass-bottom boat.

Utah-based **Meander Adventures** (☎ 888/616-7272 toll-free in the U.S. or 435/649-6015; www.meanderadventures.com) offers romantic honeymoon packages including yacht sails on the most beautiful islands, including Santorini, Rhodes, and Mykonos.

(☎ 69793/51951; www.yoga-paros.com), on the Cycladic island Paros from May to September each year. Seven-day courses take place in beachfront Piso Aliki, and participants stay in nearby Aliki; see the website for options.

Spas

Greece has many natural hot springs that have been used for therapeutic purposes since antiquity. Since the 1800s, doctors have regularly prescribed treatments—a legacy of the royal German family that once ruled Greece. Around a famous spring on Evia, at Edipsos, you can stay at a number of midclass hotels and visit the government-run GNTO facility, **Loutra Edipsou** (☎ 22260/23501 or 23502; May–Oct daily from 6/7am to 7pm; may close in the afternoon). The outdoor pool is 5€, and individual baths cost 5.50€, plus a couple of euros more for hydromassage. For a more luxe option, try **Thermae Sylla Spa Hotel** at 2 Poseidonos Street, Edipsos (☎ 22260/60100; www.thermaesyllaspa-hotel.com), which has wonderful indoor and outdoor pools.

Cruises

Big Ships

Celebrity Cruises (☎ 800/647-2251 toll-free in the U.S.; www.celebrity.com), an upscale U.S. operator of big ships, runs cruises with a culinary focus. It's a well-priced, service-oriented line that does eastern Mediterranean cruises through the year, calling on Mykonos, Rhodes, Santorini, and Athens.

Italian cruise liner **Costa Cruise Lines** (☎ 877/88-COSTA toll-free in the U.S.; www.costacruises.com), now under the Carnival umbrella, retains a distinct Italian flavor, apparent in the food, staff, and design. Cabin sizes are also noticeably large. They sail through the Greek islands each month; 7-day cruises from Italian ports stop at Corfu, Patmos, Mykonos, Rhodes, and Santorini.

California-based **Crystal Cruises** ☎ 310/785-9300; www.crystalcruises.com) is a luxury cruise company that gets top marks in the medium-size category. It's owned by Tokyo-based NYK, one of the world's largest shipping companies. The sushi restaurant has Nobu to thank for its menu; the spa was designed with *feng shui* elements; and cabins are spacious. Theme-based cruises (such as Fashion Capitals, or Emerging Artists'

Centers) venture beyond standard cruise-ship ports of call.

Greece-based **Golden Star Cruises,** at 85 Akti Miaouli, Piraeus (☎ 210/429-0650; www. goldenstarcruises.com), offers 3-, 4- and 7-day cruises from Athens to Mykonos, Patmos, Santorini, Rhodes, and Crete.

Holland America Line (☎ 206/281-3535; www.hollandamerica.com) provides relaxed premium service for the American market. Passengers can eat round-the-clock and take cooking and bar-mixing classes, while the kids can stay busy with children's facilities, games, and a library.

Louis Cruise Lines, at 8 Antoniou Ambatelou Street, Piraeus (☎ 210/458-3400; www. louiscruises.com), runs 4-, 5-, and 8-day cruises. Their short cruises on midsize, 1,200-passenger classic refurbished cruise ships take in Mykonos, Patmos, Rhodes, Iraklion, and Santorini. If you want to stop over on an island, you can re-embark from the same port, space permitting.

Smaller Ships

Building on the brand success of low-cost easyJet, Piraeus-based **easyCruise,** at 6 Astiggos Street, Karaiskaki Square, Piraeus (☎ 211/211- 6211; www. easycruise.com) offers 3- and 4-night trips to all the main Greek island ports of call—Mykonos, Santorini, Crete, Patmos, plus Kusadasi in Turkey (for ancient Greek Ephesus), and the 4-night one stops in Rhodes—from March to October.

Miami-based **Seabourn Cruise Line** (☎ 800/929-9391 toll-free in the U.S. or 305/463-3000; www.seabourn.com) takes its classy but casual clientele off the beaten path to Gythio in Mani, Hania in Crete, Katakolon on the beautiful west coast, and through the Corinth Canal. The ships seem like yachts with teak decks and an open-bar policy. The *Seabourn Spirit*'s cabins are all outside suites. Ships can offer watersports such as kayaking, snorkeling, water-skiing, and banana boating; a mesh net serves as a saltwater pool.

Sea Cloud Cruises (☎ 888-732-2568 toll-free in the U.S. or 201/227-9404; www.seacloud. com) has distinguished service and routes all over the world, including the Mediterranean. Refurbished for 64 passengers and designed down to the last detail, the *Sea Cloud*, a 1930s yacht with 36 sails owned by heiress Marjorie Merriweather Post, has a long history. Beautiful details include fireplaces in the rooms.

Cruising sophisticates will enjoy the passengers, ships, service, and itineraries of the **Sea Dream Yacht Club** (☎ 800/707-4911 toll-free in the U.S. or 305/631-6100; www.seadream yachtclub.com), founded by Seabourn executives. Their five-star mega-yachts, tall ships, and new river boats sail to lesser-charted ports of call as well as ultra-chic Hydra, Mykonos, and Santorini.

Silversea Cruises (☎ 800/722-9055 toll-free in the U.S.; www.silversea.com) offer five-star service on four elegant ships built from 1994 to 2001. Passengers are indulged by a large staff, all-suite vessels (*Silver Shadow* and *Silver Whisper*), and all-day dining. Ships hit all the interesting ports on the Italy-Greece-Turkey circuit.

Miami-based **Star Clippers** (☎ 305/442-0550; www.starclippers.com) runs 5- and 7-day cruises to the Greek isles and Turkey aboard stately but casual romantic clippers—a tall ship (69m/226 ft.) or bark (small Greek craft are called *varka*) with billowing sails, a fireplace, a library, and a writing room.

New York-based **Travel Dynamics International** (☎ 800/257-5767 toll-free in the U.S. or 212/517-7555; www.traveldynamics international.com) goes all over the world and packs in a lot of excursions, included in the cruise price. These small ships bring each destination's history and nature to life through educational programs for children and adults.

State-of-the-art computers operate the sails on the beautiful yachts of New York-based **Windstar Cruises** (☎ 800/258-SAIL toll-free in the U.S. or 206/292-9606; www.windstar cruises.com), which cater more to "resort casual" adults and their high-tech toys, including a platform for launching watersports activities and casinos. Ports of call in Greece include Rhodes, Santorini, Mykonos, Nafplion, Gythio, and Ermoupolis in the Peloponnese.

Athens-based **Variety Cruises,** at 214–216 Syngrou Avenue. (☎ 210/691-9191; in the U.S. ☎ 800/319-7776; www.varietycruises.com) hits all the big destinations and offers excursions, such as beach BBQs, and itineraries on a half-board or full-board basis, depending on the type of cruise. Passengers swim off the side of the boat, so it's more like a traditional Greek experience. It offers the upmarket Variety Cruise, Zeus Casual Cruise, and Variety Yachts, which are charter vessels for 8 to 12 passengers.

16
The Savvy Traveler

> Zooming around the Arch
of Hadrian at breakneck
speed is an experienced
best left to native drivers.

Before You Go

Government Tourist Offices

IN THE UNITED STATES **Greek National Tourism Organization** (GNTO), Olympic Tower, 645 Fifth Avenue, Suite 903, New York, NY 10022 (☎ 212/421-5777; fax 212/826-6940). IN CANADA **Hellenic Tourism Organization,** 1500 Don Mills Road, Suite 102, Toronto, Ontario M3B-3K4 (☎ 416/968-2220; fax 416/968-6533). IN THE U.K. AND IRELAND **GNTO,** 4 Conduit Street, London W1S 2DJ (☎ 020/7495-9300; fax 020/7495-4057; www.gnto.co.uk). IN AUSTRALIA AND NEW ZEALAND **GNTO,** 37–49 Pitt Street, Sydney, New South Wales 2000 (☎ 02/9241-1663; fax 02/9241-2499). IN GREECE GNTO, 7 Tsoha Street, Ambelokipi, Athens 11521 (☎ 210/870-7000; www.gnto.gr); 26 Amalias Avenue, Syntagma, Athens 10557 (☎ 210/331-0392; fax 210/331-0640; www.gnto.gr or www.visitgreece.gr.

Best Times to Go

Temperatures are most comfortable in the **fall** and full-bloom **spring,** when the country is also at its most beautiful. It is hottest in June and July, but this is also the time when **summer** festivals are in full swing. The northern *meltemi* (Etesian winds) blow from mid-July to mid-August, when chilly Aegean Sea water is warmest. In **winter,** most resorts shut down, usually by October. Museums work on a reduced schedule that lasts until April, and most hotels also go on a winterlong hiatus. Greece can get very chilly from November to March.

Festivals & Special Events

For an exhaustive list of events beyond those listed here, check http://events.frommers.com, where you'll find a searchable, up-to-the-minute roster of what's happening in cities all over the world. For performance events, including information on jazz and other concerts, see **www.ellthea.gr.** For **sports events,** see "Spectator Sports" in the Fast Facts section.

JANUARY

Feast of St. Basil (Agios Vassilios). St. Basil is the Greek equivalent of Santa Claus. His feast day, January 1, is marked by the exchange of gifts and a special cake, *vassilopita,* made with a coin in it; the person who gets the piece with the coin will have good luck. **Epiphany** **(Baptism of Christ).** On January 6, baptismal fonts and water are blessed. A priest may throw a cross into the harbor and young men will try to recover it; the finder wins a special blessing. On the 12th day of Christmas, children who have been good during the holiday thanks to the threat of *kalikantzari* (goblins) are allowed to help chase the monsters away.

Trion Ierarchon (Three Hierarchs). On January 30, churches dedicated to *Trion Ierarchon* (the Three Holy Hierarchs: St. Basil, St. Gregory, and St. John) celebrate. Stalls selling trinkets spring up at many well-known churches celebrating their namesake saints.

FEBRUARY

Carnival (Karnavali, Apokri-ES). Children dress up in costume for much of the 3-week period preceding Orthodox Lent, especially during the weekend *volta* (promenade stroll). On the last weekend, costumed revelers bash one another with plastic baseball bats and throw confetti in Athens's Plaka district. Costume parties and parades prevail. Patras's celebration is the best known, with its famous chariot parade and wild Saturnalia, private parties, and public celebrations, but other towns and villages have their own unique customs. Masked revels are widely held in Macedonia. On Skyros, the pagan "goat dance" is performed, reminding us of the primitive Dionysian nature of the festivities. Crete has its own colorful versions of Carnival, whereas in the Ionian Islands, festivities are more Italian. Tyrnavos, Thessaly, hosts a phallic festival on the first day of Lent.

MARCH

Kathara Deftera (Feb or Mar). On the first day of Lent (Clean Monday), you'll see a lot of stray kites caught in trees, and more in the air,

---

Traffic-Stopping Holidays

Greece observes a number of holidays during which museums, sites, government offices, banks, and some shops are closed. But for several days around Orthodox Easter and August 15, not only do many places shut down, but internal transportation is overwhelmed by Greeks returning to their hometowns and villages. So although it is great to be in Greece to observe these occasions, do not plan to travel around much.

specially around Filopappou Hill in Athens. Try your luck at flying your own kite from Pnyx Hill; bring a picnic lunch of canned octopus, *dolmades* (rice-stuffed grape leaves), and other Lenten foods and, of course, a kite (sold everywhere).

Independence Day and the **Feast of the Annunciation** are celebrated on the same day, March 25, the former with military parades, especially in Athens. Folk legend has it that Mary was impregnated after smelling a lily or lotus flower (a fertility symbol) that the angel Gabriel offered to her. Parades and folk dancing also celebrate the day Bishop Germanos of St. Laura Monastery hoisted the Greek flag in 1821, marking the beginning of the struggle for independence, achieved in 1829.

APRIL
See "Orthodox Easter & Holy Week" box.

MAY
Proto Maia. On May 1, May Day is celebrated with picnics and flower wreaths hung over balconies or on doors. The date marks International Labor Day as declared in Paris in 1889, to commemorate a U.S.- and Canada-wide workers' strike for the 8-hour day, when workers were killed in a crackdown in Chicago, May 1, 1886.

The Art Athina International Fair. This event takes place in May at the Faliro Pavilion, Athens, with thought-provoking and avant-garde paintings, installations, sculpture, video art, and photography. ☎ 210/330-3533; www.art-athina.gr.

Athens Epidaurus Festival. From May to October, this two-city celebration of performance features domestic and international productions of ancient drama, opera, orchestra, ballet, modern dance, and popular entertainers in the **ancient Herodes Atticus Theater**

Orthodox Easter & Holy Week

The Greek calendar revolves around religious holidays. **Orthodox Easter** (*Pascha*)—usually a week later than Western Easter, and the only holiday calculated according to the Julian calendar—is the nation's biggest. Most of the native population—97% of whom are Greek Orthodox—observe the traditions. Most people who did not fast for the 40 days of Lent begin fasting during Holy Week, which starts on the Monday before. On **Holy Tuesday,** devotees whitewash their houses and walks. On **Wednesday,** they bring holy oil home from church and use it, along with sprigs of basil, to bless the households. On **Holy Thursday,** they receive Communion, and priests in special dress read biblical accounts of the Last Supper during an all-night vigil. At home, followers boil eggs and dye them red to symbolize the blood of Christ and rebirth. Many also bake Easter bread (*tsoureki*) and biscuits (*koulourakia*). Church bells solemnly toll on **Good Friday,** and at around 8pm, a candlelit procession through the parish accompanies a decorated funeral bier (*epitaphios*) of Christ. On **Saturday,** they attempt to scare away any remaining bad spirits that might hinder the Resurrection (*Anastasi*). Most people go to their neighborhood church just before midnight with candles (*lambades*); the children carry lavishly decorated ones, often received as traditional gifts from their godparents. The lights of the church are dimmed at midnight, symbolizing Christ's death. The priest then brings out the holy flame, brought from Jerusalem for the occasion, and passes it to church members, who light one another's candles while saying "*Christos anesti*" ("Christ is risen"). Youths light fireworks, and congregants return home with their lit candles and bless their homes by "drawing" a cross on the door frame with the candle's smoke. The following day, they break the Lenten fast by cracking the eggs and eating *mageiritsa* soup, made with dill, rice, *avgolemono* (egg-lemon) sauce, and the innards of Sunday's roast lamb. **Easter Sunday** brings much feasting, drinking, and dancing. The smell of lamb permeates the air from roof-terrace spit-roasts. At church, passages on the Resurrection are read in many languages, symbolizing world unity. **Easter Monday** is a national holiday.

(☎ 210/324-2121 or 323-2771) at the foot of the Acropolis, at other venues around town, and in the **ancient Epidaurus Theater** (☎ 275/302-2026). Contact the Athens Epidaurus Festival's central box office, 39 Panepistimiou Street (sign-posted El. Venizelou), in the arcade. ☎ 210/327-2000 or 928-2900; www.greek festival.gr.

Battle of Crete. The hard-fought World War II Battle of Crete—where Allied forces were stationed, the then-king of Greece narrowly escaped capture, and civilians joined in the fighting and suffered greatly for it during occupation—is observed on the island around May 21 with events and memorial services. The 70th anniversary is in 2011.

Anthestiria Flower Festival. This celebration of spring takes place in Rhodes Town the last weekend in May. An exhibit is at Mandraki Harbor, and a flower-laden float parade proceeds along Mandraki on Sunday, complete with bands and chariots. ☎ 22410/27427; www.rhodes.gr.

Feast of St. Constantine (Agios Konstantinos). Fire-walking on hot coals and animal sacrifices—a throwback to pagan fertility rites—are practiced nowadays on May 21 in villages such as Agia Eleni in Thrace and Langada near Thessaloniki in the name of the first Orthodox emperor, Constantine, and his mother, St. Helen (Eleni).

JUNE

Medieval Rose Festival. This historical celebration takes place in May, June, or July within the walls of the Old Town of Rhodes as well as at Monolithos and Kritina (Castella) castles. A medieval fair, plays, and team games celebrate the medieval city, when the Knights of St. John held sway (1309–1522). Events from the Middle Ages are celebrated and re-created with arts and crafts, traditional products, food and drink, customs, costumes, music, sports, and games. Participation in sword fights and treasure hunts is encouraged. ☎ 22440/74405; www.medievalfestival.gr.

Ecofilms Film & Visual Arts Festival. The silver screen goes green in June, during this film festival with an environmental slant in Rhodes Town. Films are shown and prizes awarded for the most innovative works that address conservation. ☎ 210/363-6390; www.ecofilms.gr.

Nafplion Festival. This celebration in modern Greece's first capital has been running for two decades, with cultural performances taking place in venues such as the Palamidi Fortress and the Agios Giorgios Church courtyard. ☎ 27520/47030; www.nafplionfestival.gr.

International Festival of Corfu. The island Corfu celebrates its reputation for musical talent with various concert performances from June through August. ☎ 26612/00300; www.corfufestival.gr for more info.

JULY

Profitis Ilias. July 20 commemorates the life of **Profitis Ilias** (the prophet Elijah). It is celebrated especially in the Cycladic Islands at the many hilltop churches and monasteries dedicated to him.

Athens International Dance Festival. This festival includes European and American troupes, from hip-hop to experimental, and takes place during the first 2 weeks of July at the Technopolis arts complex, 100 Piraeos Street, Gazi. ☎ 210/361-2920; www.breath takingathens.com.

Epidaurus Festival. Performances of classical Greek drama take place in the famous amphitheater from July through early September. For information, contact the **Greek Festival Office,** 4 Stadiou (☎ 210/322-1459 or 322-3111, ext. 137).

Northern Greece National Theater. Classical drama is performed in the amphitheaters in Phillipi and on Thasos in July and August. You will be able to see these productions without the hassles of Athens performances. For information, call ☎ 25102/23504.

AUGUST

Assumption of the Virgin. The Assumption of the Virgin is celebrated across the country, especially at the church dedicated to the Virgin, Panagia Evangelistria, on Tinos, where believers gather to receive grace.

Santorini Festival of Classical Music. International musicians and singers give outdoor performances for 2 weeks at the end of August.

Spetses Armata. This celebration commemorates the day a Greek fire-ship sailed toward the flagship of the Turkish and Egyptian armadas in the harbor of this Saronic island. The event is commemorated on September 8 (or the nearest Sat).

International Trade Fair. This trade fair ☎ 231/012-9111; www.tif.gr) dominates Thessaloniki in early September; the economic keynote speech is made by the prime minister.

Athens International Film Festival. For the latest indie films, often before release, visit during the Athens International Film Festival ☎ 210/606-1108; www.aiff.gr.

Music in Rhodes Festival. Music ranging from classical to children's choirs and cantatas to Sephardic songs is performed by international and national ensembles at the Music in Rhodes Festival, which takes place in charming venues around the Old Town, such as the Castle of the Knights. ☎ 22410/27427 or 33343; www.musicinrhodes.gr.

OCTOBER

Fashion Week. This extravaganza takes place at the Technopolis arts center, 100 Piraeos Street, Gazi. Info on Athens events are on the city's website: www.breathtakingathens.com.

NOVEMBER

Athens Classic Marathon. This run from Marathon to Athens celebrates the heroic stamina of the 5th-century-B.C. messenger Pheidippides, who ran 42km (26 miles) to announce that the Greeks had defeated the Persians at the 490-B.C. Battle of Marathon. After proclaiming "We won!" he dropped dead. The run takes place the second Sunday in November. For information call ☎ 210/933-1113, or see www.athensclassicmarathon.gr.

Thessaloniki International Film Festival. Since 1960, this event has attracted budding filmmakers in various genres from around the Balkans for a week in Greece's second city. ☎ 23103/78400;www.filmfestival.gr.

DECEMBER

The City of Athens organizes the **Athens Running Tour** in early December. See the city's website, www.breathtakingathens.com, for more details.

Christmas. Luxury hotel restaurants vie to offer the most exotic and scrumptious menu on Christmas Eve and New Year's Eve, and Athens streets and squares are decked out in December and January for the season's festivities. Central **Syntagma Square** gets the biggest Christmas tree, a carousel, and lots of street stalls. Displays, concerts, and events are held around the city, and in the **National Gardens**, a children's circuit and Santa House are set up.

New Year's Eve. On December 31, children sing Christmas carols (kalanda) outdoors while their elders play cards, talk, smoke, eat, and imbibe.

Weather

Basically Greece has two seasons: kalo himona (good winter) and kalo kalokairi (good summer). Summer, generally starting after Easter, is very hot and dry, sometimes reaching 110°F (43°C). As the saying goes, only mad dogs and Englishmen would venture out in the midday sun, hence the siesta between 3 and 6pm. The seasonal north (Etesian) winds blow mid-July to mid-August, but it can get very windy anytime, stopping ferry transport. Rain is more frequent in western and northern Greece in the winter months, but storms and torrential rains all over the country can occur surprisingly quickly, and sometimes signal a change of season or temperature. Winter is mild and rainy with snowfall not unheard of. It can also go from warm to downright numbing. Many buildings are not insulated, and the centrally controlled heating is often intermittent, making the cold season very long indeed. In the mountainous part of the country, which means most of the mainland, snowfall can disrupt road and rail travel, though this is infrequent. Spring and fall are the best times to visit Greece for sightseeing: Sites and museums are not crowded, and the temperatures are pleasant for strolling. Prices for travel and accommodations are also lower, compared

For More Information

For more details on Greek festivals around the country, see www.greecetravel.com/holidays.

ATHENS'S AVERAGE TEMPERATURES & PRECIPITATION

	JAN	FEB	MAR	APR	MAY	JUNE	JULY	AUG	SEPT	OCT	NOV	DEC
Temp (°F)	49	50	53	60	68	76	81	80	74	65	58	52
Temp (°C)	9	10	12	16	20	24	27	27	23	18	14	11
Rainfall (in.)	1.80	1.90	1.70	1.10	0.70	0.40	0.20	0.20	0.50	1.90	2.00	2.60
Rainfall (cm)	4.57	4.83	4.32	2.79	1.78	1.02	0.51	0.51	1.27	4.83	5.08	6.60

with the peak summer season from mid-June to mid-September. If you're looking to beat the heat at the beach, head to Greece from mid-June to September.

Useful Websites

www.culture.gr: The Greek Ministry of Culture's website, for museums and sites.

www.gnto.gr: The Greek Tourism Ministry's site.

www.ticketnet.gr: See what Arts & Entertainment events are in town.

www.hnms.gr: The Hellenic National Meteorological Service (weather).

www.oasa.gr: Public transportation site, including maps.

www.poseidon.ncmr.gr: The Hellenic Centre for Marine Research's weather site, including sea-surface temperature.

Cellphones (Mobiles)

As in all of Europe, **GSM (Global System for Mobiles)** phones work in Greece, but making and receiving calls while abroad can be pricey. Check to see if you have a tri-band phone and that international calls, or at least the text message function, are enabled. You could buy a pay-as-you-go phone, equipped with a portable memory chip (SIM card), for about 35€. You can buy call time for as little as 10€.

Getting There

By Plane

Athens International Airport Eleftherios Venizelos (☎ 210/353-0000; www.aia.gr), is 27km (17 miles) east of Athens at Spata. There are two airport information desks at each end of the arrivals hall, three ATMs, free Internet spots, a pharmacy, a post office, a money exchange at the departure level, and a few shops. **The Greek**

National Tourism Organization (GNTO, or EOT in Greek; ☎ 210/353-0445) is also in the arrivals hall, alongside private tour agencies that can book hotels. **Makedonia Airport** (☎ 2310/473212), is 16km (10 miles) from the northern port city Thessaloniki. There are 32 other airports around this small country, and they receive a steady stream of international charter flights in summer.

Athens is a southern European hub and a destination airport for more than 50 airlines (many more in summer) from Europe and around the world. It also gets a steady stream of seasonal and charter flights. FROM THE UNITED STATES **Delta Air Lines** (www.delta.com) and Greece's **Olympic Airlines** (www.olympicair.com) operate direct flights from New York's JFK. In summer, **Continental** (www.continental.com) flies from Newark, Delta flies from Atlanta, and **US Airways** (www.usairways.com) flies direct from Philadelphia. European airlines departing the United States make a stop before arriving in Athens, usually at their national hub. FROM CANADA **Air Transat** (www.airtransat.ca) operates nonstop flights from Toronto and Montreal. FROM EUROPE AND THE UNITED KINGDOM There are many European airline flights to Athens (see Athens International Airport's website, www.aia.gr, for the list of airlines serving the airport), including discount airline **easyJet** (www.easyjet.com) from the U.K.

Package Tours

Package tour operator **Olympic Holidays** (☎ 0800/093-3322 in the U.K., or ☎ 22410/60749 in Rhodes; www.olympicholidays.com) has properties all over Greece and, at least in Rhodes and Symi, they're in good locations. You can also join their excursions even if you aren't staying with them at a particular resort, which is handy if there is no travel (booking) agency in the area.

Check the hotel address, or better, choose
hotel from this guidebook and cross-check
t with the package offered. Package deals can
lso be found on sites such as **travelocity.com,**
xpedia.com, last-minute.com, and **booking.**
om. Greek sites to try include **airtickets.gr,**
antasticgreece.com, and **travel.gr**.

scorted General-Interest Tours

scorted tours are structured group tours,
vith a group leader. The price usually includes
verything from airfare to hotels, meals, tours,
dmission costs, and local transportation.
See chapter 15, "Special Interest Tours.") Just
e sure the hotel is in a good neighborhood.

Two of the best-known tour operators in
thens are **Key Tours,** 4 Kallirois and Lebessi
treets (opposite the Temple of Zeus; ☎ 210/
23-3166; www.keytours.gr), and **Chat Tours,**
Xenofontos Street, Syntagma (☎ 210/322-
127; www.chatours.gr).

Two major organizers of package tours
rom outside Greece are **Homeric Tours**
☎ 800/223-5570; www.homerictours.com)
nd **Tourlite International** (☎ 800/272-7600;
vww.tourlite.com). These tours fall into the
moderate" category in pricing and accom-
nodations, and both companies carry the risk
f all charter flights—that means delays. Both
ffer some variety; often these tours provide
ocal guides, and often they include short
ruises as part of the entire stay.

A more upscale agency is **TrueGreece** (in
Jorth America ☎ 800/817-7098, or in Greece
☎ 210/612-0656; www.truegreece.com), which
scorts small groups on customized and more
ntimate tours to selected destinations.

Cosmos Tours (☎ 800/276-1241; www.
osmos.com) offers a variety of options,
ncluding 8- to 16-day tours of Greece, also
aired with Italy or Turkey, and including 3- or
-day cruises, for about 755€ to 1,737€, not
ncluding flights.

Insight Vacations (☎ 800/582-8380;
vww.insightvacations.com) offers escorted
notorcoach tours, especially of the wider
egion with cruise components in the Greek is-
ands, from about $1,000 for 7 days to $4,700
or 3 weeks.

Escorted tours can take you to the maxi-
num number of sites in the minimum amount
f time with the least amount of hassle. On
he downside, you'll have little opportunity for

interactions with locals. The tours can be jampacked with activities, leaving you little time
for individual sightseeing, whim, or adventure;
plus they often focus only on the heavily
touristed sites, so you miss out on the lesser-
known gems.

Getting to Town from the Airport

The **Metro** subway (www.amel.gr) goes to
central Athens (45 min.) from the airport,
or you can take the **Suburban** (Proastiakos)
railway (☎ 210/527-2000; www.trainose.gr)
to Larissa Station, Athens's central railway
station (40 min.), to the port of Piraeus (1 hr.),
or to Corinth and on to Kiato (bound for Patras
and other Peloponnese destinations; 1½ hr.),
but you have to change trains in Ano Liossia
en route to Athens or Piraeus. Tickets to Athens on either the Metro or the Suburban are
6€ (3€ discount), which you validate in time-
punch machines before you get to the platform. Fines up to 60 times the fare are levied
if you don't validate the ticket and get caught.
Metro and Suburban services run from about
5:30am to 11:30pm.

Public buses (☎ 185; www.oasa.gr) termi-
nate outside the arrivals hall. Tickets, which you
validate on machines on the bus, cost 3.20€.
Both no. X94 and no. X95 run to the Ethnikis
Amynas Metro station on Line 3 if you want to
take the rest of your journey into town on the
Metro from there. No. X95 continues to central
Syntagma Square, about a 70-minute trip. Bus
X96 stops at the Faliro Metro station (which
connects with the **tram**) before continuing to
the Port of Piraeus Metro station; both of those
stops are also on Metro Line 1.

A **taxi** will cost around 50€. Trip time is 30
minutes to an hour, depending on traffic. There
are additional charges—for luggage, tolls, time
and the like —which do not appear on the meter
and therefore work in (too many) dishonest
drivers' favor. The charges are usually listed on
a card mounted on the dashboard, where the
driver's ID should also be. Be on guard.

By Ferry

Boats from Ancona, Bari, Brindisi, and Venice
arrive daily in the Greek ports of Patras and
Igoumenitsa, with stops at the Ionian island
Corfu and sometimes at other islands in
summer. Trip times vary depending on the
ferry you take and your departure and arrival

points, but it takes 10 to 17 hours to get to the main arrival port of Patras, and travel is usually overnight. Schedules, ports of departure, and prices change seasonally, with tickets ranging from 33€ to 50€ for deck/economy class from Brindisi or Ancona, to 400€ for a luxury cabin in August. Eurailpass-holders should check their booklet or **www.rail europe.com** to learn which operators currently honor their passes, and then depart from the relevant port; however, on some lines (such as Superfast Ferries), expect to pay port taxes and/or fuel fees, and a season surcharge (about 30€ total), while other companies (such as Minoan) charge 30% of the regular price. Schedules, rates, and special offers for small groups are all linked through **www. greekferries.gr.** Check schedules online at **www.openseas.gr** and **www.gtp.gr.**

By Cruise Ship

Cruise-ship passengers can get from the port of Piraeus into Athens (10km/6¼ miles/20 min.) by taking bus no. 049 at the terminus on main Akti Miaouli Avenue, near the international passenger terminal, to the terminus on Athinas Street in Athens. You can also walk around the harbor (15–20 min.) to the Piraeus Metro station (20 min. to Athens) or hail a cab (15–30 min. to Athens; about 10€).

By Train

Greece is connected to the Balkans, eastern Europe, Russia, and Turkey by rail, with international trains terminating in the northern port city Thessaloniki. The trip can be a long and difficult adventure, where safety precautions may also be imperative (clip your bag to the rack, for example). It may be shorter than the traditional route (taking the ferry from Italy), but you may face long, boring border delays. Sleepers or couchettes are recommended for long journeys and overnights, and these are available for all international journeys.

The domestic train company is **OSE** (☎ 1110; www.ose.gr), and the relatively small train station in Athens is **Larissa** on Metro Line 2. There are different types of trains in Greece, notably the fast and modern **InterCity** (IC) and **InterCity Express** (ICE) trains connecting the country's urban centers, and **Regional** (R) trains that serve local and regional routes. About 10 trains a day go back and forth between Athens and Thessaloniki, and the trip takes between 4½ and 8 hours for overnights, which have sleepers.

There is also a touristic .75m-gauge rack-and-pinion railway in the Peloponnese to the mountain ski-resort village Kalavryta; a historic, revived .60m-gauge steam train route in the Pelion Peninsula that operates in summer and shoulder seasons on weekends; and the Suburban train, which plies routes from the airport to Piraeus, Athens (both with changes), and Kiato (for onward journeys to Patras via Corinth).

Apart from Larissa Station, the two **OSE ticket offices** in Athens are at 1 Karolou Street (☎ 1110 or 210/529-8829), open Monday to Friday 8am to 3:30pm, and at 6 Sina Street (international travel ☎ 210/362-7947; domestic travel ☎ 1110; from abroad ☎ 210/362-1039), open Monday to Friday 8am to 3pm. Better to call them and ask for schedule information or to get the latest time-table booklet for domestic routes if the website functions are not working.

Larissa Station has luggage storage, a restaurant, a platform cantina, and a train information counter. Only same-day tickets

---

Tips on Travel from Italy

Getting to Athens from Italy by ferry can take 3 days. With food, lodging, and transport costs, it may be cheaper, as well as faster, to fly. Check www.skyscanner.net to e-book cheap flights from Milan, Venice, or Rome; try www.flyairone.it from Rome, or check the Rome airport (☎ 06/65951; www.adr.it) for a dozen daily flights. Cheap flights in and out of Athens can also be found through www.airtickets.gr.

To get to Athens from Patras, you can take the KTEL bus (☎ 210/514-7310 in Athens, ☎ 26106/23887 in Patras) that leaves every 30 to 45 minutes; the trip takes 2½ hours. You can also take one of five daily trains that make the trek in 3½ to 4 hours. Or you can catch a bus to Delphi or to Ancient Olympia via Pyrgos. Make your connections as quickly as possible, because the last train and bus of the day usually pull out soon after the ferry arrives.

an be purchased in the building's main en-
rance. Advance tickets are available from a
cket office (daily 7am–9pm) at the south end
f the station; go around the building past the
verest Cafe and the kiosk, and enter from the
latform.

If your rail journey is limited to the Greek
nainland, buying point-to-point tickets or an
n-country pass instead of an international
ass may be cheaper. There are 25% to 50%
iscounts for children, students, families, and
eniors, and also for buying most return tick-
ts (20%).

The **Eurail Greece Pass** provides 3 to 10
ays of non-consecutive, first-class travel in
Greece. Prices start at $155 for adults.

You get 4 days of non-consecutive, first- or
econd-class travel in Greece and Italy within
 months with the **Eurail Greece-Italy Pass.**
 rices start at $315 for adults.

Ionian Travel, 1st floor, 4 Piraeos Street,
)monia Square, Athens (☎ 210/523-4774),
ffers rail-pass-holders discounts on hotels,
-day cruises, certain domestic ferry routes,
nd day trips to Delphi as well as Epidaurus.
)nian can also purchase point-to-point train
ickets for you, if you want to reserve while
ut of the country (IC trains only). Other OSE-
ffiliated travel agents may also oblige.

All of the above passes need to be pur-
hased before departing for your trip; you can
uy them from **Rail Europe** (☎ 877/456-RAIL,
00/622-8600 in the U.S., 800/361-RAIL in
Canada; www.raileurope.com).

U.K. residents and non-U.K. residents visit-
ng London should drop by the **Rail Europe**
ffice at the Europe Travel Centre, 1 Regent
treet, London SW1, U.K. (☎ 0844/848-
070; www.raileurope.co.uk). Non-U.K.
esidents should book their tickets and passes
hrough www.tgv-europe.com if they are Eu-
opean residents, or www.raileurope.fr if they
ve outside Europe.

Domestic **discount rail passes** (multiple-
ourney cards) can also be purchased through
)SE once you are in Greece. If you buy six jour-
eys on InterCity trains, you get one bonus trip.

Getting Around

By Train
Greece is served domestically by the **Hellenic**

Railways Organization, OSE (☎ 1110; www.
ose.gr), and Athens's main station is **Larissa**,
on Metro Line 2. Finding information on Greek
trains is difficult, as is getting tickets from
abroad. The website is not user-friendly even
for finding a simple schedule, and the telephone help-line, which used to be top-notch,
currently offers minimal service.

You can freely consult the English-language
page of the German website **DB Bahn** (http://
reiseauskunft.bahn.de) for international and
main domestic journeys. It also shows which
trains have sleepers—imperative for trans-
European journeys that take 2 or 3 days.

Thomas Cook (www.thomascooktime
tables.com) also issues a *European Rail Time-
table* that you can buy online for about 16€.
You can make train reservations in advance,
but you must buy your ticket at a domestic
station or OSE-affiliated travel agency, or get
someone in Greece to do it for you.

Trains leave Thessaloniki for Skopje, Macedonia; Zagreb, Croatia; Ljubljana, Slovenia;
and Belgrade, Serbia. There are also trains to
Prague, Czech Republic, and Bratislava, Slova-
kia. You can also go to Moscow, Russia; Kiev,
Ukraine; and Belarus from Thessaloniki. Check
whether the route is in service before your
journey.

Trains also go to Sofia, Bulgaria, then onward to Bucharest, Romania; and Budapest,
Hungary, and on to Vienna, Austria. Bring
food and water with you, as these may not be
offered until you reach Budapest. One train a
day, an overnight, leaves from Thessaloniki to
Istanbul, Turkey. Be open-minded when looking for cities in a schedule search on websites
such as OSE's or DB Bahn's: Some Balkan cities are not spelled the English way (Belgrade is
Beograd, Sofia is Sofija, and so forth). Athens
may be Athina, or Athene.

By Bus
Greece has an extensive long-distance bus
service (KTEL), an association of regional
operators with green-and-yellow buses that
leave from convenient central stations. For information about the long-distance-bus offices,
contact the KTEL office in Athens (☎ 210/
512-4910).

Organized and guided bus tours are widely
available. We especially recommend CHAT

Tours (www.chatours.gr), the oldest and probably most experienced provider of a wide selection of bus tours led by highly articulate guides. In the capital, the CHAT office is at 9 Xenofontos, 10557 Athens (☎ 210/323-0827).

In Athens, the KTEL regional **Bus Terminal A** (with buses to Patras, points north and south, Peloponnese, and western Greece) is at 100 Kifissou Street (☎ 14505 or 210/512-4910). The local bus no. 051 from Menandrou Street, west of Omonia Square in Athens, gets you there. **Bus Terminal B** (to central Greece, including Delphi and Meteora) is at 260 Liossion Street (☎ 14505 or 210/831-7186), and is served by bus no. 024 from Amalia Avenue, Syntagma Square. The driver usually drops passengers off near Kato Patissia Station on Line 1, however, before reaching the terminal. Buses to sites in Attica (including Cape Sounion and Marathon) leave from **Aigyptou Square** on Patission Street (☎ 210/880-8080; www.ktelattikis.gr), just past the National Archaeological Museum.

By Taxi

If you decide to take a taxi from the airport, port, or station, ask the driver for an estimate before you get in. If the driver tries to overcharge, do not pay or get out of the car unless you are in front of your hotel, and either ask a hotel clerk for assistance, or ask to be driven to a police station. If you're taking a taxi to the airport, ask the hotel desk clerk to order it for you in advance.

For info on taxis from Athens, see the "Getting Around" section in Athens Fast Facts (p. 134). For limo service and tours in Athens and all over Greece, especially suited for business travelers, call **Limotours,** 20 Syngrou Avenue (☎ 210/922-0333; www.limotours.gr), or **Athens Luxury Transportation Services** (www.athensexclusivetaxi.gr), or **George's Taxi** (☎ 210/963-7030; www.taxigreece.com) for airport pick-up, tours, and so on.

Taxis also operate on islands and in remote towns. They may often be your only option for reaching a hotel or site. Most do not have meters, so negotiate a price before setting out. Island hotels will often arrange for a taxi to pick you up at the port; ask when booking.

By Car

Driving in central Athens is not recommended because of heavy traffic and lack of parking. Greeks are expert at maneuvering into the tightest parking spot; they also know the roadside signs better than you do. Pay parking is expensive, costing from 7€ to 10€ for the first hour to 10€ for 6 hours or 20€ a day.

There are plenty of car-rental agencies that offer good deals if you want to set out for a trip into the countryside, but beware: Most cars have a manual transmission. Try and reserve ahead if you need an automatic.

The main highways are new and in good condition, some are tolled, and the posted speed limit is 120km per hour (75mph), 50km (31mph) in built-up areas, and 80km (50mph) on rural roads. Drivers are aggressive and erratic, often exceeding the limit, tail-gating (if they're flashing their headlights, move to a slower lane), and using the shoulder as an extra lane for slower traffic. Greece has an unenviable road-fatality record, and a very high accident rate. Keep alert and drive defensively. Note that drivers often pass on the right, crowd you onto the shoulder in order to pass, ignore stop signs and red lights, and fail to give the right of way. Police are increasingly vigilant, especially about driving under the influence of alcohol; offenses result in stiff fines and jail sentences.

Signs are in Greek and English, but some are easy to miss, obscured by branches, poorly placed, or neglected. Buy a good map.

Observe highway signs for how far away the next gas (petrol) station is if you need to fill up (full service), and note that in towns gas stations close in the evenings and on Sundays, but one is always open on a rotation system. Fuel is also quite expensive, and using the toilets at gas stations is uncommon.

Bring an international driver's license issued by the automobile association of your home country. You run a risk if there's an insurance claim, however. Licenses from other E.U. countries are recognized in Greece.

The Greek Automobile Association (ELPA) **road assistance** line is ☎ 10400; **Express** (another service) can be reached at ☎ 1154.

Many car-rental offices are located at the top of Syngrou Avenue in Makriyanni, Athens. Or look for the best deal through travel booking ites, or from an online supermarket such as **www.travelsupermarket.com** or **www.side tep.com.** You can get some great deals, but as lways, check the fine print, especially regarding insurance (such as the collision damage vaiver), which is often included in the booking ut "forgotten" in the paperwork at pickup. Also horoughly check the car (for the condition of he tires and such) together with the agent. As entals are so cheap lately, the maintenance, ncluding tuneups, can be a little slipshod.

Lodgings

ourism is one of Greece's primary industries, nd the country offers a full spectrum of accommodations options. They can range from nassive, all-inclusive hotel complexes at each resorts, to an extra room in a private ouse during the peak season on a heavily ouristed island, and everything in between.

Hotel categories in Greece are designated y the letters A to E (A being the nicest), but nost hotels use the familiar star-ratings to enote class (five stars being the highest). The reek categories are based more on facilities —such as public areas, pools, and in-room menities—than on any comfort or service atings.

International travelers will be familiar with najor chains like Hilton. Several historic and eluxe hotels belong to the Luxury Collection f Starwood Hotels and Resorts. Greek chains, uch as Classical Hotels, also own numerous roperties. These latter tend to be extremely pscale hotels; however, most Greek hotels are ndependent lodgings run by hands-on owners.

Booking a Room

ry to make reservations by fax or e-mail so hat you have a written record of the room nd price agreed upon. Hotel and guest rights re online at the Hellenic Chamber of Hotels www.grhotels.gr).

Be aware that a double room (*diklino*) in reece does not always mean a room with double bed (*diplo krevati*), but a room with win beds (*dio mona krevatia*). Check if you vant to be sure.

Note that in a few instances—usually at the nost expensive hotels—the prices quoted may e per person or without taxes included, which vill obviously raise the cost considerably. Note,

too, that room prices, which are regulated and must be posted in the room, usually behind the door, are often negotiable, especially in low or midseason (which can be July and August in Athens), for multiple-night stays, for cash payment, and for e-booking. Because of Greek regulations, hoteliers are often reluctant (and unable) to provide rates far in advance and may quote prices higher than their actual rates. When you bargain, don't cite our prices, which may be too high, but ask instead for the best current rate. Actual prices may be 25% (or more) lower than the lowest rates quoted, which are based on listed (rack) rates, so by all means ask.

A passport or other form of identification may be required when registering in a hotel.

Alternative Accommodations

Traditionally built guesthouses in various country villages and far-flung islands offer accommodations and "retreat"-type holidays, from stays on farms or olive picking in winter, to yoga retreats and art holidays in the summer, spring, and fall. Many of the providers are simple folk and unused to dealing in another language, which may make them difficult to locate and to see what they have to offer. But spending time in such a place is all part of the adventure. See chapter 15, "The Best Special Interest Trips," for more information.

House-Swapping

House-swapping is a cost-effective option if you are traveling with family or staying in Greece for a week or longer. You will probably have more space, a full-size, well-equipped kitchen, and a residential Greek neighborhood as your home base. The catch is that you have to be willing to reciprocate and offer your own

Hotel Bathrooms

The bathrooms in all the newer and higher-grade Greek hotels are now practically state-of-the-art, but travelers may appreciate knowing a few things that apply to all except the more upscale hotels. Washcloths are rarely provided (Greeks use sea sponges), and a small bar of soap is the standard. Many hotels don't offer generously sized towels, and many midprice hotels provide only cramped showers. Be grateful, however, if yours is enclosed by glass doors.

home to strangers. **HomeLink International** (www.Homelink.org) is a long-established home-exchange organization with many listings in Greece; www.intervac.com also has a good selection.

Religious Institutions

Some monasteries offer accommodations, often for a very low fee or even for free. Contact the ones that interest you most. For monastery listings, see p. 580, 582, and 584.

Travel Tips

Travelers with Limited Mobility

If you're planning to use the main Athens train station (Larissa) while you're pulling luggage, pushing a stroller, or wheeling a wheelchair, be warned that the Metro station that serves it is not very accessible. You have to climb a small flight of steps in order to exit the Metro station, and then you have to cross a busy street to reach the elevator to street level.

Many towns in Greece are laced with stairs, and paving can be rough and uneven. Archaeological sights can be especially difficult to navigate. Elevators and other accessibility options can be limited in many hotels and restaurants, so check ahead when booking.

Boat Schedules

Check the latest schedules to see what kind of craft, and when and where it departs, on **www.openseas.gr** or **www.gtp.gr.** Note that some island destinations are listed by the port and not the island, such as Vathy (Samos) or Aegiali (Amorgos). Santorini is the same island as Thira, and Piraeus is the port city of Athens. Remember that rough seas can severely limit boat service and boats; ferries and hydrofoils often do not operate in high winds.

Traveling with Kids

Choosing a Hotel

If you have young children, consider staying at all-inclusive hotels, where you don't have to worry about making meals. Many cater especially to families, with elaborate playgrounds, kids' clubs, and food served all day, and so on. You can also find steep discounts at those located where there is a plethora of resorts, such as areas on Rhodes and Kos, or

in mainland towns such as Ioannina. Eating at tavernas is a great experience and most are child-friendly. If you can't do it every day (meals at around 15€ per person can add up), then consider getting a studio or one-bedroom apartment with a kitchenette and sofa bed. Well-stocked minimarkets are usually located near apartments and studios, especially in beach resorts. And finally, an ice bucket or large, long-handled Greek or Turkish coffeepot (*briki*) partially filled with hot water is perfect for warming baby bottles.

Ferry Travel with Kids

The slower boats are cheaper and more pleasant out on deck. Reins or a harness are an invaluable asset with toddlers, as the ferry guard rails are widely spaced. The ferries also have snack bars on board selling snacks such as juice, grilled ham-and-cheese sandwiches, potato chips, croissants, and cookies.

Fast Facts

Apartment or Villa Rentals

For apartment-hotels, check either the long-term rates of hotels recommended in this guidebook or the classifieds in *Athens News* (www.athensnews.gr), *Athens Plus* (www.athensplus.gr), www.xpatathens.com, www.vacationhomerentals.com, www.owners direct.co.uk, or http://athens.craigslist.gr.

Area Codes

The country code for Greece is **30.** Domestically, 10 digits are needed, which includes the area code. Athens is 21# (the next digit depending on the telephone exchange) plus seven digits; Thessaloniki is 231# plus six digits, as is Patras (261#) and other urban areas. A five-digit area code is used elsewhere in the country. Cellphones do not follow the area-code rule but require 10 digits and begin with 6.

ATMs & Cash Points

ATMs are widely available, and most are open to the street. Look for the international system that your bank card belongs to (on your card and on ATMs). Both your bank and the Greek bank will charge you for the transaction. See the individual Fast Facts in each chapter for more on ATMs in each region. Bank machines ay run out of cash on weekends, so plan head, especially outside major cities.

The **Cirrus** (☎ 800/424-7787; www.master ard.com) and **PLUS** (☎ 800/843-7587; ww.visa.com) networks span the globe, cluding Greece. Go to your bank card's web te to find ATM locations at your destination.

aby-Sitting

otels usually indicate whether they can ar ange baby-sitting, but if they don't say, by all leans ask.

anking Hours

enerally, banks are open Monday to Thurs ay 8am to 2:30pm and Friday 8am to 2pm.

ike Rentals

icycle-riding is in its infancy in Greece, with he exception of the relatively flat island Kos, here bike-riding is common along country ads and bicycles are part of hotel deals. For ours and rentals, try **Pame Volta** (☎ 210/675- 386; www.pamevolta.gr), and see chapter 15, The Best Special Interest Trips."

usiness Hours

Vork hours in Greece differ by season, day f the week, and type of business. Shops are enerally open Monday, Wednesday, and Sat rday 8:30am to 2pm; Tuesday, Thursday, and riday 8:30am to 2pm and 5:30 to 8:30pm. hain stores, supermarkets, and department tores remain open through the midday siesta londays through Saturdays. In tourist areas, tores are generally open longer, as well as on undays, when other shops are closed.

ustoms

here is Customs control for flights that do ot originate in the 24 European countries that bide by the Schengen Agreement, which did way with border controls among participat g nations. A valid passport is required for ntry to Greece. No visa is needed for most reigners, including North Americans who tay less than 3 months; authorization must e obtained for longer stays. Contact the nmigration division, 24 Petrou Ralli Street, avros (☎ 210/340-5828 or 5829; garrison 210/340-5969). **U.S. CITIZENS** For specifics n what you can bring back, download the free amphlet *Know Before You Go* at **www.cbp. ov,** or contact U.S. Customs & Border Protec on (CBP), 1300 Pennsylvania Avenue NW,

Washington, DC 20229 (☎ 877/287-8667; www.cbp.gov). **CANADIAN CITIZENS** For a clear summary of Canadian rules, write for the booklet *I Declare,* issued by the Canada Border Services Agency (☎ 800/461-9999 in Can ada, or ☎ 204/983-3500; www.cbsa-asfc. gc.ca). **U.K. CITIZENS** For information, contact HM Revenue & Customs at 0845/010-9000 (or ☎ 44/2920/501-261from outside the U.K.), or consult its website, www.hmrc.gov. uk.. **AUSTRALIAN CITIZENS** A helpful brochure available from Australian consulates or Customs offices is *Guide for Travellers: Know Before You Go.* For more information, call the Australian Customs Service at ☎ 1300/363- 263, or log on to www.customs.gov.au. **NEW ZEALAND CITIZENS** Request the pamphlet *New Zealand Customs Advice to Travellers* from New Zealand Customs Service, The Customhouse, 17–21 Whitmore Street, Box 2218, Wellington (☎ 04/473-6099 or ☎ 0800/428-786; www. customs.govt.nz), or download it from the site (under Library, Publications).

Dining
See p. 653.

Electricity
Electric current in Greece is 220 volts AC, alternating at 50 cycles. Appliances from North America that are not dual voltage will require a transformer and a round, two-prong adapter plug.

Embassies & Consulates
U.S. EMBASSY 91 Vas. Sofias Ave., Athens (☎ 210/721-2951; http://athens.usembassy. gov); Metro: Megaron Mousikis. **CANADIAN EMBASSY** 4 Ioannou Gennadiou St., Athens (☎ 210/727-3400; www.athens.gc.ca); Metro: Evangelismos. **U.K. EMBASSY** 1 Plout archou St., Athens (☎ 210/727-2600; www. ukingreece.fco.gov.uk); Metro: Evangelismos. **AUSTRALIAN EMBASSY** Thon Building, Kifis sias and Alexandras aves., Athens (☎/fax 210/870-4000; www.greece.embassy.gov. au); Metro: Ambelokipi. **NEW ZEALAND CON SULATE** 76 Kifissias Ave., Athens (☎ 210/692- 4136); Metro: Ambelokipi. **IRISH EMBASSY** 7 Vas. Konstantinou St., opposite Panathenian Stadium, Athens (☎ 210/723-2771; www. embassyofireland.gr).

Emergencies

For emergencies throughout Greece, enlist the assistance of your hotel, which may have doctors it can call if needed. You can dial ☎ **100** for police assistance or ☎ **171** for the Tourist Police. Dial ☎ **199** to report a fire and ☎ **166** for an ambulance. The E.U.-wide ☎ **112** is a multilingual service for police, ambulance, and fire. English is widely spoken in this heavily tourism-reliant country, with doctors and dentists among the English speakers. Or you can call your embassy for advice. The 24-hour **SOS Doctors** (☎ 1016; www.sosiatroi.gr) makes house calls, as does **Homed** (☎ 1144; www.hospitalathome. gr). You pay by service and treatment. A house call costs about 70€ to 120€.

Etiquette & Customs

Athenians can outdo New Yorkers in their reputation for rudeness, but being polite will take you far in the direction you want to go. Remember your P's, Q's, and "Good day" greetings.

Event Listings

The most complete listings for arts or entertainment are in Greek only. Try the weekly *Athinorama* or *Time Out,* and ask at your hotel or tourist information for assistance. There are limited listings in the weekly *Athens News, Athens Plus,* and the daily *Kathimerini* section inside the *International Herald Tribune.* For festivals around the country, see **www.greecetravel. com/holidays**. See "Festivals & Special Events" at the beginning of this chapter.

Family Travel

Expect preferential treatment. Ask your hotel for special needs such as cots, bottle warming, and connecting rooms. Most restaurants, museums, and sites welcome children, but check stroller access. Children 5 and under ride free on public transport; children 17 and under and seniors get 50% off the Metro and Suburban rail fares; families with four or more children are eligible for reduced fares on buses.

Gay & Lesbian Travelers

The gay community in Greece is discreet, but there are gay-friendly places in Athens and around the country. The Gazi area of Athens has many gay-friendly bars and clubs, and the island of Mykonos is the premier destination for gays, as well as celebrities and the wealthy. Check **www.gaygreece.gr** or **www.10percent. gr** for more in-depth information and events.

Health

Greece is viewed as a "safe" destination, although problems, of course, can and do occur anywhere. You don't need to get shots, foodstuffs are generally safe, and the water in cities and towns is potable (unless you're told otherwise), but in some agricultural areas bottled water is recommended. It is easy to get a prescription filled in towns and cities.

Greece has English-speaking doctors at hospitals with well-trained medical staff. Greece adheres to most E.U.-wide practices, and some private hospitals take patients, who would otherwise be waiting in a long line, from as far away as the U.K. for elective surgeries. Foreign embassies and consulates can provide a list of area doctors who speak English.

For information on the cost of care and health insurance in Greece, see "Insurance," below. If you suffer from a chronic illness, consult your doctor before your departure. Pack prescription medications in your carry-on luggage, and carry them in their original containers, with pharmacy labels; otherwise they might not make it through airport security. Carry the generic name of prescription medicines, in case a local pharmacist is unfamiliar with the brand name.

Holidays

Greece celebrates New Year's Day (Jan 1); Epiphany (Jan 6); Clean (Ash) Monday (Feb or Mar); Independence Day (Mar 25); Good Friday and Easter Sunday and Monday (in the Orthodox calendar, Apr or May); Labor Day (May 1); Whit Monday (May or June); the Assumption of the Virgin (Aug 15); Ochi Day (Oct 28); Christmas and the day after (Dec 25–26); and unofficially, the commemoration of the student march to the U.S. Embassy (Nov 17). See "Festivals & Special Events."

Insurance

Check if you're covered already by medical, home, work, or travel policies in your home country. Automobile associations offer travel insurance, too. **Blue Cross Blue Shield** (www. bcbs.com) is an insurance company based in the U.S.; **Bupa** (www.bupa.co.uk) is a well-known U.K. provider. You can also try for the best deal and best coverage through "supermarket" websites such as **www.insuremytrip.**

m or **www.moneysupermarket.com/travel nsurance**, but do your due diligence, and at ast check the supplier via a news search ngine to see if it comes up with anything you vould know about the company. E.U. resi- ents are covered with the **European Health nsurance Card** (EHIC; www.ehic.org.uk). ote that the rates are set according to age, ealth, and other factors, and can be quite xpensive, especially for older travelers if they e traveling for extended periods.

In Greece, private-practice doctors charge bout 40€ to 70€ to examine a patient and rescribe treatment. A house call costs 70€ 120€. A simple blood test is about 12€ at a rivate lab; results are often released the ext day. State hospitals, which have well- spected and often English-speaking doctors, ven though the bricks and mortar may look bit Soviet, are highly unlikely to turn away a urist in an emergency. The payment may be ery low or free, depending on what they need do for you; otherwise they'll work some- ing out with you and your insurer.

nternet Access

lost hotels provide Internet access, and any also have Wi-Fi in the lobbies or in the ooms, free or for a fee. Every major town and esort has Internet cafes, and Wi-Fi is free in ome cafes as well as at Wi-Fi hot spots. In thens, there are hot spots at the Athens In- rnational Airport, Syntagma Square, Kotzia quare, Thissio Station, Thissio Square, and t the National Research Foundation (48 Vas. onstantinou St.; Metro: Evangelismos).

anguage

lost people speak or understand English, specially in heavily touristed places and in thens.

egal Aid

ontact your embassy or consulate if you run to trouble with the law or need legal assis- nce. People there may help with explaining e law of the land or provide you with a list attorneys, and generally assist as much as ossible, short of offering to pay for legal fees.

Lawyers in Greece are plentiful and afford- ble. As with a dentist or doctor, everyone has e. Often they don't take money for advice or ntil/unless a case goes to court, but they can harge for services.

Lost Property

For credit cards, passports, and other im- portant documents, before you leave home or upon arrival, make photocopies or scan them; keep the copies together with the phone numbers and procedures you would need in order to report them lost or stolen. For other lost items, you can file a report at the nearest police station. On trains, ask at the nearest station; on the Metro, call ☎ 210/327-9630 or go to Syntagma Station.

Mail & Postage

Overseas stamps for up to 20 grams (.7 oz.) cost .70€ and are available at many kiosks and shops selling postcards. The main post office is at Syntagma Square at Mitropoleos Street; another is at 100 Aeolou Street, just southeast of Omonia Square. The parcel post office is at 60 Mitropoleos Street. Hours are Monday to Friday 7:30am to 8pm. The Aeolou and Syntagma branches are also open Saturday 7:30am to 2pm, and Syntagma is also open on Sunday 9am to 1:30pm. Regular post offices are open Monday to Friday 7:30am to 2pm.

Money

Greece is in the Eurozone, and euros replaced the 2,500-year-old drachma in 2002. At press time, the US dollar exchange rate was 0.71€. Euro bills come in denominations of 5 (which can get pretty tatty; try not to accept it if a shop owner tries to pass you a ripped or repaired one, as it's easier for them than for you to change it at a bank), 10, 20, 50, 100, 200, and 500. Mainly bills up to 50€ are in circulation. The coins include the really use- less and tiny 1¢ and 2¢, then the bigger 5¢ (and the last of the coppers), 10¢, 20¢, 50¢, 1€, and 2€. In this cash society, most non-chain stores and restaurants do not accept credit or debit cards; try to have bills in the smaller denomi- nations. Apart from ATM withdrawals, you can get money wired through **MoneyGram** agents (www.moneygram.com) and **Western Union** (☎ 801/113-8000), located in many shops, post offices, and exchange bureaus, including in Syntagma Square. The transaction costs, however, are a bit pricey from this end.

Newspapers & Magazines

English-language newspapers are found at foreign-press newsstands, including all the kiosks at the top of Ermou Street at Syntagma

Square. The **Athens News** (www.athensnews.gr) is a weekly English-language newspaper, as is the weekly **Athens Plus. Kathimerini** (www.ekathimerini.com) is a daily found inside the *International Herald Tribune*.

There are also the monthly *Insider* and *Odyssey* magazines, as well as bimonthly tourist magazines that are widely available at hotels. The most complete listings of bar-clubs, restaurants, exhibitions, or concerts are in the Greek-language weekly *Athinorama* or in *Time Out* magazine, available at all newsstands. Get assistance from your hotel or at a tourist information desk to find what you want.

All the kiosks at Syntagma Square and Omonia Square sell foreign publications; Omonia Square has a 24-hour newsstand.

Parking

Parking is difficult and almost always bumper-to-bumper parallel. You can take your chances and park on streets where you see other cars (the signs can be confusing). Otherwise, see if your hotel has free or discounted parking, or go to a pay parking lot, though it can be quite expensive. In Athens, charges are about 8€ or 10€ for the first hour or a set 6-hour period, or 20€ a day, with similar rates in Thessaloniki.

Passes

A 12€ ticket to the **Acropolis**—a coupon booklet—is valid for 4 days, and includes admission coupons to the Acropolis, Ancient Agora, Theater of Dionysos, Kerameikos Cemetery, Roman Forum/Hadrian's Library, and the Temple of Olympian Zeus.

Many categories of visitors, including archaeology students, are admitted free (ask, or check www.culture.gr).

Passports

Most foreigners, including Canadians and Americans who stay less than 3 months, do not need a visa, just a valid passport. See Customs in this section for more information. A passport is usually required when registering in a hotel and kept until checkout.

Pharmacies

Pharmacies are marked by green and sometimes red crosses, and are usually open 8 or 10am to 2pm and 5 to 8:30pm on Tuesday, Thursday, and Friday. After-hours locations are posted (in Greek) in pharmacy windows, found by dialing ☎ 1434 (in Greek), or by looking in an **Athens News, Athens Plus,** or **Kathimerini** newspaper or on **www.ekathimerini.com**. You can get antibiotics and over-the-counter meds without a prescription, as well as advice for simple ailments. Pharmacies are often quite helpful, especially in remote areas, where the pharmacist often acts as a local health care provider. By E.U. regulations, pharmacies are only permitted to fill prescriptions issued by physicians licensed in the E.U.

Police

Dial ☎ **100.** For help dealing with a troublesome taxi driver or hotel, restaurant, or shop owner, call the **Tourist Police** at ☎ **171;** they're on call 24 hours and speak English, as well as other foreign languages.

Post Office

For post office locations, see Fast Facts at the end of each destination chapter. Post offices are generally open 7:30am to 2pm. Stamps (*grammatossima*) can be purchased at most newsstands.

Safety

Apart from averting a fall on an uneven sidewalk or giving selfish drivers the right of way, visitors have only a few minor concerns. Women may get propositioned by shopkeepers or beachcombers in tourist areas, and the unsuspecting may be scammed but not harmed. Greece has a low crime rate, and you can safely walk the streets well into the night, but some areas that are used as the collective bedroom or meeting place for drug addicts and illegal migrants are best avoided at night. Pickpocketing also occurs mostly on public transport during busy times. Motorcycle thieves also target the vulnerable by pulling up alongside and grabbing shoulder bags, pulling people over in the process. Take precautions: walk on sidewalks facing traffic and with your bag on the side farthest from the lane.

Major hospitals rotate emergency duty daily; call ☎ **1434** to hear recorded information in Greek on whose turn it is, or ☎ **112** for the multilingual European Union emergency hot line. You can also consult the English edition of the **Kathimerini** daily newspaper, distributed with the *International Herald Tribune,* sold wherever you see foreign publications and online at **www.ekathimerini.com**.

enior Travelers

eniors (60 or 65 and over) pay less at most useums and sites, on the Metro and Suburan railway (65 and over), and at organized eaches (65 and over). Always ask if discounts re available. **Elderhostel** (www.exploritas. rg) does tours. See "Special Interest Tours" . 659) for more info. For accessibility issues, ee "Travelers with Disabilities" (p. 684).

moking

moking was prohibited in public places, inuding hotels, on July 1, 2009 with some sucess, but is widely accepted.

pectator Sports

he size of the venues and relatively easy acess and low cost make it possible to see topvel track-and-field competitors and major uropean soccer clubs (Champions League) ith greater ease in Greece than elsewhere. ou can get more info on tickets for Greece's ain teams by checking the clubs' websites: **anathinaikos FC** (☎ 210/870-9000; www. ao.gr), an Athens soccer team; PAO's fierce val **Olympiakos Piraeus** (☎ 210/414-3000; ww.olympiakos.gr), based in the port city; **EK Athens** (☎ 210/612-1371; www.aekfc.gr); nd Thessaloniki's **PAOK** (☎ 23109/54050; ww.paokfc.gr). These clubs also have basetball and other sports under their respective mbrellas. Online sports sites, such as www. orldticketshop.com, also sell **tickets**.

The **Acropolis Rally** (www.acropolisrally. r) takes place in June. If you want to follow his auto race and others, check the world rally ircuit schedule at www.wrc.com.

For **track and field,** try looking up the AAF (www.iaaf.org) schedule on www.altius irectory.com for events that may be coming town, or look for annual international meets summer, such as Athens's **Tsiklitiria** (www. siklitiria.org), the **Vardinoyiannia** in Rethymon, Crete (www.european-athletics.org), nd the **Papaflessia** (www.papaflessia.gr) in alamata, Peloponnese.

Greeks aren't big **golfers,** but for tournanent info, visit www.golf.gr.

In November, if you'd like to watch (or join) **marathon** in the place that named the event, r to see the marble stadium finish line (from he 1896 Olympics), check www.athens lassicmarathon.gr.

For upcoming **windsurfing** events, check www.efpt.net.

Staying Healthy

Sunglasses and sunscreen are needed in summer, and many people also don hats and sun umbrellas. Stay in the shade as much as possible, and keep water with you; it's widely available in corner stores, kiosks, and sandwich shops. Embassies can provide info on Englishspeaking doctors if you fall ill. State hospitals treat minor emergencies free of charge; otherwise, admission is possible through a doctor.

In Greece, doctors are organized by specialty. A pathologist is the closest to a general practitioner (G.P.), but if you already know what ails you, go to a specialist. In addition to public clinics and hospitals, there are private practices throughout the city. You could also enquire at your embassy for information on doctors who speak your language, but English is widely spoken.

Taxes

A value-added tax (VAT), normally 23%, is included in the price of goods, less for items like books and food. Non-European Union residents can get VAT refunds at the airport only with a form obtained at shops with "tax free" or "duty free" signs, if they've spent a minimum of 120€. Ask for the form at the shop, and before departing Athens airport, look for the tax-refund booth (☎ 210/353-2216) at the departures level.

Telephones

For directory inquiries in Greece, dial ☎ 11888. For international calls, dial 00, then the country code. For international phone assistance, dial ☎ 139. Most public phones accept only phone cards, which are available at kiosks. **Telecards** come in denominations of 4€ and 10€. Local calls cost .03€ per minute. International rates vary, with calls to the U.S., Canada, and Australia (Zone I) costing .29€ per minute. **Prepaid calling cards** are available at kiosks, post offices, OTEshop (phone company) outlets, and money-exchange bureaus (which can also tell you what card gives the best rate for the country you want to call). Denominations are usually 5€, 10€, and 20€. Other phone companies include **AT&T** (☎ 00/ 800-1311); **MCI** (☎ 00/800-1211); and **Sprint** (☎ 00/800-1411).

Time Zone

Greece is 7 hours ahead of Eastern Standard Time (EST) in the United States; it's 2 hours ahead of London and 8 hours behind Sydney. Daylight saving time goes into effect in Greece each year from the end of March to the end of October.

Tipping

Round up to the nearest euro in a taxi; leave 10% to 20% at restaurants and bars. Restaurants include a service charge in the bill, but many people add a 10% tip on top of that. Hotel chambermaids should get at least 1€ per day and bellhops 1€ to 2€, depending on the service.

Toilets

There are public and coin-operated toilets in some locations (look for the wc sign), such as main squares, but most people use the facilities at restaurants and cafes.

Tourist Traps & Scams

Walk against the traffic to avoid motorcycle-riding purse snatchers. Don't accept offers of possibly drugged food or water from strangers at tourist sites, and avoid touts that take lone males to hostess bars, or fast friends who promise hotel-room parties. You will pay exorbitant bills if you succumb. Taxi drivers are notorious for overcharging, or giving you change for a smaller denomination bill. Put your hand over the keypad at ATMs when you enter your PIN to avoid card theft.

Travelers with Disabilities

Athens's accessibility consciousness is fledgling. The **European Network for Accessible Tourism** (☎ 210/614-8380; www.accessible tourism.org) has information, or check the relevant transport and hotel websites for accessibility. See **www.europeforall.com** or **www. sath.org** for further information on accessible travel in Greece. The Frommer's website maintains a list of U.S.- and U.K.-origin resources under "Tips for Travelers with Disabilities." The **Tactile Museum for the Blind,** by appointment only, is at 198 Doiranis and 17 Athinas streets, Kallithea (☎ 210/941-5222; www.fte.org.gr).

Visitor Information

The **Greek National Tourism Organization (GNTO)** head office is at 7 Tsochas Street (☎ 210/870-7000; www.gnto.gr); the central information desk is at 26 Amalias Street (☎ 210/331-0392).

Two good online resources are the privately maintained **www.greecetravel.com** and, for sites of interest, the Hellenic Ministry of Culture's **www.culture.gr**.

The **Tourist Police,** 43 Veikou Street (☎ 171 or 210/920-0724), south of the Acropolis, offer round-the-clock tourist information in English.

Useful Phrases & Menu Terms

When you're asking for or about something and have to rely on single words or short phrases, it's an excellent idea to use *"sas parakaló,"* meaning "please" or "you're welcome" to introduce or conclude almost anything you say.

Phrases

ENGLISH	GREEK
Airport	Aerothrómio
Automobile	Aftokínito
Avenue	Leofóros
Bad	Kakós, -kí, -kó*
Bank	Trápeza
Breakfast	Proinó
Bus	Leoforío
Can you tell me?	Boríte ná moú píte?
Cheap	Ft(h)inó
Church	Ekklissía
Closed	Klistós, stí, stó*
Coffeehouse	Kafenío
Cold	Kríos, -a, -o*
Dinner	Vrathinó
Do you speak English?	Miláte Angliká?
Excuse me.	Signómi(n).
Expensive	Akrivós, -í, -ó*
Farewell!	Stó ka-ló! *(to person leaving)*
Glad to meet you.	Chéro polí.**
Good	Kalós, lí, ló*
Goodbye.	Adío *or* chérete.**
Good health (cheers)!	Stín (i)yá sas *or* Yá-mas!
Good morning *or* Good day.	Kaliméra.
Good evening.	Kalispéra.
Good night.	Kaliníchta.**
Hello!	Yássas *or* chérete!**
Here	Ethó
Hot	Zestós, -stí, -stó*
Hotel	Xenothochío**
How are you?	Tí kánete *or* Pós íst(h)e?
How far?	Pósso makriá?
How long?	Póssi óra *or* Pósso(n) keró?
How much does it cost?	Póso káni?
I am a vegetarian.	Íme hortophágos.
I am from New York.	Íme apó tí(n) Néa(n) Iórki.
I am lost *or* I have lost the way.	Écho chathí *or* Écho chási tón drómo(n).**
I'm sorry.	Singnómi.
I'm sorry, but I don't speak Greek (well).	Lipoúme, allá thén miláo elliniká (kalá).

I don't understand.	Thén katalavéno.
I don't understand, please repeat it.	Thén katalavéno, péste to páli, sás parakaló.
I want to go to the airport.	Thélo ná páo stó aerothrómio.
I want a glass of beer.	Thélo éna potíri bíra.
I would like a room.	Tha íthela ena thomátio.
It's (not) all right.	(Dén) íne en dáxi.
Left (direction)	Aristerá
Lunch	Messimerianó
Map	Chártis**
Market (place)	Agorá
Mr.	Kírios
Mrs.	Kiría
My name is . . .	Onomázome . . .
New	Kenoúryos, -ya, -yo*
No	Óchi**
Old	Paleós, -leá, -leó* (*pronounce* palyós, -lyá, -lyó)
Open	Anichtós, -chtí, -chtó*
Patisserie	Zacharoplastío**
Pharmacy	Pharmakío
Please *or* You're welcome.	Parakaló.
Please call a taxi (for me).	Parakaló, fonáxte éna taxi (yá ména).
Point out to me, please . . .	Thíkste mou, sas parakaló . . .
Post office	Tachidromío**
Restaurant	Estiatório
Restroom	Tó méros *or* I toualétta
Right (direction)	Dexiá
Saint	Ágios, agía, (*plural*) ági-i (*abbreviated* ag)
Show me on the map.	Díxte mou stó(n) chárti.**
Square	Plateia
Station (bus, train)	Stathmos (leoforíou, trénou)
Stop (bus)	Stási(s) (leoforíou)
Street	Odós
Thank you (very much).	Efcharistó (polí).**
Today	Símera
Tomorrow	Ávrio
Very nice	Polí oréos, -a, -o*
Very well	Polí kalá *or* En dáxi
What?	Tí?
What time is it?	Tí ôra íne?
What's your name?	Pós onomázest(h)e?
Where am I?	Pou íme?
Where is . . . ?	Poú íne . . . ?
Why?	Yatí?

* Masculine ending -os, feminine ending -a or -i, neuter ending -o.

** Remember, *ch* should be pronounced as in Scottish *loch* or German *ich*, not as in the word *church*.

Numbers

	Midén
	Éna
	Dío
	Tría
	Téssera
	Pénde
	Éxi
	Eftá
	Októ
	Enyá
10	Déka
11	Éndeka
12	Dódeka
13	Dekatría
14	Dekatéssera
15	Dekapénde
16	Dekaéxi
17	Dekaeftá
18	Dekaoktó
19	Dekaenyá
20	Íkossi
21	Íkossi éna
22	Íkossi dío
30	Triánda
40	Saránda
50	Penínda
60	Exínda
70	Evdomínda
80	Ogdónda
90	Enenínda
100	Ekató(n)
101	Ekatón éna
102	Ekatón dío
150	Ekatón penínda
151	Ekatón penínda éna

152	Ekatón penínda dío
200	Diakóssya
300	Triakóssya
400	Tetrakóssya
500	Pendakóssya
600	Exakóssya
700	Eftakóssya
800	Oktakóssya
900	Enyakóssya
1,000	Chílya*
2,000	Dío chilyádes*
3,000	Trís chilyádes*
4,000	Tésseris chilyádes*
5,000	Pénde chilyádes*

Days of the Week

Monday	Deftéra
Tuesday	Tríti
Wednesday	Tetárti
Thursday	Pémpti
Friday	Paraskeví
Saturday	Sávvato
Sunday	Kiriakí

Menu Terms

arní avgolémono	lamb with lemon sauce
arní soúvlas	spit-roasted lamb
arní yiouvétsi	baked lamb with orzo
bakaliáro (skordaliá)	cod (with garlic)
barboúnia (skáras)	red mullet (grilled)
briám	vegetable stew
brizóla chiriní	pork steak or chop
brizóla moscharísia	beef or veal steak
choriátiki saláta	"village" salad ("Greek" salad to Americans)
dolmades	stuffed vine leaves
domátes yemistés mé rízi	tomatoes stuffed with rice
eksóhiko	lamb and vegetables wrapped in phyllo

garídes	shrimp
glóssa (tiganití)	sole (fried)
kalamarákia (tiganitá)	squid (fried)
kalamarákia (yemistá)	squid (stuffed)
kaparosaláta	salad of minced caper leaves and onion
karavídes	crayfish
keftedes	fried meatballs
kotópoulo soúvlas	spit-roasted chicken
kotópoulo yemistó	stuffed chicken
kouloúri	pretzel-like roll covered with sesame seeds
oukánika	spiced sausages
oukoumades	round, doughnut-hole-like pastries deep-fried, then drenched with honey and topped with powdered sugar and cinnamon
melitzanosaláta	eggplant salad
moussaká	meat-and-eggplant casserole
oktapódi	octopus
païdákia	lamb chops
paradisiako	traditional Greek cooking
pastítsio	baked pasta with meat
piláfi rízi	rice pilaf
piperiá yemistá	stuffed green peppers
revídia	chickpeas
saganáki	grilled cheese
skordaliá	hot garlic-and-beet dip
soupiés yemistés	stuffed cuttlefish
souvlaki	lamb (sometimes veal) on the skewer
spanokópita	spinach pie
stifádo	stew, often of rabbit or veal
taramosaláta	fish roe with mayonnaise
tirópita	cheese pie
tsípoura	dorado
tzatzíki	yogurt-cucumber-garlic dip
youvarlákia	boiled meatballs with rice

Index

A

Abaton (Epidaurus), 191
Abyssinia Square (Athens), 87
Academy of Athens, 75
Accommodations, 677–78. *See also*
    Where to Stay & Dine *sections*
    best, 14–15
    tipping, 684
    tips, 114, 177, 235, 302, 406, 444,
        490, 631
    with children, 678
Achaia Clauss (Patras), 224
Achilleion (Corfu), 8, 606, 610, 629
Achilleion Diving Center (Corfu), 628
Acquaplus Waterpark
    (Chersonissos), 11, 263
Acrocorinth (Peloponnese), 4, 11, 32,
    173, 176, 178, 186, 315
Acronafplia (Nafplion), 28, 176, 218
Acropolis
    Athens, 20, 30, 38, 44, 47, 69, 80
    Dodona, Ancient, 597
    Lindos, 380, 408, 410
Acropolis Museum (Athens), 6,
    44–46, 59, 249
Acropolis Walkway (Athens), 42–44,
    68, 81
Adamas, 316–17
    sea front promenade, 316
Adrianou Street (Monastiraki, Ath-
    ens), 39, 87
Adrianou Street (Plaka, Athens), 39,
    90
Adrina (Skopelos), 510
Aegean Diving College (Paros), 340
Aegean Festival (Skiathos), 507
Aegean Islands, Northeastern, 438–83
    getting around, 443, 445, 447,
        483
    getting there, 443, 445, 447, 453,
        482
    hotels & restaurants, 444, 464–
        65, 472–73, 480–81
    nightlife & entertainment, 465,
        481
    practical information, 482–83
    visitor information, 483
Aegean Maritime Museum
    (Mykonos), 358
Aegina, 140, 144–45, 148–51
Aegina Town, 148–49
Aeginitissa Beach (Aegina), 150
Aeolou Street (Athens), 86
Agathi Beach (Rhodes), 374, 386,
    403

Agathi Watersports (Rhodes), 403
Agia Aikaterina (Iraklion), 260–61
Agia Marina
    Aegina, 138, 145, 146, 150
    Spetses, 143, 146
    Symi, 415
Agia Moni (Meteora), 583
Agia Moni Convent (Nafplion), 219
Agia Paraskevi (Spetses), 146
Agia Sofia Church (Thessaloniki),
    249, 525, 550
Agia Triada (Crete), 238, 244–45,
    255
Agia Trianda (Meteora), 582
Agii Anargyri
    Poros, 161
    Spetses, 146
Agii Apostoli Solaki (Athens), 45, 76
Agii Asomati (Athens), 76
Agii Theodori (Athens), 78, 645
Agioi Pantes, 287
Agios Andreas Bay (Kefalonia), 615
Agios Antonios (Meteora), 583
Agios Dimitrias (Mystras), 204
Agios Dimitrios
    Meteora, 583
    Thessaloniki, 249, 552
Agios Dimitrios Loumbardiaris
    (Athens), 76, 81
Agios Eleftherios (Athens), 78–79
Agios Fokas (Skyros), 516–18
Agios Giorgios (Antiparos), 306
Agios Ioannis (Glossa), 487,
    490, 511
Agios Ioannis Spiliotis (Paros), 340
Agios Mammas (Naxos), 347
Agios Nikolaos
    Crete, 239, 246, 284–86, 292–93
    Kefalonia, 615
    Symi, 415
Agios Nikolaos Anapafsa (Meteora),
    582
Agios Nikolaos Padova (Meteora),
    583
Agios Panteleimon Monastery
    (Nissi), 573
Agios Sostis (Mykonos), 299, 361
Agios Stefanos
    Kos, 387, 422
    Rhodes Town, 395
Agios Stephanos (Meteora), 582–83
Agios Titos (Iraklion), 259
Agios Yeoryios
    Siros, 369
    Skyros Town, 515
Agnonda, 510
Agora, ancient

Athens, 20, 30, 42, 45, 56, 70,
    90–91, 315
Delos, 310, 315
Thera, Ancient, 329
Thessaloniki, 552
Agora of the Competialists (Delos),
    310
Agora of the Italians (Delos), 310
Agrio Livadi (Patmos), 387, 432
Airlines, 672. *See also Fast Facts for
    specific regions/islands*
Airports
    Athens, 672, 673
    Thessaloniki, 672
Akropol Theatre (Athens), 125
Akrotiri (Santorini), 23, 29, 35, 301–2,
    305, 322–24, 327–28
Akrotiri Peninsula (Crete), 238
Aktaion (Rhodes Town), 394
Alexander the Great, 26, 190–91, 249,
    336, 527, 528, 530–32, 637, 640
Aliki Beach (Poros), 9, 144, 146, 162
Ali Pasha, 248, 569, 573
Ali Pasha's Tomb (Ioannina), 565,
    568, 573, 595
Allou Fun Park and Kidom (Athens), 67
Alonnisos, 491, 494, 496–99
    getting there, 497
Alonnisos Diving School, 497
Alonnisos Walking Club, 497–98
Altis (Olympia), 181
Amari, 271
Amari Valley (Crete), 231, 238, 270–71
Ampelos (Samos), 461
Anafiotika (Athens), 80, 90
Anaktoron (Samothraki), 455
Anargyrios and Korgialenios College
    (Spetses), 142
Anavasi (maps), 541
Anavatos, 448, 470
Ancient Agora (Athens), 20, 30, 42,
    45, 70, 315
Ancient ruins. *See* Ruins &
    archaeological sites; Theaters,
    ancient
Andritsena, 28, 182, 208
Angelokastro (Corfu), 602, 610
Angistri, 145, 154–55
Anidri, 252
Ano Klima, 510–11
Ano Meara (Mykonos), 360
Ano Mera (Milos), 320
Ano Petali, 351
Ano Polis (Thessaloniki), 527, 552–53
Ano Siros, 366, 369
Antiparos, 306, 339–40
Antiparos Cave, 306, 339–40
Antoniou (Megalochori), 326

Apiranthos, 348
Apokofto (Sifnos), 307, 354
Apollonas, 347
Apollonia, 307, 350
Apollon Theatre (Ermoupolis), 368
Apothika, 471
Aptera, 279-80
Aquarium Museum (Rhodes Town), 394
Arachova, 566, 571, 576
Aradena Gorge (Crete), 254
Arcadia (Peloponnese), 28, 182
Arcadian Dipylon (Messene), 194
Archaeological and Folklore Museum (Horio), 415
Archaeological, Folklore and Historic Museum of Spetses, 164
Archaeological Museum
  Agios Nikolaos, 239, 284-86
  Argos, 181, 188
  Corfu Town, 606, 609-10, 623
  Delos, 309-12
  Ermoupolis, 368
  Fira, 301, 324
  Hania, 274-75
  Hora
    Mykonos, 358-59
    Peloponnese, 193
  Ioannina, 574
  Iraklion, 6, 35, 231, 232-33, 236, 240-41, 249, 262
  Kastro (Sifnos), 353
  Monemvassia, 201
  Mytilini, 474
  Nafplion, 176, 180, 214-15, 216
  Naxos Town, 345
  Olympia, 6, 177, 181, 195
  Parikia, 302, 306, 336
  Patras, 223
  Plaka Peninsula, 317-18
  Poros, 161
  Rethymnon, 268-69
  Rhodes Town, 381, 393-94
  Sitia, 289
  Skyros Town, 516
  Sparta, 192-93
  Thessaloniki, 6, 24, 526-27, 551
  Vathy, 440, 443, 447, 453, 458-59
Archaeological sites. See Ruins & Archaeological sites
Archaic period, 642-43
Archanes, 262
Architecture, 8, 74, 314-15, 642-49
  Byzantine, 76-79, 200-203
  Cycladic, 307
  Hellenic, 152-53
  Minoan, 240-47

Arch of Galerius (Thessaloniki), 527, 551
Area codes, 678
Areopagus (Athens), 70
Areopolis, 210-11
Argenti Museum (Chios Town), 468
Arghia Cave (Naxos), 348
Argolid Plain (Peloponnese), 186
Argos, 32, 181, 188
Argostoli, 603, 611, 614-15
Aristotelous Square (Thessaloniki), 552
Aristotelous Street (Thessaloniki), 550
Arkadi Monastery (Crete), 8, 238, 269
Arnados, 312
Arsakeion (Athens), 75
Arsinoeion (Samothraki), 455
Art, 642-49. See also specific museums and galleries
  Byzantine, 291
Artemonas, 351-52
Art Gallery (Metsovo), 568, 586
Art Gallery Museum (Rhodes Town), 381, 391
Artisan workshops (Mycenae), 189
Arts & crafts
  Athens, 39, 93, 97, 98-100
  Dion, 525, 533
  Hania, 16, 283
  Lindos Town, 408-9
  Monodendri, 589
  Nafplion, 16, 219
  Skyros Town, 519
Arvanitia (Nafplion), 28, 32, 217, 219
Asia Minor Catastrophe, 639
Asine (Gulf of Argos), 217
Askeli (Poros), 147
Asklepion
  Athens, 69
  Corinth, Ancient, 187
  Kos, 376, 385, 420-21
Aslan Mosque (Ioannina), 249, 594
Aspronisi, 324
Assos, 611, 616
Asteria Glyfada (south of Athens), 130-31
Asteri Vouliagmeni (south of Athens), 131
Athena Temple (Horio), 415
Athenian Treasury (Delphi), 579
Athens, 2, 20, 24, 30, 36-129, 134-35
  accommodation booking services, 112
  getting around, 134, 675-77
  getting there, 134, 672-74
  hotels, 14, 112-19

  movie theaters, 38, 57, 83, 125
  nightlife & entertainment, 12, 39, 120-29
  practical information 134-35
  restaurants, 13, 39, 104-11
  shopping, 16, 39, 92-103
  tours, organized, 135, 673
  visitor information, 135
  with children, 64-67
Athens Epidaurus Festival, 38, 125, 669
Athens Race Track, 129
Athens University Historical Museum, 59
Athinas Street (Athens), 39, 91
Athonos Square (Thessaloniki), 550
Athos Sea Cruises (Ouranoupolis), 537
ATMs, 678-79
Atsitsa, 495, 516
Attica Zoological Park (Athens), 67

B
Baby-sitting, 679
Badminton Theater (Athens), 129
Balkan Wars, 638-39
Banking hours, 679
Bars & clubs
  Athens, 121-25, 126-27
  Corfu, 625
  Faliraki, 374, 407
  Hydra, 158
  Kos, 427
  Lindos, 411
  Mykonos, 365
  Rhodes Town, 397
  Samos, 465
  Santorini, 333
  Skiathos, 507
  Thessaloniki, 557
Basilica of St. Andrew (Patras), 223-24
Bassae, 4, 28, 34, 153, 182, 194-95, 208
Bathhouse of the Winds (Athens), 59
Battle of Marathon, 637
Battle of Navarino, 638, 641
Battle of Salamis, 457, 637
Beaches, 9. See also specific beaches
  Aegina, 138, 146, 147, 149-50
  Alonnisos, 491, 494, 497
  Angistri, 138, 145, 147, 154
  Athens, 130-33
  Chios, 444, 471
  Corfu, 607, 610
  Crete
    Chryssi Island, 289
    Elafonisi, 9, 251-52
    Falasarna, 251

Kliopatria, 293
Komos, 255
Makriyialos, 288
Marmara Beach, 254
Matala, 237, 255
Palm Beach, 237, 270
Red Beach, 255
Rethymnon, 268
Stavros, 280
Sweetwater Beach, 253-54
Vai, 290
Gulf of Argos, 217
Hydra, 158
Ithaca, 617
Kefalonia, 9, 611, 615
Kos, 387, 388, 422-25
Lesbos, 9, 441, 445, 449, 479
Milos, 9, 17, 318, 319
Mykonos, 299, 303, 360, 361
Naxos, 9, 346, 347
Northern Greece, 529, 536-37
Paros, 306, 340
Patmos 9, 387, 388, 432-33
Peloponnese, 9, 28, 32, 208, 217, 219
Poros, 9, 144, 146-47, 162
Rhodes, 9, 374, 380, 384, 386, 387, 402-4, 409
Samos, 443, 446, 460
Santorini, 302, 328
Sifnos, 307, 354
Siros, 369
Skiathos, 9, 486-87, 488-49, 492-93, 503-4, 505
Skopelos, 490, 510, 511
Skyros, 495, 516-18
Spetses, 143, 146
Symi, 415
Beach resorts
Kos, 422-25
Rhodes, 402-7
Bema (Ancient Corinth), 187
Benaki Museum (Athens), 50-51, 62-63
Beulé Gate (Athens), 47
Biking, 660, 679
Blessed David Church (Osios David; Thessaloniki), 7, 525, 553
Boating/Sailing, 661
Central & Western Greece, 568, 569, 595
Crete, 230-31, 287
Cyclades, 2, 319, 328
Dodecanese, 376, 384, 415, 432
Ionian Islands, 603
Northern Greece, 537
Saronic Gulf Islands, 17, 138-39
Sporades, 487, 491, 498

Bouboulina, Laskarina, 166
Bouboulina Museum (Spetses Town), 139, 142-43, 165
Bouleterion
Delos, 310
Dodona, Ancient, 597
Bourgo (Naxos Town), 305, 344
Bourtzi
Nafplion, 176, 219
Skiathos Town, 502
Boutari (Megalochori), 326
Bouzoukia
Athens, 128
Thessaloniki, 525, 557, 559
Bros Therma (Kos), 376-77, 385, 387, 422
Business hours, 679
Bus travel, 673, 675-76
Byzantine and Christian Museum (Athens), 63, 79
Byzantine and Folklore Museum (Panormitis), 412
Byzantine and Post-Byzantine Collection (Hania), 7, 276
Byzantine Empire, 7, 76-79, 200-204, 248-49, 637, 644-45
Byzantine Museum
Chios Town, 466
Corfu Town, 610, 621, 623
Ioannina, 568, 573, 595
Byzantine Road (Paros), 306, 338-39

C
Caldera path (Santorini), 324
Calypso Bay (Poros), 147
Campiello (Corfu Town), 621
Camping Mitkas (Litochoro), 529
Car travel, 676-77, 682. See also Fast Facts for specific regions/islands
Casa Romana (Kos Town), 420
Cash points, 678-79
Casinos
Athens, 126
Rhodes, 397
Thessaloniki, 557
Castalian Spring (Delphi), 27
Castel di Morea (Patras), 224
Castello dei Franchi (Nafplion), 218
Castello dei Greci (Nafplion), 218
Castello del Torrione (Nafplion), 218
Castle (Samos), 463
Castle of Mina (Gerolimenas), 212
Castle of St. John (Horio), 415
Castle of the Knights (Kos Town), 377, 385, 418
Cave of the Apocalypse (Patmos), 377, 385, 430
Cave of the Bear (Crete), 280

Cave of the Nymphs (Ithaca), 611, 617
Caves
Crete, 256, 280
Ithaca, 611, 617
Kefalonia, 603, 611, 616
Naxos, 348
Paros, 306, 339-40
Patmos, 377, 385, 430
Peloponnese, 211
Skiathos, 486, 493, 504
Zagori, 574-75
Cellphones, 672
Central & Western Greece, 17, 562-99
getting around, 599
getting there, 598
hotels & restaurants, 576, 580-81, 591, 596
practical information, 598-99
visitor information, 599
Central court (Knossos), 243
Central Market (Athens), 54, 91, 101
Centre of Contemporary Art (Rhodes Town), 391
Ceramics (Skyros), 519
Chalki, 348
Changing of the Guard (Athens), 51, 64
Chersonissos, 263
Children. See Family travel
Children's Museum (Athens), 65
Chios, 2, 7, 15, 440-41, 444, 447-48, 466-73
getting there & around, 445, 482-83
mastic villages, 2, 441, 444, 447, 469, 471, 473
Chios Town, 444, 447, 466-68
Chrissi Akti (Paros), 340
Christian catacombs (Milos), 317
Christos Go-Carts (Kos), 424
Christos sto Daos (Paros), 339
Chrysopigi, 307, 353-54
Chryssi Island, 289
Churches. Including basilicas, cathedrals, chapels, etc.
Aegina, Agios Nektarios, 145
Agiassos, Church of the Panagia Vrefokratousa, 476
Angistri, Church of Agii Anargyri, 154
Ano Siros, Basilica of San Giorgio, 369
Apollonia, Panagia Ouranophora, 350
Artemonas, Panagia tou Barou, 352
Athens
Agii Apostoli Solaki, 45, 76

Agii Asomati, 76
Agii Theodori, 78, 645
Agios Dimitrios Loumbardiaris, 76, 81
Agios Eleftherios, 78–79
Kapnikarea, 78, 86
Panagia Chrysospiliotissa Church, 69
Panagia Gorgoepikoos, 7, 78–79
Sotira Likodimou, 79
Chalki, Church of Panagia Protothrone, 348
Corfu Town
Cathedral of Agios Lakavos, 621
Cathedral of Agios Spyridon, 605, 619, 621
Mitropolis, 621
Dion, Christian basilica, 535
Dodona, Ancient, 597
Filoti, Church of Kimisis tis Theotokou, 348
Folegandros, Church of Kimisis tis Theotokou, 320
Glossa, Agios Ioannis, 487, 490, 511
Hora (Mykonos)
Church of Agia Kyriaki, 360
Church of the Paraportiani, 303, 359–60
Hora (Patmos)
Chapel of St. Artemios, 430
Chapel of the Saints Apostles, 431
Church of St. John the Divine, 377, 431
Horio, Panagia Church, 415
Iraklion
Agia Aikaterina, 260–61
Agios Marcos Church, 259
Agios Titos, 259
Kastro (Sifnos), Church of the Eftamartyres, 353
Krista, Panagia Kera, 287, 291
Lefkes, Church of Agia Triada, 338
Lindos
Church of Our Lady, 380, 409
Church of St. John, 410
Mandamadhos, Church of the Taxiarchis, 477
Mesta, Megas Taxiarchis, 471
Meteora, St. John the Baptist Chapel, 582
Moni, Church of Panagia Drosiani, 348
Mystras, Agios Dimitrias, 204
Nafplion

Agia Sofia, 216
St. Spyridon Church, 216
To Sotiros (Church of the Transfiguration), 217
Naoussa, Church of Agios Nikolaos Mostratou, 337
Naxos, Agios Mammas, 347
Parikia, Panagia Ekatontopylani (Church of the Hundred Doors), 302, 306, 334–35
Patras, Basilica of St. Andrew, 223–24
Petra, Glykophilousa Panagia, 449, 479
Polyrinia, Ancient, Church of the Holy Fathers, 250
Potami, Church of Metamorphosis, 460
Pyrgi, Church of Agii Apostoli, 471
Skiathos
Church of Trion Ierarchon, 502
Yeni Nisi tou Khristou, 505
Skopelos Topwn
Agia Barbara, 490, 510
Agios Athanasios, 509
St. John the Baptist, 510
Stemnitsa, Church of Moni Agiou Ioannitou, 208–9
Thera, Ancient, Chapel of Agios Stefanos, 329
Thessaloniki
Agia Sofia Church, 249, 525, 550
Agios Dimitrios, 249, 552
Church of Osios David, 7, 525, 553
Panagia Achiropiitos, 552
Panagia Chalkeon, 548
St. George Church, 249, 527, 552
Tinos Town, Church of Panagia Evangelistria tes Tenou, 312
Vrisses
Church at Samonas, 254
Church of the Panayia, 254
Church of Agii Anargyri (Angistri), 154
Church of Osios David (Thessaloniki), 7, 525, 553
Church of Our Lady (Lindos Town), 409
Church of St. John the Divine (Hora, Patmos), 377, 431
Church of the Hundred Doors (Panagia Ekatontopylani; Parikia), 302, 306, 334–35
Church of the Transfiguration (To Sotiros; Nafplion), 217

Cinema, 652
City of Athens Museum, 62
Civilizations of Greece, 248–49
Classical era, 248–49, 637, 642, 644
Clothing (fashion), 649
Athens, 97
Hora (Mykonos), 363
Colossus of Rhodes, 637
Consulates, 679
Convent of Pantanassa (Mystras), 204
Corfu, 501, 600–602, 604–10, 618–33
getting around, 633
getting there, 632–33
hiking & watersports, 628
hotels & restaurants, 624–25, 631
nightlife & entertainment, 12, 625
practical information, 632–33
visitor information, 633
Corfu Golf Club, 628
Corfu Town, 3, 10, 602, 604–6, 607, 608–610, 618–25
nightlife & entertainment, 12, 625
Old Town, 605, 609, 619, 621
Corfu Trail, 628
Corinth, Ancient, 4, 29, 32, 176, 178, 184–86, 187
Coronet Theatre (Athens), 129
Council chamber (Ancient Dodona), 597
Cretaquarium (Crete), 11, 263
Crete, 2, 35, 228–95, 501
accommodations booking services, 235
bus travel, 232–35
getting there & around, 260, 267, 275, 286, 295
hotels & restaurants, 231, 235, 257, 264–65, 272–73, 282–83, 292–93
mythology of, 245
nightlife & entertainment, 12, 265
practical information, 295
visitor information, 260, 267, 275, 286, 295
Cruise lines, 664–65
Currency, 681
Customs regulations, 679
Cyclades, 296–371
accommodations booking services, 302
architecture of, 307
beaches, best, 299, 340, 346, 361
getting around, 309, 318, 323, 370–71
getting there, 305, 309, 318, 323, 335, 342, 351, 358, 366, 370
hotels & restaurants, 302, 313,

321, 330–33, 341, 349, 355, 362–64, 369
nightlife & entertainment, 333, 365, 369
practical information, 370–71
tours, organized, 302
visitor information, 371
Cycladic Art Museum (Athens), 63, 249
Cycladic Collection (Athens), 49

D

Dante's Gate (Spinalonga), 287
Daphni Monastery (Athens), 79
Dapia (Spetses), 142, 164
Dark Ages, 637
Dark Cave (Skiathos), 486, 493, 504
Daskalopetra (Vrontados), 468
Decorative Arts Collection (Rhodes Town), 381, 391–92
Delian Agora (Delos), 310
Delos, 5, 299, 303, 306, 308–12, 315, 352
getting there & around, 309
Delphi, 5, 20–22, 27, 34, 153, 249, 564, 567, 570–71, 576–79
Delphi Archaeological Museum, 27, 564, 567, 570, 576–77
Department stores (Athens), 96–97
Dexia Beach (Ithaca), 617
Diakofto, 181
Dimini, 636
Dimitsana, 28, 182, 209
Dining, 13, 398–99, 653–57, 684. *See also* Where to Dine for specific towns/islands
Dio Horia, 312
Dion, 26, 525, 528–29, 532, 535
shopping, 525, 533
Disabilities, travelers with, 678, 684
Diving, 660
Alonnisos, 497
Corfu, 628
Mykonos, 361
Paros, 340
Skiathos, 505
Dodecanese, 372–437
beaches & beach resorts, 386–88, 402–7, 415, 422–25, 432
getting around, 436–37
getting there, 436
hotels & restaurants, 396–97, 404, 405–7, 411, 416–17, 422–27, 432, 434–35
nightlife & entertainment, 374, 397, 407, 411, 427
practical information, 436–37
visitor information, 437

Dodona, Ancient, 5, 565, 574, 595, 597
Dolphin Diving Center (Skiathos), 505
Domus Venetian Museum (Naxos Town), 345
Dora Stratou Theater (Athens), 57, 125
Doric Temple of Aphaia (Aegina), 138, 140, 145, 150
Doric Temple of Asklepios (Kos), 421
Drachondoschisma Peninsula (Skopelos), 510
Drama, Greek, history of, 456–57
Drogarati (Kefalonia), 611, 616

E

Eastern Orthodox religion, 248–49, 536–39, 584–85, 637, 640, 669
E. Averoff (Metsovo), 568, 586
Ecclesiastical Museum (Panormitis), 412
Economou Mansion (Spetses Town), 139, 167
Ecotourism, 662–64
Educational travel, 661–62
Efpalinio Orygma (Efpalinio Tunnel; Samos), 8, 440, 462
Eftalou (Lesbos), 477
Egnatia Street (Thessaloniki), 527, 552
Egyptian Collection (Athens), 49
Egyptian commandant's house (Ancient Thera), 329
Elafonisi
Crete, 9, 251–52
Peloponnese, 9, 202
Elderhostel, 683
Electricity, 679
Eleftherias Gate (Rhodes Town), 390
Elena Votsi, 649
Athens, 101
Hydra, 157
El Greco (Kyriakos Theotokopoulos), 260–61, 647–48
Elia (Mykonos), 303, 306, 360–61
Elias (Skiathos), 492, 503
Elios (Skopelos), 511
Elounda, 286
Elounda Peninsula (Crete), 231, 239
Embassies, 679
Emergencies, 680
Ephesus (Turkey), 449, 452, 463
Epidaurus, 4–5, 29, 32, 38, 125, 173, 177, 180, 191, 249
Epigraphical Museum (Rhodes Town), 394

Epta Piges (Rhodes), 401
Erechtheion (Athens), 47, 153
Eressos Women's Festival (Lesbos), 481
Ermou (Mytilini), 474
Ermoupoleia (Siros), 369
Ermoupolis, 366
Ermoupolis Industrial Museum, 368–69
Ermou Street (Athens), 39, 56, 86
Esplanade
Corfu Town, 604–5, 609, 618–19, 621
Hora (Mykonos), 306
Etiquette & customs, 680
Etz Hayyim Synagogue (Hania), 276–78
Eurail passes, 675
Eurozone, 639, 641, 681
Evans, Sir Arthur, statue of (Knossos), 243
Event listings, 668–71, 680
Evia, 501
Exambala, 352
Exarchia Square (Athens), 48
Eye Clinic (Athens), 74–75

F

Falasarna, 251
Faliraki, 374, 379, 380, 384, 388, 402
nightlife & entertainment, 12, 374, 379, 407
Faliraki water park, 384, 403
Family travel, 11, 678, 679
Athens, 64–67
Thessaloniki, 553
Faros, 354
Fashion (clothing), 649
Athens, 96
Hora (Mykonos), 363
Ferry travel, 3, 673–74
with children, 678
Festival of the Aegean (Siros), 369
Festivals & special events, 668–71, 680. *See also* Performing arts
Fetiye Mosque
Athens, 56, 91
Ioannina, 249, 565, 568, 573, 595
Filerimos, 400–1
Filopappou Hill (Athens), 81
Filoti, 348
Fira, 23, 35, 301, 304, 322–24
Firkas fortress (Hania), 235, 277
Firostefani, 324–25
Fiskardo, 611, 616
Flisvos Marina (Athens), 67
Flora & fauna, 389, 499, 501
Foki (Chios), 444, 471

okos (Mykonos), 361
olegandros, 320, 321
olk Art Museum (Athens), 59
olklore Museum
  Agios Nikolaos, 286
  Hania, 275
  Hora (Mykonos), 303, 359
  Sitia, 289–90
  Skopelos Town, 494, 508
olk Museum (Kipi), 589
ood & drink, 653–57
  feta, 612–13, 656
  honey, 16
  meze, 398–99, 654
  ouzo, 399, 460, 657
  shops
    Athens, 97–98
    Hora (Mykonos), 363
    Metsovo, 568
    Nafplion, 219
    Naxos Town, 344
    Nissi, 569
  wine, 16, 326, 460, 656–57
ood & wine trips, 661–62
ortezza (Rethymnon), 268
ortress (Lindos), 410
ortress of Kales (Ierapetra), 288
oti Rapakousi Museum (Ioannina),
  565, 594
ountain of Arethusa (Ithaca), 611, 617
ountain of Lerna (Ancient Corinth),
  187
ountain of Peirene (Ancient Corinth),
  187
ourfouras, 271
ranchthi Cave, 636
rangokastello, 254–55
reedom Gate (Rhodes Town), 390
rikes, 611, 617
telia (Mykonos), 361
2 Windsurfing Center (Paros), 340

G

Galatas, 146
Galerian Complex (Thessaloniki),
  527, 550–51
Galissas, 369
Gavdos, 501
Gay & lesbian travelers, 680
  beaches, 361, 479
  nightlife & entertainment
    Athens, 127–28
    Mykonos, 365
Gazi (Athens), 84, 87
Gazi Flea Market (Athens), 39,
  92, 101–2
Geraki, 201
Gerolimenas, 212

Giustiniani mansion (Chios Town), 466
Glauke Fountain (Ancient Corinth), 187
Glossa, 490, 494, 511
Gods & goddesses of Mount
  Olympus, 544–47
Golden Beach (Kos), 425
Golfing, 683
  Athens, 129
  Corfu, 628
Gortyna, 237, 246, 255
Goudouras, 288
Gournes, 263
Gournia, 246, 288
Gouverneto, 238
Granary (Mycenae), 189
Grand Meteoro (Meteora), 583, 585
Grand staircase (Knossos), 243
Granite Palaestra (Delos), 310
Grave circle (Mycenae), 189
Greco-Turkish War, 639
Greek National Opera, 125
Greek National Tourist Organization,
  445, 482
Greek Travel Pages, 445, 482
Grikos (Patmos), 432
Gritsa Beach (near Litochoro), 529
Grotto (Ancient Thera), 329
Gulf of Argos, 180, 217
Gymnasium
  Olympia, 196
  Thera, Ancient, 329
Gymnasium of the Ephebes (Ancient
  Thera), 329
Gythion, 212

H

Hadrian's Arch (Athens), 46, 68
Halikiada (Angistri), 154
Hania Gate (Iraklion), 261
Hania, 10, 231, 234–35, 238, 274–83
  shopping, 16, 283
Happy Train (Athens), 66
Haraki Bay (Rhodes), 2, 403
Health concerns, 680, 683
Health insurance, 680–81
Hellenic Festival (Epidaurus), 177, 190
Hellenistic-era theater (Dion), 535
Heracles (Ancient Dodona), 597
Heraion (Ancient Samos), 443, 444,
  452–53, 463
Heraklion Archaeological
  Museum, 636
Hercules (Ancient Dodona), 597
Herodes Atticus Theater (Athens),
  30, 69, 120, 125, 669–70
Hieron (Samothraki), 455
Hiking, 660–61, 662
  Alonnisos, 497–98

Corfu, 628
Crete, 2, 17, 230, 235, 238, 252,
  253
Mount Olympus, 17, 525, 529,
  540–41
Patmos, 430
Samos, 440, 459–60
Sifnos, 17, 298, 307, 353
Zagori, 565, 568, 573, 581, 589
Hill Memorial School (Athens), 90
Hippocrates, 385, 418, 420
Hippodrome (Olympia), 196
Historical and Folk Art Museum
  (Rethymnon), 269
Historical Museum
  Hania, 278
  Hydra port, 144
Historical Museum of Crete (Iraklion),
  233, 261–62
History of Greece, 248–49, 636–41
Holidays, national, 668, 669, 680
Holy Mount Athos Pilgrim's Bureau,
  538
  Ouranoupolis branch office, 539
Holy Trinity (Agia Trianda; Meteora),
  582
Holy Week, 669
Homer, 457, 468, 470, 651,
Hora
  Alonnisos, 487, 491, 494
  Folegandros, 298, 320
  Mykonos, 10, 302, 306, 356–60
  Patmos, 385, 429
  Peloponnese, 193
Hora Sfakion, 254
Horio, 384, 415
Horseback riding, 661
  Mykonos, 361
Hot springs
  Kos, 376–77, 385, 387, 422
  Lesbos, 441, 445, 449, 477
House of Dionysus (Delos), 310
House of Priests (Ancient Dodona),
  597
House of the Columns (Mycenae), 189
House of the Dolphins (Delos), 310
House of the Masks (Delos), 310
House on the Lake (Delos), 310
House-swapping, 677–78
Hovolo (Skopelos), 490, 511
Hydra, 29, 139, 141, 156–59
  history of, 158
  nightlife & entertainment, 158
  port, 139, 143–44, 156–58
  seawall promenade, 158
Hydra Historical Archaeological
  Museum, 158
Hyselotera (Meteora), 583

I

Ia, 10, 23, 301, 304, 325
Ialyssos, Ancient, 400-1
Iera Odos
    Delphi, 571, 579
    Samos, 453
Iera Oikia (Ancient Dodona), 597
Ierapetra, 288
Ifestou Street (Athens), 87
Ikos (Kokkinokastro), 494, 497
Iliad, the, 249, 636-37, 651
Iliou Melathron (Athens), 62, 74
Imbros Gorge (Crete), 254
Imerovigli, 301, 325
International Hippocratic Foundation
    (Kos), 421
Internet access, 339, 681
Ioannina, 568-69, 573, 574, 592-96
    shopping, 16, 569, 573
Ionian Islands, 600-633
    getting around, 633
    getting there, 632-33
    hotels & restaurants, 617, 624-25,
        631
    nightlife & entertainment, 625
    practical information, 632-33
    visitor information, 633
Iraklidon Street (Athens), 56
Iraklion, 6, 35, 232-33, 236, 249,
    258-65
    city walls, 236, 261
    nightlife & entertainment, 265
Iron Gates (Samaria Gorge), 253
Islands of Greece, 500-501
Isthmus of Corinth, 11, 174-75, 178
    getting there, 175
Ithaca, 603, 611, 614, 617
Its Kale (Ioannina), 249, 568, 573,
    594

J

Jewelry & silver, 649
    Athens, 16, 101
    Hania, 16, 283
    Hora (Mykonos), 363
    Hydra port, 157
    Ioannina, 16, 569, 573
    Nafplion, 16, 219
Jewish Community of Thessaloniki,
    554
Jewish Museum of Greece (Athens),
    59
Jewish Museum of Thessaloniki, 554
Jewish Quarter (Corfu Town), 621

K

Kainouryia Gate (Iraklion), 261
Kaiser's Throne (Pelekas), 607

Kalafati Dive Center (Mykonos), 361
Kalafi (Mykonos), 361
Kalambaka, 567, 571, 580-81
    monasteries, 580-81
Kalambaka-Meteora footpath, 567,
    571, 581
Kalamitsa, 495
Kalavria, 146-47
Kalavrita, 181
Kalavrita Express (Peloponnese),
    11, 181
Kalikatsou (Patmos), 432
Kalliopi Papalexopoulos statue
    (Nafplion), 216
Kallithea Spa (Rhodes), 401
Kalogeriko Bridge (near Kipi), 590
Kalogria, 208
Kalo Livadi (Mykonos), 303, 306,
    360-61
Kalpaki 1940-41 War Museum, 588
Kalymnos, 385, 424
Kamari
    Kos, 422-23
    Santorini, 302
Kambos
    Chios, 440-41, 444, 447, 469
    Patmos, 9, 388, 432
Kamilari, 255
Kamiros, Ancient, 400
Kanapitsa Water Sports Center
    (Skiathos), 505
Kanoni, 607, 627-28
Kapnikarea (Athens), 78, 86, 645
Karathonia (Gulf of Argos), 217
Kardamena (Kos), 388, 423
Kardamena Watersports Center, 423
Kardamyli, 183, 210
Kare Gorge (Crete), 254
Karitena, 28, 172, 182, 208
Karzama fortress (Sitia), 289
Kastani, 511
Kastaraki (Naxos), 346
Kastelli Hill (Hania), 277
Kastro
    Folegandros, 320
    Ioannina, 568, 573, 592-95
    Naxos Town, 305, 344-45
    Parikia, 336
    Patras, 222
    Sifnos, 307, 353
    Skiathos, 505
    Skopelos Town, 487, 489-90
Kastronisia, 505
Kategogeion (Epidaurus), 191
Kato (Patmos), 432
Kato Klima, 511
"Kebab Street," (Athens), 39, 107
Kefalonia, 611, 614-16, 617

Kefalos (Kos), 422-23
Kerameikos Cemetery (Athens),
    56, 87
Kerkyra, 606. *See* Crete
Kimboloi Museum (Nafplion), 219
Kimolos, 319
Kioni, 611, 617
Kipi, 568, 573, 588-59
Klima
    Milos, 318
    Skopelos, 490, 494, 510-11
Kliopatria (Agios Nikolaos), 293
Knossos, 5, 35, 233, 236, 241-43, 249,
    262, 636
Kokkari, 443, 459
Kokkinokastro (Alonnisos), 491,
    494, 497
Kolimbithres (Paros), 340
Kolonaki Square (Athens), 50, 99
Kolona Site & Archaeological
    Museum (Aegina Town), 148-49
Kolymbada, 495
Kolymbia, 404
Komboloi Museum (Nafplion), 219
Komninaki Kralli mansion (Molyvos),
    448, 478
Komos, 255
Konstantinos-Irini (Symi), 415
Kontodimos Bridge (near Kipi), 590
Korgialenio History and Folklore
    Museum (Argostoli), 611, 614
Kos, 385, 389, 418-27
    beaches & resorts, 422-25
    nightlife & entertainment, 427
    salt marsh, 385, 389
Kos Archaeological Museum, 385,
    418-20
Kos Town, 385, 418-20
Koukounaries, 492, 503
Koukounaries Beach (Skiathos),
    486-87, 492
Koules (Iraklion), 8, 236, 262
Kounopetra (Kefalonia), 615
Krista, 287
Kyra Panagia
    Alonnisos, 499
    Skyros, 516
Kyria Vryssiani (Exambala), 352

L

Lake Pamvotis (Zagori), 569, 573
Lake Voulismeni (Agios Nikolaos),
    239, 284
Lalaounis Jewelry Museum (Athens),
    59, 649
Lalaria (Skiathos), 9, 486, 489,
    492-93, 504
Lambi (Kos Town), 385, 423-24

Langada Pass (Peloponnese), 193
Language, 681
 schools, 662
 useful words & phrases, 685–89
Lasithi Plateau (Crete), 231, 238, 256
Laskaris Mansion (Mystras), 204
Lato, 288
Lazarides Bridge (near Kipi), 590
Lefkes, 302, 306, 338
Legal aid, 681
Leonidaion (Olympia), 196
Leonidas statue (Sparta), 183, 192
Lepeda (Kefalonia), 615
Leros, 385
Lesbos, 441, 444–45, 448–49, 474–81
Liberty Gate (Rhodes Town), 390
Lido Water Park (Kos), 424
Lighthouse in Alexandria, 637
Limenaria, 154
Limonki Xerxes (Skiathos), 492, 503
Lindos, 9, 10, 374, 379–80, 384, 388, 408–11
 nightlife & entertainment, 411
Lindos Beach, 9, 380, 388, 409
Lindos Town, 10, 408
Linear A, 241, 244, 249, 637
Linear B, 193, 240–41, 637, 651
Lion Gate (Mycenae), 181, 189, 315
Lipsi, 385
Lissos, 252–53
Liston (Corfu Town), 605, 621
Literature, 651–52
Lithostroto (Argostoli), 614
Litochoro, 529, 540–41, 542–53
Little Banana (Skiathos), 503–4
Little Monastery (Athens), 87
Little train tour (Rhodes Town), 379, 394–95
Little Venice (Hora, Mykonos), 302–3, 306, 359
Lixouri Peninsula (Kefalonia), 9, 611, 615
Loggia (Iraklion), 259
Loggia Mosque of Hassan Pasha (Kos Town), 249, 418
Lost property, 681
Loutra Yeras (Lesbos), 449, 477
Loutro, 253–54
Loutropolis Thermis (Lesbos), 477
Loutro ton Aeridon (Athens), 59
Lycabettus Hill (Athens), 50, 66, 83
Lycabettus Theater (Athens), 125
Lysicrates monument (Athens), 90

M

Macedonia, 530–32, 637, 639
Macedonia Museum of Contemporary Art (Thessaloniki), 551
Magazia, 516
Magic Beach (Kos), 425
Magic Park (Thessaloniki), 553
Mail & postage, 681
Makriyialos, 288
Malia, 245–46
Mandamadhos, 444, 477, 449
Mandraki Harbour (Rhodes Town), 394
Mandraki Peninsula (Skiathos), 489
Mani Peninsula, 172, 183
Manolates, 461
Manos Faltaits Historical and Folklore Museum (Skyros Town), 495, 515–16
Marathi, 306
Marathi Quarries (Paros), 337–38
Marathonas (Aegina), 144, 147, 149–50
Marathonas Beach (Aegina), 150
Marathounda (Symi), 415
Marble (Paros), 298–99, 306, 337–38
Maritime Museum
 Chios Town, 466
 Hania, 276
 Yialos, 414
Markellos Tower (Aegina Town), 149
Markets
 Athens, 39, 54, 91, 92, 101–2
 Hania, 274
 Iraklion, 260
 Mytilini, 474
 Rhodes Town, 378
 Thessaloniki, 527, 548–50
Marmara Beach (Loutro), 254
Marmari (Kos), 385, 424
Martinengo Bastion (Iraklion), 233, 261
Martyr's Square (Rhodes Town), 393
Mastic villages (Chios), 2, 441, 444, 447, 469, 471, 473
Mastihari (Kos), 424
Matala (Crete), 35, 237, 255
Mausoleum at Halicarnassus, 637
Mavra Volia (Chios), 444, 471
Mavromati, 194
Medical insurance, 680–81
Medjitie Djami (Chios Town), 466
Megali Idea, 638
Megalohori, 154
Megalo Seitani (Samos), 443, 446, 460
Megaro Gyzi Cultural Centre (Fira), 322

Megaron Mousikis (Athens), 125–26
Megas Lakkos (Kefalonia), 615
Mega Spileo (Pelopponese), 181, 207, 585
Megisti Lavra (Mount Athos), 585
Megistis Lavras (Kyra Panagia), 499
Melanes Valley (Naxos), 305, 345
Meloi (Meli; Patmos), 432
Meroi, 516
Messene, Ancient, 193–94, 249
Mesta, 471
Metals Collection (Athens), 49
Metamorphosis (Skopelos), 510
Meteora, 7, 26–27, 564, 567, 571, 580–83, 585
 footpath, 567, 571, 581
 monasteries, 7, 26–27, 567, 571, 580–83, 585
Methoni, 172, 182, 210
 fortress, 172, 210
 octagonal castle, 210
Metro (Athens), 134, 673
Metroon (Olympia), 196
Metsovo, 564, 567–68, 572, 586, 591
Mikro Seitani (Samos), 446, 460
Milia (Skopelos), 510
Milos
 Angistri, 154
 Cyclades, 17, 298, 316–21
  getting there & around, 318
Mining Museum (Adamas), 317
Minoan civilization, 231, 240–47, 248–49, 636, 642
Mithymna, 441, 444–45, 478
Mitropoleos Street (Athens), 39, 107
Mitropolis (Corfu Town), 621
Mobile phones, 672
Modiano Market (Thessaloniki), 527, 548–49
Molossi (Zagori), 589
Molyvos, 10, 441, 444–45, 478
Monasteries, 539, 584–85
 Alonnisos, 499, 585
 Athens, 79, 87
 Chios, 441, 444, 448, 469–70
 Corfu, 610
 Crete, 8, 231, 237, 238, 239, 251, 269–70, 271, 280, 290
 Ithaca, 617
 Meteora, 580–83
 Mount Athos, 525, 536–39
 Mykonos, 360
 Naxos, 347
 Nissi, 573
 Paros, 340
 Patmos, 377, 385, 429–30, 431, 585
 Peloponnese, 181, 204, 207, 585

Poros, 138, 140, 144, 161
Rhodes, 400–1
Samos, 461, 462
Santorini, 301, 327
Sifnos, 307, 352, 353–54
Skiathos, 489, 504
Skopelos, 509–10
Skyros, 515
Symi, 384, 412–14
Tinos, 312
Monastery Beach (Poros), 147
Monastery of Moni Panagias
   Tourlianis (Mykonos), 360
Monastery of Panagia Chrysopigi
   (Sifnos), 307, 353–54
Monastery of St. John the Divine/the
   Theologian (Hora, Patmos), 377,
   385, 429–30, 431, 585
   museum, 431
Monastery of the Taxiarchis
   Evangelistrias (Vathy), 354
Monastery of Zoodochos Pigi (Poros),
   138, 140, 144, 161
Monastic life, 584–85
Monastiraki Square (Athens), 87
Monastiri, 312
Monastirioton Synagogue
   (Thessaloniki), 554
Monemvassia, 7, 11, 183, 200–1
Monemvassia Gate, 172, 204
Money, 681
Moni, 348
Moni Agia Triada (Crete), 280
Moni Asomaton (Crete), 271
Moni Chrysoskalitissa (Crete), 251
Moni Evangelismou (Skopelos), 509–10
Moni Evangelistrias (Skiathos), 489,
   504
Moni Gouverneto (Crete), 231, 280
Moni Katheron (Ithaca), 617
Moni Kechrouvni (Tinos), 312
Moni Panagias Spillanis (Samos), 462
Moni Preveli (Crete), 237, 269–70
Moni Toplou (Crete), 239, 290
Moni Vronta (Samos), 461
Monodendri, 568, 573, 589
Mon Repos (Corfu), 602, 606, 623,
   626–27
Monte Smith Hill (Rhodes Town), 395
Mosque of Aga Pasha (Nafplion), 216
Mosque of the Janissaries (Hania),
   277
Mount Athos (Northern Greece),
   525, 536–39
Mount Enos (Kefalonia), 611, 616
Mount Ida (Crete), 271
Mount Ithomi (Peloponnese), 194
Mount Kynthos (Delos), 310

Mount Olympus, 525, 529, 540–47
   gods & goddesses, 544–47
Mount Pantokrator (Corfu), 628
Mount Parnassus (Central Greece),
   576
Mount Poulouki (Skopelos), 490, 494
   monasteries, 509
Mount Profitis Elias
   Antiparos, 306, 340
   Naxos, 347
Mount Tsiknias (Tinos), 312
Mouse Island, 627–28
Moutsouris (Pelion), 564, 575
Municipal Museum (Ioannina), 594
Museum
   Corinth, Ancient, 187
   Dion, 535
   Hora (Patmos), 431
   Mycenae, 177, 181, 190
   Nissi, 569, 573, 595
Museum of Asian Art (Corfu Town),
   607, 610, 622
Museum of Byzantine Culture
   (Thessaloniki), 7, 24, 249, 525,
   527, 551
Museum of Childhood Emotions
   (Athens), 67
Museum of Cretan Ethnology (Vori),
   237
Museum of Greek Children's Art
   (Athens), 65
Museum of Greek Popular Musical
   Instruments (Athens), 58–59, 66
Museum of Iannoulis Chalepas
   (Pyrgos), 313
Museum of Marble Crafts (Pyrgos),
   313
Museum of Natural History (Mytilini),
   463
Museum of Prehistoric Thera (Fira),
   301
Museum of Tenos Artists (Pyrgos), 313
Museum of the History of the
   Excavations (Olympia), 195
Museum of the History of the
   Olympic Games in Antiquity
   (Olympia), 195
Museum of the Olympic Games
   (Olympia), 195
Museums, best, 6
Music, 650–51. See also Bouzoukia;
   Performing Arts
Mycenae, 4, 29, 32, 173, 177, 181,
   188–90, 315
   civilization, 49, 248–49, 636–37
Mycenaean Collection (Athens), 49
Mykonos, 34–35, 302–3, 306,
   356–65

getting there, 358
   nightlife & entertainment, 365
   shopping, 16, 363
   windmills, 360
Mykonos Diving Center, 361
Mykonos Horse Riding, 361
Mykonos Windsurfing Center, 361
Myli, 154
Myrtiotissa (Corfu), 607, 610
Myrtos (Kefalonia), 611, 616
Mystras, 7, 11, 183, 201–4
   Lower Town, 204
Mytikas (Mount Olympus), 541
Mytilini, 445, 449, 474

N

Nafplion, 2, 10, 16, 28–29, 32, 176,
   180, 186, 214–21, 249
   Old Town, 28, 176, 180, 214, 216
   shopping, 16, 219
Nafplion Promenade, 172, 219
Nanou Bay (Symi), 415
Naoussa, 302, 306, 336–37
National Archaeological Museum
   (Athens), 6, 30, 46–49, 63 188,
   249
National Bank of Greece (Nafplion),
   216
National Gardens (Athens), 11, 52, 65
National History Museum (Athens),
   62
National Library (Athens), 75
National Marine Park of Alonnisos
   Northern Sporades, 17, 487, 491,
   494, 496–99
Naval Maritime Museum (Ia), 325–26
Navarinou Square (Thessaloniki),
   527, 550
Naxos, 249, 305, 342–49
   beaches, 346
   getting there, 342
Naxos Town, 342–45
Nea Kaimeni, 324, 328
Nea Moni (Chios), 7, 441, 444, 448,
   469–70
Necropolis (Samothraki), 455
Nemea, Ancient, 32, 181, 190–91
Nemean Games, 181, 190
Neo Frourio (Corfu Town), 605,
   609, 623
Neolithic Collection (Athens), 49
Neorio (Poros), 161
Nestor's Palace (Hora, Peloponnese),
   193
New Art Gallery (Rhodes Town), 391
New Fortress (Corfu Town), 605,
   609, 623
New Market (Rhodes Town), 378, 390

Newspapers & magazines, 681–82
Nightlife & entertainment. See also Performing arts
  Athens, 12, 121–29
  Corfu, 12, 625
  Iraklion, 12, 265
  Hydra, 158
  Lindos, 411
  Mykonos, 12, 365
  Rhodes, 12, 374, 379, 397, 407, 411
  Samos, 465
  Santorini, 333
  Skiathos, 12, 507
  Thessaloniki, 557
Nikis Street (Athens), 88–90
Nissi, 569, 573–74, 595
  shopping, 569
Nissyros, 423
Northeast Citadel (Ioannina), 573, 594
Northern Greece, 522–61
  getting around, 561
  getting there, 560–61
  hotels & restaurants, 533, 538, 542–43, 555–59
  nightlife & entertainment, 557
  practical information, 537, 560–61
  shopping, 533
  visitor information, 561
Northern Pindus National Park Information Center (Zagori), 590
NOS Beach (Symi), 415
Numismatic Museum (Athens), 62, 74
Nymphaeum (Olympia), 196
Nymphaeum of Nike (Samothraki), 455

O

Odeion (Dion), 535
Odeon, Ancient (Kos Town), 420
Odus 1866 (Iraklion), 233
Odyssey, the, 249, 617, 651,
Old Fortress (Corfu Town), 605, 610, 621, 622
Old Synagogue (Ioannina), 592–94
Old Turkish Quarter (Thessaloniki), 552–53
Olimbi, 471
O Loutros (Thessaloniki), 13, 525, 559
Olus, 231, 286, 288
Olympia, 4, 28, 34, 172–73, 177, 181, 195–96
Olympia Theatre (Athens), 125
Olympic Athletic Center of Athens, 129
Olympic Games, 198–99, 639, 641
Olympic Stadium (Athens), 53

Open-Air Water Power Museum (Dimitsana), 209
Opera (Athens), 125. See also Performing arts
Orthodox Culture and Information Center (Skala, Patmos), 428
Orthodox Easter, 669
Ottoman Empire, 248–49, 637, 640–41
Ouranoupolis, 536–37
Outdoor activities, 17, 660–61, 662

P

Palace (Mycenae), 189
Palace of Kato Zakro (Crete), 247, 289
Palace of Knossos (Crete), 5, 35, 233, 236, 241–43, 249, 262
Palace of Malia (Crete), 245–46
Palace of St. Michael and St. George (Corfu Town), 605, 610, 621
Palace of the Despots (Mystras), 204
Palace of the Grand Masters (Rhodes Town), 7, 23, 381, 384, 392–93
Palaestra
  Delos, 310
  Olympia, 196
Palaikastro (Crete), 247, 289
Palamari, 516
Palamidi Fortress (Nafplion), 28, 176, 217
Palea Kaimeni, 324, 328
Paleochora
  Aegina, 145
  Crete, 252
Paleochoria (Milos), 319
Paleo Frourio (Corfu Town), 605, 610, 621, 622
Paleokastritsa (Corfu), 603, 607, 610, 630
Paleopolis (Corfu), 610
Pallas Beach (Rhodes), 409
Palm Beach (Crete), 237
Pamponas (Naxos), 344
Panagia Achiropiitos (Thessaloniki), 552
Panagia Chalkeon (Thessaloniki), 548
Panagia Ekatontopylani (Parikia), 302, 306, 334–35
Panagia Filerimos, 400-1
Panagia Gorgoepikoos (Athens), 7, 78–79
Panathenian Stadium (Athens), 53, 65
Pandrossou Street (Athens), 86
Panormitis Monastery (Symi), 384, 412–14
Panormos (Mykonos), 361

Panormos Bay
  Mykonos, 361
  Skopelos, 510
  Tinos, 313
Papadiamantis Museum (Skiathos Town), 502
Papalexopoulos, Kalliopi, statue of (Nafplion), 216
Paradise (Mykonos), 303, 360, 361
Paradise Beach (Kos), 424
Paralia Kokkini (Santorini), 328
Paralia Thermis (Lesbos), 449, 477
Paranga (Mykonos), 351
Parian Chronicle (Parikia), 336
Parikia, 302, 305–6, 336
Parking, 682
Parko Flisvos (Athens), 67
Parliament building (Athens), 72
Paros, 298–99, 302, 334–41
  beaches, 340
  getting there, 335
Parthenon (Athens), 4, 8, 47, 70, 80, 249
Passports, 682
Patitiri, 497
Patmos, 385, 428–35
  footpaths, 377, 385, 430
Patras, 222–25
Pefkos, 404
Pelekas, 607, 610, 629–30
Pelion, 571
Pella Archaeological Museum, 524, 527–28, 530–31
Pella, 26, 527–28, 530–31
Pelopeion (Olympia), 196
Peloponnese, 170-227
  getting around, 227
  getting there, 175, 226–27
  hotels & restaurants, 177, 197, 205, 213, 220–21, 225
  practical information, 205, 224, 226–27
  shopping, 219
  visitor information, 227
Peloponnesian Folklore Foundation (Nafplion), 176, 180, 215–17, 219
Peloponnesian War, 637, 640
Perama Cave (Zagori), 574–75
Perdika, 140, 144, 150
Performing arts. See also Festivals & special events; Opera
  Athens
    Akropol Theatre, 125
    Badminton Theater, 129
    Coronet Theatre, 129
    Dora Stratou Theater, 57, 125
    Epidaurus Festival, 125
    Greek National Opera, 125

Herodes Atticus Theater, 30, 69, 125
Lycabettus Theater, 125
Megaron Mousikis, 125–26
Olympia Theatre, 125
Pericles Odeon, 69
Technopolis, 57, 87
Terra Vibe, 129
Epidaurus
Epidaurus Theater, 29, 32, 38, 125, 173, 180, 191
Hellenic Festival, 177, 190
Lesbos
Eressos Women's Festival, 481
Theater Festival, 481
Rethymnon, Rethymnon Renaissance Festival, 268
Siros
Apollon Theatre, 368
Ermoupoleia, 369
Festival of the Aegean, 369
Skiathos, Aegean Festival, 507
Skopelos
Trata, 513
Valch's Wedding, 513
Skyros, festival, 517
Thessaloniki, Thessaloniki Concert Hall, 557
Pergamon (Turkey), 449, 452, 478
Pericles Odeon (Athens), 69
Perikleous Street (Athens), 91
Peristera, 499
Perivleptos Monastery (Mystras), 204
Petaloudes, 401
Petra
Lesbos, 445, 479
Patmos, 432
Petrakis Workshop for Icons (Elounda), 291
Petrified Forest (Lesbos), 449, 479
Phaestos (Crete), 35, 237, 244, 249, 255
Phaestos Disk (Crete), 244
Pharmacies, 682
Philip II of Macedonia, 6, 26, 524–25, 528, 530–31
Philippeion (Olympia), 196
Philosophy, 651
Phylakopi (Milos), 318–19
Piperi (Alonnisos), 499
Pirates, 495
Pirgis Frankopolous (Chalki), 348
Pirgos Bellonia (Naxos), 305, 346
Pirgos Dirou Caves (near Areopolis), 211
Pirgos Tower (Naxos), 346
Pitsidia, 255

Plaka
Athens, 46, 66, 80, 88, 90
Naxos, 9, 346
Plaka Beach (near Litochoro), 529
Plaka Peninsula (Milos), 317
Plakidas Bridge (near Kipi), 590
Plane Tree of Hippocrates (Kos Town), 385, 418
Planetarium (Athens), 66–67
Platanakia mountain villages (Samos), 443, 459–60, 461
Platani (Kos Town), 420
Plateia Eleftheriou Venizelou (Iraklion), 258–59
Plateia Iroon (Apollonia), 350
Plateia Kornarou (Iraklion), 260
Plateia Miaoulis (Ermoupolis), 366–68
Plateia Olga (Patras), 222
Plateia Rupert Brooke (Skyros Town), 515
Plateia Syntagma (Nafplion), 2, 28, 173, 176, 180
Plateia Vallianou (Argostoli), 614
Plato Ornos (Mykonos), 361
Plato Yialos (Mykonos), 361
Pnyx Hill (Athens), 39, 82
Police, 682. See also Fast Facts for specific regions/islands
Pollonia, 318, 319
Polychnitou (Lesbos), 445, 449, 477
Polykleitou Street (Athens), 91
Polyrinia, Ancient, 250
Pontikonisi, 627–28
Popular and Folk Art Museum (Apollonia), 350
Porinos Naos (Delos), 310
Poros, 138–39, 140, 144, 146–47, 160–63
modern history of, 163
port, 160–61
Portara (Naxos Town), 153, 299, 305, 342–44
Portara Maggiora (Chios town), 466
Post office, 682. See also Fast Facts for specific regions/islands
Potami, 443, 460
waterfall, 443
Pouria, 516
Prehistoric Exhibit (Rhodes Town), 393
Prodomos, 338–39
Prodromos (Meteora), 583
Profitis Elias (Santorini), 301, 327
Profitis Elias o Pilos (Sifnos), 298, 307, 353
Promodos, 306

Propylaea (Lindos), 410
Propylaia (Athens), 47
Propylon (Samothraki), 455
Propytheria (Delos), 310
Prytaneion
Delos, 310
Dodona, Ancient, 597
Olympia, 196
Psalidi (Kos), 425
Psaromachalas Quarter (Nafplion), 216
Psarou (Mykonos), 361
Psathoura, 499
Psili Ammos (Patmos), 432
Psychro Cave (Crete), 256
Psyrri (Athens), 39, 54, 88, 91
Pylos, 182, 193, 209–10
Pyrgaki (Naxos), 346
Pyrgi, 471
Pyrgos
Santorini, 301, 305, 327
Tinos, 313
Pyrgos of Mistras, 14, 205
Pythagorio (Samos), 11, 446–47, 450–52, 462

Q
Queen's apartments (Knossos), 243

R
Rail Europe, 675
Red Beach (Matala), 255
Regency Casino Thessaloniki, 557
Religious institutions, lodging at, 678
Renieri Gate (Hania), 277
Rethymnon, 234, 238, 249, 266–73
Old Town, 234, 238, 266
Rethymnon Renaissance Festival, 268
Rhodes, 23, 372, 374–76, 378–84, 386, 388, 390–97, 408–411
beach resorts, 402–7
getting around, 436–437
getting there, 436
hotels & restaurants, 396–97, 404, 405–7, 411
nightlife & entertainment, 12, 374, 379, 397, 407, 411
practical information, 436–37
visitor information, 437
Rhodes Town, 374–76, 378–79, 382–84, 390–97
city walls, 8, 381, 392
excursions from, 400–1
little train tour, 379, 394–95
nightlife & entertainment, 397
Old Town, 10, 23, 374–76, 378, 381, 390–94, 374–76

Rizarios Exhibition Center (Mono-
dendri), 589
Roman Agora (Athens), 56, 90–91
Roman baths
Corfu, 610
Dion, 535
Kos, 421
Thera, Ancient, 329
Thessaloniki, 552
Roman forum
Corinth, Ancient, 187
Thessaloniki, 552
Roman temple (Lindos), 410
Roman theater (Dion), 535
Ropa Valley (Corfu), 607, 628
Rotunda (Thessaloniki), 249, 527, 552
Roussanou (Meteora), 583
Royal Road (Knossos), 243
Ruinenviereck (Samothraki), 455
Ruins & archaeological sites, 4–5,
30–35. *See also* Theaters, ancient;
and specific sites
Acrocorinth, 4, 11, 32, 173, 176,
178, 186, 315
Aegina, 138, 140, 144, 145, 148–
49, 150
Argos, 32, 181, 188
Athens
Acropolis, 20, 30, 38, 44, 47,
69, 80
Agora
Ancient, 20, 30, 42, 45, 70,
315
Roman, 56, 90
Areopagus, 70
Erechtheion, 47, 153
Herodes Atticus Theater, 30,
69, 125
Kerameikos Cemetery, 56, 87
Panathenian Statium, 53, 65
Parthenon, 4, 8, 47, 70, 80,
249
Syntagma Station, 51
Temple of Olympian Zeus,
52–53, 68
Tower of the Winds, 56, 86, 90
Bassae, 4, 28, 34, 153, 182,
194–95, 208
Corfu, 602, 606, 610, 623, 626–27
Corinth, Ancient, 4, 29, 32, 176,
178, 184–86, 187
Crete, 35
Aptera, 279–80
Gortyna, 237, 246, 255
Gournia, 246, 288
Iraklion, 6, 35, 232–33, 236,
258–65
Kato Zakro, 247, 289

Knossos, 5, 35, 233, 236,
241–43, 249, 262
Lato, 288
Lissos, 252–53
Malia, 245–46
Olus, 288
Palaikastro, 247, 289
Phaestos, 35, 237, 244, 249,
255
Polyrinia, Ancient, 250
Thronos, 271
Tylissos, 244
Delos, 5, 299, 303, 306, 308–12,
315
Delphi, 5, 20–22, 27, 34, 249, 567,
570–71, 576–79
Castalian Spring, 27
Sanctuary of Apollo, 27, 34,
564, 567, 577, 579
Sanctuary of Athena, 27, 153
Dion, 26, 528–29, 532, 535
Dodona, Ancient, 5, 574, 595, 597
Epidaurus, 4–5, 29, 32, 38, 125,
173, 177, 180, 191, 249, 670
Hora (Peloponnese), 193
Kos, 376, 377, 385, 420–21
Lesbos, 449
Messene, Ancient, 193–94, 249
Milos, 318–19
Mycenae, 4, 29, 32, 173, 177, 181,
188–90, 249, 315
Naxos, 153, 299, 305, 342–44,
347
Nemea, Ancient, 32, 181, 190–91
Olympia, 4, 28, 34, 172–73, 177,
181, 195–96
Pella, 26, 527–28, 530–31
Poros, 140, 144, 161, 162
Rhodes, 23, 380, 382–84, 391,
395, 400–1, 408, 410
Samos, Ancient, 8, 11, 440, 443–
44, 446–47, 450–53, 462–63
Samothraki, 449, 453–55
Santorini
Akrotiri, 23, 29, 35, 301–2, 305,
322–24, 327–28
Thera, Ancient, 23, 29, 302,
305, 315, 322–24, 328–29
Sounion, 30, 53
Sparta, 183, 191–93
Thessaloniki, 249, 527, 550–51,
552
Tiryns, 32, 180, 188, 249, 315
Vergina, 6, 26, 249, 528, 531, 533
Zagori, 589
Russian Bay (Poros), 144, 147,
161–62

S
Sacred Lake (Delos), 310
Sacred Way
Delos, 310, 315
Delphi, 571, 579
Safeti (Dion), 525, 533
Safety, 682. *See also Fast Facts for
specific regions/islands*
St. George Church (Thessaloniki),
249, 527, 552
St. Stephen (Agios Stefanos/Monte
Smith Hill; Rhodes Town), 395
Samaria Gorge (Crete), 2, 230, 235,
238, 252, 253
Sami Caves (Kefalonia), 611, 616
Samos, 440, 442–44, 446–47,
458–65
getting there & around, 443, 445,
482–83
nightlife & entertainment, 465
Samos, Ancient, 443–44
Samos Wine Museum, 460
Samothraki, 449, 453–55
Sanctuary of Apollo
Delos, 310, 345
Delphi, 27, 34, 564, 567, 577, 579
Sanctuary of Artemidoros of Perge
(Ancient Thera), 329
Sanctuary of Artemis Orthia (Sparta),
183, 192
Sanctuary of Asklepios (Epidaurus),
177, 180, 191
Sanctuary of Athena (Delphi), 27, 153
Sanctuary of Isis (Dion), 529, 535
Sanctuary of the Bulls (Delos), 310
Sanctuary of the Great Gods
(Samothraki), 453–55
Sanctuary to the Egyptian gods
(Ancient Thera), 329
Sangri, 347
Santa Maria (Paros), 340
Santo (Pyrgos), 326
Santorini, 22–23, 29, 35, 298, 300–2,
304–5, 322–33, 501
caldera, 2, 298, 324
getting there & around, 305, 323,
370–71
nightlife & entertainment, 333
Sarakiniko (Milos), 9, 318, 319
Saronic Gulf Islands, 136–69
beaches, best, 146–47
getting around, 141, 165, 169
getting there, 141, 168
hotels & restaurants, 145, 151, 155,
159, 163, 167
nightlife & entertainment, 158
practical information, 168–69
visitor information, 169

School of Greek Letters (Dimitsana), 209

Scropios Museum (Paros), 340

Sculpture Collection (Athens), 49

Senior travelers, 683

Seven Springs (Rhodes), 401

Shoes & leather goods (Athens), 39, 56, 86, 103

Sifnos, 17, 298, 307, 350–55
getting there & around, 351, 370–71

Sigri, 449, 479

Sigri's Natural History Museum of the Lesbos Petrified Forest, 479

Silos, underground (Knossos), 243

Silver Beach (Patmos), 432

Silver Hall (Ioannina), 565, 568–69, 573, 595

Siros, 366–69
getting there, 366

Sitia, 239, 289–90

Sivas, 255

Skala
Angistri, 138, 145, 147, 154
Patmos, 385, 428

Skala Beach (Rhodes), 409

Skala Eressos (Lesbos), 9, 441, 445, 449, 479

Skaros, 325

Skiathos, 11, 488–89, 492, 502–7
getting there & around, 489, 503, 520–21
nightlife & entertainment, 507
south coast, 503–4
tips on accommodations, 490

Skiathos Town, 502–3

Skiing (Central & Western Greece), 566, 567–68, 571, 572, 576, 586

Skliri (Angistri), 154

Skolio (Mount Olympus), 541

Skopelos, 489–90, 493–94, 501, 508–13
getting there, 509, 520
southeast coast, 510

Skopelos Town, 10, 487, 489–90, 508–9

Skyrian Horse Project (Skyros), 517

Skyros, 494–95, 514–19
getting there & around, 515, 520–21
shopping, 519

Skyros Town, 487, 514–16

Smoking, 683

Smudgy the Pelion Steam Train, 564, 575

Soccer, 683
Athens, 129

Sotira Likodimou (Athens), 79

Sotos Watersport Center (Faliraki), 402

Souda Bay (Crete), 279

Soufari-seraglio (Ioannina), 594

Sougia, 252–53

Sparta, 183, 191–93, 197

Spas (Athens), 81

Spectator sports, 683
Athens, 129

Spetses, 142, 164–67
getting there & around, 165, 168–69

Spetses Museum, 143, 164

Spianada (Corfu Town), 604–5, 609, 618–19, 621

Spilia Galazia (Skiathos), 504

Spilia Halkini (Skiathos), 504

Spilia Skotini (Skiathos), 486, 493, 504

Spili Melissani (Kefalonia), 603, 611, 616

Spinalonga, 11, 239, 286–87

Sporades, 484–521
getting around, 521
getting there, 489, 497, 503, 509, 515, 520
hotels & restaurants, 490, 498, 506–7, 512–13, 518–19
nightlife & entertainment, 507
practical information, 520–21
visitor information, 503, 509, 521

Stadium
Delos, 310
Delphi, 567
Dodona, Ancient, 597
Olympia, 196

Stafylos, 510

Stathatos Mansion (Athens), 63

Statue of Sir Arthur Evans (Knossos), 243

Statue of Zeus, 153, 196, 199, 637

Stavrinides, 461

Stavros, 280

Stefanos Ski School (Skiathos), 505

Stemnitsa, 28, 182, 208–9

Stoa
Lindos, 410
Samothraki, 455

Stoa Basilike (Ancient Thera), 329

Stoa of Attalos (Athens), 45

Stoa of Eumenes (Athens), 69

Street of the Knights (Rhodes Town), 381, 392

Subway (Athens), 134, 673

Sunshine Express (Athens), 66

Super Paradise (Mykonos), 303, 360, 361

Sweetwater Beach (Loutro), 253–54

Symi, 23, 376, 384, 412–17
footpaths, 377

Synagogue (Delos), 310

Syntagma (Athens), 84–86

Syntagma Square
Athens, 84, 88
Nafplion, 2, 28, 173, 176, 180

Syntagma Station (Athens), 51, 64

T

Ta Liontaria (Iraklion), 233, 258–59

Taxes, 683

Taxis, 673, 676

Taygetos Mountains (Peloponnese), 193

Teacher's Rock (Vrontados), 468

Technopolis (Athens), 57, 87

Teleferik (Athens), 66

Telephones, 683

Temenos (Samothraki), 455

Temperatures, 672

Temple at Lissos, 252–53

Temple of Aphaia (Aegina), 138, 140, 144, 145

Temple of Aphrodite
Corinth, Ancient, 186
Rhodes Town, 391

Temple of Apollo
Corinth, Ancient, 187
Delphi, 579
Rhodes Town, 395

Temple of Apollo Epicurius at Bassae, 4, 28, 34, 153, 182, 194–95, 208

Temple of Artemis, 637

Temple of Athena Nike (Athens), 47

Temple of Athena Pronaia (Delphi), 579

Temple of Demeter (Sangri), 305, 347

Temple of Hera (Olympia), 195, 196

Temple of Olympian Zeus (Athens), 52–53, 68

Temple of Poseidon
Poros, 161
Sounion, 30, 53

Temple of Zeus
Nemea, Ancient, 153, 181, 190
Olympia, 52–53, 68, 181, 195, 196

Temples of Dione (Ancient Dodona), 597

Temples to Hera and Poseidon (Corfu Town), 610

Temple to Aphrodite (Ancient Dodona), 597

Temple to Apollo
Kos, 421
Thera, Ancient, 329

Temple to Apollo Karneios (Ancient Thera), 329

Temple to Asklepios (Kos), 421
Temple to the goddess Athena (Lindos), 410
Temple to Zeus (Ancient Nemea), 190
Tennis, 661
Tériade Museum (Varia), 475-76
Terrace of the Festivals (Ancient Thera), 329
Terrace of the Lions (Delos), 310
Thalassea (Athens, south coast), 131-33
Theater Festival (Lesbos), 481
Theater, Greek, history of, 456-57
Theater of Dionysos (Athens), 68-69
Theater performances. See Performing arts
Theaters, ancient
    Argos, 32, 181, 188, 315
    Athens, 30, 38, 68-69, 125
    Corinth, Ancient, 187
    Delos, 310
    Delphi, 579
    Dion, 535
    Dodona, Ancient, 597
    Epidaurus, 4, 29, 32, 125, 173, 177, 180, 191, 249, 670
    Knossos, 243
    Samothraki, 455
    Sparta, 183, 192
    Thera, Ancient, 329
    Thessaloniki, 552
Themis's Ionic temple (Ancient Dodona), 597
Theodorou Beach (Kos), 425
Theokoleon (Olympia), 196
Theophilos Museum (Varia), 475
Theotokou Monastery (Paleokastritsa), 610
Thera, Ancient, 23, 29, 302, 305, 315, 322-24, 328-29
Thera Collection (Athens), 49
Thera Foundation: The Wall Painting of Thera (Fira), 35, 301, 324
Therasia, 324, 328
Theriade Museum (Varia), 445
Thermal springs
    Kos, 376-77, 385, 387, 422
    Lesbos, 441, 445, 449, 477
Thermopylae, 191, 637, 640
Thessaloniki, 24, 526-27, 548-59
    nightlife & entertainment, 557
    Upper City (Ano Polis), 24, 552-53
    with children, 553
Thessaloniki Concert Hall, 557
Thessaloniki Science Centre and Technology Museum (Thessaloniki), 553

Thisseion (Athens), 45
Thissio (Athens), 88, 91
Thission Open-Air Cinema (Athens), 57, 83, 125
Thissio Square (Athens), 20, 39, 42
Tholos
    Delphi, 579
    Epidaurus, 191
Throne of Zeus (Mount Olympus), 541
Throne room (Knossos), 243
Thronos, 271
Tigaki (Kos), 385, 425
Time zone, 684
Timios Stavros (Naxos), 347
Tinos, 299, 308, 312-13
    getting there & around, 309
Tinos Town, 312
Tipping, 684
Tiryns, 32, 180, 188, 249, 315
Toilets, 684
Tolo (Gulf of Argos), 217
Tomb of the Unknown Soldier (Athens), 72
To Sotiros (Nafplion), 217
Tourist offices, 668. See also Fast Facts for specific regions/islands
Tourist passes, 682
Tourist season, 668
Tourist Police, 682. See also Fast Facts for specific regions/islands
Tourist traps & scams, 684. See also Safety
Tours, package & escorted, 658-65, 672-73
Tower of Prosforion (Ouranoupolis), 537
Tower of the Winds (Athens), 56, 86, 90-91
Town Hall (Corfu Town), 621
Traditional Handicraft Center (Ioannina), 569, 573
Traditional Lindian House Souvenir Shop (Lindos), 408-9
Tragaea Villages (Naxos), 305, 347, 348
Train travel, 674-75
Trata (Skopelos), 513
Traveling to Greece from abroad, 672, 674
Treasuries (Olympia), 196
Treasury (Ioannina), 565, 568-69, 573, 595
Treasury of Atreus (Mycenae), 189
Trekking Hellas (Athens), 17, 581
Trianon (Nafplion), 216
Tria Pagadia (Hora, Mykonos), 358
Tripia Petra (Skiathos), 504

Trips, special interest, 658-65
Tris Boukes Bay (Skyros), 495, 518
Trizina, Ancient (Poros), 140, 144, 162
Tsambica (Rhodes), 388
Tumulus of Philip II at Vergina, 524-25, 528, 530-31
Turkish bazaar (Ioannina), 2, 249, 569, 574
Turkish House (Rhodes Town), 393-94
Turkish Neokastro (Pylos), 210
Tylissos (Crete), 244
Tzisdarakis Tzami (Athens), 58, 86

U
Unification of the Archaeological Sites of Athens, 68, 647
University of Athens, 75

V
Vai (Crete), 291
Valch's Wedding (Skopelos), 513
Valley of Petaloudes (Valley of the Butterflies; Paros), 339
Valley of the Nightingales (Samos), 461
Vaporia (Ermoupolis), 368
Vareltzidhena Mansion (Petra), 479
Varia, 445, 449, 475
Varlaam (Meteora), 583
Vase and Minor Objects Collection (Athens), 49
Vatera (Lesbos), 445, 449, 476
Vathia, 212
Vathy
    Ithaca, 617
    Sifnos, 307, 354
Vayionia (Poros), 147
Velania (Skopelos), 510
Venetian arsenali (Hania), 277
Venetian Harbor (Hania), 231, 249, 276, 277
    fortifications, 277
Venetian Kastro (Skyros Town), 515
Vergina, 6, 26, 249, 528, 531, 533
Vikos Gorge (Zagori), 565, 568, 573, 589
Villa of Dionysos (Dion), 535
Visitor information, 684. See also Fast Facts for specific regions/islands
Vlaherna, 627
Volax, 313
Volissos, 448, 470
Vori, 255-56
Voukourestiou Street (Athens), 99
Voula A (Athens, south coast), 131-33
Vounakiou (Chios Town), 444
Vouno, 518

Vouraikos Gorge (Peloponnese), 181, 206–8
Vourliotes, 461
Vradeto Steps, 590
Vrisses, 254
Vrontado (Siros), 366, 369
Vrontados (Chios), 448, 468
Vrontokhion Monastery (Mystras), 204

W

Wall Painting of Thera (Fira), 35, 301, 324
War Museum (Athens), 63
War of Independence, 637–38, 641
Watermania (Mykonos), 361
Water park (Faliraki), 384, 403
Water Sports Club Platos Yialos (Mykonos), 361
Weather, 671–72
Weddings, 331, 501, 664
Weiler Building (Athens), 75
West court (Knossos), 243
Western Excavation site (Kos Town), 377, 420
Western Greece. *See* Central & Western Greece
West wing (Knossos), 243
White Tower (Thessaloniki), 8, 526, 551
Windsurfing, 661
   Mykonos, 361
   Paros, 340
Wine & wineries, 656–57
   Mykonos, 363
   Nafplion, 16, 219
   Naxos, 344
   Patras, 224
   Pyrgos, 301
   Samos, 460
   Santorini, 301, 326
Workshop of Phidias (Olympia), 196
Woven goods
   Dion, 525
   Hania, 16, 283
   Hora (Mykonos), 16, 363
   Krista, 287
   Nafplion, 219
   Skyros Town, 519

X

Xi (Kefalonia), 615
Xombourgo, 313

Y

Yabanaki Varkiza (Athens, south coast), 133
Yad Lezicaron Synagogue (Thessaloniki), 554
Yeni Hamam (Rhodes Town), 381, 394
Yialos, 384, 414, 416–17
Ypapanti (Meteora), 583

Z

Zagori, 586–91
   stone roads & bridges, 564, 590
Zappeion (Athens), 72–74
Zappeion Gardens (Athens), 52, 65, 83

Photo Credits

Note: l= left; r= right; t= top; b= bottom; c= center

Cover Photo Credits: Front cover (l to r): Ann Rayworth/Alamy; © Georgios Makkas; © Georgios Makkas. Back cover (t and b): © Cindy Miller Hopkins/DanitaDelimont.com; © Yannis Lefakis. Cover flap (t to b): © ACE STOCK LIMITED/Alamy; © Kevin Beebe/age fotostock; James Burke/Time Life Pictures/Getty Images; © Mark Sunderland/age fotostock; © Hemis.fr/SuperStock. Inside front cover (clockwise from tr): Northern Greece: © Photononstop/SuperStock; The Sporades: © Yannis Lefakis; Northeastern Aegean Islands: © Georgios Makkas; The Cyclades: Yannis Lefakis; Rhodes & The Dodecanese: © Georgios Makkas; Crete: © Yannis Lefakis; Saronic Gulf Islands: © Yannis Lefakis; Peloponnese: © Rolf Richardson/Alamy; Corfu & The Ionian Islands: © Georgios Makkas.

Interior Photo Credits: Adrian Hotel: p115; AGE: © Stefan Auth/age fotostock: p478; © Andrew Bain/age fotostock: p638; © Kevin Beebe/age fotostock: p314; © Walter Bibikow/age fotostock: p278(r); © Tibor Bognar/age fotostock: p46(t); © Spyros Bourboulis/age fotostock: p64; © Moirenc Camille/age fotostock: p546(br); © DEA/A Garozzo/age fotostock: p454; © Hermann Dobler/age fotostock: p153(3rd from tl); © Nevio Doz/age fotostock: p vii(t), p492; © Guizou Franck/age fotostock: p168; © H Goethel/age fotostock: p501; © Jiri Hubatka/age fotostock: p546 (4th from tl); © KEENE/age fotostock: p598; © Katja Kreder/age fotostock: p365; © Alvaro Leiva/age fotostock: p84; © Stefano Lunardi/age fotostock: p130, p132; © Rene Mattes/age fotostock: p564; © Moustafellou/IML/age fotostock: p162(t); © Josef Müllek/age fotostock: p544(3rd from bl); © Adrian C Nitu/age fotostock: p536; © T. Papageorgiou/age fotostock: p214(t); © Doug Pearson/age fotostock: p270(b), p271; © Ingolf Pompe/age fotostock: p356; © The Print Collector/age fotostock: p530, p643; © Rfcompany/age fotostock: p304; © Juergen Richter/age fotostock: p3(r); © Ellen Rooney/age fotostock: p630; © Spyropoulos/IML/age fotostock: p334; © Mark Sunderland/age fotostock: p546(2nd from bl); Alamy: © Ace Stock Limited/Alamy: p198; © Aegean Images/Alamy: p319; © Vladimir Alexeev/Alamy: p585(2nd from l); © Ancient Art & Architecture Collection Ltd/Alamy: p181, p46(tl and 3rd from bl); © Arco Images GmbH/Alamy: p183(r); © Jon Arnold Images Ltd/Alamy: pp228-29, p260, p412; © The Art Archive/Alamy: p153(tr), p248(3rd from t); © Art Directors & TRIP/Alamy: p315(c); © The Art Gallery Collection/Alamy: p544(tl); © Erin Babnik/Alamy: p544 (2nd from tl); © Banana Pancake/Alamy: pp522-23; © Nathan Benn/Alamy: p544(tr); © Bon Appetit/Alamy: p533, p657; © David Cameron/Alamy: p482; © CuboImages srl/Alamy: p345(l), p453(b), p455, p491; © dk/Alamy: p543(t); © Peter Eastland/Alamy: p192; © Rod Edwards/Alamy: p300; © Eyebyte/Alamy: p279; © FORGET Patrick/SAGAPHOTO.COM/Alamy: p291(b); © Robert Fried/Alamy: p612; © Greece/Alamy: p172, p529; © Robert Harding Picture Library Ltd/Alamy: p318; © terry harris just greece photo library/Alamy: p128, p207, p398-99(tl), p520, p613(tl), p651(l); © Hemis/Alamy: p71; © Peter Horree/Alamy: p248(t); © imagebroker/Alamy: p328(r), p329, p331; © Images & Stories/Alamy: p499; © IML Image Group Ltd/Alamy: pp xii-1, p321, p510, p557, p656; © INTERFOTO/Alamy: p546(3rd from tl, bl), p641(t); © International Photobank/Alamy: p156; © Wolfgang Kaehler/Alamy: p315(t); © Justin Kase zsixz/Alamy: p560; © Kuttig-Travel/Alamy: p iv(b), p208, p347(t); p348; © Tony Lilley/Alamy: p160; © Lonely Planet Images/Alamy: p127, p202(l), p226, p346(r); © mauritius images GmbH/Alamy: p211(r); © Gareth McCormack/Alamy: p254; © John Norman/Alamy: p554; © Alan Novelli/Alamy: p619(l), p620; © Werner Otto/Alamy: p538; © Steve Outram/Alamy: p613(bl); © Michael Owston/Alamy: p390; © PCL/Alamy: p178, p632; © Tom Pfeiffer/Alamy: p9; © Nicholas Pitt/Alamy: p328(l); © PjrTravel/Alamy: p294; © PRISMA ARCHIVO/Alamy: p248(3rd from b); © Ann Rayworth/Alamy: p408(t); © R A Rayworth/Alamy: pp484-85, p500; © Simon Reddy/Alamy: p507; © ReligiousStock/Alamy: p585(l); © Rolf Richardson/Alamy: p183(l); © Thomas Semmler/Alamy: p450, p483; © Steve Taylor ARPS/Alamy: p17; © Nevena Tsvetanova/Alamy: p544(3rd from tl); © World Pictures/Alamy: p425; Aliki Hotel: p417; AP Images: AP Photo: p641(c); AP Photo/Elise Amendola: p641(b); AP Photo/Jacques Brinon: p648; AP Photo/Space Imaging: p199(b); Art Archive: The Art Archive: p544(2nd from bl); The Art Archive/Archaeological Museum Piraeus/Gianni Dagli Orti: p546(4th from bl); The Art Archive/Archaeological Museum Venice/Alfredo Dagli Orti: p544(bl); The Art Archive/Fitzwilliam Museum Cambridge/Alfredo Dagli Orti: p544(br); The Art Archive/Museo Statale Metaponto/Gianni Dagli Orti: p546(2nd from tl); Athens Studios: p116; Avalon Boutique-Suites Hotel & Klimt Hotel: p396; Bratsera Hotel: p159; Bridgeman: Illustration from *The Story of Greece* by Mary Macgregor, 1st edition, 1913 (color print), Crane, Walter/Private Collection/The Stapleton Collection/The Bridgeman Art Library: p199(t); *Voyage to Athens and Constantinople: Nickolaki Mitropolos taking the standard of the Cross at Salona on Easter Day in 1821*, 1825 (litho), Dupre, Louis/Private Collection/Photo © The Fine Art Society, London, UK/The Bridgeman Art Library: p248(b); Byzantino Hotel: p225; Capsis Hotel Thessaloniki: p555; Casa Delfino: p282; Casa Lucia: p631; Cavo Tago: p15; Chateau Zevgoli: p349; Corfu Palace Hotel: p624; Divani Palace: p113; Electra Palace: p117; Elounda Beach Hotel: p14, p230; Esperides Hotel: p405; Faliraki, Alexis Sofianopoulos Photography: p384; Gaia Garden: p426; Getty: James Burke/Time Life Pictures/Getty Images: p456; Karin Iden/